INVESTMENT
STRATEGY

McGRAW-HILL
SERIES IN FINANCE

PROFESSOR CHARLES A. D'AMBROSIO
University of Washington
CONSULTING EDITOR

INVESTMENT STRATEGY

C. Robert Coates

Department of Finance
Southern Methodist University

McGraw-Hill Book Company

New York   St. Louis   San Francisco   Auckland   Bogotá   Düsseldorf
Johannesburg   London   Madrid   Mexico   Montreal   New Delhi
Panama   Paris   São Paulo   Singapore   Sydney   Tokyo   Toronto

This book was set in Garamond by Progressive Typographers.
The editors were J. S. Dietrich, Bonnie E. Lieberman, Michael Elia,
Theresa J. Kwiatkowski, and Ellen Warren;
the designer was Joan E. O'Connor;
the production supervisor was Leroy A. Young.
The drawings were done by J & R Services, Inc.
R. R. Donnelley & Sons Company was printer and binder.

INVESTMENT STRATEGY

1234567890 DODO 78321098

Library of Congress Cataloging in Publication Data
Coates, C   Robert,   date
Investment strategy.

(McGraw-Hill series in finance)
Bibliography: p.
Includes index.
1. Investments. I. Title.
HG4521.C523   332.6'7   77-16520
ISBN 0-07-011471-4

to Suzanne

CONTENTS

PART TWO   RISK, INFLATION, AND RATES OF RETURN

PART THREE   TAXES

PART FOUR   INSTITUTIONS

PREFACE

What makes *Investment Strategy* so different from the hundreds or perhaps even thousands of other books on investments? The answer is its unique blend of both traditional and modern investment concepts, its easy-to-read style, and its focus on the individual investor.

Today's investor lives in a complex and contradictory world. Making money has never been easier. But at the same time, holding on to it has probably never required more ingenuity. Taxes, inflation, a stop-and-go economy, a mind-boggling array of investments, and the high cost of "expert" advice all create a formidable obstacle course to investment success.

To make matters still more perplexing, technology has finally begun to turn investing into a science. Research centers like the University of Chicago, MIT, Stanford, the University of California at Berkeley and at Los Angeles, and the University of Rochester continue to pile up important new findings about investments. But because of their limited mathematical expertise, few investors or Wall Street professionals can benefit from these results. Indeed, faculties at many business schools remain unaware of the results.

Investment Strategy reaches out to the individual investor and explains how these new findings can be used to develop successful investment strategies. It introduces important concepts without the use of mathematics. The analyses and sometimes earthy anecdotes are based on facts rather than on market folklore. *Investment Strategy* also tells about the important fine print of federal and state taxes, pension plans, insurance, and Social Security. As a result, investors gain all of the tools needed to make their own investment decisions.

ORGANIZATION OF THE BOOK

In the first part of *Investment Strategy* the reader is taken behind the business scene to witness the birth of a corporation, the efforts to raise money by the sale of stock, the regulations surrounding new stock issues, and the sometimes hilarious attempts by shareholders to influence corporate policy.

Then the investor travels to New York to the so-called Big Board—the biggest auction market in the world. Afterwards he or she learns how to open an account, how to read the financial pages, and how to use sophisticated trading techniques like short selling and limit orders. Next, a variety of investments ranging from bonds to options and commodity futures are discussed.

Chapter 5, the "Efficient-Market Concept," closes out the first part on the investment environment. It gives people an important new philosophy on which to base their investment decisions.

Part Two of the book—"Risk, Inflation, and Rates of Return"—marks a significant departure from the traditional approach to investments. It shows the individual how to eliminate much of the risk of investing by using new portfolio techniques. And it describes in detail the impact of inflation on investments. Finally, the chapters on rates of return and valuation strip away the many myths about the returns on various investments and show how to use actual returns to calculate investment values.

The third part of *Investment Strategy* is devoted to taxes. Despite the clamor about high taxes, the average investor often pays taxes needlessly. The chapters "Income Taxes" and "Tax-sheltered Retirement Plans" provide a number of strategies for reducing taxes—no matter who the individual is or how much money he or she takes home.

After mastering taxes, the reader moves on to the institutional investment arena. More and more of today's dollars are going into mutual funds, life insurance, and Social Security. Part Four of *Investment Strategy* tells the investor how to wend his or her way among these financial giants without being trampled. These chapters include discussions on the proper selection of mutual funds, a new financial product called the index fund, methods of buying the right amount of insurance at the lowest possible price, and techniques for estimating Social Security benefits.

The fifth part of this book covers the costs of investing—a topic often avoided because of its controversial nature. Here, the investor will discover dozens of ways to save both money and time. And some individuals will probably even acquire a flair for bargaining, once they learn the secrets.

Most books never mention the most crucial ingredient in the entire investment process—the investor. Part Six of *Investment Strategy* remedies that oversight. First, the investor learns about risk taking and the assessment of risk-return preferences. Then a chapter on consumption-investment decisions aids in the always painful process of allocating too few dollars to too many needs. The final chapter of this book shows the investor how to put all these separate pieces together into a complete investment strategy.

ACKNOWLEDGMENTS

Investment Strategy took several years to make into a reality. During that time I received help and encouragement from a number of people. My greatest debt is to my wife, Suzanne, who did everything but actually write the book. She researched many of the ideas, obtained all of the permissions, wrote all the bibliographies and footnotes, edited the manuscript, and typed many drafts. Perhaps even more important, she provided me with the incentive to develop a new approach to the investments course. Whatever credit *Investment Strategy* receives, I gratefully share with her.

I would also like to thank my reviewers for their insightful comments and for their complimentary remarks (the latter provided me with a much-needed push to finish the book). I consider myself fortunate to have worked with John Aber (Boston University), Charles D'Ambrosio (University of Washington), Jack Clark Francis (City University of New York), Nancy Jacob (University of Washington), Robert Persons (University of Bridgeport), Patrick Regan (BEA Associates), Michael Rozeff (University of Iowa), Andrew Senchack (University of Texas), and Jack Treynor (*Financial Analysts Journal*). Charles D'Ambrosio also deserves a special thank-you for first talking me into writing a textbook and then providing me with quick, detailed reviews.

In addition, I am grateful to the University of New Orleans and Southern Methodist University for providing an environment conducive to writing and research. My department chairmen, Professors Terry Wilford and Bill Townsend, helped considerably to ease my burdens. And students like Steve Anderson, Scott Beazley, Wayne Chenault, Judy Delaney, Leslie Doerfer, Don Lalonde, David Parrott, Quentin Stumpf, and Tom Thompson all provided much needed research assistance.

Publishing companies ask authors not to mention their staff, but I am going to break that rule for Mike Elia and Stephen Dietrich. Mike spent months working with me on the manuscript, much to the reader's benefit. And Stephen signed the contract, counseled me, and forgave me for almost all of my missed deadlines.

Finally, I want to thank the hundreds of students and participants in my classes and seminars for their helpful comments.

WHY INVESTMENT STRATEGY?

One of the things this book emphasizes is the value of time. Before you invest any more of it in *Investment Strategy,* please answer the following questions:

1 Do you completely understand the wide variety of investments available to individuals including stocks, bonds, preferred stocks, options, futures, mutual funds, insurance, and pension plans?
2 Can the small investor match the performance of professionals?
3 Is the advice of brokers worthless, at least in selecting undervalued securities?
4 Do you trade stocks, bonds, options, and real estate at a substantial discount from regular commissions?
5 Do you know how to diversify your portfolio in order to increase returns while at the same time reducing risk?
6 Can someone who invests $10,000 make $1 million within a lifetime without doing any work at all?
7 Do you know how to measure the financial risk you expose yourself to?
8 Do you know the returns on various investments?
9 Can you calculate the real value of a stream of retirement benefits consisting of $20,000 a year for twenty-five years?
10 Do you have a tax-sheltered retirement plan?
11 Do you know how to match your objectives to those of a mutual fund?
12 Do you agree with the saying that "You never go broke by taking a profit"?
13 Does a high rate of inflation guarantee large profits in real estate?
14 Does straight life insurance provide a return exceeding 5 percent?
15 Do Social Security benefits depend solely upon the amount of your contributions?
16 Do people behave consistently in different risky situations?
17 Do you ever buy stocks on inside tips?
18 Do you have a personal cash flow statement and balance sheet?
19 Do you have an investment strategy?

If you answered yes to questions 1–11, no to questions 12–16, and yes to questions 17–19, you fall in the financially enlightened category. Otherwise, read on, since this book will save you money and, perhaps more important, considerable anxiety.

C. Robert Coates

INVESTMENT
STRATEGY

PART ONE

THE INVESTMENT ENVIRONMENT

CHAPTER ONE

STOCKS

A t last count more than 25 million Americans—1 in every 6 adults—had the staggering sum of $800 billion invested in stocks. What do these stockholders get for their money? The answer is ownership of corporations ranging in size from the local gas station to giant AT&T, with a work force larger than the active U.S. Army.

Altogether corporations employ 47% of this country's total work force and provide 60% of all goods and services purchased by the American consumer. Last but not least, they pay 16% of all taxes. Despite these impressive statistics, few people really know much about stocks or about the corporations that sell these stocks.

SUCCESS STORIES

The signs hanging on every McDonald's outlet steadily tick away the billions of hamburgers sold. At the end of 1976 the scorecard read over 21 billion, enough to keep a hamburger lover eating nonstop for 200,000 years. No wonder *Time* magazine credits McDonald's with "the burger that conquered the country."

Ray Kroc tasted his first McDonald's hamburger in 1955. Afterward, he talked the McDonald brothers into letting him franchise their name and golden arches nationally.

Within five years the hard-driving Kroc had helped open more than 200 outlets around the country. Kroc then offered to buy out the McDonald brothers. He met their asking price of $2.7 million by borrowing from a variety of lenders and taking on partners.

McDonald's sold stock to the public for the first time in 1966. Investors who put their money where their mouth was enjoyed some spectacular gains. A $5,000 investment soared to $320,000 in only 7 years. As a result, Ray Kroc's personal fortune is estimated at about $500 million, and his secretary retired with $64 million.

Other than success, Texas Instruments and McDonald's have little in common. Texas Instruments (TI) symbolizes the "electronics era." The company produced the world's first commercially feasible transistor radio. And millions of people keep track of time and numbers with digital watches and pocket calculators from TI. Moreover, complex electronic components manufactured by TI go into computers, television sets, traffic lights, vending machines, appliances, airport landing systems, and a host of other products consumers now take for granted. At the end of 1975 company sales comfortably exceeded $1 billion.

The two young scientists who founded the company in 1930 probably never dreamed of such success. The nation's economy had just collapsed. With businesses failing every day and soup lines commonplace, merely surviving was an accomplishment.

TI made it through the Depression and emerged from World War II with annual sales of about $3 million. A $5,000 investment in the company's stock in 1953 had grown to nearly $200,000 by 1965.

STARTING A BUSINESS

Every year more than 300,000 new companies are formed. Some of these will become the Texas Instruments and McDonald's of the future.

How does someone start a business? First the would-be entrepreneur needs an idea or concept. Although originality helps, many of the greatest business successes resulted from simply popularizing and/or modifying an already existing product. Neither Pizza Hut nor Pizza Inn—the two largest sellers of pizza in the United States—invented pizza. But they did open the first chains of restaurants specializing in pizza. Now their sales total hundreds of millions of dollars each year.

Suppose a prospective businesswoman, Sally Smith, decides that a drive-in restaurant specializing in natural foods offers tremendous potential. She researches the idea and finds that people are becoming increasingly aware of the importance of a balanced diet. Although this trend promises to continue in the future, not one fast-food chain currently offers natural foods.

TABLE 1-1   MAJOR CHARACTERISTICS OF CORPORATIONS,
PARTNERSHIPS, AND SOLE PROPRIETORSHIPS

Characteristics	Corporations	Partnerships	Sole Proprietorships
1 Method of creation	Charter issued by state	Agreement by partners	Created by an individual
2 Liability of owners	Limited liability	Unlimited liability	Unlimited liability
3 Duration	May be perpetual	Termination by death, agreement, or withdrawal of a partner	Termination by death or withdrawal
4 Management	Shareholders elect directors who set policy	All partners in absence of agreement have equal vote	Proprietor sets policy
5 Taxation	Income taxed to corporation	Income taxed to partners	Income taxed to sole proprietor
6 Ownership	Easily transferable; shares bought and sold	Not transferable	Not transferable

With the help of several friends, Sally designs a low-priced menu and finds a building to rent. For the sake of simplicity, and because the name appeals to her, she decides to call her restaurant Sally's.

Forms of Business Organization

Next Sally must select a form of organization for the company. Enterprises generally fall into 1 of 3 categories: (1) sole proprietorships, (2) partnerships, or (3) corporations. The major characteristics of these forms of business organization are compared in Table 1-1.

Most of the businesses in the United States are **sole proprietorships**; i.e., they are owned by one person. Usually the owner also manages the business. A sole proprietor reports all business income on his or her individual income tax return.

In contrast to a sole proprietorship, a **partnership** involves two or more owners. Partners usually sign a written agreement setting forth guidelines for the operation and eventual dissolution of their business. And they always report their respective shares of the firm's profits on their own income tax returns.

The **corporation** represents the most complex form of business organization. It is created by filing **articles of incorporation** with the proper state authorities. Most state laws require these articles to include at least the following:

1 Name of the corporation
2 Principal place of business
3 Nature of business
4 Amount of stock authorized for sale (called **authorized shares**)
5 Names of **incorporators** (persons filing for incorporation)
6 Provisions for the regulation of the business and the conduct of the affairs of the corporation

After approving the proposed articles of incorporation, the state grants the business a **charter** or license to operate.

The act of incorporation makes the company a separate **legal entity**. That is why the name of a corporation must always include one of the following words: corporation, company, incorporated, or limited. As a legal entity, a corporation pays taxes on its income, owns property, and can sue or be sued. In addition, the corporation theoretically possesses immortality. This perpetual existence stands in marked contrast to a partnership or sole proprietorship, which may be dissolved upon the death or withdrawal of an owner.

The corporate form of organization offers two outstanding advantages over a partnership or sole proprietorship. The first is **limited liability**. In other words, the owners of a corporation can never lose more than they invest in the company. On the other hand, partners and sole proprietors are completely liable (legally responsible) for the unpaid debts of their businesses. The second advantage of a corporation is the ease of transferring ownership. For both of these reasons, only corporations ever achieve wide public ownership.

Of course, there are also some disadvantages to the corporate form of organization. The most important is **double taxation**. First the corporation pays tax on its income. And then the shareholders pay taxes on any income they receive from the corporation. In effect, taxes are paid twice on the same income.

After discussing the different forms of organization with her lawyer, Sally decides to incorporate the business. So Sally's becomes Sally's, Incorporated (usually abbreviated Inc.).

Raising Capital

Before even attempting to raise any money, Sally makes up a **cash budget** for the first year of operations. Judging from this forecast of future expenditures and receipts, the company needs $100,000. This will pay for legal fees, licenses, rent, interior decoration, equipment, supplies, advertising, Sally's salary, and the employees' salaries, as well as providing some extra cash for emergencies.

In order to obtain the **capital** (money or funds) needed to carry on its business, Sally's, Inc., can borrow money and/or sell securities. **Securities** consist of all types of stocks and bonds. A **bond** resembles an IOU. Companies sell bonds to the public and agree to pay the bondholders a fixed income. And, of course, they promise to eventually repay the money. Both bonds and borrowed money fall under the general category of debt.

In contrast to debt, **common stock** represents **equity,** or ownership, in a corporation. Louis Engel, author of the best-selling *How to Buy Stocks,* says: "There's nothing commonplace about common stock. It's the number one security in our system, basic to all corporate business and to our whole free enterprise system. If you own a share of stock in a company, you own part of that company. You and other shareholders own the company in common."[1]

Sally, with the advice of a lawyer and an accountant, decides to raise the full $100,000 needed for the company through the sale of common stock. Why common stock? Because no investor wants to buy the bonds of a small, unknown company. The risk of nonpayment is just too great. And the local bankers see little or no promise in a restaurant specializing in natural foods.

Sally originally planned to sell 100 shares in the company at $1,000 a share. That way, each person buying one share would have owned one-hundredth of the company. But many of the people she talked to could afford to invest only a few hundred dollars. A $1,000 price tag on a share would have eliminated all of these small investors and left Sally far short of the needed $100,000. So, instead of issuing 100 shares, she decides to sell 10,000 shares at $10 each. Anyone buying one of these shares would own one ten-thousandth of the company.

There is an important difference between the number of **shares outstanding** (owned by investors) and the number of shares authorized. Although Sally plans to sell only 10,000 shares, she listed the number of authorized shares in the articles of incorporation as 20,000. This makes it possible for the company to sell as many as 10,000 additional shares in the future.

Before attempting to sell a single share, Sally makes absolutely certain she has satisfied all state and federal regulations concerning the sale of new securities. Otherwise, she could be fined heavily and/or end up in jail. Then she makes up a list of friends and acquaintances and starts calling them one by one and telling them of her ideas. A few of them laugh so hard that she hangs up. But many of the others listen carefully and ask detailed questions. They all want to know what they stand to gain and lose on their investments.

"Quite frankly," she tells them, "you could lose every penny you put into Sally's, Inc. But the corporate form of organization protects you from losing any more. In my opinion the potential rewards more than justify the risk. I think you have to agree that there is a growing market for natural foods. And if my projections of sales are correct, profits from just this one location could easily amount to $25,000 a year. Of course, if we expand regionally or nationally, you could make a fortune on your investment. Just look at Kentucky Fried Chicken—the original shareholders made millions of dollars."

Soon the money comes pouring in from friends and acquaintances, and by the end of the month Sally sells the last 100 shares. Each of the new shareholders receives a printed **stock certificate** as evidence of part ownership in the company. A typical share certificate is shown in Figure 1-1. In addition, Sally **registers** the name and address of each shareholder in the company's books, just as all large corporations do. This way the firm can maintain contact with its shareholders and also have proof of who owns the shares.

FIGURE 1-1 Typical common stock certificate. (Reprinted with permission of American Telephone and Telegraph Company.)

About a week after the stock certificates go out in the mail, Sally gets a phone call from Dr. John Williams, one of the larger shareholders. "Sally, I just got my certificate in the mail and I think there has been a mistake," says the doctor. "According to my certificate, my shares have a par value of $1 each. But I paid $10 for each of them. It seems like I paid too much."

Sally, who has known Dr. Williams for a long time, laughs and says, "Doctor, I know how closely you watch your golf scores. So I can understand why you are concerned about coming in at par. But the **par value** of a stock no longer has any real meaning. It is just the value printed on the face of the stock certificate. In fact, many firms today issue shares which have no designated par value."

INVESTMENT BANKERS

Sally's, Inc., is not the only firm needing money. Each year United States corporations raise billions of dollars in equity capital by selling new shares to the public. Sometimes a single offering totals several hundred million dollars. For example, AT&T sold $658,500,000 of stock during 2 weeks in 1976—a far cry from the $100,000 needed by Sally's, Inc.

With large sums of money like this to raise, corporations usually seek the help of professionals called, for some obscure reason, **investment bankers.** Actually these people are neither bankers nor investors. Instead they devote themselves to merchandising securities.

What do investment bankers do to earn their money? According to one corporate executive, they go through extraordinary amounts of "toil, sweat, frustrations, problems—yes, and tears." In short, raising money, regardless of the purpose, is never easy. Investment bankers provide corporations with three types of services in their search for new funds: (1) advice and counsel, (2) underwriting, and (3) selling. Naturally, investment bankers prefer to provide all three of these services, but they sometimes sell only part of the package.

Advice and Counsel

Advice and counsel involves more than just handholding. Most financial executives view the equity market almost as a last resort. Their distaste for new stock issues probably stems from the high costs of floating (selling) new stock and the enormous amount of red tape placed in their way by state and federal regulations governing the sale of new securities.

Whatever the reason, most companies obtain additional funds by retaining earnings, selling bonds, or borrowing from banks rather than by selling new stock. According to one detailed study of corporate financing, only 2 out of 20 large manufacturing corporations issued common stock more than once over a 20-year period. As a result, most executives have little or no familiarity with new stock issues. The investment banker, on the other hand, specializes in new issues of both stocks and bonds. For example, Salomon Brothers, a large investment banking firm, participated in over 700 offerings during 1975.

As an adviser, the investment banker reviews the financial plans of the firm and offers detailed suggestions about the timing and terms of the offering and the satisfaction of legal requirements. Companies planning their first public offering of stock always receive special scrutiny. In the words of one investment banker:

> *The key thing we look at in deciding whether a company is ready for an initial public offer [of stock] is whether that offering is the best way to solve the company's present problems and the best way to take advantage of its present opportunities. In other words, having considered all the other alternatives for raising capital and gaining liquidity, is this the right solution at the time?*
>
> *After that we next look at the company's management. Are they proven? Do they have a good track record? Is the company selling mostly new stock or is there a risk of a bailout [in other words, do the original owners plan to sell their stock]? There must be a good earnings record, or at a minimum, great expectations of such record.*[2]

Underwriting

Investment bankers also provide an underwriting service. Most people think of underwriting as the exclusive province of insurance companies. But it has its place on Wall Street too. Investment bankers **underwrite**, or guarantee, the price of the new stock to the issuing corporation. In doing so, they bear the risk that the public may be unwilling to buy all the stock at the asking price. For that reason, they are often referred to as underwriters.

Underwriting transfers the uncertainty about the success of the new issue from the firm making the offering to the investment banker. Once an investment banker agrees to underwrite an issue, the firm knows it has the full amount of money, less the underwriter's fees, of course. Underwriting fees average about 3% of large issues and perhaps as much as 10 to 20% or more on small issues.

Selling

The final step in the investment banking process involves the sale of the securities to the public. For large issues, investment bankers usually form temporary coalitions, or **syndicates.** Each of the investment bankers in the syndicate agrees to underwrite and/or sell a specific number of shares to the public. By spreading the risks this way, the investment bankers obtain a better market distribution and reduce their individual risks.

REGULATION OF NEW ISSUES

The great stock market crash of 1929 and the backbreaking depression which soon followed ruined many investors. Outraged by its enormous losses, the public demanded a congressional investigation of the securities industry. Congress and the new administration responded vigorously. The Senate Committee on Banking and Currency collected 11 volumes of testimony and evidence relating to fraud, manipulation, and embezzlement in stocks—a virtual "parade of horribles."

In an effort to cleanse the markets of some of these defects, Congress passed the **Securities Act of 1933**. The Securities Act of 1933—often referred to as the **Truth in Securities Act**—is designed primarily to ensure that prospective investors in new issues receive adequate information. It requires issuers and their underwriters to file registration statements with the SEC before making a public distribution of securities. And prospective purchasers of the new issue must be provided with a prospectus describing the issuer and the securities.

Over the years the **registration statement** has become longer and longer. It includes details on the company issuing the securities, its **capitalization** (the total amount of money invested in the business), its officers and directors, the purpose of the financing, the terms of the underwriting, and a wide assortment of financial statements and legal agreements. Few investors ever see the entire registration statement, which is filed with the Securities and Exchange Commission. Instead, potential investors receive a **prospectus** consisting of the first part of the registration statement. According to *Webster's Eighth New Collegiate Dictionary* the word "prospect" implies "an extensive view." The prospectus conveys "a mental picture of something to come."

By law, at least 20 days must pass between the filing of the registration statement and the sale of new securities. During this waiting period, the staff at the SEC carefully reviews all the required documents to ensure their accuracy and completeness. At the same time, the company and its underwriters often provide interested investors with a **red herring**, or preliminary prospectus.

Why the name "red herring?" Some writers claim it refers to the warning printed in red ink on the front page of the preliminary prospectus. The SEC requires the following declaration:

> *A registration statement relating to these securities has been filed with the Securities and Exchange Commission but has not yet become effective. Information contained herein subject to completion or amendment. These securities may not be sold nor may offers to buy be accepted prior to the time the registration statement becomes effective.*

Other sources more familiar with Wall Street say the red herring refers to the old practice of drawing a red herring across a trail to confuse hunting dogs. Apparently some of the prospectuses published during the infancy of the SEC actually served to distract attention from the real facts about the new issue.

If the registration statement receives SEC approval, the actual prospectus, usually identical with the preliminary one except for the addition of the offering price, goes to the public. Every buyer of new securities must receive this prospectus.

The Truth in Securities Act imposes large costs on issuers of new securities.

In order to avoid placing an unfair burden on small companies, the SEC exempts certain issues from registration and prospectus requirements. A simplified registration procedure applies to issues of $500,000 or less. The issuers need to provide buyers with only a brief circular describing the offering instead of a detailed prospectus. **Intrastate issues** (new issues sold within the boundaries of a single state) also qualify for exemptions, as do **private offerings** (issues not sold to the general public) and securities offered by the federal, state, and local governments.

CONTROLLING THE CORPORATION

Ninety people expressed their confidence in Sally's, Inc., by purchasing shares. Each of these stockholders owns a fractional interest in the company and its profits and therefore has a say-so in its operations. But imagine 90 owners voting on every action the corporation takes. Just getting the bills paid would take months. So shareholders of every corporation elect a **board of directors** to oversee the company's activities and to represent their interests. Although the rules for electing directors differ from corporation to corporation, most companies give their shareholders one vote for each share of stock owned. The directors then select officers to manage the everyday operations of the firm. (Nothing prevents the officers from also serving as directors, and many do.) The chain of command in corporations is illustrated in Figure 1-2.

At General Electric, shareholders elect a total of 18 directors. General

FIGURE 1-2   Chain of command in corporations.

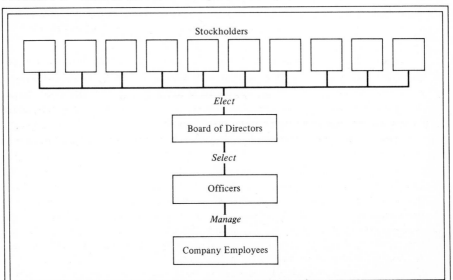

Motors has 24 directors. Smaller firms usually have fewer directors. Sally's, Inc., has only 4. Sally and her father invested a total of $30,000 in the company's shares; so they own 3,000 of its 10,000 shares. With 30% ownership of the firm, they are almost certain to control the election of the directors. Sally, her father, and two close friends all campaign for the director's positions. They run unopposed and win by a margin of 9,000 votes to 5, with the 5 votes going to a write-in candidate one of the shareholders jokingly added to his ballot.

Annual Meetings

The directors of Sally's, or of any other corporation, meet periodically—perhaps once every month or every 3 months. And they are called into session whenever a matter of crucial importance arises. In addition, the directors conduct an **annual meeting** every year for the purpose of electing directors and making a report to the shareholders. Annual meetings seldom attract a very large crowd, even though they are open to all shareholders.

The annual meeting symbolizes corporate democracy in action. John Brooks, a financial writer for *The New Yorker,* tells of his own experience with meetings in the "Stockholder Season":

> *Leafing through some papers on the plane going out there [Detroit], I learned that the number of AT&T stockholders had increased to an all-time record of almost three million, and I fell to wondering what would happen in the unlikely event that all of them, or even one-half, appeared in Detroit and demanded seats at the meeting. At any rate, each one of them had received by mail, a few weeks earlier, a notice of the meeting along with a formal invitation to attend. . . . My fears on the first score were put to rest when I got to Cobo Hall, a huge riverfront auditorium, where the meeting was to take place. The hall was far from filled: the Yankees in their better days would have been disgusted with such a turnout on any weekday afternoon. (The papers next day said the attendance was four thousand and sixteen.)*[3]

But the 4,016 included a very vocal minority. Probably much to the dismay of management, several professional stockholders, including Wilma Soss and Lewis Gilbert, both of New York, appeared at the meeting. **Professional stockholders** like these two devote their full time to buying stock in companies, often only a few shares, and attending annual meetings to ask piercing questions and/or propose resolutions. Brooks describes the role of the professional stockholder as follows:

> *Something I did not know, and learned at the AT&T meeting (and at others I attended subsequently), was that, apart from the prepared speeches of management, a good many big company meetings really consist of a dialogue—in some cases it's more of a duel—between the chairman and the few professional stockholders. The contributions of non-professionals run strongly to ill-informed or tame questions and windy encomiums of management, and thus the task of making cogent criticisms or asking embarrassing questions falls to the professionals. Though largely self-appointed, they become, by default, the sole representation of a huge constituency that may badly need representing.*[4]

Soss and Gilbert take their self-appointed tasks seriously enough to have gained recognition in *Who's Who in America.* They made themselves heard in Cobo Hall that night. According to the official report of the meeting,

> *The greater portion of the discussion period was taken up by questions and statements of a few individuals on matters that can scarcely be deemed relevant. . . . Two individuals interrupted the opening statement of the chairman. . . . The chairman advised the individuals who had interrupted to choose between ceasing their interruption or leaving the meeting.*

Apparently most of the shareholders present at the AT&T meeting heartily wished the professional shareholders had stayed in New York. A Detroit shareholder concluded the night's comments by telling AT&T, "I hope you won't let the abuse you've been subjected to by a few malcontents keep you from bringing the meeting to the great Midwest again!"

Proxies

Small attendance does not necessarily mean lack of interest. Most shareholders mail in proxies rather than attend in person. A **proxy** is a signed slip of paper authorizing a particular person or group of persons to act on the shareholder's behalf. One example of a proxy is shown in Figure 1-3. In this case, the shareholder casts votes for the directors and for the selection of an independent public accounting firm and grants management the right to vote his or her shares on any other matters which may be raised at the annual meeting.

FIGURE 1-3   Sample proxy. (Reprinted with permission of Trans World Airlines, Inc.)

PROXY   **TRANS WORLD AIRLINES, INC.**

FOR COMMON STOCK   ANNUAL MEETING OF STOCKHOLDERS, APRIL 27, 1977

The undersigned hereby appoints L. EDWIN SMART, CHARLES N. KIMBALL and C. E. MEYER, JR., proxies, with power of substitution, to vote at the Annual Meeting (including adjournments) of stockholders of TRANS WORLD AIRLINES, INC., to be held April 27, 1977, with all powers the undersigned would possess if personally present, as specified on the ballot below on the election of directors, on the proposal set forth and on any other business that may come before the meeting.

ELECTION OF DIRECTORS: ☐ For   ☐ Refrain from voting
Management recommends a
vote FOR:

PROPOSAL: The proposal to approve the selection by the Board
Management recommends a   of Directors of Messrs. Haskins & Sells as the
vote FOR: principal independent public accountants.

                                 ☐ For   ☐ Against

Unless a contrary specification is made, this proxy is to be voted FOR the election of directors and FOR the proposal above.

This proxy is solicited on behalf of the Management.

REWARDS TO OWNING STOCKS

At the end of the first year of operations, the officers of Sally's, Inc., sit down and prepare the **annual report.** Nowadays most large companies provide their shareholders with glossy, picture-packed reports. But Sally's, Inc., sends only a two-page summary of operations to its shareholders. It includes a short letter from the president of the company, Sally Smith, as well as an income statement and balance sheet. With only 90 shareholders, a more detailed description would be a waste of money.

The annual report includes a balance sheet and income statement. The company's **balance sheet** lists the **assets** (what is owned) and **liabilities** (what is owed) of the corporation. It also shows the stockholders' equity, i.e., the amount of money the owners have contributed to the operation of the company. The **income statement** measures the company's economic performance. The word **income** refers to the difference between sales and expenses. Sales at Sally's totaled $200,000 the first year, and expenses amounted to $175,000; so profits equaled $25,000.

This $25,000 profit belongs to the shareholders, who partake in any profit in the same proportion as they own shares. Sally owns 1,000 shares, or one-tenth, of the company's shares; so she is entitled to one-tenth of the company's profits, plus her salary as an officer. Bob Clark owns only 5 shares; so his portion comes to five ten-thousandths, a tiny fraction of the profits. Since the firm has a total of 10,000 shares outstanding, the company's **earnings per share** equal $2.50; i.e.,

$$\frac{\$25,000 \text{ earnings of company}}{10,000 \text{ shares outstanding}} = \$2.50 \text{ earnings per share}$$

Dividends

Very few companies pay out all their earnings to their stockholders, and Sally's is no exception. Most of the profits must be retained in the form of increased inventories, equipment, accounts receivable, etc. Just because a company makes a $25,000 profit does not mean it has $25,000 lying around in idle cash.

The board of directors of a company always decides how much of the profits to distribute to shareholders as **dividends** and how much to retain. The directors of Sally's, Inc., vote to pay a year-end dividend of 20¢ on each share of stock, a total dividend of $2,000. So, for each share the owner receives 20¢ in cash. For example, a person holding 60 shares collects $12.

Companies follow a standard procedure in paying dividends. First, the directors meet and declare a dividend. Unlike Sally's, most companies pay dividends every 3 months rather than just once a year. Then the company prepares a final list of its stockholders on the **holder-of-record date.** Only stockholders on this list receive a dividend check.

But the holder-of-record date is not the real cutoff date for receiving a dividend. There are always delays in registering new shareholders on the company's books and in removing the names of the old shareholders. In order to avoid any confusion about who receives the upcoming dividend, the investment community has established a simple rule. Anyone buying stock more than 4 days before the holder-of-record date receives the dividend. On the fourth day before the holder-of-record date the stock goes **ex-dividend,** meaning it sells without the right to the dividend. Anyone buying the stock on or after this **ex-dividend date** misses the forthcoming dividend.

> EXAMPLE   After deciding upon the dividend, the directors of a large company often release a formal statement to the financial press. Typically the notice says something like, "The board of directors has this day declared a quarterly dividend of 25¢ per share on the common stock, payable September 30, 1978, to shareholders of record September 14, 1978."
>
> In this case the **payment date** is September 30, 1978, and the holder-of-record date is September 14. But the ex-dividend date is September 10. So anyone who wants to receive the dividend must buy the stock no later than September 9. By the way, stock prices usually drop by the full amount of the dividend on the ex-dividend date. And for good reason. Investors buying shares on or after that date no longer receive the dividend.

Very few companies pay a dividend in the first year of their operations. Either they lose money or their rapid growth makes them "cash poor." In other words, all their money goes into the purchase of additional supplies and equipment. Sally's, Inc., pays a token dividend because many of its small shareholders expect some cash return.

Dividends versus Appreciation

Most of the shareholders receive the annual report and the notice of the dividend with enthusiasm. But one elderly lady calls and "demands" to speak to the president.

"I just got your report in the mail, Sally, and I must say I am very disappointed," the woman says. "Apparently you and the other directors don't know very much about money. This 20¢ dividend amounts to a return of only 2% on my investment of $10. My bank pays me much more than that! And I know my money is safe with them!"

Sally hesitates for a moment, wondering how to explain the world of high finance in one easy lesson. "Mrs. Nelson, your stocks are very different from a bank account," she says slowly. "The banker always pays you the full amount your deposit earns. Right now, if you have a long-term bank deposit, you are probably making 7 to 8%.

"But most firms reinvest part of their profits. These reinvested profits are called **retained earnings.**

"Now the important figure for you to look at with stocks is the company's profit. At Sally's, Inc., we earned a profit of $2.50 on each share."

There is a long pause at the other end of the phone, and then Mrs. Nelson says, "That all sounds very well and good. But I don't see any $2.50 sitting here in my hand. All I see is a check for 20¢!"

"Mrs. Nelson," Sally replies patiently, "you really get two returns from owning stock. One is in the form of cash dividends. The other is **appreciation**—an increase on the market price of the stock. By reinvesting most of our company's earnings, we are providing for a more profitable future and eventually much larger cash dividends. This usually causes stock prices to increase. Look at McDonald's. Until recently they paid absolutely no dividends, but the stock has made many people millionaires by going up in value."

"Well now, that sounds pretty good," exclaims Mrs. Nelson. "If I can make a million dollars, I don't mind these small dividends!"

Sally groans. "I just want to remind you," she continues, "that stock prices do not travel on one-way streets. They go down in value as well as up."

EXAMPLE   Sally's explanation of dividends and appreciation also applies to Texas Instruments and other corporations. In 1975 profits at TI totaled $62,142,000. With 22,925,089 shares outstanding, the earnings per share equaled $2.71. TI paid a dividend of $1 in 1975. It retained the other $1.71.

The **current yield** on any investment equals the cash income received during the year divided by the price of the investment. On December 31, 1975, one share of TI sold for $95; so the current yield equaled about 1% ($1 divided by $95).

Why buy Texas Instruments? Primarily for possible appreciation in the value of the shares and secondly because of current dividends.

Stock Dividends

How do companies satisfy the Mrs. Nelsons of the world? Most companies adopt reasonably stable dividend policies. In that way firms paying high dividends attract an income-oriented clientele, and those paying no or low dividends attract investors seeking appreciation. A sample of high- and low-dividend-paying stocks, together with their current yields, is shown in Table 1-2.

Some firms try to pacify both groups of investors by paying **stock dividends.** With a stock dividend, the firm distributes additional shares of stock rather than cash. For example, the board of directors of a company might declare a stock dividend of 10% and then give the shareholders 1 new share for every 10 they already own. That way the shareholders get a dividend and the company retains the earnings.

This financial sleight of hand appeals to some people. But it in no way benefits the stockholders. Even though they own more shares after the stock dividend, the total market value of all the shares remains the same. Therefore, the stockholders still own the same average percentage of the company and its prof-

TABLE 1-2   STOCKS PAYING HIGH AND LOW DIVIDENDS*

Company	Annual Dividend, $	Stock Price, $	Current Yield, %
High Dividends			
American Can	2.40	39.25	6.1
Household Finance	1.20	20.50	5.9
Royal Dutch Petroleum	3.26	52.50	6.2
Texaco	2.00	27.88	7.2
Foremost-McKesson	1.00	15.75	6.3
Low Dividends			
Houston Natural Gas	0.70	33.25	2.1
Kresge	0.32	39.13	0.8
Smith International	0.52	37.25	1.4
Texas Instruments	1.00	97.88	1.0
Hewlett Packard	0.30	82.50	0.4

* Dividends paid during 1976. Stock prices as of January 11, 1977.

its. And the stock dividend in no way affects the basic characteristics of the firm—there is no change in the amount of cash it holds or its plant and equipment or its sales, etc.

A **stock split** closely resembles a stock dividend. But a stock split usually involves the issuance of more new shares than a stock dividend. Many investors view a distribution of stock totaling less than 25% of the already existing shares as a stock dividend. A distribution involving 25% or more of the outstanding shares qualifies as a stock split.

Companies split their stocks in order to provide a broader market for their shares. Take the case of Dow Chemicals, for example. Because of the company's consistent profitability, the stock climbed to more than $100 in 1976. Dow then declared a 2 for 1 split and exchanged 2 new shares for every 1 old share. (In the case of a split, the company exchanges new shares with a lower par value for the old shares. In the case of a stock dividend, the shareholders simply receive additional shares with the same par value.)

What is the effect of a stock split? Probably not much. Are two $50 bills better than a $100 bill? Of course not. By the same token, a stock split simply divides the fixed value of the company into a larger number of lower-priced shares. Suppose the directors of a company with a total market value of $100 million and with 1 million shares outstanding declare a 2 for 1 stock split. As a result, every shareholder receives 1 additional share for each share already owned. Now there are 2 million shares outstanding. With the total market value of the firm unchanged, share prices fall from $100 to $50. Are two $50 shares better than a $100 share? Apparently some investors and managers think so.

KEYWORDS

sole proprietorships
partnership
corporation
articles of incorporation
authorized shares
incorporators
charter
legal entity
limited liability
double taxation
cash budget
capital
securities
bond
common stock
equity
shares outstanding
stock certificate

registers
par value
investment bankers
underwrite
syndicates
Securities Act of 1933
Truth in Securities Act
registration statement
capitalization
prospectus
red herring
intrastate issues
private offerings
board of directors
annual meeting
professional stockholders
proxy

annual report
balance sheet
assets
liabilities
income statement
income
earnings per share
dividends
holder-of-record date
ex-dividend
ex-dividend date
payment date
retained earnings
appreciation
current yield
stock dividends
stock split

QUESTIONS

1 Describe the role of the corporation in the American economy.
2 Discuss the possible reasons for the success of companies like McDonald's and Texas Instruments. How did the shareholders in these companies fare?
3 Each year entrepreneurs start hundreds of thousands of new businesses. What steps do they take in creating these firms?
4 What are the advantages of a corporation compared with a partnership or sole proprietorship? What about the disadvantages?
5 What services do investment bankers provide to corporations? Why do corporations use these services?
6 What are the major provisions of the Securities Act of 1933?
7 Are all new issues of securities subject to the Securities Act of 1933?
8 Do securities regulations eliminate losses from fraud?
9 Do professional stockholders serve any useful purpose? Should shareholders take a more active role in the management of corporations?
10 Explain the corporate procedure for paying dividends to shareholders, beginning with the initial declaration and ending with the actual payment.
11 Do most corporations pay out all their earnings to shareholders? Why or why not?
12 Tru-Tone, Inc., a manufacturer of stereo systems, earned $2 million last year. It paid $1 million in dividends to shareholders. There are 600,000 shares outstanding, and shares sold for $20 each at the end of the year. What are the earnings per share, dividends per share, and current yield?
13 Do shareholders benefit from stock dividends? Explain why or why not.

REFERENCES

Baumol, William J.: *The Stock Market and Economic Efficiency,* Fordham, New York, 1965.

*Brooks, John: *Business Adventures,* Weybright and Talley, New York, 1969.

"The Burger That Conquered the Country," *Time,* Sept. 17, 1973, pp. 84–86, 89–90, 92–93.

Corley, Robert N., and Robert L. Black: *The Legal Environment of Business,* 3d ed., McGraw-Hill, New York, 1973.

*Engel, Louis: *How to Buy Stocks,* 5th ed., Bantam, New York, 1972.

How to Read a Financial Report, 4th ed., Merrill Lynch, Pierce, Fenner & Smith, New York, 1973.

Klein, Frederick C.: "The Middle Men: As New Stock Issues Increase, Underwriters Scramble for Business," *The Wall Street Journal,* Apr. 18, 1972, pp. 1, 32.

Manne, Henry G., et al.: *Wall Street in Transition: The Emerging System and Its Impact on the Economy,* New York University Press, New York, 1974.

Mason, Edward S.: "Corporation," in *International Encyclopedia of the Social Sciences,* vol. 3, Macmillan, New York, 1968.

The New York Stock Exchange: 1976 Fact Book, New York Stock Exchange, 1976.

The Specialist: Key Man in the Exchange Market, New York Stock Exchange, 1973.

West, Richard R., and Seha M. Tinic: *The Economics of the Stock Market,* Praeger, New York, 1971.

White, Shelby: "The New Central Market Place: The Debate Goes On," *Institutional Investor,* August 1976, pp. 30–31.

Winter, Elmer L.: *Complete Guide to Making a Public Stock Offering,* 2d ed., Prentice-Hall, Englewood Cliffs, N.J., 1972.

Investments textbooks also provide an abundance of material on stocks and other assorted topics. Four of the most widely used texts are:

Christy, George A., and John C. Clendenin: *Introduction to Investments,* 6th ed., McGraw-Hill, New York, 1974.

Cohen, Jerome B., Edward D. Zinbarg, and Arthur Zeikel: *Investment Analysis and Portfolio Management,* 3d ed., Irwin, Homewood, Ill., 1977.

D'Ambrosio, Charles A.: *Principles of Modern Investments,* Science Research Associates, Chicago, 1976.

Francis, Jack Clark: *Investments Analysis and Management,* 2d ed., McGraw-Hill, New York, 1976.

* Publications preceded by an asterisk are highly recommended.

CHAPTER TWO

BUYING AND SELLING STOCKS

John Brooks, writing in *The New Yorker* magazine, aptly described the stock market as the "daytime adventure serial of the well-to-do."[1] Aside from its entertainment value, the stock market serves two important economic functions. First, it offers a ready outlet for existing shares of stock. Second, it provides price signals which help allocate the country's **real capital** resources—its factories, machinery and equipment, natural resources, and other long-lived assets.

Firms seldom repurchase their shares; so without a stock market, investors would presumably have to marry themselves to the stocks they purchased, for better or worse, until the end of time. Instead, prospective buyers and existing shareholders simply transact with each other in the stock market, where a share can be bought or sold on a moment's notice. This makes it possible to mesh the short-term investment goals of the public with the long-term capital requirements of companies. In the words of William Baumol, a past member of the President's Council of Economic Advisers, "The market performs an act of magic, for it permits long-term investments to be financed by funds provided by individuals, many of whom wish to make them available for only a very limited period, or who wish to be able to withdraw them at will."[2] Without this "act of magic," funds for long-term investments would be extremely difficult to raise and the economy would suffer.

The stock market also aids in the distribution of real capital. The stock market is a **secondary market,** meaning that only shares already in existence change owners. So money does not flow directly from the stock market into the hands of people buying factories and other capital goods, but the prices set in the stock market largely determine the terms and conditions in **primary markets,** like the new-issue market, where investors deal directly with the ultimate users of funds.

NEW YORK STOCK EXCHANGE

At 10 A.M. on most weekdays a bell rings announcing the opening of the world's largest auction market—the **New York Stock Exchange.** By the time trading ends 6 hours later, close to $1 billion of shares in America's largest corporations has usually exchanged hands.

The New York Stock Exchange (NYSE) traces its ancestry back almost 200 years. In 1792 a group of merchants met under a Buttonwood tree near Wall Street and signed what turned out to be an incredibly long-lasting agreement. These merchants agreed to trade only among themselves and to always charge identical commission rates. In 1817 the group adopted a constitution and the name New York Stock & Exchange Board. Thirteen years later, on March 16, 1830, the group celebrated "the dullest day in the history of the Exchange"—only 31 shares traded. Afterward business grew steadily, and by 1886 the exchange had experienced its first million-share day.

Daily Auction

Today the daily auction at the NYSE takes place in a large building on the corner of Wall and Broad Streets in lower Manhattan. Inside, the sightseer finds an enormous trading room, almost the size of a football field, with 50-foot-high ceilings. Scattered about the floor of this room are a number of horseshoe-shaped counters called **trading posts.** Every post serves as the exclusive trading area for about 75 stocks. For example, RCA always trades at post 12. Above each of the counters small signs carry the names and current prices of the different companies. A diagram of the exchange floor is shown in Figure 2-1.

Customers' orders come into the exchange via the telephones and teletypes located in special booths along the edge of the trading floor. These booths are staffed by clerks employed by the various brokerage firms. Once an order reaches a booth, the clerk notifies a floor broker. The floor broker then takes the order and walks toward a specific trading post.

If the order covers General Motors, the broker goes to post 4. Arriving at the exact position along the counter where GM trades, the broker inquires in a noncommittal way, "How's GM?" One of the other brokers in the crowd may

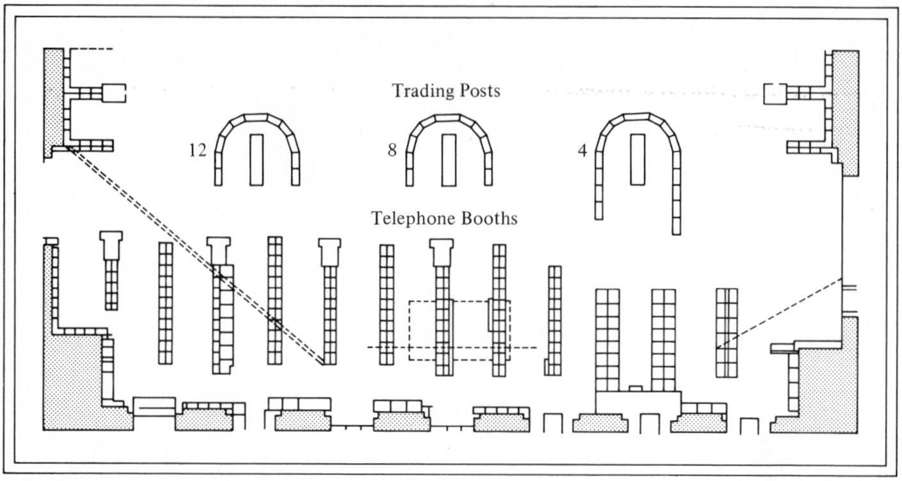

FIGURE 2-1   Floor of the New York Stock Exchange. (From Louis Engel, *How To Buy Stocks,* 5th ed., Bantam, New York, 1972, p. 65.)

answer, "Seventy and one-quarter to seventy and one-half," meaning someone wants to buy GM at $70^1/_4$ and someone else wants to sell at $70^1/_2$. Then the broker with the buy order makes an offer, saying, "Three-eighths for 100," meaning $70^3/_8$ per share for 100 shares. If someone replies "sold," the deal is completed solely on a word-of-mouth basis.

An exchange employee called a **reporter** immediately records the details of the transaction on a precoded card and feeds it into an **optical scanner.** This electronic reading device deserves a place in the *Guinness Book of World Records*—it can "read" the New York City phone book in less than 3 minutes. The scanner transmits the information on the card to a computer, which in turn relays it to investors across the country.

The **continuous trading** action on the exchange floor sets the NYSE apart from most auctions. Prospective buyers and sellers experience almost immediate execution of their orders rather than having to wait for an auctioneer to call off items one by one. Inveterate auctiongoers know how time-consuming and tedious the usual "call process" can be.

But continuous trading imposes heavy information costs on any market. The NYSE has reduced these costs by:

1 Imposing strict rules and procedures to eliminate confusion. For example, identical bids for a stock are always resolved by tossing a coin. And only members of the exchange and its employees are allowed on the trading floor.
2 Establishing trading posts, which in effect make the exchange a multi-auction. As a result, anyone transacting in a particular stock knows exactly where to find other interested parties.
3 Permitting only **listed stocks** to trade on the exchange. In order to list its

shares, a company must pay a fee and satisfy strict requirements concerning the number of shareholders, the number of shares outstanding, and earnings. Why impose these conditions? Because the NYSE wants to avoid inactively traded stocks.

4   Appointing a **specialist** in every listed stock. The specialist is a broker who makes a market in a specific stock. In other words, he or she provides a continuous market in a stock by stepping in and buying and selling for his or her own account whenever necessary.

5   Only allowing members of the NYSE to trade on the exchange. To some extent the NYSE resembles a very exclusive private club. Prospective members must first be approved by the Board of Governors of the exchange and then they must buy a **seat.** Back in 1793 the brokers actually occupied seats in the Tontine Coffee House. Now the word "seat" simply refers to a membership in the NYSE.

The Specialist

Because of the specialist, every buyer on the exchange finds a seller and vice versa. Suppose a floor broker arrives at post 12 with an offer to sell 100 shares of RCA. At the time, no one wants to buy RCA. So the specialist makes an offer, knowing the stock will eventually be resold, probably at a slight profit.

The specialist's activities in a stock usually ensure price continuity and liquidity. In other words, prices fluctuate very little from transaction to transaction, and investors can buy and sell at a moment's notice.

The specialist performs another service, functioning as a sort of "broker's broker" by executing orders for other brokers. Suppose a customer wants to buy 100 shares in XYZ when it drops to $18. The stock currently sells for $20. The customer's broker takes this order to the appropriate trading post. Rather than wait around for XYZ to drop to $18, the broker gives it to the specialist in XYZ. The specialist then enters the order in the **book,** a 4 × 11 inch loose-leaf binder. If XYZ ever falls to $18, the specialist buys the shares and collects a part of the other broker's commission.

The specialist serves as both a dealer—buying and selling for his or her own account—and a broker. A dealer attempts to profit from transactions with the public, while a broker strives to obtain the best prices for the public. Richard Ney, an investment adviser and author of the *Wall Street Jungle* and the *Wall Street Gang,* strikes out at this inherent conflict of interest. Studies by the U.S. Securities and Exchange Commission and congressional committees also comment upon the difficulty of "wearing two very different hats" at the same time.

Odd Lots

The NYSE and most of the other exchanges trade orders only in **round lots,** i.e., orders for 100 shares or a multiple of 100 shares. Any order for less than 100 shares, usually called an **odd lot,** must be bought or sold off the floor of the exchange.

Suppose an investor wants to buy five shares of AT&T. The broker relays the order to an **odd-lot dealer,** a firm specializing in the purchase and sale of odd lots. At the present time only SIAC (Securities Industrial Automation Corporation) performs this service on the NYSE. It may fill this order simply by selling the customer 5 of its own shares of AT&T, or it may actually buy 100 shares of AT&T on the floor of the exchange and sell 5 to the small investor, while keeping the other 95 for future sale. Odd-lot orders are always stamped with the time of receipt and filled at the same price as the next round-lot transaction executed on the exchange.

The odd-lot buyer or seller pays the odd-lot dealer a fee of 12.5¢ for every share priced at $50 or less. The fee for shares priced over $50 is 25¢ per share. Carlisle, DeCoppet adds this fee to the purchase price of the share and subtracts it from the sale price. So if an investor buys one share for $40, the amount actually paid is $40.125. If one share is sold for $40, the investor receives only $39.875.

OVER-THE-COUNTER MARKET

The New York Stock Exchange, the so-called Big Board, dominates exchange trading. The American Stock Exchange (AMEX), located only blocks away from the NYSE, comes in a distant second. And until recently regional markets like the Midwest, Pacific, Philadelphia, Boston, and Cincinnati Stock Exchanges traded only a tiny fraction of the volume of the NYSE or AMEX.

Not all shares trade on organized exchanges. At the end of 1976 more than 40,000 companies, ranging in size from only a few thousand dollars in sales to financial giants like American Express, traded in the **over-the-counter market** (OTC). Unlike the exchanges, the OTC market possesses no central location. Instead, a loose-knit network of telephones and teletypes connects numerous dealers who stand ready to buy and sell shares in specific stocks. In the old days, they actually bought and sold share certificates over the counter. Now a broker simply calls a dealer and places an order.

By the way, a dealer in securities is often called a wholesaler or market maker, whereas a broker is referred to as a retailer. Why the distinction? Because the broker sells directly to the ultimate consumer, the investor. On the other hand, the dealer serves as an intermediary and sells to brokers. To make matters still more confusing, some brokers also act as dealers and vice versa.

Richard West, an expert on the stock market and dean of Dartmouth's School of Business, describes the OTC market as follows:

Among the factors responsible for shaping the over-the-counter market's character and distinguishing it from that of the exchanges, the most important is freedom of access and behavior.

*The securities traded in the over-the-counter market do not have to meet any listing require-
ments. Nor is it necessary for those who perform the broker and dealer functions to buy a seat
or in some analogous way obtain formal entry to the market place. Anyone with a telephone,
some capital, a measure of intestinal fortitude and a registration with the Securities and Exchange Commission is free to become a participant in the over-the-counter market.*[3]

NASDAQ

For years the OTC market labored under an antiquated communications system.
Brokers often had to call as many as 10 or more dealers to get quotes on OTC
issues. But in 1971 **NASDAQ,** the National Association of Securities Dealers
Automated Quotations System, thrust Wall Street into the space age. Now, anyone interested in an OTC issue simply pushes a button to obtain a visual display
of dealers and their bid-and-asked prices.

How does NASDAQ work? It consists of a sophisticated communications
network designed around two large computers. According to Lawrence Armour,
a writer for *Barron's,* these computers are housed in a "fortress-like complex" in
Connecticut and linked by "30,000 miles of high-speed transmission lines" to
other computers located around the country. Thousands of brokerage offices and
security dealers are in turn tied into these communication channels.

Subscribers to the NASDAQ service rent three basic systems. Armour
described them as follows:

*Level I, the simplest, is designed for the customers' man [securities salesman] who merely
wants to quote an OTC issue; by pushing the proper buttons on his desk-top interrogator, the
rep gets a TV screen read-out of the median bid and asked price for any issue in the system.
Level II, which is designed for OTC retailers, provides a visual picture of the bid and asked
prices of the firms making markets in a particular issue. Level III, designed for the market
makers themselves, has an extra keyboard attachment which enables traders to change their
quotes as conditions dictate.*[4]

STOCK MARKET OF TOMORROW

Technology has a way of eroding time-honored traditions and humbling the most
powerful of institutions. Even the New York Stock Exchange—a symbol of
power and tradition—may soon be steamrollered by progress.

The price of a seat on the exchange reflects this possibility—it fell from a
40-year high of $515,000 in 1969 to about $70,000 in 1976. Why the sudden
doubts about the Big Board's ability to survive in its present form? There are primarily three reasons:

1   The increasing importance of institutional investors relative to individual investors

2   The more active role of the government in promoting competition in the se-
    curities market
3   The development of extremely sophisticated computers and high-speed com-
    munications systems

Institutional Investors

To some extent the decline of the NYSE coincides with the increasing strength of
institutional investors like mutual funds, pension funds, bank trust departments, and insurance companies. At the start of the sixties these institutions accounted for only 15 to 20% of all trading in NYSE listed stocks. Now they dominate the market, placing nearly 70% of all orders (in terms of value).

Many of these institutions count their assets in the billions of dollars. Unlike
most individuals, they often buy and sell **blocks** of 10,000 or more shares. The
growth in this block trading created problems for the NYSE. From its founding
in 1792 until 1975 the Big Board rigidly adhered to fixed commissions. As a result, institutions found themselves paying the same price per share as a small investor, even though their enormous orders should have been much more eco-
nomical to execute.

Dissatisfied by this state of affairs, some of the institutions helped create a
third market. The so-called third market is actually an over-the-counter market
for stocks listed on the exchanges, predominately those on the NYSE. Firms like
Weeden and Company make markets in many of these listed stocks. They also act
as agents in matching the orders of different institutions. By transacting in the
third market, institutions sometimes save as much as 75% of the commissions
charged by the exchanges.

But price is not the only reason institutions use the third market. According
to Donald Weeden, the third market possesses another advantage over the
specialist-dominated exchanges. Weeden says, "The hard truth is that the economic interests of the institutional investor are better served by a negotiated
market than by an auction market. The institutional investor prefers to control
his own order; he wants direct access to the market makers."[5] Weeden is essentially saying that the continuous auction process is not consistent with block
trading by institutions. Instead, the only way to satisfy a big seller is to find a big
buyer. The third market satisfies this need.

Although the third market caters primarily to institutions, thousands of
broker-dealers who are not members of any exchange also use the market. By
doing so, they are often able to offer their customers lower commissions than
they pay to members of the exchange.

Some institutions liked the third market concept so much that they decided
to carry it one step further to a **fourth market,** a market of direct trades. In this
market securities are bought and sold directly without the use of a broker or a
dealer.

Competition and Technology

Brokerage firms nicknamed May 1, 1975, "Mayday"—the international distress signal. On that date the exchanges, under tremendous pressure from the SEC, the courts, and the Justice Department, eliminated fixed commission rates. The switch to competitive rates ended nearly 2 centuries of price fixing, begun with the signing of the Buttonwood Agreement in 1792. Despite predictions of widespread bankruptcy among member firms and chaotic market situations, the transition occurred smoothly.

The Buttonwood Agreement signed by the original members of the NYSE included another monopolistic device. The original founders agreed to trade only among themselves. Now the government wants to eliminate barriers to competition and promote a **central marketplace**—a national market system open to all investors, dealers, and brokers.

The first step toward a central marketplace was the implementation of a **composite tape** which reports all transactions in listed securities, regardless of their place of execution.

The second step will be the establishment of a **composite-quotation system.** This quotation system (probably somewhat similar to NASDAQ) will make it possible to immediately communicate all bids and offers on exchange-listed stocks throughout the country.

The composite-quotation system frightens many members of the NYSE. In their worst dreams they see Wall Street swallowed by a giant computer. And if the government has its way, their dreams may come true. Who needs an exchange floor when one can communicate electronically? Moreover the SEC wants to include a **consolidated limit-order book** in the system. No doubt this centralized, computerized depository for all limit orders would eliminate the specialist.

Other changes envisioned by the government include the development of a more efficient mechanism for transferring stock certificates and a thorough review and revision of regulations governing all participants in all securities markets.

The central marketplace has some obvious virtues and some very vague costs. As Gustave Levy, former chairman of the board of the New York Stock Exchange and a senior partner of a prestigious investment banking and brokerage firm says: "This central market system idea is like motherhood. No one can be, or is, against it. On the other hand, no one has defined exactly what it is, what it will cost, and who will pay for it." [6]

OPENING AN ACCOUNT

Suppose you want to become a part owner in General Motors, IBM, McDonald's, or some other company. How do you buy shares?

First, you contact a stockbroker. Turning to the Yellow Pages of the phone book and looking under "stockbrokers," you will find dozens of names like Bache

Halsey and Stuart, Dean Witter, A. G. Edwards, E. F. Hutton, Kidder Peabody, Merrill Lynch, etc. These are just a few of the nearly 500 brokerage firms doing business in this country.

After narrowing the list to two or three firms, you call each brokerage house and talk to one of the company's **registered representatives,** or **account executives,** as these salespersons are frequently called. The first question almost always concerns the goals of the investor.

"Well," says the representative, "I am certainly glad you thought of our company. Just what are your investment plans?"

"I want to buy five shares of General Motors," you say eagerly.

There is a pause at the other end of the line as the representative digests this fact. Depending upon his or her personality and the policy of the brokerage firm, one of two things will happen next. Brokerage firms do not make money on small accounts. In fact, they often lose money. So registered reps at some brokerage firms either discourage small investors from opening an account or direct them into investments paying higher commissions and/or requiring less of the representative's time. Other brokerage firms recognize the fact that small accounts often grow into substantial sums of money and actively encourage the participation of small investors.

In this case the investor is in luck. After offering encouragement, the representative says, "As you probably know, you must open an account with our firm before you can buy or sell any stock. I will send you the necessary forms right away. Please sign them and return them as soon as possible. Then you can place your order for the GM stock."

Many beginning investors make their first mistake at this point. They simply say "Thank you" and sit back and wait for the forms to arrive in the mail. Given the close personal relationship between the broker and the client and the large sums of money involved, they would be better off arranging a personal interview. By meeting with the representative, the investor gets a much better idea of how the two of them will work together and a closeup view of the firm's facilities and method of operation.

Brokerage offices almost always look the same. They consist of a large open room, usually called a **boardroom,** filled with desks for the registered representatives. Letters and numbers describing the ups and downs of the stock market silently slide across the long, narrow sign on the front wall of each office. Whenever anyone buys or sells shares of a company listed on an exchange, the news of the transaction appears on this **tape.** By the way, the word "tape" is a holdover from the old days when brokerage offices all had paper tape rather than electronic displays.

Some of the letters and numbers moving across the tape are:

PRD   38   X 2s56   GM 8s70&M

To save time and space, the tape carries abbreviations instead of the full name of the company. PRD stands for Polaroid. One hundred shares just sold at $38 a share. The X represents U.S. Steel. Spectators can always tell the oldest and best-known companies by their symbols—they usually have only one letter. According to the tape, 200 shares of U.S. Steel just traded at $56 a share—the "2s" in front of the "56" indicates the volume. The next symbol always receives instant recognition. It is "GM" for General Motors, and 800 shares just sold at $70 a share. The "M" after the ampersand (&) indicates that the GM trade took place on the Midwest Stock Exchange rather than the NYSE.

TYPES OF ORDERS

Investors have a great deal of flexibility in placing their orders. If they simply instruct their broker to buy or sell shares at **market,** the order is executed almost immediately at the best price available.

Some investors use **limit orders** rather than market orders. For example, they might ask the broker to buy 100 shares of XYZ for $20 or less. With a limit order they know they will never pay more than the specified price. With a market order, they could theoretically end up paying almost any price.

Actually, stock prices seldom fluctuate by more than a fraction of a point during the few minutes required to fill a market order. But cautious investors prefer limit orders, especially in inactive securities. And they usually pay a lower price because of their willingness to wait. Of course, they also run the risk of letting the stock "get away" from them when the price moves past their limit.

Stop Orders

Stop orders gained a great deal of publicity with the publication of Nicholas Darvas' book *How I Made $2,000,000 in the Stock Market.* Darvas, a professional dancer turned speculator, claims to have made millions by employing stop-loss orders together with several other techniques.

A stop order is nothing more than a delayed market order. The broker is instructed to buy or sell the stock at market if it reaches a certain price. Suppose an investor owns 100 shares of XYZ purchased at $20. To guard against a substantial loss, the stockholder places a stop order to sell the stock at $18. This order remains in a state of suspended animation until XYZ drops to a market price of $18 or lower. When it does, the specialist executes the order at the market price.

Stop-loss orders sound very attractive. But investors delude themselves if they think stop-loss orders prevent losses. Stop-loss orders make sense only if stock prices move in one direction for long periods of time. Recent research on the behavior of stock prices indicates just the opposite—prices bounce up and down like a rubber ball. As a result, the investor is often "stopped" out of desirable stocks simply because of minor fluctuations and thus pays unnecessary commissions and perhaps extra taxes. Both of these topics are discussed in later chapters.

A stop-order-to-buy works on the same principle as a stop-order-to-sell. It remains suspended until the stock hits a specified price. For example, an individual might want to delay a purchase of XYZ until it moves up to $24, perhaps in the belief that this large increase indicates tremendous underlying strength in the stock. Whatever the reason, the person places a stop-order-to-buy at $24. Any move by the stock to $24 or above triggers the order to buy at the market price.

Time Orders

Market, limit, and stop orders all involve prices. The investor can also specify the period of time allowed for the execution of the order. Two of the usual options with respect to time are good for the day only and good-till-canceled. **Day orders** expire at the end of the trading day, whereas a **good-till-canceled order** remains on the books until canceled by the investor.

Brokers prefer good-till-canceled orders. With a day-only order they must keep asking the individual whether or not to submit the order again. And then they must contact their agent on the floor of the exchange. A good-till-canceled order eliminates these extra steps and saves the broker time and effort. It does the same for the investor but at a cost. Too many investors forget about their good-till-canceled orders. The surprise execution of one of these orders sometimes disrupts their financial plans. Or by then they no longer find the stock desirable.

Good-till-canceled orders suffer from another drawback. Important news about the market in general and about individual stocks often appears over the weekend or at night. Before the investor even finds out about this news, the good-till-canceled order gets executed because of the resulting movement in share prices.

Discretionary Orders

A **limited discretionary order** allows the broker to select the time, place, and price for the completion of a transaction. A **complete discretionary order** carries this freedom one step further and grants the broker the privilege of selecting even the stocks which are bought and sold.

Supposedly an investor using a discretionary order gains from the broker's experience. But the technique closely resembles giving a stranger a signed blank check. For this reason, investors should avoid the use of discretionary orders except under extraordinary circumstances.

SHORT SELLING

Probably no investment activity attracts more attention with less understanding than **short selling.** And with good reason, since short selling violates the everyday rules of common sense.

The short seller performs a seemingly impossible act, that of selling stock the *shortsell 3step Process* 1) BORROW 2) SELL 3) REPAY

person does not own. This sounds vaguely reminiscent of the activities of the fast-talking con artists who used to sell the Brooklyn Bridge. But there is an important difference. The investor selling stock short first arranges to borrow the shares, then sells the borrowed stock, and at some later date completes the transaction by buying the stock and replacing the borrowed shares. This is called covering a short sale.

What does the investor gain from this three-step process? A profit, if the price of the stock falls after the short sale. Suppose an individual sells short 100 shares of a stock at $20 a share. The stock then drops to $16 a share, where the investor buys it back. After the borrowed shares have been replaced, the gain on the short sale is:

$20 price of stock sold short
− 16 price paid to cover short sale
$ 4 profit on each share

The profit on each share equals the difference between the price received for the short sale and the price paid to cover the sale. The profit on the 100 shares totals $400.

Unlike ordinary investors, short sellers make money when prices decline and lose money when prices rise. For that reason, a prolonged increase in stock prices usually gives short sellers insomnia. Take the example of one brokerage firm. According to *The Wall Street Journal,* members of the firm sold short a substantial number of shares of Fairchild Camera at $50 a share. The stock immediately ascended to new highs. Instead of covering their short sale and taking their losses, the partners waited. When it hit $150 a share, the firm declared bankruptcy. They simply could not cover their short sales at these prices.

Short sellers must cover their sales or face the consequences. In the famous words of Daniel Drew: "He who sells what isn't his'n, must buy it back or go to prison." Drew is better known for his speculative exploits during the 1870s than for his poetry.

Drew probably coined his verse on short selling during a **short squeeze** in the Harlem Railroad. He and his associates sold short thousands of shares in the railroad, a predecessor of the New York Central. These forced sales, combined with rumors of impending failure, panicked many of the stockholders. Prices dropped substantially. But Commodore Vanderbilt bought every share sold and then some, obtaining a **corner** on the market in Harlem shares. Unable to deliver the shares they had sold, Drew's group finally surrendered to Vanderbilt's outrageous terms.

Partly because of the manipulations of men like Drew, short selling gained an unsavory reputation. Congressional investigations after the great stock-market crash of 1929 reinforced this view. One of the first rules enforced by the newly created Securities and Exchange Commission was the **uptick rule.**

Just how does the uptick rule work? Suppose an investor wants to sell short some shares. If the stock last sold for $30, the short sale can be executed only at $30^1/8$ or higher. By permitting short sales only on an uptick, i.e., an increase in price, the SEC makes it impossible for short sellers to drive prices lower and lower. There is one exception to this rule: If the most recent change was upward, the stock need not be sold at an increase in price. Suppose a number of trades have taken place at $30 a share, but the preceding price was $29³/₄. Then shares can be sold short on an "even tick" at $30. Obviously this exception to the rule still makes it impossible to drive prices lower by selling short.

Many people still view short selling as un-American. Apparently pessimism wins few followers. And short selling seems to serve no productive purpose. But, in reality, the short seller plays an important role in a properly functioning market. A report by a special study group of the SEC emphasizes the virtues of short selling:

> *The classic theory has held that short selling occurs when the market advances, thereby acting as a brake to the rise, and conversely, that the resulting covering transactions, which represent the only compulsory buying power in the market, take place as prices decline, and thus act as a cushion breaking the force of the decline.*[7]

Whatever the advantages or disadvantages, short selling represents only a tiny fraction of the total sales occurring on the exchange.

READING THE FINANCIAL PAGES   omit

Most investors keep track of their stocks by reading the financial pages of a newspaper. To the uninitiated, these pages appear about as meaningful as ancient hieroglyphics. A sample of stock quotations titled "NYSE-Composite Transactions" is shown in Figure 2-2. It summarizes all transactions in stocks listed on the New York Stock Exchange. The word "composite" indicates that orders executed on the NYSE, as well as on the regional exchanges, the over-the-counter market, and Instinet (a fourth market system), are included in these figures.

Stocks   There are three entries on the sample page referring to General Motors (abbreviated GnMot). Only the first refers to the common stock of GM. The other two represent preferred stocks. Since preferred stocks resemble bonds more than they do common stocks, they are described in Chapter Three on bonds.

1976 High-Low   Look at the first entry for General Motors. According to the headings at the top of the first two columns, GM stock traded as high as $75 a share and as low as $57³/₄ during the past months. Judging from these figures, even the stocks of large, well-known companies fluctuate widely in price.

Dividend   To the right of "GnMot" stands "5.55e." The "5.55" indicates the annual dividend paid on a share of GM stock. The letter "e" after the "5.55" is a **footnote.** The explanatory notes at the end of the stock pages tell the reader that

NYSE-Composite Transactions

Monday, November 22, 1976

Quotations include trades on the New York, Midwest, Pacific, Philadelphia, Boston and Cincinnati stock exchanges and reported by the National Association of Securities Dealers and Instinet.

(Stock quotation table — columns: 1976 High Low, Stocks Div., P-E Ratio, Sales 100s, High, Low, Close, Net Chg.)

EXPLANATORY NOTES

(For New York and American Exchange listed issues)

Sales figures are unofficial.

Unless otherwise noted, rates of dividends in the foregoing table are annual disbursements based on the last quarterly or semi-annual declaration. Special or extra dividends or payments not designated as regular are identified in the following footnotes.

a – Also extra or extras. b – Annual rate plus stock dividend. c – Liquidating dividend. e – Declared or paid in preceding 12 months. i – Declared or paid after stock dividend or split up. j – Paid this year, dividend omitted, deferred or no action taken at last dividend meeting. k – Declared or paid this year, an accumulative issue with dividends in arrears. n – New issue. r – Declared or paid in preceding 12 months plus stock dividend. t – Paid in stock in preceding 12 months, estimated cash value

on ex-dividend or ex-distribution date. x – Ex-dividend or ex-rights. y – Ex-dividend sales in full. z – Sales in full.

cld – Called. wd – When distributed. wi – When issued. ww – With warrants. xw – Without warrants. xdis distribution.

vj – In bankruptcy or receivership or being reorganized under the Bankruptcy Act, or securities assumed by such companies.

Year's high and low range does not include change in latest day's trading.

Where a split or stock dividend amounting to 25 cent or more has been paid the year's high-low r and dividend are shown for the new stock only.

MOST ACTIVE STOCKS

	Open	High	Low	Close	Chg.	Volume
Kauf Broad......	9¼	9⅝	9¼	9½	+⅛	249,700
Am Tel&Tel......	62	62½	61¼	62¼	+⅜	230,900
Occiden Pet......	19¾	19⅞	19½	19¾	–¼	193,000
Texaco Inc......	26¼	26½	26¼	26¾	+⅛	160,500
IntlTelTel	30¾	31⅜	30¼	31¼	+½	152,500
Chrysler	19¾	20¼	19½	20	+½	151,800
Southern Co......	15½	15½	15¾	15⅜	+⅛	150,400
Gulf Oil	26½	27¼	26¾	27¼	+½	149,500
Citicorp	29¾	29¾	29½	29½	–⅛	146,100
Tandy Corp......	38	38⅝	38	38¾	+¾	146,150

FIGURE 2-2   Sample stock quotations. (Reprinted with permission of *The Wall Street Journal*, © Dow Jones & Company, Inc., Nov. 23, 1976, p. 46. All rights reserved.)

"e" means "declared or paid in the preceding 12 months." So anyone holding one share of GM for a full year collected a total of $5.55 in dividends.

High, Low, Close, and Net Change   Now skip past the P-E ratio and sales figures to the high, low, close, and **net change.** GM sold for as high as $71⅝ on Monday, November 22, and as low as $70⅜. The last trade took place at $71⅝. The + 1 in the net change column simply indicates that GM closed $1 higher on Monday than it did on the previous day. In other words, it closed at $70⅝ on

Friday. Anyone holding 100 shares over the weekend made $100 as the stock climbed from $70⅝ on Friday to $71⅝ on Monday.

Sales 100s   In order to save space, *The Wall Street Journal* and other newspapers print the number of shares traded in hundreds. To find the total number of GM shares bought and sold, simply add two zeros to the number 1,401. That means 140,100 shares changed hands—considerable trading activity. In fact, GM just missed making the list of "Most Active Stocks" shown in the *Journal.*

But this 140,100 shares represents only the tip of an iceberg. Altogether, GM has 287,617,000 shares outstanding. The day's trading represents less than one-twentieth of 1% of all GM shares.

P-E Ratio   Instead of showing a firm's earnings, the *Journal* and most local papers print its **P-E ratio.** "P-E" stands for price earnings. The P-E ratio equals the closing price of a stock divided by its earnings per share for the most recent 12 months. GM's P-E ratio is 8 to 1 (shown as 8). In other words, anyone buying GM at $71⅝ pays about $8 for every $1 of current earnings.

> EXAMPLE   General Motors earned $9.45 a share during the 12 months ending in September 1976. The stock closed at $71⅝.
>
> The exact P-E ratio is calculated as follows:
>
> $$\frac{\$71.63 \text{ closing market price of stock}}{\$9.45 \text{ earnings per share}} = 8 \text{ price-earnings ratio}$$
>
> The newspapers round off the P-E ratios to the nearest whole number.
>
> The *Journal* does not report current earnings of firms. But any investor can estimate these earnings by dividing the closing price by the P-E ratio:
>
> $$\frac{\$71.63 \text{ closing price}}{8 \text{ price-earnings ratio}} = \$8.95 \text{ earnings per share}$$
>
> Because of the rounding error, the estimate is off by 50¢.

Many investors mistakenly associate low P-E ratios with better values. Nothing could be further from the truth. Generally speaking, low P-E ratios indicate a lack of future growth possibilities, whereas high P-E's suggest great growth potential. For example, Texas Instruments and McDonald's often sport P-E ratios of 26 or more. Why the high price of these companies relative to their current earnings? Because investors buy stocks for their future earnings and dividends, not current earnings. The faster a company grows, the larger these dividends and earnings become and the more valuable the stock.

Should investors buy high P-E or low P-E stocks? The answer depends upon their objectives. Fast-growing companies with high P-E ratios usually reinvest most of their earnings. As a result, the shares of these stocks often appreciate considerably in price. On the other hand, stocks with low P-Es often pay large dividends because of their lack of investment opportunities. Anyone buying these shares usually sacrifices appreciation for current income.

Over-the-Counter Quotations

Now suppose an investor wants to buy 100 shares of Anheuser-Busch, the maker of Budweiser beer. The recent quotes in the over-the-counter section of the financial pages provide the following information:

Stock Div.		Sales 100s	Bid	Asked	Net Change
Anheuser-B	.68	796	$22^{3}/_{4}$	$23^{1}/_{4}$	. . .

The annual dividend on Anheuser-Busch equals 68¢ a share. During the day 79,600 shares changed hands (796 times 100). Instead of showing the open, high, low, and close, *The Wall Street Journal* displays the **bid-and-asked prices**.

The dealers in Anheuser-Busch stock are asking $23^{1}/_{4}$ for a share and offering or bidding $22^{3}/_{4}$. So anyone buying shares must pay $23^{1}/_{4}$; anyone selling receives only $22^{3}/_{4}$.

The difference between the bid-and-asked prices, usually called the **bid-ask spread,** represents the dealer's profit on a transaction. This bid-ask spread is a reimbursement for the dealer's time and effort in making a market and provides a return on the money the dealer invests in the inventory of securities.

STOCK AVERAGES AND INDEXES

Stock prices attract considerable attention. After all, millions of people have billions of dollars invested in the stock market. And changes in the level of stock prices often foreshadow dramatic changes in the economy.

Dow Jones Averages

The most publicized measure of stock prices is the **Dow Jones Industrial Average** (DJIA). Despite the public's long exposure to this average, few investors really understand how it is calculated or what it means. Actually, there are four Dow Jones averages: the widely quoted industrial average and the transportation, utility, and composite averages. The industrial average measures the price movements of 30 manufacturing and retail companies, like American Telephone and Telegraph, Eastman Kodak, General Motors, and Sears Roebuck. The transportation average traces the performance of 20 transportation companies, including Consolidated Freightways, Southern Pacific, and TWA. The utility average reflects the price action of 15 public utilities, such as Commonwealth Edison, Houston Lighting and Power, and Philadelphia Electric. The composite average represents a combination of the other three averages. All the stocks included in the Dow Jones averages trade on the New York Stock Exchange.

The Dow Jones Industrial Average first appeared in 1884. It carries the name of Charles H. Dow and Edward Jones, the two founders of *The Wall Street Journal*. They were newspapermen, not mathematicians, and the average they designed so many years ago reflected their background. They simply wanted to follow movements in the average price of stocks. So they selected 11 well-known companies, added the prices all together, and then divided by 11.

Adjusting the Averages

For a while the original Dow Jones average actually measured the average price of the stocks included in the average. But stock splits soon created a problem. As previously explained, when a stock splits, the company exchanges new shares for old shares: with a 2 for 1 split, every shareholder receives 2 new shares for every 1 old share. Even though these new shares probably sell for one-half the price of the old shares, no fundamental economic change has occurred. There are simply twice as many shares outstanding. So the Dow Jones average must somehow be adjusted for this artificial price change.

One way of adjusting the DJIA for stock splits is to reduce the *divisor* used in calculating the value of the average. Imagine a three-stock average computed in the same fashion as the Dow Jones averages. Table 2-1 shows the effect of a stock split on this average. It drops from 60 to 40—a ridiculous result, since the total market value of all shares remains the same and shareholders experience no losses. In order to compensate for this stock split and leave the average unchanged, the divisor must be arbitrarily reduced from 3 to 2. As more and more splits occur in the future, the divisor, which began as simply the total number of stocks in the average, will be progressively whittled down to a smaller and smaller number.

The Wall Street Journal publishes the current divisor for the DJIA every Monday morning. On December 13, 1976, it equaled 1.504. The decline in the divisor from 30 to $1\frac{1}{2}$ reflects the large number of stock splits which have occurred over the past decades. As a result, the DJIA now bears a closer relation-

TABLE 2-1   IMPACT OF A STOCK SPLIT
ON A HYPOTHETICAL STOCK AVERAGE

| Stock | Before Split | | After Split | |
	Number of Shares	Price	Number of Shares	Price
A	4,000,000	40	4,000,000	40
B*	2,000,000	120	4,000,000	60
C	8,000,000	20	8,000,000	20
		$\frac{180}{3} = 60$		$\frac{120}{3} = 40$

* Stock B splits 2 for 1. This reduces the average from 60 to 40.

TABLE 2-2   COMPUTATION OF THE DOW JONES INDUSTRIAL AVERAGE

Stock	Price on Dec. 10, 1976	Price on Dec. 17, 1976
Allied Chemical	$36^5/_8$	39
Alcoa	$54^3/_4$	$54^1/_8$
American Brands	$43^1/_8$	43
American Can	$36^7/_8$	$38^5/_8$
AT&T	$63^7/_8$	$63^1/_4$
Bethlehem Steel	$39^1/_4$	$40^5/_8$
Chrysler	$19^3/_8$	$18^7/_8$
Du Pont	$131^3/_4$	$135^1/_2$
Eastman Kodak	$84^1/_2$	83
Esmark	$33^1/_2$	$33^1/_8$
Exxon	$52^5/_8$	$52^1/_2$
General Electric	$53^1/_4$	$52^3/_8$
General Foods	$32^1/_8$	$30^3/_4$
General Motors	$73^3/_4$	75
Goodyear	$22^7/_8$	$23^1/_4$
Inco	29	$30^1/_4$
International Harvester	$31^1/_8$	$31^3/_4$
International Paper	$66^3/_8$	$67^1/_2$
Johns Manville	$34^3/_4$	$34^1/_2$
Minnesota Mining & Mfg.	$55^5/_8$	$55^3/_8$
Owens-Illinois	$54^1/_8$	55
Procter & Gamble	$93^3/_4$	91
Sears Roebuck	$69^3/_4$	$67^3/_4$
Standard Oil California	$38^1/_2$	$38^7/_8$
Texaco	$26^3/_4$	$27^3/_8$
Union Carbide	$57^7/_8$	61
U.S. Steel	$48^5/_8$	$50^5/_8$
United Technologies	$37^3/_4$	$36^7/_8$
Westinghouse	$16^1/_4$	$16^7/_8$
Woolworth	$24^1/_4$	$23^3/_4$

$$\frac{1463.63}{1.504} = 973.15 \qquad \frac{1472.50}{1.504} = 979.06$$

---

ship to the total price of the stocks than it does to the average price, as can be seen from the figures in Table 2-2, which shows how to calculate the DJIA.

Other Stock Averages and Indexes

The DJIA possesses one virtue—a familiarity bred from nearly 100 years of publicity. But it also has several shortcomings. When there are thousands of stocks, why look at only 30 to determine whether prices are going up or down? Unlike the original creators of the Dow Jones average, today's computers possess the ability to quickly process large numbers of stock prices. For that reason, newer stock averages and indexes include hundreds or even thousands of stocks. Despite this difference in coverage, the behavior of the DJIA closely parallels the other measures of market prices. After all, the 30 stocks in the DJIA constitute nearly 30% of the total market value of all stocks in the country.

The DJIA suffers from another shortcoming. It gives the greatest weight to high-priced stocks. A quick glance at the figures in Table 2-2 reveals that a 10% gain in a high-priced stock like Du Pont has a much greater impact on the averages than a 10% gain in a low-priced stock like Westinghouse Electric.

But why weight the performance of the individual stocks in the average by their price? The **Standard and Poor's 500 Index,** another widely publicized measure of market activity, weights each stock by its total market value. So stocks with the greatest value (and therefore of the greatest economic importance) receive the greatest weight.

Actually, the S&P 500 is an index of total market values at two different times, rather than a simple average of prices. The "market diary" in *The Wall*

Friday, December 10, 1976

MARKET DIARY

	Fri	Thurs	Wed	Tues	Mon	(a)
Issues traded	1,928	1,924	1,917	1,958	1,937	2,107
Advances	904	1,039	968	855	1,169	1,545
Declines	594	482	505	662	353	401
Unchanged	430	403	444	441	415	161
New highs, 1976	137	169	128	150	146	402
New lows, 1976	5	6	9	5	6	20

(a) Summary for the week ended December 10, 1976.

DOW JONES CLOSING AVERAGES

	– – – – FRIDAY – – – –			
	1976	–Change–		1975
Industrials	973.15	+ 2.41	+0.25%	832.81
Transportation	230.88	– 0.22	–0.10%	164.78
Utilities	105.70	+ 0.13	+0.12%	81.00
Composite	316.08	+ 0.44	+0.14%	253.90

Ex-dividend of Detroit Edison Co., 36¼ cents, lowered the Utility Average by 0.10.

The above ex-dividend lowered the Composite Average by 0.05. Dividend yields last week on the stocks used in th averages; Industrials 4.20%, Transportation 3.83%, Utilities 7.10%.

OTHER MARKET INDICATORS

		1976	–Change–		1975
N.Y.S.E.	Composite	56.33	+ 0.12	+0.21%	46.26
	Industrial	61.49	+ 0.07	+0.11%	51.34
	Utility	40.63	+ 0.20	+0.49%	32.47
	Transportation	41.52	–0.06–	–0.14%	31.00
	Financial	57.86	+ 0.32	+0.56%	42.92
Amer. Ex. Mkt Val Index		103.20	+ 0.40	+0.39%	81.92
Nasdaq	OTC Composite ..	94.62	+ 0.52	+0.55%	74.91
	Industrial	96.40	+ 0.64	+0.67%	78.40
	Insurance	103.98	+ 0.53	+0.51%	79.04
	Banks	90.02	+ 0.47	+0.52%	70.22
Stand. & Poor's 500		104.70	+ 0.19	+0.18%	87.83
	400 Industrial ..	116.31	+ 0.18	+0.15%	98.33

TRADING ACTIVITY

Volume of advancing stocks on N.Y.S.E., 13,090,000 shares; volume of declining stocks, 7,960,000. On American S.E., volume of advancing stocks, 1,350,000; volume of declining stocks, 1,060,000. Nasdaq volume of advancing stocks, 4,651,900; volume of declining stocks, 1,662,700.

FIGURE 2-3 "Market Diary." (Reprinted with permission of *The Wall Street Journal,* © Dow Jones & Company, Inc., Dec. 11, 1976, p. 31. All rights reserved.)

Street Journal, reproduced as Figure 2-3, shows the various market indicators. On this date the S&P 500 Index stood at 104.70. It is calculated by taking the total market value of the stocks in the index, dividing by the average market value of these stocks during 1941 to 1943, and then multiplying by 10. In other words, stocks now sell for 10.47 times their value during 1941–1943. No wonder so few investors really understand price indexes! But everyone can understand the change in the S&P 500. The increase from the preceding day equaled 0.19 or 0.18%; i.e., the market value of stocks included in the index increased by about one-fifth of 1% from the previous day. The movement of stock prices, as measured by the S&P 500, is shown in Figure 2-4.

New York Stock Exchange Composite Index   The **New York Stock Exchange Composite Index** covers all common stocks traded on the NYSE. Each stock is weighted by its market value, so in this respect it resembles the S&P 500. In addition to the composite, the NYSE publishes specialized indexes for industrial, utility, transportation, and financial companies. The composite index was equal to 50 on December 31, 1965. On December 10, 1976, it still equaled only 56.33, as can be seen by referring to Figure 2-3. Obviously, the stock market turned in less than a sterling performance over this 11-year period.

American Stock Exchange Price Level Index   The **American Stock Exchange Price Level Index** includes all stocks traded on the American Stock

FIGURE 2-4   Movements in Standard and Poor's 500. (From the Board of Governors of the Federal Reserve System, *Historical Chart Book,* Washington, D.C., 1976, p. 92.)

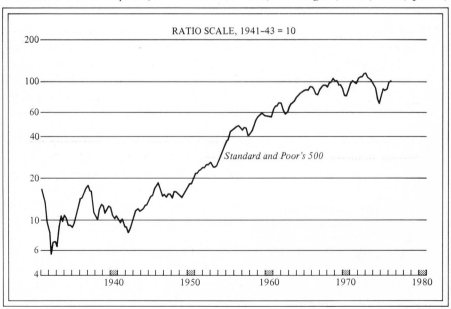

Exchange. In effect, it weights stocks by their prices; so it resembles the Dow Jones averages in this respect.

NASDAQ Index The **NASDAQ Index** provides the investing public with a wide variety of indexes measuring the performance of over-the-counter stocks quoted on its NASDAQ system.

Advances and Declines Investors desiring a simple approach to viewing market performance often turn to the number of **advances** (stocks going up) **and declines** (stocks going down). On Friday, December 10, 1976, 904 stocks advanced and 594 declined.

Which stock average or index should the investor use? The answer depends upon the goals. The S&P 500 probably provides the best broad-based measure of overall market performance. At least, that is the yardstick many professional investors now use to judge their performance relative to the overall stock market.

INVESTOR PROTECTION

Investors in United States securities should consider themselves fortunate. They are protected by a wide variety of laws and by the self-regulation of the stock exchanges and securities dealers. But no set of rules and regulations can completely eliminate losses from fraud and other dishonest activities. When all else fails, the courts provide investors with the opportunity to recover their lost money.

Securities Exchange Act of 1934

The Securities Act of 1933 requires the disclosure of information on new issues. The **Securities Exchange Act of 1934** extends the disclosure concept to outstanding securities. This legislation also provides for the regulation of credit, the prevention of fraud, and the establishment of the Securities and Exchange Commission. Critics of the act describe it as an ill-conceived catchall patched together during a few months. Here are the major provisions of this legislation:

1 Established the Securities and Exchange Commission as a watchdog for the securities industry. The SEC assumed the duties of administering the provisions of both the Securities Act of 1933 and the Securities Exchange Act of 1934.
2 Required the registration of all stock exchanges and gave the SEC the authority over short selling, floor-trading techniques, the listing and delisting of securities, and the procedures and rules of the exchanges.
3 Forbade market manipulation, misrepresentation, deception, and other fraudulent practices.
4 Prescribed operating standards for securities brokers and dealers, including registration with the SEC.

5   Required most large corporations to file registration statements and financial data with the SEC and to provide up-to-date reports.

6   Required all officers, directors, and major stockholders of registered corporations to file an initial report disclosing the number of company shares owned. Also required these so-called **insiders** to file a monthly report of any changes in their holdings. Moreover, the act prohibits short selling by insiders of their company's securities and gives stockholders the right to sue insiders for the return of any profits made on company securities bought and sold in less than 6 months.

7   Gave the SEC power to set rules governing proxy statements.

8   Granted the Board of Governors of the Federal Reserve System the authority to set credit standards for the purchase of securities.

Securities and Exchange Commission

Congress gave the SEC enormous powers. But, until recently, the commission has relied heavily on self-regulation by the securities industry itself. William O. Douglas, an early chairman of the SEC and later a Justice of the U.S. Supreme Court, described this philosophy as one of "letting the exchanges take the leadership with Government playing a residual role. Government would keep the shotgun, so to speak, behind the door, loaded, well oiled, cleaned, ready for use but with the hope it would never have to be used."

To date, most of the public applauds the activities of the SEC. But several well-known economists and lawyers question its real usefulness. In a scathing criticism of the SEC, Henry Manne, a distinguished professor of law, suggests the abolishment of the agency. According to Manne, the famous Senate hearings held before the adoption of the securities acts of 1933 and 1934 "were carefully designed and professionally staged to create public mistrust in our financial institutions and to pave the way for the adoption of extensive securities regulation."[8] We have absolutely no proof of significant fraud problems in the pre-1933 stock market, he argues.

Manne cites studies by Professor Benston of the University of Rochester in support of his argument. Benston examined corporate accounting data prior to 1934 and found the incidence of fraud to be almost negligible. And despite the drastic downward slide of stock prices, the stock markets appeared to incorporate new information.

In 1964 economist George Stigler, one of the champions of the free enterprise system, asked a seemingly simple question: Have investors benefited from 30 years of the SEC? Stigler answered no. Other economists, equally qualified, questioned the accuracy of his results, but to date, no economist has demonstrated that the SEC has significantly benefited investors.

Perhaps the SEC is requiring disclosure of the wrong information. A leading securities lawyer has suggested that "the SEC filings generally have an artificial and unreal quality." And a United States district court judge says "even the moderately well informed investor is almost as much at the mercy of the issuer as was his pre-SEC parent." Finally, a law professor named Homer Kripke reluctantly concludes, "The real problem with the statutory prospectus is not that it is unreadable, but that it is unread. It is unread because it does not contain the information which the investors consider crucial to the investment decision."[9]

Manne also criticizes the high costs imposed on firms by the disclosure requirements. He feels the SEC is forcing risk-taking entrepreneurs out of the capital markets and seriously diverting the flows of capital to firms. With today's requirements, the country's mining industry would never have been developed, he argues. Finally, the SEC and securities legislation do not eliminate fraud, as evidenced by the disasters of large, well-known companies like National Student Marketing and Equity Funding.

Manne and other critics probably have some valid points. But the common view among economists and investors appears to be that some information is better than none. As Baumol says, "*caveat emptor* [let the buyer beware] is not really . . . an acceptable rule for public welfare."[10]

Other Securities Legislation

Not ready to rest on its laurels, Congress continued to add to the new securities laws during the Depression. Between 1935 and 1940 Congress passed the following legislation affecting investors:

1 Public Utility Holding Company Act of 1935
2 Maloney Act of 1938
3 Bankruptcy Act of 1938
4 Trust Indenture Act of 1939
5 Investment Company Act of 1940
6 Investment Advisers Act of 1940

Public Utility Holding Company Act The **Public Utility Holding Company Act of 1935** severely restricts the use of a holding company structure to control different utilities. A holding company controls other corporations through the ownership of some of their common stock. During the booming 1920s, Samuel Insull and other individuals used holding companies to control hundreds of electric and gas utility companies. The stock-market crash shook these elaborate corporate empires like houses of cards. Bankrupt investors, determined to settle the old scores, demanded and received restrictive legislation against holding companies.

Maloney Act The **Maloney Act of 1938** permits brokers and dealers to form national associations. Only one association, the National Association of Securities Dealers, NASD for short, exists at the present time. But NASD counts most of the nation's securities dealers among its members. Most of the activities of the

NASD involve establishing and policing efficient and fair operating procedures. In addition, the NASD initiated NASDAQ, the automated stock-quotation system for over-the-counter securities.

Bankruptcy Act   The Bankruptcy Act of 1938 revised federal bankruptcy laws concerning the reorganization of corporations and authorized the SEC to advise the courts on large reorganizations.

Other Acts   The Trust Indenture Act of 1939 specifically covers bonds; so it is discussed in detail in Chapter Three. The **Investment Company Act of 1940** provides for fair management of mutual funds and other investment companies. It is summarized in Chapter Thirteen, where investment companies are discussed. Finally the **Investment Advisers Act of 1940** requires investment advisers to register with the SEC and to file specific information about themselves and their business. In addition, it sets forth rules on business conduct.

Securities Investors Protection Corporation

Despite all this legislation, investors still found themselves losing money through no fault of their own. The sixties and seventies proved to be up and down years for brokerage firms as well as for stocks. Hundreds of brokerage firms went bankrupt or were forced to merge with other companies. Success killed many of these firms when mountains of paperwork literally buried them.

The New York Stock Exchange protected customer accounts at its own member firms with the proceeds from a special trust fund. But other brokerage firms who were not members of the NYSE sometimes dragged their customers' savings down with them. To remedy this situation, Congress passed the **Securities Investors Protection Corporation Act of 1970,** creating a special insurance fund to protect investors' accounts. SIPC insures brokerage firm customers against the loss of their securities or cash for up to $50,000, with no more than $20,000 of this amount covering cash left in the account (as opposed to customers' securities held by the firm). The fund comes from special assessments made against the commissions of brokerage firms and is backed up by an optional $1 billion line of credit from the U.S. Treasury.

SIPC has already paid investors for millions of dollars lost in brokerage firm failures. But investors complain of the many months it often takes to receive reimbursement. These delays sometimes result in substantial losses, since no interest is paid on the money tied up in the closed accounts and SIPC does not cover changes in the value of the securities held in the account during this period.

Self-Regulation by the Exchanges

The stock exchanges, especially the New York Stock Exchange, closely regulate their own member firms and the trading taking place on their floors. The NYSE has even installed a computerized stock-surveillance service which monitors the trading in all listed stocks. When the computer pinpoints any unusual movements in the price or volume of a stock, an employee of the exchange investigates the reasons for the activity.

Not everyone abides by exchange rules. Once a month the New York Stock Exchange discloses the violations and fines. For example, the NYSE occasionally announces disciplinary actions against members for violation of its net capital rules. Under Big Board rules, a brokerage firm's total debt cannot exceed 15 times its real capital. Any more than the stipulated debt supposedly endangers the firm.

The February 15, 1974, issue of the *Journal* adds to the list of infractions. According to the *Journal*:

> *The exchange also disclosed disciplinary steps against eight individuals, mainly former registered representatives from various firms. Their offenses ranged from misstating their educational attainments to transferring stock from customer's accounts to their own. Three individuals were fired, another was barred permanently from employment with any member firm and others were suspended.*[11]

One of the most interesting revelations about rule violations concerned a college sophomore who managed to place orders for $200,000 of stock "without paying a cent, signing a paper, or setting foot in a brokerage office," according to an editorial in the *Journal*. The exchange disciplined five brokerage-firm executives and five salesmen for this oversight. The executives "were charged with supervisory failures while the salesmen were accused of failing to comply with the exchange's 'know your customer' rules."

Court Actions

If all else fails, investors can always seek damages in the courts of law. In 1972 a Wisconsin court ordered a large, well-known brokerage firm to refund $25,000 in commissions to 47 customers. Apparently one of the firm's brokers executed orders for 210,000 shares of Chris Craft stock in the customers' accounts over a 14-month period. These transactions accounted for 88% of all stock purchased by his customers. The court concluded that the registered representative "failed to make the necessary inquiry to determine whether the recommendations were suitable for all such customers."

Another court case involved a widow who watched her stock account dwindle from $600,000 to $6,500 in a little over a year. She filed a complaint in federal court, claiming she came "under the complete domination and control" of her broker and asking for damages of $1.3 million. Apparently she paid the broker over $122,000 in commissions. Obviously a case of both "love and money."

KEYWORDS

real capital
secondary market
primary markets
New York Stock Exchange
trading posts
reporter
optical scanner
continuous trading
listed stocks
specialist
seat
book
round lots
odd lot
odd-lot dealer
over-the-counter market
(OTC)
NASDAQ
institutional investors
blocks
third market
fourth market
central marketplace
composite tape
composite-quotation
system

consolidated limit-order
book
registered representatives
account executives
boardroom
tape
market order
limit orders
stop orders
day orders
good-till-canceled order
limited discretionary order
complete discretionary
order
short selling
covering a short sale
short squeeze
corner
uptick rule
footnote
net change
P-E ratio
bid-and-asked prices
bid-ask spread

Dow Jones Industrial
Average (DJIA)
Standard and Poor's 500
New York Stock Exchange
Composite Index
American Stock Exchange
Price Level Index
NASDAQ Index
advances and declines
Securities Exchange Act of
1934
insiders
Public Utility Holding
Company Act of 1935
Maloney Act of 1938
Bankruptcy Act of 1938
Investment Company Act
of 1940
Investment Advisers Act
of 1940
Securities Investors Pro-
tection Corporation Act
of 1970 (SIPC)

QUESTIONS

1   What are the two major economic functions of the stock market?
2   Trace the history of the New York Stock Exchange.
3   How does continuous trading on the NYSE benefit investors?
4   Continuous trading imposes heavy costs on any market. How has the NYSE reduced these costs?
5   Describe the two duties of the specialist. Does the specialist face a possible conflict of interest? Is there any way to resolve this conflict?
6   List the differences among the organized exchanges, the over-the-counter market, and the third and fourth markets.
7   Discuss the recent changes in the stock market. What will the stock market of tomorrow look like?
8   Before opening an account at a brokerage house, investors should always meet with whom? Why?
9   Explain the following: Stop orders don't always eliminate extremely large losses on any one stock. And they definitely do not protect the investor from losses suffered over a long period of time.

10   What are the advantages and disadvantages of using a market order? What about limit orders?

11   Should short selling be permitted? Why or why not?

12   Look up the quotation for Jantzen in Figure 2-2. Is the stock trading nearer to its high or its low for the year? What is Jantzen's P-E ratio? About how much did the company earn last year?

13   Find three common stocks in Figure 2-2 with a current yield of 6% or more.

14   Compare the P-E ratios of General Signal and General Steel. What probably accounts for the striking difference?

15   Suppose the divisor for the Dow Jones Industrial Average equals 1.5. How much does a 3-point gain in General Motors shares affect the average?

16   What are the shortcomings of the DJIA? Which stock average or index provides a better measure of overall stock-market movements?

17   Discuss the major provisions of the Securities Exchange Act of 1934.

18   Why doesn't Congress allow insiders to sell short or take profits on stocks held for less than 6 months?

19   How effective has the SEC been in regulating the securities markets? Should it extend its powers still further?

20   What protection do investors have against the failures of brokerage firms? Does this protection also apply to the failures of companies issuing securities?

REFERENCES

Baumol, William J.: *The Stock Market and Economic Efficiency,* Fordham, New York, 1965.

Benston, George: "Required Disclosure and The Stock Market: An Evaluation of the Securities Exchange Act of 1934," *American Economic Review,* March 1973, pp. 132–155.

"Big Board Disciplines 3 Firms for Violations of Net-Capital Rules, *"The Wall Street Journal,* Feb. 15, 1974, p. 18.

Bogen, Jules I., ed.: *Financial Handbook,* 4th ed., Ronald, New York, 1964.

*Brooks, John: *Business Adventures,* Weybright and Talley, New York, 1969.

*Engel, Louis: *How to Buy Stocks,* 5th ed., Bantam, New York, 1972.

Farrar, Donald E.: "Towards a Central Market System: Wall Street's Slow Retreat into the Future," *Journal of Financial and Quantitative Analysis,* November 1974, pp. 815–827.

Gapay, Les: "Little Guy's Friend? Snags Develop in Fund Set Up to Aid Investors in Brokerage Collapses," *The Wall Street Journal,* May 12, 1972, pp. 1, 20.

How to Invest: What Everybody Ought to Know about This Stock and Bond Business, Merrill Lynch, Pierce, Fenner & Smith, New York, 1971.

Lorie, James H., and Mary T. Hamilton: *The Stock Market: Theories and Evidence,* Irwin, Homewood, Ill., 1973.

Manne, Henry G., et al: *Wall Street in Transition: The Emerging System and Its Impact on the Economy,* New York University Press, New York, 1974.

The New York Stock Exchange: 1976 Fact Book, New York Stock Exchange, New York, 1976.

Ney, Richard: *The Wall Street Jungle,* Grove Press, New York, 1970.

* Publications preceded by an asterisk are highly recommended.

Penn, Stanley: "Of Love and Money: The Case of the Lady and the Stockbroker Could Affect Many," *The Wall Street Journal,* Apr. 21, 1972, pp. 1, 27.

Rustin, Richard E.: "Big Board Disciplines 10 Brokers, Citing Student's Phony Orders for $200,000 Stock," *The Wall Street Journal,* May 8, 1972, p. 6.

_____: "Wisconsin Orders Walston to Refund Fees for Allegedly Disregarding Investor Aims," *The Wall Street Journal,* Jan. 17, 1972, p. 5.

"The Small Investor Is Still Stock-Shy," *Business Week,* Aug. 9, 1976, pp. 58–59.

The Specialist: Key Man in the Exchange Market, New York Stock Exchange, 1973.

Welles, Chris: *The Last Days of the Club,* Dutton, New York, 1975.

West, Richard R., and Seha M. Tinic: *The Economics of the Stock Market,* Praeger, New York, 1971.

"What If Your Broker Goes Broke?" *Changing Times,* August 1973, p. 6.

White, Shelby: "The New Central Market Place: The Debate Goes On," *Institutional Investor,* August 1976, pp. 30–31.

CHAPTER THREE

FIXED-INCOME SECURITIES

Much to the dismay of anyone who still believes in Shakespeare's dictum to "neither a borrower nor a lender be," the total debt in the United States surpassed the $1 trillion mark in 1975. And it continues to grow as corporations, the federal government and its agencies, and state and local governments all vie with each other in borrowing more and more money.

The securities issued by these borrowers include corporate bonds, convertible bonds, preferred stock, United States government bonds and notes, Treasury bills, municipal bonds, bankers' acceptances, commercial paper, and negotiable certificates of deposit. All these securities share one characteristic—they pay a fixed income. For that reason, they are generally referred to as fixed-income securities.

For years the public viewed these investments as safe but stodgy. However, the events of recent years have changed its mind. The news that United States government securities outperformed the stock market during the 10-year period ending in 1975 sparked widespread attention. And high interest rates, sometimes tax free, have helped to attract record numbers of individual investors. In fact, bondholders now total 25 million.

CORPORATE BONDS

Investors familiar with bonds speak a language all their own. They frequently use words and phrases like sinking fund, conversion ratio, collateral trust, basis point, and protective covenant. Some people find this terminology so forbidding that they forgo the profitable opportunities offered by bonds.

General Characteristics

Actually a bond resembles an ordinary IOU. Everyone knows that an IOU is simply a signed paper with the letters IOU and a stated amount of money written on it. The letters "IOU" stand for "I owe you."

Like an IOU, a bond represents a promise to repay a specific amount of money. This promise is usually engraved on a **bond certificate** similar to the one shown in Figure 3-1. But, unlike an IOU, bonds are bought and sold. The original issuer of bonds borrows money by selling these pieces of paper. Take, for example, Union Oil's offering of $150 million of bonds in 1974. The company urgently needed long-term funds for its share of construction costs for the Alaska pipeline. It raised the money by selling thousands of individual bonds.

Face Value   Most of the bonds sold by corporations carry a **face value** (a value on the face of the certificate) of $1,000. The corporation promises to eventually repay this sum of money to the bondholder. Bond traders often refer to the face value as the **principal amount,** the par value, or the **denomination** of the bond. Some corporations issue bonds in denominations as low as $100 and as high as $25,000 or more. Although low-denomination bonds appeal to small investors, they should be avoided, because their uniqueness makes them difficult to resell.

New bonds usually sell for very close to their face value, whereas older bonds often trade at much higher or lower prices. When the market price of the bond exceeds the face value, the bond is said to sell at a **premium.** A bond going for less than the face value sells at a **discount.**

Maturity Date   Companies promise to repay the face value after a specific period of time. Most bonds issued today mature in 20 to 30 years. On the **maturity date,** or **expiration date,** the company pays the bondholder the face amount of the bond. For example, some of the bonds issued by Consolidated Edison, a company supplying New York City with most of its electricity and gas, mature in the year 2002. The patient and long-lived bondholder will collect the full face value of the bond—in this case $1,000—at that time. Of course, since bonds are marketable, no one is compelled to hold them until they mature.

Coupon Rate   Why does anyone hold bonds? Because issuers pay stated rates of interest on the face value of their bonds. This rate is usually referred to as the **coupon rate,** or **nominal rate,** of interest. The Consolidated Edison bonds of 2002 carry a coupon rate of 7.9%; so the bondholder collects interest income

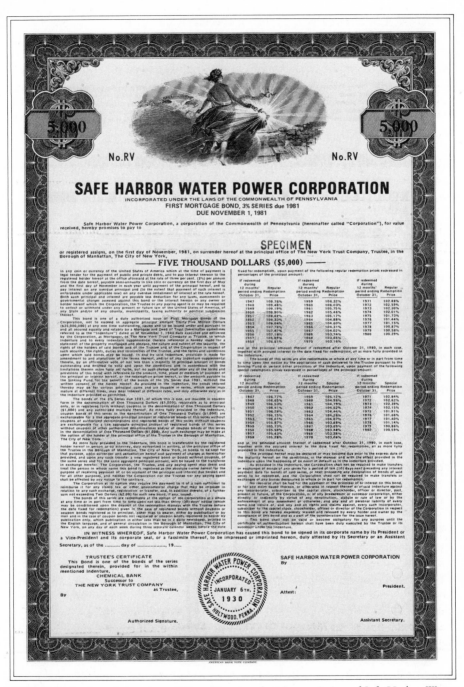

FIGURE 3-1 Sample bond certificate. (Reprinted with permission of Safe Harbor Water Power Corporation.)

totaling $79 during the year (7.9% of the face value of $1,000). Consolidated Edison, like most corporations, sends a check to its bondholders every 6 months for half the annual amount of interest.

Over the years the coupon rate on new bonds has varied tremendously. In addition to the 7.9s of 2002, Consolidated Edison has issues like the 4s of 1988 still outstanding. Why the tremendous difference in the coupon rates? Because Consolidated Edison, despite its large size, must follow the dictates of the bond market. Changes in economic conditions, especially in the rate of inflation, cause interest rates to move up and down. When the company sold the 4s of 1988, interest rates were low. When it sold the 7.9s of 2002, interest rates were much higher.

Bearer and Registered Bonds   Bonds come in two forms: bearer and registered. The name of the owner of a **registered bond** is recorded in the company's books. This protects the investor against theft or loss. The company also mails interest payments directly to the owner of a registered bond.

Bearer bonds are owned by the holder or bearer of the bond. The old saying that "possession is nine-tenths of the law when it comes to ownership" applies completely to bearer bonds. By definition, anyone possessing a bearer bond is the owner, no matter how the bond was acquired (unless theft can somehow be proven). For that reason, bearer bonds should be protected as carefully as cash.

Since a company never knows the identity of the owner of a bearer bond, special procedures must be used to pay interest. A strip of coupons, each **coupon** representing one interest payment, is attached to every bearer bond. When the interest comes due, usually every 6 months, the holder of the bond clips off the appropriate coupon and mails it to the company or its paying agent. Years ago, people referred to the life of the idle rich as one of "clipping coupons," i.e., living off the interest income from bonds.

Security

Bond buyers are by nature a cautious group. Before lending any money, they always insist upon a legally enforceable contract. This **bond indenture** states the rights of the bondholders and the obligations of the issuer—especially the prompt repayment of principle and interest. In addition, the bond indenture usually contains a number of **protective convenants,** including limits on the payments of cash dividends and on the sale of new debt.

There are three parties to the bond contract: the issuer, the bondholders, and the **trustee.** The trustee, usually a large, well-known bank or trust company, is appointed by the corporation to act on behalf of the bondholders. Why do bondholders need a trustee? Because no one else truly represents their interests. The officers and directors of the company owe their allegiance to the stockholders, not to the bondholders.

The trustee performs a variety of duties for the bondholders, including:

1   Authenticating the bonds in order to protect against forgeries and overissues
2   Enforcing the terms of the indenture
3   Handling administrative details like interest payments and bond redemptions

During the Depression bondholders discovered that some bond indentures provided them with little or no protection. And trustees, because of their intimate banking relationships with corporations, often served the corporations' interests rather than those of the bondholders. In an effort to provide additional protection for bondholders, Congress passed the **Trust Indenture Act of 1939.** This legislation requires firms to (1) include standard safeguards in their bond indentures, (2) reveal the major provisions of the indentures to bond buyers, and (3) appoint truly independent trustees.

The law now provides bondholders with several powerful remedies for **default,** i.e., the failure of a corporation to fulfill its legal obligations under a bond contract. Possible actions include a court order forcing the company to perform, the foreclosure and sale of a company's property, and bankruptcy proceedings. The severity of these actions usually ensures the prompt payment of interest and principal.

Some companies offer bondholders additional guarantees of repayment in the form of **secured bonds.** These bonds are backed by a specific type of security, perhaps real estate or equipment. If the company defaults, the bondholders are entitled to first claim on this property. Some of the secured bonds, together with their backing, are as follows:

Mortgage bonds. Buyers of a **first mortgage bond** have first claim on specific real estate. Buyers of a **second mortgage bond** must wait until the first mortgageholders recover all the money owed to them.

Equipment certificates. Railroad cars and airplanes provide especially attractive security because of their easy marketability. Bonds backed by **equipment certificates** are also called **chattel mortgages.**

Collateral trust bonds. **Collateral trust bonds** are rarely issued. The security consists of specific stocks or bonds pledged by the borrower.

Over the years bond buyers have come to realize that the best security for a bond is the intangible earning power of the company. After all, the money to pay the company's obligations must eventually come from its earnings, and the physical property of most corporations tends to become almost worthless when the company ceases operations. Either the property and equipment get tied up in bankruptcy proceedings for years or no buyer can be found because of its specialized nature. So most large corporations issue only unsecured bonds called **debentures.** These bonds are backed by the general credit of the company rather than

Debenture – based on earning power of firm

by any specific collateral. Debentures have performed admirably since World War II—less than one-tenth of 1% of all debentures have defaulted.

Call Provisions

When it comes to forecasting the future, human beings often appear to be remarkably shortsighted. Back in 1964, interest rates on most bonds stood at about 4%. In 1974, many firms considered themselves lucky to borrow at rates of 9% or more. In an attempt to compensate for this uncertainty about future interest rates, most corporations insert a **call provision** in their bonds. This provision gives them the right to call or buy back their bonds before the maturity date.

Suppose a company issues $100 million of 30-year bonds with a coupon rate of 9%. Within 5 years interest rates drop to 5%. Rather than continue to pay high rates of interest, the company calls in its bonds and sells a new issue with a lower interest rate. By **refunding** its debt, it saves $4 million a year in interest payments, or a total of $100 million over the life of the original bond.

Bond buyers object strenuously to the call provision. After all, they want to lock in those high returns. So they often bargain with the issuer for a **deferred call feature,** which delays any call for 5 to 10 years. And they demand to be paid a **call premium** when the bonds are called. This premium generally amounts to 1 year's interest and is paid in addition to the face value of the bond. As the years go by, the call premium usually declines gradually to zero.

Sinking Fund   *retirement of bonds*

When people borrow money from a bank, they usually agree to repay the loan gradually. By the same token, many corporations retire a small amount of their issues each year. They do so through a **sinking fund.**

Despite the unfavorable connotations, bondholders generally benefit from a sinking fund. Once a year the corporation pays an agreed amount of money into a special fund. The trustee then uses this money to retire some of the outstanding bonds. Or the trustee invests these funds until the bonds mature and then retires the entire issue all at one time. In most cases the trustee retires the bonds from year to year rather than waiting until they mature.

A 1972 report by Salomon Brothers, one of the nation's leading investment bankers, shows the popularity of sinking funds. Nearly two-thirds of the bonds in the study required the creation of a sinking fund.

Why so many sinking funds? Because bondholders like them. A sinking fund provides for the orderly retirement of an issue. Second, it tends to support the market price of the bonds. Third, it reduces the bondholders' exposure to risk by reducing the amount of outstanding debt. But there is one disadvantage to a sinking fund. Instead of buying bonds on the open market, the trustee sometimes calls in the necessary amount of bonds.

Selling New Bonds

In recent years corporations have gone on an unprecedented borrowing binge. By the end of 1974, corporate bonds outstanding totaled nearly $275 billion. And in 1974 alone corporations sold nearly $40 billion of new bond issues.

Selling billions of dollars of new bonds is no easy task. Most corporations rely upon investment bankers to do this job. Investment bankers handle new bond issues in more or less the same way as new stock issues—first providing advice and then underwriting and distributing the securities.

Because of the tremendous demand for bonds by large institutional investors, investment bankers often arrange a **private placement.** When this happens, the entire bond issue is sold to only a few buyers. Today nearly one-third of all new bond issues are privately placed. Private placements offer several advantages over sales to the general public, including (1) confidentiality, (2) convenience, and (3) reduced cost. Why the differences between public and private placements? Because the strict requirements imposed on issues of new securities by the Securities Act of 1933 do not apply to private offerings.

The amounts of new bonds (both public and private offerings) sold by corporations during the years from 1947 to 1975 are shown in Figure 3-2.

FIGURE 3-2   Public and private offerings of new corporate bonds. (From the Board of Governors of the Federal Reserve System, *Historical Chart Book,* Washington, D.C., 1976, p. 59.)

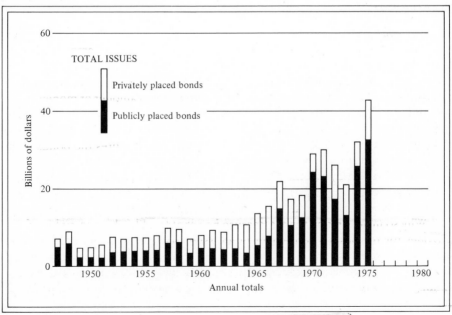

Bond Quotations

Bonds offer prospective investors an enormous variety of possibilities. But the investor must first learn how to buy and sell bonds. At the end of 1976, nearly 2,000 bonds were listed for trading on the NYSE and 200 on the AMEX. Despite these large numbers, the two exchanges place a distant second and third to the trading volume on the over-the-counter market.

A section of *The Wall Street Journal* titled "New York Stock Exchange Bonds" is shown in Figure 3-3. The first quotation on the page reads as follows:

Bonds	Cur Yld	Vol	High	Low	Close	Net Chg
AMF 10s85	9.4	5	106$^7/_8$	106$^7/_8$	106$^7/_8$	+1$^1/_4$

The column labeled "Bonds" lists the abbreviated name of the issuer, the coupon rate, and the maturity date. "AMF" stands for AMF, Incorporated—a manufacturer of a wide variety of recreational equipment, including Head skis and Harley Davidson motorcycles. The AMF bonds are referred to as the tens ("10s") of 1985 ("85"), meaning they carry a coupon rate of 10% and mature in 1985.

Skipping past the "Cur Yld" column for a moment, the volume column (Vol) tells the reader that only five bonds traded during the day. The next three columns indicate the high, low, and closing prices for the day. Bond quotations differ greatly from stock quotations. Bonds are always quoted as a percentage of their face value. The AMF bonds have a face value of $1,000, so the closing price of 106$^7/_8$ actually stands for 106$^7/_8$% of $1,000, or $1,068.75. The dollar price of bonds with a face value of $1,000 can be found by multiplying the figure quoted in the newspaper by 10.

The last column, "Net Chg," shows how much the closing price differs from the previous day's closing price. In this case the net change equals 1$^1/_4$% of the face value of $1,000, or $12.50. So the AMF bonds must have closed at $1,056.25 on the previous day ($1,068.75 minus $12.50 equals $1,056.25).

Prospective bond buyers need to know how much they can make on their investments. According to the *Journal,* the AMF bonds provide a current yield ("Cur Yld") of 9.4%. This is equal to the annual interest of $100 divided by the closing price of $1,068.75.

Why is the current yield on the AMF bonds less than the coupon rate of 10%? Because the bonds are selling at a slight premium over the face value. And the higher the bond price, given the fixed income of $100, the lower the current yield.

By the way, most bonds trade for the market price indicated in the *Journal* or elsewhere plus accrued interest. If 3 months have passed since the last interest payment, the buyer must pay the seller the interest accrued during that period. The AMF bonds pay $50 every 6 months; so in this case the accrued interest totals about $25. A few bonds trade **flat,** meaning that the buyer need not pay accrued interest.

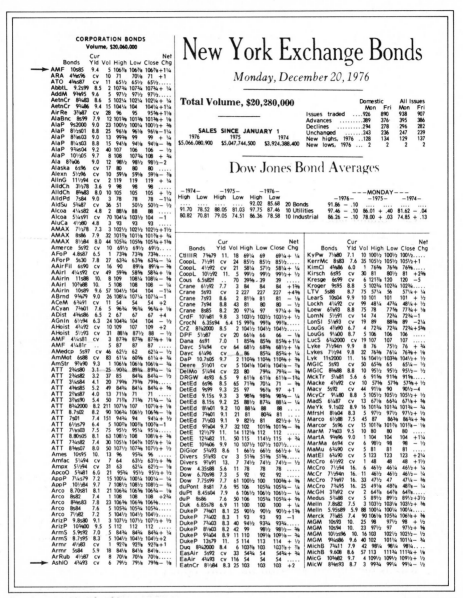

FIGURE 3-3 Sample NYSE bond quotations. (Reprinted with permission of *The Wall Street Journal,* © Dow Jones & Company, Inc., Dec. 21, 1976, p. 30. All rights reserved.)

Bonds versus Stocks

Bonds differ from stocks in numerous ways. By far the most important difference is in the nature of the rewards offered to investors. Bonds pay a fixed income. Stocks offer a share in the profits and losses of the company. The price behavior

TABLE 3-1 BONDS VERSUS STOCKS

Bondholders	Stockholders
1 Receive a fixed income	1 Share in the profits and losses of the corporation
2 Lend money to the corporation	2 Own the corporation
3 Have no voice in management	3 Are entitled to vote for directors
4 Are paid with before-tax dollars	4 Are paid with after-tax dollars
5 Are repaid their principle on the maturity date	5 Are never repaid their initial investment
6 Accept repayment at the option of the corporation (through the call process)	6 Are never required to sell their shares
7 Receive prior claim to assets in the case of bankruptcy	7 Receive last priority in the event of bankruptcy

of stocks and bonds reflects the relative uncertainty about these payments. Stock prices fluctuate tremendously as the prospects for future profits change from year to year. Bond prices fluctuate too, but over a much narrower range.

Some of the other differences between bonds and stocks are summarized in Table 3-1. They all appear to stem from the fact that stocks represent ownership, whereas bonds represent debt. For example, the government allows a company to deduct interest payments from its income before paying taxes. But dividends are not deductible, presumably because the stockholders own the company. (This obviously provides a tremendous incentive to use debt rather than equity.) Moreover, stockholders stand last in line for both the income and the assets of the corporation. Lenders must be repaid completely before stockholders receive even a cent.

If stockholders had to choose a theme song, it would probably be the "Impossible Dream." Bondholders would undoubtedly select "He's Got the Whole World in His Hands."

CONVERTIBLE BONDS

Some companies attempt to offer investors the best of both the bond and the stock worlds. They sell hybrid securities called **convertible bonds**—bonds convertible into shares of stock. These bonds provide investors with a steady income and the opportunity to participate in rising stock prices.

The Ashland Oil convertible debentures of 1993 provide a good example of convertibility. The Ashland Oil quotation in Figure 3-3 carries the letters "cv" in the current yield column, an abbreviation for the word "convertible." *Moody's Industrial Manual,* a standard guide to corporate securities, describes this conversion feature as follows:

CONVERTIBLE—Into com. [common] *at any time (if called, on business day next preceding redemption date)* at $50 a sh [share]. *No adjustment for interest or divs [dividends]. Cash paid in lieu of fractional shs. Conversion privilege protected against dilution.*[1]

According to *Moody's,* the Ashland Oil bonds are convertible into common shares at $50 a share. At this **conversion price,** the investor can exchange 1 bond for 20 shares of Ashland Oil,

$$20 \text{ shares } = \frac{\$1,000 \text{ face value of bond}}{\$50 \text{ conversion price}}$$

The **conversion ratio** for the bond equals 20 to 1, 20 shares of stock for 1 bond.

Because of the conversion feature, convertible bonds possess a "split personality." At times they behave like stocks and at times like bonds. Therefore, it makes sense to analyze a convertible bond first as a bond and then as a stock. Strip away the conversion feature from a convertible bond and all that remains is an ordinary bond. This "straight" bond possesses an **investment value** based solely on its bond characteristics. Regardless of what happens to the price of the company's stock, a convertible bond can never sell for less than this investment value. In effect, the investment value sets a floor to the price of the convertible bond.

The Ashland Oil convertible bonds carry a coupon rate of $4^3/_4\%$ and mature in 1993. Suppose bonds without a conversion feature but with the same coupon rate and maturity date currently sell for $700. Then the investment value of the Ashland Oil convertible equals $700.

Convertible bonds almost always sell for more than their investment value. The difference between the actual market price of the bond and its investment value is called the **investment premium.** This premium reflects the value of the conversion feature. If the Ashland Oil convertible sells for $830, then the investment premium equals $130,

$$
\begin{array}{rl}
\$830 & \text{market price of bond} \\
-\,700 & \text{investment value of bond} \\
\hline
\$130 & \text{investment premium}
\end{array}
$$

Next the convertible bond can be analyzed solely as a claim on the company's stock. Suppose Ashland Oil stock sells for $30 a share in the market. Then the **conversion value** of the Ashland convertible—its value when converted into shares of common stock—equals $600. This conversion value is found by multiplying the $30 market price of a share of common stock by 20 shares. Changes in the price of the stock raise or lower the conversion value, which in turn pulls the price of the bond up or down.

Convertible bonds usually sell for more than their conversion values, since convertibles offer more than just an indirect investment in stocks. The difference between the market price of the bond and its conversion value is called the **con-**

version premium or **exchange premium.** If the Ashland Oil bonds fetch $830 at the same time the stock goes for $30, the conversion premium amounts to $230:

$830   market price of bond
−600   conversion value of bond (20 shares times $30)
$230   conversion premium

By the way, convertible bonds rarely sell for less than their conversion value. If they did, sharp-eyed investors would immediately purchase the bonds and convert them into shares with a higher market value.

Now it is time to put together the investment and conversion values. Figure 3-4 displays the relationship between the price of a convertible bond and the price of the underlying common stock. At very high stock prices, the conversion value dominates totally. At very low stock prices, the conversion feature is almost worthless and the bond sells for close to its investment value. Why does the bond sell for even 1¢ more than its investment value at low stock prices? Because the conversion feature provides bondholders with the hope, no matter how faint, of some day participating in a rise in the stock price.

Because of the complexity of convertible bonds, simple rules about the selection of the "best" issues are almost always wrong. A case in point is the oft-offered advice to buy convertibles with low conversion premiums. Actually, the correct choice depends upon the investors' objectives. If they want income, they should buy convertibles selling for close to their investment value. These bonds probably sport a hefty conversion premium because they possess little value as a stock. If investors prefer to take an active role in the movement of the underlying

FIGURE 3-4   Relationship between convertible bond price and stock price.

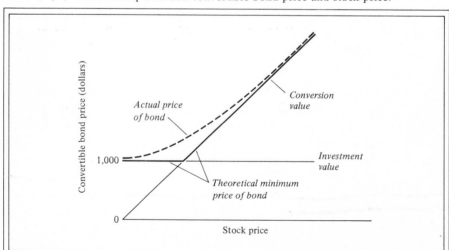

stock, they should buy convertibles selling for close to their conversion values and therefore carrying a low conversion premium. Obviously, there is no right answer for everyone. One last point: Investors pay for the conversion feature in one way or another. Consequently no one should buy a convertible without being at least mildly optimistic about the prospects for the stock market and the company's stock.

PREFERRED STOCKS

Technically speaking, **preferred stock** represents a share of ownership in a corporation. The word "preferred" refers to the fact that preferred stockholders receive priority over common stockholders in terms of dividends and assets if the company goes bankrupt.

But preferred stock differs from common stock in one crucial respect. Preferred stockholders do not share directly in the profits of the company. Instead, they receive a fixed income, just like any bondholder. As a result, the price behavior of preferred stock parallels the price behavior of bonds much more closely than it does that of common stock. This is illustrated in Figure 3-5 for the common stock, preferred stock, and bonds of General Motors. In terms of economic reality, a preferred stock deserves to be thought of as a bond.

Although corporations must always pay interest on their bonds, they can omit the dividend on preferred stock. What protects preferred stockholders from an arbitrary decision by management to stop paying dividends? First, preferred shares usually pay **cumulative dividends.** With this cumulative dividend feature, unpaid dividends carry over into future years until completely repaid. Moreover, a company cannot pay any dividends to its common stockholders until it pays preferred stockholders their accumulated dividends.

Most companies also give preferred stockholders the right to elect several directors when preferred dividends go unpaid for a specific period of time. Unlike bondholders, the owners of preferred shares do not have the power to force a company into bankruptcy for nonpayment of interest. So this right to elect directors gives the preferred stockholders some badly needed clout in making the company pay preferred dividends.

Preferred stocks trade in the same way as common stocks. The only difference between common and preferred stock quotes in a newspaper is the addition of the letters "pfd" after the name of the company and the absence of a P-E ratio. This can be seen by referring to the General Motors $3.75 preferred in Figure 2-2. The quote reads as follows:

High	Low	Stocks Div.	P-E Ratio	Sales 100s	High	Low	Close	Net Chg.
$54^1/_2$	$49^1/_4$	GMot pf 3.75	. . .	60	$53^1/_8$	53	53	$+^1/_2$

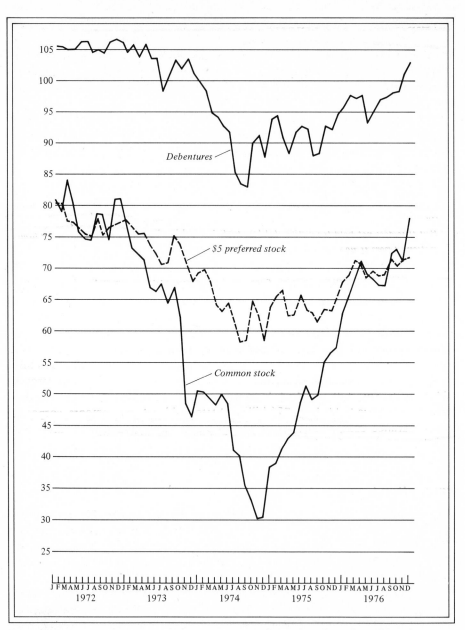

FIGURE 3-5   Price behavior of **GM** common stock, preferred stock, and bonds.

GOVERNMENT SECURITIES

One short word describes the government securities market—big. At the end of 1974 the public debt, the amount of money owed to the public by the government, totaled nearly $500 billion. And each year the U.S. Treasury issues an additional $30 to $40 billion of new securities.

Some pessimists prefer to describe the public debt with two words—too big. They fear the eventual collapse of government under this enormous burden. Enlightened economists like Abba Lerner long ago dispelled most of these doubts. Lerner says:

> By far the most common concern about the national debt comes from considering it as exactly the same kind of thing as a private debt which one individual owes to others. . . .
>
> But this does not hold for national debt which is owed by the nation to citizens of the same nation. There is no external creditor. "We owe it to ourselves."[2]

Who owns the vast amount of government securities currently outstanding? The largest owner of government debt is the government itself: at the end of 1973 United States government investment accounts held nearly $130 billion of securities, and the Federal Reserve Bank accounted for another $80 billion. Perhaps because of the frequent ads to "buy savings bonds at the place you work," individuals hold about $60 billion of savings bonds plus another $16 billion of other government securities. Commercial banks are the next largest holder, with $60 billion. And foreign investors still think enough of the American dollar to hold about $56 billion. State and local governments, corporations, insurance companies, mutual savings banks, and miscellaneous investors hold the rest.

Savings Bonds

Probably the best-known government securities are the familiar **United States savings bonds.** First issued in 1935, these bonds gained widespread acceptance during World War II, when they were called Victory Bonds. Nowadays the United States Treasury offers two types of savings bonds: **Series E bonds** and **Series H bonds.**

Series E bonds appeal to small investors. As nearly every schoolchild knows, they can be purchased for as little as $18.75. Series E bonds do not pay interest directly. Instead, they are issued at a discount from their face value. As time goes on, the redemption value gradually increases. At the end of 5 years, the redemption value equals $25. This increase in value is equivalent to an annual return of 6%. On the other hand, the U.S. Treasury pays interest on Series H bonds every 6 months. Series H bonds sell for $500, $1,000, and $5,000.

Savings bonds cannot be sold to another investor, nor can they be pledged or used as security for a loan. All bonds are registered in the owners' names. When a savings bond is lost, stolen, mutilated, or destroyed, the government replaces it with a duplicate.

The United States government backs every savings bond with its "full faith and taxing power." As taxpayers well know, this is an awesome power. For that reason, investors view savings bonds, as well as all other government securities, as among the safest investments in the world.

Treasury Bills

Treasury bills form the backbone of the American financial system. Not only are they guaranteed by the United States government, but they are also extremely marketable.

Like Series E savings bonds, T-bills, as they are usually called, are discounted. Instead of paying interest, they are issued for less than face value. T-bills normally mature in 3, 6, 9, or 12 months.

The U.S. Treasury sells 3- and 6-month (actually 91- and 182-day) T-bills at a weekly auction; 1-year bills are offered every 4 weeks. Despite the enormous amounts of money involved, such auctions probably qualify as the quietest in the world. Rather than appear in person, the buyers and/or their agents submit written bids on forms like the one in Figure 3-6.

Prospective buyers must decide whether to bid on a competitive or noncompetitive basis. The experts enter **competitive bids,** or **tenders,** as they are usually called. Competitive bids must be expressed on the basis of 100, with not more than three decimals, say 99.646. The Treasury accepts the highest bids (the higher the bid, the lower the interest rate the government pays). It fills all **noncompetitive bids** up to $200,000 at the weighted average price of the competitive bids. Amateurs interested in buying Treasury bills would do well to avoid the guessing game and submit noncompetitive bids.

Small investors suffer from two disadvantages when buying Treasury bills. First, T-bills must be purchased in amounts of $10,000 or more. Second, they are bearer securities. Therefore, a $10,000 T-bill must be guarded as carefully as a $10,000 bill. Despite these obstacles, T-bills occasionally attract large numbers of small investors. During 1974, interest rates on T-bills soared to 10%. Meanwhile, commercial banks and savings and loans continued to pay 5 to 5¹/₄% interest on passbook accounts, the maximum allowed by law. Before long, thousands of people withdrew their savings and marched down to one of the Federal Reserve banks to submit noncompetitive tenders. In 1 month, the commercial banks lost several hundred million dollars in deposits.

Two years later new T-bills returned only 4.5%. By then, most small investors had deserted T-bills and returned to their favorite savings institutions. No doubt, rates will rise again someday and lure them back into these short-term government securities.

The Wall Street Journal and most newspapers report the daily prices of Treasury bills in their financial section. The quotations look like the ones in Figure 3-7. Instead of quoting dollar prices, traders state the yields on the bills. The

GB 52

IMPORTANT—(a) This is a standard form. Its terms are subject to change at any time by the Treasury. You may call Tel. No. 212-791-5823 (or 716-849-5046 in the Buffalo area) for current information on Treasury securities offerings. (b) This tender will be construed as a bid to purchase the securities for which the Treasury has outstanding an invitation for tenders on the date received by the Federal Reserve Bank of New York or its Buffalo Branch.

TENDER FOR 3-MONTH TREASURY BILLS

To FEDERAL RESERVE BANK OF NEW YORK,
    Fiscal Agent of the United States
    New York, N.Y. 10045

Dated at...

...., 19____

Pursuant and subject to the provisions of Treasury Department Circular No. 418 (current revision) and to the provisions of the public notice issued by the Treasury Department inviting tenders for the current offering of 3-month Treasury bills, the undersigned hereby offers to purchase such currently offered Treasury bills in the amount indicated below, and agrees to make payment therefor at your Bank on or before the issue date at the price indicated below:

COMPETITIVE TENDER	*Do not fill in both Competitive and Noncompetitive tenders on one form*	NONCOMPETITIVE TENDER
$............................... (maturity value) or any lesser amount that may be awarded. Price: .... per 100. *(Price must be expressed with not more than three decimal places, for example, 99.925)*		$............................... (maturity value) *(Not to exceed $500,000 for one bidder through all sources)* at the average price of accepted competitive bids.

Subject to allotment, please issue, deliver, and accept payment for the bills as indicated below:

Pieces	Denomination	Maturity value			
	$ 10,000				
	15,000				
	50,000				
	100,000				
	500,000				
	1,000,000				
	Totals				

☐ 1. Deliver over the counter to the undersigned

☐ 2. Ship to the undersigned

☐ 3. Hold in safekeeping (for member bank only) in—
    ☐ Investment Account
    ☐ General Account
    ☐ Trust Account

☐ 4. Hold as collateral for Treasury Tax and Loan Account *

(No changes in delivery instructions will be accepted)

Payment will be made as follows:

☐ By charge to our reserve account

☐ By cash or check in *immediately available funds*

☐ By surrender of eligible maturing securities

(Payment cannot be made through Treasury Tax and Loan Account)

☐ 5. Special instructions:

* The undersigned certifies that the allotted securities will be owned solely by the undersigned.

Insert this tender in envelope marked "Tender for Treasury Bills"

(Tel. No.)

(Name of subscriber—please print or type)

(Address—incl. City and State)

(Signature of subscriber or authorized signature)

(Title of authorized signer)

(Banking institutions submitting tenders for customer account must list customers' names on lines below or on an attached rider)

(Name of customer)   (Name of customer)

INSTRUCTIONS:

1. No tender for less than $10,000 will be considered, and each tender must be for a multiple of $5,000 (maturity value).

2. Only banking institutions, and dealers who make primary markets in Government securities and report daily to this Bank their positions with respect to Government securities and borrowings thereon, may submit tenders for customer account; in doing so, they may consolidate competitive tenders *at the same price* and may consolidate noncompetitive tenders, provided a list is attached showing the name of each bidder and the amount bid for his account. Others will not be permitted to submit tenders except for their own account.

3. If the person making the tender is a corporation, the tender should be signed by an officer of the corporation authorized to make the tender, and the signing of the tender by an officer of the corporation will be construed as a representation that such officer has been so authorized. If the tender is made by a partnership, it should be signed by a member of the firm, who should sign in the form "..., a copartnership, by ...., a member of the firm."

4. Payment must be completed by the issue date. If payment is by check drawn on a bank in this District, it must be received by the third business day before the issue date; checks drawn on a bank in another District must be received by the fifth business day before the issue date. All checks must be drawn to the order of the Federal Reserve Bank of New York; checks endorsed to this Bank will not be accepted.

5. If the language of this tender is changed in any respect, which, in the opinion of the Secretary of the Treasury, is material, the tender may be disregarded.

Rev. 11/76

FIGURE 3-6 Sample Treasury bill bid. (Reprinted with permission of the Federal Reserve Bank of New York.)

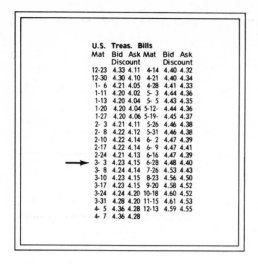

U.S. Treas. Bills					
Mat	Bid	Ask	Mat	Bid	Ask
	Discount			Discount	
12-23	4.33	4.11	4-14	4.40	4.32
12-30	4.30	4.10	4-21	4.40	4.34
1- 6	4.21	4.05	4-28	4.41	4.33
1-11	4.20	4.02	5- 3	4.44	4.36
1-13	4.20	4.04	5- 5	4.43	4.35
1-20	4.20	4.04	5-12-	4.44	4.36
1-27	4.20	4.06	5-19-	4.45	4.37
2- 3	4.21	4.11	5-26	4.46	4.38
2- 8	4.22	4.12	5-31	4.46	4.38
2-10	4.22	4.14	6- 2	4.47	4.39
2-17	4.22	4.14	6- 9	4.47	4.41
2-24	4.21	4.13	6-16	4.47	4.39
3- 3	4.23	4.15	6-28	4.48	4.40
3- 8	4.24	4.14	7-26	4.53	4.43
3-10	4.23	4.15	8-23	4.56	4.50
3-17	4.23	4.15	9-20	4.58	4.52
3-24	4.24	4.20	10-18	4.60	4.52
3-31	4.28	4.20	11-15	4.61	4.53
4- 5	4.36	4.28	12-13	4.59	4.55
4- 7	4.36	4.28			

FIGURE 3-7 Sample Treasury bill quotations. (Reprinted with permission of *The Wall Street Journal,* © Dow Jones & Company, Inc., Dec. 21, 1976, p. 30. All rights reserved.)

buyer of the bills maturing on March 3 earns 4.15%; that is, the asked price paid provides a yield of 4.15%. These discount rates can be translated into dollar prices by referring to a special table or by using the following formula:

$$\text{Dollar price of } \$10{,}000 \text{ bill} = \$10{,}000 - (\text{discount rate in basis points} \times \text{days to maturity} \times \$0.00277778)$$

A **basis point** refers to one one-hundredth of a percentage point, or 0.01%. A quote of 4.15% equals 415 basis points. The nice round figure of $0.00277778 in the preceding formula corresponds to the amount of money earned per day on a Treasury bill for each basis point of interest.

If 90 days remain before the March 3 Treasury bills mature, the selling price is $9,896 and the buying price is $9,894. In this case, the dealer's bid-ask spread amounts to $2, a tiny fraction of the amount invested. So, in order to make any money, Treasury bill dealers must buy and sell enormous amounts of bills. A good dealer buys and sells $100 million of government securities on a typical day. Any trades for less than $1 million are viewed as odd lots.

Notes and Bonds

The Treasury also issues notes and bonds. **Treasury notes** range in maturity from 1 to 7 years. **Treasury bonds** may be issued with any maturity but generally mature in over 7 years. Both bonds and notes are available in bearer or registered form and pay interest every 6 months. Bonds and notes come in denominations of $1,000, $5,000, $10,000, $100,000, and $1,000,000 (for the really big spenders); notes are also available in the denomination of $500,000.

Because of the lower denominations and the registered form, notes and bonds appeal to knowledgeable small investors. In the summer of 1974, people stood in line for hours to buy $1,000 Treasury notes yielding 9%. Not since the Civil War had the United States government paid so high a rate.

There is really no need for prospective note and bond buyers to stand in line at the local office of the Federal Reserve Bank. The Treasury follows more or less the same auction procedures as it does for bills. The government generally announces an offering 1 to 3 weeks in advance of the issue date. Investors submit either a competitive or noncompetitive tender and then wait for the results. Those 9% Treasury notes attracted so much demand that investors ended up paying $1,010 for a note with a face value of $1,000. This reduced the effective yield to 8.59%—still a bonanza for the little guy otherwise unable to compete with large investors.

Now and then the Treasury experiments with different auction techniques. One of the most unique methods involves the **Dutch auction** scheme. Under this system, bidders still submit their best offers, but, instead of paying these prices, the successful bidders all pay the lowest acceptable price, the so-called **stop-out price**. This supposedly encourages the participation of smaller, nonprofessional investors who need not worry about submitting ridiculously high bids. The Dutch auction also seems fairer, because all buyers pay the same price for the same securities.

Most of the Treasury's new offerings of notes and bonds involve a refunding rather than a cash sale. In an **exchange refunding,** the Treasury offers new securities in exchange for securities about to mature. With an **advance refunding,** the government issues new securities in exchange for outstanding securities not immediately due to mature. And a **cash refunding** involves the sale of notes or bonds for cash, with the money immediately used to refund a maturing issue. These refunding techniques provide the Treasury with considerable flexibility in financing its needs and, of course, eliminate considerable bookkeeping.

Treasury notes and bonds trade actively in the over-the-counter markets. The AMEX also provides a market for odd lots of these securities. A typical newspaper quotation for a Treasury bond or note is shown in Figure 3-8. These quotes bear no similarity to those for T-bills and also differ considerably from those for corporate bonds. For example, the following quotation refers to the 9% Treasury notes maturing in August 1980:

9s   1980 Aug n   107.4   107.12   − .2   6.54

The small letter "n" indicates that the security is a note rather than a bond. Government note and bond prices are always expressed as a percentage of par or face value just as other bonds are. But the number after the decimal refers to thirty-seconds of 1%. For example, 107.12 means $107^{12}/_{32}\%$ of the face value. With a $1,000 note, this amounts to $1,073.75; so this particular issue sells at a premium over the face value.

The government quotations also refer to **yield to maturity** rather than to current yield. This figure provides a much more realistic picture of the return earned on the investment, since it includes the change in price as well as the interest income. Take the August 1980 notes, for example. Anyone buying one of

Government Securities

Wednesday, Mar. 23
Over-the-Counter Quotations: Source on request.
Decimals in bid-and-asked and bid changes represent 32nds 101.1 means 101 1-32. a-Plus 1-64. b-Yield to call date. d-Minus 1-64.

Treasury Bonds and Notes

Rate	Mat.	Date	Bid	Asked	Bid Chg.	Yld.
6½s,	1977	Mar n	100	100.2	.....	2.62
7⅜s,	1977	Apr n	100.7	100.9	− .1	4.40
6⅞s,	1977	May n	100.8	100.10	.....	4.53
9s,	1977	May n	100.18	100.20	.....	4.39
6¾s,	1977	May n	100.11	100.13	.....	4.43
6½s,	1977	Jun n	100.13	100.19	.....	4.43
7½s,	1977	Jul n	100.28	101	.....	4.70
7¾s,	1977	Aug n	101.2	101.6	− .1	4.65
8¼s,	1977	Aug n	101.11	101.15	.....	4.75
8⅜s,	1977	Sep n	101.20	101.24	− .1	4.90
7½s,	1977	Oct n	101.11	101.15	.....	4.99
7¾s,	1977	Nov n	101.17	101.21	.....	5.10
6⅝s,	1977	Nov n	100.27	100.31	− .1	5.17
7¼s,	1977	Dec n	101.12	101.16	.....	5.29
6⅜s,	1978	Jan n	100.24	100.28	.....	5.31
6¼s,	1978	Feb n	100.21	100.25	.....	5.35
8s,	1978	Feb n	102.8	102.12	− .1	5.36
6¾s,	1978	Mar n	101.6	101.10	− .1	5.41
6½s,	1978	Apr n	100.30	101.2	.....	5.49
7⅛s,	1978	May n	101.20	101.24	+ .1	5.52
7⅞s,	1978	May n	102.13	103.17	.....	5.56
7⅛s,	1978	May n	101.21	101.25	+ .1	5.55
6⅞s,	1978	Jun n	101.12	101.16	.....	5.63
6⅞s,	1978	Jul n	101.13	101.17	.....	5.68
7⅝s,	1978	Aug n	102.13	102.17	.....	5.71
8¾s,	1978	Aug n	103.27	103.31	− .1	5.75
6⅝s,	1978	Aug n	101.3	101.7	.....	5.73
6¼s,	1978	Sep n	100.17	100.21	− .1	5.79
5⅞s,	1978	Oct n	99.31	100.3	.....	5.81
6s,	1978	Nov n	100.2	100.6	− .1	5.88
5¾s,	1978	Nov n	99.22	99.26	− .1	5.87
5¼s,	1978	Dec n	98.24	98.28	.....	5.93
8⅛s,	1978	Dec n	103.17	103.21	.....	5.92
5⅞s,	1979	Jan n	99.24	99.28	.....	5.95
7s,	1979	Feb n	101.23	101.27	.....	5.96
5⅞s,	1979	Feb n	99.23	99.25	.....	5.99
7⅞s,	1979	May n	103.16	103.20	− .1	6.05
7¾s,	1979	Jun n	103.11	103.15	.....	6.09
6¼s,	1979	Aug n	100.4	100.8	.....	6.14
6⅞s,	1979	Aug n	101.15	101.19	.....	6.15
8½s,	1979	Sep n	105.4	105.8	.....	6.21
6¼s,	1979	Nov n	99.29	100.1	.....	6.24
6⅝s,	1979	Nov n	100.23	100.27	.....	6.28
7s,	1979	Nov n	101.22	101.26	+ .2	6.25
7½s,	1979	Dec n	102.29	103.1	− .2	6.29
4s,	1980	Feb	93.30	94.14	− .2	6.13
6½s,	1980	Feb n	100.8	100.12	− .2	6.35
7½s,	1980	Mar n	102.29	103.5	− .2	6.33
6⅞s,	1980	May n	101.6	101.14	.....	6.36
7⅝s,	1980	Jun n	103.4	103.12	− .2	6.46
→ 9s,	1980	Aug n	107.4	107.12	− .2	6.54
6⅞s,	1980	Sep n	100.26	101.2	− .1	6.52
3½s,	1980	Nov	90.30	91.14	.....	6.16

n− Treasury notes.

FIGURE 3-8 Sample Treasury bond and note quotations. (Reprinted with permission of *The Wall Street Journal,* © Dow Jones & Company, Inc., Mar. 24, 1976, p. 38. All rights reserved.)

those notes pays $1,073.75. When the note matures, the government repays the bondholder only $1,000. So the investor loses $73.75. This considerably reduces the total return on the bond. In fact, by using bond tables the investor can calculate the total annual return. The yield to maturity is only 6.54%, a lot less than the stated rate of 9%.

UNITED STATES GOVERNMENT AGENCY SECURITIES

Investors in government agency securities enter the world of **Fannie Mae, Freddie Mac, Sallie Mae,** and **Ginnie Mae.** Anyone looking for the Wall Street version of the Beverly Hillbillies will be disappointed to learn that these names refer to government agencies and not to countrified bond dealers. Here are the official names of these agencies:

Fannie Mae—Federal National Mortgage Association
Freddie Mac—Federal Home Loan Mortgage Corporation
Ginnie Mae—Government National Mortgage Association
Sallie Mae—Student Loan Marketing Association

Government agencies offer a perplexing variety of securities. Altogether more than 40 agencies are empowered, most often by an act of Congress, to independently raise money in the capital markets. Although these securities are not the direct obligations of the United States government, they generally involve federal sponsorship or guarantees. By 1974 the amount of these agency securities had burgeoned to a total of nearly $100 million.

Government-sponsored Enterprises

Actually, there are two distinct groups of agencies. The first of these, **government-sponsored enterprises,** consists of the following publicly owned organizations:

Banks for Cooperatives (Co-ops)—make loans to farmers' cooperatives

Federal Intermediate Credit Banks (FICB)—advance funds to specialized banks and financial institutions which lend money to the agricultural sector

Federal Home Loan Banks (FHLB)—provide money to savings and loan associations and similar savings institutions

Federal Home Loan Mortgage Corporation (FHLMC, or Freddie Mac)—buys residential mortgages from federally insured savings institutions

Federal Land Banks (FLBs)—provide funds to Federal Land Bank associations, which in turn lend money to farmers for real estate and other purchases.

Federal National Mortgage Association (FNMA, or Fannie Mae)—purchases residential mortgages, most of them insured or guaranteed by another government agency and other financial institutions

These six government-sponsored agencies account for nearly 75% of all issues of all agencies. Although none of their obligations is guaranteed by the United States government, investors regard them very highly.

Federal Agencies

The second group of government agencies is generally referred to as **federal agencies.** The United States government owns many of these agencies; so most of their obligations carry a government guarantee. At the rate new federal programs are springing up, this group may soon have a cast of hundreds. The largest and best-known agencies are the Export-Import Bank (Exim Bank), Farmers Home Administration (FHA), Federal Housing Administration (FHA), Government National Mortgage Association (GNMA, or Ginnie Mae), Tennessee Valley Authority (TVA) and the U.S. Postal Service.

The Wall Street Journal and other newspapers publish quotations on many of the federal agencies and government-sponsored enterprises. These quotations are identical in form with other government issues. Agency securities pay slightly higher returns than government securities. Investors interested in details on available issues should consult David Darst's *The Complete Bond Book.*

MUNICIPAL BONDS

In recent years **municipal bonds** have attracted record numbers of individual investors. These bonds offer a sure-fire way of beating the tax collector—they pay tax-free interest. Moreover, interest rates on municipals, or tax-exempt bonds as they are often called, reached new highs in 1974 and 1975.

The tax-free-interest feature means that more dollars stay in the pockets of the bondholders. This is because the United States government does not tax the interest earned on municipal bonds. Nor do state and local governments tax the income earned on their own bonds.

Why this relief for the hard-pressed taxpayer? The answer has nothing to do with the charitable nature of the IRS. The exemption arises from a long series of rulings by the United States Supreme Court. In 1819 the court set the first legal precedent in the case of *McCulloch v. Maryland.* The Chief Justice of the court, the renowned John Marshall, summarized the opinion of this court by saying that the power to tax was the power to destroy. Therefore, neither the federal government nor state governments possessed the power to tax each other. Subsequent rulings have reaffirmed this opinion, even though the Treasury occasionally creates an uproar by recommending the elimination of this exemption.

Who issues municipal bonds? States, cities, towns, villages, school districts, and a wide variety of other governmental bodies (excluding those of the United States government). No wonder more than 120,000 different municipal bond issues are currently outstanding.

General Obligations

Despite the enormous number of issues, tax-exempt municipal bonds can be classified as either general obligation bonds or revenue bonds. **General obligations** make up nearly three-quarters of the total. They are aptly named, since they are an obligation or debt backed by the full faith, credit, and taxing power of the issuer.

Theoretically, the holders of a general obligation have first claim on the revenues of the state or local government. But some skeptics question whether a city or state would actually pay interest to bondholders before paying the salaries of its fire fighters, police officers, and other employees. Fortunately, few investors have had to find out the answer the hard way. General obligations have had an outstanding record since World War II, with only a tiny number defaulting. As a result, most investors rank "G.O.'s" as only slightly more risky than the securities of the United States government and its agencies.

Some general obligations are not backed by the full taxing power of the issuer. These **limited-tax general obligations** are secured by the pledge of a tax limited in either amount or rate, such as a maximum property tax. Naturally, investors consider this obligation to be inferior to the more common unlimited general obligation.

Revenue Bonds

Revenue bonds constitute the second major category of municipal bonds. These securities are backed by the earnings of a specific income-producing facility, like a toll bridge, turnpike, airport, or utility system. Since they are not secured by the full faith, credit, and taxing power of the issuer, investors generally rate them below general obligations in quality.

Now and then the earnings from the public facility fail to cover the interest payments and/or the repayments of principle. The Chesapeake Bay Bridge and Tunnel District provides an example. The district first defaulted on its interest payments on a $100 million bond issue back in July 1970. Since then, it has met only two semiannual payments. Apparently, far fewer drivers use the 18-mile bridge tunnel across the lower Chesapeake Bay than had been expected. Investors in this issue not only lost income, they also experienced a drastic decline in the value of their bonds. The price of the issue fell from $700 to $180 after the announcement of the default.

State and local governments sometimes commit themselves to providing additional revenues to assist projects financed by revenue bonds. This commitment usually takes one of two forms: (1) a legally binding contract or (2) a moral obligation. In the case of a **moral obligation bond** the state or local government reimburses the bondholders only if its lawmakers approve the necessary appropriation. Investors should never confuse moral obligation bonds with general obligation bonds.

Apparently some institutional investors are now asking the question, "Why should I buy the moral obligations of immoral politicians?" The reason for this cynicism is the recent unpleasant experience with New York City bonds. New York's Urban Development Corporation, the largest public-housing developer in the country, defaulted on some of its moral obligation bonds in 1975. This default, coupled with the fact that the City of New York has $6 billion of moral obligation issues outstanding, provoked a sudden reassessment of moral obligations.

The moral obligation bond is the brainchild of a former bond attorney named John Mitchell. Mitchell is better known for his service as the country's Attorney General during the Nixon administration. He designed the moral obligation bond as a device for avoiding a public vote on new public-housing financing. Apparently, voters too often turned down requests by the housing authority for additional funds.

Two other types of revenue bonds are **industrial revenue bonds** and **pollution-control bonds**. Industrial revenue bonds (IDRs) gained considerable popularity in the 1960s. Cities and towns issued billions of dollars of these tax-exempt bonds and used the funds to build factories, office buildings, and industrial sites for companies. By doing so, they lured companies into the area, thereby creating new jobs and eventually higher income and property tax collections.

Alarmed by this distortion of the tax-exemption provision (in effect, taxable corporations were receiving the benefits intended for state and local governments), Congress restricted the use of industrial revenue bonds in 1968. But Congress left two loopholes. It continued to permit IDR issues of under $5 million. As a result, many small municipalities continue to issue these bonds. Unlike general obligations and most revenue bonds, IDRs seldom carry any guarantees by the local governments. Instead, they are backed only by a lease signed by the company using the facilities. This vital point of information usually gets buried in the fine print of the bond indenture.

The results have been disastrous for some small investors. In the state of Oklahoma alone, 21 IDR bond issues defaulted in the 2-year period ending in 1976. And some of these defaults appear to have been the direct result of fraud.

At the same time that Congress outlawed issues of industrial revenue bonds in excess of $5 million, it authorized the sale of tax-exempt pollution-control bonds. Companies sell pollution-control bonds through a state or municipal agency. The firms use the proceeds to buy pollution-control equipment. The interest saved by going the tax-exempt route often adds up to millions of dollars. As a result, this type of financing has grown spectacularly over the 6 years from 1971 to 1976—from $88 million in 1971 to $5 billion in 1976.

There is one other type of revenue bond. Local authorities issue **housing authority bonds** to finance low-rent housing projects. These bonds also have the backing of a United States government agency, the Housing Assistance Administration. Investors justifiably view them as a very safe investment.

Buying and Selling Municipal Bonds

A decade ago only 15% of new municipal bonds were purchased by individuals. Now individuals dominate this market. Despite this popularity, tax-exempt municipal bonds still present special problems to the small investor.

Until recently, the tax-exempt municipal bond market was virtually unregulated by the government. As a result, full disclosure of information or even reasonable disclosure does not yet exist. The recent scandals in the tax-exempt markets attest to some of the resulting problems.

The enormous number of tax-exempt bond issues creates additional problems. Just obtaining a bond price sometimes takes a day or more—none of the newspapers carries quotes. As a result, prices for the same bond can and do vary from dealer to dealer. Government investigations reveal occasional overcharges of 20% or more.

Later chapters provide detailed strategies for investors to employ in such markets. For now, individual investors should remember to:

1   Study their own tax situation carefully before buying tax-exempt bonds. These bonds pay much lower interest rates than non-tax-exempt bonds of similar quality. Therefore, not all taxpayers benefit from the tax-exempt feature. As a general rule, the individual must be in at least a 25 to 30% tax bracket to justify the purchase of tax exempts.
2   Buy large, well-known issues.
3   Consider bonds issued by their own state or one of its municipalities or authorities. By doing so they usually avoid state and local taxes.
4   Plan to hold on to the bonds for a long time because of the lack of ready marketability.
5   Refuse to buy bonds unless they have an unqualified legal opinion attached approving the bond. These opinions are usually provided by bond attorneys with recognized expertise in municipal bonds.

MONEY MARKET INSTRUMENTS

Institutional investors and wealthy individuals looking for a place to park their excess cash often turn to the money market. The term **money market** refers to a market for loans or securities maturing in 1 year or less, not to a market for money. But the name seems justified in view of the extremely short-term nature and ready marketability of these investments. They are the next best thing to cash, and they pay interest.

Commercial paper, negotiable certificates of deposit, bankers' acceptances, and Treasury bills all qualify as **money market instruments.** (They are generally called instruments rather than securities because of their short lives.) Treasury bills have already been described in the section on government securities. **Commercial paper** basically consists of short-term debt, especially the unsecured promissory notes (IOUs) of large, well-known companies. Commercial paper seldom comes in denominations of less than $250,000. Investors endowed with this much money enjoy the privilege of being able to personally specify any maturity from 5 to 270 days.

Negotiable certificates of deposit also attract large investors. Banks usually issue these receipts in exchange for the deposit of funds of $100,000 or more. Most certificates range in maturity from 1 to 12 months, but some extend

---

TABLE 3-2   SAMPLE MONEY MARKET RATES

NEW YORK   Bankers' acceptance offered rates quoted by one dealer: 30 days, 4.55%; 60 days, 4.55%; 90 days, 4.55%; 120 days, 4.60%; 150 days, 4.60%; 180 days, 4.60%

Commercial paper sold through dealers: 30 to 270 days, $4^5/_8$ to $5^1/_2$%.

Certificates of deposit ($100,000 or more): top rates paid by major banks in the newly issued market—1 month, 4.65%; 2 months, 4.65%; 3 months, 4.65%; 6 months, 4.75%; 1 year, 5%.

---

to 18 months or more. Negotiable certificates trade in active secondary markets and should not be confused with the smaller-denomination, nonnegotiable savings certificates also issued by banks.

Bankers' acceptances represent a form of short-term financing used in this country since the 1800s. Bankers' acceptances arise primarily from foreign trade. Before an exporter ships goods to another country, he or she insists upon a check or draft on the buyer's bank account. But the buyer dates the check with the expected date of arrival, perhaps many months into the future. The exporter, unable to cash the postdated check immediately, sells it to a bank at a discount. The bank can then (1) hold the check until the payment date or (2) guarantee (accept) the check for future payment and sell it to still another investor. A guaranteed check bears the bank's name and the stamped word "accepted."

These bankers' acceptances trade actively in a secondary market. They offer a broad range of maturity dates, generally from 1 to 270 days, and they come in a wide variety of sizes, ranging in face values from $5,000 to $1 million or more.

The Wall Street Journal and other papers quote the rates on money market instruments every day. A sample quote is presented in Table 3-2.

PRICE FLUCTUATIONS

Bondholders sometimes forget one of the most important facts of investment life—prices fluctuate. Apparently the promise of a safe, steady income lulls them into a false sense of security. Figure 3-9 serves as a painful reminder of the fact that even the obligations of the United States government, of thriving American cities, and of profitable blue-chip corporations have their frequent ups and downs. For example, the United States government 4's of 1980 ranged between a high of 101 and a low of 72.14 during the period from 1960 to 1975.

Changes in Interest Rates

Why do bonds fluctuate in price? Because interest rates fluctuate. During 1960, interest rates on new government bonds hovered around 4%. At the time, this appeared to be a reasonable return. Fifteen years later, with double-digit inflation rocking the economy, the government found itself forced to pay 8% or more on

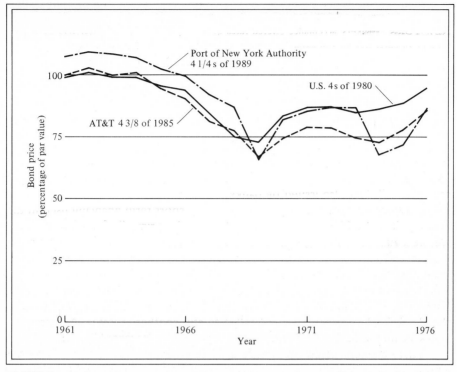

Bond price (percentage of par value)

100
75
50
25
0

Port of New York Authority
4 1/4 s of 1989

U.S. 4s of 1980

AT&T 4 3/8 of 1985

1961   1966   1971   1976
Year

FIGURE 3-9   Price fluctuations in United States government, municipal, and corporate bonds.

its new obligations. As a result, the prices of existing government bonds plunged lower and lower. This decline in price served to raise the return to buyers and to make the old bonds competitive with the new bonds.

EXAMPLE   Suppose the government sells long-term bonds paying 4%. Then, as the years go by, interest rates climb higher and higher until they reach 8%. As a result, all new government securities carry an 8% coupon rate.

With new $1,000 bonds yielding $80 a year in interest, no investor wants to pay $1,000 for a bond returning only $40 a year. In fact, old bonds with a 4% coupon must sell for $500. At that price, the prospective bond buyer can buy two 4% coupon bonds and earn $80 on the $1,000 investment—the same income offered by a new security selling for $1,000.

In general, an increase in market interest rates causes a decline in the price of outstanding bonds. On the other hand, a decrease in rates produces a rise in bond prices. In other words, bond prices move in the opposite direction from interest rates.

Not all bonds fluctuate with changes in interest rates to the same degree. As a rule, the amount of the price change in a bond depends upon the maturity of the bond. The longer the maturity, the greater the change in price for a given change in the interest rate. There is an explanation for this phenomenon. A bond basically represents a long-term contract between the issuer and the bondholder. The bondholder lends the issuer money in exchange for a fixed income. Regardless of what happens to the market rate of interest, this income remains unchanged. Now if interest rates fall, the bondholder benefits from the contract by having a high income. But if interest rates rise, the investor is locked in by the contract and loses the opportunity to make a higher income elsewhere. The longer the term of the contract, the greater the loss. And since the bond markets reflect these events, the greater the resulting decline in the value of the bond.

Potential bond buyers who find the mechanics of bond prices difficult to grasp can always imagine themselves about to sign an ironclad job contract lasting for many years. If salaries go higher after they sign the contract, they obviously lose money. The amount of the loss equals the difference between their contractual salary and the going salary for similar jobs multiplied by the length of the contract. On the other hand, if salaries fall below their contractual salary, they gain.

> EXAMPLE   Tom Johnson signs a 10-year contract for $30,000 as a center fielder on a professional baseball team. At the time he signs, this is the going rate for good center fielders. The next year, because of unexpectedly high inflation and an upturn in TV contracts, salaries for unsigned center fielders jump to $40,000. In effect, the contract costs Tom $90,000, the $10,000 more he could have been earning for each of these 9 years. If he wants to play for another team, he will probably have to pay his club about $90,000. Then it can hire another center fielder without losing money.
>
> Nancy Rogers invests $10,000 in 30-year bonds paying 6%. The next year, interest rates unexpectedly climb to 8%. By buying the bond when she did, she sacrificed additional interest income of $200 a year for 30 years. In order to sell the bond, she will have to settle for a price which reflects this loss.

To summarize, the longer the time remaining until the bond matures, the greater the price fluctuation for a given change in interest rates. This is shown in

TABLE 3-3   *PRICE FLUCTUATIONS FOR VARIOUS MATURITIES*

Rising Interest Rates and Falling Securities Prices

Time to Maturity	Price at 7%, $	Price at 8%, $	Percentage Change
6 months	100	99$^1/_2$	−0.50
1 year	100	99	−1.00
2 years	100	98$^1/_8$	−1.88
5 years	100	96	−4.00
10 years	100	93$^1/_4$	−6.75
20 years	100	90	−10.00

Table 3-3. According to the figures in this table, a 1% increase in interest rates causes a ¹/₂% decrease in the value of a 6-month security and a 10% decrease in the value of a 20-year bond. Obviously investors who dislike surprises should concentrate their holdings in short-term bonds.

Changes in Future Prospects

Bond prices, especially those of corporations and of state and local governments, fluctuate for another reason. As time goes on, the financial prospects of the issuers change. Take the case of Grolier, long recognized as one of the leading publishers of encyclopedias. The Grolier 9¹/₂% debentures traded between 100 and 112 ($1,000 and $1,120) from 1971 through 1973. Then during 1974 the price of the bond collapsed to 24 ($240). Much of this downward slide was caused by the company's misfortunes. Grolier incurred a loss of nearly $30 million in 1974. Apparently many of the bondholders feared almost immediate bankruptcy, because at a price of $240 the Grolier bonds were yielding nearly 40% a year ($95 interest divided by a price of $240).

YIELD SPREADS

Bargain-hunting investors usually find the bond market very disappointing. But sometimes it takes them years to discover the nature of the old saying that "you get what you pay for."

Bond yields differ greatly among various issues. Some pay high returns and others low returns. Almost without exception, the difference in yields reflects the underlying strengths and weaknesses of the individual bonds. Bond traders refer to these differences between the returns on fixed-income securities as **yield spreads** or **yield differences.** They frequently talk about the yield spread between government bonds and high-grade industrial bonds. At the end of 1976, the yield spread between these two types of securities equaled 78 basis points (0.78%) as can be seen in Figure 3-10. Over the years, the difference between these securities widened and narrowed as market conditions changed. In 1974 corporate bonds offered nearly 2% more than government bonds.

Investors must learn to match their objectives with the bonds they buy. In order to do so, they need to understand why yields vary among fixed-income securities. Although bonds differ in innumerable ways, three characteristics play an overwhelmingly important role in determining yields. These three factors are (1) quality, (2) maturity, and (3) income taxation.

Quality

The bond market functions in basically the same way as any other market—the better the quality of the merchandise, the higher the price. Of course, since most

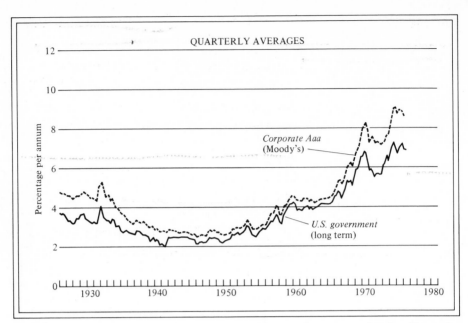

FIGURE 3-10 Yield spreads between government and corporate bonds. (From the Board of Governors of the Federal Reserve System, *Historical Chart Book,* Washington, D.C., 1976, p. 97.)

new bonds sell for the same price, what differs is the income offered to the investor. The higher the quality, the lower the return, and vice versa.

Quality means different things to different people. Fortunately, several companies publish widely used bond ratings. The two best-known rating services are Moody's Investor Services, Inc., and Standard and Poor's Corporation. An article in *The Wall Street Journal* summarizes the importance of these agencies as follows: "Their evaluations of the credit worthiness of debt issuing corporations and governmental bodies not only are strongly influencing investment decisions but also, in the case of municipal securities, are provoking headlines in newspapers and heartburn in politicians."[3] The *Journal* goes on to say that the ratings largely determine the interest rate an issuer must pay. And this ultimately influences the building of schools and factories.

The highest quality bonds (rated AAA by Standard and Poor's and Aaa by Moody's) pay the lowest returns. This is because the investor is much more certain of collecting the full amount of the promised interest payments and the principal. As the ratings drop, the returns go higher. For example, the Carnation Company 8.5% sinking-fund debentures maturing in 1999 were yielding 8.56% in December 1976. At the same time the Pfizer, Inc., 8.5% sinking-fund debentures due in 1999 were returning 9%. What accounts for this yield spread of 44 basis points? A slight difference in quality. The Carnation bonds received the highest rating, the Pfizer securities the second highest rating.

Judging from these results, the investor must choose either high returns or high quality—the two very seldom go together. Just how that vital decision is made is the subject of later chapters.

Maturity

During most of the past few centuries, interest rates on short-term securities have been less than those on long-term securities. Nearly everyone with a bank deposit is aware of this relationship. Passbook accounts, which can be withdrawn immediately with no penalty, pay the least. Ninety-day accounts earn a slightly higher rate. One-year savings certificates pay still more, and so on. The same is true of bonds. Look at the serial bonds issued by the Department of Water and Power of the City of Los Angeles. The bonds maturing in 5 years yield 4.4%, in 10 years 5.25%, and in 20 years 6.3%.

As always, there is a very sound explanation for these higher returns on longer term securities. Remember, the longer the maturity, the greater the change in price for a given change in interest rates. Most investors purchase bonds so they can sleep well at night. If they wanted to watch their dollars perform gymnastic feats, they would buy stocks instead. So they need to be induced to hold longer term securities. The higher returns provide that incentive.

Taxation

Because of the desirability of tax-exempt interest, municipal bonds pay much lower interest rates than non-tax-exempt bonds of similar quality and maturity. Usually the difference amounts to at least 2%. So the taxpayer buying tax-exempt bonds sacrifices a higher taxable return elsewhere in order to obtain tax-free interest.

Other Factors

Numerous other factors affect the yield on fixed-income securities. These include:

1 *Marketability* The more marketable or liquid the security, the lower the yield it carries. Marketability usually hinges upon the size of the issue. For example, corporate bond issues of less than $30 million lack a ready market.
2 *Sinking funds* Bonds with sinking funds generally pay lower returns.
3 *Call protection* Securities with call protection yield less than securities with little or no protection against calls.
4 *Seasoned issues* **Seasoned issues** (bonds which have been outstanding for a while) generally pay less than new issues. Underwriters usually sell new securities at higher yields in order to move them more quickly.
5 *Currency* Some bonds are expressed in foreign currency rather than dollars. Depending upon the attractiveness of the currency, the yield can be higher or lower.

KEYWORDS

bond certificate
face value
principal amount
denomination
premium
discount
maturity date
expiration date
coupon rate
nominal rate
registered bond
bearer bonds
coupon
bond indenture
protective covenants
trustee
Trust Indenture Act of
    1939
default
secured bonds
first mortgage bond
second mortgage bond
equipment certificates
chattel mortgages
collateral trust bonds
debentures
call provision
refunding
deferred-call feature

call premium
sinking fund
private placement
flat
convertible bonds
conversion price
conversion ratio
investment value
investment premium
conversion value
conversion premium
exchange premium
preferred stock
cumulative dividends
United States savings
    bonds
Series E bonds
Series H bonds
Treasury bills (T-bills)
competitive bids
tenders
noncompetitive bids
basis point
Treasury notes
Treasury bonds
Dutch auction
stop-out price
exchange refunding
advance refunding

cash refunding
yield to maturity
Fannie Mae
Freddie Mac
Sallie Mae
Ginnie Mae
government-sponsored en-
    terprises
federal agencies
municipal bonds
general obligations
    (G.O.'s)
limited-tax general obliga-
    tions
revenue bonds
moral obligation bond
industrial revenue bonds
    (IDRs)
pollution-control bonds
housing authority bonds
money market
money market instruments
commercial paper
negotiable certificates of
    deposit
bankers' acceptances
yield spreads
yield differences
seasoned issues

QUESTIONS

1   Describe a bond.
2   Given a choice, should individual investors buy bearer bonds or registered bonds? Why?
3   Discuss the different types of direct security offered by corporations on their bonds.
4   Explain the following statement: "Strangely enough, the best security for a bond is the company's earning ability."
5   How do sinking funds operate? What advantages do they offer bondholders? Are there any possible disadvantages?
6   Explain why bond buyers usually seek call protection.
7   Refer to Figure 3-3. What is the closing price of the MGM 10s of 1993? Are these bonds selling at a discount or a premium? What is the current yield? What additional information can be obtained from the quotation?

8   How do bonds differ from stocks?

9   Why do investors buy convertible bonds?

10 The conversion ratio for a convertible bond equals 30 and the market price of the underlying stock equals $40. What is the conversion value? If the bond sells for $1,500, what is the conversion premium?

11 Look up the American Airlines (abbreviated A Airl) and the Air Reduction (abbreviated Air Re) convertible bonds in Figure 3-3. Which bond should an investor seeking considerable price appreciation purchase? What type of investor would be interested in the other bond? Be certain to use the following information on these two bonds in your answers to the questions:

	American Airlines	Air Reduction
Face value	$1,000.00	$1,000.00
Conversion price	$44.25	$31.25

12 Is preferred stock more like common stock or a bond? Explain.

13 List the various types of government securities. What type of investor purchases each of these securities?

14 How do investors buy Treasury bills and notes? Do these investments offer any special advantage over savings accounts during times of unusually high interest rates?

15 Look at the quotation for the United States government 9s of 1980 in Figure 3-8. How much income does the holder of a $10,000-denomination bond collect? How much does the bondholder collect when the government redeems the bond? Why is the yield to maturity less than the coupon rate?

16 What are the real names of Fannie Mae and Freddie Mac? Are they federal agencies or government-sponsored enterprises? What do they do?

17 What are the two major categories of municipal bonds? How do they differ?

18 What happened to the Chesapeake Bay Bridge and Tunnel District bonds? How did this affect the bondholders?

19 Should companies be allowed to benefit from tax-exempt industrial revenue and pollution-control bonds? Why or why not?

20 What steps should individual investors take in buying municipal bonds?

21 Why do bond prices fluctuate? Do the prices of government bonds fluctuate more or less than corporate bonds?

22 Why do long-term bonds fluctuate more than short-term bonds?

23 Interest rates soared to new highs in 1974. Why did bond prices drop to new lows at the same time?

24 Explain the impact of quality, maturity, and taxation on yield spreads.

25 Does anyone benefit from the tax-exempt interest feature of municipal bonds besides rich taxpayers?

26 Do money market instruments provide attractive investment media for small investors? What about large institutional investors?

REFERENCES

The Bond Book, Merrill Lynch, Pierce, Fenner & Smith, New York, 1975.

Buchanan, James M.: *Public Principles of Public Debt,* Irwin, Homewood, Ill., 1958.

Clark, Lindley H., Jr.: "Speaking of Business: Buying Bonds," *The Wall Street Journal,* Dec. 18, 1973, p. 20.

*Darst, David M.: *The Complete Bond Book: A Guide to All Types of Fixed-Income Securities,* McGraw-Hill, New York, 1975.

Elia, Charles J.: "Chances Grow of Companies Calling in Bonds as Long-Term Rates Decline, Analyst Notes," *The Wall Street Journal,* Feb. 12, 1976, p. 31.

Expanded Bond Tables, Financial Publishing, Boston, 1970.

"First U.S. Corp. Accused by SEC of Bilking Client," *The Wall Street Journal,* Aug. 23, 1973, p. 4.

Gezci, Michael L.: "The Rating Game: Credit-grading Firms Wield Greater Power in Public Debt Market," *The Wall Street Journal,* Oct. 26, 1976, pp. 1, 37.

Handbook of Securities of the United States Government and Federal Agencies and Related Money Market Instruments, 26th ed., First Boston Corporation, 1974.

Homer, Sidney, and Martin L. Leibowitz: *Inside the Yield Book: New Tools for Bond Market Strategy,* Prentice-Hall and the New York Institute of Finance, Englewood Cliffs, N.J., 1972.

Klapper, Byron: "Crisis of Confidence: Just How Binding Is a 'Moral Obligation'? Bond Market Nervously Awaits Answer," *The Wall Street Journal,* Feb. 28, 1975, p. 32.

Laing, Jonathan R.: "The Trader: Treasury-Bond Dealer Finds Job More Hectic as the Market Gyrates," *The Wall Street Journal,* Aug. 13, 1975, pp. 1, 11.

Leger, Richard: "Borrowing Cheaper: More Companies Sell Tax-exempt Bonds for Pollution Control, Saving Millions," *The Wall Street Journal,* July 8, 1974, p. 24.

Nagdeman, Julian J.: "Behind the Tombstones: Lies a Thriving Capital Market in Private Placements," *Barron's* Dec. 6, 1976, pp. 5, 18, 20.

Richert, Lindley B.: "Better Safe than . . . Mutual Funds Dealing Exclusively in Bonds Catch Investors' Eye," *The Wall Street Journal,* Jan. 31, 1973, pp. 1, 29.

_____: "One Man's Junk Is Another's Bonanza in the Bond Market," *The Wall Street Journal,* Mar. 27, 1975, pp. 1, 19.

Roche, Peter B.: "Municipal Funds Are Thriving as Woes Hit Other Types of Tax-exempt Securities," *The Wall Street Journal,* June 9, 1975, p. 23.

Shaffer, Richard A.: "Suspicious Issues: Rising Bond Failures Are Being Investigated for Possible Swindles," *The Wall Street Journal,* July 21, 1976, pp. 1, 27.

*Sherwood, Hugh C.: *How to Invest in Bonds,* McGraw-Hill, New York, 1974.

U.S. Department of the Treasury: *United States Savings Bonds: A Quick-Reference Guide,* U.S. Savings Bonds Division, 1973.

* Publications preceded by an asterisk are highly recommended.

CHAPTER FOUR

OPTIONS AND FUTURES

Despite drastic changes in our society and economy, people still dream about becoming millionaires. How can investors achieve this goal? The old-fashioned way is through patience and frugality. Anyone who began investing $1,000 a year in the stock market 40 years ago has by now made at least $1 million.

But patience has become less of a virtue in today's fast-moving world. Options and futures represent the newest approach to making a million—sometimes in less than a year.

OPTIONS

Options differ radically from other investments. The holder of an **option** merely possesses the right to buy or sell a specific asset, perhaps 100 shares of stock or 50 acres of land. The option contract specifies both the period of time allowed to exercise this right and the price.

Supposedly the first recorded use of options dates back to the Old Testament, when Jacob was granted the right to marry Rachel. The price of the option was 7 years of labor. The ancient Greeks, Phoenicians, and Romans also used options, but in affairs of money rather than of the heart.

Real Estate Options

Real estate investors sometimes use options to limit their losses. Imagine a developer trying to assemble enough land for a new community. In order to obtain the necessary acreage, a number of different parcels must be purchased. The old saying that "half a loaf is better than no loaf" definitely does not apply to large-scale real estate projects. Nothing could be worse than spending an enormous amount of money only to find out that several key properties cannot be obtained.

Instead of buying each of the properties outright, the developer acquires options on the land and pays a fee to the landowners, who in return promise to sell the developer their property on or before a specific date at a predetermined price. The option in no way commits the developer to the purchase of the parcels. But it does commit the landowner to selling if and when the developer decides to exercise the right to buy. If the developer can assemble all the necessary acreage and appropriate financing, he purchases each of the properties. Otherwise, the options expire, with a loss of only the cost of the options.

Why do the owners of the land demand to be paid for granting options to the developer? Because they not only sacrifice the possibility of selling the land to someone else during the period of the option, but they also tie their money up in the property.

Besides limiting the possible loss on an investment, options serve another purpose. They temporarily magnify the buying power of the investor. Again, take the case of real estate. Suppose someone discovers that a major highway system is planned for a remote part of the country. Knowing that land values will jump dramatically once the news becomes widely known, she decides to invest every penny of her savings in property along the proposed right of way. Her $10,000 does not buy much real estate—the raw land costs $500 an acre, and financing is not readily available. One alternative is to spend the $10,000 for options on the land. By agreeing to pay a slightly higher price of $550 per acre and limiting her option to only 1 year, the land speculator in effect lays claim to 1,000 acres for that period. In return, she pays the owners a token fee of only $10 an acre for the options. Six months later officials announce the construction of a new highway system, and the land optioned by the investor doubles in price to $1,000 an acre. Rather than go to the trouble of acquiring the land and then selling it, she simply sells the options to another investor who wants to acquire the land. The options sell for $450 an acre, i.e., the difference between the agreed-upon price for the land ($550) and the going market price ($1,000). Total profit from the option play comes to $440,000, quite a return on an investment of $10,000.

No doubt some millionaires owe their fortunes to just this type of strategy. But option investments seldom end so happily. Suppose the highway system fails to materialize, land prices stay at $500 an acre, and at the end of the year the options expire without any value. Goodbye $10,000.

LISTED STOCK OPTIONS

The investment success story of the 1970s focuses on listed stock options. Only a few years ago the stock options market was the exclusive domain of the sophisticated speculator. Now options trading exceeds the activity on the American Stock Exchange, the second largest stock exchange in the country.

Why the sudden surge of interest in options? Because the **Chicago Board Options Exchange** (CBOE for short) completely changed the rules of the game. Prior to the establishment of the CBOE in 1973, speculators purchased so-called **conventional options** in the over-the-counter market. One of these conventional options is displayed in Figure 4-1. A conventional stock option is custom-designed to meet the exact requirements of the buyer, just like a real estate option. So it is almost impossible to resell the option. Like the captains of ships in days gone by, purchasers of conventional options generally stay with them until they sink beneath the waves. Or they exercise the option and buy the stock.

The organizers of the CBOE decided to correct this situation by standardizing options. They accomplished their objective by limiting options to certain dates, prices, and stocks. They also simplified the exchange of options by establishing a special clearing house and by declaring that the seller of options always retains any dividends paid on stocks.

By standardizing options, the CBOE and the other exchanges not only provided investors with a ready market but also reduced the cost of the options. Apparently, the public liked the end result. The CBOE opened on April 26, 1973, with options on only 16 stocks. By 1976 the number had expanded to 90. And the American, Midwest, Pacific, and Philadelphia Stock Exchanges now trade options on another 100 or more stocks. Volume on just the CBOE increased more than 2,000% in the $3^{1}/_{2}$-year period ending in 1976.

The Language of Options

Option terminology often confuses beginning investors. The phrase **striking price** refers to the specific price at which the underlying stock (the stock specified in the option contract) can be bought or sold. The option contract expires or ceases to exist after the **expiration date**. The price of an option is usually called the premium. Finally, there are two types of stock options—calls and puts. A call gives the holder the right to buy 100 shares of a particular stock, whereas a put gives the holder the right to sell.

EXAMPLE   Suppose the Polaroid July 40 calls sell for $5. This option gives the holder the right to buy (call) 100 shares of Polaroid, the pioneer company in instant

U.S. OPTION INTERNATIONAL, INC.

PUT AND CALL OPTIONS

GUARANTEED BY MEMBERS N. Y. STOCK EXCHANGE

New York, N. Y. ______________ 19____

For Value Received, the BEARER may CALL on the endorser for ONE HUNDRED (100) shares of the ______________

stock of the ______________

at ______________ Dollars ($______________) per share

ANY TIME WITHIN ______________ days from date.

THIS STOCK OPTION CONTRACT MUST BE PRESENTED, AS SPECIFIED BELOW, TO THE ENDORSING FIRM BEFORE THE EXPIRATION OF THE EXACT TIME LIMIT. IT CANNOT BE EXERCISED BY TELEPHONE.

DURING THE LIFE OF THIS OPTION:

1. (a) — the contract price hereof shall be reduced by the value of any cash dividend on the day the stock goes ex-dividend; (b) — where the Option is entitled to rights and/or warrants the contract price shall be reduced by the value of same as fixed by the opening sale thereof on the day the stock sells ex-rights and/or warrants.

2. (a) — in the event of stock splits, reverse splits or other similar action by the above-mentioned corporation, this Option shall become an Option for the equivalent in new securities when duly listed for trading and the total contract price shall not be reduced; (b) — stock dividends or the equivalent due-bills shall be attached to the stock covered hereby, when and if this Option is exercised, and the total contract price shall not be reduced.

Upon presentation to the endorser of this Option attached to a comparison ticket in the manner and time specified, the endorser agrees to accept notice of the Bearer's exercise by stamping the comparison, and this acknowledgment shall constitute a contract and shall be controlling with respect to delivery of the stock and settlement in accordance with New York Stock Exchange usage.

EXPIRES ______________ 19____
3:15 P. M., NEW YORK, N. Y. TIME

6525

The undersigned acts as intermediary only, without obligation other than to obtain a New York Stock Exchange firm as Endorser.

U. S. Option International, Inc.

CALL OPTION

FIGURE 4-1 A conventional option agreement. (Reprinted with permission of U.S. Option International, Inc.)

photography, for $40 a share (striking price) until the third Saturday in July (expiration date). The premium equals $5 a share. Since 1 option covers 100 shares, the option costs $500.

All CBOE options expire on the Saturday following the third Friday in 1 of 4 months. For example, options on Polaroid expire in January, April, July, and October. Other options expire on a February, May, August, and November cycle. The striking price of an option is determined by the market price of the underlying stock at the time the option is issued. Striking prices on CBOE options always end with a 5 or a 0. They vary in intervals of $5 for stocks selling below $50, $10 for those selling between $50 and $200, and $20 for stocks selling above $200. Trading begins in a new series of options with a different striking price whenever a stock moves past the midpoint of a new interval. For example, suppose Polaroid falls from $41 to $36. Then the CBOE will open trading in options with a striking price of $35.

Option Quotations

The Wall Street Journal carries a daily summary of option trading on the various exchanges. A sample page is shown in Figure 4-2. According to the column titled "-July-Last," the Exxon July 45 calls closed at $8³/₄. Each July 45 option gives the holder the right to buy or call 100 shares of Exxon at a striking price of $45 a share until the third Saturday in July. Since the premium equals $8³/₄ a share and an option covers 100 shares, each option costs $875. Judging from the figures in the column marked "July Vol.," only nine of these options changed hands on December 20. The last column labeled "N.Y. Close" indicates that shares of Exxon closed on the New York Stock Exchange at $51⁵/₈.

On the same day, 83 of the Exxon January 55s were bought and sold. The closing price of these short-lived promises equaled $¹/₄ a share or $25 an option. None of the Exxon July 55s is outstanding, which is indicated by the letter "b." And the Exxon January 60 options did not trade, which is shown by the letter "a."

Why the wide variety of striking prices on the Exxon options? Because Exxon had fluctuated sharply during the previous months. The CBOE initiates a new series of options each time a stock moves substantially. For example, if Exxon drops to 42, the CBOE will open trading in Exxon options with a striking price of 40.

Buying Calls

Optimistic investors purchase calls. A call gives them the right to buy 100 shares of stock at a fixed price, regardless of the actual market price. Ideally the market price of the underlying stock moves considerably higher after the investor buys the call.

Suppose someone buys a January call on IBM when IBM stock is selling for

Chicago Board

Option &	price	Jan Vol.	Jan Last	Apr Vol.	Apr Last	Jul Vol.	Jul Last	N.Y. Close
Alcoa	... 50	55	3½	4	5	a	a	53⅜
Alcoa	... 55	59	1⅛	b	b	b	b	53⅜
Alcoa	60	18	1-16	3	1	5	2	53⅜
Am Tel	..55	51	8¼	2	8⅜	a	a	63⅛
Am Tel	..60	276	3⅜	412	3⅞	248	4¼	63⅛
Am Tel	..65	b	b	158	1⅛	71	1¾	63⅛
Atl R	... 40	10	17½	b	b	b	b	57⅜
Atl R	... 45	28	12¼	a	a	b	b	57⅜
Atl R	50	112	7⅝	24	8½	8	9¼	57⅜
Atl R	60	281	⅞	164	2⅝	97	3¾	57⅜
Avon	 40	175	6⅜	44	7¼	35	8	45⅞
Avon	 45	475	1 15-16	109	3⅞	99	4¾	45⅞
Avon	 50	377	5-16	375	1½	228	2 7-16	45⅞
BankAm	.25	43	3¼	27	3⅝	16	4	28⅛
BankAm	.30	27	3-16	30	1	14	1½	28⅛
Beth S	.. 35	27	5⅝	13	6⅛	4	6¼	40½
Beth S	.. 40	127	1 1-16	95	2⅛	13	2¾	40½
Beth S	...45	103	⅛	148	11-16	b	b	40½
Bruns	10	7	5¼	b	b	b	b	15⅜
Bruns	... 15	186	⅞	84	1 9-16	165	2 1-16	15⅜
Bruns	... 20	43	1-16	315	5-16	122	11-16	15⅜
Burl N	...40	13	7	a	a	a	a	46⅜
Burl N	.. 45	33	2⅛	18	3⅞	a	a	46⅜
Burl N	.. 50	31	¼	18	1½	b	b	46⅜
Citicp	25	15	5⅞	a	a	18	7⅛	30¾
Citicp	... 30	123	1	64	2 1-16	64	2⅞	30¾
Citicp	... 35	122	1-16	54	½	24	1	30¾
Citicp	40	5	1-16	13	⅛	b	b	30¾
Delta	 35	a	a	17	4⅛	a	a	37½
Delta	... 40	106	½	7	1⅝	12	2½	37½
Delta	 45	a	a	1	5-16	b	b	37½
Dow Ch	. 40	321	2⅛	150	3⅞	40	4⅞	41¾
Dow Ch	. 45	115	5-16	284	1⅝	94	2½	41¾
Dow Ch	. 50	11	1-16	106	⅜	b	b	41¾
Eas Kd	..80	484	3⅞	339	6¾	27	8⅞	82
Eas Kd	..90	810	⅜	703	2⅝	201	4⅛	82
Eas Kd	.100	188	1-16	601	¾	b	b	82
Eas Kd	110	a	a	17	⅛	b	b	82
Eas Kd	120	30	1-16	b	b	b	b	82
Exxon	.. 45	62	7	4	7⅛	9	8¾	51⅝
Exxon	.. 50	184	2½	102	3½	25	4⅜	51⅝
Exxon	.. 55	83	¼	208	1 3-16	b	b	51⅝
Exxon	.. 60	a	a	1	5-16	14	11-16	51⅝
F N M	..15	274	1½	36	1¾	56	2 1-16	16½
F N M	..20	a	a	50	¼	37	⅜	16½
Fluor	 30	12	6⅝	a	a	a	a	36⅜
Fluor	35	25	2¼	2	3⅝	2	5⅛	36⅜
Fluor	40	73	⅜	50	1⅝	66	2½	36⅜
Fluor	... 45	12	1-16	18	½	b	b	36⅜
Ford	 50	91	9	91	9¾	25	10⅝	58⅞
Ford	 60	244	1	70	2½	79	3⅝	58⅞
Gen El	..50	149	3⅜	119	4¾	25	5¾	52⅞
Gen El	..55	92	11-16	87	1 15-16	25	2¾	52⅞
Gen El	.. 60	70	1-16	47	⅝	b	b	52⅞
G M	60	284	15¼	5	15¼	b	b	75⅛
G M	70	619	5⅜	99	6⅜	85	7⅛	75⅛
G M	80	121	⅜	126	1 9-16	54	2½	75⅛
Gt Wst	...15	177	7⅛	a	a	a	a	22¼
Gt Wst	..20	147	2¼	80	3⅛	43	3⅞	22¼
Gt Wst	..25	81	¼	86	1	32	1 7-16	22¼
Glf Wn	..15	204	2 15-16	156	3⅜	86	4	17¾
Glf Wn	..20	131	⅛	376	11-16	362	1 3-16	17¾
GfWn O	..16	138	2 1-16	b	b	b	b	b
GfWn O	..20	22	3-16	b	b	b	b	b
Halbtn	.. 50	4	12¾	b	b	b	b	63
Halbtn	.. 55	19	7¾	b	b	b	b	63
Halbtn	...60	62	3⅞	13	5¾	6	7¼	63
Halbtn	...70	1	¼	82	1 7-16	6	2¾	63
Homstk	..25	5	11½	1	11½	b	b	36¾
Homstk	..30	63	6⅝	20	7⅛	22	8⅜	36¾
Homstk	..35	138	2¼	65	3¾	34	4¾	36¾

Total volume 75,271 Open interest 1,462,071

a-Not traded. b-No option offered.

Listed Options Quotations

Monday, December 20, 1976

Closing prices of all options. Sales unit usually is 100 shares. Security description includes exercise price. Stock close is New York Stock Exchange final price.

Option &	price	Feb Vol.	Feb Last	May Vol.	May Last	Aug Vol.	Aug Last	N.Y. Close
Boeing	.. 45	161	2	35	3⅜	6	4¼	45
Bois C	...25	23	7	5	7⅜	a	a	32⅛
Bois C	...30	158	2⅝	41	3⅜	36	4⅛	32⅛
Bois C	...35	61	9-16	29	1¼	99	1 13-16	32⅛
C B S	... 60	40	1	5	2¾	a	a	57½
Coke	 70	165	6¼	1	8¾	1	9¼	73½
Coke	 80	234	1⅜	121	3⅜	95	4⅜	73½
Coke	90	127	⅛	91	⅞	b	b	73½
Colgat	.. 25	5	1⅞	5	2¾	1	3	26½
Colgat	.. 30	28	3-16	21	9-16	2	1	26½
Cmw Ed	30	5	1¼	16	1⅝	5	2	31⅛
Cmw Ed	.35	a	a	32	¼	18	⅜	31⅛
C Data	..20	104	4⅝	36	5⅝	5	6⅛	24⅛
C Data	..25	638	1 3-16	313	2¼	65	2⅞	24⅛
Gn Dyn	..45	8	8⅜	2	9⅝	b	b	52½
Gn Dyn	. 50	37	4½	9	6½	11	7¾	52½
Gn Dyn	. 60	63	11-16	53	2⅛	19	3⅛	52½
Gn Dyn	..70	20	⅛	b	b	b	b	52½
Gen Fd	..30	176	1⅝	12	2½	30	2 11-16	30¾
Gen Fd	..35	130	¼	a	a	8	¾	30¾
Hewlet	...80	65	6	5	9	a	a	83¼
Hewlet	.. 90	120	1 9-16	5	4	8	6¼	83¼
Hewlet	. 100	33	5-16	36	1¾	22	2⅝	83¼
Hewlet	..110	4	⅛	36	11-16	b	b	83¼
Hewlet	..120	12	1-16	b	b	b	b	83¼
H Inns	.. 10	20	3⅜	37	3⅝	13	3⅞	13¼
H Inns	.. 15	190	⅜	93	¾	76	1 1-16	13¼
Honwll	...40	83	6⅛	a	a	a	a	44¾
Honwll	.. 45	246	2½	96	4⅛	21	5	44¾
Honwll	.. 50	317	⅝	196	1⅞	85	2⅞	44¾
In Flv	... 20	30	2	a	a	a	a	21⅛
In Flv	...25	47	¼	17	¾	8	1 3-16	21⅛
J Manv	..25	1	8½	5	8⅝	b	b	33
J Manv	. 30	103	3½	117	4¼	14	5⅛	33
J Manv	. 35	352	¾	109	1¾	15	2½	33
MGIC	... 15	1	5⅛	7	5½	29	5⅞	19⅜
MGIC	... 20	245	1⅛	126	2 1-16	116	2 11-16	19⅜
Mobil	... 50	4	13	a	a	a	a	62½
Mobil	... 55	38	7½	2	8¼	b	b	62½
Mobil	60	64	3	46	4	33	4⅝	62½
N Semi	..25	1078	2⅜	910	3⅝	605	4⅝	25
N Semi	..30	1853	13-16	761	1¾	353	2⅝	25
N Semi	..35	457	3-16	839	13-16	b	b	25
N Semi	..40	120	1-16	530	5-16	b	b	25
N Semi	..45	45	1-16	b	b	b	b	25
N Semi	..50	10	1-16	b	b	b	b	25
Occi	15	52	7⅝	48	8⅛	7	8⅛	22¾
Occi	20	1173	3	380	3⅝	204	4⅛	22¾
Occi	25	541	9-16	647	1¼	522	1 11-16	22¾
Raythn	.. 60	25	2⅜	47	4¼	a	a	59⅞
Raythn	.. 70	a	a	88	15-16	b	b	59⅞
Rynlds	...50	22	14⅞	b	b	b	b	64⅝
Rynlds	...60	14	5⅛	2	5½	a	a	64⅝
Rynlds	...70	a	a	4	⅞	127	1½	64⅝

FIGURE 4-2 Sample options quotations. (Reprinted with permission of *The Wall Street Journal,* © Dow Jones & Company, Inc., Dec. 21, 1976, p. 27. All rights reserved.)

$272. The striking price equals $280, the expiration date is the third Saturday in January, and the call sells for $5 a share. Now a skeptic might ask: Why pay $5 a share for an option to buy IBM at $280 when the stock sells for only $272? The answer in one word is—hope. The call-option buyer hopes IBM will jump in price. If it does, the option will also increase in price, since it represents a claim on this stock. But why not just buy the stock outright? Because 100 shares cost $27,200—a much larger amount of money than the $500 required for an option.

The option buyer runs a race against time. In order to just break even on the call, IBM must reach $285. At that price the holder of the option makes $5 a share on the stock, buying the stock at the striking price of $280 and selling it on the market for $285. But since the option costs $5 a share, the gain on the stock exactly offsets the cost of the option. The following numbers show why the investor just breaks even on the call:

Total cost of purchasing one share
of IBM with a January 280 call:
Striking price	$280
Call premium	+ 5
Total cost	$285

Profit on each share covered
by a call:
Market price of IBM	$285
Cost of IBM purchased with call	− 285
Profit	$ 0

Profit on call: $0 × 100 shares = $0

Regardless of how the stock performs, the option buyer pays the option premium. This option entitles the holder to buy IBM for $280 a share from the investor who sold the option. Obviously, no one exercises a call unless the market price of the stock exceeds the striking price.

If IBM goes to $290, the option buyer makes a 100% return on the money invested in the option. Ignoring all commission costs, the buyer calculates the profit as follows:

Total cost of purchasing one share
of IBM with a January 280 call
(see preceding example): $285

Profit on each share:
Market price of IBM	$290
Cost of IBM purchased with call	− 285
Profit	$ 5

Profit on call: $5 × 100 shares = $500

A $500 profit on a $500 investment translates into a 100% profit in only a few months. So the investor's money doubles in no time at all.

In reality, option buyers seldom buy and sell the stock underlying the option. They prefer to simply trade the options, which always reflect the price of the stock. By dealing only in options, they save considerable commission costs and also avoid putting up the large sums of money necessary to trade the stocks. Otherwise, imagine the plight of small investors who purchased the call on IBM for $500. In order to call the stock, they must come up with $280 times 100 shares, or $28,000. This scramble for large sums of money to purchase the stock would eliminate one of the main advantages of trading options.

A call buyer interested in IBM might have selected a call with a different striking price. For example, options with a striking price of $260 traded side by side with the 280s. The IBM January 260 calls sold for $17—a much higher price than the January 280 calls. The reason for this is not hard to see. Even though IBM currently sells for $272, the January 260 call option gives the holder the right to buy shares at a price of $260. Anyone buying shares of IBM at $260 and selling them in the market for $272 makes $12. The option premium reflects this fact. The relevant question is: How much is the option buyer paying above this immediate exchange value? The answer is $5, the premium of $17 minus the current exchange value of $12.

The prospective option trader needs to know how much the underlying stock must move before a profit can be made at the expiration date. The per-share cost of purchasing 100 shares of IBM with a January 260 option is calculated as follows:

> Cost of purchasing one share of
> IBM with a January 260 call:
>
> | | |
> |---|---|
> | Striking price | $260 |
> | Call premium | + 17 |
> | Total cost | $277 |

With IBM already selling at $272, a move of only five points takes the call buyer up to the break-even point of $277, assuming all commissions are again ignored. If IBM closes at $290 on the final day of trading in the January options, the January 260 calls must close at exactly $30—the difference between the striking price and the market price. The investor sells an option originally purchased at $17 for $30, a gain of $13. This $1,300 profit on a $1,700 investment represents a tidy return of nearly 76% in a few months.

Returns on Calls

Options provide investors with roller-coaster-like results. During the week of April 7, 1975, the Monsanto April 60 calls dropped to a low of $$^1/_4$. At that price the investor with $1,000 could have purchased calls on 4,000 shares of Monsanto. With Monsanto stock selling at 54^3/_4$, those 4,000 shares represent a total market value of $219,000. So the option buyer suddenly possesses the same clout as a millionaire.

The option buyer's time in these exalted ranks is limited. The options expire in a few weeks, and unless Monsanto moves to at least $60, they expire worthless. Actually Monsanto did even better than that. It jumped by nearly 25% to close at

$68^5/\!s$. And the April 60s catapulted from $1/4$ to $8^3/\!4$—an increase of 3,400% in less than 1 month! After selling the options and paying all commissions the fortunate option buyer cleared over $30,000 on an original investment of $1,000.

Option buyers seldom fare this well. Max Ansbacher, a writer for a widely read financial newspaper called *Barron's,* described the situation well when he said:

> *When the New York Stock Exchange sneezes, the CBOE catches cold; when Big Board stocks contract a serious illness, CBOE calls just about roll over and die.*
>
> *To illustrate, of the 89 July options which were available on July 26, 1974—the last day they were traded—all but nine were worthless.*[1]

Ansbacher goes on to say that a $1,000 investment in all the calls available on May 1 shrank to a paltry $110 by the end of July.

Buying Puts

Pessimistic investors purchase puts. A put gives an investor the right to sell 100 shares of stock at a fixed price, regardless of the actual market price. Ideally the underlying stock drops considerably after the investor buys the put.

Imagine an investor buying a put on IBM with a striking price of $260. If the stock falls to $240, the investor buys the stock for that price and then sells it to the individual who promised to buy it for $260. Or, still simpler, the holder of the put just sells it back for $20.

Writing Options

Not everyone buys options, of course. In fact, for every buyer there must obviously be a seller, or, in the lingo of options, a **writer.** Option writers issue the contracts promising to buy or sell stock for a fixed price. The option premium reimburses them for standing ready to buy or sell.

Option writers experience returns vastly different from those realized by option buyers. Buyers seek unlimited profits, whereas option writers settle for a limited income in the form of a fixed premium. Option writing also appears to be much more of a sure thing than option buying. Most option writers make a good return—some people say 15 to 20% a year—on their capital. On the other hand, most option buyers lose money, according to studies done by the Securities and Exchange Commission. Buyers seem to feel the opportunity of making really large profits justifies these losses.

Who buys options and who writes them? According to a study commissioned by the CBOE, most of the traders are clients of large brokerage firms. The sellers appear to be much better off financially than the buyers. Most buyers earn $15,000 to $50,000 a year in their jobs and have a net worth ranging from $25,000 to $100,000. Salaries of option writers range from $25,000 to $100,000 annually, and they usually have a net worth of from $50,000 to $500,000. That probably explains why many Wall Streeters believe option sellers are wealthy and market-wise, while buyers are "marks."

A survey conducted by Louis Harris and Associates for the American Stock Exchange contradicts these findings. According to the Harris poll, the typical options investor earns an income of $35,000 a year and owns investments worth $104,000. This description holds true for both buyers and sellers of options.

As time goes on, more and more institutions will probably join individual investors in selling options. Already some insurance firms, banks, and retirement funds write options on stocks held in their portfolios.

Mechanics of Option Writing

The mechanics of option writing differ very little from option buying. Suppose an individual owns 500 shares of Polaroid and is thinking of writing options on the stock. The options quotations yield the following information:

DATE: DECEMBER 20								
	Jan.		April		July			N.Y.
Option & Price	Vol.	Last	Vol.	Last	Vol.	Last		Close
Polar 30	323	$7^1/_4$	b	b	b	b		37
Polar 35	510	$2^7/_8$	236	$4^1/_2$	69	$5^1/_2$		37
Polar 40	871	$^9/_{16}$	405	$2^3/_{16}$	95	$3^1/_4$		37

The investor decides to sell five April 35s at a premium of $4^1/_2$ on each share and calculates the hoped-for return on this transaction as follows:

Step 1   Option premium $4^1/_2$
          Less immediate exchange value -2
          Excess of premium over exchange value $2^1/_2$

Explanation of Step 1: Since shares of Polaroid are currently selling for $37 and the striking price is only $35, the immediate exchange value of the option equals $2. Therefore, the option writer really makes only $2^1/_2$ on the option.

Step 2   Investment in shares of Polaroid
          at market price $37
          Less cash received for option $-4^1/_2$
          Actual investment $32^1/_2$

Explanation of Step 2: The option writer immediately receives the premium of $4^1/_2$ and so needs to invest only an additional $32^1/_2$ in each share of Polaroid.

Step 3   Return on sale of options: $\dfrac{\$\ 2^1/_2}{\$32^1/_2} = 7.7\%$

Explanation of Step 3: At the most the writer earns $2½ on a $32½ investment, a return of 7.7%. This return is based upon the assumption that the stock remains at $37 and either it is "called away" from the writer at the exercise price of $35, or the option writer buys the option back just before expiration for $2.

Step 4   Annual return on sale of options: $7.7\% \times 3 = 23.1\%$

Explanation of Step 4:   The option writer earns 7.7% in a 4-month period. This amounts to 23.1% a year, since there are three 4-month periods in a year.

Prospective writers must balance their returns from writing options against the potential gains from simply holding the stock. If they sell the options, they forgo these gains. They must also consider the possibility of the market declining sharply. The income from the sale of the options provides a buffer against small declines in the underlying stock. But a large drop would eradicate the premiums and cut deeply into investment values.

Not all option writers own the underlying stock. Some of the more aggressive traders write **naked options,** i.e., options not covered by the ownership of stock. Naked-option writers expose themselves to tremendous risk, but the profits can be rewarding. They collect a premium without ever having to buy the stock. (They do have to deposit some good-faith money, thus ensuring their satisfactory completion of the contract.) If the stock price stays the same or goes down, they pocket the full amount of the option premium. If the stock price goes up by only the amount of the option premium, they break even. And if the stock goes still higher, they face some very difficult decisions.

Option Prices

The variety of expiration dates and striking prices offered with options bewilders many investors. How does anyone select the "best" expiration date and striking price? The answer depends upon an investor's goals, forecasts of the future, and pocketbook.

Volatility   Option premiums reflect the personal beliefs of both buyers and sellers. Buyers of options thrive on changes in stock prices and gladly pay higher premiums for options on volatile stocks. The more stock prices fluctuate in the future, the better their chances for making money. And the buyers' losses are limited to the amount of the premium. On the other hand, sellers detest volatility, since it can only work against them. As a result, option sellers usually demand much higher prices for writing options on volatile stocks. The willingness of buyers to pay higher premiums combined with the reluctance of sellers to write them produces higher premiums on options of more volatile stocks.

Expiration Date   The expiration date of the option also affects the premium. The odds of a stock making a profitable move increase with time. The option buyer resembles a broad jumper. The longer the run, the better the chances of making a good jump. Because buyers benefit from extended periods of time and sellers suffer, buyers and sellers agree to higher premiums for longer-lasting options. For this reason, options are a wasting asset. As time goes on, the value of the option decreases, and the decline usually occurs at a faster and faster pace.

Striking Price   Striking prices add a further complication to the analysis of options. The striking price remains the same during the entire life of the option contract. The nearer this striking price is to the market price of the underlying stock, the greater the buyer's chances of making money on the option. In effect the striking price serves as a hurdle placed in front of an investor sprinting after profits. Higher hurdles or striking prices make it more difficult for option buyers to finish the race on time. In fact, many of the runners fall flat on their faces. No wonder calls with striking prices far above the current market price sell for so little.

Dividends   Dividends also affect option premiums. Generally speaking, firms paying high dividends seldom increase very much in price. So prospective call buyers avoid options on these stocks. Since option writers collect these dividends in addition to their premium income, they naturally prefer to write options on high-dividend stocks. Buyers and sellers compromise and agree to lower premiums for options on high-dividend-paying stocks.

Interest Rates   Interest rates have the exact opposite impact on premiums. At higher interest rates, option writers sacrifice considerable income by holding stocks instead of bonds. As a result, they usually demand and get higher premiums for writing options during times of high interest rates.

WARRANTS AND RIGHTS

Warrants and **rights** bear a close resemblance to call options. Like calls, they enable the holder to purchase a stated number of shares at a specified price, but unlike calls, the holder of a warrant or right purchases the stock from the company issuing the warrant or right rather than from another investor.

Speculators grow misty eyed when they reminisce about the performance of warrants. The warrants of Tri-Continental (a firm providing investment advice) hit bottom at $\$^1/_{32}$ in 1942. By 1946 they rebounded to $\$5^5/_8$, and in 1969 they reached $\$75^3/_4$. No wonder warrants often foster dreams of great wealth. Anyone cashing in on this 27-year price increase made $2,424 on every dollar initially invested. A $1,000 investment eventually transformed itself into nearly $2.5 million dollars.

Of course, for every success story in warrants, there are numerous failures. Warrants often expire worthless. The TWA warrants provide one of the more celebrated collapses. They took a crash dive from $25 a share to $0 in about 6 months, when the price of TWA's common stock dropped substantially.

TABLE 4-1 *EXPIRATION DATES OF WARRANTS*

Time Period	Number of Warrants	Percentage of Warrants
0 to 1 year	27	23
1 to 2 years	25	21
2 to 3 years	24	21
3 to 4 years	13	11
4 to 5 years	6	5
5 to 10 years	12	10
10 to 30 years	6	5
No expiration date	4	4
	117	100

Source: All warrants listed in the *Value Line Convertible Survey* on December 13, 1976.

Warrants differ greatly in their expiration dates. Tri-Continental and Allegheny warrants never expire. Most of the other warrants available today expire in 3 to 5 years. The expiration dates for warrants traded on the NYSE and AMEX as of December 1976 are shown in Table 4-1.

Why does a company issue warrants? Usually to "sweeten" a debt financing. Supposedly a combination of warrants and bonds appeals to prospective buyers of new bond issues. The warrant provides the staid bond investor with a chance to participate in the growth of the company.

Warrants generally last considerably longer than options. But rights are short-lived, with most expiring in 2 to 3 weeks. Companies issue rights in connection with new stock issues. The corporate charters of many firms and the laws of 22 states guarantee shareholders a preemptive, or first, right to new shares. This preemptive right makes it impossible for management to sell new shares without first offering them to existing stockholders.

EXAMPLE The XYZ company decides to sell 1 million shares of new stock. It already has 5 million shares outstanding. The company makes the sale through a rights offering, giving stockholders 1 right for every 1 share they already own. At the end of 2 weeks the stockholders can exchange their rights together with the specified amount of cash for new shares. The new shares are sold for a reduced price in order to attract buyers, and it takes 5 rights to purchase each new share.

If stockholders do not want to buy the new shares, they simply sell their rights to someone else. But at least they had the opportunity to retain their proportion of the ownership in the company.

FUTURES

A **futures** contract involves future delivery of some asset or service. The exact terms of that future delivery, including the time and place of delivery, are fixed in the contract. Take, for example, the futures contracts in wheat traded on the Chicago Board of Trade. Anyone buying one of these contracts agrees to purchase 5,000 bushels of No. 2 soft red winter wheat or some reasonably close substitute.

Reading Futures Quotations

The Wall Street Journal and many other local newspapers carry daily information on futures trading in a variety of commodities ranging from wheat to plywood. A sample page from the *Journal* is shown in Figure 4-3.

The *Journal* shows the abbreviated name of the exchange, the size of the contract, and the price per unit for each commodity. Wheat futures trade on the Chicago Board of Trade and on the Kansas City and Minneapolis Exchanges. On Monday, November 22, the December wheat contracts opened on the Chicago

FIGURE 4-3   Sample commodity futures quotations. (Reprinted with permission of *The Wall Street Journal,* © Dow Jones & Company, Inc., Nov. 23, 1976, p. 40. All rights reserved.)

Board of Trade (CBT) at 260¢, or $2.60, a bushel. The December futures hit a high for the day of $2.65 a bushel, a low of $2.60, and closed at $2.63 ¹/₂–$2.64. The closing price for the day topped the previous day's close by 4¢ to 4 ¹/₂¢. The *Journal* also shows the season's high and low for each type of contract. The December futures contract in wheat has ranged between a high of $4.23 and a low of $2.50 ¹/₂.

Futures traders, like options traders, confront a variety of contract dates. On November 22, wheat futures for delivery in the months of December 1976 and March, May, July, September, and December of 1977 exchanged hands. Altogether, 6,827 contracts were bought and sold.

The commodity exchanges limit all futures contracts to specific months and permit the seller to deliver the commodity anytime during the month. For example, anyone selling December 1976 wheat on the Chicago Board of Trade agrees to deliver 5,000 bushels of No. 2 soft red winter wheat or some close substitute at a specific location any day during the month of December 1976. The agreed-upon price equals the sales price of the contract, say $2.64 a bushel.

The world sugar contract provides another example of commodity futures. Sugar contracts trade on the New York Coffee and Sugar Exchange (CSE). Each contract covers 112,000 pounds of sugar, and the contract price is stated in cents per pound. No one purchased any of the January contracts, but someone did offer to sell for 8.5¢ a pound. Sugar for delivery in March opened at 8.95¢ a pound and apparently moved sharply higher to 9.10¢ a pound. The low for the day equaled 8.95¢, and the contracts closed at 9.08¢ to 9.10¢ for a gain of 0.2 to 0.22 of 1¢ (about one-fifth of 1¢) from the previous day.

A daily gain of one-fifth of 1¢ sounds like penny ante. But this contract covers an enormous amount of sugar. The total gain on the contract equals one-fifth of 1¢ times 112,000 pounds, or more than $200. And when sugar really gets moving, daily price fluctuations of 1¢ a pound or $1,000 a contract become commonplace.

The season's high and low for the older sugar contracts reflects the volatile nature of sugar prices. March sugar contracts have traded as high as 16.20¢ a pound and as low as 7.94¢.

Finally, the *Journal* indicates estimated sales of 2,656 contracts on Monday (it usually takes at least 24 hours to tally all of the sales) and actual sales of 2,598 contracts on Friday.

Trading Futures

The very thought of trading commodities futures terrifies some beginning investors. After all, what in the world does anyone do with 5,000 bushels of wheat? That's a lot of bread. And it comes at a cost of about $13,000—also a lot of bread!

Actually very few investors ever take delivery of commodities. They sell their contracts before delivery occurs. If they do take delivery, the commodities are stored in bonded warehouses, rather than being dumped on their front yard.

And they seldom pay the full amount of the contract value. Instead they deposit 6 to 10% of the purchase price as good-faith money. On November 22, an investor could have purchased a wheat contract with only $1,250.

> EXAMPLE Liz Jones thinks sugar prices will increase during the coming year. In November she buys one October sugar contract, paying a price per pound of 9.40¢. Although the total value of the contract equals $10,528, her broker asks for a deposit of only $2,000.
>
> Over the following 3 months sugar steadily moves higher in price. At the end of January the October sugar contract closes at 18¢, and Liz sells her contract. Since she paid 9.4¢ a pound and now sells it for 18¢, the gain on each pound of sugar equals 8.6¢. Total profit on the contract amounts to 8.6¢ times 112,000 pounds, or $9,632—a pretty sweet showing.

> EXAMPLE Unfortunately, Liz's gain is Bob Smith's loss. Bob Smith originally sold Liz Jones the sugar contract (both parties to a transaction remain anonymous until delivery). Like Liz, his only interest in sugar stems from the profit potential inherent in futures. He has no intention of ever delivering sugar to anyone. Long before his commitment comes due, he plans to buy back his contract, at a much lower price he hopes.
>
> By the end of January, Bob thoroughly regrets his sale of October sugar. He has lost $9,632, and lately he has been lying awake at night, unable to sleep. If sugar goes much higher, he will be squeezed right out of the market and most of his life savings.

Speculators, Floor Traders, and Hedgers

Participants in the commodities futures game fall into one of three general categories: (1) **speculators,** (2) **floor traders,** and (3) **hedgers.**

Speculators trade solely for fun and/or profit. They have no intention of ever taking or making delivery of any of the commodities. Most speculators in commodity futures trade actively and seldom maintain a position in any one contract for any length of time. Some of them even concentrate on daily price moves and get out the same day they get in. These so-called **scalpers** settle for small profits (and losses).

Floor traders buy and sell futures contracts on the floor of a commodity exchange. Because of their membership on the exchange, they pay reduced commissions on their trades. Or they execute orders from brokerage houses for a small commission.

Hedgers provide the economic justification for futures markets. They use the futures markets to reduce risk. Many of these hedgers hold large inventories of commodities. For example, soft-drink manufacturers always maintain considerable supplies of sugar in order to satisfy production needs. Large fluctuations in sugar prices translate into substantial gains or losses in raw-sugar inventories. Not only are these inventory gains and losses extremely unpredictable, but they are almost certain to eventually create a financial crisis for any company. For that reason, soft-drink manufacturers prefer to transfer the commodity price risk of sugar to speculators and concentrate on more productive and predictable operations like bottling and canning soda.

Hedging

Hedgers reduce their exposure to inventory risk by selling futures contracts. Suppose a soft-drink manufacturer keeps 10 million pounds of sugar in stock. Sugar prices fluctuated between 10¢ and 60¢ in 1974 and 1975; so the firm might have lost millions of dollars during those 2 years. Instead, the management of the company maintained a short position in 90 sugar futures; i.e., it sold sugar futures contracts. The gains or losses on these futures contracts nearly offset the gains or losses on the company's sugar inventories.

> EXAMPLE   The Cola Company holds an inventory of 10 million pounds of sugar. In order to reduce its exposure to the risk of falling sugar prices, management sells 90 sugar-futures contracts. Each contract covers 112,000 pounds of sugar; so 90 contracts involve slightly more than 10 million pounds of sugar. The previous month cash sugar prices plunged by 10¢ a pound, creating a $1 million loss on the sugar inventory. But the futures contracts declined by 9¢ a pound from 40¢ to 31¢. Management sold these contracts at 40¢ a pound and now buys them back at 31¢, a 9¢ profit. The profit on the sugar futures contracts almost offsets the inventory loss. The actual results are:
>
> | | |
> |---|---:|
> | 10,000,000 pounds × −$0.10 inventory loss | − $ 1,000,000 |
> | 90 contracts × 112,000 pounds × $0.09 | |
> | profit on futures | 907,200 |
> | Total loss on sugar | − $ 92,800 |

Hedging through the futures markets seldom eliminates all risk of price fluctuations. In the previous example the firm still lost $92,800, even though it had hedged its position in sugar. Complete protection from price changes is difficult to achieve for several reasons. Futures contracts often differ in size, duration, and quality from the hedger's own commitments. And futures prices seldom move exactly in unison with cash prices. Futures traders refer to the difference between cash prices and futures prices for the same commodity as the **basis**. On November 22, 1976, No. 2 soft red wheat sold in the cash markets for $2.62 a bushel. On the same day the July 1977 wheat contract closed at $2.80. So the basis in this case equals 18¢. Anyone hedging wheat hopes this basis moves in her or his favor or at least remains the same.

Some firms and individuals face another type of risk. They must agree to deliver goods in the future even though they hold no inventories. Take the case of a builder who agrees to construct a home at the end of 1 year. The prospective buyer insists upon knowing the exact price immediately and wants it to be as low as possible. The builder finally quotes a price, but does so knowing that the entire profit on the house could easily be lost by a mistaken prediction of future lumber

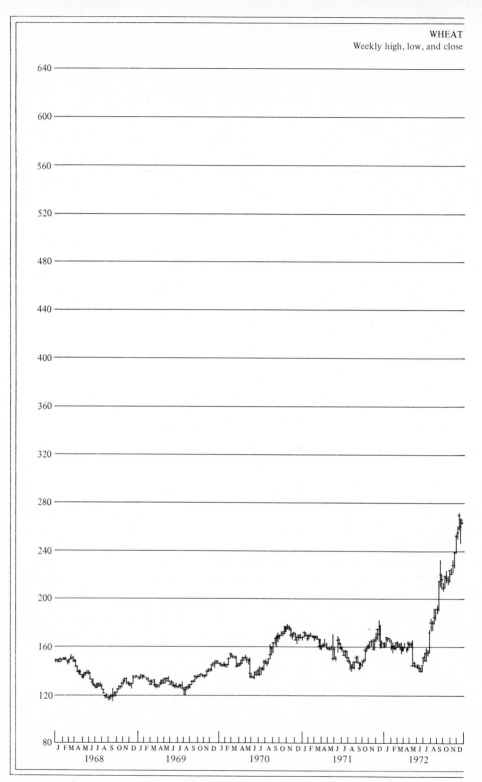

FIGURE 4-4 Behavior of wheat futures prices. (From Commodity Research Bureau, Inc., New York, *1977 Commodity Year Book,* p. 366.)

CHICAGO
of nearest futures (in cents per bushel)

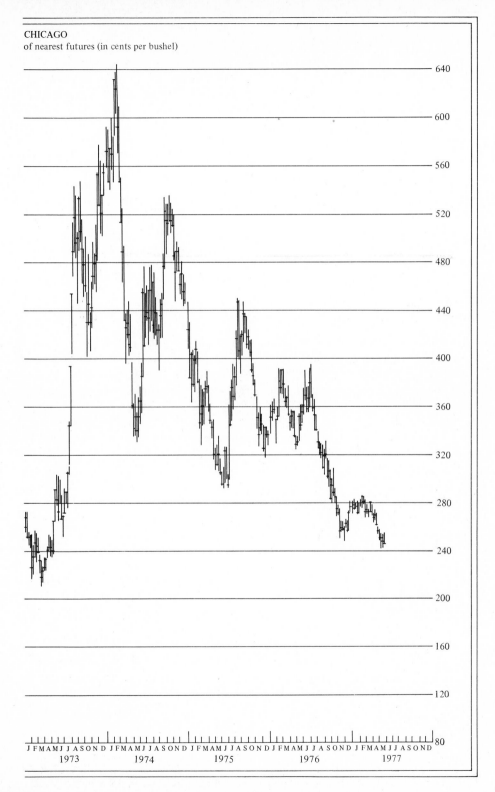

costs. To hedge against this possibility, the builder decides to buy lumber futures. If lumber prices increase during the year, the gain on the futures contract will protect against the increased construction costs.

> EXAMPLE   A builder signs a contract in June guaranteeing to construct a house for $90,000 in 1 year's time. Although the quote reflects expected increases in materials and labor, a dramatic rise in lumber prices would easily wipe out the small profit.
>
> To protect against this contingency, the builder purchases a lumber contract with delivery in 1 year. At $200 per 1,000 board feet (a board foot of lumber is 1 foot long × 1 foot wide × 1 inch thick), the contract covers 100,000 board feet for a total cost of $20,000. But the builder needs to deposit only $700 on the contract.
>
> Now if cash lumber prices increase, the futures contract does also. Therefore, gains on lumber futures more or less offset losses on the purchase of materials for the home. And the usual profit is made for managing the construction.

Supply and Demand of Commodities

When asked for advice about the future behavior of stock prices, the famous banker J. P. Morgan supposedly replied, "They will fluctuate." Morgan's comment is doubly true of commodities futures. Figure 4-4 illustrates the behavior of wheat futures prices over the 10-year period from 1968 through 1977. In most years wheat futures fluctuated by at least 25%. And from March 1973 to March 1974, they nearly tripled in price, going from about $2.20 a bushel to $6.40.

To the uninitiated, these tremendous changes in price appear to be caused by the speculative excesses of commodity traders. After all, what else could cause such enormous fluctuations in a staple crop like wheat? The answer is basic changes in supply and demand. Not even futures prices are immune from these underlying economic forces. Many traders recognize this fact of life and base their trading on detailed information about weather conditions, governmental purchases, exports, harvests, etc.

A detailed analysis of wheat provides an example of some of the information used by traders. Wheat grows around the world. The map in Figure 4-5 shows that major growing areas exist within the boundaries of the United States, Canada, Argentina, Australia, India, China, and large parts of Europe and Russia. Most United States wheat comes from the Midwest, with Kansas accounting for the largest percentage of the total crop.

Futures traders and farmers classify wheat in two ways: first according to physical characteristics and second by the time of planting. The three basic types of wheat are hard, soft, and durum. Hard wheat is the essential ingredient in most of the bread made in the United States. Soft wheat goes into biscuits, cakes, crackers, pastries, etc. Durum wheat is used in spaghetti, macaroni, and similar products.

Wheat also varies with the time of planting. The United States wheat crop consists of winter and spring wheat. Farmers plant winter wheat in the fall, let it lie in the ground during the winter, and harvest it in the early summer. They sow

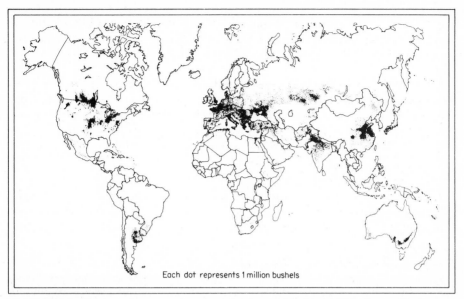

Each dot represents 1 million bushels

FIGURE 4-5   Major wheat-growing areas in the world. (From *The Commodity Futures Game: Who Wins? Who Loses? Why?* by Richard J. Teweles, Charles V. Harlow, and Herbert L. Stone, © 1974 by McGraw-Hill, Inc., p. 363. Used with permission of McGraw-Hill Book Company.)

the spring wheat as soon as they can in the early spring and harvest the crop in the late summer.

The **supply** of wheat or any other similar commodity equals the current harvest or production plus the carry-over from the previous growing season and any imports. The United States government controls most of the carry-over through the Commodity Credit Corporation, an agency of the United States Department of Agriculture. Once the crop is planted, weather has a crucial effect on the total amount of wheat harvested. Futures traders pay especially close attention to the evening weather reports. The better the weather conditions, the larger the harvest and the lower the commodity prices. The worse the weather, the smaller the harvest and the higher the commodity prices. Speculators hoping for larger crops and lower prices find a silver lining in every cloud, providing it does not rain so much that it floods the crops.

Demand also plays a role in futures prices. The United States is one of the world's leading exporters of wheat. The Russian wheat purchase of 400 million bushels in 1972 made the headlines. Because of the low price received by the United States, some witty observers labeled it the Great Grain Robbery. Wheat exports totaled more than a billion bushels in each of the years from 1972 to 1976. In addition to commercial exports, the United States sends millions of bushels of wheat overseas under government programs such as Public Law 480 and Aid for International Development.

Wheat exports usually account for more than half of the total wheat production. American consumers and farmers use the rest. About 5 to 10% of domestic consumption (or disappearance, as traders sometimes call it) comes from seed usage. Another 1 to 5% goes to feed livestock, and the remainder goes into food.

Most brokerage firms issue periodic reports on supply-and-demand conditions in each of the major commodities. For example, Bache Halsey Stuart Shields, Inc., issued the following analysis of wheat in November 1976:

> *A very demoralized situation is about the best way to describe the futures market as repeated attempts to pick the bottom have failed. Farmer holding has at times provided a prop under the market but slow export business has generally overshadowed this, particularly in recent days as Argentina has substantially underbid United States prices on any origin tenders. Weakness in other grain futures has weighed on wheat with commercial selling also a recent market factor. Outside participation has been very light as it appears that speculators, who are most generally bullish, prefer to trade other commodities. The thinness of the market then compounds the problem with little in the way of support on dips.*
>
> *On the export front PL-480 business continues to progress while outright cash deals remain very slow. Competition is stiffening from countries that produced better crops than expected while potential buyers are more selective in their shopping.*
>
> *Winter wheat seeding is now virtually completed with stands generally in good condition and while moisture would be welcome in many areas, the situation is far from critical. We look for further weakness over the near term, but would be very cautious about selling at these levels.* [2]

Who Speculates in Futures and Why?

If futures trading sounds either too risky or too complicated to appeal to the average person, guess again. The Commodity Exchange Authority occasionally conducts studies of the types of people who speculate in futures. According to the CEA, students, homemakers, farmers, physicians, salespeople, maids, and the unemployed all speculate in futures. Judging from the CEA figures, farmers and farm managers far outnumber participants from any other profession. Apparently they believe they have special insights into the economics of crops. Physicians also play a surprisingly active role in the futures markets.

Very few of these speculators risk much money on one commodity. One CEA study of the corn futures market shows 40% of the speculative accounts holding only one contract and another 35% with only two or three contracts.

Many speculators approach commodity futures trading as they would a game, and most of the present books on the subject reinforce this view. Thomas Hieronymus, author of the scholarly *Economics of Futures Trading,* says "People are drawn to markets by the mystery, glamour, and excitement and many stay to play the game." [3] Bruce Gould begins his book, the *Dow Jones–Irwin Guide to Commodities Trading,* by saying "Trading commodities is like playing bridge or poker." [4] Gould claims to have played the game extremely well. After graduating from law school he supposedly turned a $5,000 investment into $80,000 in less than 7 months. He concludes his introduction with the words, "For those who make it, commodities is the only game in town." Teweles, Harlow, and Stone even call their best-selling guide to futures *The Commodity Futures Game: Who Wins? Who Loses? Why?*

Investors in stocks, bonds, and real estate seldom describe their activities as a game. What makes the investor in futures so different? Probably the inherent conflict present in every futures trade. To some extent, futures markets resemble the ancient gladiator pits. The buyer of a futures contract stands in direct opposition to the seller. If prices increase, the buyer benefits and the seller suffers. And when prices decline, the tables are turned. So for every winner in the futures market, there is a loser.

Mathematicians describe futures trading as a zero-sum game. In other words, the total wealth of the traders always remains the same. As the game progresses, players simply redistribute this wealth among each other. In this respect futures trading resembles poker. Once all the poker chips have been placed on the table, successive hands merely determine who wins the available chips. Neither poker nor futures trading directly creates new wealth.

Actually futures trading more closely resembles a negative-sum game, at least for investors. All the players pay commission costs, so over the very long run all players lose. In other words, the payoffs to all players sum to less than zero.

Despite the gladiatorlike aspect of futures trading, or perhaps because of it, numerous people participate in the markets. Futures trading offers several advantages. First and foremost, a speculator can go to bed poor and wake up a millionaire. Enormous gains occur surprisingly frequently. And the entry fee into this long-shot contest seldom exceeds several thousand dollars. Some of the contracts require a deposit of only $300. But individual brokerage firms usually set minimum account sizes for their customers. A 1977 survey of 13 brokerage firms showed the following requirements for trading commodities futures:

Size of Account	Number of Brokerage Firms
No minimum	3
$0 to $3,000	5
$5,000	5

In addition, several of the firms require their customers to have a minimum net worth of $20,000 or more. And Merrill Lynch, the largest brokerage firm in the country, authorizes trading only for investors with a net worth of at least $75,000, exclusive of home and life insurance.

Speculation in futures offers other benefits. Instead of facing a myriad of stocks and bonds and properties, traders confront only about 50 different commodities. These commodities are relatively easy to follow. And there are no quarterly reports, annual reports, dividends, tender offers, proxies, coupons, taxes, certificates, or other financial complications. Finally, commissions account for only a small percentage of the value of the goods traded.

Perhaps all these advantages offset the two outstanding shortcomings of futures—the negative-sum aspect of the game and the great risk of losing the entire amount invested. Only the investor can decide.

Stop Orders and Trading Limits

Futures trading sometimes bankrupts people. In order to guard against this unpleasant possibility and to conserve capital, most traders make it a practice to place stop orders. Suppose a trader buys a copper contract in the hopes of an upturn in worldwide economic activity. Every 1¢ move in a 25,000-pound copper contract results in a loss or gain of $250. If copper drops by 10¢, the speculator loses $2,500 on an initial investment of $750.

To protect against this possibility the investor places a stop order and instructs the broker to sell the contract if the price ever drops by more than 5¢ below the price originally paid for the contract. This stop-loss order prevents large losses from accumulating during protracted downturns and frees the trader from the necessity of following the market closely.

Unfortunately, stop-loss orders do not completely eliminate the possibility of extremely large losses. The rules of every commodities exchange set daily **trading limits** on commodities prices. No trading is permitted at prices outside these limits. For example, the Commodity Exchange limits fluctuations in copper contracts to 5¢ above or below the preceding day's close.

Presumably trading limits prevent overly large fluctuations in commodities prices. But they often result in traders being locked into their contracts. Suppose a major copper producing country suddenly announces its intention to lower its copper prices by 20¢ a pound. The price on the exchange reflects this news and immediately falls by 5¢ a pound under a barrage of sell orders. No further trading takes place, since exchange rules limit fluctuations to 5¢. Although trading is permitted within the 5¢ limit, no one wants to buy until prices fall further than the daily limit. After 2 more days of limit-price moves, the speculator's stop-loss order gets filled, with a loss of $5,000, considerably more than planned. Obviously no one should ever rely completely on stop-loss orders to protect against loss.

Spreads

Cautious futures speculators (some do exist) enter **spreads** rather than simply buying or selling contracts. The investor buys one commodity contract and simultaneously sells a similar but not identical contract. For example, he or she sells 10,000 bushels of December wheat and buys 10,000 bushels of September wheat.

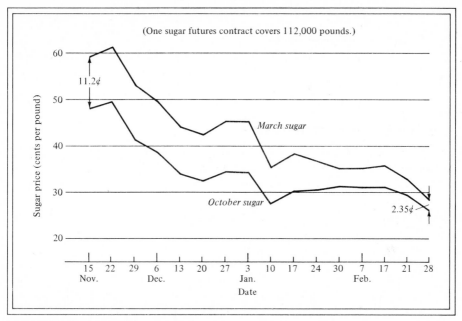

FIGURE 4-6   A spread in sugar futures.

A spread immunizes the trader from the ups and downs of commodity prices. Now the worry is about the difference between prices and not just prices. This refinement in the trader's tastes apparently comes with experience, just as many people first learn to like wine and then come to appreciate the difference in various wines.

Turn the clock back to November 15, 1974. In the preceding months, sugar futures had surged upward on the news of a sugar shortage. An investor following sugar decides prices are headed much lower during the next year. She considers several alternative strategies for cashing in on this move. The simplest and most obvious is to just sell some sugar contracts. But in a volatile market like sugar, catastrophic losses sometimes occur even with stop orders. Instead she decides to take a lower risk strategy and establishes a spread in sugar. She sells a March contract at 59.2¢ and purchases an October 1975 contract for 48¢.

As long as the prices of these two contracts move exactly in tandem, the trader remains in the eye of the price hurricane. Only a change in the price spread between the two contracts can produce a profit or loss. During the first weeks, prices jump by several cents a pound, but the spreader breaks even. In the following weeks the spread narrows and produces a substantial profit. The week-by-week prices of both contracts are displayed in Figure 4-6. And the total profits or losses from the spread are calculated as follows:

Contract	Profit or Loss per lb., ¢
March Sugar, ¢	
Sold at 59.20 and bought at 28.70	30.50
October Sugar, ¢	
Bought at 48.00 and sold at 26.35	−21.65
Total profit	8.85
Total profit on spread	8.85¢ × 112,000 lb = $9,912

CURRENCY FUTURES

For a long time the ads in Barron's read: "Money Grows Faster in Mexico." With promises of 10 to 14% on special savings certificates, hundreds of millions of dollars flowed south of the border.

On the evening of August 31, 1976, the Mexican government devalued its currency. This break in a 22-year tradition of stable currency shocked many American investors with peso savings accounts. In the next 2 weeks, they watched the peso plummet in value from about 8¢ to 5¢. Anyone converting pesos back into dollars suffered a 36% loss, a high price to pay for a lesson in currency fluctuations.

Other people paid a still higher price. The **International Money Market** (IMM) in Chicago offers investors a chance to participate in international finance on a grand scale. Credit-worthy customers can buy and sell **currency futures** contracts involving hundreds of thousands of dollars in Mexican pesos, German deutsche marks, Dutch guilders, Italian lira, Japanese yen, British pounds, Swiss francs, and Canadian dollars.

Take, for example, the Mexican peso contract. The contract covers 1 million pesos for delivery in the future. Prior to the devaluation *The Wall Street Journal* showed the following quote in its section of futures prices:

	Open	High	Low	Close	Change	Season's High	Low
Dec.	0.07785	0.07810	0.07765	0.07770	−0.00010	0.07919	0.06622

At the closing price the buyer of a single peso contract pledges to pay $77,700 in December for a million pesos. But the amount of money required as a good-faith deposit totals only $3,000. Unexpected devaluations make some currency futures traders rich and others poor—almost overnight. Eight days later the *Journal* quoted the December peso contract as follows:

	Open	High	Low	Close	Change	Season's High	Low
Dec.	0.04700	0.04815	0.04650	0.04810	−0.02547	0.07919	0.04650

Between Tuesday of one week and Wednesday of the next, the peso contract dropped in price by nearly 3¢, falling from $0.07770 to $0.04810. To make matters worse, most speculators found themselves "locked" into their contracts because of trading limits. Anyone holding a single peso contract lost nearly $30,000.

Currency futures trading attracts a special breed of speculator. These people apparently ignore the frequent tales of financial disasters. For example, foreign-exchange losses caused the collapse of the large Herstadt Bank of West Germany and forced the reorganization of the $1 billion Franklin National Bank of New York. And the losses of financial giants like the Lloyds Bank, the Vatican, and the Union Bank of Switzerland were huge. In currency trading, even the gnomes of Zurich, Switzerland, occasionally lose money.

The shining example of success at foreign-exchange trading is provided by Lord Keynes. Keynes, one of the world's outstanding economists, reputedly made a fortune, lost it, and then made it again by trading currencies. And he did so while at the same time having a leisurely breakfast in bed each morning.

KEYWORDS

option	naked options	basis
Chicago Board Options Exchange (CBOE)	warrants	supply
	rights	demand
conventional options	futures	trading limits
striking price	speculators	spreads
expiration date	floor traders	International Money Market (IMM)
call	hedgers	
put	scalpers	currency futures
writer		

QUESTIONS

1   Give two reasons why investors purchase options on real estate.
2   Define the following terms: call, put, expiration date, striking price, premium.
3   Refer to the quotations on the Atlantic Richfield options in Figure 4-2. Why are there so many different striking prices? What are the expiration dates on these options? What was the closing price of the January 60 options? How many of these option contracts changed hands in 1 day? What was the closing price of Atlantic Richfield on the New York Stock Exchange?
4   Suppose a stock is selling for $40. Explain why an option on the stock with a striking

price of $30 must sell for at least $10. (The term *arbitrage* refers to the simultaneous buying and selling of the same good at different prices. The *arbitrageur* makes a profit by exploiting this price difference.)

5 Anyone buying the Eastman Kodak April 80 calls shown in Figure 4-2 hopes Eastman Kodak will sell for at least what price before the expiration date?

6 What risk does the covered writer of options confront? What about the writer of naked options? Why do investors write options?

7 What is the maximum annual return a writer can expect to earn on the National Semiconductor February 25 calls? Assume the individual buys the stock for cash and writes the option at the closing prices shown in Figure 4-2. There are 61 days before the option expires.

8 Explain how the following factors affect option prices: volatility of the underlying stock, expiration date, striking price, dividends, and interest rates.

9 How do warrants and rights differ from options?

10 Look at the fresh eggs quotation in Figure 4-3. Where do future contracts for eggs trade? How many eggs does one contract cover? What is the dollar value of December eggs at the high for the day? How much would a speculator in the December eggs have made by buying at the season's low and selling at the season's high?

11 Look at the closing prices of the different egg contracts. If speculators guess the future correctly on the average, what do these prices imply about prices consumers will pay for eggs in the future?

12 Do most investors take delivery on futures contracts? Why or why not?

13 Explain the difference between hedging and speculating.

14 Suppose a textile-manufacturing company signs a contract with the United States government to deliver 100,000 uniforms at the end of 1 year. The cloth in each uniform consists of 5 pounds of cotton. How could the company hedge its risk in the commodity futures market? What are some alternative actions it could take?

15 Poor weather conditions usually cause an increase in commodity futures prices. Explain why.

16 Read the brokerage house comment on page 104. List the demand-and-supply factors mentioned in the article.

17 Why do investors view commodity futures as a game?

18 "For every winner in the commodity futures game, there is a loser." Explain.

19 Why do trading limits in commodity futures make it nearly impossible for stop orders to eliminate sudden large losses?

20 High interest rates usually indicate substantial risk. Why did Mexican savings accounts pay such high interest rates? Did investors benefit from these rates?

REFERENCES

Ansbacher, Max G.: "Near-Total Wipe-Out," *Barron's,* August 1974, pp. 9, 18.

Black, Fischer: "Fact and Fantasy in the Use of Options," *Financial Analysts Journal,* July-August 1975, pp. 36–41, 61–72.

Browne, Harry: *You Can Profit from a Monetary Crisis,* Bantam, New York, 1975.

Cirino, Robert J.: "Options: What the New Game Is All About," *Investing,* February 1974, pp. 6–9.

Collins, Stephen H., and Alan J. Wax: "Business Mushrooms on the CBOE: Volume up

1,000 Per Cent; Success Spurs Competition," *The Commercial and Financial Chronicle,* Apr. 28, 1975, pp. 3, 32.

"Commodity Trading," *Business Week,* Mar. 15, 1976, pp. 50–57.

Ehrbar, A. F., ed.: "Gold's Rather Dubious Glitter," *Fortune,* January 1975, pp. 51–52, 54.

*Gastineau, Gary L.: *The Stock Options Manual,* McGraw-Hill, New York, 1975.

Gould, Bruce G.: *Dow Jones–Irwin Guide to Commodities Trading,* Dow Jones–Irwin, Homewood, Ill., 1973.

Guide to Commodity Fundamentals, Bache Halsey Stuart, New York, 1974.

Guide to Commodity Futures Trading, Bache Halsey Stuart, New York, 1974.

Guide to Technical Analysis of Commodity Futures, Bache Halsey Stuart, New York, 1975.

Hershman, Arlene: "The Action in Auctions," *Dun's Review,* August 1974, pp. 38–41.

Hieronymus, Thomas A.: *Economics of Futures Trading,* Commodity Research Bureau, New York, 1971.

"How to Trade in Commodities," *Business Week,* Sept. 20, 1976, pp. 129–131, 136, 138.

Karp, Richard: "Vanishing Breed: The Old Put and Call Dealers Are Shutting Up Shop," *Barron's,* June 16, 1975, pp. 9, 23–25, 28.

"Leveraging the Leverage," *Forbes,* Apr. 1, 1976, pp. 64, 66.

McInnes, Neil: "Whither Gold? Experts Are Sharply Divided in Their Appraisal," *Barron's,* Jan. 12, 1976, pp. 5, 67.

The Options Clearing Corporation, Prospectus of the Clearing Corporation, Chicago, 1976.

"The Options Investor: Well Heeled," *The Commercial and Financial Chronicle,* July 5, 1976, p. 32.

"Personal Business: Investing in Art and Antiques," *Business Week,* Oct. 27, 1973, pp. 105–109.

Robertson, Wyndham: "Gold Bugs Are On the March," *Fortune,* June 1974, pp. 150–153, 262, 265–266.

Rodolakis, Antony, and Nicholas Tetrick: *Buying Options: Wall Street on a Shoestring,* Reston Publishing, Reston, Va., 1976.

Rush, Richard H.: "Connoisseur's Corner: You Can Still Afford an Old Master," *The Wall Street Transcript,* Dec. 17, 1973, pp. 35, 329; 35, 365.

Serfass, William D., Jr.: "You Can't Outguess the Foreign Exchange Market," *Harvard Business Review,* March-April 1976, pp. 134–137.

Shakin, Bernard: "Commodities Options: They're Available from London through Some N.Y. Brokers," *Barron's,* Jan. 27, 1975, pp. 11–12.

The Silver Outlook, Monex International, Ltd., 1975.

Stinson, Richard J.: "Can You Win at Currency Trading?" *Financial World,* May 15, 1976, pp. 21–24.

*Teweles, Richard J., Charles V. Harlow, and Herbert L. Stone: *The Commodity Futures Game: Who Wins? Who Loses? Why?* McGraw-Hill, New York, 1974.

Trading in International Currency Futures, International Monetary Market of the Chicago Mercantile Exchange, Chicago, 1973.

Trading in Tomorrows, Chicago Mercantile Exchange and International Monetary Market, Chicago, 1974.

Ways, Max, ed.: "Thoroughbreds for Fun and Money," *Fortune,* September 1974, pp. 63, 66, 70, 74, 78, 82, 84, 86.

* Publications preceded by an asterisk are highly recommended.

CHAPTER 5

EFFICIENT-MARKET CONCEPT

People compete. They compete on the playing field, in the classroom, at work, and in the investments markets. This competition has an important effect—it makes it difficult for any person to consistently outperform everyone else. The few who do are usually talented, work hard, and/or take abnormally large risks.

Competition in the investments markets is especially fierce. Not only is it very easy to participate in these markets, but also the potential payoff from selecting the right investments can be enormous. Investors who double their money every year for 10 consecutive years will turn $1,000 into $1,024,000. Even if they earn only 15% a year, their $1,000 will still grow to more than $267,000 in 40 years. As a result, there are numerous individuals and institutions competing for investment profits. For example, there are approximately 25.2 million stockholders in the United States. By comparison, large-scale investment opportunities are limited in number. The stocks of the 50 largest companies account for nearly one-half of the total value of all common shares in the United States.

Many academicians, including Nobel-Prize-winning M.I.T. economist Paul Samuelson, argue that all this competition has an important effect on the investments markets. In particular, they believe that the competitive drive for profits eliminates excess profits and results in fair prices for individual stocks and bonds. A **fair price** means that (at any one point in time) the price reflects the intrinsic value of the investment. This is because undervalued investments are so sought after that their prices are quickly bid up by eager purchasers seeking to make a profit. On the other hand, overvalued investments are so avoided that their prices decline until they are no longer overvalued. Because of the intense competition among buyers and sellers, these adjustments occur very rapidly.

EFFICIENT MARKETS

Just what is an **efficient market?** Eugene Fama, a distinguished professor of finance at the University of Chicago, describes it as a market in which prices always fully reflect available information. If that is true, nothing that investors read or hear can help them select stocks that will do any better than average. In fact, investors who know nothing about stocks will do no worse than investors who are well informed.

In a completely efficient market, all investors have an equal opportunity to make (or lose) money, regardless of their background, knowledge, or resources. If a contest were staged matching experts against beginning investors, the beginners would be just as likely to select the best performing stocks as the experts. And it would be irrelevant how much time or effort either group spent in selecting stocks. This conclusion may sound too incredible to be true. Certainly it is a direct contradiction of the beliefs of most investors and professional advisers. But each year an increasing amount of research is added to the already substantial body of evidence that the securities markets are reasonably efficient. Much of this research compares the performance of experts with that of investors who know nothing about stocks. So far, these "naive" investors are tied with the experts.

This does not imply that the experts know nothing. Far from it. It simply means that the competition of so many investors results in prices which quickly reflect all known information. In other words, stock prices don't deviate for very long from their true value. For example, a natural disaster may result in the sudden destruction of a company's plant and equipment. By the time a stockbroker's clients have been notified, the stock of the company has dropped sharply in value. And it goes no lower in the following days.

Competition in the investments markets implies that no one can plan to make above-average profits unless that person possesses information which is not known to others or takes above-average risks. Competition for profits does not eliminate high returns on high-risk investments, and large profits do accrue to those who have special talents or knowledge.

Of course, the words "average" and "above-average profits or returns" mean different things to different people. The average investor who purchased and held stocks over a 40-year period covering the Great Depression and several wars watched his or her investments increase in value about 50 times. The newer gen-

eration of investors who bought stocks during the 1950s and 1960s probably quadrupled its money in less than 10 years. These returns are not unique to stocks.
During the period from 1951 to 1969, art collectors saw their old-master prints
soar in value to 39 times what they had originally paid for them. And investors in
farmland and other real estate sometimes double their investment in several
years. Obviously, people can make fortunes just by chance in an efficient market.
For this reason, it seems best to interpret the efficient-market concept as simply
saying that, because of competition, prices reflect all known information. Prices
are neither too high nor too low, and they adjust almost immediately to any new
information. As a result, it is almost impossible to earn an above-average return
in the sense of outperforming other investors.

Everyday Competition

Although the idea of an efficient market sounds radical, it is difficult to argue
against. The rationale behind the efficient-market concept—that people compete
for and thus eliminate abnormal profits—is a simple one and can be observed
every day. Even shoppers in a crowded store behave in this way. Despite the very
small payoff (a few minutes more or less of waiting in a line), shoppers quickly
judge the length of the checkout lines and the size of the parcels carried by people in the different lines and then move determinedly to the lines in which they
believe they will have the shortest wait. As a result of this competition among
shoppers, the average waiting times are roughly the same in all lines. There is
never an obviously fast or slow line. Of course, there is a possibility that one line
will move more quickly than others for reasons which cannot be foreseen. But
there is no way for a shopper to consistently select that particular line beforehand. In effect, the lines are priced fairly in terms of waiting time.

Another example of the effect of competition on profits is the betting at a
racetrack. The racetrack crowd is a mixed one, consisting of careful students of
the sport as well as casual bettors out for an evening's amusement. Because winning is more fun than losing, even the casual bettors usually equip themselves
with racing forms showing the favored entries. As the money comes in at the
windows, the odds on each horse often fluctuate considerably. However, by the
time the last bets have been placed, the odds on each horse are an excellent reflection of the chances that the horse will win or lose. Any habitual racetrack-goer
can testify that it is very difficult to beat the odds and consistently make a profit.
The choice is usually one of either taking high risks and betting on the long shots
or playing it safe and wagering on the favorites at low odds. Regardless of how
good or bad a horse is, the odds on that horse usually reflect its chances of winning. In effect, horses are priced fairly in that the odds are neither too low nor too
high.

Auctions are no different. Despite the excitement of the auction and boasts
of items bought at extraordinarily low prices, auction prices at large, well-attended
auctions are usually neither too low nor too high. Most sales are made at fair
prices. Any opening price which is obviously too low is quickly met with a num-

ber of shouted offers at higher and higher prices. As the bidding goes higher, fewer and fewer bids are made, until finally the bidding is closed out on the item. Again, competition results in prices being fair in that they are neither too low nor too high, assuming that no bidders have compulsive psyches and/or unlimited funds. As a result, it is very difficult to make above-average profits at auctions.

TESTS OF MARKET EFFICIENCY

As convincing as these conclusions may appear, some people still do not accept the efficient-market concept. Nevertheless, many people now believe in it who only a few years ago laughed at it. The evidence that the stock market is reasonably efficient is very convincing. This evidence was developed by testing the value of three different types of information used in buying investments to determine whether or not each type would produce an above-average return. The types of information are (1) information on past prices; (2) other public information such as the earnings of firms, tender offers, and announcements of stock splits and of changes in government economic policy; and (3) inside information possessed by employees of brokerage firms and by investment advisers, mutual fund managers, and corporate officers and directors.

In a truly efficient market, information is eagerly sought after and is used as a basis for buying and selling investments. This competition for information makes it very unlikely that any one individual will be able to consistently find information which helps him in purchasing undervalued investments or in selling overvalued investments. It also virtually guarantees that any information which is found is quickly acted upon by the finders, so that the prices of securities are bid up or down and reflect that information almost immediately. Of course, this is not to say that prices are always exactly right, but it does imply that these prices are neither consistently too low nor too high on the average and that they adjust very quickly to new information.

Tests of the efficient-market concept are essentially tests of whether the three general types of information—past prices, other public information, and inside information—can be used to make above-average returns on investments. In an efficient market, it is impossible to plan on making above-average returns regardless of the information available, unless abnormal risk is taken. Moreover, no investor or group of investors can consistently outperform other investors in such a market.

These tests of market efficiency have also been termed **weak-form** (price information), **semistrong-form** (other public information), and **strong-form** (inside information) **tests.** In a sense, past prices provide a weak test of market efficiency, because prices are readily available to everyone, and these prices do not contain any detailed information about the underlying investment. For these reasons, it seems unlikely that past prices can be used to reap abnormally large returns.

Other public information provides a semistrong test of efficiency, since this category includes accounting statements, detailed analyses of investments and of the economy, and published forecasts. Most investors rely almost exclusively on this type of information in buying and selling securities, and they seem to believe that this information can be used in selecting undervalued investments.

The most severe test of the efficient-market concept is based on the study of inside information, which is why it is termed a strong-form test. If the securities markets were completely efficient, even the knowledge possessed by a company's officers and directors would be valueless in buying and selling investments. However, there is reason to doubt that any market is that efficient. Markets are efficient because of competition, and competition is based on large numbers of people striving to make a profit. But, by its very definition, inside information is known to only a few people. Therefore, it seems very unlikely that any market is completely efficient.

PRICE (WEAK-FORM) TESTS

If an investment market is efficient, past prices or price changes will provide no profitable clues about future price changes. It makes absolutely no difference whether investment prices are hitting new highs each day or have been declining steadily over a long period of time. In other words, price changes have no memory. To quote Fama, "the past history of the series (of stock price changes) cannot be used to predict the future in any meaningful way."

Technical analysts would argue strongly against this conclusion. Technical analysts, often called chartists, analyze past price action in order to develop projections of future prices. They do so because they think that there are long-term trends in future stock prices which can be discovered by the careful study of past prices. A **trend** is defined as a general tendency to move in a well-defined pattern. Market technicians believe that a knowledge of these trends can be used effectively to buy and sell securities and to make above-average rates of return.

The study of past prices, especially stock prices, has a long history. Most technical analysts credit Charles H. Dow, the cofounder and editor of *The Wall Street Journal,* with being the father of technical analysis. After Dow's death in 1902, William P. Hamilton succeeded him as the editor of the *Journal.* Over a period of 27 years, Hamilton organized and expanded Dow's principles into the so-called **Dow theory,** which forms the foundation of technical analysis. According to the theory, stock prices swing in primary, secondary, and minor trends. **Primary trends** are extensive up and down movements which usually last for 1 or 2 years. They are often interrupted by **secondary trends** in the opposite direction. These secondary movements are termed "corrections," since they are believed to occur because the market has gotten ahead of itself. Finally, there are small day-to-day fluctuations in stock prices which are called **minor trends.** These movements are illustrated in Figure 5-1.

The Dow theory is often "explained" by comparing the stock market to the

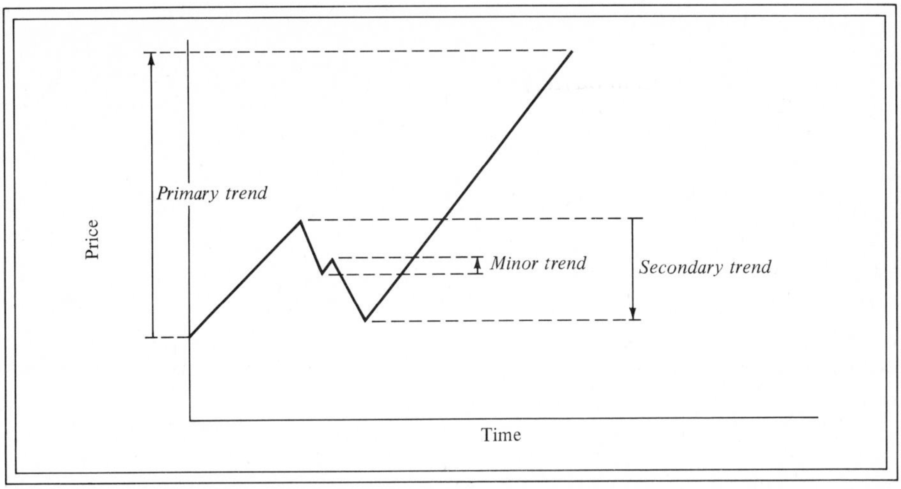

FIGURE 5-1   Primary, secondary, and minor trends in stock prices.

ocean. The tides are the primary trends, the waves are the secondary trends, and the ripples are the minor trends. Believers in the Dow theory attempt to swim with the tide and ignore the waves and ripples, since the last two can't be accurately predicted. Dow theorists determine which way the tide is running by watching for a sequence of successive highs or lows in the stock averages.

Although the analogy between the market and the ocean is appealing, there is no reason why stocks should behave analogously to the ocean. Despite the lack of any convincing explanation of why trends exist, most technicians believe that individual stocks, as well as the overall market, do move in trends. Many technicians believe that if a stock descends by more than a given percentage from a previous low, it will probably go down still further and should be sold. On the other hand, if a stock increases by a given percentage above a previous high, it will probably go up still more; so it should be purchased.

At first, this may seem contrary to common sense, since anyone who follows such a policy will buy stocks only after they have gone up and sell them only after they have already declined in price. But a technician would argue that it is best to buy stocks that are showing strength by their increasing prices and to sell stocks that are showing weakness by their decreasing prices. It is probably no coincidence that such a policy results in an investor buying more when he or she is making money and buying less or selling when losing money. And, of course, such a view is also consistent with a belief in trends.

With a computer, it is relatively easy to determine whether or not past stock prices can be used to predict future prices. The technician's advice is to buy a stock after it has gone up by some specified percentage from a previous low and to sell it or to sell it short when it has gone down by some percentage from a previous high. If the stock fluctuates within a small range, no action is taken. This no-action region is called a **filter test,** since it serves to screen out price changes

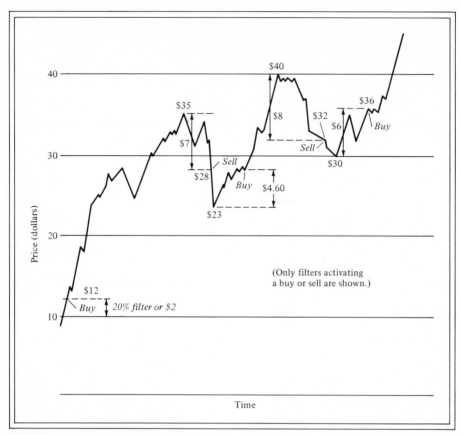

FIGURE 5-2   Application of the filter test.

which technicians believe should have no effect on the investor's buy-or-sell decision.

In order to test this belief, researchers selected a large number of arbitrary
percentages, or filters, which they applied to stocks. When a stock's price passed
through a filter, i.e., went up or down by more than some fixed percentage, the
stock was assumed to have been either bought or sold. This filter test is illustrated
for actual stocks in Figure 5-2. Each successive low and high is labeled, and the
filter or no-action region is indicated. Once the total price change goes beyond
this no-action region, the stock is either bought or sold, depending upon which
direction it leaves the filter. The effects of using a 10% no-action region or filter
and a 20% filter are shown in Table 5-1. The smaller the no-action region, the
more likely that stock prices will quickly pass through this region and the stock
will be bought or sold. The results of these tests are very interesting. They show
that a person who buys or sells stocks frequently can make above-average profits
with certain filters as long as no commissions are paid to a broker. But once commissions are considered, above-average profits are eliminated. In fact, it appears

TABLE 5-1   RESULTS FROM USING A FILTER RULE

Preceding Low, $	Preceding High, $	Current Stock Price, $	Action
20% Filter Rule			
10*	NA†	12	buy
NA	35	28	sell
23	NA	28	buy
NA	40	32	sell
30	NA	36	buy
10% Filter Rule			
10	NA	11	buy
NA	28	25	sell
24	NA	26	buy
NA	35	32	sell
31	NA	34	buy
NA	34	31	sell
23	NA	25	buy
NA	40	36	sell
30	NA	33	buy
NA	35	31	sell
31	NA	34	buy

* All prices are rounded to the nearest dollar. The smaller the filter, the more frequent the action.
† NA—not applicable.

that individuals who follow a filter rule often make less than average profits or even lose all their money, with the bulk of it going to their stockbrokers.

RANDOM WALK

The filter test is a direct test of the efficient-market concept. There is other evidence on prices which is not quite so direct but which is still very relevant to the question of market efficiency. For the past 20 years, numerous researchers have been using computers to analyze the behavior of stock prices and, to a much lesser extent, the prices of other investments. The results of this research indicate that stock prices follow a **random walk**. Although a random walk is a complex statistical concept, it can be described very simply. It is the movement which can be observed when a drunk is left in the middle of a vacant field. Almost all the evidence on the stock market indicates that stock prices behave just like a drunk, weaving first in one direction and then in another, in no predetermined fashion.

A random walk can also be described in more technical terms. If stock prices follow a random walk, changes in the price of the same stock are **independent** and **identically distributed random variables.** The description of a stock price change as a variable means that the actual price change which is observed varies from time to time. Everyone agrees that stocks fluctuate, but the random-walk concept states that these changes are random or uncontrolled, meaning that changes in prices cannot be determined beforehand. In addition, the fact that price changes are independent means that past price changes have absolutely no effect on future price changes; i.e., they are independent of each other. If this is the case, price changes have no memory of what has happened in the past. They do not follow previous patterns or move in trends. A large price increase on one day does not in any way suggest that there will be another large increase the next day. And the fact that a stock has gone down or up every day for the last 10 days is no indication that future price changes will continue in the same direction.

There is one final condition which price changes must satisfy if prices are to follow a random walk—the changes must be identically distributed. Even though price changes are due to chance, it is possible to state the probable size of future price changes For example, in the past, a stock might have experienced a weekly price change of less than $1 in about 75% of the weeks. If the weekly price changes are identically distributed, this will also be true of price changes in future weeks.

Efficient Market and Random Walk

It must be emphasized that the efficient-market concept does not require that stock prices or any other prices follow a random walk. Nothing in that concept requires that price changes be independent of each other or identically distributed, but the fact that they are provides further support for the efficient-market concept, since it is impossible to profit from the study of price changes which are independent.

Implications of Random Walk

Stock price changes are not the only independent, identically distributed random variables. A more obvious example is the outcome of tossing a coin. The outcome is variable, since it can be either a head or a tail, and, since the result of tossing a coin cannot be controlled, it is random. Moreover, if the coin is a fair coin, successive outcomes are independent of each other in that the results from previous coin tosses have absolutely no impact on the outcome of any future coin toss. Even if the last 5, 10, 100, or 1,000 coin tosses all fell heads or all fell tails, the outcome of the next toss is just as likely to be heads as it is tails. Finally, since the odds of getting heads or tails remain the same for each coin toss (1 out of 2), the variable is identically distributed.

The news that stock prices follow a random walk created a considerable controversy on Wall Street. As one member of the investment community has noted, it became a popular Wall Street practice to schedule two luncheon speakers, one who was for random walk and the other who was against, and then sit back and watch the fight. Numerous indignant letters and comments were also written criticizing the academicians and their findings. But the research continued and the findings were always the same—securities prices are best described as a random walk. Eventually, the protests gave way to silent disregard.

Most investors find it very difficult to accept the idea that stock prices are a random walk and that stock price changes are independent, identically distributed random variables. But they usually reject the random walk for the wrong reasons. They often mistakenly interpret random to mean chaotic, or they incorrectly believe that randomness in price changes implies the absence of any rational price formation. Actually, randomness in price changes implies nothing about the exact nature of those changes. That is determined by the fundamental characteristics of the company and the overall economy. Nor does randomness in price changes alter the fact that the price of a company's stock is determined by its earning power, its management, its products, etc. What it does mean is that people do their best to forecast the future and that investment prices are based upon those forecasts. Since no one has perfect foresight, there are usually errors in the forecasts. It is these unforeseen errors which cause prices to change randomly.

Stock price changes have been compared to the results from tossing a coin. That is hard to believe. But if it is correct, it should be possible to use a coin to create a series of artificial stock prices which look like real stock prices. This can be done by studying an imaginary random walker. Before taking a step in either direction, the random walker tosses a coin. If the coin lands heads, he takes a step forward; if it lands tails, he takes a step backward. His path for one series of tosses is traced in Figure 5-3. Daily stock prices for IBM are also charted on the same diagram. It is impossible to distinguish between the random walker and stock prices.

There are several statistical techniques which can be used to determine whether or not there are trends in stock prices. One technique is called a **runs test**. Changes in price, or for that matter changes in almost any other quantity, can be classified as being positive (+), negative (−), or zero (0). A run consists of any unbroken sequence of one type of change, i.e., all positive, all negative, or all zero. For example, the sequence of price changes, + +|0|− − − − −|+ consists of four runs. A trend is defined as a general tendency to move in one direction. If there are trends in stock prices, as technicians argue, price changes will be predominantly positive as stocks move up and predominantly negative as they move down. As a result, price changes would exhibit a much smaller number of runs than would be expected if there were no trends and stock prices followed a random walk.

A number of researchers have performed tests on stock price data for numerous firms over long periods of time. Each researcher found that the number of runs for the stocks studied did not differ significantly from the number that one would expect if stock prices followed a random walk. In other words, price changes for a stock appear to be independent of each other and random.

Correlation tests and spectral analysis have also been applied to stock prices. These sophisticated statistical techniques make it possible to measure the exact relationship between stock price changes at different points in time. For example,

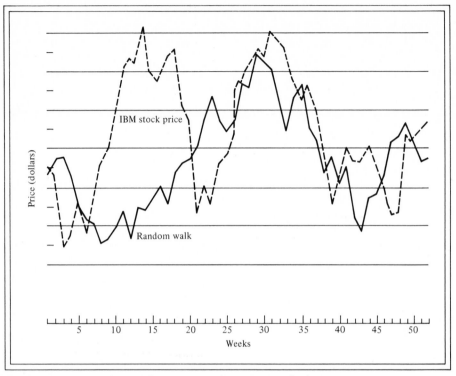

FIGURE 5-3   "Random walker" compared to IBM stock prices.

if stock prices tend to rally during the month of June, there will be a positive correlation in the June price changes for different years. The daily, weekly, and
monthly price changes of thousands of stocks have been studied by numerous
individuals and by the employees of several investment advisory firms. The results are almost completely identical—there are no significant trends. Although
there does appear to be a slight degree of dependence in daily price changes, it
cannot be exploited to make a profit.

Trends in Stock Prices

The one outrageous exception to these results was reported in a study by a very
large, nationally known brokerage firm. According to the brokerage firm, investors could buy the stocks of companies in certain industries during particular
times of the year and make unusually large profits. The suggested technique involved buying shares when a company's sales and earnings were at seasonal lows
and selling them when they were at seasonal highs. For example, shares of firms
making air conditioners would be purchased in the winter, when sales and profits
and supposedly share prices were at their lows for the year, and then sold in the
summer, when sales and profits and supposedly share prices were at their highs

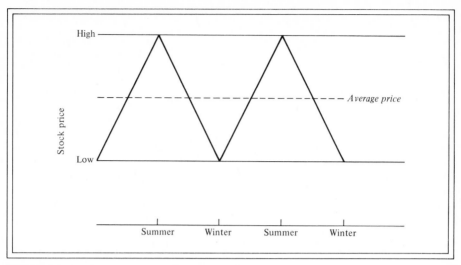

FIGURE 5-4   Imaginary seasonal price trends.

for the year. If this were actually true, monthly price changes for the same month in different years would be related to each other, as shown in Figure 5-4. And this would in turn imply that prices did not reflect the knowledge that the firm would do well at certain times of the year and badly at others. On the other hand, any investor who knew this would obviously take a long-run view of the investment and consider the full-year results. Based on the long-run view, the price would be the same regardless of the season of the year, other things being equal.

The brokerage firm study was severely criticized by members of both the academic and investment communities. The authors of the report eventually agreed that the study had been poorly executed and that the results were incorrect.

This example also serves to illustrate why a technical approach which is well known could never be used to produce above-average profits, even if there were trends in stocks. Suppose that for some reason stock prices actually followed a trend similar to that in Figure 5-4. Technicians would detect the trend almost immediately and start buying shares at the lows and selling at the highs. When they bought at the lows they would bid up prices, and when they sold at the highs they would bid down the prices. It wouldn't take many technical analysts very long to completely level out the stock price.

The absence of trends relates to future prices. Viewed with hindsight, the prices of many stocks appear to be best described by a trend. For example, Rosario Resources, an important producer of silver and gold, had an almost uninterrupted increase in price between March 1972 and December 1974 from $8 a share to $32. At the same time, shares in Fruehauf, Inc., the largest U.S. manufacturer of trucks, declined from $45 to $13. The price behavior of these two stocks presents investors with a good test of their belief in the random walk and

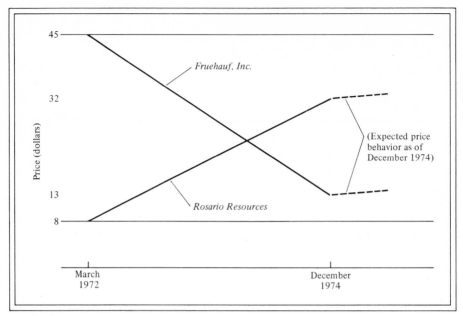

FIGURE 5-5   Test of investor's belief in the "random walk."

the efficient market. If investors accept the random-walk and efficient-market concepts, they will argue that such stock behavior is the result of an almost unbroken string of unexpected good news about Rosario, whereas the opposite was true with Fruehauf. Moreover, they will argue that the prices at the end of 1974 reflect all that is currently known or foreseeable about each of these firms. For that reason, the future price behavior of both stocks would best be described by the dotted lines in Figure 5-5. In other words, the most recently observed price plus some increase is the best forecast of future prices, since the current price fully reflects all known information. The expected increase in price provides investors with an incentive to hold their shares.

Most technical analysts would debate this conclusion. They would say that Rosario was in an uptrend and should be purchased, whereas Fruehauf was in a downtrend and should be avoided. On the other hand, other investors might argue that Rosario was overpriced and should be avoided, whereas Fruehauf was cheap in terms of past prices and should be purchased. If the results of the research done to date are correct, and they appear to be, neither of these opinions is justified.

Individuals who still want to argue that the study of past stock prices is worthwhile must somehow show that they can relate patterns in past prices to future prices and then use this knowledge to make above-average profits in the stock market. So far, no technical analyst has done this very convincingly, and, unfortunately, it seems unlikely that anyone will ever meet this challenge. For all the investing public knows, a technical analyst may be unable to tell the price history of a real stock like IBM from the trail of a random walker.

TESTS BASED ON OTHER PUBLIC INFORMATION (SEMISTRONG TESTS)

The findings from the weak-form or price tests could be shrugged off by most of the investing community. After all, there are relatively few investors who base their decisions solely upon past prices. Instead, most investors rely on **fundamental analysis.** Fundamental analysis is an attempt to determine the intrinsic value of an investment. This is done by studying profit and loss statements, balance sheets, dividend records, sales data, managerial ability, economic indices, and numerous other factors which affect investment value. Investors who practice fundamental analysis believe that the market price does not always provide a good measure of the intrinsic value of an investment, i.e., that the market is not efficient. But at the same time, they are also convinced that market prices eventually do adjust to intrinsic values; otherwise it would be pointless for them to buy stocks on the basis of estimates of the intrinsic value. Although fundamental analysis appears to differ completely from technical analysis, the two approaches have one similarity. Both are based on the belief that prices gradually adjust to new information.

The semistrong-form or other public-information tests of market efficiency are a direct inquiry into the usefulness of fundamental analysis in selecting investments providing above-average returns. These tests are designed to see how well and how quickly public information is incorporated into stock prices. The question is, Can investors study public information, such as earnings reports and other financial statements, economic data, repurchase offers, and secondary distributions, and by doing so make an above-average profit for the risk undertaken? If they can, the market is not efficient. The answer so far has been that above-average profits cannot be made by using public information, which confirms the efficient-market concept.

In one of the best-known studies of public information, the impact which stock splits have on future stock prices was examined. When a stock split occurs, investors in a company receive new shares for their old shares. For example, if there is a 2 for 1 stock split, stockholders receive 2 new shares for each old share they hold. Since there has been no fundamental change in the company and each investor still owns the same proportion of the company, the 2 new shares would be equal in value to 1 old share. Many investors once believed that stocks which were split would outperform the market after the split. Fama, Fisher, Jensen, and Roll tested this belief with detailed information on 940 splits over a 33-year period. They calculated the monthly abnormal returns on each of these split stocks for the 60 months surrounding the date of the split. The **abnormal return** is the return on the stock (i.e., the increase in price) in excess of that

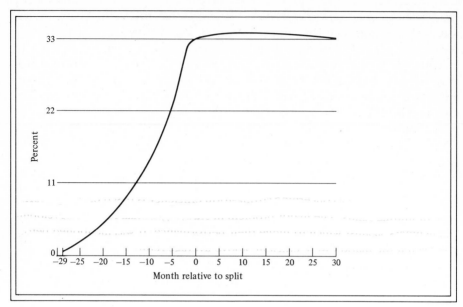

FIGURE 5-6 Abnormal returns before and after stock splits.

caused by changes in the overall market. In other words, an abnormal return is attributable solely to factors which are unique to the individual firm.

The total abnormal return which could have been earned by purchasing stocks which had split is shown in Figure 5-6. By the time of the split, the average stock had increased in value by about 34%, a high abnormal return. After the split, however, there were no additional abnormal returns. Judging from these results, investors do not make excess returns by buying stocks after they have split. Why? Because the efficient market has already incorporated news of the split into the stock price before the split occurs.

The results from tests of other public information are almost identical with those made by Fama, Fisher, Jensen, and Roll.[1] Perhaps the most striking results are reported in a study of **tender offers** to repurchase shares. Occasionally the management of a firm will offer to buy back its company's shares at a price in excess of the current market price. For the firms in the study, the adjustment of market price to the new higher tender price was almost immediate, a finding which supports the efficient-market concept.

INSIDE-INFORMATION TESTS (STRONG FORM)

The final category of tests, the strong-form tests, is concerned with whether or not certain individuals or groups of individuals possess inside information which can be used to make above-average profits. If they could make such profits, it would indicate that stock prices did not reflect all information and that the market was not totally efficient. The results of these tests are mixed, but, on the whole, seem to support the idea of the efficient market. On the one hand, it appears that individuals who manage mutual funds are not able to obtain information which they can use to consistently realize above-average returns. Nor do brokerage firms or other investment advisers provide advice which does any better than average. On the other hand, officers and directors of companies do appear sometimes to use inside information to make above-average profits for themselves.

Performance of Mutual Funds

Much of the evidence concerning strong-form efficiency is based on the performance of mutual funds. The major problem in studying mutual funds is developing a benchmark against which to judge their performance. It was mentioned before that even if the market were efficient, above-average returns could still be earned by investing in stocks which were more risky than average. For this reason, the performance of mutual funds must be judged relative to the riskiness of these funds.

This has been done in several studies. Jensen evaluated the performance of 115 mutual funds over the 10-year period from 1955 through 1964. He concluded that even when the sales charges and other expenses associated with mutual funds are ignored, the funds do no better or worse than any investor could have done by holding a combination of Treasury bills and a random selection of stocks. If the sales charges and expenses of the funds are taken into consideration, the funds do far worse than the investor who simply bought Treasury bills and a selection of stocks representative of the entire market. In fact, such an investor would have outperformed the average fund by a total of 15% over a 10-year period. More recent studies of mutual funds, including one done by the Securities and Exchange Commission, have confirmed that mutual funds do no better on the average than the overall market.

As a group, the managers of mutual funds obviously have no special information or skills. But the averages may conceal the fact that the managers of several funds do consistently better than average, and, correspondingly, that others do consistently below average. To determine whether or not this was so, the performances of the individual funds were compared over different periods of time. It was found that the actual performances of funds fluctuated greatly from period to period. Success or failure in one period was no guarantee of similar results in the next period. In fact, a fund that had performed badly in one period was just as likely to do well in the next period as a fund that had a record of above-average performance. The inconsistent performance of mutual funds can be seen by comparing the 1968 and 1969 rankings of 10 mutual funds shown in Table 5-2. Rather than rely on past accomplishments in selecting a successful fund, it appears that an investor could as easily have drawn the name of a mutual fund out of a hat.

TABLE 5-2   MUTUAL FUND RANKINGS IN 2 SUCCESSIVE YEARS

Name of Mutual Fund	1968 Rank	1969 Rank
Neuwirth Fund	1	259
Gibraltar Fund	2	169
Mates Investment	3	307
First Sierra Fund	4	77
Pennsylvania Mutual	5	328
Puerto Rican Investment	6	30
Crown-West.-Dallas	7	279
Franklin Dynatech	8	337
First Participating	9	49
Enterprise Fund	10	329

Performance of Investment Advisers

Every year the performance records of mutual funds are published, and every year the funds fail to outperform the overall market. Perhaps because of these disappointing results, many investors prefer to invest their own money and pay professional investment advisers and/or financial services for guidance. These fees are usually justified on the basis that professional advice improves investment results. However, in an efficient market, the information provided by advisers and services is already reflected in stock prices, so that no additional gains are possible.

One of the earliest studies of the forecasting ability of professional investors was published in 1933 by Alfred Cowles. It couldn't have appeared at a more appropriate time. The stock market had reached record highs in 1929 and then came crashing down. By the end of 1932, the average stock had fallen in price by nearly 90% from the highs set 3 years earlier and the Great Depression had become an undeniable fact.

Cowles examined 7,500 separate stock recommendations made by 16 leading financial services during the $4^1/2$ year period ending in July 1932. He compared the percentage gain or loss on each stock that was recommended with the percentage gain or loss on the overall market during the exact same period. Subscribers to the financial services who invested equal dollar amounts in the recommended stocks would have made 1.4% less than the return on the overall market, without even taking into account commission costs and taxes.

Cowles then scored 24 publications on their success in forecasting future movements in the overall market. These publications included 18 professional financial services, 4 financial weeklies, 1 bank letter, and 1 investment-house letter. The advice provided on market movements was no better than the stock recommendations. In 1928, the only year in which the market showed a net gain, the smallest number of optimistic forecasts was recorded. In contrast to this, optimistic forecasts outnumbered pessimistic forecasts by more than 5 to 1 in 1931—a year in which the market plunged by 54%.

Despite the poor overall performance of the publications, several of them had excellent forecasting records. In order to determine whether this success could be explained solely by chance, one set of cards was assigned numbers corresponding to the different weeks in the $4^{1}/_{2}$-year period, and another set was given numbers corresponding to different investment policies. Cards were then drawn from each set to create 24 random forecasting records. The results from following the random forecasting records are compared with those achieved by following the advice of the professional investors in Figure 5-7. The professionals did no better than amateurs armed with decks of cards.

Cowles performed one more analysis. He examined the 26-year forecasting record of William P. Hamilton from 1903 to 1929. During his 27 years as editor of *The Wall Street Journal,* Hamilton wrote 255 editorials based on the Dow theory. Cowles had five readers determine whether these editorials expressed a bullish, bearish, or doubtful view of the market. Altogether, Hamilton recommended 90 changes in investment position, of which 45 were profitable and 45 were not. Anyone who followed Hamilton's editorials faithfully for the entire period and interpreted them in the same way as the panel did would have multiplied his or her invested money by a factor of 19. Although that is a very substantial gain, the same investor who simply invested an equal dollar amount in each of the stocks included in the Dow Jones Industrial Average would have increased her or his wealth by more than 42 times—more than double the gain from Hamilton's recommendations.

FIGURE 5-7   Random selection compared with expert advice. (From Alfred Cowles, III, "Can Stock Market Forecasters Forecast?" *Econometrica,* July 1933, p. 320.)

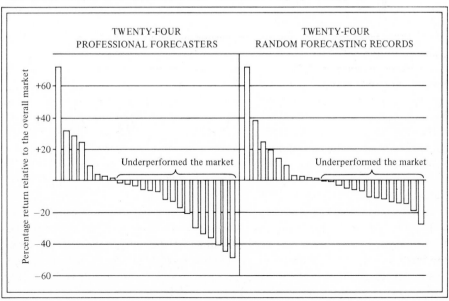

In a later study, which appeared in 1944, Cowles reported that an examination of the forecasting records of 11 leading financial periodicals and services over periods ranging from 10 to $15^1/2$ years disclosed no ability to foresee the future. However, he did change his conclusions about the relative success of Hamilton. Hamilton died in December 1929. His last editorial on the future course of the market appeared on October 25, 1929, and was titled "A Turn in the Tide." In that article Hamilton predicted a change from the great bull market to a bear market. Three days later the market dropped by more than 13%, and in the next three years it dropped a total of 90%. When the forecasts made by Hamilton and successive editors of *The Wall Street Journal* are extended to 1944, the overall results from following their advice during the 40-year period were 3.3% per year better than a policy of buying and holding stocks. Apparently, this substantial difference in the overall results is completely due to the accuracy of the last forecast ever made by William P. Hamilton.

Although the two studies by Cowles have several shortcomings and were done many years ago, his findings have never been disputed. In fact, in the last decade numerous researchers have presented evidence which supports Cowles's point of view. These researchers have focused their attention on a firm's own earnings forecasts rather than on stock recommendations. Most brokerage houses, investment institutions, and advisers base their investment decisions on earnings projections. In addition, the managements of many companies often make public forecasts of their firms' future earnings. Unlike stock recommendations, earnings forecasts are usually well defined, so that the forecaster's accuracy is easily measured. A review of these results suggests that the professionals' crystal balls are clouded. Their earnings forecasts are no better than the forecasts that a naive investor could have made by using simple techniques.

Performance of Insiders

Judging by the evidence presented so far, the stock market is remarkably efficient. But the question remains whether insiders—corporate officers, directors, and large shareholders—can profit from information about their companies which is known only to themselves. Since insiders do have access to classified information, they are required by law to report their stock purchases or sales to the Securities and Exchange Commission. These reports are then published by the government in summary form in the *Official Summary of Insider Trading*.

Jaffe has recently presented the results of an extensive analysis of these published insider transactions. He first computed the abnormal returns earned by insiders on all their transactions. The excess returns during the 8-month period following purchases and sales by insiders were only about 1.4% more than could have been earned by simply buying a random selection of stocks with the same risk as those traded by insiders. This small difference indicates that even company insiders are unlikely to make abnormally large profits during the ordinary course of events.

Next Jaffe looked at the returns on transactions made during "intensive trading months." These are defined as months in which there are a disproportionate number of buyers or sellers. This one-sided trading activity indicates that insiders are probably aware of some news which is associated with a single important event, such as an oil discovery, a tender offer, or a dramatic change in reported earnings. Insiders made about 5% more on these trades during an 8-month period than could have been made by simply buying a random selection of stocks with the same risk.

Prospective investors might well wonder whether they could have taken advantage of the information in the *Official Summary* to make an above-average profit. Surprisingly, the answer seems to be yes. According to Jaffe, the returns that could have been earned by reading the *Official Summary* and then duplicating the actions of the insiders are almost identical with those earned by the insiders. But this does not imply that investors should actively buy and sell stocks that are being intensively traded by insiders. The commission costs and taxes associated with such a policy would probably exceed the extra returns. Instead, information about insider trading should be used to decide which of several stocks should be bought or sold.

OTHER EVIDENCE ON MARKET EFFICIENCY

Most of the research on investment prices and on investment performance has been based on stocks. There are three reasons for this: (1) stocks account for a large percentage of total invested wealth; (2) stock prices fluctuate considerably; and (3) stocks are publicly traded, so that prices are readily available. The extensive research on stocks has begun to stimulate interest in the characteristics of other types of investments. It will probably not be long before large computerized information files on other investments, such as real estate, bonds, commodities, and art, will be readily available.

A considerable amount of work has already been done on Treasury bills and commodity futures. Richard Roll, a professor of finance at Carnegie-Mellon, has shown that the price changes of Treasury bills are completely consistent with the efficient-market concept if adjusted. He also explains why the prices of some investments exhibit trends or patterns even in an efficient market. For example, the prices of cantaloupes and other perishable commodities decline steadily because they deteriorate. Moreover, since this type of commodity deteriorates at a faster and faster rate, the downward price changes become larger and larger until the price eventually reaches zero. By the same token, investments such as Treasury bills and bonds and commodity futures contracts may display some dependence in price changes because of the ever-decreasing time to maturity. None of this implies that excess profits can be made by trading in cantaloupes or other commodities or in Treasury bills, bonds, and commodity futures.

THE STOCK MARKET, A COIN-TOSSING CONTEST, AND HUNGRY BIRDS

The securities markets are reasonably efficient. As a result, efforts on the part of investors to seek out undervalued stocks and bonds will probably go unrewarded and experts will do no better or worse than casual investors. Moreover, from the evidence on the random walk, it appears that investors are about as likely to predict future price changes as they are to select the outcome of a coin toss.

Given these facts, the actions of many investors appear somewhat ridiculous. In fact, long before the efficient-market concept was publicized, one disgruntled observer of investors' behavior suggested the following analogy between the stock market and a coin-tossing contest.[2]

Let 400,000 men and women engage in a contest based upon pure chance. They are lined up, facing each other in pairs, across a table miles long. Each player is going to play a series of games with the person opposite. In this case, they are all going to match coins.

The referee gives a signal for the first game to start, and 400,000 coins flash in the sun as they are tossed. The scorers make their tabulations and discover that 200,000 people are winners and 200,000 are losers. Some players drop out of the game, others are added, and still others change opponents. Then the second game is played. Of the original 200,000 winners, about one-half win again. There are now about 100,000 contestants who have won both games.

The third game is played, and, of the 100,000 who have won both games, half are again successful. In the fourth game, these 50,000 are reduced to 25,000 and, in the fifth, to 12,500. These 12,500 players have by now won five straight games without a loss and are beginning to believe that they are experts. They may even feel that they have a special instinct for coin tossing. However, in the sixth game, 6,250 of them are shocked and disappointed to find that they have finally lost. Some of them even start a congressional investigation into coin tossing.

But the victorious 6,250 play on and are successively reduced in number until fewer than 1,000 are left. This small group has won nine straight games without a single loss, and by this time many of them have acquired at least a local reputation for their ability. People come from some distance to consult them about their method of calling heads and tails. Some of the experts modestly give explanations of how they have achieved their success. Others charge high fees for their advice and assure their clients that such fees are justified by the high profits that will result. The contest continues. Eventually there are about a dozen men and women who have won every single time for about 15 games. They are regarded as the greatest experts on coin tossing in history—the coin tossers who never lose. They have their biographies written and/or they begin to publish books and articles on how to best toss coins.

If the efficient-market concept is correct, the coin-tossing contest is a good analogy to the investments markets. But there are several differences. The first is that coin tossing, like any other form of gambling, is at best a zero-sum game. In other words, for every winner, there is a loser—the only result is a transfer of money from the losers to the winners. With stocks, bonds, real estate, etc., every investor can make money, since there is usually a real increase in the wealth of a country as a result of productive investments. The second difference between coin tossing and investing is that investors can benefit considerably from spending time on certain aspects of investing even in efficient markets. This is the topic of later chapters.

The example of the coin-tossing contest emphasizes the importance of judging the performance of so-called experts very carefully. Many investors have excellent records for short periods of time, but that could easily have resulted just from chance. The true test of expertise must always be based upon an examination of the techniques used as well as of performance over a long time.

Some critics of the efficient-market concept will probably never accept the concept regardless of the evidence in support of it. They will ask, and perhaps with good reason, why so many investors behave the way they do if the markets are efficient. There are several possible answers. One of the best has been presented by a psychologist. According to him, investors will discover what appear to them to be meaningful patterns upon which to base their forecasts even if prices follow a random walk. That is because many investors behave in the same way as hungry birds which are given food at brief, random intervals during laboratory experiments. These birds develop very peculiar habits, with the precise form of behavior varying from bird to bird.

The strange behavior of the hungry birds can be explained in terms of the concept of **positive reinforcement,** made famous by another psychologist named B. F. Skinner.[3] The delivery of food increases the chances of the birds' behaving in the same way they did just before the food was delivered. Food is then presented again. Because the reinforced behavior occurs more frequently, it is more likely to be reinforced again. The second reinforcement causes a further increase in the frequency of the particular behavior, which further improves its chances of being reinforced again and again. After a short time, the birds are "turning rapidly counterclockwise about the cage, hopping from side to side, making odd head movements, etc.," in an effort to obtain more food. Of course, since the food is supplied at random intervals, none of this behavior has the slightest effect on the amount of food the birds receive.

Much of what investors do appears to have as much impact on their chances for success as the birds' strange behavior does on their being fed again. For the most part, prices change randomly and so does the investor's wealth. But the reinforcement is both positive and negative, since prices go down as well as up. These price changes are the result of a tremendously complicated market mechanism which reflects the different opinions of millions and millions of investors. Faced with this complexity, even intelligent investors will begin finding patterns in prices or will evolve complicated theories "explaining" why certain investments have gone up or down in price. Moreover, if they happen to make large profits they will probably decide that they have special insights and will devote more and more time to buying and selling securities. On the other hand, if they lose money, they will think that they are either unlucky or inept and will completely withdraw from the market or simply become uninterested.

There is another important lesson which can be learned from the study of animal behavior. A particular response can persist for a very long time. Since behavior patterns are reinforced less than 100% of the time, they often persist even after reinforcement has completely stopped. Some animals have been known to make as many as 10,000 attempts to obtain a reward that was no longer forthcoming. The efficient-market concept is still a relatively new theory. It will probably take some investors a very long time to accept the concept.

IMPLICATIONS OF THE EFFICIENT-MARKET CONCEPT

In an efficient market, as has been noted, intense competition ensures that information is efficiently incorporated into prices, which means that prices adjust very quickly and without error to any new information. Since the stock market appears to be reasonably efficient, traditional investment techniques and philosophies are probably useless. In fact Richard West, the dean of the Dartmouth College Tuck School of Business and an outstanding academician, has stated that the traditional approach to investing closely resembles witchcraft.

Unlike traditional methods, the efficient-market concept is a very positive approach to investing. It implies that most investors pay a fair price for their investments. Because securities are fairly priced, there is no need for individuals to spend considerable time and effort in selecting particular securities. Moreover, beginning investors will probably do as well as the professionals.

Investors who want to make above-average profits in an efficient market must concentrate their efforts on selecting investments which have above-average risk or somehow obtain inside information. Since no market is completely efficient, they also have a small chance of finding undervalued securities. But to do so they will have to adopt a unique approach. Because of competition, simply predicting the future is not enough.

None of this means that investors can't make large amounts of money in an efficient market. Many people have made fortunes over long periods of time by simply making so-called average returns on their investments. And, of course, some investors have earned still higher returns just by chance.

The efficient-market concept makes it apparent that investors have only themselves to blame for not doing better. For most investors, the desire to select undervalued securities is an unrealistic and/or unimportant goal. Instead, every effort should be made to (1) define individual investment objectives, (2) reduce taxes, (3) reduce commissions and other investment costs, (4) select the proper risk-return combination of assets, and (5) eliminate unnecessary risk. By following these guidelines, investors can create a winning investment strategy for themselves.

Of course, not every market is as efficient as the stock market. Individuals who want to spend their time and effort in the quest for undervalued or overvalued investments should select an inefficient market. But because competition exists even in an inefficient market, many of the techniques which are designed for efficient markets will still be applicable.

KEYWORDS

fair price	Dow theory	identically distributed
efficient market	primary trends	random variables
weak-form tests	secondary trends	runs test
semistrong-form tests	minor trends	fundamental analysis
strong-form tests	filter test	abnormal return
technical analysts	random walk	tender offers
trend	independent	positive reinforcement

QUESTIONS

1 Define an efficient market. What makes markets efficient?
2 Do so-called experts enjoy any advantages over amateurs in selecting investments in a completely efficient market?
3 What are the general implications of an efficient market?
4 Why are tests of the efficient market described as weak-, semistrong-, and strong-form tests?
5 Discuss the price tests of market efficiency.
6 Do prices have to follow a random walk for markets to be efficient?
7 What does the evidence on stock prices imply about the technicians' attempts to foretell future prices?
8 Discuss other public-information tests of the efficient market.
9 Evaluate the following statement: "I would have made a fortune if I had only bought real estate back in the early 1950s. Now it's too high in price—just look how much property values have increased." (Hint: Do past changes in prices imply anything about future prices?)
10 Are the stock prices of companies manufacturing air conditioners higher in the summer, when earnings are at a peak than in the winter?
11 What do the results from the other public-information tests imply about the attempts of security analysts to predict future prices?
12 How have mutual fund managers and investment advisers performed? Is there any evidence that these professionals can do better than the ordinary investor?
13 Why do some insiders outperform the market? How serious a setback is this finding to the efficient-market concept?
14 Should insiders be allowed to trade on the basis of inside information? (Believe it or not, there are some valid reasons for permitting insider trading.)
15 Before purchasing stocks, investors should probably check the insider trading reports. Why?

16   How do investment markets differ from a coin-tossing contest?

17   *a*   What might cause investors to behave like the hungry birds studied by B. F. Skinner?

    b   Should investors closely follow the daily fluctuations in the prices of their investments?

18   Why is the following statement not true: "If markets are efficient, investors will earn nothing on their money."

19   The efficient-market concept has a strange impact on some people. Realizing that they have almost no control over stock prices, they conclude that investing is no different from gambling. Explain why this view is not justified. (Hint: Do individuals have any control over the interest rates banks pay on savings accounts or the prices stores charge for clothes? Is there any uncertainty associated with bank accounts and clothes?)

20   Most investors spend very little time analyzing stocks, bonds, or other securities. Explain why the efficient market should come as good news to these people.

21   A small number of individuals (the author of this book included) spend inordinate amounts of time analyzing securities. Can these people expect to earn above-average returns? Why do they continue to pursue these activities?

22   The chapter on efficient markets appears at the end of most investments textbooks, if it appears at all. Apparently the authors asked themselves, "If everything is so efficient, why read a book on investments?"

    Actually the need for knowledge about investments and for the formulation of investment strategies becomes all the more important in such a world. Only the emphasis changes. Look briefly at each of the chapters in this book and explain why this is so.

23   Discuss the following: In an efficient market all investors have the opportunity to become millionaires. But they can considerably improve their chances of attaining this goal (or perhaps other, more worthwhile objectives) by learning about risk and return, valuation, taxes, investment media, the costs of investing, their own personal objectives and resources, and investment strategies.

REFERENCES

*Arbit, Harold L., and James E. Rhodes: "Performance Goals in a Generally Efficient Market," *The Journal of Portfolio Management,* Fall 1976, pp. 57–61.

Ball, R.J., and P. Brown: "An Empirical Evaluation of Accounting Income Numbers," *Journal of Accounting Research,* Autumn 1968, pp. 159–178.

Bar-Yosef, Sasson, and Lawrence D. Brown: "A Reexamination of Stock Splits Using Moving Betas," forthcoming in *The Journal of Finance.*

*Brealey, Richard A.: *An Introduction to Risk and Return from Common Stocks,* M.I.T., Cambridge, Mass., 1969.

    ————: *Security Prices in a Competitive Market: More about Risk and Return from Common Stocks,* M.I.T., Cambridge, Mass., 1971.

Coates, C. Robert, and Albert J. Fredman: "Price Behavior Associated with Tender Offers to Repurchase Common Stock," *Financial Executive,* April 1976, pp. 40–44.

* Publications preceded by an asterisk are highly recommended.

Cowles, Alfred, III: "Can Stock Market Forecasters Forecast?" *Econometrica,* July 1933, pp. 309–324.

Edwards, Robert D., and John Magee: *Technical Analysis of Stock Trends,* 5th ed., Magee, Springfield, Mass., 1966.

Ellis, Charles D.: "The Loser's Game," *Financial Analysts Journal,* July–August 1975, pp. 19–26.

Fama, Eugene F.: "The Behavior of Stock Market Prices," *Journal of Business,* January 1965, pp. 34–105.

*———: "Efficient Capital Markets: A Review of Theory and Empirical Work," *Journal of Finance,* May 1970, pp. 383–417.

———, and Marshall Blume: "Filter Rules and Stock Market Trading Profits," *Journal of Business,* Special Supplement, January 1966, pp. 226–241.

———, et al.: "The Adjustment of Stock Prices to New Information," *International Economic Review,* February 1969, pp. 1–21.

Granger, Clive W. J., and Oskar Morgenstern: *Predictability of Stock Market Prices,* Heath Lexington, Lexington, Mass., 1970.

Hamilton, William Peter: *The Stock Market Barometer,* Harper, New York, 1922.

Jaffe, Jeffrey: "Special Information and Insider Trading," *Journal of Business,* July 1974, pp. 410–428.

Jensen, Michael: "The Performance of Mutual Funds in the Period 1945–1964," *Journal of Finance,* May 1968, pp. 389–419.

*Lorie, James, and Richard Brealey, eds.: *Modern Developments in Investment Management: A Book of Readings,* Praeger, New York, 1972

———, and Mary T. Hamilton: *The Stock Market: Theories and Evidence,* Irwin, Homewood, Ill., 1973.

Madrick, Jeffrey: "Gremlins That Harry the 'Efficient Markets,'" *Business Week,* Aug. 23, 1976, p. 59.

Malkiel, Burton G.: *A Random Walk down Wall Street,* Norton, New York, 1973.

"Money Management: Wall Street Goes Slow," *Business Week,* Oct. 11, 1976, pp. 100–104, 109.

Nelson, S. A.: *The ABC of Stock Speculation,* Fraser Publishing, Wells, Vt., 1964. First published in 1903.

Rinfret, P. A.: "Investment Managers *Are* Worth Their Keep," *Financial Analysts Journal,* March-April 1968, pp. 163–170.

Roll, Richard: *The Behavior of Interest Rates: An Application of the Efficient Market Model to U.S. Treasury Bills,* Basic Books, New York, 1970.

Rolo, Charles J., and George J. Nelson, eds.: *The Anatomy of Wall Street: A Guide for the Serious Investor,* Lippincott, Philadelphia, 1968.

Samuelson, Paul A.: "Proof That Properly Anticipated Prices Fluctuate Randomly," *Industrial Management Review,* Spring 1965, pp. 41–49.

Schwed, Fred, Jr.: "Where Are the Customer's Yachts?", rev. ed., Simon and Schuster, New York, 1955.

Sharpe, William F.: "Mutual Fund Performance," *Journal of Business,* January 1966, pp. 119–138.

Skinner, B.F.: "Superstition in the Pigeon," *Journal of Experimental Psychology,* April 1948, pp. 168–172.

*Slovic, Paul: "Psychological Study of Human Judgment: Implications for Investment Decision Making," *Journal of Finance,* September 1972, pp. 779–799.

Tabell, Anthony W.: "Down a Blind Alley with a Random Walker," Review of *Random Walk down Wall Street,* by Burton Malkiel, *Business Week,* Nov. 3, 1973, pp. 10–11.

"A Turn in the Tide," *The Wall Street Journal,* Oct. 25, 1929, p. 1.

U.S. Securities and Exchange Commission: *Institutional Investor Study Report of the Securities and Exchange Commission,* vol. 2, 92d Cong., 1st Sess., 1970.

U.S. Securities and Exchange Commission: *Official Summary of Security Transactions and Holdings,* monthly.

Waud, R. N.: "Public Interpretation of Discount Rate Changes: Evidence on the Announcement Effect," *Econometrica,* March 1970, pp. 231–250.

West, Richard R.: "The Teaching of Investments—Is Witchcraft Still Appropriate?" *Journal of Financial and Quantitative Analysis: 1974 Proceedings,* November 1974, pp. 789–793.

Zweig, Martin E.: "Clouded Crystal Ball," *Barron's,* Dec. 18, 1972, p. 9.

PART TWO

RISK, INFLATION, AND RATES OF RETURN

CHAPTER SIX

RISK

T oday's investor resembles the ancient hero forced to choose between two unmarked doors. Behind one door stands his beautiful bride-to-be. Behind the other a hungry tiger paces restlessly.

The lady and the tiger symbolize the close relationship between good and bad or success and failure. The old tale of the lady and the tiger suggests that storytellers long ago recognized that great success can be achieved only by risking great losses.

Until recently, most investors seemed oblivious to this fact. But the dreadful experiences of recent years have cured many investors of their blind optimism. In addition, the efficient-market concept has played a role in the spreading awareness of the close tie between risk and return. According to this concept, high returns can be earned in efficient markets only by taking on high risks.

Because of the intimate relationship between risk and return, risk is very important. However, risk is so vague and at the same time so complex, that few investors fully understand the concept.

DESCRIPTION OF RISK

Most people possess an intuitive understanding of **risk,** but they have a difficult time explicitly defining or measuring it. Many of them probably associate risk with an action which can easily result in substantial monetary loss or personal injury. For example, driving a car at 100 miles an hour seems risky because the driver might easily be killed, and investing $10,000 in a new company planning to convert iron into gold appears risky, since the firm will almost certainly go bankrupt.

This commonsense definition of risk suffers from two shortcomings. First, the words "easily" and "substantial" mean different things to different people. Some beginning drivers cringe at the thought of driving a car even at 60 miles an hour. On the other hand, some entrepreneurs optimistically invest thousands of dollars in new companies, regardless of their products.

The usual definition of risk has another shortcoming. Imagine blindfolding someone and asking the person to draw a piece of paper from 1 of 2 hats. One hat contains an equal number of $1 bills and $10,000 bills; the other holds $5,000 bills. Even though there is no cost for the drawing and only different degrees of good fortune can result, many people would consider this a risky situation.

For these reasons, it seems preferable to define risk in a more general fashion. Risk is best described as uncertainty about the actual outcome of an action. Driving a car at any speed may result in one of two outcomes—the driver either gets to his or her destination or becomes involved in an accident. The possibility of an accident and the subsequent loss always exists, but the chance of having an accident varies directly with the speed. Obviously, the uncertainty about the actual outcome becomes greater at higher speeds.

What is the risk of an investment? Since risk involves uncertainty about the eventual outcome, the risk of an investment must be related to the uncertainty about future values of the investment. If for some reason the investor knows the future value, there is no uncertainty and therefore no risk. The more uncertain the future value, the greater the risk.

Probability   *expectations play large role as well*

One way of describing the uncertainty associated with making an investment is to list all the possible outcomes. The greater the number of possible outcomes, the greater the uncertainty. Suppose an investor must select one of two stocks. Both are currently priced at $9, and neither pays a dividend. The first stock is expected to sell for $6, $7, $8, $9, $10, $11, or $12 at the end of 1 year. The second stock seems much more stable. The investor believes it will sell for $8, $9, or $10 after 1 year. Based on the definition of risk as uncertainty about the final outcome, the first stock appears considerably more risky than the second. This can be seen by referring to Figure 6-1.

Often a listing of possible outcomes provides a good measure of risk, but the simple enumeration of possibilities suffers from an important shortcoming. Some

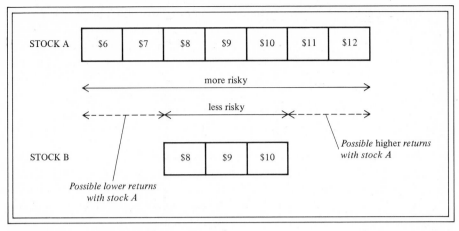

FIGURE 6-1   Uncertainty about two stocks.

outcomes are usually much more likely to occur than others. In order to give greater weight to the more likely events, an investor can assign probabilities to each possible outcome. For instance, an individual may believe a particular property selling for $20,000 will go to $10,000, $22,000, or $30,000 after 1 year and attaches the following probabilities to each of these possible prices:

Outcome, $	Probability
10,000	1 in 10, or 10%, or .1
22,000	8 in 10, or 80%, or .8
30,000	1 in 10, or 10%, or .1

There are several ways of explaining these probabilities. Many people adopt a frequency approach to **probability.** According to this view, a probability indicates the relative frequency with which a particular event will occur. Since there are 2 sides to a coin and only 1 side can appear at any one time, the probability of tossing a head is 1 in 2. In other words, given a sufficiently large number of coin tosses, one-half of the tosses will turn up heads.

Two interpretations of the investor's probabilities are possible with this frequency approach. One is that if the investor continues to buy and sell properties exactly like those described in the preceding example, 10% of the time the properties will go to $10,000, 80% of the time to $22,000, and 10% of the time to $30,000. Another way of viewing these probabilities is to imagine that, at any one time, there exist numerous properties identical with each other in terms of investment prospects. If the investor buys a very large number of these identical properties, 10% of them will go to $10,000, 80% to $22,000, and 10% to $30,000.

Some statisticians disagree vehemently with the frequency approach to probability. They ask, What meaning does frequency have when an event occurs only once in a lifetime? They prefer to interpret probabilities simply as subjective weights assigned to alternative events. According to this view, the investor who believes a price of $22,000 is 8 times as likely as a price of $10,000 or of $30,000 assigns a probability of .8 (80%) to the $22,000 price and a probability of .1 (10%) to each of the other two prices.

Whatever the interpretation of probabilities, these numbers should always add up to 1. Since the investor has described every possible outcome from taking a specific action, one of these outcomes must always occur; i.e., 100% (1.0) of the time the actual result will be one of the possible outcomes. For the same reason, the probability of any one outcome can never be greater than 1 or less than 0.

Even the most optimistic investors have doubts about how their investments will do. For instance, imagine a person who buys a stock for $10 and believes it will probably go to $11–$12 in 1 year. But it may stay in the range of $10–$11 or even drop as low as $9–$10. These all-inclusive possibilities are shown in Figure 6-2.

These outcomes can also be expressed in terms of how well the investor fares in terms of the profit, or loss on a share of stock. If the stock price is $9 to $10, the profit is − $1 to $0; if the price is $10 to $11, the profit is $0 to $1; if the price is between $11 and $12, the profit varies from $1 to $2.

Still another way of describing the possible outcomes is to record the different rates of return on the investment. These rates of return are from − 10 to 0%, from 0 to 10%, and from 10 to 20%.

The investor now knows how to describe the risk or uncertainty associated with an investment. But the question remains as to how to use that knowledge to make better investment decisions. One possible answer to this question is suggested in the following section.

FIGURE 6-2   Probabilities and stock prices.

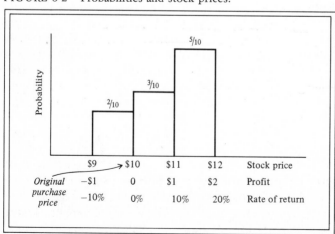

DECISION MAKING UNDER UNCERTAINTY

Rain falls steadily on two hunters and their decoys. Suddenly a formation of ducks appears. The ducks swoop to join their silent comrades, their paths traced by raised gun barrels. For the hunters, the seconds go by even more slowly than the long, cold, wet hours spent waiting for the ducks. Then the guns go off almost simultaneously, ending the suspense.

The black numbers on the white signs passing by the driver's window are all the same—55. They don't match the numbers on the car's speedometer—80. But then again, why should they? It is already 1 P.M., the appointment is for 3 P.M., and the city is still 150 miles away.

Young men in rented formal wear ceremoniously lead well-dressed families into the church. People talk quietly to each other and occasionally turn and look expectantly at the main entrance at the back of the room. Finally everyone is seated and the woman at the organ begins to play. Bridesmaids and their escorts step carefully down the central aisle. Then the groom strides to the altar. Everyone waits in silence. Finally the music resounds and the bride-to-be enters gracefully. The bride and groom stand facing each other. For them it had been love at first sight. A 6-month engagement followed a whirlwind courtship, and now they will become husband and wife—exactly 1 year after they met.

These three events may seem only remotely related to investments. But they share important similarities. Human beings are decision makers. During a lifetime a person makes thousands, perhaps even millions, of decisions. The outcomes of most of these decisions are cloaked in uncertainty. Look again at the three scenarios just described. Each one has at least two possible outcomes. And no one can predict for certain the eventual result.

Human decision making is complicated by another aspect of life. Only by taking on more risk can a higher return be earned. The duck hunters, automobile driver, and bride and groom all confront trade-offs between risk and return. The closer the ducks come to the hunters, the better the hunters' chances of making a killing shot, but, at the same time, the greater the chance the ducks will detect the hunters and escape before a shot is fired. The driver speeding to an appointment must also balance the good with the bad. The higher the speed, the better the chance of being on time. However, high speeds are accompanied by the possibility of being involved in an accident or of being stopped for speeding and heavily fined. Even the bride and groom must balance the good with the bad. The amount of time they have known each other may have an important impact on the success of their marriage.

Expected-Value Concept

Despite their preoccupation with decision making, not much is known about how people actually make up their minds. One of the earliest scientific theories about decision making evolved in the 1600s. It is called the theory of **expected value**. According to this theory, the individual first mentally lists the possible outcomes of each action. Then he or she assigns probabilities and monetary values to each possible outcome and takes the action with the maximum expected value. The expected value of each action is calculated by multiplying the probability of each outcome by its value and then summing up all possible outcomes. Expected-value maximizers never pay more than the expected value of an action.

Gambling   Expected-value maximizers have no trouble in selecting different bets. For example, sports fans in the United States often take an active interest in football cards. These cards cost $1 each, and the hopeful participant attempts to select the winners of the 1 to 10 games listed on the cards. By assigning suitable point spreads, or handicaps, the promoters of the cards ensure that the chances of each team winning are equal, no matter how mismatched they may be.

Since each of the two teams in a game has an equal chance of winning, the odds of correctly selecting the winner in 1 game are $1/2$. The odds of picking 2 winners in 2 games are $1/4$ ($1/2 \times 1/2$), of selecting 3 out of 3 games are $1/8$ ($1/2 \times 1/2 \times 1/2$), etc. The real optimist can attempt to select 10 winners out of 10 games. But the odds of succeeding in this endeavor amount to only 1 in 1,024.

Suppose a person decides to bet on either 3 teams or 10 teams. Each of these bets can be described by the following **payoff matrix** showing the possible outcomes and the probability and payoff of each outcome:

Bet on 3 Teams			Bet on 10 Teams		
Outcome	Probability	Payoff, $	Outcome	Probability	Payoff, $
Lose	7/8	−1	Lose	1,023/1,024	−1
Win	1/8	5	Win	1/1,024	300

Both bets are characterized by only two possible outcomes: win or lose. The bettor loses if any of his or her selections fail to win. If the bettor selects each of 3 teams correctly, the take is $5. If the bettor somehow manages to pick all 10 winning teams, the take is $300.

The expected value of the 3-game bet or of any other action can be found by multiplying the probability of each outcome by its value and then summing up these products. Therefore, the expected value of a 3-game bet equals −25¢ [(7/8 × −$1) + (1/8 × $5)]. By the same token, the expected value of the 10-game bet is about −70¢ [(1,023/1,024 × −$1) + (1/1,024 × $300)]. The 3-game bet has a greater expected value than the 10-game bet (the player loses less). For that reason the expected-value maximizer will always select the 3-game bet over a 10-game bet.

In actuality, no self-respecting expected-value maximizer would ever place bets on football cards, and for a very good reason. Any bet on these cards has a negative expected value. In other words, the average person loses money on football cards. One hundred thousand bettors will lose a total of $25,000 on their 3-game bets, an average loss of 25¢. And any player gifted with immortality but not common sense will lose an average of 25¢ on each card, providing he plays forever.

Most bets, whether legal or illegal, have an expected value of less than zero—meaning that players lose money on the average. So bettors pay to take on uncertainty.

Insurance   Insurance also has a negative expected value. But with insurance, people pay to eliminate risk. Fire insurance is a case in point. Suppose fire insurance for 1 year on a $50,000 frame house costs $100. In addition, assume that previous experience indicates that an average of 1 house in every 1,000 burns down each year. The payoff matrix in deciding whether or not to buy fire insurance can be described as follows:

	Buy Fire Insurance		Don't Buy Fire Insurance	
	Probability	Payoff, $	Probability	Payoff, $
No fire	999/1,000	−100	999/1,000	0
Fire	1/1,000	−100	1/1,000	−50,000

Any purchaser of fire insurance can completely eliminate the risk of a $50,000 fire loss. This peace of mind costs $100 a year; i.e., the expected value of buying fire insurance is − $100. The expected value of not buying fire insurance comes to only (999/1,000 × $0) + (1/1,000 × −$50,000) = −$50. Why the difference? Because insurance companies charge enough to completely absorb home losses and also to cover their expenses. Since insurance companies return only part of their premiums to homeowners, no expected-value maximizer would ever purchase fire insurance. After all, the expected value of not insuring the home exceeds the expected value of buying insurance (− $50 versus − $100).

Expected-Utility Concept

If everyone were an expected-value maximizer, the world would be a strange place. No one would ever gamble or buy insurance. Daniel Bernoulli, a famous mathematician, came to this same conclusion about 1728 and at the same time solved the **St. Petersburg paradox.** The St. Petersburg paradox puzzled the leading scholars of the day, all of whom believed in expected-value maximization.

The paradox concerns a special gamble which can be described as follows: Take a coin. Choose one side of the coin, say heads. Keep tossing the coin until the other side turns up. When this happens, the game is finished. Until then the casino doubles your money on each consecutive winning-coin toss. As a result, if you toss heads and then tails you collect $2; if you toss 2 heads in a row and then a tail, you collect $4; 3 heads in a row and then a tail, $8; 4 heads in a row and then a tail, $16; and so on. The fortunate player who manages to go 16 consecutive rounds makes $65,536.

The question is, How much should a person be willing to pay the casino to play this game? If the individual adheres to expected value, the answer is an infinite amount—an amount so large that it cannot even be expressed. After all, the expected value of the game is infinitely large [$(1/2 \times \$2) + (1/4 \times \$4) + (1/8 \times \$8) + (1/16 \times \$16)$ and so on], and expected-value maximizers are always willing to pay the expected value of an action.

Despite its enormous expected value, most bettors refuse to pay more than $20 to play the St. Petersburg game. To those who believed deeply in expected value as a prime motivator in human decision making, this was paradoxical. But Bernoulli had a sensible explanation. Money means different things to different people, he argued. Indeed money means different things to even the same person. For example, a man down to his last $1 values it very highly, whereas the same man with $1 million finds $1 to be almost meaningless. According to Bernoulli, gamblers refuse to pay much to play the St. Petersburg game because the almost certain loss of their small stakes outweighs the tiny chance of winning a huge sum of money.

Bernoulli's explanation of the St. Petersburg paradox displays the simplicity characteristic of so many ingenious solutions. According to Bernoulli, man is still a maximizer. But he maximizes **expected utility, not expected value**. He first translates all dollar outcomes into highly personal quantities called utilities and then selects the particular decision which maximizes expected utility. Some people judge the loss of $10,000 to be 100 times as painful as a loss of $1,000, even though it involves only 10 times as much money, or a loss of $10,000 may cause someone 5 times as much displeasure as a gain of $10,000 causes pleasure. For that reason, people use utilities rather than the actual dollar values in making decisions.

Risk Averters, Risk Neutrals, and Risk Lovers

To better understand these ideas, imagine investors living in a truly mechanistic world governed by the concept of expected utility. Each investor accurately records his or her beliefs about the probability of various possible investments. After doing this the investor assigns personal values to different amounts of money. These highly subjective personal values or utilities are then summarized in a **utility function**. A utility function is simply a mathematical relationship which describes the utility obtained from different amounts of money. The utility functions of three different types of people are displayed in Figure 6-3. The three general types of people depicted there are usually referred to as being risk-neutral, risk-averse, and risk-loving.

Anyone who adheres to the philosophy of expected-value maximization is a **risk neutral**. To such a person, a dollar is a dollar no matter how many or how few he or she already possesses. The satisfaction accompanying the gain of $1 exactly equals the dissatisfaction associated with the loss of it. That is why the utility function is a straight line. On the other hand, **risk lovers** experience much greater pleasure in winning a sum of money than displeasure in losing an equal

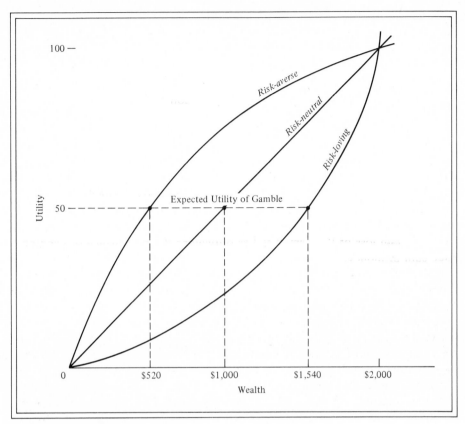

FIGURE 6-3 Three types of investors: risk-averse, risk-neutral, and risk-loving.

sum. For that reason, their utility functions increase with money at a faster and faster rate. **Risk averters** are just the opposite: they regret their losses much more than they enjoy their gains. Their utility functions increase at a slower and slower pace with each increase in money.

Gambling and Insurance

All this probably seems very confusing. But several examples can demonstrate the differences between people who are risk-averse, risk-neutral, and risk-loving. The first question is, Who will pay to gamble? The answer is, Only the risk lover. To see why, consider an itinerant coin tosser who approaches three people, each representing one of the three types, and offers to toss coins with them for rather high stakes—$1,000 for calling the toss correctly. Since the risk averter, risk neutral, and risk lover each possess only $1,000, the coin-tossing game will leave them with either $0 or $2,000.

By combining the probabilities of winning and losing with the individual utilities for the particular sums of money involved, the expected utility of playing the coin-tossing game can be calcuiated for each person. Since the utility of $0 equals 0 and the utility of $2,000 equals 100, the expected utility of the game $(1/2 \times 0) + (1/2 \times 100) = 50$ for each individual. But a utility of 50 corresponds to different sums of money, as can be seen in Figure 6-3. The risk averter assigns a utility of 50 to $520. The risk neutral associates a utility of 50 with the sum of $1,000. And it takes $1,540 to provide the risk lover with a utility of 50 units.

Judging from these utilities, only the risk lover eagerly matches coins. This is illustrated in Figure 6-4, which summarizes the feelings of each type of individual. The expected value of the coin-tossing game $(1/2 \times \$1,000) + (1/2 \times -\$1,000) = \$0$. In other words, players neither win nor lose on the average. Since the game provides the risk lover with the same utility as $1,540 in cash, the risk lover would willingly pay the coin tosser as much as $540 a toss just for the opportunity to play the game. Perhaps this explains the success of only slightly more attractive games in Las Vegas.

On the other hand, the risk neutral assesses the gamble at its expected value of $0 and so takes a completely unemotional view of the opportunity—this person may or may not toss coins depending upon his or her whims. But the coin tosser could easily talk the risk-neutral character into playing by offering to pay a few extra dollars on each toss.

In order to interest the risk averter, the coin tosser would have to pay him or her to play. In fact, the risk averter demands an additional fee of at least $480 be-

FIGURE 6-4   Different attitudes toward gambling.

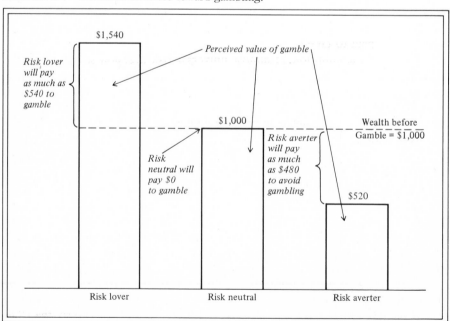

fore taking part in a single coin toss. This fee is usually referred to as a **risk premium.** It is a bonus or incentive which any risk averter demands before taking a risk. The risk premium compensates for the mental turmoil the risk averter experiences while exposed to a risky situation.

This same type of analysis can be used to show that only the risk averter will purchase insurance.

↳ *not so!*

Human Behavior toward Risk

The three general types of investors can now be described as follows:

Type of Person	Behavior
Risk averters	Pay less than the expected value of an uncertain action
Risk neutrals	Pay an amount equal to the value of an uncertain action
Risk lovers	Pay more than the expected value of an uncertain action

The preceding rules show the maximum amount each type of person will pay to take an uncertain action. Of course, if people can pay less, they will do so.

In actuality, the same people often buy insurance and make small bets. Milton Friedman and Leonard Savage argue that this behavior indicates that individuals are simultaneously risk-averse and risk-loving. But the risk preference usually applies only to small gambles. When substantial sums of money are involved, it seems reasonable to assume that most investors are risk-averse; i.e., they must be paid to take on the risk.

Why is this assumption of almost universal risk aversion so generally accepted? Because very few people behave in a way which directly contradicts the assumption. Risk-loving investors would willingly stake their life's savings on the toss of a coin. In fact they would even pay for the privilege of doing so. And risk-neutral investors would be indifferent about betting their total savings on a coin toss. If they were offered a penny incentive to take this bet, they would do so.

Application of the Expected-Utility Concept

Bernoulli's concept of expected utility still stands at the center of decision-making theory. Of course, the concept has been embroidered with elaborate and mathematically sophisticated theorems, and Bernoulli's argument that $1 means more to an impoverished person than to a millionaire has been rejected and more general assumptions about utility functions substituted. Any taxicab driver or other worker who depends upon tips can understand why this change was necessary. Apparently the rich can be just as frugal, sometimes even more so, than the not-so-rich.

Otherwise, the expected-utility theory is as theoretically appropriate as it was hundreds of years ago. But so far it appears to have had only a limited impact on investors. Why have investors ignored the expected-utility concept? R. Sinsheimer, a computer expert, provides one possible explanation in an article provocatively titled "The Brain of Pooh: An Essay on the Limits of the Mind." Everyone knows that Winnie the Pooh lacked much in the way of intellectual capabilities. But few realize that people have a very limited ability to process information on probabilities. Sinsheimer argues that people are primarily trial-and-error learners, who usually ignore uncertainty and rely upon either habit or simple rules. And there is now considerable evidence to support Sinsheimer's view.

Whatever the shortcomings of the human brain, there seems to be little doubt that people can improve their decision-making ability by being better informed. According to the expected utility concept, information on probabilities and utilities is vital to decision making. For that reason simplified techniques for understanding and estimating risk are provided in the remainder of this chapter. And several methods for determining personal preferences are outlined in later chapters. By incorporating these probabilities and preferences into simple rules, investors can improve their investment decision making.

MEASURING RISK

Every investment traded in an efficient market carries an invisible seal of approval. It has been carefully inspected by millions of investors, and the price is right. But individuals must still select the particular investments which satisfy their own personal needs and objectives.

Probably no other factor has a more important impact on their emotional well-being than risk. And yet very few investors know how to measure the risk of stocks, bonds, real estate, mutual funds, gold, silver, coins, or even their own bank accounts. Those who do know have often gained their knowledge the hard way by personally experiencing unexpected ups and downs in poorly selected investments.

The simplest way to measure risk is to study the past price behavior of the investment. Investments appear to display reasonably consistent patterns of behavior. In particular, securities exhibiting large price fluctuations in the past can be expected to vary considerably in the future. The monthly changes in the prices of AT&T, General Motors, and Polaroid are given in Figure 6-5. All these stocks behave fairly consistently, despite the fact that their price histories span a 15-year period of time. Judging from past price behavior, investors seeking security would do well to avoid investing all their money in Polaroid, which had an average monthly price change of 20%. Sleep would probably come much more easily if they bought AT&T instead, which had an average monthly price change of only 4%.

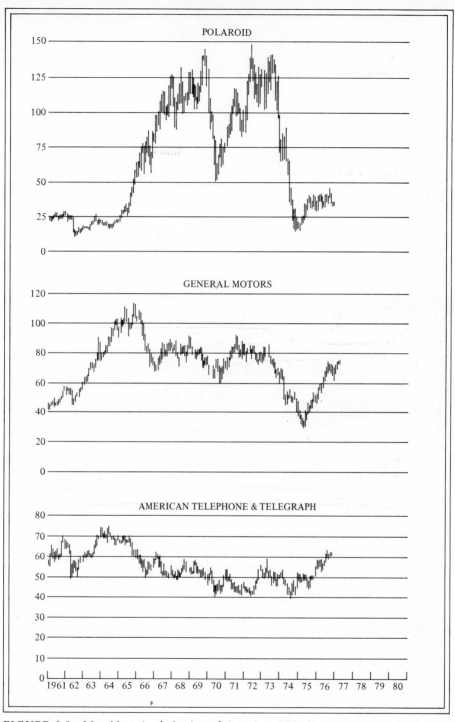

FIGURE 6-5   Monthly price behavior of American Telephone & Telegraph, General Motors and Polaroid.

Range, Variance, and Standard Deviation

The careful observer can learn much about the risk of an investment simply by studying a chart of past prices. For that reason, a picture of prices can be worth 1,000 words. But a numerical measure of risk can be worth 10,000 words, especially in comparing different investments. The **range** of past prices of an investment offers the simplest numerical measure of risk. It is defined as the difference between the high and low prices of the investment over a particular period of time. Many newspapers report the yearly highs and lows of stocks, bonds, commodities, etc. For example, the price of a share in AT&T in 1974 ranged between a low of $44 and a high of $52. During the same year Xerox fluctuated between $50 and $88. The range for AT&T was $8; for Xerox it was $38. Xerox appears about 5 times as volatile as AT&T.

Although highs and lows in prices are readily available and easy to use, the range suffers from several shortcomings. First, it gives undue emphasis to extreme results. A stock may have dipped to a new low only to shift immediately to a much higher price. Secondly, the range gives no consideration to price behavior in earlier years, despite the fact that price behavior in any given year often differs considerably from that in previous years. The range has another drawback. It must be adjusted for stocks with different prices. The adjustment should reflect the fact that a $4 change in a stock originally selling for $200 has a much smaller impact on the investor's total wealth than a $4 change in a $4 stock. In the first case the investor gains or loses 2%; in the second either the money is all lost or a 100% gain is made. The difference between these two stocks is shown in Figure 6-6.

These problems in determining volatility can be eliminated by using a measure based upon a large number of observations on rates of return. Unlike the price range, rates of return are independent of investment prices; so it makes no difference whether a stock sells for $4 or $200. And by basing the risk measure

FIGURE 6-6   Price ranges for different stocks.

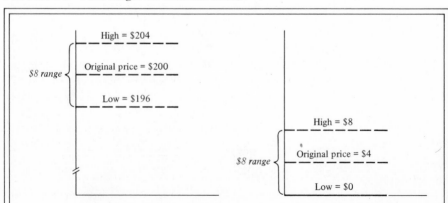

upon numerous observations, the importance of extreme and unusual price changes is reduced.

However, a new problem arises. Percentage price changes for numerous different time periods must somehow be condensed into one measure. The problem can be solved by calculating the variance or standard deviation of the rates of return. The **variance** can be computed in four steps: (1) determine the average or expected return; (2) calculate the deviation or difference between each observed return and the average; (3) square each deviation; and (4) add all the squared deviations together and divide by the number of observations. The result is called the variance. Now, to find the **standard deviation** (Step 5 in table below), which is an intuitively more appealing measure of risk, take the square root of the variance. Although this may sound complicated, the following example shows how easy it is to do.

EXAMPLE   The annual rates of return on a stock during a 6-year period were 20%, 25%, −60%, 15%, 20%, and 10%. The variance and standard deviation of annual returns are computed as follows:

Step 1 *Determine average returns*			Step 2 *Calculate the deviations*	Step 3 *Square each deviation*
Actual Returns		*Average Return*		
20	−	5	+15	225
25	−	5	+20	400
−60	−	5	−65	4,225
15	−	5	+10	100
20	−	5	+15	225
10	−	5	+5	25

$\dfrac{30}{6} = 5$ average return

Step 4   *Add the squared deviations and divide by the number of observations* $\dfrac{5,200}{6} = 867$ variance

Step 5   *Take the square root of the variance* $\sqrt{867} = 29.3\%$

In Step 1 of the preceding example, the expected return is determined. Then in Step 2 the differences between the actual returns and this expected return are calculated. Each of these deviations represents a surprise to the investor. In this case the individual expected a 5% return in the first year but actually earned 20%. So the difference between the actual and the expected return equals 15%. Step 3 consists of squaring each of these deviations. By squaring these numbers the investor assigns additional weight to large deviations or surprises. This implies special concern about substantial surprises and the desire to avoid them if at all possible. For example, a deviation of 65 is only $3^{1}/_{4}$ times as large as a deviation of 20. But the squaring process assigns it a value more than 10 times as great (4,225 versus 400). The variance is found in Step 4 by taking the average of the squared deviations.

29.3% of what?

The variance has one shortcoming. It does not provide an intuitive measure of risk, since it is expressed in terms of squared numbers. This problem is eliminated by taking the square root of the variance. The resulting measure is called the standard deviation. In the preceding example the standard deviation equaled 29.3%.

One obvious question still remains unanswered: What do investors do with a standard deviation? One hopes they use it to form a mental image of investment risk, but before doing so, they should make two crucial assumptions. Both concern the distribution of investment returns.

The returns on most investments appear to be almost normally distributed. In order to better understand the concept of a **normal distribution,** imagine an inexperienced but ambitious investor who wants to describe all possible outcomes from a future investment. He or she buys a set of building blocks, and as the price of the investment changes from one period to the next, writes each return on a single building block. When this investor runs out of building blocks, he or she stops recording the rates of return. He or she then draws a straight line on the floor and marks off increasing rates of return. Sorting the blocks along this line, the investor finds them distributed just like the set in Figure 6-7. The smaller the building blocks, the closer the distribution resembles the bell-shaped curve characteristic of normal distributions.

FIGURE 6-7   Normally distributed rates of return.

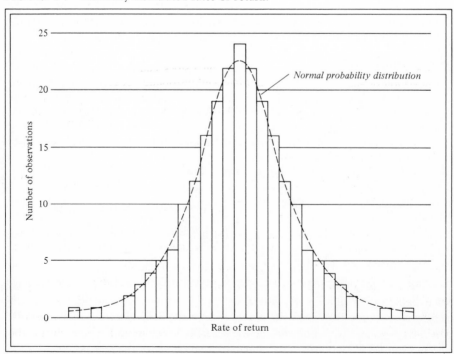

$$\overline{X} - M$$

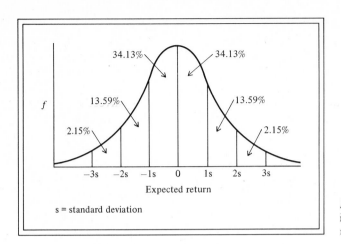

FIGURE 6-8 Probabilities associated with a normal distribution.

The investor now makes a second assumption, that the distribution of returns is **stationary**, rather than shifting in one direction or another or changing shape over time. If the distribution of returns is both normal and stationary, the investor can safely assign probabilities to future results.

The investor knows that the probabilities in Figure 6-8 hold true. For example, 68%, or approximately two-thirds, of all returns should cluster within one standard deviation of the expected value, and 95% should fall within two standard deviations. Consequently only 5% should fall outside this range.

EXAMPLE   The expected annual return on a stock equals 10%, and the standard deviation of annual returns equals 15%. The distribution of returns appears to be both normal and stationary. Therefore, the investor can be reasonably confident that two-thirds of all future annual returns will fall within one standard deviation of the expected return (between − 5 and 25%) and 95% of all returns will fall within two standard deviations (between − 20 and 40%). These beliefs can be expressed in terms of **confidence intervals** as follows:

| −5%   10%   25% | 68% confidence interval |
| −20%   10%   40% | 95% confidence interval |

The confidence intervals can also be interpreted in terms of odds. A 95% confidence interval corresponds to odds of 95 to 5 (or 19 to 1) that the annual return on the stock will fall between − 20 and 40%.

The use of prices to measure risk need not be limited to stocks. The past price behavior of gold, silver, stamps, coins, options, and other investments usually serves as a portent of the future risk of these investments. For example, past prices can be used to determine the volatility of gold. Gold prices during the 12 months of 1975 are shown in Table 6-1. The range for the year is $42.50, indi-

TABLE 6-1. *GOLD PRICES DURING 1975*

Month	Price per Ounce, $*
January	175.80
February	181.75
March	177.25
April	167.00
May	167.00
June	166.25
July	166.70
August	155.00
September	139.25
October	143.75
November	141.10
December	141.75

* London gold prices from *The Wall Street Journal* for the end of each month.

cating that investors can expect a substantial fluctuation in the value of their gold investments. The standard deviation of monthly rather than annual percentage returns is 13%. This provides still stronger support to the statement that gold is risky when held as the sole investment.

Stability Index

Fortunately, investors can avoid making detailed calculations of risk measures by subscribing to an investment advisory service. For example, Value Line publishes a risk measure called a **stability index** for approximately 1,600 stocks. The stability index is expressed as a number ranging from 5 to 100 in multiples of 5—the higher the number, the more stable the stock. In order to determine the stability index for a stock, Value Line first calculates the standard deviation of a stock's weekly percentage price changes from the most recent 5 years of stock prices. Then the stocks are ranked by the magnitude of their standard deviations. The stocks at the top of the list have the smallest standard deviations; the stocks at the bottom of the list, the largest. The list is then divided into 20 categories, with each category containing 5% of the stocks. At the end of 1976, the stability indexes for AT&T, General Motors, and Polaroid were 100, 85, and 20. These figures indicate that AT&T is in the top 5% of stocks with regard to stability. General Motors stock is also relatively stable. It is in the top 15%. On the other hand, Polaroid stock fluctuates considerably. It is in the lowest 20% in terms of stability.

So far it has been assumed that investors passively accept the risks and rewards available to them in the investments markets. Actually many investors modify these risks and returns by:

1   *Investing with borrowed money.* This borrowed money adds financial risk to the already present market risk, but it also increases the expected returns. Finan-

cial risk, often called financial leverage, is explained in the next section of this chapter.

2   *Combining different assets into a portfolio.* This diversification usually reduces the total risk without reducing the expected returns. Diversification is discussed in the next chapter on portfolios.

FINANCIAL RISK

The existence of debt opens up an exciting but risky possibility to investors. By using Other People's Money, or **OPM,** they can greatly magnify their own profits and losses. Many self-made millionaires attribute their success to OPM.

How does OPM turn ordinary investors and small businesspeople into millionaires (or paupers)? The answer is simple. Lenders demand a fixed return for the use of their money. So investors who employ OPM experience the full amount of any gain or loss (over and above this fixed return) on every dollar invested.

A couple who purchase a $40,000 home with a $4,000 down payment are relying heavily on OPM. If they guess right and the home increases in value by only 10%, their own $4,000 investment increases in value by 100%. On the other hand, a 10% decline in the value of the home, a relatively small percentage change, completely wipes out their $4,000 investment. Obviously the more OPM relative to Owner's Money, or OM, the larger the percentage gains and losses the investor experiences. By the way, most people call the owner's money **equity.** Equity is usually defined as the amount of money left over from the market price of an investment after all debts have been repaid.

Since debt provides the investor with a lever to multiply gains and losses, the use of debt is referred to as leverage or **financial leverage.** The degree of leverage or multiplication depends upon the amount of debt employed by the investor. The greater the debt relative to the equity, the larger the investment an individual can swing. This leverage is illustrated in Figure 6-9. If an individual's own money in a $2 investment is $1, the leverage factor is 2 to 1. Every 1% change in the overall value of the investment produces a 2% change in the amount of the investor's own money, if one ignores for the moment any interest charges. If the investor's own money constitutes only $1 of every $10 invested, the leverage factor is 10 to 1. A 1% change in prices causes a 10% change in the investor's equity. In general, the **leverage factor** is calculated as follows:

$$\text{Leverage factor} = \frac{\text{total investment}}{\text{equity}}$$

Or the leverage factor can be computed as follows:

$$\text{Leverage factor} = \frac{1}{\text{equity as a percentage of total investment}}$$

The greater the leverage, the greater the possibility of making really large profits. Commodities futures provide an extreme example of the immense

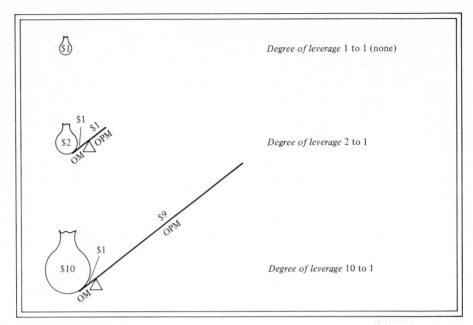

FIGURE 6-9   Financial leverage.

rewards possible with OPM. Investors usually purchase sugar futures contracts with very small down payments of 5% to 10% of the contract value. During 1974 the price of sugar futures went from about 12¢ a pound to more than 65¢. Any investor who risked $10,000 of his or her own money to buy $200,000 worth of sugar contracts made close to $1 million. The exact results would have been as follows:

$$\begin{array}{ll} \$200,000 & \text{invested in sugar futures contracts} \\ \times \quad 4.42 & 442\% \text{ increase in price of sugar futures} \\ \hline \$884,000 & \text{increase in value} \end{array}$$

This represents an enormous return of 8,840% on the investor's $10,000—far more than the 442% that would have been earned by buying $10,000 of futures contracts for cash. Of course, very few speculators ever reap such returns. Most futures traders find themselves quickly eliminated from the game by small fluctuations in contract prices. After all, leverage works in both directions.

So far nothing has been said about how the return promised to lenders affects the success or failure of leveraged investments. Obviously, the return an investor expects to earn on an investment should at least equal the cost of borrowed money. But sometimes the actual return on an investment falls below the return promised to lenders. During the tight-money times of 1975, numerous real estate projects collapsed for this very reason. One of the most publicized bankruptcies involved William Zeckendorf, a world renowned builder, whose huge projects helped reshape the skyline of New York City. Zeckendorf's unexpected plight resulted from the high cost of his extremely heavy borrowings coupled with his inability to find prime tenants for several new office buildings and a sharp drop in real estate prices.

Zeckendorf was not alone. In the early seventies real estate investment trusts (REITs) became the Cinderellas of the investment world. These companies pooled the investment funds of millions of investors and then lent this money, together with even larger sums borrowed from banks, to real estate promoters. The success of the REITs was short-lived. As interest rates on the money borrowed from banks soared higher and higher and returns on investments plunged, these companies faced the same impossible situation as did Zeckendorf. After paying the high cost of borrowed money, the first adverse change in the value of their investments completely wiped out the owners' equity.

Margin Requirements

Despite occasional mishaps in the real estate industry, most investors have no difficulty borrowing 80% or even 90% and 100% on income properties or homes. However, investors hooked on the beauty of OPM face greater difficulties in borrowing money for stocks, bonds, and other securities. Suppose an individual decides to buy stock on **margin,** meaning that she or he provides only a fraction of the total investment. In a sense the investor's margin is the down payment on the investment. The remaining amount comes from a loan with a brokerage firm or bank. The margin is usually expressed as the fraction of the investment paid for with the investor's own money; i.e.,

$$\text{Percentage margin} = \frac{\text{investor's own money or equity}}{\text{total investment}}$$

The Federal Reserve Bank sets **initial margin requirements** in an attempt to prevent unwise speculation by investors. The initial margin requirement applies only on the day of purchase. When the initial margin requirement on stock is 50%, an investor must provide cash or acceptable securities totaling 50% of the purchase price of the stock, borrowing the other 50% from the broker or bank. When the initial margin requirement is 60%, investors must pay at least 60% of the purchase price out of their own funds and the other 40% can be borrowed. The higher the initial margin requirement, the greater the proportion of equity that must be put up for a purchase and the smaller the proportion of OPM.

The Federal Reserve has mandated initial margin requirements for so long that even the most vocal advocates of free markets seldom complain about this limitation on economic freedom. Congress gave the Federal Reserve this authority in 1933, while the speculative frenzies of the 1920s were still fresh in the minds of the people. During the 1920s, many investors had purchased stocks on margins of only 10 to 20%. The margin requirements established by the Federal Reserve over the years are given in Figure 6-10.

Investors who want to employ substantial leverage in securities suffer from

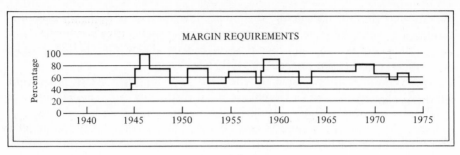

FIGURE 6-10   Federal Reserve margin requirements.

another handicap. Securities prices fluctuate daily and are widely publicized. Before surrendering their money, most lenders demand that the borrower pledge securities as protection against default. When these securities drop in value, lenders become very nervous, and understandably so. Suppose a banker or broker lends an investor $50,000 and the investor puts up the other $50,000. Since the loan is secured by $100,000 of readily marketable stocks, the lender charges a relatively low interest rate. Should the total value of those securities suddenly fall to $40,000, the lender has a serious problem. If the borrower fails to repay the loan, the lender loses $10,000—the difference between the unpaid loan and the market value of the securities.

Lenders usually solve the problem of falling securities prices by asking for more collateral. In polite circles this request is termed a **margin call.** Careful bankers and brokers issue margin calls long before the value of securities drops below the amount of the loan. If investors refuse to meet a margin call, their investments are immediately sold and the proceeds used to pay off the loan. Any money left over is returned to the investors.

In order to avoid as many unpleasant surprises to investors as possible, banks and brokerage houses set **maintenance margin requirements.** Borrowers must always maintain at least this much equity in all margined investments. At the present time, most brokerage houses require a maintenance margin on stocks of 30%. In other words, the investor's own money, or equity, must always make up at least 30% of the total market value of the stocks. Since 30% is considerably less than the initial margin requirement of 50%, stocks can decline by a large amount before an investor receives a margin call.

Suppose an individual purchases $10,000 of stock on margin. At least $5,000 must initially be OM. If the stock then drops 20% in value to $8,000, the equity in the investment decreases to $3,000; i.e.,

$8,000	new value of stock
−5,000	loan
$3,000	equity, or the amount of the investor's own money that would be left after repaying the loan

Despite the considerable decline in price and equity, the 30% maintenance requirement is still satisfied ($3,000 is 37.5% of $8,000). But if the stock continues to drop in price until the total market value sinks to $7,142, the maintenance requirement is just barely satisfied. And when the stock goes below this value, the investor has one of two choices: put up more money or watch the broker or banker sell the stock.

Pyramiding

As prices decline, the investor may continually be asked to put up additional money to satisfy margin requirements. On the other hand, when prices rise steadily, the investor may be able to pyramid. **Pyramiding** refers to the continuous borrowing of additional money as investments increase in value and the reinvesting of this borrowed money. Most get-rich-quick schemes rely upon pyramiding techniques.

Commodity futures provide tremendous opportunities for pyramiding. An investor can buy $20,000 of some commodity futures with only a 5% margin of $1,000. If the value of the futures contract jumps by 5% to $21,000, the investor then has an equity of $2,000, the initial $1,000 of OM plus a $1,000 profit. A $2,000 investment can support $40,000 of futures; so the investor buys another contract. (Actually, the investor must put up another $100 in cash, since two contracts are worth $42,000.) Now if the market goes up by still another 5%, the equity will be $4,200—the previous $2,100 plus the $2,100 profit on $42,000 of futures. With 4,200 the investor can hold $84,000 of futures and so buys two more contracts (again putting up a few hundred extra dollars).

As long as the market continues to go up, the investor can keep buying contracts. The initial $1,000 investment supports a larger and larger dollar invest-

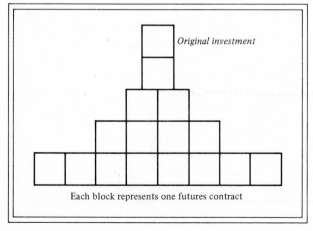

Original investment

Each block represents one futures contract

FIGURE 6-11   Pyramiding.

ment. And with each increase in the value of the futures contracts, an increasingly larger dollar amount can be added to the investment. In this case, successive 5% increases in the value of the futures contracts result in the additions shown in Figure 6-11. Anyone successfully pyramiding sugar contracts in 1974 obtained truly amazing results. One hundred dollars invested at the right time grew to millions of dollars.

These same pyramiding techniques can be applied to real estate. First the investor buys a property with 20% down. The property increases in value. Then she or he refinances the property or borrows additional money through a second mortgage and buys another property. Both properties go up in value. And the process of refinancing, buying, refinancing, buying goes on and on.

Unfortunately, success stories like this are very rare—much rarer than brokers and those who dabble in commodities futures and highly leveraged real estate would have investors believe. After all, prices fluctuate both up and down, and falling prices can quickly topple pyramids.

RUIN

Financial leverage increases risk. This in turn increases the probability that an investor will be ruined. The word **ruin** possesses considerable emotional overtones for most people. But statisticians objectively define ruin as the complete loss of an initial sum of money, and they have calculated the exact probability of ruin occurring in different situations.

These calculations are too complicated to present here. But the same general results can be obtained by computer **simulation.** A simulation is a make-believe process. A computer is programmed to generate possible outcomes based on assumed probabilities. In the simulation described in Table 6-2 the probabilities associated with an investment in a risky asset were used together with different investment strategies. The conservative strategy consisted of investing half the available funds in a risky asset like stocks and the other half in a very low risk asset like a bank account. The average strategy involves investing all the money in the risky asset. The speculative strategy consists of putting all the investor's savings plus an equal amount of borrowed money into the risky asset. The simulation results presented in Table 6-2 tell a sad story. Most of the people who invest considerable amounts of borrowed money in volatile investments eventually go bankrupt, even though they may initially enjoy great success.

The general experience of investors in commodity futures, stock options, and other highly leveraged investments supports this conclusion. According to studies by Stewart, by Hieronymus, and by Teweles, Harlow, and Stone, 65 to 75% of all investors in commodity futures lose money. For this reason, the commodities investor's dash for profits closely resembles the Charge of the Light Brigade. But in the case of commodity trading, new recruits continually fill the rapidly thinned ranks. As P. T. Barnum put it, "There's a sucker born every minute."

TABLE 6-2   LEVERAGE AND RUIN*

| Month | Total Amount Invested | | |
	Conservative Strategy, $	Average Strategy, $	Speculative Strategy, $
0	1,000	1,000	1,000
10	930	810	520
20	1,120	1,180	1,040
30	1,510	2,420	3,770
40	1,950	3,260	5,520
50	1,830	2,760	3,420
60	1,720	2,390	2,350
70	1,450	1,620	850
80	1,830	2,490	1,800
90	2,260	3,770	3,400
100	2,640	4,880	5,430
150	2,400	3,310	1,030
200	2,850	3,720	760
250	2,860	3,290	220
300	3,790	5,050	290
350	9,530	27,360	4,620
400	11,980	37,490	4,800
450	6,720	10,020	160
500	7,540	10,580	80

* The conservative strategy consists of investing only half the funds in a risky asset. The average strategy puts all the funds into the risky asset. And with the risky strategy one-half of the money invested is borrowed.
Source: These figures are reprinted from Harry Markowitz, *Portfolio Selection: Efficient Diversification of Investments,* Wiley, New York, 1959.

But the problem does not lie with commodities per se. When combined with sufficient leverage, any investment poses the risk of ruin. Even home buyers must beware. Von Furstenberg has demonstrated that leverage is intimately related to foreclosures. According to him, the number of homes foreclosed increases by nearly 300% when the down payment declines from about 20 to 10%. And buyers purchasing homes with a down payment of only 3% experience foreclosure 18 times more often than buyers with down payments ranging from 20 to 24%.

SUMMARY

We live in a world of uncertainty. But strangely enough, we seem to be primarily trial-and-error learners who usually ignore uncertainty. No wonder so many people bemoan the results of their investment decisions!

Fortunately, investors can improve their investment decision making. The first step in this self-improvement process is the explicit recognition of risk. Next, investors must accept the fact that risk and return are inseparably intertwined. And then investors must learn how to measure and control risk.

Probabilities provide one means of describing the risk of any investment. At the present time very few investors know how to assign probabilities to alternative events. But the day will probably come when members of investment-advising firms sit down with their clients and guide them in these assessments. Already some large financial institutions have incorporated probabilities into their own decision making.

Investment decision making requires more than just probabilities. People must attach values to each of the possible outcomes and then combine those values with the probabilities. In doing so, they can select either money values or highly subjective utilities. Judging from human behavior, people tend to base their decisions on utilities rather than strict monetary values.

This utility-oriented decision making has a very important consequence. It implies that each person must make his or her own investment decisions. Experts can explain the alternatives and make recommendations, but they cannot experience the individual's personal feelings about the possible outcomes. And, to date, no one has had very much success in communicating utilities to other people. So investors should never completely delegate the decision-making authority to another person. The moral of utility theory is obviously, "Different strokes for different folks."

How can the investor measure risk? Range, variance, and standard deviation provide indicators of uncertainty or risk. And several advisory services supply ratings and indexes which can be used to estimate market risk.

Investors have nearly complete control over another type of risk—financial risk. By borrowing money, they can greatly increase their expected returns, but of course they do so only by undertaking more risk. Apparently some investors focus almost exclusively on the chances for large profits and overlook the accompanying chances of large losses.

Investors intrigued by the possibility of making a fortune will want to employ considerable leverage. They can do so by borrowing large sums of money. But they should never forget that the probability of ruin increases with leverage. And the longer they employ leverage, the greater the likelihood that they will eventually be ruined.

So far people have relied upon trial and error to guide themselves through an uncertain world. But they show great ability to adapt simple tools to the evaluation of risk. And the efficient-market concept emphasizes the importance of this task. Since return is tied to risk by an umbilical cord, all investors must seek out the degree of risk and rate of return which best satisfies their personal objectives.

KEYWORDS

risk	expected utility	risk premium
probability	utility function	range
expected value	risk neutral	variance
payoff matrix	risk lovers	standard deviation
St. Petersburg paradox	risk averters	normal distribution

stationary	financial leverage	maintenance margin re-
confidence intervals	leverage factor	quirements
stability index	margin	pyramiding
OPM	initial margin requirements	ruin
equity	margin call	simulation

QUESTIONS

1   Define risk. Now describe some risky situations you face in everyday life.

2   Suppose an individual assigns the following probabilities to tomorrow's weather:

	Rain	*No Rain*
Probability	.3	.7

Explain these probabilities in terms of (1) the frequency approach and (2) the subjective approach. Why do the probabilities add to 1?

3   What is the probability of tossing a head on a coin toss? Why? What is the probability of drawing an ace out of a deck of playing cards? Why? (What did you probably assume about both the coin and the deck of cards?)

4   An investor attaches the following probabilities and monetary outcomes to a commodity futures trade:

	Profit of $1,000	*Profit of $0*	*Loss of $600*
Probability	.4	.3	.3

What is the expected value of the trade?

5   Remember the television series called "The Millionaire"? Now imagine the following updated version: You are offered a no-strings-attached check for $1 million. Or you can toss a coin. If the coin lands heads, you win $5 million. If it lands tails, you receive nothing.

Do you take the $1 million check or toss the coin? (Before you make a decision, think long and hard about how $1 million would change your life.) Is your decision consistent with the expected-value concept? Why or why not?

6   Why do risk averters buy insurance? (Explain this in terms of a utility function.) Why do they demand to be paid for taking on risk?

7   Alfred Hitchcock tells the chilling story of a madman who offered people the following gamble: Take your cigarette lighter. If it lights the next time, I pay you a large sum of money. If it fails to light, I cut off your finger.

Hitchcock's tale serves as a dramatization of the fact that people often risk life and/or limb in the pursuit of monetary gain. How large a payoff would it take for you to accept the madman's wager? (Does knowing that 1 in every 200 people in the United States is seriously injured in auto accidents each year affect your answer?)

8   Do you think the expected-utility concept can actually help you make better decisions? Why or why not?

9   Compute the standard deviation in annual returns for the following stock:

Year	Price, $
1	20
2	23
3	22
4	25
5	26

10   Compute the 50, 75, and 95% confidence intervals for an investment with an expected return of 10% and a standard deviation of annual returns of 30%. (A 50% confidence interval corresponds to .67 standard deviations on each side of the expected return and a 75% confidence interval to 1.15 standard deviations.)

11   Calculate the leverage factor when the equity equals 10, 25, 50, 75, and 100% of the total investment.

12   Brokers often use the term "buying power" to refer to the additional amount of stock which can be purchased with the equity in an account. Compute the buying power in the following brokerage accounts:

Account	Amount Invested, $	Equity, $
Jones	0	10,000
Smith	10,000	5,000
Thompson	20,000	15,000
Zellner	60,000	20,000

Assume the initial margin requirement equals 50%. (Hint: The Jones account has $20,000 of buying power.)

13   Do you think the Federal Reserve Bank should regulate margin requirements? Why or why not?

14   Suppose the maintenance margin requirement equals 25%. An investor purchases $20,000 of stock with $12,000 of equity. How much can the value of the stock drop before the investor receives a margin call?

15   How does pyramiding depend upon initial margin requirements? (Compare the pyramiding possible with 10 and 100% margin requirements.)

16   How does leverage affect the probability of ruin?

REFERENCES

Bernhard, Arnold: *Investing in Common Stocks with the Aid of the Value Line Rankings and Other Criteria of Stock Value,* Arnold Bernhard, New York, 1975.

Bernoulli, Daniel: "Exposition of a New Theory on the Measurement of Risk," translated by Louise Sommer, *The Theory of Business Finance: A Book of Readings,* edited by Stephen H. Archer and Charles A. D'Ambrosio, Macmillan, New York, 1967.

Fama, Eugene F., and Merton H. Miller: *The Theory of Finance,* Dryden Press, Hinsdale, Ill., 1972.

Friedman, Milton, and Leonard J. Savage: "The Utility Analysis of Choices Involving Risk," *The Theory of Business Finance: A Book of Readings,* edited by Stephen H. Archer and Charles A. D'Ambrosio, Macmillan, New York, 1967.

Lapin, Lawrence L.: *Statistics for Modern Business Decisions,* Harcourt Brace Jovanovich, New York, 1973.

Leuthold, Stephen C.: "The Causes and Cures of Market Volatility," *Journal of Portfolio Management,* Winter 1976, pp. 21–25.

Logue, Dennis: "Are Stock Markets Becoming Riskier," *Journal of Portfolio Management,* Spring 1976, pp. 13–19.

McDonald, John G., and Richard E. Stehle: "How Do Institutional Investors Perceive Risk?" *Journal of Portfolio Management,* Fall 1975, pp. 11–16.

Markowitz, Harry M: *Portfolio Selection: Efficient Diversification of Investments,* Wiley, New York, 1959.

Officer, Robert: "The Variability of the Market Factor of the New York Stock Exchange," *Journal of Business,* July 1973, pp. 434–453.

Robertson, Wyndham: "How the Bankers Got Trapped in the REIT Disaster," *Fortune,* March 1975, pp. 113ff.

Teweles, Richard J., Charles V. Harlow, and Herbert L. Stone: *The Commodity Futures Game: Who Wins? Who Loses? Why?* McGraw-Hill, New York, 1974.

CHAPTER SEVEN

PORTFOLIOS

Many people believe that stocks are a very risky investment, and they can often substantiate their beliefs by describing their own unfortunate experiences in the stock market. Most of these stories have a common theme. A considerable amount of money is invested in a single stock. The market declines. The stock drops sharply, and in desperation the frightened investor sells it for a fraction of its cost. Or the overall market may even go up, but, for some reason, the price of the particular stock that was purchased turns down, and the end result is the same.

Investors can largely eliminate these unhappy results, but they need a general knowledge of portfolio concepts. A **portfolio** is defined as a combination or collection of securities or other investments. By diversifying their holdings and owning several stocks instead of just one, investors can considerably lower the risk they expose themselves to without reducing the amount of money they make. The same is true for other investments besides stocks.

EFFECT OF DIVERSIFICATION

Diversification involves spreading or distributing money among a number of different investments. Therefore, the key to diversification is variety. Just how does diversification reduce risk? The answer lies in the fact that when there are numerous investments, the gains usually more than offset the losses. On the other hand, when there is only one investment, the investor is often faced with either feast or famine.

Diversification is not a new concept. In fact the old saying, "Don't put all your eggs in one basket," is simply advice to diversify. But many people have a difficult time understanding exactly how diversification works or why it is so important to the investor.

There are two simple tests of whether or not an investor has an intuitive understanding of diversification.[1] The first test consists of the following question:

> A certain town is served by two hospitals. About 45 babies are born each day in the large hospital and about 15 in the small hospital. Approximately 50% of all babies are girls. However, the exact percentage of baby girls varies from day to day. Sometimes it may be higher than 50%, sometimes lower.
>
> For a period of 1 year, personnel at both the large and the small hospital recorded the days on which more than 60% of the babies born were girls. At which hospital were more of these 60% days recorded?
>
> Check one:
>
> a   The large hospital   _____
>
> b   The small hospital   ___✓___
>
> c   About the same (i.e., the number of days were within 5% of
>   each other)   _____

The second test also consists of a single question. The question is as follows:

> There are two large opaque jars filled with red and white marbles. In each jar, two-thirds of the marbles are one color and one-third are another. One person draws 5 marbles from the first jar and finds that 4 are red and 1 is white. Another individual draws 20 marbles from the second jar and finds that 12 are white and 8 are red.
>
> Check the statement most likely to be true:
>
> a $2/3$ of the marbles in the first jar are red and
> $1/3$ are white
>   (4 out of the 5 marbles drawn from this jar were red)   _____
>
> b $2/3$ of the marbles in the second jar are white and
> $1/3$ are red
>   (12 out of the 20 marbles drawn from this jar were white)   ___✗___
>
> c   Both statements are equally likely to be true   ___✓___

Law of Large Numbers

The correct answer to the question about baby girls is the smaller hospital. The explanation is based upon the law of large numbers. According to the **law of large numbers,** the larger the sample, the more representative it is of the underlying total from which it was drawn. Since one-half of all babies born are girls, the larger the sample of actual births, the greater the chances that the number of baby girls will be equal to one-half of the births.

The answer to the second question also depends upon the law of large numbers. Despite the higher proportion of red marbles in the first drawing of 5, considerably greater weight must be given to the sample of 20 marbles. Therefore, statement *b* is more likely to be true. Again, the reason is because the larger the number of observations, the more representative the sample is of the underlying total from which it was drawn.

Many of the people who take these two tests appear to be unaware of the law of large numbers and incorrectly believe that a small sample provides a very good indication of the state of the real world. As a result of this belief, they ignore the difference in the sizes of the two hospitals and put great faith in the finding that a high percentage of the five marbles was red, thus overlooking the small size of the sample. If carried to an extreme, this belief in the validity of small numbers would imply that a drawing of two marbles, both red, is still stronger evidence that the first jar contains two-thirds red marbles.

Diversification is based upon the law of large numbers. The larger the number of investments an investor owns, the more certain the investor can be of the eventual outcome and the less risk assumed. For example, if all stocks return 10% on the average, the larger the number of stocks held by an investor, the greater the likelihood that the investor's portfolio will actually earn 10%. The law of large numbers also holds true for other types of investments. Suppose apartment buildings in a particular city have an average vacancy rate of 5%. Then the more units an apartment building has, the greater the possibility that the actual vacancy rate will be 5%. For that reason the owner of a 100-unit apartment complex would be very surprised to have a 30% vacancy rate during any 1-month period. On the other hand, the owner of a 4-unit dwelling should expect to occasionally experience a 25 to 50% vacancy rate. And yet, many small real estate investors appear to be amazed when that actually happens.

Potential Gains from Diversification

How much does diversification reduce risk? In a world of independent investments, diversification into larger and larger numbers of investments eventually eliminates all risk. Investments are independent of each other if the outcome of one is in no way linked to the outcome of any other.

In reality very few investments are completely independent of each other, since changes in overall economic conditions cause more or less simultaneous changes in the prices of investments. Diversification cannot completely eliminate the risk of dependent investments, for reasons soon to be explained. Nevertheless, the assumption of independence provides a convenient starting point for analyzing the gains from diversification. First, the calculation of portfolio risk is much easier for independent investments. Second, independent investments provide a reasonable benchmark for measuring the potential gains from diversification.

The reduction in risk which can be achieved by spreading money over several independent investments is substantial, and the investor does not need to hold numerous investments to gain these benefits. In fact, much of the reduction in the total risk of the portfolio occurs when a second investment is added to the first. Additional investments produce smaller and smaller reductions in risk.

This makes sense. After all, by holding two investments rather than one, the investor is doubling the number of investments. On the other hand, if the individual already has eight different investments and then adds one more, he or she has increased the number of investments by only one-eighth. As a result, the increase in safety obtained by diversifying into one more investment becomes very small after 8 to 16 different assets have been acquired.

Random Diversification

The reduction in risk which can be achieved by random diversification can be easily calculated when investments are independent of each other. **Random diversification** simply involves investing an equal amount of money in each of a number of different assets. When the variance in returns is used as a measure of risk and is the same for every investment, the risk of a randomly diversified portfolio equals the risk of any one investment divided by the number of investments in the portfolio. If half the investor's money is put into each of two investments, the variance of the portfolio is one-half of what it was when only one investment was held. If one-fourth of the money is put into each of four investments, the variance is one-fourth of what it was with only one investment. With eight investments, it is one-eighth, etc. Figure 7-1 shows both the variance and standard deviation of the returns from investing an equal amount of money in different numbers of independent investments. Total risk drops sharply in the early rounds of diversification, but the reduction in risk which occurs after 16 to 32 investments have been acquired is relatively small.

> EXAMPLE   An investor can purchase a large tract of land for $40,000 or can invest in four small lots, each costing $10,000. The variance in annual returns on the large lot and on each of the small lots equals 36%. (So the standard deviation in returns amounts to 6%.)
>
> The investor believes that the lot prices will move almost independently of each other in the future. Therefore, the variance in returns experienced by holding four small lots totals only 36%/4, or 9%. (So the standard deviation in returns equals 3%.) This is just one-fourth of the variance in returns associated with an investment in the single large lot.

Some investors act as though they were completely unaware of these results and almost always purchase the single stock, bond, or property which appeals to them the most. In 1962 the Federal Reserve Bank conducted a survey of consumer finances. One of the questions asked of each household was how many dif-

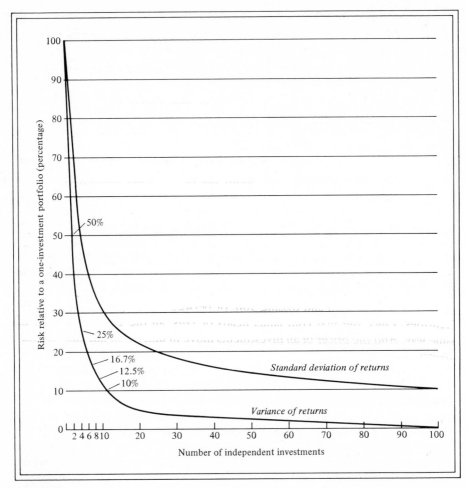

FIGURE 7-1   Reduction in risk from diversification among independent investments.

ferent stocks were held in total by all members of the household. Considering the potential advantages of diversification, the answers were surprising. The average number of stocks held by all families owning stock was only 3.41, and 50% owned only 1 or, at most, 2 stocks. A 1972 study conducted by the Internal Revenue Service supports these findings. The IRS analyzed a special sample of 17,056 individual income tax forms filed for the 1971 tax year. Of the individuals who owned stock, 34% listed shares in only one company and 51% listed no more than two stocks. Only 5% of the taxpayers in the sample had achieved the same degree of diversification which could be obtained by random diversification in seven securities.

DIVERSIFICATION IN THE REAL WORLD

Until now it has been assumed that investments can be found which are completely independent of each other. If that were the case, events which affect one investment would have absolutely no impact on any other investment. As noted earlier, investments are rarely independent of each other. When one stock has done well, it is quite likely that many other stocks have also gone up in value. Or when one apartment building suffers from high vacancy rates, others in the area do also. This tendency for the prices and/or income from different investments to move together reduces the gains that are possible from diversification.

When investments are independent, the results from holding several different investments for any one period of time can be compared with the results from tossing a number of coins. The larger the number of coins that are tossed at one time, the more certain it is that the outcome will be one-half heads and one-half tails. Similarly, the larger the number of investments in the portfolio, the more certain the investor can be of the final return. But if for some reason the coins or investments are dependent upon each other, the total result is much more uncertain. In the case of complete dependence, there is no difference between tossing 1 coin and tossing 500, or between holding 1 security and 500 securities. Once the first coin lands heads or tails, all the other coins land the same way. And the prices of all investments move in unison. In this extreme case, diversification is useless.

Fortunately, very few investments are completely dependent. Most show some independence and fluctuate in fairly unique ways. Judging from past history, between one-half and two-thirds (depending upon the time period studied) of the price changes in stocks are independent of each other. The other one-third to one-half of the movements are tied together. The independent fluctuations in investment values can be eliminated by diversification, whereas the dependent movements cannot. Therefore, sufficient diversification can eliminate from one-half to two-thirds of the fluctuations in stocks.

Actual Risk Reduction from Diversification

Several studies of the effects of diversification on stocks have been done to determine the actual reduction in risk which is possible. The most complete study, done by Professors Lawrence Fisher and James Lorie of the University of Chicago, examines the variability in the returns of all stocks listed on the New York Stock Exchange for the 40-year period 1926–1965. Some of the results from the Fisher-Lorie study are shown in Table 7-1. Their computations are based upon the assumption that at the start of every year, $1 was invested in each of the stocks on the NYSE. The figures in the first line of the table show the actual outcomes from this one-stock strategy: 95% of the stocks (the one-stock portfolios) were worth $1.975 or less at the end of 1 year; the other 5% were worth more than $1.975. In other words, fewer than 5% of the stocks doubled in 1 year. On

TABLE 7-1   RESULTS FROM HOLDING DIFFERENT PORTFOLIOS OF NYSE STOCKS, 1926–1965*

Number of Securities in Portfolio	5% of the Portfolios Had Values Equal to or Less Than:	95% of the Portfolios Had Values Equal to or Less Than:	Standard Deviation
Results for 1-Year Holding Periods, $			
1	.466	1.975	.554
2	.539	1.855	.451
8	.582	1.719	.354
128	.576	1.606	.318
Results for 5-Year Holding Periods, $			
1	.201	4.875	2.064
2	.418	4.533	1.623
8	.678	4.278	1.190
128	.851	4.335	1.019

* It was assumed that $1 was invested in each of the portfolios at the start of the holding period.
Source: Lawrence Fisher, and James H. Lorie, "Some Studies of Variability of Returns on Investments in Common Stocks," *Journal of Business,* © 1970 The University of Chicago Press, April 1970, p. 110.

the other hand, the worst 5% of the stocks lost more than 50% of their value and were worth $.466 or less.

The second line of Table 7-1 demonstrates that diversification reduces the range of investment returns. It shows the outcome of investing $1 in portfolios containing two different stocks at the start of each year: 95% of these two-stock portfolios were worth $1.855 or less at the end of a year; 5% were worth $.539 or less.

If $1 were invested in each possible combination of eight stocks, the results would be similar to those shown on the third line. Again, the outcomes are less extreme. Finally, the fourth line shows the results of investing $1 in combinations of 128 stocks. The end-of-year values are the least extreme of the four different portfolios, the results varying between $.576 and $1.606.

The range is one measure of the risk an investor experiences. The standard deviation is another, more accurate measure of risk. The standard deviations for 1-year investments in 1-, 2-, 8-, and 128-stock portfolios are also shown in Table 7-1. The conclusions which can be drawn from these figures are similar to those reached from an examination of the range of investment results. On a per-stock basis, the largest reduction in risk occurs in going from a 1-stock to a 2-stock portfolio. By holding 8 stocks instead of 1, the investor achieves a considerable degree of diversification. During the period from 1926 to 1965, 1-stock portfolios provided a standard deviation of $.554, whereas 8-stock portfolios offered a standard deviation of $.354. Therefore, the reduction in risk amounted to almost 40% (the difference between $.554 and $.354 divided by $.554). Adding another 120 stocks to the portfolio only reduced the standard deviation to $.318.

This reduction in risk by diversification has a very important effect over a period of several years, as can be seen in the second part of Table 7-1. This part of the table shows the actual results of investing $1 in 1-, 2-, 8- and 128-stock portfolios for distinct 5-year periods. The lowest 5% of the 1-stock portfolios were worth $.201 or less at the end of the 5 years. That is a disastrous loss of $.799 or more on the dollar. The lowest 5% of the 2-stock portfolios were worth more than twice as much, or $.418. The lowest 5% of the 8-stock portfolios were worth $.678 or less, and the lowest 5% of the 128-stock portfolios sold for $.851 or less.

Investors who bought only one stock did very badly when they did badly. What did they gain by their daring? Not very much. After 5 years, the top 5% of the 1-stock portfolios were worth $4.875 or more, of the 2-stock portfolios $4.533, of the 8-stock portfolios $4.278, and of the 128-stock portfolios $4.335. And the top 10% of the 128-stock portfolios (this is not shown in Table 7-1) were actually worth more than the top 10% of the 1-stock portfolios—$3.987 compared with $3.581. Moreover, the average returns (also not shown in Table 7-1) were almost identical, no matter how many stocks were held in the portfolio.

What can investors conclude from all these numbers? First, they would be wise not to expect to make a fortune in the stock market overnight. Fewer than 5% of the portfolios quintupled in value in any 5-year period. Second, diversification reduces risk without reducing average returns and results in a marked reduction in losses without reducing opportunities for substantial gains. Third, a portfolio of 8 stocks provides substantial diversification, and even a 2-stock portfolio is a much less risky investment than a 1-stock portfolio. Fourth, even diversification does not eliminate all losses.

Another striking example of the importance of diversification to investors is provided by the famous Morgan silver-dollar series. More than 570 million Morgan silver dollars were minted between the years of 1878 and 1921. Many of these silver dollars were still circulating in the United States in the early 1960s before the price of silver began its steady climb upward. The prices of three dates of uncirculated Morgan dollars—the 1892-S, 1903-O, and 1903-S dollars—are shown in Figure 7-2 for a 25-year period.

Pity the investors who bought just the scarce 1903-O dollars, especially if they purchased them near their historic high of $1,500 in 1963! Prices dropped to $35 the following year when the United States government announced the discovery of several thousand of these 1903-O silver dollars in one of the old mint buildings. This sad turn of events could have been avoided by random diversification. There are 112 different Morgan dollars, if different dates as well as mint marks are counted. The results of investing an equal dollar amount in each Morgan dollar, i.e., random diversification, are shown in Figure 7-2.

It should be obvious by now that diversification can eliminate much of the extreme price fluctuation in any investment portfolio. For that reason, safety-conscious investors should be certain to diversify their holdings. But conservative investors are not the only people who diversify. Even gamblers at a racetrack or a

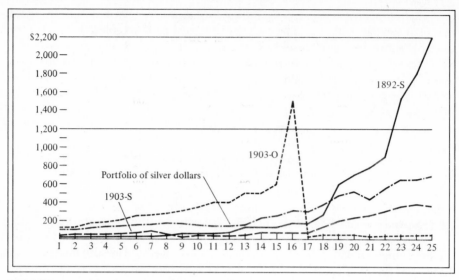

FIGURE 7-2   Price behavior of Morgan silver dollars. (From R. S. Yeoman, *A Guide-book of United States Coins,* Western Publishing Co., Inc., Racine, Wisconsin, 1973).

casino reduce their risks by wagering only a fraction of their money at any one time. People seldom go to the track and bet all their money on a single horse. Instead, they usually place bets on several horses in each of several races. By doing so, they eliminate the possibility of being wiped out during just one race. Of course, they also reduce the chances for a really large win.

Diversification and Returns

Why do some investors refuse to diversify their investments? Because diversification diminishes the possibility of extremely high returns on a single investment at the same time that it reduces the chances of suffering extremely large losses. As long as there is a chance—no matter how small it is—of making a very large profit, these investors prefer to plunge all of their money into a single investment.

These investors point to the fact that every year several stocks, coins, stamps, properties, etc., display tremendous increases in value. At the same time, they admit that the prices of a small number of investments plummet to zero. The figures in Table 7-2 demonstrate how extreme some of the returns can be for stocks traded on the New York Stock Exchange. In 3 out of the 40 years—1928, 1933, and 1936—at least one stock increased in value by more than 1,000%. For example, in 1928 a stock jumped 1,223% in price. And in most of the other years at least one stock increased in value by 200 to 300%. Judging from these figures, any investors who can pick the best performing stock for 5 or 6 years in a row can

TABLE 7-2   RESULTS FROM INVESTING IN THE BEST- AND WORST-PERFORMING STOCKS ON THE NYSE, 1926–1965

Year	Best Stock, $*	Worst Stock, $*
1926	2.97	.07
1927	7.89	.00
1928	13.23	.40
1929	1.85	.00
1930	2.11	.05
1931	2.20	.00
1932	3.31	.00
1933	20.84	.00
1934	9.48	.90
1935	6.08	.00
1936	17.23	.18
1937	1.37	.11
1938	7.19	.00
1939	2.83	.00
1940	2.75	.00
1941	2.94	.00
1942	5.91	.56
1943	7.47	.29
1944	4.39	.42
1945	4.70	.65
1946	2.23	.25
1947	2.58	.35
1948	4.54	.34
1949	2.89	.10
1950	3.29	.65
1951	4.05	.14
1952	1.87	.11
1953	2.14	.00
1954	5.44	.61
1955	2.89	.16
1956	4.28	.14
1957	2.27	.27
1958	5.08	.80
1959	3.37	.43
1960	2.38	.25
1961	3.81	.00
1962	1.74	.15
1963	3.21	.00
1964	3.13	.33
1965	5.43	.29

* Value at the end of one year of a $1 investment in the particular stock.

Source: Lawrence Fisher, and James H. Lorie, "Some Studies of Variability of Returns on Investments in Common Stocks," Journal of Business, © 1970 The University of Chicago Press, April 1970, pp. 119–127.

easily transform a $1,000 investment into $1 million, but they also run the risk of losing all their money. At least one stock went bankrupt in 13 out of the 40 years, and in most of the other years some stocks fell by 50% or more.

Unfortunately, investors who refuse to diversify are following an inferior investment strategy. Since they are willing to take on considerable risks, they could earn a much higher return by investing their money properly. By failing to diversify, they are taking on unnecessary risk and will receive no additional return for bearing this risk.

Until now, it has been assumed that the greater the risk of an investment, the greater the return that could be expected. But why should any borrower pay a lender to assume extra risk which the lender can easily eliminate through diversification? Similarly, why should any lender in good conscience demand more for taking on a risk which can be eliminated? The answer is that higher returns should not and will not be paid for taking on **diversifiable risk,** i.e., risk which can be avoided simply by diversifying.

EFFICIENT PORTFOLIOS

Despite their diverse backgrounds and distinct personalities, most investors share two common objectives: They want to make as much money as possible on their investments and to avoid taking on risk. But it is impossible for investors to completely satisfy both objectives. In order to make more money, they must take on more risk. In order to reduce risk, they must sacrifice some return. As a result, every investor faces a trade-off between risk and return.

By combining different amounts of various investments, an investor can create millions of unique portfolios. Each of these portfolios provides a particular combination of risk and return. Somehow the investor must balance the risk and return of each portfolio and select the one which is best suited to his or her needs.

But how can any investor select one portfolio from among millions? The answer is provided by the **efficient-portfolio concept.** The efficient-portfolio concept should not be confused with the efficient-market concept. The efficient-portfolio concept is simply a screening device for separating efficient portfolios from inefficient portfolios. A portfolio is said to be efficient if there are (1) no other portfolios with the same expected return and less risk and (2) no other portfolios with the same risk and a greater expected return. Since investors prefer more return and less risk, every investor should attempt to hold an efficient portfolio. Investors holding inefficient portfolios can increase their return without increasing their risk, or reduce their risk without reducing their return, by switching to efficient portfolios. This results in an improvement in their financial well-being.

The difference between efficient and inefficient portfolios is best described in a diagram. The risks and expected rates of return for four different portfolios—A, B, C, D—are shown in Figure 7-3. The investor has analyzed the

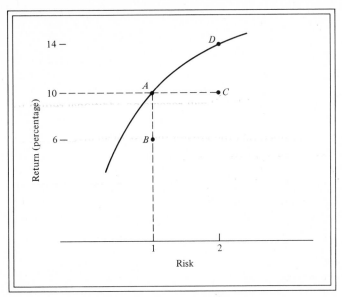

FIGURE 7-3 Risk and return for different portfolios.

investments in each portfolio and feels reasonably certain that the points on the diagram represent the risks and the expected returns of the portfolios. For example, portfolio A has one unit of risk and an expected return of 10% a year. Portfolio B has the same risk but is expected to return only 6%. Portfolio A is obviously a more efficient combination of assets than B—it offers considerably more return without being any more risky. Given a choice between only these two portfolios, investors should select A rather than B.

The same analysis can be applied to portfolios A and C. In this case both portfolios offer the same expected return, but C is riskier. Investors should again select A. By doing so, they reduce the risk they are exposed to while maintaining their return. In other words, A is more efficient than C because it offers the same return with less risk.

Just because portfolio A is better than portfolio B or C does not mean that A is an efficient portfolio. To be efficient, portfolio A must satisfy two conditions. First, it must offer the highest expected return of any portfolio with the same degree of risk. If there is no point directly above A on the vertical line, it satisfies this condition. Second, it must have the least risk of any investment offering the same return. If there is no point on the left-hand side of the horizontal line passing through A, it satisfies this condition. Only then can portfolio A be called an efficient portfolio.

Can an investor now use the efficient-portfolio criterion to decide whether to select between portfolios A and D in Figure 7-3? The answer is no. Portfolio D offers more return than A, but it is also more risky. For that reason, neither portfolio is obviously superior. If both portfolios are efficient, an investor must rely on his or her own personal preferences in choosing between the two. If high returns are most desired, D should be chosen. If the preference is to avoid risk, A should be selected.

By using the efficient-portfolio concept, it is possible to compute what is known as the **efficient frontier.** The efficient frontier illustrates the different combinations of risk and return that can be obtained from efficient portfolios. The efficient frontier is the curved line passing through A, D, and all other points representing efficient portfolios. This frontier is simply the boundary line marking off the best risk-and-return combinations available to the investor. In order to maximize return and minimize risk, the investor should operate on this efficient frontier. The territory above the frontier is a sort of "no-man's land." No investor can achieve a risk-return combination represented by a point in this area. On the other hand, the area below the frontier corresponds to combinations that no well-informed investor would ever find acceptable, since all these portfolios are inefficient.

Risk-free Assets and the Efficient Frontier

The consideration of zero-risk assets changes the efficient frontier described in Figure 7-3. **Zero-risk investments** have guaranteed outcomes. United States government Treasury bills come very close to being zero risk. They mature in as little as 3 months' time at a fixed value, and they are backed by the full taxing power of the United States government. Other short-term obligations, such as passbook accounts, resemble a zero-risk investment. These accounts pay interest daily, are insured by an agency of the federal government for up to $40,000, and can be withdrawn at any time. Point A on Figure 7-4 represents a zero-risk investment. Three risky investments, B, C, and E, are also shown on the diagram.

The addition of a risk-free investment has an important effect on the investor's selection of assets. In particular, many of the portfolios deemed suitable when there was no risk-free asset now cease to be efficient. As a result, investors should spread their money between a combination of risky investments and the risk-free asset. The line connecting point A with point C shows the different returns and risks which can be obtained by investing in Treasury bills or a bank account and a risky combination of assets represented by point C. At point A, 100% of the money is invested in the risk-free asset. At point C, 100% is in investment C. At D, which is one-half the way along the line, half of the total funds are in the risk-free asset and half in the risky combination. Portfolio D appears to be a considerable improvement over portfolio B. By holding combination D rather than B, the investor earns a higher return without taking on any more risk. Indeed, combinations along the line between A and C are clearly superior to combinations along the old efficient frontier formed with no risk-free asset. So the new efficient frontier consists of the straight line connecting points A and C and the curved line extending from C to E.

The addition of a zero-risk asset has a profound impact on the efficient fron-

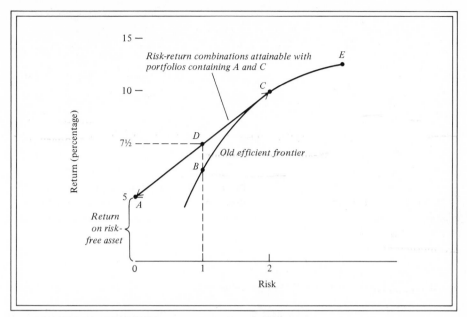

FIGURE 7-4   A risk-free asset and the efficient frontier.

tier and consequently on investment decision making. Investors must now focus on a combination of risky assets, represented by point C in Figure 7-4, and a risk-free asset. Their investment decisions fall neatly into two categories: (1) determination of the best combination of risky assets and then (2) the division of the available funds between the risky combination and the risk-free asset.

Borrowing and the Efficient Frontier

So far nothing has been said about investing with borrowed money. If the individual can borrow at the risk-free rate shown in Figure 7-5, the efficient frontier consists of the solid line from points A to E. Suppose people expect to earn 10% a year on combination C. By borrowing money at 5% and using it to purchase combination C, they can achieve a return greater than 10% on their own money. But this financial leverage increases risk as well as return. Point E represents the risk and return of an investment in combination C financed half with the investor's own money and half with borrowed money. In this case the investor expects to earn 15% on his or her own money, while at the same time assuming twice as much risk as another investor who invests no borrowed money in combination C.

In reality most investors must pay considerably more than the risk-free rate for their borrowed money. Suppose an investor pays 8% a year for a loan backed by securities. Then the efficient frontier will consist of the line connecting points A, C, D, and extending through F in Figure 7-5. Where does an individual in-

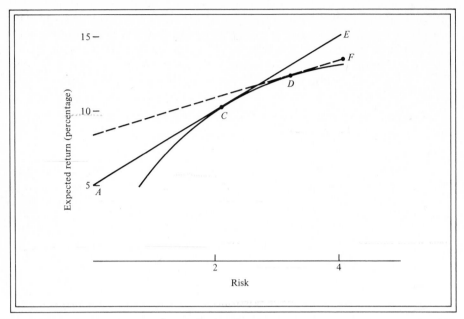

FIGURE 7-5   Borrowing and the efficient frontier.

vestor end up on this frontier? The answer depends upon personal feelings about risk and return and to some extent upon a knowledge of modern investment concepts.

> EXAMPLE   Diana Jones has always purchased stocks on margin. She usually borrows one-third of the purchase price of each investment. At the start of the year, she had $15,000 in the market, $10,000 of it her own money. But the market declined by 40% during the year, and Diana lost $6,000. As a result, she has only $9,000 invested and $5,000 of that amount is borrowed money.
>
> Diana has probably made a big mistake by not selling off some of her securities. Though she may have been satisfied with the risk-return combination of the first portfolio, she should be totally disenchanted with the existing portfolio. It implies a much higher risk, since a greater percentage of the total investment consists of borrowed money. To attain the previous risk-return combination, she should sell $3,000 of securities and pay off this much debt.

Computing the Risk and Return of Portfolios

The efficient-portfolio concept is a very logical device for screening out inferior portfolios, but its actual application to portfolio selection is not as easy as it may appear to be. For one thing, how does an investor estimate the expected returns and risks of the various portfolios?

The expected return of a portfolio is fairly easy to calculate, once the expected return on each investment in the portfolio is known. The expected return on a portfolio is simply the weighted average of the expected returns on every investment in the portfolio. The weight given to a particular investment is equal to the proportion of the total market value of the portfolio held in that investment. For example, an investor might own shares in General Motors, Polaroid, and Trans World Airlines. Estimates of expected returns on each investment can be based upon historical figures, the investor's judgment, etc. The market value and expected returns are as follows:

Investment	Market Value, $	Proportion of Total Portfolio	Expected Return, %	Weighted Return, %
General Motors	5,000	5,000/20,000 = .25 ×	10 =	2.5
Polaroid	10,000	10,000/20,000 = .50 ×	20 =	10.0
Trans World Airlines	5,000	5,000/20,000 = .25 ×	14 =	3.5
Portfolio	20,000	1.00		16.0

The expected return on the entire portfolio is equal to 16%. If the investor's expectations are realized, the $20,000 will earn $3,200 in a year's time.

The risk of a portfolio is much more difficult to calculate than the expected return. It is definitely not a simple weighted average of the risk of each investment, since the results on diversification prove that the total risk of a portfolio is often less than the sum of its parts. This is because fluctuations in one investment partially offset the fluctuations in other investments. As a result, some investments which are very risky when held by themselves carry little or no risk when they are part of a large portfolio.

Much of the analysis of the risk of investments ignores this fact. Each stock or bond or parcel of land is treated as being a unique asset, and absolutely no consideration is given to the other investments held by an individual. Actually a potential investment should be viewed as an addition to a combination of other assets, i.e., to a portfolio. The risk of an investment should be measured in terms of how it affects the risk of the entire portfolio held by an investor.

Portfolio Risk

The portfolio approach represents a total approach to investments. The investor no longer focuses on single securities, properties, etc., but instead concentrates on the overall performance of the portfolio. Although the specific characteristics of any one investment still interest the investor, the possible interactions between the different assets play a far more important role. To some extent, the investor's attempts to select the appropriate securities for a portfolio resemble a coach's efforts to find the right players for a team. Just as each player's talents and abilities must contribute to a total team effort, so each security must contribute to the total portfolio.

Very few investors fully appreciate the importance of the portfolio approach. They have some good excuses for their ignorance. The concept is relatively new. Harry Markowitz' justly renowned book, *Portfolio Selection: Efficient Diversification of Investments,* did not appear until 1959, and most of the relevant research on portfolios first surfaced in the 1960s.

Of course, technology often spreads very quickly among the populace. However, the portfolio approach suffers from two distinct handicaps. It deals with the future—a rather intangible product, and most of the explanations of the concept have been couched in complex statistical terms. No wonder the pocket calculator has caught on more quickly.

Despite the rather forbidding mathematics necessary to solve portfolio problems, the concepts could not be simpler. Imagine a person planning a dinner party. The success or failure of the party depends primarily upon whether the participants get along together and only secondarily upon the exact nature of the individual personalities. The hostess decides to invite nine people. She makes up a list of the possible participants. The individual's personality—in a sense, how well one gets along with oneself—is one consideration. But there are eight other factors to consider, namely the person's ability to interact with each of the other eight guests. So interactions with other people assume a much greater weight than the individual's personality.

Finally by the process of elimination and guesswork the hostess selects nine individuals. Her final guest list looks like the one in Table 7-3, where the guests' personalities and compatibilities are rated on a 10-point scale.

At the last minute one of the guests calls and says he has broken a leg skiing and cannot come to the party. The hostess mentally lists her possibilities. Jim has a reasonable personality; so he scores 8 out of 10; and he gets along well with everyone, another score of 8. Ken has a sparkling personality (a score of 9) but sometimes offends people; so he gets an average compatibility factor of only 6. Therefore, Jim scores a total party factor of $8 + (8 \times 8) = 72$, and Ken only $9 + (8 \times 6) = 57$. The hostess invites Jim.

TABLE 7-3   A "PORTFOLIO" OF DINNER GUESTS

	John	Mary	Bob	Sue	Tom	Chris	Linda	Debbie	Dave
John	10	9	8	9	8	7	6	10	10
Mary	9	9	9	9	9	9	9	9	9
Bob	8	9	7	9	9	10	10	10	10
Sue	9	9	9	9	9	10	9	10	9
Tom	8	9	9	9	10	10	10	9	10
Chris	7	9	10	10	10	9	8	10	8
Linda	6	9	10	9	10	8	8	8	8
Debbie	10	9	10	10	9	10	8	6	7
Dave	10	9	10	9	10	8	8	7	5

The numbers along the diagonal line measure personality. The numbers off the diagonal line measure compatibility.

As farfetched as this method of selecting guests might seem, it does demonstrate the importance of interaction between investments. One measure of this interaction is called the **covariance.** The prefix "co" means together, or jointly. The covariance indicates how two investments (or any other objects) vary together, whereas the variance just measures the variation in an individual investment. The larger the covariance, the greater the extent to which the two sets of numbers tend to move up and down together. The variance of a portfolio is a weighted average of all the individual variances and covariances. The number of covariances to be considered increases very rapidly as the number of investments in the portfolio increases.

> EXAMPLE   An investor wants to measure the risk of a 9-stock portfolio. In order to do so the variance of each investment and the covariances of each investment with every other investment must be considered. There are 9 variances (1 for each security) and 72 covariances (8 pair-wise comparisons for each security). Only one-half of the covariances are unique. For example, the covariance of IBM with Ford is identical with the covariance of Ford with IBM, since the same 2 stocks are involved.
>
> In order to measure the risk of a portfolio containing 100 securities instead of 10, 100 variances (1 for each security) and 9,900 covariances (99 pair-wise comparisons for each of 100 securities) must be considered. Again, only one-half of the covariances are unique.

Judging from the preceding example, any investor attempting to calculate the variability of different portfolios must first specify millions of covariances. The impatient and/or uninformed individual must find an alternative. Markowitz realized this and suggested a much simpler approach to the selection of assets. This simplicity is gained with only a small sacrifice in accuracy. Suppose the covariance of investment returns can be explained by a single factor which affects all investments to some degree. Then the investor needs to know only the relationship between each individual asset and the underlying factor. The next section on the market model provides an explanation of this comovement in investment prices.

MARKET MODEL

Many people suffer from investor's myopia—a special type of nearsightedness. They see only the impact of their own actions. A truly myopic investor views every profit as evidence of her or his innate wisdom in selecting specific investments. Losses fall into a more nebulous category. But most myopic investors bemoan their mistaken selections and assume full responsibility for their failures.

In reality the actions of the general public often overshadow the individual's attempts to select specific stocks, bonds, or properties. When the overall stock market moves up, most stocks also increase in value, and when real estate booms, the prices of even the worst lots usually edge upward. On the other hand, few winners emerge from a declining market, regardless of how cleverly they analyze specific investments. The investor who ignores these powerful market forces does so at a high cost.

Alphas and Betas

The **market model** provides one technique for explicitly recognizing general market factors. It relates the percentage return on a specific investment to the return on all other investments.

$$\text{Rate of return on investment} = \text{constant} + \text{beta} \times (\text{market return}) + (\text{error term})$$

$$K = A + BX + e$$

The central feature of the market model is the explicit recognition of the fact that market movements propel individual investments upward and downward. **Beta** measures this relationship between the return on an individual investment and the return on the overall market. In effect, beta answers the question, How much does a particular security respond to a 1% change in the market? For example, if a stock has a beta of 2, the stock goes up by 2% when the market goes up by 1%. Conversely, when the market goes down by 1%, the stock goes down by 2%. The higher the beta, the more volatile the stock, since small changes in the market cause large changes in the return on the stock. If the stock has a beta of 3 and the market goes up by 1%, the stock goes up by 3%. Since the market consists of every stock, the average beta of all stocks must equal 1; that is, the beta of the market equals 1.

The constant term in the market model, often called **alpha,** measures the average return not explained by movements in the overall market. Suppose that alpha equals 5% a year. Then this particular asset provides a return of 5% a year, regardless of what the market does.

Not all the return on a specific investment can be explained by overall market conditions and the constant term. The death of a key executive, the discovery of an important new product or new technology, an antitrust suit, and numerous other events more or less peculiar to each firm have an important impact on stock prices. By the same token, real estate prices fluctuate not only with economic conditions but also with demographic changes in local areas, the construction of new roads and highways, and the relocation of industry. No attempt is made to include each of these unique factors in the market model. Instead, a single **error term** is added to reflect the combined effect of all these factors. The expected value (not the actual value) of this error term is usually assumed to be zero. The efficient-market concept provides one justification for this assumption. In an efficient market, prices provide unbiased estimates of future events; so the errors average out over time.

The relationship between the annual returns on a particular stock and the returns on the overall stock market are shown graphically in Figure 7-6. The Standard and Poor's 500 Index provides a measure of overall market returns. The beta for the stock is 2, implying that every 1% movement in the market pro-

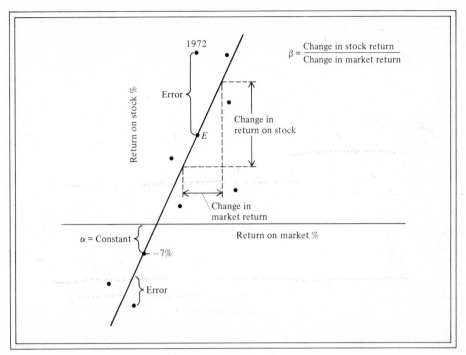

FIGURE 7-6   Market model for a stock.

duces a 2% change in the value of the stock. The beta can also be interpreted as the slope of the line which best fits the scattered points in Figure 7-6. The steeper the line, the greater the slope and the greater the change in the stock for each 1% change in the market. This line of "best fit" is called the characteristic line. The constant term or alpha is also shown in Figure 7-6. The constant term of -7% indicates that the stock returned an average of -7% each year, even when there was no change in the overall market. Finally, the error term summarizes the specific influences on the stock's return which cannot be attributed to overall market conditions.

The market model seldom provides a perfect explanation of the return on an investment. In 1972 the market increased 14% and the stock rose by 42%. Given a 14% return on the market, this security should have increased by only 21%, since beta times the market return equals 28% ($2 \times 14\%$) plus the constant term of -7%. The predicted return of 21% can be read off the market line displaying the traditional relationship between the stock and the overall market. First, a market return of 14% is located on the lower axis of the diagram. Then a vertical line is drawn until it touches the market line at point E. This point corresponds to a stock return of 21%.

The point labeled 1972 represents a return of 14% on the market and 42% on the stock. The difference between the actual return of 42% on the stock and the return predicted by the market model amounts to 21%. This difference equals the error in attempting to explain the total price behavior of the stock solely in terms of the overall market. Obviously there are special forces influencing the security which cannot be explained by general market conditions. The error term reflects these forces.

Market and Residual Risk

The market model provides investors with a technique for judging the risk of their own portfolios, as well as for attempting to adjust these portfolios to anticipated market movements. The higher the beta of an investment, the higher its volatility. This type of risk cannot be diversified away, since it is due to general market forces. In other words, no matter how many investments an individual holds, overall market conditions will still make them fluctuate. And the larger the betas of the investments, the larger these movements will be.

The total risk of any investment can now be broken down into two categories: (1) the risk associated with general movements in the market (measured by beta) and (2) the risk caused by factors peculiar to the investment. Most people refer to the first type of risk as **systematic, market,** or **nondiversifiable risk,** since it results from movements in the overall market. This systematic, or nondiversifiable risk, depends upon the variability of the overall market and the beta of the security. The higher the beta, the greater the nondiversifiable risk. The second type of risk is usually called **residual, unsystematic,** or **diversifiable risk.** It is related to the variability of the error term. Residual risk results from independent fluctuations in factors unique to each investment. Diversification eliminates residual risk, but it does not eliminate systematic risk. The relationship between the number of assets in a portfolio, its systematic or market-related risk, and its residual risk is illustrated in Figure 7-7. The risk of the portfolio can never be reduced below its systematic risk.

CAPITAL-ASSET PRICING MODEL

Investors, of course, want to know about future returns. While crystal balls remain in limited supply, most of these people will have to settle for the **capital-asset pricing model,** or **CAP model** for short.

Academicians generally credit William Sharpe with the creation of the earliest version of the CAP model. He published his conclusions in a 1964 article titled, "Capital Asset Prices: A Theory of Market Equilibrium under Conditions of Risk." Prior to this time, numerous authors had discussed risk and return, expected utility, and the selection of portfolios of assets, but no one had combined all these elements into a coherent explanation of the formation of investment (capital asset) prices.

Sharpe answered the following vital question: What is an investment worth? He did so by assuming that investors are all risk averters who can borrow at the

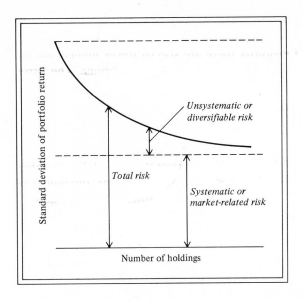

FIGURE 7-7 Diversifiable and nondiversifiable risk.

risk-free rate and have the same expectations about the future. In addition, it is probably necessary to assume that markets are reasonably efficient.

Rather than use actual prices, Sharpe compares the rates of return on different investments. This not only provides a much more general explanation, but it also tells the investor exactly what return can be expected by holding a particular asset.

Sharpe demonstrated that the expected return on an asset depends upon: (1) the risk-free rate of return, (2) the expected return on the overall market, (3) and the nondiversifiable risk (beta) of the asset. The exact relationship can be expressed as follows:

Expected return
on an asset $=$ risk-free return + beta × expected market-risk premium

The expected **market-risk premium** is a bonus the investor expects to receive for bearing risk. It is equal to the difference between the expected return on the market and the risk-free rate of return; i.e.,

Market-risk premium = expected return − risk-free return
on overall market

Suppose the comovement of investment returns can be explained by a single factor which affects all investments to some degree. This dominant factor can be loosely referred to as "general economic conditions." If the CAP model provides an adequate representation of this situation, the predicted return on any asset equals the risk-free return plus the expected market-risk premium times

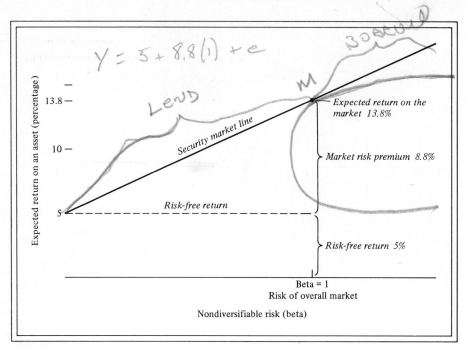

FIGURE 7-8   Relationship between risk and return.

beta. In other words, the higher the nondiversifiable risk (beta) of an investment, the higher the expected return. This relationship between risk and return is illustrated in Figure 7-8.

The CAP model provides a convenient format for interpreting the return on any asset. Investors are paid for their patience and frugality by the risk-free return and receive an additional reward for bearing risk in the form of a risk premium.

> EXAMPLE   Treasury bills will probably yield a risk-free rate of return of 5% during the coming year. Investors expect the return on the overall stock market to be about 11%. Therefore, the market-risk premium or return in excess of the risk-free rate equals 6%.
>
> In order to earn 17% a year on a particular investment or portfolio of investments, the investor must purchase assets with an average beta of 2. By doing so, the individual expects to earn the risk-free return of 5% plus twice the market-risk premium of 6% for a total of 17%.

The CAP model no doubt comes as a great disappointment to investors interested in making a killing in the market. Since the CAP model is based upon the assumption of an efficient market, it can provide no magic formula for selecting superior investments. Indeed, the CAP model indicates that above-average returns can be obtained only by taking on additional risk.

What good then is the CAP model? First, it aids investors in selecting assets which provide the returns necessary to achieve their goals. Second, it provides guidelines for evaluating the performance of these assets in reaching their goals.

Evaluating Portfolio Risk and Performance

In order to achieve a high return, an investor with no special knowledge must take on nondiversifiable risk. Many individuals lose sight of this objective when selecting their investments. For example, one investor assembled the following $50,000 portfolio:

Investment	Market Value, $	Proportion of Total Portfolio	Beta
Polaroid	15,000	.3	1.50
Trans World Airlines	5,000	.1	1.70
General Motors	10,000	.2	1.05
IBM	20,000	.4	1.05

Several questions can be raised immediately. The first is, How much nondiversifiable risk is the investor assuming with this portfolio? Only someone who understands the CAP model can answer that question.

The nondiversifiable risk of the sample portfolio can be found by taking a weighted average of the individual betas. The weight given to each beta equals the proportion of the total market value of the portfolio accounted for by the stock. The market value of Polaroid shares totals $15,000. This amounts to approximately .3 of the total value of all stocks in the portfolio. Since the beta for Polaroid is 1.50 and .3 of the value of the portfolio has that beta, Polaroid makes a contribution of 0.3 times 1.50, or 0.45 to the nondiversifiable risk of the portfolio. The contribution of each of the other securities to the overall beta of the portfolio can be calculated in a similar fashion. The overall beta of the portfolio equals the sum of these individual contributions:

$$.3 \times 1.50 = 0.45$$
$$.1 \times 1.70 = 0.17$$
$$.2 \times 1.05 = 0.21$$
$$.4 \times 1.05 = \underline{0.42}$$
$$\text{portfolio beta} = 1.25$$

Since the beta of the portfolio equals 1.25, the portfolio should move 1.25% with each 1% change in the market.

Suppose an investor holding this exact same portfolio wants to measure his or her performance during the year. This can be done by comparing the return on the portfolio to the return on a randomly selected portfolio with the same beta. The randomly selected portfolio can be created by buying on margin the shares in the Standard and Poor's 500. Why assume that the S&P 500 is purchased with borrowed money? Because that is one easy way to increase the beta of the market portfolio to 1.25 from 1.

Now assume that the individual earned 20% more than the risk-free return on the four-stock portfolio consisting of Polaroid, TWA, GM, and IBM. Does a return of this magnitude reveal any special insights into the market? The answer is a resounding no. During the year the overall market also surpassed the risk-free return by 20%. Therefore, a portfolio with a beta of 1.25 should have provided a return 25% higher than the risk-free rate. Judging from these results, the investor holding the four-stock portfolio considerably underperformed the market. At the same time, this misguided individual undertook a substantial amount of unnecessary risk by holding an inadequately diversified portfolio.

Investors can use betas as a guidepost for expected future returns and as a benchmark for assessing their own performance in the market. If they believe that they can select undervalued and overvalued stocks or can predict future movements in the market, they can find a third use for betas. In selecting among investments which appear especially promising, they can use beta as a screening device to eliminate unusually risky investments. If several investments have good prospects but only one can be purchased, it makes sense to select the one with the lowest beta and therefore the lowest risk. On the other hand, some investors may simply have strong convictions about the future movement of the market. If they believe that the market is about to move sharply higher in price, they may decide to select a portfolio of high-beta stocks. If instead it appears the market will decline, a shift into low-beta stocks or into bonds would be in order.

Altering Portfolio Risk

Investors who attempt to shift into high- or low-beta investments face a serious problem. Stocks with extremely high or low betas constitute a rare species. The highest beta of any stock on the New York Stock Exchange in 1975 was 3.0. The lowest beta was 0.3.

Moreover, stocks in the same industries tend to have similar betas. As a result, investors who decide to adopt a high-beta portfolio may be forced to buy stocks in only one or two industries. Not only does this make it difficult to diversify a portfolio, it may also limit the investors to industries which they believe to be overpriced. The limited range of betas and the similarity in the betas for stocks in the same industry are displayed in Figure 7-9.

Fortunately investors do not need to shift money into higher- or lower-beta investments in order to change the beta of a portfolio. Instead they can sell part of their securities and hold a zero-risk investment such as Treasury bills or borrow additional funds and increase their investment in the portfolio. The beta for the revised portfolio can be computed just as it was in an earlier section.

For example, if the beta of a portfolio of stocks was 1, it will be 0.5 when half the portfolio is sold off and invested in a zero-beta asset, such as T-bills.

On the other hand, if enough money is borrowed to double the amount in-

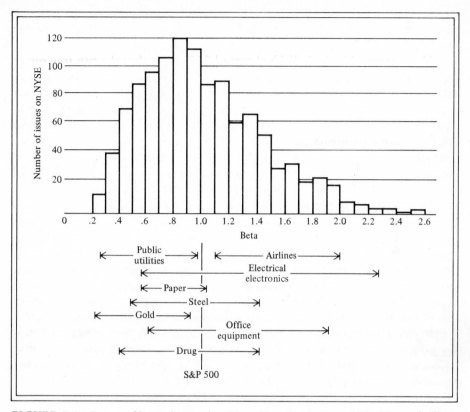

FIGURE 7-9 Range of betas for stocks. (From Douglas A. Love, "The Use and Abuse of Leverage," *Financial Analysts Journal,* March-April 1975, p. 55.)

vested in the portfolio, the beta for the investor's own money will be equal to 2, because for every 1% change in the portfolio, that money experiences a 2% change. However, the margin requirements on securities are seldom less than 50%. That means that debt may be of only limited use in increasing the beta of a portfolio beyond a certain range.

Regardless of how betas and the market model are used, it must be emphasized that the market model is not infallible. It must be remembered that in calculating the beta, past results are used. For this reason there is no assurance that the beta is a good predictor of future price movements. This is especially true of the betas of individual investments. The world is just too dynamic to be able to place much confidence in beta estimates for single investments. Only when they are combined and used for portfolios consisting of several investments can the beta be relied upon. As a general rule, the portfolio beta is more accurate the larger the number of securities in the portfolio. This is because errors in predicting the individual betas offset each other.

PORTFOLIO STRATEGIES

The portfolio-selection techniques presented so far describe investor behavior in an imaginary world. This imaginary world resembles utopia in that there are no taxes, no costs of buying and selling investments, and no information costs. Perhaps even more important, people live in economic harmony, since they all have the same expectations. In addition, everyone exhibits risk aversion. Finally, every investor has the opportunity to borrow money at the lowest interest rate available.

Life in this utopian world is simple but dull. Every investment trades in a completely efficient market. As a result, investment prices reflect all current information, and people readily accept this fact of life.

Investing in such a world is a very easy task. Each investor selects the most appealing combination of risk and return. If conservative, the investor then divides the money between a risk-free asset and the market portfolio. Otherwise, money is borrowed and invested in the market portfolio.

In this perfect world every investor diversifies completely. This is because there is no return for bearing nondiversifiable risk and no cost for eliminating such risk. As a result, investors bear only nondiversifiable risk. And the return depends solely on the actual amount of nondiversifiable risk assumed.

Today's investment environment differs greatly from utopia. As a result, few investors diversify completely, despite their distaste for uncertainty. One obvious reason for their failure to do so is ignorance. Beginning investors seem particularly prone to investing in only one or two stocks.

Even experienced investors display a surprising disregard for the advantages of diversification. It is easy to see why. Most of the investment information available today emphasizes returns rather than risk.

Forecasting Ability and Diversification

Mere knowledge of the mechanics of diversification does not guarantee that an individual will diversify completely. Many investors believe they possess special insights into future prices, and some of them no doubt do. Anyone who could forecast the future perfectly would have no reason to diversify, since the future would hold no uncertainty. Such a person would simply select the best available investment.

There is convincing evidence that no one alive today has perfect foresight, or at least no one who is playing the stock market. According to figures released by one brokerage house, an omniscient individual could have made a profit of $23 billion in 20 years with an initial investment of only $1,000!

Investors gifted with perfect foresight would not diversify at all. On the other hand, those who sincerely believe in the efficient-market concept always diversify as completely as possible (if there are no costs to diversification). That leaves a very large middle ground occupied by stock-market gurus, real estate pundits, insiders, hard-working analysts, and a wide variety of experts. How should they diversify? The answer depends upon their forecasting ability. The greater their ability, the more justified they are in concentrating their money in just a few outstanding investments. Professional money managers apparently have little faith in their forecasting abilities, since many mutual funds hold 200 or more stocks.

Unless the investor possesses a crystal ball or an intuitive feeling for the market, the selection of investments takes time and effort. These forecasting costs also affect the investor's decision about diversification. As a general rule higher forecasting costs imply less diversification. Again, the evidence indicates that professional money managers spend little time or effort in the selection of individual securities.

> **EXAMPLE** Expertise in one narrow area often leads business people into poorly diversified portfolios. Take the the case of Jean Clements, who owns a very successful photo-finishing firm. She uses Eastman Kodak film exclusively. During her years of experience with Eastman Kodak she has gained deep respect for the company and its technological and marketing prowess.
>
> Kodak has just developed an instant camera. Convinced of the future success of the camera, Jean decides to invest all her savings in Eastman Kodak. She buys 700 shares at $110 each. She borrows $37,000 of the total purchase price of $77,000 from her broker.
>
> Jean's knowledge of the photo industry has distorted her investment decision making. Shares of Eastman Kodak trade in a very efficient market; so it is unlikely that Jean enjoys much of an advantage over the average investor. In order to achieve this questionable advantage in the stock market, she has completely sacrificed diversification. Every penny she has, and then some, is now invested in the photography industry, either through her interest in the photo-finishing firm or the shares of Kodak.
>
> Within 8 months after her purchase, Kodak drops by $40 a share to $70. Kodak is experiencing production difficulties with the new camera and faces a patent infringement suit from another company. Jean sells her Kodak shares at a $28,000 loss (including commissions). Fortunately the economy remains stable. Otherwise her photo-finishing business might have incurred substantial losses at the same time. The combination of losses on both the stock and her own company could have forced her into bankruptcy.

Diversification into Different Types of Investments

Portfolio techniques provide a totally new perspective on investment risk. Covariance, rather than variance, becomes all-important. Just because a single investment demonstrates large fluctuations in price does not mean it adds to the risk of a portfolio. The important question is, How does it move with changes in the prices of other investments?

Experienced investors often lose sight of this fact. Because of the time and effort required to develop expertise, they usually tend to concentrate their money in one particular type of investment. Some invest in stocks, others in real estate. But seldom does one person invest in both stocks and real estate. Instead,

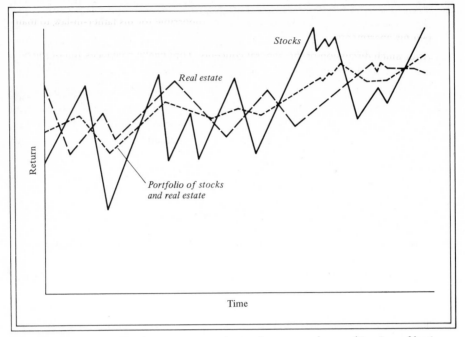

FIGURE 7-10   Simulated returns on stocks, real estate, and a combination of both.

the investments community often resembles two opposing armies, with the adherents of stocks on one side and the believers in real estate on the other. Small bands of uncommitted investors hover around these two armed camps, shifting their allegiance as first one side and then the other gains an illusory advantage in the battle for investment profits.

It is to be hoped that portfolio theory will someday unite these two warring factions. Portfolio theory demonstrates the tremendous advantage of combining dissimilar investments. Their very dissimilarity results in a significant reduction in the risk the investor confronts. The simulated results from investing in the overall stock market, the overall real estate market, and a combination of both stocks and real estate are presented in Figure 7-10. By spreading money into both real estate and stocks, the investor greatly reduces the risk of the portfolio without sacrificing any returns.

EXAMPLE   Jim Simmons retired 2 years ago after a very successful career as a contractor. During the last few years, he built or purchased five small apartment buildings, which now provide him with a reasonable income. He also has $50,000 in a bank account. Until now, Jim has refused to buy any stocks, since he knows nothing about the stock market and several of his friends have lost large amounts of money in the market.

But his son-in-law, Tom, has recently been converted to portfolio theory. He sees the unnecessary risk Jim and his wife are exposing themselves to by investing in only one type of asset—even though apartment buildings have a relatively low risk. And he is also convinced that ill health would make it impossible for his father-in-law to maintain his apartments.

After much discussion of the general concepts, Tom finally convinces Jim of the possible advantages of diversification, and obtains permission to suggest alternative investments. The next day he returns with the following possibilities:

Present Portfolio

Bank	$ 50,000
Apartments	450,000
Total	$500,000

Total expected return $48,000
Total risk (measured by standard deviation of return) 15%

Proposed Portfolio

Bank	$ 50,000
Apartments	350,000
Mutual funds	100,000
Total	$500,000

Total expected return $50,000
Total risk 12%

The new portfolio provides a higher total return with less total risk. And Jim has one less apartment building to maintain.

In their quest for low covariance assets, investors are beginning to look beyond their own national boundaries. Presumably, the economic forces affecting investments differ from country to country. As a result, diversification into the assets of several countries should reduce risk. A recent study of the re-

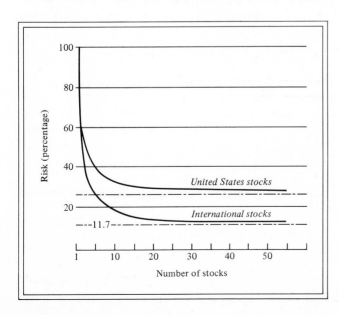

FIGURE 7-11 Gains from international diversification. (From Bruno Solnik, "Why Not Diversify Internationally Rather than Domestically?" *Financial Analysts Journal,* July-August 1974, p. 51.)

turns on stocks in different countries supports this belief. The gains from international diversification are presented in Figure 7-11. A well-diversified portfolio of stocks selected from different countries exhibits about one-half the risk of a portfolio containing an equal number of United States stocks. As a result, investors can reduce risk and/or increase return simply by selecting stocks from different countries.

Investors unwilling to diversify their portfolios by purchasing foreign securities have another alternative. They can buy shares in ITT, Caterpillar Tractor, Coca-Cola, Colgate Palmolive, and other multinational companies with large overseas markets. Some of these companies derive more than one-half their sales from foreign operations, as can be seen in Table 7-4.

SUMMARY

When investments move independently of each other, the potential gains from diversification are enormous. Unfortunately, few investments are completely independent of each other. But diversification still produces a considerable reduction in risk. For example, diversification eliminates from one-half to two-thirds of the risk associated with individual stocks, thus sparing the investor from many unnecessary losses.

Once the advantages of diversification have been recognized, most investors will want to hold an adequately diversified portfolio. However, they face a difficult problem. Somehow they must select one portfolio from among the infinite

TABLE 7-4   SALES AND NET INCOME OF MULTINATIONAL COMPANIES

	Sales, $*		Net Income, $*	
Company	Domestic	Foreign	Domestic	Foreign
Borden	2,130	424	59	14
Caterpillar Tractor	1,600	1,582	113	134
Coca-Cola	1,201	944	88	127
Colgate Palmolive	982	1,213	28	61
Gillette	545	520	34	53
Honeywell	1,444	965	49	48
IBM	5,851	5,143	723	853
ITT	4,888	5,295	248	280
Pfizer	640	667	49	72

* All figures for 1973, in millions.
  Source: Ruben Shobet, "Investing in Foreign Securities," Financial Analysts Journal, September–October 1974, p. 56.

number available to them. Each of these portfolios offers a specific combination of risk and return.

The efficient-portfolio concept provides a general framework for comparing different portfolios. Portfolios are first classified as being either efficient or inefficient. An efficient portfolio satisfies two conditions: (1) no other portfolio provides a greater return with the same risk, and (2) no other portfolio offers less risk with the same return. Risk-averse investors should always select an efficient portfolio.

Although the individual preferences of the investor determine the actual portfolio selected, every investor should use the same approach to portfolio selection. First investors choose the best possible combination of risky assets. Then they allocate their money between a risk-free asset such as Treasury bills and the risky combination or borrow additional money and invest it in the risky combination. More conservative investors will choose the first course of action.

Of course, this leaves a very obvious question unanswered. How does an investor select the best combination of risky assets? Anyone who completely accepts the efficient-market concept finds the task easy and just buys the market portfolio—or any other portfolio consisting of a very large number of assets. Most large mutual funds provide a good approximation to a market portfolio of stocks. Then the investor borrows or lends the appropriate percentage of her or his funds to obtain the desired risk-and-return combination.

Many investors reject this passive approach to investments. They prefer to select a limited number of assets promising above-average prospects for gain. They must somehow determine the risks and returns of alternative portfolios.

The expected return of a portfolio is simple to calculate. On the other hand, portfolio risk presents some very difficult computational problems. The interactions between all the investments in the portfolio must be considered. As a general rule, these interactions become more and more important relative to the individual variations as the portfolio becomes larger and larger. So investors seeking adequate diversification must pay special attention to the covariances of potential additions to a portfolio.

The market model provides a simple technique for judging the risk of any portfolio. The total risk of any investment consists of two components: (1) the risk associated with general movements in the market and (2) the risk caused by factors unique to each investment. The first type of risk is called systematic, non-diversifiable, or market risk. The second type of risk is called unsystematic, diversifiable, or residual risk.

Besides providing a simplified technique for measuring risk, the market model highlights a very important truth about investment selection. Financial success or failure depends primarily upon general economic conditions. Many investors ignore this fact and concentrate solely upon the selection of individual assets and ignore this broad economic panorama. Their emphasis is misplaced. Few stocks, bonds, properties, coins, stamps, or other assets move counter to the overall market. For this reason the investor should first concentrate on the direction of the market and then upon the selection of individual assets.

But which of these individual assets pay the highest returns? The capital-asset-pricing model provides an answer to this important question. According to the CAP model, the expected return on any asset equals the risk-free return plus the expected risk premium on the overall market times beta. In a sense investors receive two entirely distinct returns—one for patience and the other for courage (or perhaps just plain audacity). Patience is rewarded by the risk-free return and courage by the risk premium. The greater the amount of systematic risk (measured by beta) assumed by the investor, the greater the expected return.

The CAP model has a number of important implications. First, the market rewards only the right type of risk taking. Investment daredevils who take on unnecessary risk receive no returns for their efforts. Second, performance and risk are intimately related.

Despite the advantages of diversification, many investors refuse to adequately diversify their portfolios. They believe their experience and insights provide them with substantial advantages in a particular category of investments, such as stocks or real estate, but unless they possess considerable foresight, they are making a costly mistake. The dissimilarities in major-asset categories, such as stocks and real estate, virtually ensure that their returns will move somewhat independently of each other. As a result, the combination of stocks and real estate reduces portfolio risk without reducing returns.

Given the substantial benefits of such a policy, it seems amazing that so few investors follow this course of action. Apparently many of them focus on the total risk of each asset rather than on nondiversifiable risk. Familiarity with a specific type of investment, far from breeding contempt, creates in these people a sense of security. As a result, they perceive lower total risk in each real estate investment than in each stock investment.

But the really relevant question is, How does the investment affect the risk of the overall portfolio? No one is going to argue with Gertrude Stein's statement that "A rose is a rose is a rose." But investors who believe that a "risky investment is a risky investment is a risky investment" are mistaken. Every investment must be judged relative to a portfolio of investments. And it just so happens that some stocks that appear to be very risky by themselves actually reduce the risk of an overall portfolio consisting largely of real estate. The same is true of other types of assets.

One obvious extension of this philosophy involves foreign stocks, bonds, etc. Because economic conditions often vary from country to country, asset prices often diverge between countries. This divergence creates considerable opportunities for risk reduction in a portfolio.

KEYWORDS

portfolio	random diversification	efficient frontier
diversification	diversifiable risk	zero-risk investments
law of large numbers	efficient-portfolio concept	covariance

market model	systematic, market, [or]	capital-asset pricing model
beta	nondiversifiable risk	(CAP model)
alpha	residual, unsystematic, [or]	market-risk premium
error term	diversifiable risk	

QUESTIONS

1   A portfolio is defined as a combination or collection of securities or other investments. List the investments in your own portfolio.

2   Many investors completely ignore nonmarketable assets such as human capital (education) and claims on the government (Social Security) and pension benefits. How important are these investments to you?

3   Explain the law of large numbers. How does it apply to investors? How does it apply to insurance companies?

4   Imagine a world in which (1) stocks all move independently of each other, and (2) the standard deviation of annual returns equals 20% for every stock. Draw confidence intervals for portfolios containing 1, 8, and 128 stocks. (Hint: The variance of a randomly diversified portfolio of independent investments equals 1 divided by the number of investments times the variance of any one investment.)

5   Do you think the average investor fully understands the importance of diversification? Why or why not?

6   Most investments display some price dependence. Discuss the possible reasons for dependence within each of the following four categories of investments: (1) stocks, (2) bonds, (3) farmland, and (4) apartment buildings.

7   How much of the variability in stock prices can be eliminated by diversification?

8   Does diversification reduce the expected return of a portfolio? What about extreme returns?

9   Describe the efficient-portfolio concept. Why should an investor always attempt to hold an efficient portfolio?

10   How does the existence of a risk-free asset change the shape of the efficient frontier?

11   The Federal Reserve Bank imposes margin requirements on the purchase of stocks and bonds. Draw the efficient frontier with unlimited borrowing opportunities. Next show how the Federal Reserve requirements impose substantial costs upon some investors. (Assume that investors seeking extremely high returns always find some way to satisfy their desires.)

12   What is the expected return on the following portfolio:

Type of Investment	Value, $	Expected Return, %
Stocks	20,000	14
Education	50,000	10
Bonds	10,000	8

13   The expected return of a portfolio equals the weighted average of the returns on each investment. Why is the variance of a portfolio usually not equal to the weighted average of the variances of each investment?

14   Suppose an investor wants to calculate the variance of a 20-security portfolio. How many variances does one need to know? How many covariances?
15   Explain the market model.
16   Do investors receive a risk premium for bearing diversifiable risk? Why or why not?
17   Compute the expected return for the following portfolio:

Stock	Beta	Total Portfolio, %
Revlon	0.85	30
Rockwell International	0.75	40
Homestake Mining	0.45	30

The risk-free return equals 5% and the expected market premium amounts to 6%.

18   Suppose you are given $10,000 to invest in the stock market. In addition, assume you know nothing at all about stocks and there are no costs to diversifying. How much do you diversify?

REFERENCES

Black, Fischer: "Can Portfolio Managers Outrun the Random Walkers?" *The Journal of Portfolio Management,* Fall 1974, pp. 32–36.

Blume, Marshall E.: "On the Assessment of Risk," *Journal of Finance,* March 1971, pp. 1–10.

Blume, Marshall, and Irwin Friend: "The Asset Structure of Individual Portfolios and Some Implications for Utility Functions," *Journal of Finance,* May 1975, pp. 585–603.

Brennan, M. J.: "The Optimal Number of Securities in a Risky Asset Portfolio When There Are Fixed Costs of Transacting: Theory and Some Empirical Results," *Journal of Financial and Quantitative Analysis,* September 1975, pp. 483–496.

Cass, Roger: "A Global Approach to Portfolio Management," *Journal of Portfolio Management,* Winter 1975, pp. 40–48.

Ehrbar, A. F.: "It Can Pay to Send Money Abroad," *Fortune,* August 1974, pp. 121ff.

Evans, John L., and Stephen H. Archer: "Diversification and the Reduction of Dispersion: An Empirical Analysis," *Journal of Finance,* December 1968, pp. 761–767.

Fisher, Lawrence: "Using Modern Portfolio Theory to Maintain an Efficiently Diversified Portfolio," *Financial Analysts Journal,* May–June 1975, pp. 73–85.

——— and James H. Lorie: "Some Studies of Variability of Return on Investment in Common Stocks," *Journal of Business,* April 1970, pp. 99–134.

Ittensohn, Jacques: "How to Structure Efficient International Portfolios," *The Journal of Portfolio Management,* Fall 1976, pp. 62–66.

Jacob, Nancy: "A Limited Diversification Portfolio Selection Model for the Small Investor," *Journal of Finance,* June 1974, pp. 847–856.

King, Benjamin: "Market and Industry Factors in Stock Price Behavior," *Journal of Business,* January 1966, pp. 139–190.

Lorie, J. H.: "Diversification: Old and New," *Journal of Portfolio Management,* Winter 1975, pp. 25–28.

Markowitz, Harry M.: *Portfolio Selection: Efficient Diversification of Investments,* Wiley, New York, 1959.

Sharpe, William F.: "Adjusting for Risk in Portfolio Performance Measurement," *The Journal of Portfolio Management,* Winter 1975, pp. 29–34.

————: "Capital Asset Prices: A Theory of Market Equilibrium under Conditions of Risk," *Journal of Finance,* September 1964, pp. 425–442.

————: "Risk, Market Sensitivity, and Diversification," *Financial Analysts Journal,* January–February 1972, pp. 74–79.

Sohet, Ruben: "Investing in Foreign Securities," *Financial Analysts Journal,* September–October 1974, pp. 55–72.

Solnik, Bruno: "Why Not Diversify Internationally Rather than Domestically?" *Financial Analysts Journal,* July–August 1974, pp. 48–54.

Tversky, Amos, and Daniel Kahneman: "Judgment under Uncertainty: Heuristics and Biases," *Science,* September 27, 1974, pp. 1124–1131.

Upson, Roger B., Paul F. Jessup, and Keishiro Matsumoto: "Portfolio Diversification Strategies," *Financial Analysts Journal,* May–June 1975, pp. 86–88.

Wagner, Wayne H., and Stuart R. Quay: "Ten Myths about Beta," *The Journal of Portfolio Management,* Fall 1974, pp. 37–40.

CHAPTER EIGHT

INFLATION

Times change. And so do prices. The 1905 Sears, Roebuck & Company catalog lists men's shirts for 40¢, wicker rocking chairs for $2.65, a solid-oak dining room table for $4.25, and a complete set of Dickens's writings in 15 bound volumes for $2.69.

Today's high prices reflect decades of slow but steady price increases, interrupted only occasionally by a dramatic upsurge or a small decline. As a result, most shoppers now recognize the constantly changing value of a dollar. But to many investors and the Internal Revenue Service a dollar is a dollar regardless of what it will purchase.

Investors can ill afford to ignore inflation and deflation. Changes in the overall price level often have an important impact on investment values and on the economic well-being of individuals. To make matters worse, the usual dollar measures of profit, loss, and rates of return lose much of their meaning during inflation.

MEASURING PRICE-LEVEL CHANGES

Inflation has been called many things by many people. *Webster's Eighth New Collegiate Dictionary* provides one of the simplest definitions of **inflation**—"A substantial and continuing rise in the general price level." To some extent this definition raises more questions than it answers. How long must price changes persist to be termed "continuing"? And what exactly is a substantial "rise" or "decline"? Still more important, how does one measure the "general price level"?

The answers to the first two questions depend upon the individual's perspective. During most of the 1950s and early 1960s overall prices in the United States increased by only 1 to 2% every year. Some economists describe this phenomenon as "creeping inflation." Others view the period as one of relatively stable prices.

The concept of a general price level sounds more concrete, at least until someone tries to measure it. Individuals interested in simply comparing today's prices with yesterday's prices can always do so on an item-by-item basis. For example, suppose a curious homemaker wishes to compare today's grocery prices with those existing 10 years ago. She writes down the following columns:

Shopping List	Today's Prices, $	Prices 10 Years Ago, $
T-Bone steak (lb)	1.68	.89
Ground beef (lb)	1.08	.49
Bacon (lb)	1.89	.85
Loaf of bread	.53	.26
Coffee (lb)	3.83	.69
Sugar (lb)	.20	.08
Eggs (doz)	.83	.47
Milk (gal)	1.44	.69
Potatoes (lb)	.25	.10
Total cost	$11.73	$4.52

At first glance, it appears as though overall prices have nearly tripled.

But two very important factors have been overlooked. First, shoppers seldom purchase an equal dollar amount of every item. The average individual only uses 6 pounds of coffee each year, but consumes nearly 200 pounds of meat. As a result, a simple item-by-item comparison of prices provides a misleading picture of the cost of living.

The other difficulty with an item-by-item comparison of prices concerns quality changes. In many cases, the products sold today represent considerable improvements over yesterday's products. For example, substantial improvements in the technology of refrigerator manufacturing have resulted in marked increases in both overall refrigerator capacity and in freezing-compartment capacity, with no increase in refrigerator size. And few people would want to revert to shopping in the drugstore of 10 years ago. Price comparisons should be adjusted for these changes in quality.

Consumer Price Index

Experienced price watchers follow numerous price indexes for hints about the future and comparisons with the past, but the **Consumer Price Index** (CPI) probably attracts the most attention.

The CPI provides a monthly measure of the cost of living for the "average urban American." According to detailed statistical studies published by the Bureau of Labor Statistics, this individual consumes an enormous variety of goods. At the end of 1976, the bureau included more than 400 different items in the CPI. These items, in specific quantities, represent the **market basket** consumed by the average American.

Assume this market basket of goods and services costs $564 in 1975 and $610 in 1976. The cost of maintaining a particular standard of living increased during 1 year by $46, or about 8%. As a result, a dollar spent in 1976 buys about 8% fewer goods than a dollar spent in 1975.

Anyone watching the cost of living is primarily interested in price changes. For that reason, the government provides a price index rather than actual prices. An index is a ratio of two numbers. In the case of the CPI, these numbers are the total costs of the goods and services in the market basket (a given standard of living) at two different points in time. The government selects one of these points in time and calls it the **base year.** This base year serves as a reference point for future price levels. The CPI for any year equals:

$$CPI = \frac{\text{current price of market basket}}{\text{price of market basket for base year}} \times 100$$

Suppose the government selects 1967 as the base year for computing the index. There is nothing magical about this particular year. It simply serves as a convenient reference point. Moreover, the government changes the base year about every 10 years. Assume the price of the market basket during 1967 totaled $350. The same market basket cost $610 in 1976. The Consumer Price Index for 1976 is calculated as follows:

$$CPI\ 1976 = \frac{\$610 \text{ price of market basket in } 1976}{\$350 \text{ price of market basket in } 1967} \times 100$$

$$CPI\ 1976 = 174.3$$

In other words, the market basket cost 74.3% more in 1976 than in 1967, the base year. This in turn implies that the cost of maintaining the same standard of living increased by approximately 74.3%.

Viewed in another way, the purchasing power of the dollar declined by approximately 43% between 1967 and 1976. A shopper in 1967 needed only $1 to buy the same goods purchased by a shopper in 1976 with $1.74. In terms of today's dollars, $1 in 1976 purchased what 57¢ did in 1967. So shoppers lost 43¢, or 43%, of every dollar during this period.

EXAMPLE   The price of the market basket equaled $300 in 1967. In the year 1991, the price of the same market basket will total $4,500. The CPI for 1991, using 1967 as the base year, will equal

$$\frac{4,500}{300} \times 100 = 1,500$$

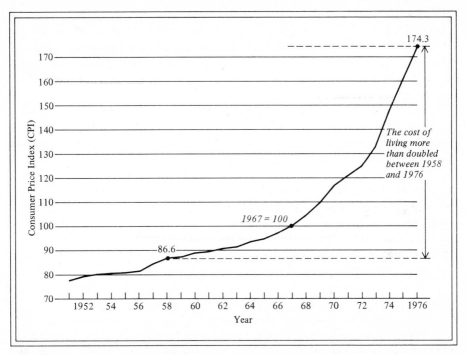

FIGURE 8-1   Consumer Price Index.

In other words, the cost of living will have increased by 1,400%, that is, from 100 to 1,500.

The decline in the purchasing power of the dollar amounts to 93.4%. It will take $15 in 1991 to buy the same amount of goods as $1 purchased in 1967. So $1 in 1991 will equal $1/$15, or 6.6¢ in 1967.

The CPI for the 26 years from 1951 to 1976 is presented in Figure 8-1. These numbers portray a relatively low rate of inflation until 1966. After that, inflation accelerated, reaching the double digits by 1974.

INFLATIONARY EPISODES

Inflation was not invented in the twentieth century. According to historical evidence, price increases have been going on for thousands of years. And the United States experience dates back to the founding of the country.

Continental Congress

"No taxation without representation!" served as the rallying cry for independence in the 13 colonies. Unfortunately for the Continental Congress and its fledgling army, citizens of the new republic soon shortened the slogan to "No tax-ation."

As incredible as it may now seem, Americans in 1776 passionately refused to be taxed. Congress and the individual states soon employed the usual alternative —the printing of money. In less than a year, millions of dollars of Continental and state currency circulated throughout the United States.

Some members of the Continental Congress showed a surprising grasp of the inflationary consequences of this increased money supply. For example, one resolution to Congress stated: "No truth being more evident than that, where the quantity of money of any denomination exceeds what is useful as a medium of commerce, its comparative value must be proportionately reduced." The cor-rectness of this principle soon became apparent. Prices of goods increased stead-ily and the value of the Continental dollar declined drastically. By April 1779, a paper dollar was worth only 5¢ in gold, and in the spring of 1781, 525 Continen-tal dollars equaled just $1 in gold, completely justifying the then-popular expres-sion, "not worth a Continental."

Most governments vehemently deny any responsibility for inflation. The Continental Congress was no exception to the rule. In May 1779, it issued a proc-lamation to all United States citizens. According to Congress, inflation was partly caused by "the artifices of men who have hastened to enrich themselves by mo-nopolizing the necessaries of life, and to the misconduct of inferior officials em-ployed in the public service." Additional pronouncements by Congress served to reinforce the popular opinion that monopolizers and extortioners had caused the inflation. These official pronouncements on the supposed causes of inflation were accompanied by a record-breaking issuance of 140 million Continental dollars.

The end of the Revolutionary War marked the end of paper money. All Con-tinental dollars were eventually replaced with gold or silver.

Civil War Finance

Not much more than 100 years ago, members of the United States Congress actively debated the wisdom of issuing a paper currency not backed by gold or silver. One opponent of the concept emphatically declared it "not in the power of this Congress . . . to accomplish an impossibility in making something out of nothing." Even an ardent supporter of paper currency stated "that only with ex-treme reluctance, only with fear and trembling as to the consequences, can we have recourse to a measure like this of making our paper a legal tender in pay-ment of debts." But because of the difficult financial conditions imposed by the Civil War, Congress passed the Legal Tender Act, and the United States govern-ment almost immediately began issuing new paper dollars.

During 1862 and 1863, hundreds of millions of these so-called greenbacks poured from the printing presses. At the same time, the average prices of goods nearly doubled. This dramatic rise in prices created a speculative environment. The Commissioner of Revenue at the time stated that because of the "high profits realized in trading during the period of monetary expansion . . . the spirit of trading and speculation pervade the entire country."

Hyperinflation in Germany

Post-World War I Germany provides the classic example of inflation. Like the Allies, Germany mobilized forces in 1914, certain of quick victory. But hopes of being "home by Christmas" faded rapidly. Heavy wartime spending, financed mostly by debt, combined with the Allied blockade of German foreign trade soon pushed prices higher. By the end of the war, 4 years later, prices stood at more than twice their prewar level.

The armistice ended the war, but not the German inflation. Between October 1918 and February 1920, the prices of domestic goods increased more than 500% and the prices of imported goods by nearly 1,900%. After a short period of relative stability in 1920, prices resumed their upward climb. Between May 1921 and July 1922 domestic prices increased by over 700%. Then, in the following year, they jumped by an incredible 18,000%.

But the worst was still to come. Prices increased so much in the 6 months between July 1923 and December 1923 that the numbers almost defy meaning. Before the great inflation subsided at the end of the year, prices had soared upward until the cost of living index equaled 1 quadrillion, that is, 1 million millions (1,000,000,000,000). By the end of November 1923, a loaf of bread cost 428 billion paper marks—up from one-fourth of a mark at the start of the war. Newspapers sold for 20 billion marks, a bus ticket 150 billion, a stamp for a local letter 100 billion, and a pound of butter 2 trillion. Economists coined the word **hyperinflation,** meaning super inflation, to describe these conditions.

All this time the German printing presses were creating more and more money. The wild printing of paper money created some ridiculous sights. Money shops refused to give change for 10,000-mark notes. Housewives carried bushel baskets of money to the store and returned with hardly enough food to last for a day. Children used old bank notes to make kites. And eventually the blank back of a million-mark note became more useful as a scratch pad than as currency.

DEFLATIONARY EPISODES

In contrast to inflation, deflation appears to be a nearly extinct species of economic phenomenon. **Deflation** is the exact opposite of inflation—it is a continuing decline in the general price level. In the last 30 years, prices in the United States have declined only twice and then by only 1 or 2%. If present trends continue, future generations of investors may read about price-level declines with the same awe as today's children view the bones of dinosaurs.

Surprising as it may now seem, the United States once experienced long periods of deflation. For example, the end of the Civil War marked the start of a 30-year decline in prices. In 1866, the wholesale price index (another widely used measure of price levels) stood at 168. By 1896, it had plummeted to a low of 67.

Many people associate price declines with unemployment and reduced growth in the economy. But the deflation of 1866 to 1896 occurred during a period of unparalleled growth and, at times, of great prosperity. In fact, the rate of growth in income and net national product has never been equaled in this country.

After 1896, wholesale prices increased almost every year until the index reached 101 in 1910. A sharp drop to 93 occurred during the next year. Then World War I drove prices rapidly upward. Prices more than doubled in the 5 years from 1916 through 1920. But unlike today's prices, prices in the 1920s moved down as well as up. They dropped by about 40% in 1921 and 1922.

The next deflation coincided with the Great Depression. Wholesale prices fell by 2% in 1930, 7% in 1931, 10% in 1932, and 6% in 1933. Considering the severity of the Depression, many economists express surprise at the small declines in prices.

CAUSES OF INFLATION AND DEFLATION

Economics lacks the precision of the physical sciences. Anyone who asks three economists for their opinions on an important topic usually gets four answers. And if the question concerns the causes of inflation, the differences in opinion become even more pronounced.

Despite the wide range of views about inflation, the careful observer of economic debates eventually recognizes a distinct pattern. Most economists believe inflation is caused primarily by (1) monetary factors, (2) demand pull, or (3) cost push.

$$\sqrt{MV} = \sqrt{PQ}$$

Monetary View of Inflation

Monetarists view inflation as "too much money chasing too few goods." One of the chief advocates of the monetary view of inflation is Nobel Prize winner Milton Friedman. According to Friedman, "Inflation is always and everywhere a monetary phenomenon."

Friedman's view of money represents a modern interpretation of the very old **quantity theory of money**. This theory dates back at least to the eighteenth century and the writings of the philosopher David Hume. Even certain members of the Continental Congress apparently understood the concept.

Quantity theorists attach great importance to the quantity of money as the determinant of the overall price level. They base their belief on the study of the relationship between the quantity of money and the price level over the course of hundreds of years.

People hold money—namely, currency and balances in checking accounts—for a reason, and it must be a very good reason, since money pays no explicit returns. Money serves primarily as a medium of exchange. It can be easily exchanged for other goods, whereas barter requires considerable time and effort. So money reduces exchange costs.

The average amount of money held by an individual or a business depends upon several factors. Friedman believes the demand for money depends primarily upon (1) the level of income and (2) the cost of holding money. Since money pays no explicit return, the cost of holding money equals the return that could be earned by investing this cash in interest-bearing bonds or real goods. The higher that return, the higher the cost of holding money.

Not all monetary economists agree with Friedman about the importance of income to the demand for money. Many of them emphasize the dollar amount of transactions rather than income. Since people use money to transact with, this seems only natural.

According to quantity theorists, people attempt to hold a relatively constant proportion of their incomes (or transactions) in cash. If for some reason the available quantity of money changes, individuals make every attempt to restore their cash balances to the habitual relationship. For example, an increase in the supply of money results in attempts by individuals to get rid of their excess cash balances, probably by buying additional goods or investments. But society as a whole cannot eliminate excess money. As in a game of musical chairs, the dollars are simply passed from person to person without any change in the total number.

Individual efforts to purchase additional goods eventually cause higher prices. These in turn result in increased dollar incomes and transactions. Of course, this in no way implies higher real incomes. But at these higher levels of income and transactions, people are content to hold the increased quantity of dollars and prices stop rising.

Demand Pull

Many economists and business people disagree with the quantity theory of money. They believe the quantity theorists have ignored the truly important economic forces that create price movements. After all, they argue, "dollar bills do not walk into stores and spend themselves."

Well then, what does happen? According to adherents of the **demand-pull** school of thought, increased prices result primarily from increased demand. This increased demand comes from business, consumers, or the government.

For example, suppose a country goes to war. Suddenly there is a tremendous increase in the government's demand for tanks, ships, airplanes, and other materials of war. But, for a while, the supply of goods remains more or less constant. The increased demand for goods without an increase in supply pulls prices higher. In effect, the government bids away resources from the consumers and business by offering higher prices.

The United States consumer price index provides some evidence of the impact of wars on price levels. Prices increased by 10% during the Korean war and by 16% during the Vietnamese war. And when price controls were removed after World War II, pent-up demand exploded and prices increased by more than 18% in 1 year.

Government deficits are not the only cause of inflation. According to the demand-pull school, excessive investment by businesses in plant and equipment and/or inventories also fans the inflationary fires. This increased spending supposedly results from low interest rates and/or an ebullient economic picture.

Cost Push

Another large group of economists and business people take a **cost-push** view of inflation. Cost pushers have thrived in the troubled times of the 1970s. The Arab oil embargo, widespread labor unrest, and disturbed commodity markets all made numerous converts to the cost-push way of thinking.

Whereas believers in demand-pull inflation focus on demand, cost-push theorists explain inflation primarily from the supply side. They believe prices rise because the costs of goods increase. The Arab oil embargo provides a widely quoted example of cost-push inflation. Prior to the oil embargo, crude oil sold for about $2.50 a barrel. After the embargo, the Organization of Petroleum Exporting Countries (OPEC) succeeded in raising prices to $11 a barrel. Since crude oil constitutes an essential ingredient in thousands of products, this nearly 400% price increase rippled throughout the economies of the world.

OPEC's aggressive pricing policies represent a relatively new cost-push factor. In the past, labor unions and big business have borne the brunt of the blame for cost-push inflation.

One of the favorite examples of wage push concerns the construction unions. During the 3 years from July 1968 to July 1971, wages in the construction industry shot upward by 32%, far outdistancing the cost-of-living and average-wage increases. At the same time, unions instituted a number of restrictive work practices.

Despite the multitude of forces pushing costs upward, price increases are not inevitable. Technology tends to counteract many of these cost factors by increasing productivity. For example, Eli Whitney's cotton gin greatly reduced the amount of labor needed to clean cotton. In a letter written to his father in 1793, Whitney says his first cotton gin "required the labor of one man to turn it and will clean ten times as much cotton as he can in any other way before known and also clean it much better than in the usual mode."

IMPACT OF INFLATION AND DEFLATION ON RATES OF RETURN

Inflation and deflation refer to changes in the overall price level, nothing more and nothing less. But inflation and deflation often coincide with drastic changes in the overall economy. In fact, inflation and deflation may even cause some of these changes.

Because of the complex interactions between price-level changes and economic conditions, attempts to unravel the impact of pure price-level changes on investments often fail. For that reason, individuals sifting through the scattered economic debris surrounding actual inflations and deflations should have some guidelines to follow.

Real versus Nominal Returns

Irving Fisher provides those guidelines in the *Theory of Interest,* published in 1930. Fisher distinguishes between two types of interest rates—nominal and real. With interest rates, as with many other things in life, what a person sees is not necessarily what he or she gets. Investors see **nominal interest rates,** since these rates measure changes in the dollar (or nominal) value of investments. But because of inflation and deflation, dollar rates of return seldom reflect economic reality. Only **real interest rates** measure changes in economic well-being. Paradoxically, investors never directly observe real rates of interest.

If all this sounds too preposterous to be true, imagine the curious plight of investors who held government savings bonds during 1974, 1975, and 1976. In nominal or dollar terms, these investors earned 6% on their money each year. And they had the dollars and their income tax returns to prove it. But the consumer price index rose by 11% in 1974, by 9.1% in 1975, and by 8% in 1976. As a result, every investor holding government savings bonds during these years experienced a loss in real terms.

What ultimately counts to every investor is not how many dollars he or she has, but how much can be bought with those dollars. With the overall price level increasing by 11% in 1974, individuals had to have 11% more money at the end of the year just to stay even. Instead they had only the 6% more provided by interest payments. Therefore, the net result of 1 year of savings actually amounted to a loss of 5%; that is, the real rate of interest on savings bonds in 1974 equaled minus 5%. Since the 1975 increase in the price level totaled 9.1%, the increased cost of living exceeded the interest received on these bonds by 3.1%. That is, the real rate of interest in 1975 equaled minus 3.1%. With an 8% increase in the CPI in 1976, the real rate amounted to minus 2%. Altogether frugality cost the individual a loss of more than 10% in real terms over the 3-year period 1974–1976.

Bond investors were not the only ones to suffer from inflation. Many people purchased stocks in the 1960s because of their glowing prospects. Judging from the graph of the Dow Jones averages in Figure 8-2, the actual results fell far below these great expectations. The Dow Jones Industrial Average reached a high of 969.26 at the end of 1965. Nine years later, it sagged to 616.24, and then rebounded to 947.22 at the close of 1976. At this point in time, many shareholders breathed a sigh of relief at having recouped their original investment.

In actuality, these unfortunate investors suffered an enormous loss in real terms over the years from 1965 to 1976. True, they eventually ended up with about the same number of dollars they started with. But a 1976 dollar bore only a

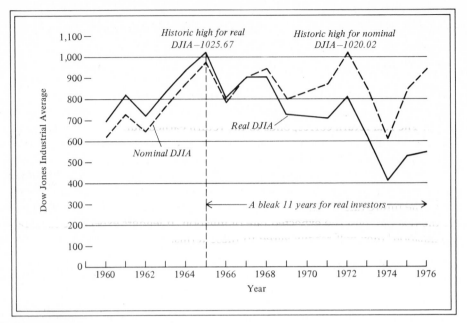

FIGURE 8-2   The real and nominal Dow Jones Industrial Average.

faint resemblance to the 1965 dollar. In 1965 the CPI stood at 94.5. In the next 11 years the CPI bounded upward to 174.3. As a result of this 84% increase in the cost of living, the investor needed $1.84 to buy the same goods once purchased for $1.

The Dow Jones Industrial Average can be expressed in terms of real purchasing power at any point in time simply by dividing the average by the CPI at the same date. The "real" DJIA for the period 1964–1976 is also shown in Figure 8-2. These figures tell a sad story of the decline in the true value of most shareholders' savings.

PRICE-LEVEL ANTICIPATIONS AND RATES OF RETURN

At first glance these returns on stocks and bonds defy understanding. Is the real reward for patience and risk-bearing a negative return? In other words, do investors pay for the privilege of lending their money to government, business, etc.?

No one can deny the fact that the real return from investing is often negative over a long period of time. But this is an **ex post** view of the world, meaning after the fact. In a world of uncertainty, most economists and financiers prefer to take an ex ante approach to investment. **Ex ante** means before the fact. Unless they are clairvoyant, investors must base their decisions on incomplete knowledge. They act on an ex ante basis and then mourn or celebrate the ex post results.

Fisher's Theory of Interest Rates

According to Irving Fisher, investors expect to make a nominal return on their investments equal to the real return plus the expected rate of change in the price level. The real return corresponds to the return earned during times of complete price-level stability. It measures the real change in wealth. Many economists believe the real return hovers around 3% per year on an average.

Suppose investors demand a real return of 3% on their money. They can achieve this goal by asking borrowers to guarantee this return. Or they can estimate the future rate of inflation and then demand a nominal or dollar return equal to the real rate plus the expected rate of inflation. If lenders expect the same rate of inflation, they will readily agree to these terms.

> EXAMPLE   An investor wants to make a real return of 3% on a $10,000 investment. He believes the rate of inflation during the coming year will equal 5% and thus demands and in this case receives a nominal return of 8%.
>
> The forecast of inflation is correct. Reviewing the results for the year, he finds that the interest on the $10,000 was actually 8%, or $800. This is a nominal return, since it is stated in dollars.
>
> But the decline in the purchasing power of the $10,000 partially offsets this interest income. Since the cost of living increased by 5%, each dollar now purchases 5% less than it did a year ago. So the real return on the investment equals 8% minus 5%, or 3%; that is, the investor is able to purchase 3% more goods.

Fisher believed that the real return on an investment is determined by the productivity of capital and the impatience of people to spend their money. In other words, fundamental economic factors determine the real return. Abundant examples of capital productivity exist. Probably the most appealing concerns the aging of wine. Many wines grow finer and therefore more valuable with time. A 1-year-old burgundy tastes better than a brand-new burgundy. For this reason, older burgundies sell for higher prices. If a 1-year burgundy sells for 5% more than a new burgundy, the real return on investments in wine equals 5%.

According to Fisher, the relationship between nominal returns, real returns, and expected changes in the price level is:

Nominal return = real return + expected rate of change in price level

Or, rearranging terms,

Real return = nominal return − expected rate of change in price level

Fisher's expression demonstrates the folly of shifting funds into bonds simply because they pay high nominal returns. These high returns merely reflect high rates of inflation, not an improvement in real returns. And if people underestimate the

P↑ NR↓ than real
218   CHAPTER EIGHT
P↓ NR↑ than real

rate of inflation, even these high returns may fail to compensate investors for the loss of purchasing power. After World War I, one American bank offered to lend money to German companies at an annual rate of interest of 100%, with the interest and loan to be repaid in German currency. Fortunately for the bank, the Germans refused the offer. Even this exorbitant rate failed to come close to compensating lenders for the tremendous decline in purchasing power of the German currency during the German hyperinflation.

The real return provides investors with a meaningful target. But because of changes in the price level, the target is a moving one. Every investor must somehow estimate future changes in the price level or, as an alternative, accept the opinions of others in the marketplace. When people expect high inflation rates, nominal interest rates should be much higher than usual. And the nominal rate ought to greatly exceed the real rate of return. When people expect no price-level changes, the nominal return should equal the real return. And when people believe prices will decline, the nominal return should be less than the real return.

Most economists and financial theorists agree with this part of Fisher's theory of the interest rate. The debate centers on his explanation of the formation of people's expectations. Fisher believed that people adapt very gradually to price changes and that their expectations reflect only the past. Leaving aside the question of how people form expectations, Fisher's theory does provide a definite link between real and nominal rates of interest.

Inflation and Interest Rates in Efficient Markets

Fisher's concept of nominal rates of interest is widely accepted by economists and financiers. But Richard Roll questions the actual existence of the **Fisher effect,** i.e., the relationship between nominal interest rates and expected rates of inflation or deflation. According to Roll, the Fisher effect is valid only when markets display considerable inefficiency. In a world of truly efficient commodity and security markets, commodity prices adjust immediately rather than trending upward.

Suppose, for example, that gold sells for $100 an ounce. Suddenly the government agrees to a program of steadily increasing the price it pays for gold by 10% a year. Moreover, it promises to buy all gold offered for sale. Does the price of gold rise steadily by 10% a year, or does it immediately increase in price until the market price reflects the future growth in government prices? If the gold market is efficient and the interest rate equals 5%, gold doubles in price the same day of the announcement. At that price, anyone holding gold earns exactly 5% a year on the money invested.

Now what if the government declares a policy of every year paying 20% more for all goods? Perhaps it plans to implement this policy by printing additional money and using the money to purchase goods and services. If Roll is correct, the resulting change in expectations about inflation or deflation will cause tremendous shifts in the prices of assets. Overnight the inhabitants of the country come to believe that prices will rise 20% each year. This implies an annual increase of 20% in the prices of all real goods such as houses, art, antiques, stamps, coins, gold, other metals, stocks, and even canned foods. In the morning, crowds roam the streets searching out and making offers on all these items. Prices jump astronomically. Paintings of the old masters that only 1 day ago were valued at $5,000 each are quickly bid up to $20,000 or more. Gold and silver prices also quadruple in the first few hours, and stocks surge upward.

Are these price rises justified? Based on expectations of the future, yes. After all, with the general price level increasing by 20% a year, the prices of real goods will more than double in value every 5 years.

The flight into real goods and out of dollars, bonds, insurance policies, etc., cannot go on forever. Attempts by individuals and institutions to liquidate dollar assets result in plunging bond prices and greatly increasing interest rates. At the same time, the quest for real goods drives up their prices and lowers their expected future returns. Eventually, a point is reached where bonds and other money market instruments become attractive because of their higher returns. At that point, shifts in assets end and there are no further bursts in asset prices.

Something similar to this scenario occurred in 1973 and 1974 in the United States and other countries of the world. Suddenly, the population grew concerned about inflation and dire forecasts of runaway prices became popular. In 1 year art, antiques, etc., quadrupled in value. At the same time, the prices of Treasury bills and bonds plunged to new lows, and interest rates soared to new highs. All this was in keeping with expectations of inflation.

Unfortunately, salespersons of investment media seldom recognize the reasons for the success of their products. Once prices have adjusted to expectations of inflation, there is no reason for further change. Only if people change their minds about future inflation rates will these real assets score large gains again. In point of fact, governments regained partial control of their economies and reduced the rate of inflation. This resulted in a decline in expected price-level changes and, with it large declines in the prices of gold, silver, commodities, and other real goods.

Stocks and Inflation

Real-value goods such as stocks, gold, and real estate seldom provide complete protection against inflation. Most of the studies done to date show very little relationship between stock prices and inflation. In fact, United States stocks turned in one of their worst performances during the inflationary years from 1966 to 1974.

Why the great chasm between perceived theory and reality? Because the perceived theory is oversimplified. Stocks provide a complete hedge against inflation only when inflation increases product prices by at least the same percentage as product costs. This is shown in Figure 8-3. In other words, a 10% rate of inflation must translate into at least 10% higher profits, a 20% rate of inflation into 20% higher profits, etc. But profits seldom move exactly in tandem with inflation. The figures in Table 8-1 illustrate that fact of economic life. Dollar profits

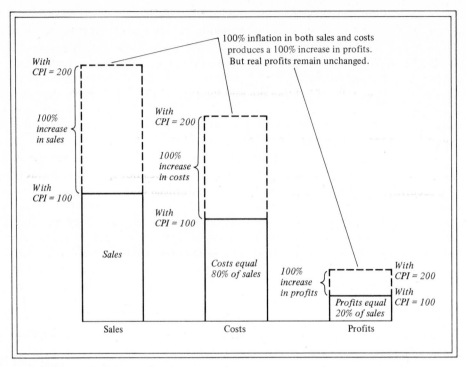

FIGURE 8-3   Inflation and company profits.

earned on each dollar employed by American industry barely increased over the 10-year period 1966–1975. And real profits declined by more than 33%. In order to keep pace with inflation, dollar profits should have increased by 61%. No wonder the real value of stocks declined.

The American experience with stocks is in no way unique. Constantino

TABLE 8-1   *DOLLAR PROFITS AND REAL PROFITS OF UNITED STATES CORPORATIONS*

Year	Dollar Profits*	Real Profits*
1966	82.5	84.9
1967	79.3	79.3
1968	85.8	82.3
1969	81.4	74.1
1970	67.9	58.4
1971	77.2	63.6
1972	92.1	73.5
1973	99.1	74.5
1974	84.8	57.4
1975	91.6	56.8

* In billions of dollars.

Bresciani-Turroni spent 9 years in post-World War I Germany, serving first as a member of the Reparations Commission, then as director of German Exports Control, and finally as economic adviser to the Agent-General of Reparations. His book, *The Economics of Inflation,* provides the classic summary of German hyperinflation. According to Bresciani-Turroni, much of the German public eventually realized the folly of holding the rapidly depreciating paper mark. By 1919 these unhappy citizens had transferred a substantial part of their wealth to the Berlin Bourse, the major stock exchange. From then until currency reform ended inflation in 1923, a speculative fury characterized the exchange. One newspaper columnist of the day noted, "Today there is no one—from lift boy, typist, and small landlord to the wealthy lady in society—who does not speculate in industrial securities and who does not study the list of official quotations as if it were a most precious letter."[1]

Because of the tremendous fluctuations in prices, some people quickly made a fortune. But the average investor suffered sizable losses over the 5 years of inflation. These investors had only one consolation—investors who held only bonds and other fixed-dollar assets during these same years lost everything.

South America provides another testing ground for the impact of inflation on stock prices. During the inflationary period from 1950 to 1971 stock prices declined sharply in real value in Chile, Argentina, and Peru. In Brazil, stocks performed admirably, but it is no mere coincidence that the profits of Brazilian companies also increased substantially during the same period.

Judging from past events, stocks do provide protection against inflation if profits increase correspondingly. Unfortunately, the price controls, social upheaval, and economic distortions so often associated with inflation frequently create an unfavorable business climate. As a result, profits and stock prices often lag behind inflation.

Real Estate, Gold, and Inflation

Next to stocks, real estate provides the most popular form of real-value investment. But real estate differs from stocks in that comparatively little is known about the long-run returns on different types of real estate. During the German hyperinflation, commercial properties and farmland supposedly provided an excellent hedge against inflation. Both commercial property rents and farm prices increased with the inflation. At the same time, the mortgage payments remained fixed in amount and declined tremendously in real terms.

The owners of residential rental properties found themselves in a much less enviable position. The German government soon imposed rent controls on nearly all apartments. As a result, the owners of apartment buildings faced ever-increasing costs with little or no increase in revenues. At the same time, the tenants, neighbors, and passersby stripped most apartment buildings of stair carpets, doorhandles, all metal fixtures, and even electric light bulbs. After all, these real-value items appreciated in price every day. Eventually the financial and psychological pressures forced many landlords who owned six- or eight-flat build-

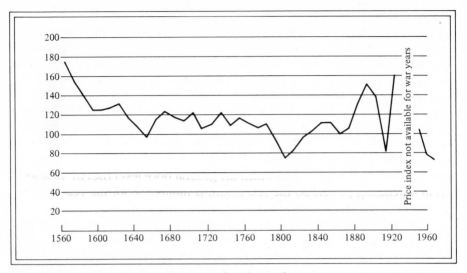

FIGURE 8-4   The real price of 1 ounce of gold over four centuries. (From Roy Jastram, *The Golden Constant,* Wiley, New York, 1977.)

ings to sell. For example, it was estimated that one-third of the apartment build-ings in Berlin changed owners during this period. Foreigners bought many of them. Again, the moral of the story appears to be that no real-value asset provides complete protection against inflation.

Gold represents the last refuge of inflation-wary (and -weary) investors. Harry Brown, Franz Pick, James Dines, and at least a score of other investment advisers wax poetic when discussing gold. According to them, the inflationary tendencies of modern-day governments almost guarantee a steady rise in the price of gold.

The past record of gold prices fails to substantiate these optimistic predic-tions. Professor Roy Jastram of the University of California at Berkeley has stud-ied the price of gold from 1560 to 1973. According to Jastram, the purchasing power of gold changed by less than 1% during this period—leading him to refer to the precious metal as the "golden constant." But there were many times during those four centuries when gold prices fluctuated in unexpected ways. For ex-ample, the Napoleonic wars produced hyperinflation and political instability. Given this environment, gold prices should have jumped. In actuality, gold bugs lost much of their purchasing power (and sometimes their lives, since owning gold was a crime punishable by death in France). The real price of 1 ounce of gold from 1560 to 1973 is displayed in Figure 8-4.

SUMMARY

Today's investor lives in an inflationary environment. During the last 10 years, the general price level—as measured by the Consumer Price Index—increased by more than 70%. Most economists predict further increases in the future.

What causes this inflation? Judging from past history, money plays a key role. There is not a single instance of a prolonged inflation unaccompanied by a substantial increase in the money supply. Perhaps for that reason, many investment managers closely monitor changes in the money supply for clues to future price increases. Economists also believe that demand pull and cost push cause increases in the price level.

Inflation considerably complicates investment decisions. Investors must learn to distinguish between real and nominal returns. Dollar (nominal) returns lose their meaning in an inflationary world. What matters is how much these dollars will actually buy (the real return). For example, someone making 8% on corporate bonds during a year in which the general price level rises by 10% loses 2% in purchasing power. So the real return is minus 2% for the year. Anyone who believes differently is the victim of an optical illusion.

Investors' expectations about future inflation have a substantial impact on the prices of stocks, bonds, and other assets. As a general rule, forecasts of increased inflation drive bond prices lower and the prices of real-value goods like stocks, real estate, art, and gold higher. However, prices also depend upon politics. If investors believe the government will impose price controls or in some other way limit the nominal increase in the profits of corporations, stocks can actually decline in price.

KEYWORDS

inflation	hyperinflation	nominal interest rates
consumer price index (CPI)	deflation	real interest rates
	quantity theory of money	ex post
market basket	demand pull	ex ante
base year	cost push	Fisher effect

QUESTIONS

1   Suppose the market basket cost $500 during the base year and $800 5 years later. Calculate the CPI for each of these 2 years.

2   If the CPI increases from 180 to 190 during the year, what is the annual rate of inflation?

3   Explain why the purchasing power of the dollar can never decline by more than 100%, whereas the rate of inflation can be astronomical.

4   Find the current CPI in a copy of the *Survey of Current Business*. Compare it to the CPI shown in Figure 8-1 for 1976.

5   Are there any similarities between the inflationary episodes in the United States during the Revolution and the Civil War and in Germany following World War I? What are they? Do you think these factors caused the runaway inflation?

6   Have deflationary periods been very common in the United States since the turn of this century?

7   Suppose labor unions demand and receive a 25% increase in wages during the year. Analyze the effect of this action from the cost-push and monetary points of view.

8   Compute the real returns on a passbook savings account for the years 1972–1976, using the following information:

Year	CPI	Maximum Interest Rate on Savings Account, %
1972	125.3	5
1973	133.1	5
1974	147.7	5
1975	161.2	5
1976	174.3	5

9   Now assume the saver pays income taxes at a 30% rate. In other words, 30¢ of every dollar of interest income goes to the government. What is the real after-tax return to the investor during each of the 5 years?

10   On December 31, 1965, an investor bought 100 shares of stock at $20 a share. At that time the CPI equaled 94.5. Eleven years later the stock sells for $30 and the CPI equals 170. Has the investor's real wealth increased?

11   Suppose corporate bonds yield 11% at the same time that everybody expects an 8% increase in the general price level. What is the expected real return on these bonds?

12   The CPI increased from 97.2 to 170 during the 10-year period ending in 1976. The Dow Jones Industrial Average showed almost no change over the exact same period: it closed at 990 in 1966 and at 970 in 1976. What should the DJIA have closed at in 1976 in order for stocks to have just stayed even with inflation? (Ignore dividends.)

13   Apartment properties proved to be a terrible hedge against hyperinflation in Germany (and in New York City during the 1960s and 1970s). Why?

14   Are so-called risk-free investments like Treasury bills and savings accounts truly risk-free? What is one possible measure of their real risk?

15   Evaluate the following statement from a sales brochure: "Inflation is here to stay. As a result, rare coins can be expected to show steady increases in value." (Hint: Apply Roll's analysis of the impact of inflation on asset prices.)

16   Discuss the following statement from a syndicated newspaper column: "Home buyers benefit from inflation, since they repay their mortgages with cheaper dollars." (Hint: Do interest rates on mortgages reflect this decline in the purchasing power of the dollar?)

17   Devise a beat-inflation investment strategy. Concentrate on eliminating the risks of inflation while at the same time earning a positive real return. Be certain to differentiate between expected and unexpected rates of inflation.

REFERENCES

Ball, R. J., and Peter Doyle, eds.: *Inflation: Selected Readings,* Penguin, Harmondsworth, England, 1969.

Bender, Marylin: "When You Think about Inflation, It Gets Worse," *The New York Times,* Aug. 25, 1974.

Branch, Ben: "Common Stock Performance and Inflation: An International Comparison," *The Journal of Business,* January 1974, pp. 48–52.

Bresciani-Turroni, Constantino: *The Economics of Inflation: A Study of Currency Depreciation in Post-War Germany 1914–1923,* translated by Millicent E. Sayers, G. Allen, London, 1937.

The Consumer Price Index: A Short Description, U.S. Department of Labor, Bureau of Labor Statistics, Washington, D.C., 1971.

Fisher, Irving: *The Theory of Interest,* Macmillan, New York, 1930.

Friedman, Milton: *Inflation: Causes and Consequences,* Asia Publishing, Bombay, 1963.

*_____: "Money: Quantity Theory," *International Encyclopedia of Social Sciences,* Vol. 10, pp. 432–446, Macmillan, New York, 1968.

_____, ed.: *Studies in the Quantity Theory of Money,* University of Chicago Press, Chicago, 1956.

Giersch, Herbert, et al.: *Correcting Taxes for Inflation,* American Enterprise Institute for Public Policy Research, Washington, D.C., 1975.

Guttmann, William, and Patricia Meehan: *The Great Inflation: Germany 1919–1923,* Saxon House, D.C. Heath Ltd., Westmead, England, 1975.

Klein, Roger, and William Wolman: *The Beat Inflation Strategy,* Simon and Schuster, New York, 1975.

Laden, Ben E.: "The Impact of Inflation on the Investor," *Trust and Estates,* January 1975, pp. 22–25.

Levine, David A.: "The Causes and Dangers of Interest Rate Volatility," *The Journal of Portfolio Management,* Fall 1976, pp. 14–21.

Lintner, J.: "Inflation and Security Returns," *Journal of Finance,* May 1975, pp. 259–280.

Reilly, Frank: "How to Use Common Stocks as an Inflation Hedge," *Journal of Portfolio Management,* Summer 1975, pp. 38–43.

_____, Glenn L. Johnson, and Ralph E. Smith: "Inflation, Inflation Hedges, and Common Stocks," *Financial Analysts Journal,* January–February 1970, pp. 104–110.

Roll, Richard: "Assets, Money, and Commodity Price Inflation under Uncertainty," *Journal of Money, Credit, and Banking,* pp. 904–919.

_____: "Interest Rates on Monetary Assets and Commodity Price Index Changes," *The Journal of Finance,* May 1972, pp. 251–277.

Rom, Martin M.: *Nothing Can Replace the U.S. Dollar . . . and It Almost Has: How You Can Multiply Your Money during Runaway Inflation and Depression,* Thomas Y. Crowell, New York, 1975.

Sumner, William Graham: *The Financier and the Finances of the American Revolution,* vol. I, Dodd, Mead, New York, 1891.

* Publication preceded by an asterisk is highly recommended.

CHAPTER NINE

RATES OF RETURN

T here are two approaches to understanding the bewildering array of available investments. The traditional method is to view each type of investment as unique and to describe in detail its characteristics. The new approach, and the one used here, is to select several attributes which are common to all investments and then attempt to measure to what extent a particular investment possesses these attributes. Two attributes or characteristics are extremely important to all investors: expected return and risk.

CALCULATING RATES OF RETURN

Suppose one person invests $1,000 and another person, $1 million. Or perhaps an individual makes two different investments, one for $1,000, and the other for $1 million. How can the results of these investments be compared in some way that abstracts from their difference in size? The answer is, with the rate of return.

The rate of return shows how fast an investment is changing in value, regardless of the amount of money invested. Investment values change for two reasons. First, they increase when money or other valuable goods are paid to the investor. For example, stockholders receive dividends, and bondholders receive interest.

These receipts give rise to a change in wealth as a result of income paid in money. However, income sometimes takes other forms. For instance, during the Depression several companies that had no cash paid dividends in merchandise. A few liquor firms even gave bottles of liquor to their shareholders as dividends.

An investor's wealth fluctuates for another reason besides the receipt of income. The market price of an investment can go up or down. Whether or not the investment is sold after this price change is irrelevant. The investment has changed in value and so has the investor's wealth. People often talk about their **paper losses,** as if they weren't real. For example, someone buys shares in a company at $80. One year later the market price is $20, but the owner decides to hold the stock, perhaps in the belief that the loss is not real until the stock has actually been sold. Until then, the loss is viewed as only "on paper." In calculating rates of return, however, changes in market value should be used, whether or not the gain or loss has been realized. This is because the buying and/or borrowing power of the investor's wealth has changed.

As was already stated, an individual's wealth changes in two ways as a result of holding a particular investment:

1 Wealth can change because of income derived from the investment, or
2 Wealth can change because of fluctuations in the market price of the investment.

These two amounts taken together measure the total change in wealth associated with an investment. The rate of return for any specific period can be calculated from this total change. The first step is to determine the change in price and the income received during the period in question. Then this figure is divided by the price of the asset at the start of the period, which makes the change in wealth relative to the size of the investment. This relationship can be expressed as:

$$\text{Rate of return} = \frac{\text{price at end of period} - \text{price at start} + \text{income during period}}{\text{price at start of period}}$$

or

$$= \frac{\text{change in price} + \text{income during period}}{\text{price at start of period}} \qquad R = \frac{\Delta P + I}{P}$$

where the change in price equals the price at the end of the period minus the price at the start of the period.

The figures in Table 9-1 are the prices of General Motors stock at different dates in the past. The annual rates of return, that is, how fast wealth invested in GM changed over each 1-year period, are also shown in the table. Investors who purchased shares of GM at the closing price on July 31, 1970, would have earned nearly 18% on their money during the following year; i.e.,

$$\frac{\text{Rate of return for year}}{\text{ending July 20, 1971}} = \frac{\$76.75 - \$68.00 + \$3.40}{\$68.00}$$

$$= 17.9\%$$

TABLE 9-1   PRICES, DIVIDENDS, AND RATES OF RETURN FOR GM

Date	Price per Share, $	Price Change during the Year, $	Dividends per Share, $	1-Year Rate of Return, %
July 31, 1970	68.00			
July 30, 1971	76.75	8.75	3.40	17.9
July 31, 1972	74.88	−1.87	4.45	3.4
July 31, 1973	67.63	−7.25	5.25	−2.7
July 31, 1974	41.13	−26.50	3.40	−34.2
July 31, 1975	51.38	10.25	2.40	30.8

In 1970 they invested $68 in each share. During the year they collected $3.40 in dividends on each share. And a year later shares sold for $76.75. The annual rates of return for the 4 years ending on July 31, 1972, 1973, 1974, and 1975 were 3.4, −2.7, −34.2, and 30.8%, respectively.

The price of GM shares fluctuated greatly during this 5-year period. Investors who desired a more stable investment and a larger income could have purchased government bonds. One of the best-known issues of government bonds are the $4\frac{1}{4}$'s of 1987–1992. The United States government pays interest at the rate of $4\frac{1}{4}\%$ on the face value of these bonds and promises to redeem them between 1987 and 1992. The actual prices of these bonds together with the amount of interest paid on each are shown in Table 9-2. Investors who purchased the $4\frac{1}{4}$'s on July 31, 1970, paid $710. By the end of 1971, they had collected $42.50 in interest on each bond and their bonds had increased in value by $42.20 to $752. So the rate of return for that year was 11.9% ($84.70/$710). In the following year, the bonds increased in value to $810 and the bondholders again received $42.50 in interest. Therefore, the annual return for the year ending in 1972 was 13.3%. But for the year ending on July 31, 1973, the bonds dropped sharply in price to $724. As a result, the return on holding a bond that year was −5.4%. Bondholders lost money that year despite the fact that they were paid interest. Then, in the next 2 years, they earned 7.5 and 17.4%, respectively.

Most investors who purchase bonds think only about the interest they receive and ignore price changes. But the figures in Table 9-2 reveal that changes in the prices of bonds often exceed the interest earned on the bonds. On the other hand, many investors who purchase stocks concentrate on price changes and pay little attention to dividends. Perhaps as a result, popular stock indexes such as the Dow Jones Averages and Standard and Poor's measure only price changes. And yet the figures in Table 9-1 illustrate how important dividends can be to shareholders. Obviously, performance measurements of either stocks or bonds should reflect both price changes and income; i.e., they should be based upon rates of return. The rate of return provides a measure of the total performance of any investment. It reflects both price changes and income.

TABLE 9-2   PRICES, INTEREST PAID, AND RATES OF RETURN FOR
THE 4¹/₄'s OF 1987–1992

Date	Price per Bond, $	Price Change during the Year, $	Interest Paid per Bond, $	1-Year Rate of Return, %
July 31, 1970	710.00			
July 30, 1971	752.20	42.20	42.50	11.9
July 31, 1972	810.00	57.80	42.50	13.3
July 31, 1973	724.00	−86.00	42.50	−5.4
July 31, 1974	736.00	12.00	42.50	7.5
July 31, 1975	821.90	85.90	42.50	17.4

Compounded Rates of Return

A rate of return for a single period of time is relatively unambiguous. If the return on an investment is 40% over 1 year, investors have 40% more money than
they had invested a year earlier. But difficulties arise with rates of return for different periods of time. In particular, several rates of return cannot be added
together to determine how much an investment has changed in value. For example, a stock may have gone up by 100% in the first year and then down by
50% in the second. Plus 100% and minus 50% equals 50%. However, the stock
did not increase by 50% over the 2 years, nor did it increase by 25% a year. The
actual change over the 2-year period was 0%, as can be seen in Figure 9-1.

When comparing investments over different periods of time, it is necessary
to convert rate-of-return figures to **compounded rates of return,** or, as they are
sometimes called, **geometric rates of return.** These compounded rates of return
are often calculated on an annual basis. The annual compounded rate of return is
defined as the steady growth rate per year. The annual compounded rate of return for an investment which increased by 100% in one year and then declined
by 50% the next is simply 0%, since growth was zero. The average annual com-

FIGURE 9-1   Comparing rates of return over different periods of time.

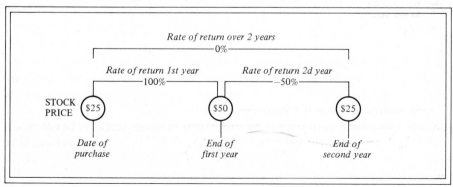

TABLE 9-3   *GROWTH IN VALUE OF $1,000 INVESTED AT 8% A YEAR*

Year	Amount at Start of Year, $		Interest Rate, %		Amount of Interest, $	Amount at End of Year, $
1	1,000	×	0.08	=	80	1,080
2	1,080	×	0.08	=	86	1,166
3	1,166	×	0.08	=	93	1,260
4	1,260	×	0.08	=	101	1,360
5	1,360	×	0.08	=	109	1,469
6	1,469	×	0.08	=	118	1,587
7	1,587	×	0.08	=	127	1,714
8	1,714	×	0.08	=	137	1,851
9	1,851	×	0.08	=	148	1,999
10	1,999	×	0.08	=	160	2,159

Note: All numbers have been rounded to the nearest dollar.

pounded rate of return for **GM** for the period 1970–1975 was 0.5%, and for the $4^{1}/_{4}$'s of 1987–1992 it was 8.6%. In other words, investors who held **GM** stock for the full 5 years (and reinvested their dividends in additional stock) would have been just as well off if they had put their money in a special account which increased in value by 0.5% for each of the 5 years. And bondholders would have done as well by earning 8.6% a year on their money for each of the 5 years.

Growth rates are widely misunderstood. In fact, one survey reveals that consumers have little understanding of the true meaning of the interest rates that they earn on their investments or pay on their loans. Someone who buys a $1,000 certificate of deposit paying 8% interest annually receives $2,159 at the end of 10 years. The 10-year rate of return is 116% ($1,159/$1,000). Many investors mistakenly conclude that the steady annual growth rate is simply 116% divided by 10 years or 11.6%. But the real annual growth rate is only 8%. Not only the original investment, but the accumulated interest is increasing at that rate, as can be seen in Table 9-3.

Because of this "interest on the interest," it is difficult to visualize the tremendous impact that a small increase in growth rates has on wealth. An individual who earns 16% a year for 30 years is nearly 30 times better off at the end of that period than someone who earns 4%. And yet, 16% is only 4 times as much interest as 4%. These results, together with the change in the value associated with a $1,000 investment at different rates of growth, are displayed in Figure 9-2.

Investors who want to determine how long it takes to double their money at different interest rates can use a simple rule. According to the rule of 69, the number of time periods required for money to double equals,

69/interest rate + 0.35

If the interest rate is 5% a year, it takes 14.15 (69/5 + 0.35) years for the investor to double his money. At 20% a year, investments double in value every 3.8 (69/20 + 0.35) years.

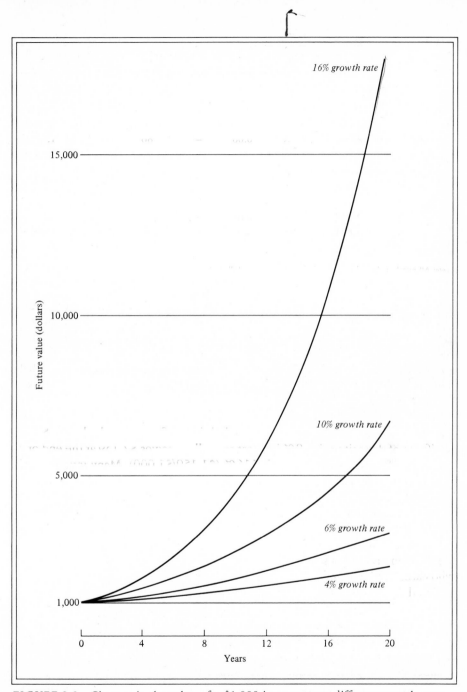

FIGURE 9-2   Changes in the value of a $1,000 investment at different growth rates.

HISTORICAL RATES OF RETURN
ON STOCKS AND BONDS

An investment strategy is based on expectations about returns on alternative investments. The emphasis is on the word "expected," since the best an investor can do is to make educated guesses about the future. Before searching out particular investments, it is helpful to form some expectations about the return on several very general types of assets. For instance, an individual should know what return can be expected on stocks or real estate as opposed to bonds or insurance.

Stocks

How much can investors reasonably expect to make on their investments? That is a difficult question. One answer has been to describe the returns that have been earned during previous years in the hope that the past will be repeated in the future. Perhaps the best-known study of historic rates of return is that by Fisher and Lorie on stocks. Fisher and Lorie calculated the returns that could have been earned by buying and holding stocks during the 40-year period 1926–1965. They found that an investor would have earned an average annual compounded rate of return of 9.3% if the dividends received were reinvested and no taxes paid.

Since this rate of return is quoted so often, it is important to understand how Fisher and Lorie computed that particular figure as well as the other rates of return they reported. They assumed that an investor bought an equal dollar amount of each stock listed on the New York Stock Exchange on a particular day. December 31, 1928, is one of the dates from which they calculated returns. The assumption that the investor bought an equal amount of each stock has an important implication. On that day in 1928 firms like GM and AT&T were listed on the exchange. These firms were large and well known even then. At the same time, some of the other firms trading on the NYSE were small and unknown and had to be regarded as being somewhat questionable investments. Despite this difference in quality, the investor was assumed to have invested the same amount of money in the stock of each of these companies.

Investors doing this would be displaying complete impartiality in their selection. Moreover, they would need no investment advice. If these investors could not buy all the stocks traded on the exchange, they would no doubt buy them randomly, since random selection implies complete impartiality. One device used as an example of random selection is a bowl filled with marbles, each of which carries the name of one of the stocks on the NYSE. Each marble has an equal chance of being drawn; so each stock has an equal chance of being purchased. This is certainly impartiality on the part of the buyer, since there is absolutely no control over which shares are purchased. Another such device, albeit a more dramatic one, is to blindfold a chimpanzee and have the animal throw darts at the financial pages from *The Wall Street Journal.* Shares in a particular firm are purchased if a dart hits the name of the firm.

When the Fisher and Lorie study first appeared, many individuals in the

FIGURE 9-3   Stock selection with a dart-tossing chimp. (From John Lane, *Business Week,* Nov. 3, 1973, McGraw-Hill, New York, p. 10.

financial community viewed it as implying that investors should buy dart boards instead of financial advice. Since dartboards are considerably cheaper than financial advice and worked so well (9.3% was considered to be a very good return), this was very threatening to investment advisers. As a result, a number of critical comments of the study were soon published. In addition, numerous cartoons featuring dart-tossing chimps, like the one in Figure 9-3, appeared in newspapers and magazines. But Fisher and Lorie had done their work competently, and such comments had little impact. Indeed, the financial community soon realized that there was a good point to the study, which they had at first overlooked. This point was that over a very long period of time, which covered the Great Depression, wars, booms, and recessions, people could have bought stocks and still made a very high return.

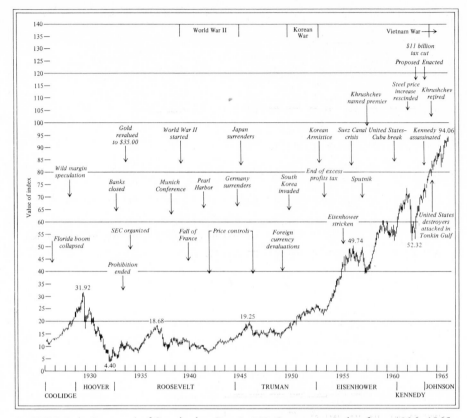

FIGURE 9-4   Portrayal of Standard & Poor's 500 Composite Index from 1926–1965.

Figure 9-4 portrays the S&P 500 Composite Index over the period 1926–1965. Under the portrayal, a description of major historical events has been written in. It seemed incredible that a person could have bought stocks just before the Depression and the terrible decline in stock prices which accompanied it and still have made a great deal of money by holding these stocks. Even more impressive were the post-World-War-II results. Stocks purchased at almost any time after the war had appreciated in very large amounts by the 1960s. In fact, the rates of return were so large (13 to 15%) and so consistent that it seemed like a new era had been ushered in.

With this information a broker could confidently tell her or his customers that all they had to do was buy stocks and they had a very good chance of becoming rich. Of course, there might be temporary downturns. But the important point seemed to be that if an investor were only patient, high returns and great wealth would some day be forthcoming. For example, by investing a single amount of $5,000 and earning 15% a year, a person would accumulate $81,830 by the end of 20 years or $1,339,315 by the end of 40 years. Of course, if some part of the person's salary were saved each year and invested in stocks, the re-

Top section — From years:

To	1/26	12/26	12/27	12/28	12/29	12/30	12/31	12/32	12/33	12/34	12/35	12/36	12/37	12/38	12/39	12/40	12/41	12/42	12/43	12/44
12/26	−1.6																			
12/27	15.3	(30.0)																		
12/28	23.9	37.7	(45.5)																	
12/29	7.8	9.6	0.1	−30.0																
12/30	−2.3	−3.5	−13.0	−31.7	−37.2															
12/31	−11.1	−13.5	−21.7	−36.3	−40.8	−47.8														
12/32	−11.0	−12.7	−19.0	−30.3	−32.1	−31.0	−11.1													
12/33	−2.7	−3.2	−7.7	−15.6	−11.8	−1.3	36.9	108.4												
12/34	−1.2	−1.6	−5.2	−11.3	−7.0	2.4	28.2	55.0	13.8											
12/35	2.2	2.1	−0.8	−5.7	−0.5	9.3	32.9	53.5	31.2	50.4										
12/36	6.6	5.5	3.1	−0.4	5.3	15.3	37.5	54.5	40.9	56.8	63.9									
12/37	0.5	0.1	−2.3	−6.2	−2.8	3.3	16.1	23.1	8.2	6.6	−10.9	−46.0								
12/38	2.8	2.5	0.4	−2.9	0.9	7.0	18.7	25.1	12.9	12.4	1.1	−16.2	30.7							
12/39	2.6	2.3	0.3	−2.6	0.9	6.0	15.7	20.5	10.1	9.0	0.4	−11.2	12.9	−3.3						
12/40	1.9	1.6	−0.2	−3.0	0.2	4.7	13.0	16.9	7.9	6.4	−1.1	−9.8	6.3	−5.0	−9.9					
12/41	1.2	0.9	−0.8	−3.3	−0.5	3.5	10.8	13.8	5.8	4.2	−1.9	−9.2	2.6	−5.5	−9.0	−10.2				
12/42	2.0	1.9	0.4	−1.9	0.9	4.8	11.6	14.3	7.2	6.0	0.9	−4.9	6.1	0.6	1.1	7.6	31.1			
12/43	3.5	3.6	2.2	0.2	3.1	7.2	13.8	16.5	10.2	9.7	5.5	0.9	12.3	9.4	12.1	22.2	47.1	56.7		
12/44	4.6	4.7	3.5	1.7	4.7	8.7	15.2	17.9	12.3	12.0	8.4	4.6	15.7	13.7	17.1	26.8	45.6	49.3	38.1	
12/45	6.3	6.5	5.5	3.9	7.0	11.3	17.6	20.4	15.4	15.5	12.4	9.3	20.3	19.4	23.7	33.6	51.4	55.4	50.1	59.8
12/46	5.5	5.7	4.7	3.2	6.0	9.9	15.6	18.0	13.3	13.1	10.2	7.2	16.3	15.0	17.8	24.2	34.8	34.5	26.0	20.2
12/47	5.3	5.6	4.6	3.1	5.8	9.3	14.6	16.8	12.4	12.1	9.4	6.7	14.7	13.6	15.5	20.3	27.5	26.3	18.9	13.2
12/48	5.1	5.2	4.2	2.8	5.2	8.5	13.5	15.5	11.3	11.0	8.4	5.8	12.7	11.7	13.3	17.0	22.5	20.8	14.2	9.1
12/49	5.7	5.8	4.9	3.6	6.0	9.1	13.8	15.7	11.7	11.5	9.1	6.8	13.3	12.3	13.9	17.3	22.2	20.8	15.2	11.4
12/50	6.3	6.7	5.9	4.6	7.0	10.2	14.9	16.7	12.9	12.8	10.6	8.5	14.8	14.1	15.6	19.0	23.5	22.4	17.9	15.0
12/51	6.9	7.1	6.4	5.1	7.5	10.6	15.1	16.7	13.1	13.1	11.0	9.0	14.8	14.1	15.6	18.6	22.6	21.6	17.7	15.2
12/52	7.0	7.2	6.5	5.3	7.6	10.5	14.8	16.4	13.0	13.0	11.0	9.0	14.5	13.8	15.1	17.9	21.5	20.4	16.8	14.5
12/53	6.6	6.8	6.1	5.0	7.1	9.8	13.9	15.3	12.2	12.1	10.2	8.3	13.3	12.5	13.7	16.1	19.3	18.1	14.8	12.5
12/54	8.0	8.2	7.6	6.4	8.7	11.4	15.5	17.0	14.0	14.1	12.2	10.5	15.5	14.8	16.2	18.7	21.9	21.0	18.2	16.4
12/55	8.4	8.6	8.0	6.9	9.2	11.9	15.9	17.4	14.5	14.6	12.7	11.1	15.9	15.2	16.6	18.8	21.8	21.1	18.6	16.9
12/56	8.5	8.7	8.1	7.0	9.2	11.8	15.7	17.1	14.4	14.4	12.6	11.1	15.6	15.1	16.2	18.2	20.8	20.2	17.9	16.4
12/57	7.8	7.9	7.3	6.3	8.3	10.7	14.3	15.5	12.9	12.9	11.2	9.7	13.9	13.2	14.2	15.9	18.3	17.5	15.1	13.6
12/58	8.8	9.0	8.4	7.5	9.5	11.9	15.5	16.7	14.3	14.4	12.7	11.3	15.5	15.0	16.0	17.8	20.2	19.4	17.3	16.0
12/59	8.9	9.1	8.5	7.6	9.7	12.1	15.6	16.8	14.4	14.5	12.8	11.5	15.6	15.0	16.0	17.6	19.9	19.1	17.1	15.8
12/60	8.8	9.0	8.3	7.5	9.4	11.6	14.9	16.1	13.9	13.9	12.3	11.1	14.8	14.2	15.1	16.6	18.7	17.9	15.9	14.6
12/61	9.3	9.5	8.9	8.9	9.9	12.2	15.4	16.6	14.4	14.5	13.0	11.8	15.4	15.0	15.8	17.3	19.3	18.5	16.5	15.4
12/62	8.6	8.8	8.2	7.3	9.1	11.2	14.3	15.3	13.2	13.3	11.8	10.7	14.0	13.5	14.3	15.6	17.3	16.5	14.6	13.5
12/63	8.9	9.1	8.5	7.7	9.5	11.6	14.6	15.6	13.5	13.6	12.2	11.1	14.3	13.8	14.6	15.8	17.4	16.7	14.9	13.9
12/64	9.1	9.3	8.8	7.9	9.6	11.6	14.5	15.6	13.6	13.7	12.4	11.3	14.4	14.0	14.7	15.8	17.4	16.7	15.0	14.0
12/65	9.3	9.5	9.0	8.2	10.0	12.0	14.9	15.9	13.9	14.0	12.6	11.6	14.6	14.2	14.9	16.0	17.5	16.9	15.4	14.4

Bottom section — From years:

To	12/45	12/46	12/47	12/48	12/49	12/50	12/51	12/52	12/53	12/54	12/55	12/56	12/57	12/58	12/59	12/60	12/61	12/62	12/63	12/64
12/46	−10.6																			
12/47	−4.9	−1.5																		
12/48	−3.8	−1.5	−4.0																	
12/49	1.6	5.1	7.6	18.0																
12/50	7.6	12.1	16.2	26.4	34.5															
12/51	9.2	13.1	16.1	22.8	24.6	13.8														
12/52	9.3	12.7	15.0	19.5	19.4	11.9	7.8													
12/53	7.7	10.3	11.9	14.8	13.4	7.1	2.9	−4.3												
12/54	12.4	15.4	17.6	21.1	21.4	17.6	18.1	22.2	53.2											
12/55	13.3	16.1	18.1	21.2	21.6	18.3	18.8	21.8	36.5	17.8										
12/56	13.2	15.5	17.1	19.7	19.8	16.8	16.7	18.3	26.3	12.8	5.4									
12/57	10.5	12.2	13.4	15.2	14.6	11.8	10.9	10.9	14.2	3.0	−4.2	−13.9								
12/58	13.2	15.1	16.6	18.6	18.5	16.4	16.3	17.3	21.6	14.2	12.6	16.8	56.1							
12/59	13.2	15.2	16.6	18.5	18.5	16.5	16.5	17.4	20.9	14.8	13.7	17.2	35.2	13.2						
12/60	12.2	13.9	15.1	16.7	16.4	14.7	14.7	15.2	17.6	12.2	11.0	12.8	21.4	5.8	−3.1					
12/61	13.1	14.8	16.0	17.4	17.2	15.9	15.9	16.5	18.8	14.4	13.3	15.9	23.3	13.2	12.3	26.2				
12/62	11.3	12.7	13.6	14.8	14.4	13.0	12.7	12.9	14.5	10.3	9.2	10.2	14.8	6.0	3.4	5.2	−14.4			
12/63	11.7	13.2	14.0	15.1	14.8	13.4	13.2	13.4	14.9	11.2	10.3	11.3	15.5	8.5	7.1	10.0	1.4	16.3		
12/64	12.0	13.4	14.1	15.2	15.0	13.6	13.4	13.7	15.2	11.8	11.1	12.2	16.0	10.2	9.4	12.5	7.2	17.8	15.0	
12/65	12.6	14.1	14.8	15.9	15.7	14.4	14.3	14.6	16.2	13.0	12.4	13.5	17.5	12.5	12.3	15.7	12.6	22.2	22.7	26.9

FIGURE 9-5 Rates of return on stocks from 1926 to 1965. (From Lawrence Fisher, and James H. Lorie, "Rates of Return on Investments in Common Stocks: The Year by Year Record 1926–1965," *Journal of Business,* © 1968 The University of Chicago Press, July 1968, pp. 296–297.)

turns would be even greater. An investment of only $1,000 every year at 15% would produce $117,810 in 20 years and $2,045,953 in 40 years.

These results are even more impressive because they were calculated after commission costs had been taken out. Actually there would be very few purchases and sales, since Fisher and Lorie assumed that once a stock was bought it was held. All the investor had to do was reinvest the dividends. Some of the results from the Fisher and Lorie study are given in Figure 9-5. The numbers along the top of the columns show the year-by-year rates of return.

For example, the annual rate of return for the year starting at the end of 1926 (12/26) and finishing at the end of 1927 (12/27) equaled 30.0%. The next year, the rate of return totaled −45.5%. Strangely enough the best year in the entire 40-year period was 1933. In the midst of the Depression, stocks rebounded by 108.4% (but remember, they increased from a very low base).

In order to find the annual compound rate of return over a longer period of time, the reader simply selects the intersection of a particular column and row in Figure 9-5. The 9.3 at the intersection of the 1/26 column with the 12/65 row indicates an annual compound rate of return equal to 9.3% for the period from January 1926 to December 1965.

Returns on Bonds

Corporate stocks account for a substantial part of the invested wealth of this country. But numerous institutions and individuals have large amounts of money in bonds and other fixed-income obligations, such as bank accounts, mortgages, and life insurance. How have these investors fared? Fisher and Weil have done a study of the rates of return on corporate bonds. Since the yields on these bonds are substantially greater than those on bank accounts and insurance policies and are about equal to those on mortgages, they provide a good indication of how well an investor could have done by buying and holding fixed-income obligations.

The methods used by Fisher and Weil to calculate the returns on bonds are considerably more complicated than those used for stocks. They assumed that investors always held a portfolio of the highest-grade 20-year bonds. After 1 year, 20-year bonds become 19-year bonds, which in turn become 18-year bonds after another year, etc. Eventually, they are redeemed at face value. For that reason, Fisher and Weil also had to assume that bondholders reinvested their money in 20-year bonds at the end of every year. The average annual compounded rate of return on a portfolio of the highest quality (AAA) corporate bonds was 3.7% for the period 1926–1965. This means that the growth rate of stocks was 5.6% higher than the growth rate of bonds over the same 40-year period.

Recent Returns on Stocks and Bonds

The Fisher and Lorie results end with 1965. Roger Ibbotson and Rex Sinquefield have just published rate-of-return figures on stocks and bonds for the period 1926–1976. Ibbotson is an assistant professor of finance at the University of Chicago and Sinquefield is a vice-president of the American National Bank and Trust Company of Chicago. Whereas Fisher and Lorie based their calculations on a random selection of stocks, Ibbotson and Sinquefield attempt to measure the performance of an average investor. The basic difference is that an average investor does not hold an equal dollar amount of each of the stocks listed on the NYSE. Since some companies are larger than others, this would be impossible to do. Instead, most investors have their money in IBM, GM, AT&T, or several of the 80 or 90 other companies which account for the largest part of the total market value of all stocks.

According to Ibbotson and Sinquefield, the average investor earned an annual compounded rate of return on stocks of 10.4% during the 40 years from 1926 to 1965 (this figure does not reflect commissions, which would have been very small). The annual compounded rate of return on stocks for the entire period from 1926 to 1976 equaled 9.2%. Viewed in another way, a $1 investment in stocks in 1926 had grown to $53.01 by the end of 1965. And by 1972, that $1 investment had grown in value to $84.96. It declined sharply to $53.30 at the end of 1974 and then jumped to $90.57 in 1976.

The Ibbotson-Sinquefield performance index of stocks is shown in Table 9-4, together with their performance indexes for bonds and Treasury bills. These performance indexes reflect both price changes and income and are based upon the assumption that all income is reinvested. There is a striking difference between the investment performance of stocks and bonds. The average annual compounded rate of return on bonds was only 3.9% for the period from 1926 to 1965, which is very close to the Fisher and Lorie estimates, and 4.1% for the

TABLE 9-4   IBBOTSON-SINQUEFIELD PERFORMANCE INDEXES FOR STOCKS AND CORPORATE BONDS, 1925–1976

End of Year	Common Stocks, $	Long-Term Corporate Bonds, $	U.S. Treasury Bills, $
1925	1.00	1.00	1.00
1926	1.12	1.07	1.03
1927	1.54	1.15	1.07
1928	2.20	1.19	1.10
1929	2.02	1.23	1.15
1930	1.52	1.32	1.18
1931	.86	1.30	1.19
1932	.79	1.44	1.20
1933	1.21	1.59	1.21
1934	12.0	1.81	1.21
1935	1.77	1.98	1.21
1936	2.37	2.12	1.21
1937	1.54	2.17	1.22
1938	2.02	2.31	1.22
1939	2.01	2.40	1.22
1940	1.81	2.48	1.22
1941	1.60	2.55	1.22
1942	1.93	2.61	1.22
1943	2.43	2.69	1.23
1944	2.91	2.82	1.23
1945	3.97	2.93	1.23
1946	3.65	2.98	1.24
1947	3.85	2.91	1.24
1948	4.07	3.03	1.25
1949	4.83	3.13	1.27
1950	6.36	3.20	1.28

Note: These indexes reflect both price changes and dividends. Each index is based upon an initial investment of $1.00 at the end of 1925.
Source: Roger G. Ibbotson, and Rex A. Sinquefield, *Stocks, Bonds, Bills, and Inflation: The Past (1926–1976) and the Future (1977–2000)*, Financial Analysts Research Foundation Monograph, 1977.

TABLE 9-4   (Continued)

End of Year	Common Stocks, $	Long-Term Corporate Bonds, $	U.S. Treasury Bills, $
1951	7.89	3.11	1.30
1952	9.34	3.22	1.32
1953	9.24	3.33	1.35
1954	14.11	3.51	1.36
1955	18.56	3.53	1.38
1956	19.78	3.29	1.42
1957	17.65	3.57	1.46
1958	25.30	3.49	1.48
1959	28.32	3.46	1.53
1960	28.46	3.77	1.57
1961	36.11	3.96	1.60
1962	32.96	4.27	1.64
1963	40.47	4.36	1.70
1964	47.14	4.57	1.75
1965	53.01	4.55	1.82
1966	47.67	4.56	1.91
1967	59.10	4.34	1.99
1968	65.64	4.45	2.09
1969	60.06	4.09	2.23
1970	62.47	4.84	2.38
1971	71.41	5.37	2.48
1972	84.96	5.76	2.58
1973	72.50	5.83	2.76
1974	53.30	5.65	2.98
1975	73.13	6.47	3.15
1976	90.57	7.68	3.31

period from 1926 to 1976. At 4.1% each year, the investor winds up with only $7.68 after 51 years for each $1 originally invested. In contrast to this, $1 invested in stocks was worth $90.57 at the end of 1976.

Ibbotson and Sinquefield also measured the performance of Treasury bills. A $1 investment in T-bills, with all interest reinvested, grew to $3.31 over this 51-year period.

REAL RETURNS ON STOCKS AND BONDS

How have investors fared in real terms over the years? Surprisingly few people ask this vital question, and fewer still know the answer.

Fortunately, Ibbotson and Sinquefield have provided some important insights into real returns. Not content to merely report the dollar results from investing in stocks, bonds, and Treasury bills, they also looked behind the monetary veil at real returns. What they found will shock most people.

What could a patient investor actually buy with money invested in 1926 after waiting 51 years? Not much if all of it were squirreled away in government bonds and bills. That initial $1 investment in T-bills grew to $3.31, but those new dollars purchased the equivalent of only one 1926 dollar. In other words, the investor gained nothing for 51 years of deprivation.

Of course, a true measure of a person's economic welfare must also take into consideration the taxes paid on all interest income over those years. Ibbotson and Sinquefield have not performed those calculations—perhaps because they want to avoid completely breaking the investor's spirit. Judging from their figures, it appears that anyone in a 30% or higher tax bracket for this entire period would have ended half a century with a considerable loss of funds.

Investors who purchased and held marketable long-term government bonds fared only slightly better. Very few small investors purchase marketable government bonds, concentrating instead on lower-paying and smaller-denomination savings bonds. Marketable government bonds are almost the exclusive territory of large sophisticated investors and financial institutions such as banks and insurance companies. A $1 investment in marketable government bonds increased to $5.44 over a 51-year holding period. But the purchasing power of this end-of-period wealth amounted to only $1.64. So the real return equaled only 1.0% a year.

Stocks performed much better in real terms than bonds or Treasury bills. Even after the disastrous decline of the Great Depression, the annual compounded real return on stocks totaled a healthy 6.9%. At that rate a $1 investment grows to $27.57 of real purchasing power over a 51-year period. And since much of the increase represents unrealized capital gains, the investor pays relatively low taxes on these returns.

Implications of Ibbotson-Sinquefield Study

The Ibbotson and Sinquefield study spans a very long period of time. By now most of the people old enough to have participated in the stock and bond markets in 1926 are seventy to eighty years old. But the Ibbotson-Sinquefield study is more than a performance record for septuagenarians and octogenarians with a passion for buying and holding investments. It presumably measures the rates of return available to today's investors.

Why look at 51 years of investor experience? Because actual returns for short periods of time seldom have much meaning, despite the emphasis sometimes given to them. The rates of return on stocks are a case in point. Investors unfortunate enough to have held stocks for the 10 years from 1929 through 1938 lost 0.8% a year. On the other hand, investors who purchased stocks at the end of 1938 and sold them 10 years later made 7.3% a year.

The Ibbotson-Sinquefield study also illustrates the dangers of concentrating on nominal rather than real returns. Judging from the past returns on Treasury bills, investors gained nothing from their frugality. These safety-conscious investors sacrificed all real return in order to avoid risk. This finding stands in stark contrast to the assumption made by many economists and investors that the real return on risk-free investments approximates 3%. Apparently the financial world pays only for risk bearing, and the reward varies directly with the amount of risk.

So ambitious investors seeking their fortunes must turn to stocks rather than T-bills and bonds. As a general rule, the return on stocks exceeds that on T-bills by about 6.7% a year.

RETURNS ON REAL ESTATE

So far, only the historical rates of return on a select group of stocks and bonds have been described. Ideally, the investor should compare the returns on stocks and bonds with the returns on other investments such as real estate, commodities, education, etc. However, detailed rates of return for long periods of time are not available for many of these other investment categories. Despite the importance of real estate, the returns on this type of investment are among the least documented. Because there is no central marketplace, it has been impossible until recently to obtain the actual sales prices of a large number of properties.

To some extent, the Department of Agriculture has avoided this problem by constructing an index based upon estimated farm values rather than market prices. Every 6 months the Department conducts a survey of its thousands of crop reporters and asks them to estimate the market value of farms in their areas. The estimates are used to compute an index of average value per acre of farmland. The values in this index for the 55-year period from March 1920 to March 1975 are shown in Figure 9-6. The Department of Agriculture farm-price index indicates that, contrary to public belief, real estate prices can and do go down at times. In particular, the average value of an acre of farmland fell by 59% during the 13-year period ending in 1933.

The farmland-price index has several shortcomings. The most obvious is that it is not based on actual prices. Another is that the estimated value of farm property includes buildings as well as land, so that a substantial part of the increase in value may be accounted for by new construction rather than by a true increase in farmland value. A third shortcoming is that the index does not include the rental income earned on farms. Annual rents have averaged about 3% of market value. According to one study, the annual compounded rate of return on farm properties (including rental income) for the 19-year period 1951–1969 works out to about 9.5% a year. However, the costs of buying and selling farmland were not considered in calculating this figure. Therefore, the true return was probably somewhat less than 9.5%.

The return on farmland is considerably less than the return of 12.5% which would have been earned by holding stocks during that same period. (According to Ibbotson and Sinquefield, stocks increased in value from $6.36 to $60.06 during 1951 to 1969. This is equivalent to an annual compounded rate of return of 12.5%.) At a 9.5% rate of growth, the value of an investment triples every 12 years. On the other hand, any investor who makes 12.5% every year for 12 years quadruples his money.

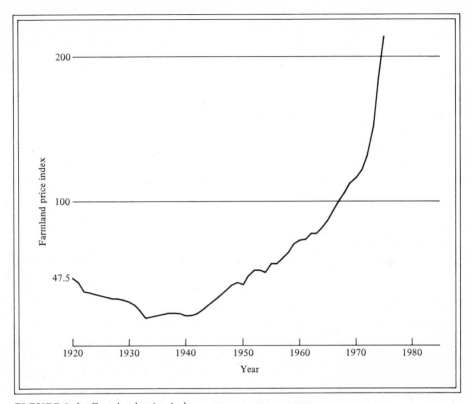

FIGURE 9-6   Farmland price index.

Homes

One of the first investments most people make is a down payment on a home. Despite the relatively large amount of money invested, apparently few home buyers think of their residences as an investment. According to one survey, only 5% of the homeowners in a particular area bought a home as an investment. The failure to consider the investment characteristics of homes is probably due in part to the lack of publicity about the returns from owning a home. A price index for homes can be computed for the period 1947–1976 by combining information from two different sources.

The information for 1963–1976 is published by the Bureau of the Census and is based on the actual market values of new single-family homes with essentially the same characteristics from year to year. The other prices were calculated from estimates of the market value of both new and old homes. In order to obtain a complete picture of the investment performance of homes, it would be necessary to obtain estimates of property taxes, insurance, maintenance, and repairs as well as the value of living in the home. Unfortunately, these figures are not avail-

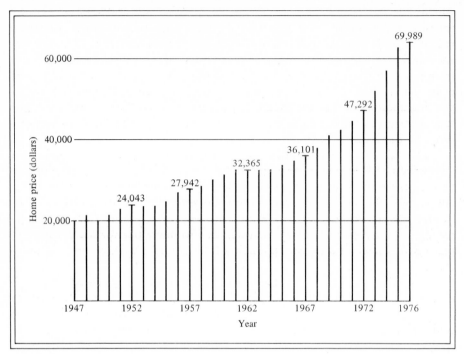

FIGURE 9-7   Home price index.

able. The price index for homes is shown in Figure 9-7. Judging from these figures, few people can expect to make enormous profits by buying homes. But there were several years in which homes increased in value by more than 10%. Given the small down payments which most people make on homes, a 10% return on the house price is often equivalent to a 50% return on their down payments.

RETURNS ON COMMODITY FUTURES

Stocks, bonds, and real estate are the traditional investments. However, commodity futures have been gaining increasing attention recently. Although some brokers claim the returns are very high, there is little evidence to substantiate this belief. Actually, commodity futures must provide a zero return on the average. A commodity futures contract is an agreement to buy or sell a commodity such as corn, wheat, or copper at a specified price in the future. Buyers and sellers of futures contracts simply exchange promises to buy and sell in the future—they do not really invest in a productive enterprise. The money that they are required to hold against a contract is only a small fraction of the value of the contract. It merely serves to guarantee that they will fulfill their contractual obligations.

There has been a long debate among academicians and practitioners about whether or not hedgers in commodities pay speculators to invest in futures contracts. According to one school of thought, hedgers pay speculators to assume the risk of possible price changes for them. In effect, speculators sell hedgers insurance against price changes. Suppose a speculator purchases a futures contract from a hedger. Since the speculator holds none of the commodity and has no plans to purchase any for future use, he or she experiences a profit or loss, depending upon which way the commodity price moves. For assuming this risk, the speculator presumably collects some payment from the hedger in the form of a profit on the futures contract.

The other school of thought is that hedgers pay speculators nothing for taking the opposite side of their transactions. They don't have to pay them anything because the wild price action in the commodities markets attracts speculators, even though the average returns are zero. These speculators view the futures trading market as a socially acceptable gambling casino. Instead of demanding compensation for risk bearing, they willingly pay for the privilege of playing the game. As time goes on, new arrivals replace the losers and the disenchanted.

A special survey by the Commodity Exchange Authority of traders in pork belly (sides of bacon) futures suggests that this is true of at least some types of commodities. On January 31, 1969, there were 5,835 traders who had bought or sold pork bellies. Out of these 5,835 traders, 5,772 declared themselves to be speculators and only 113 as hedgers. And the contracts held by speculators far outnumbered those held by hedgers. The speculators in pork bellies seem more interested in playing the game among themselves than they do in providing insurance to hedgers and being paid for their speculative services.

But the question remains: How much money do speculators make on their futures-trading activities? Here are some of the findings:

1   Blair Stewart, a consulting economist for the Commodity Exchange Authority, analyzed the complete trading records of 8,922 customers over the 9-year period 1924–1932. Traders were classified as either hedgers or speculators. Stewart concluded that the vast majority (75%) of speculators lost money. The most successful speculator traded only once during the 9-year period—he purchased contracts on corn, wheat, and rye in 1924 and made a profit of $300,000.

2   Thomas Hieronymus examined the trading records of customers at one brokerage firm for the single year 1969. Sixty-five percent of the 462 customers lost money during the year, and dollar losses (including very substantial commissions) of the group far exceeded gains.

3   Teweles, Harlow, and Stone studied customer accounts at another brokerage house for a 10-year period. On the average only 1 in 4 traders made money.

4   Charles Rockwell, an economist with the Food Research Institute, sifted through 7,900 semimonthly observations on 25 different commodities for the period 1947–1966. According to Rockwell, speculators as a group netted more than $175 million during the 18 years. But Rockwell completely ig-

nored commissions, which could easily have exceeded the profits on the contracts.

5   The most recent study, completed by Katherine Dusak while she was a doctoral student at the University of Chicago, measured both the risk and return on futures. According to Dusak, the returns are zero (again ignoring commissions). But the betas are also zero, implying that commodity futures add little to the risk of a large, well-diversified portfolio.

RETURNS ON ART

Most people purchase stocks, bonds, real estate, and commodities solely for income or a hoped-for increase in value. For those individuals who want to indulge their aesthetic tastes as well as pursue profits, art provides an excellent investment. And the returns can be very high. A price index published by *The London Times* and by Sotheby's, one of the world's largest auction houses, is shown in Table 9-5. In the period 1950–1969, the Dow Jones Industrial Average tripled. During that same time, the average price of an old master print soared upward by 39 times. The worst-performing art object on the *Times* list was English porcelain, which quadrupled in value.

The *Times*-Sotheby index spans only a 20-year period. But Richard Rush, an investment banker and art collector, has carefully compiled an art-price index for the years from 1925 to 1960. As Rush points out, computing a price index for art is much more difficult than for stocks. There are three reasons for this: (1) artists' works far outnumber listed stocks; (2) shares of a company's stock are identical, whereas no two paintings by the same artist are exactly comparable; and (3) the market for paintings is imperfect, so that market prices are difficult to establish. Despite these difficulties, Rush was able to calculate a price index for interna-

TABLE 9-5   TIMES-*SOTHEBY ART INDEX*

	Number of Times the Price Index Multiplied, 1950–1969
Dow Jones Industrial Index	3
Old master prints	37
Modern pictures	29
Chinese porcelain	24$1/2$
Old books	13
Modern books	9
Old master drawings	22
Impressionist pictures	18
Old master pictures	7
English glass	9
French furniture	5
English porcelain	4
English pictures	10$1/2$
English silver	8$1/2$

Source: Lee Berton, "Art as Investment Outpaces Stocks," *Financial World,* May 23, 1973, p. 22.

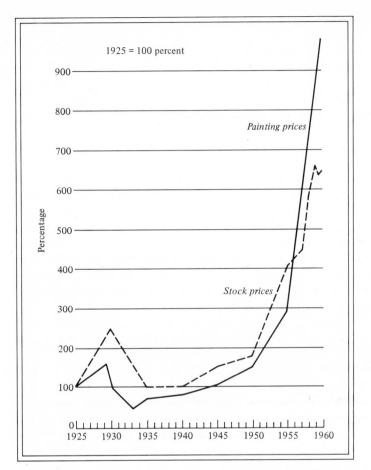

1925 = 100 percent

FIGURE 9-8 International art prices compared with stock prices. (From *Art as an Investment* by Richard H. Rush, © 1961 by Richard H. Rush. Published by Prentice-Hall, Inc., Englewood Cliffs, New Jersey, p. 385.)

tional art. This index does not represent the vast majority of paintings, since most paintings are of only national or local interest and sell for under several thousand dollars. Rush's international art index is compared with a stock-price index in Figure 9-8.

Art and stock prices seem to move very closely together, but art prices considerably outpaced stocks in the 5 years from 1955 to 1960. And the *Times*-Sotheby index indicates that they continued to do so in the decade of the 1960s. But the comparison is somewhat unfair. Stocks pay dividends, whereas art provides no monetary income. According to Fisher and Lorie, more than half the returns on stocks come from dividends. These dividends are not included in the stock price index. There are also large costs in selling art, and there are storage and insurance fees. These costs are not reflected in Rush's index.

Finally, there seems to be a serious bias in art-price indexes in that they reflect only the art objects which have performed the best. For instance, Rush eliminated nineteenth-century British art from his index, since it had declined in price to a very low point. And he put a heavy weight on modern art, since that school of art has become extremely important in dollar sales. If the same approach were taken with stock indexes, it would result in stocks like IBM being given a very heavy weight, which would in turn produce much higher values in the stock-price index. In the period 1950–1969, IBM, one of the largest United States corporations, increased in value by 49 times, considerably more than old master prints. And this figure does not include any of the dividends paid to shareholders.

All things considered, the monetary return on collectors' items, such as art, coins, stamps, and antique cars, should be less than that on ordinary investments, such as stocks. The reason for this is a familiar one—competition. Collectors' items provide a psychic income as well as the possibility of an increase in value. Stocks provide only a monetary return. If the dividends and price appreciation on stocks didn't exceed the price appreciation on paintings, most investors would buy paintings. After all, if both paintings and stocks provided a 10% return, most people would prefer to have a painting hanging on a wall rather than a stock certificate sitting in a safe-deposit box.

RELATIONSHIP BETWEEN RISK AND RETURN

The average annual compounded rate of return on a portfolio of high-grade corporate bonds was 4.1% for the period 1926–1976. The average return on an investment in a random selection of stocks traded on the New York Stock Exchange was 9.2% per year during the same period. That is a difference of 5.1% a year over an identical 51-year period. At these rates of return an investor who bought $1,000 of bonds and reinvested all interest payments over the year would have accumulated $7,681. If instead the investor had bought $1,000 of stock and reinvested the dividends, $90,567 would have been available at the end of the 51 years. There has to be some explanation for a difference of this magnitude.

Probably the most convincing explanation is that investors don't have the advantage of hindsight but must instead rely on intuition. No investor could be certain that stocks would return 9.2% and bonds 4.1%. In fact, during that 51-year period there was one year when stocks declined by 47.8%, and there was another when they were down by 46%.

Moreover, numerous stocks fared still worse than the overall market. Many firms went bankrupt. On the other hand, the overall return on bonds was never less than −9.2% in any one year. Of course, there were also extremely good years in the stock market, even during the Great Depression. In 1933, the stock market rebounded by 108.4%, and in 1936, it was up by 63.9%. There were also gains of 53.2% in 1954 and 56.1% in 1958. Again, the returns on certain stocks often far outpaced the market. Bonds never came close to matching these returns: the best year for bonds was 1934, when they returned 15.3%.

Stocks obviously differ from bonds in one very important respect—the returns on stocks fluctuate much more than those on bonds. There is a reason for this. Bondholders are promised a fixed amount of interest each year. If the interest is not paid, they can force the company into bankruptcy. In addition, most bonds have a definite maturity date, at which time the company must redeem the bonds for their full face value. Again, if the company fails to do this, the bondholders can force it into bankruptcy. Shareholders are more exposed to the vagaries of the business world. They have a claim on company earnings, but these earnings are only what is left after all company costs, including the interest on its bonds, have been paid. Moreover, the shareholders have the last claim on the assets of the firm. If a firm goes bankrupt, the government, bondholders, and other creditors are paid off first, and then the shareholders receive whatever is left.

Risk and Return—Stocks

Most investors appear to dislike uncertainty. They want to know what their investments will be worth next week, next year, etc. For this reason, they demand a higher return on more risky investments, if they will even take on such investments. As a result, the rule when investing sizable amounts of money seems to be: the greater the risk, the greater the expected return. Numerous studies of investments have shown that this relationship holds true. For example, in one study by Sharpe and Cooper stocks were grouped according to their betas and the average annual return on each group of stocks was computed. The results are shown in Figure 9-9.

Each group contains 10% of the stocks listed on the New York Stock Exchange from 1931 to 1967. Group 1 contains the 10% of the stocks with the lowest betas (companies like Abbott Labs, Homestake Mining, and Minnesota Power and Light) and Group 10 consists of the 10% with the highest betas (companies like Bell & Howell, Braniff Airways, and Eastern Airlines). The average annual return (not the annual compounded rates of return) on the most risky stocks traded on the NYSE was 22.7% during this 36-year period—nearly twice the 11.6% that could have been earned by buying a portfolio of the least risky stocks. There also appears to be a close relationship between the risk of each group and the average return of the stocks in that group. In general, the riskier the stocks, the higher the average return, but the relationship does not hold exactly true.

Risk and Return—Bonds

The same is true of bonds. Bonds are rated by Moody's and by Standard and Poor's. Judging from their wide acceptance, these ratings have proven to be a good indication of the riskiness of bonds. The lower the ratings assigned by these agencies, the better the chance that the company issuing the bond will default on payments of interest or will fail to repay the loan. The average returns actually

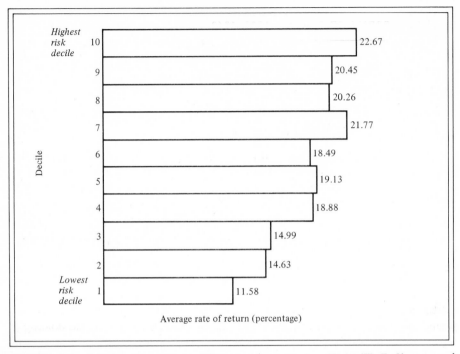

FIGURE 9-9   Returns on stocks in different risk categories. (From W. F. Sharpe, and G. M. Cooper, "Risk-Return Classes of NYSE Common Stocks, 1931–1967," *Financial Analysts Journal,* March-April 1972, p. 51.)

realized on different categories of bonds during the period from 1900 to 1943 are given in Table 9-6.

Ibbotson and Sinquefield have presented newer evidence which supports these findings. They compare the returns on the highest-grade long-term corporate bonds with those on long-term government bonds and on U.S. Treasury bills. The government obligations are less risky than the corporate bonds. And since Treasury bills mature in 3 to 6 months, they are less risky than long-term government bonds. For that reason one would suspect that the return from holding Treasury bills would be lower than that on long-term government bonds and that the return on government bonds would be lower than that on long-term corporate bonds.

In fact the annual compounded rate of return during the period 1926–1976 was 2.4% for Treasury bills, 3.4% on long-term government bonds, and 4.1% on long-term corporate bonds—exactly as predicted. Investors who maintained a continuous investment in T-bills from 1926 to 1976 tripled their money. On the other hand, those who invested in long-term corporate bonds multiplied their money by a factor of eight. This is a remarkably large difference, considering the fact that not one single company whose bonds were rated the highest quality has defaulted in the last 20 years. It serves to emphasize the importance that investors attached to the possibility of loss.

TABLE 9-6 ANNUAL COMPOUNDED RATES OF RETURN ON DIFFERENT RISK CATEGORIES OF BONDS,* 1900–1943

Rating	Return, %	Amount of All Issues of Bonds in Billions of Dollars
9 (least risky)	5.1	6,482
8	5.0	10,809
7	5.0	11,813
6	5.7	8,955
5	5.6	3,748
4	9.2	811
3	23.4	467
2	} 28.1	} 210
1 (most risky)		

* Includes railroad, public utility, and industrial bonds.
Source: W. Braddock Hickman, *Statistical Measures of Corporate Bond Financing since 1900,* National Bureau of Economic Research, New York, 1960, p. 394.

Differences in the riskiness of bonds also result in differences in the yields to maturity that are available on bonds. The yield to maturity is the annual compounded rate of return which can be earned by purchasing a bond and holding it until it matures. At the end of September 1975, the average yield to maturity on the four highest quality categories of bonds were 8.95, 9.10, 9.74, and 10.38%. Any investor purchasing a bond on that date could have earned nearly $1^1/2\%$ more each year on the higher-risk bonds. Since these bonds don't mature for 20 or 30 years, that is a sizable difference. It exists because the lower the grade of the bond, the greater the risk that the company issuing the bond will someday default on the interest or principle. However, this risk is very small for any bond ranked in the top four categories.

Risk and Return—Real Estate

Apparently real estate is no different from stocks and bonds—the riskier the real estate investment, the higher the return that can be expected. Maury Seldin and Richard Swesnik, the authors of a well-known book on real estate, have declared that it is not unreasonable to expect the following results from investing in different types of real estate:[1]

1   A tripling of the investor's money in eight to twelve years in garden apartments—a growth rate of $9^1/2\%$ to 15% a year.
2   A quadrupling in eight to twelve years in high rise apartments—a growth rate of $12^1/2\%$ to 19% each year.
3   A quintupling in eight to twelve years in office buildings—a growth rate of $14^1/2\%$ to $22^1/2\%$ a year.
4   A quadrupling in five to seven years in shopping center investments—a growth rate of 22% to $32^1/2\%$ a year.
5   A tripling in three years in land investment—a growth rate of 45% each year.

By now it will come as no surprise that land investment is considered to be very speculative, whereas garden apartments are considered to be a low-risk investment.

According to Seldin and Swesnik, the return on low-risk garden apartments supposedly averages between $9^1/_2$ and 15% a year. The return on land, which is usually a very high-risk investment, is presumably about 45% a year. These projected real estate returns are considerably in excess of the historical returns reported in this chapter. They illustrate the ease with which even reputable investment advisers fall into the trap of quoting unrealistic rates of return. Seldin and Swesnik probably based their estimates upon the following assumptions:

1   Real estate is financed mostly with borrowed money. The historical returns reported earlier in this chapter were on the total investment, not just the investor's own money. Borrowed money not only increases the expected returns on the investor's own money, it also increases the risk.
2   The high growth rates realized on real estate in the early 1970s would continue in the future. When real estate prices soared between 1970 and 1974, some investors realized returns on their money equal to or greater than those cited by Seldin and Swesnik.

The real estate story has an unhappy ending. Widespread claims of high returns lured many investors into highly leveraged projects. When real estate prices stagnated in late 1974, many of these investors awoke to find their money gone.

Risk and Return—Consumer Loans

So far only the risk-return relationship for investments has been summarized. But perhaps the most striking comparison between risks and returns is displayed in consumer loans. The type of collateral offered by a borrower greatly affects the riskiness of the loan. For example, most lenders view a loan which is secured by marketable securities as being the least risky. If a borrower doesn't meet the terms of the loan, the securities can be easily sold at a well-defined price. Home loans which are backed by a down payment and a deed to the property have the next lowest risk. Then come new-car loans, mobile-home loans, consumer-goods loans, personal loans, and credit-card loans. In April 1973, banks were charging 8.5% for loans on stocks and bonds, 9.25% for home loans, 10.04% for new-car loans, 12.74% for personal loans, and 17.19% for credit-card loans. At the same time, many borrowers with low credit ratings had to rely upon finance companies instead of banks. These people paid much higher rates in April: 11.88% on new-car loans, 16.44% on used-car loans, and nearly 21% on personal loans. Consumers paying 21% a year for their loans lose a tremendous amount of money—a dollar invested at 21% a year multiplies tenfold in 12 years.

Application of the Risk and Return Relationship

Almost all the studies to date confirm that there is a positive relationship between risk and return, i.e., the greater the risk of the investment, the greater the return. But that does not mean that every investor is assured of making a high return on a high-risk investment. Obviously, the investment would not be risky if that were the case! Nor does it mean that investors can purchase risky investments and by holding on to them for a long time ensure themselves of high returns.

Many investors have deluded themselves into believing that this is the implication of the Fisher and Lorie study on rates of return on stocks, which concluded that investors who held stocks for 40 years earned an average return of 9.3%. But that does not mean that the next 40 years will produce the same results in the stock market or even that there will be a stock market in 40 years. After all, history has shown that no country remains prosperous and successful forever. And investment returns have varied dramatically from country to country. This can be seen by referring to Table 9-7, which shows the average rates of return on the common stocks of 28 countries during the 19-year period 1951–1969.

There is one qualification to the general rule that the greater the risk of the investment, the higher the potential return. Individuals are compensated only for taking on risk which cannot be avoided. For that reason, every investor should attempt to eliminate unnecessary risk by the proper diversification of investments.

Given the fundamental relationship between risk and return, it is important that the investor be able to determine the riskiness of an investment. There is one very simple rule for judging the degree of risk (the techniques for doing this are the subject of earlier chapters). If the promised or prospective return is high, the

TABLE 9-7   AVERAGE RATES OF RETURN ON COMMON STOCKS OF 28 SELECTED COUNTRIES, 1951–1969

Country	Rate of Return, %	Country	Rate of Return, %
Australia	5.0	Mexico	17.4
Austria	14.5	Netherlands	19.0
Belgium	3.6	New Zealand	14.7
Canada	8.4	Norway	12.5
Ceylon	−0.2	Peru	12.1
Chile	3.8	Philippines	39.4
Denmark	5.4	Portugal	17.7
Finland	9.5	South Africa	19.0
France	8.6	Spain	17.2
Germany	17.1	Sweden	12.8
India	0.1	Switzerland	21.0
Israel	3.5	United Kingdom	15.9
Italy	10.6	United States	11.6
Japan	17.9	Venezuela	15.8

Source: Reprinted from Haim Levy and Marshall Sarnat, *Investment & Portfolio Analysis,* Wiley, New York, 1972, p. 532.

risk is probably also high. Unfortunately, the investor's desire for a large profit too often results in overlooking the risk associated with making that profit.

IMPLICATIONS FOR INVESTMENT STRATEGY

Investors face a trade-off between risk and return. As a rule, the greater the risk of an investment, the higher the return which can be expected. But there is always the possibility that a substantial amount of money will be lost. The more risky the investment, the more likely is the loss. For that reason, every investor must decide what risks he or she is willing to accept. Long ago, Baron Rothschild advised prospective investors to first decide whether they wanted to eat well or sleep well. Rothschild's advice is still appropriate today. Potential millionaires should accept the fact that they will probably never sleep well until they have made their millions.

An individual's investment strategy is based upon a desired combination of risk and return. Investors who want to earn high returns and are willing to accept the accompanying risks should invest in stocks, land, and art. If past returns are an indication of the future, they can expect to triple their money every 8 to 12 years. But there will be many times when these expectations fail to materialize. The investments markets, like Mother Nature, can be extremely fickle.

On the other hand, investors seeking safety should invest in fixed-income obligations such as bonds, bank accounts, and insurance. However, judging from past results, they can look forward to little real growth in the value of their investments.

KEYWORDS

paper losses
compounded rates of return
geometric rates of return
rule of 69

QUESTIONS

1 Discuss the following statement: "I bought Polaroid at $180 a share. Now it's at $40. But since I still own it, I really haven't lost any money."
2 Calculate the annual rates of return on the following stocks:

Year	Year-End Price, $	Dividend, $
1	20	1
2	25	1
3	22	1

3   What is the average annual compounded rate of return for the stock described in question 2? (Assume the price of the stock at the start of year 1 was $19.)

4   How long does it take to quadruple your money (doubling it twice) if the annual rate of return equals 5, 10, 15, or 20%?

5   Why did the Fisher-Lorie study on rates of return create so much controversy?

6   Discuss the following statement from a sales brochure, "Coin prices increased by 100% during the last four years. Therefore, we expect similar gains in the future."

7   Average returns on high-grade bonds differ by how much from the returns on stocks traded on the NYSE?

8   Discuss the following statement: Judging from the Ibbotson-Sinquefield results, the real return for simple frugality is zero. And once taxes are considered, the real return is less than zero.

9   Myths about the returns on real estate abound, probably because of the dearth of published sales prices. What return can investors reasonably expect to earn on land?

10   During the last 40 to 50 years, bonds returned from 3 to 4% a year and stocks from 9 to 10%. But now bonds offer 9 to 10%. Should stockholders still expect to earn only 9 to 10%? Why or why not? What accounts for the change?

11   According to one school of thought, hedgers pay commodity futures speculators to assume risk. According to another, speculators happily settle for zero or negative returns just for the chance to participate in a socially acceptable form of gambling. Which view do you think is correct?

12   Some of the long-run returns on art look simply fantastic. But are these returns realistic estimates?

13   Rank the following investments by their expected returns: stocks, high-grade corporate bonds, Treasury bills, options (buying and selling), land, homes, apartment properties, art, antiques, commodity futures, bank accounts. (Not all these investments were discussed in this chapter.)

14   Now rank these same investments by risk.

15   By how much do the average returns on different risk categories of stocks differ over the long run?

16   Check the current yield spreads on the four highest-quality categories of bonds in Standard and Poor's or Moody's. What accounts for the difference?

17   Rank the various consumer loans by their cost to the borrower. Devise a borrowing strategy based upon these differences in rates.

18   Your brother asks you for advice on investing $2,000 in stocks. During the course of the conversation, you find out that he owes $2,000 on a credit card. What course of action do you recommend to him? (Hint: Compare the expected returns on stocks with the cost of borrowing money on credit cards.)

19   Actual returns often deviate from expected returns. For example, investors holding stocks from 1972 to 1976 realized an annual rate of return of only 3%. In the light of results like these, discuss the meaning of the words "expected return."

REFERENCES

Bergstrom, Gary L.: "A New Route to Higher Returns and Lower Risks," *Journal of Portfolio Management,* Fall 1975, pp. 30–38.

Berton, Lee: "Art as Investment Outpaces Stocks," *Financial World,* May 23, 1973, pp. 22ff.

Bhatia, K. B.: "A Price Index for Nonfarm One-Family Houses, 1947–1964," *Journal of the American Statistical Association,* March 1971, pp. 23–32.

Durkin, Thomas A.: "Consumer Awareness of Credit Terms: Review and New Evidence," *Journal of Business,* April 1975, pp. 253–263.

Dusak, Katherine: "Futures Trading and Investor Returns: An Investigation of Commodity Market Risk Premiums," *Journal of Political Economy,* November/December 1973, pp. 1387–1406.

Ehrbar, A. F., ed.: "The Long-Term Case for Stocks," *Fortune,* December 1974, pp. 97, 100, 102.

Fisher, Lawrence, and James H. Lorie: "Rates of Return on Investments in Common Stock: The Year by Year Record, 1926–65," *Journal of Business,* July 1968, pp. 291–316.

———, and Roman Weil: "Coping with the Risk of Interest Rate Fluctuations: Returns to Bondholders from Naive and Optimal Strategies," *Journal of Business,* October 1970, pp. 408–431.

Gould, John P., and Roman L. Weil: "The Rule of 69," *Journal of Business,* July 1974, pp. 397–398.

Hickman, Braddock: *Corporate Bond Quality and Investor Experience,* National Bureau of Economic Research, New York, 1958.

———: *Statistical Measures of Corporate Bond Financing Since 1900,* National Bureau of Economic Research, New York, 1960.

Hieronymus, Thomas A.: *Economics of Futures Trading,* Commodity Research Bureau, New York, 1971.

*Ibbotson, Roger G., and Rex A. Sinquefield: "Stocks, Bonds, Bills, and Inflation: Year-by-Year Historical Returns (1926–1974)," *Journal of Business,* January 1976, pp. 11–47.

*———: *Stocks, Bonds, Bills, and Inflation: The Past (1926–1976) and the Future (1977–2000),* Financial Analysts Research Foundation Monograph, 1977.

Levy, Haim, and Marshall Sarnat: *Investment and Portfolio Analysis,* Wiley, New York, 1972.

Ricks, R. Bruce: "Imputed Equity Returns on Real Estate Financed with Life Insurance Company Loans," *Journal of Finance,* December 1969, pp. 921–937.

Rockwell, Charles S.: "Normal Backwardation, Forecasting, and Returns to Commodity Futures Traders," *Food Research Institute Studies,* supplement, 1967, pp. 107–130.

*Roulac, Stephen E.: "Can Real Estate Returns Outperform Common Stocks?" *Journal of Portfolio Management,* Winter 1976, pp. 26–43.

Rush, Richard: *Art as an Investment,* Prentice-Hall, Englewood Cliffs, N.J., 1961.

———: "You Can Still Afford an Old Master," *The Wall Street Transcript,* Dec. 17, 1973, pp. 35, 329ff.

Seldin, Maury, and Richard Swesnik: *Real Estate Investment Strategy,* Wiley-Interscience, New York, 1970.

Sharpe, William F., and Guy M. Cooper: "Risk-Return Classes of New York Stock Exchange Common Stocks, 1931–1967," *Financial Analysts Journal,* March–April 1972, pp. 46–54, 81.

Stewart, Blair: *An Analysis of Speculative Trading in Grain Futures,* U.S. Department of Agriculture, Technical Bulletin No. 1001, October 1949.

Teweles, Richard J., Charles V. Harlow, and Herbert L. Stone: *The Commodity Futures Game: Who Wins? Who Loses? Why?* McGraw-Hill, New York, 1974.

* Publications preceded by an asterisk are highly recommended.

CHAPTER TEN

VALUATION

Deciding how much an investment is worth is a difficult task. And yet every investor must eventually make this decision. The question is, How?

One way to determine value is simply to find out the going price. To some extent, the old saying that something is worth whatever a person will pay for it is true. When an investment is traded in an efficient market, this adage gains even more validity. But it still does not provide any explanation of why an investor is willing to pay a particular price for a specific investment.

MONEY NOW VERSUS MONEY LATER

By definition, every **asset** is expected to provide some kind of income or benefit in the future, even though it may never actually fulfill this expectation. Stocks pay dividends, bonds pay interest, homes provide shelter and perhaps status and psychological gratification, apartment buildings yield rent to their owners, art kindles certain aesthetic feelings, etc. Even with this short list it can be seen that the income or benefits provided by an asset can be primarily monetary, such as dividends and interest, or largely nonmonetary. Usually nonmonetary benefits can be converted into monetary terms. For instance a home can be rented at a well-defined monthly cost as easily as it can be purchased. Putting a price tag on a fine collection of paintings available for private viewing and showing to friends is more difficult, but the benefits are real nonetheless and can be determined if necessary.

Since an asset provides income and/or other benefits, it might seem logical to conclude that the value of an asset is equal to the sum of all income or benefits it is expected to provide in the future. This conclusion would be correct if it weren't for two complications. The first is the **time value of money**—a dollar received today is worth more than a dollar received tomorrow. The second complication is uncertainty about the receipt of future dollars.

The most straightforward reason why a dollar today is worth more than a dollar tomorrow is that money can be invested to earn interest. The longer the money is kept invested, the more interest accumulates. At 5% interest per year $1 put aside today will grow to $2.65 in 20 years. So anyone who gives up $1 now in exchange for only $1 in 20 years is shortchanged by $1.65.

Some economists and psychologists have tried to provide another explanation of why a dollar today is worth more than a dollar in the future. They have called this reason **time preference** and have asserted that most people would prefer to spend money now rather than later. Although this thinking may be consistent with some people's feelings, it seems more reasonable to assume that the average person would prefer to spread expenditures evenly over time and thus avoid spending too much now at the cost of having too little to spend in the future.

Aside from the time value of money, there is another reason why an investment is not worth the sum of all its future income or benefits. At least some of these receipts are uncertain. They may never be collected or perhaps only some part of the money will be received. In general, people dislike uncertainty about the future and seem willing to pay to avoid it. Many will eagerly trade a stock that is expected to pay a dividend of $1 a year for a bond which pays only $.80 because the $.80 is much more likely to be received than the $1. And these same people will probably trade the bond for a bank account which guarantees them only $.60 a year, again because the payment is even more certain than payment from a bond.

TIME VALUE OF MONEY

Investment decisions usually involve a choice between dollars at different points in time. Students pursue graduate degrees at a considerable sacrifice in present income in the hopes of higher future incomes. Taxpayers eagerly seek out tax shelters in an attempt to defer taxes to a later date. Businesspeople risk their life savings on new products for the chance of receiving large profits in the future.

Families budget part of their earnings for insurance against a possible loss in later years. And workers plan for their retirement by saving some money.

Somehow every investor must decide which combination of present and future incomes provides the greatest satisfaction. This decision-making process is complicated by the fact that savings usually earn interest. As a result, a dollar now is worth more than a dollar in the future. Present- or future-value techniques make it possible for people to explicitly incorporate this time value of money into their investment decisions.

With the **present-value concept,** all sums of money are brought back to the present. With the **future-value concept,** all sums are carried forward to the same point in the future. Either way, all sums of money are translated into dollars at a single point in time.

Future-Value Concept

Future values are simpler to understand than present values. Suppose an investor wants to find out how much an investment will be worth at some date in the future. When the future is considered to be only 1 year away, the answer can be found by first determining how much $1 invested at different rates of interest is worth after 1 year. Invested for a year at 10%, $1 earns $.10 interest, so the year-end value is $1.10—the initial investment of $1 plus interest of $.10. Invested at 5% for a year, $1 earns only $.05 interest; so the year-end value is $1.05. The beginning (present) and ending (future) values for a $1 investment at 10 and 5%, and also for rates of 4, 3, 2, and 1% are shown in Table 10-1.

Table 10-1 is a future-value table. It shows the value at the end of a year of $1 invested at different rates of interest. This value is simply equal to 1 plus the interest rate expressed in decimal form. Once the future value of a $1 investment is known, the future value of any other amount of money can easily be found by just multiplying the future value of $1 by the amount invested. For example, an investor who sets aside $500 at 3% will have $500 × $1.03, or $515, at the end of 1 year.

TABLE 10-1   VALUES OF $1 IN 1 YEAR INVESTED
AT DIFFERENT INTEREST RATES

Beginning Value, $	Interest Rate, %	Interest on $1	Ending Value, $
1	1	.01	1.01
1	2	.02	1.02
1	3	.03	1.03
1	4	.04	1.04
1	5	.05	1.05
1	10	.10	1.10

The following examples may be helpful in understanding future-value concepts:

Question: An investor sets aside $800 in a bank account and earns 8% a year on the savings. How much is in the account at the end of 1 year?

Answer: At 8% a year, $1 grows to $1.08. Therefore, $800 grows to $864 ($800 × 1.08).

Question: An individual obtains a personal loan for $2,000. The interest rate on the loan is 18% a year, and the loan and interest must be paid in full at the end of 1 year. How much money must be repaid to the lender?

Answer: At 18% a year, $1 grows to $1.18. Therefore $2,000 invested now would accumulate to $2,360 ($2,000 × 1.18) in 1 year . This is the amount that must be repaid.

Present-Value Concept

The present value of any sum of money that is paid out or received in the future can be found by answering the following question. Given a particular rate of interest, how much money must be invested right now in order to grow to a specific amount in the future? When the interest rate is 10% a year, $1 invested now will be worth exactly $1.10 in 1 year. Therefore, the present value of $1.10 in 1 year, given a 10% rate of interest, is $1. Investors who accept this 10% rate of interest as a fair measure of their investment opportunities will not care whether they receive $1 immediately or wait 1 year for $1.10.

In order to determine the present value of any future amount of money, a specific rate of interest must be used. Usually the interest rate selected is the best available rate which the investor can earn. The lower the interest rate a person can earn, the higher the present value of a future dollar. At first this may seem paradoxical. But the lower the interest rate, the less the interest sacrificed by waiting for the money. If the rate is 10%, an investment of $.91 together with the $.09 interest will total $1 at the end of the year. Therefore, the investor should be willing to trade $.91 today for $1 a year from now; i.e., the present value of $1 which will be received 1 year from now is $.91.

On the other hand, if the rate of return is 4%, approximately $.96 must be invested in order to have $1 at the end of the year. So the present value of $1 received in 1 year is $.96—only $.04 is earned by waiting for the money for 1 year.

As the rates of return become lower and lower, the present value of $1 a year from now becomes higher and higher. Finally, at a zero rate of interest, $1 received in 1 year has a present value of $1. Since no interest can be earned on money that is invested, $1 invested today will be worth only $1 in 1 year.

The impact of interest rates on present values can be shown as follows:

Annual Interest Rate, %	Present Value, $	Value in 1 Year, $
10	.91	1.00
8	.93	1.00
6	.94	1.00
4	.96	1.00
0	1.00	1.00

The present value of $1 received in 1 year is equal to $1 divided by 1 plus the interest rate. Therefore, high interest rates produce low present values, and low interest rates produce high present values.

The following example may be helpful in understanding present- and future-value concepts:

Question: An individual has a choice between receiving either $10,000 immediately or $12,000 in 1 year's time. If 10% can be earned on the $10,000, which of the two alternatives should be selected?

Answer: Comparing dollars received or paid out at different points in time is like comparing apples with oranges—do 10 apples equal 10 oranges? By the same token, $1 today is different from $1 a year from now. The difference between the two is measured by the amount of interest that can be earned on $1 today.   *TV = 10,000*

The present- and future-value concepts make it possible to compare sums of money at various points in time. With the present-value concept, all sums of money are brought back to the present. With the future-value concept, all sums are carried forward to the same point in the future. Either way, all sums of money are translated into dollars at a single point in time.

First, let's evaluate $10,000 now versus $12,000 in 1 year using the future-value method. The future value of $1 at 10% for 1 year is $1.10. Therefore, the value of $10,000 in 1 year from now is $11,000 ($10,000 × $1.10). This $11,000 value can be compared directly with the promise of $12,000 in 1 year. Viewed in this light, the individual is obviously better off waiting for 1 year to receive $12,000 than taking the $10,000 immediately.

Second, let's evaluate $10,000 now versus $12,000 in 1 year using the present-value technique. The present value of $1 received 1 year from now is simply 1 divided by 1 plus the interest rate, or $.91 ($1/$1.10). Since the present value of $1 is $.91, the present value of $12,000 is $10,920 ($12,000 × $.91). That is the amount of money that would have to be invested immediately in order to have $12,000 at the end of 1 year. Since the individual receives only $10,000 and not $10,920 by taking immediate payment, it would be better to wait a year to collect the money.

P.V. of $1 which will be received one year from now is .91

VALUE OF SINGLE SUMS

Present- and future-value techniques are not restricted to finding the value of payments or receipts 1 year in the future. They can be used to find the value of any payment or receipt at any time in the future. Again, it helps first to find the future values of $1 invested at different rates of interest. The figures in Table 10-2 show the result of investing $1 at 6% for a number of years. In this case, the interest is assumed to be **compounded interest;** i.e., interest is calculated on the previous years' interest as well as on the initial investment. This payment of interest on the interest becomes more and more important as time goes on and the amount of interest accumulates. After a number of years have passed, it completely dominates the income earned on the original investment. For example, the Indians supposedly sold Manhattan for $24 in 1626. If that small sum of money had been immediately invested at 6% with all interest reinvested annually, it would have grown to more than $18 billion by the end of 1977.

Future Value

Look at the figures in Table 10-2. At the end of 1 year (Year 1), an investment of $1 is worth $1.06, the initial investment of $1 and $.06 interest on $1. The $1.06 is then reinvested, so that at the end of another year (Year 2) there is $1.124. This amount consists of the $1.06 that was invested at the start of the second year plus 6% interest, or about $.064. Notice that interest of about $.004 is earned on the previous interest of $.06.

The continued reinvestment and accumulation of interest can go on indefinitely if so desired. If $1 is kept invested for a full 10 years, it will grow to $1.791—the initial $1 plus a total of $.791 interest. This future value is sometimes described as a compounded sum, because interest is paid on the interest. Without this compounding or payment of interest on interest, $1 would have

TABLE 10-2 $1 INVESTED NOW AT 6%

Year	Value at Start of Year, $		Interest Earned during Year, $		Value at End of Year, $
1	1.000	+	.060	=	1.060
2	1.060	+	.064	=	1.124
3	1.124	+	.067	=	1.191
4	1.191	+	.071	=	1.262
5	1.262	+	.076	=	1.338
6	1.338	+	.081	=	1.419
7	1.419	+	.085	=	1.504
8	1.504	+	.090	=	1.594
9	1.594	+	.095	=	1.689
10	1.689	+	.102	=	1.791

TABLE 10-3   FUTURE VALUE, OR COMPOUND SUM, OF $1

Value at End of Period	$1 Invested Now at			
	1%	5%	10%	15%
1	1.010	1.050	1.100	1.150
2	1.020	1.103	1.210	1.323
3	1.030	1.158	1.331	1.521
4	1.041	1.216	1.464	1.749
5	1.051	1.276	1.611	2.011
6	1.062	1.340	1.772	2.313
7	1.072	1.407	1.949	2.660
8	1.083	1.477	2.144	3.059
9	1.094	1.551	2.358	3.518
10	1.105	1.629	2.594	4.046
15	1.161	2.079	4.177	8.137
20	1.220	2.653	6.727	16.367
25	1.282	3.386	10.835	32.919
30	1.348	4.322	17.449	66.212

Note: Investors earning 15% a year on their investments will approximately double their money every 5 years.

grown to only $1.60 ($1 plus 10 years' interest of $.06 a year). Approximately $.191 of the final amount of $1.791 is interest earned on the interest.

Tables showing the future value, or compound sum, of $1 at different interest rates and time periods are readily available. Table 10-3 is an example of these tables. It shows the future value of $1 when invested at 1, 5, 10, and 15% for periods from 1 to 30 years. The higher the interest rate, the more interest that accumulates and the greater the future value of the investment. For example, $1 invested at 1% a year will be equal to only $1.105 at the end of 10 years; at 5% it accumulates to $1.629; at 10% it becomes $2.594; and finally at 15% the investment of $1 more than quadruples to $4.046. Judging from these future values, a small change in the rate of interest can have a tremendous effect on the long-term value of an investment—a fact often forgotten by small investors. The future values of $1 invested for different lengths of time and at different interest rates are also shown graphically in Figure 10-1.

The following example may be helpful in understanding future-value concepts:

Question: An individual invests $1,000 in a special account paying 10%. How much will be in the account at the end of 5 years?

Answer: The future value of $1 at 10% in 5 years is shown in Table 10-3 as $1.611. The future value can also be worked out with a calculator. If $1 is invested for a year at 10%, it grows to $1.10; that is, the investor gets the initial $1 back and also earns $.10 interest. If this $1.10 is reinvested for a second year, it grows to $(1 + .10) \times (1 + .10) = 1.21. In other words, the investor gets back $1.10 and earns

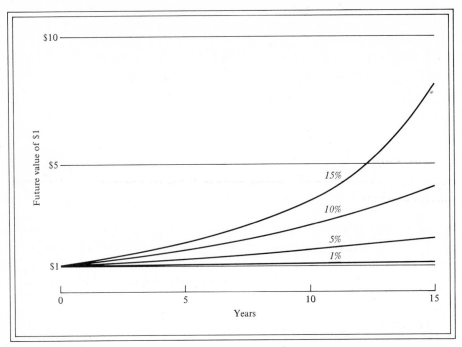

FIGURE 10-1   The impact of time and rate of return on future values.

10% interest on the $1.10. If the $1.21 is reinvested in the third year, it grows to $(1 + .10) \times (1 + .10) \times (1 + .10)$; that is, the investor gets back $(1.10) \times (1.10)$ and earns 10% on the investment.

As a general rule, the future value of $1 for any number of years is determined as follows:

Multiply the future value after 1 year by itself for as many times as there are years.

In this case, the value 5 years from now is

$$1.10 \times 1.10 \times 1.10 \times 1.10 \times 1.10 = \$1.611$$

As a result, the account will contain $1.611 in 5 years.

Despite the fact that the investor is earning 10% interest a year, many people conclude that the interest earned is really at least 12% a year. After all, $1,000 was invested and $1,611 accumulated. And that is a gain of $122.20 each year, or more than 12% a year. But such an argument completely ignores the fact that financial institutions pay interest on any interest income left in an account. If that interest is withdrawn immediately after it is paid, the account will be worth only $1,500 at the end of 5 years.

Future values demonstrate the enormous impact interest rates have on investment values. At an interest rate of 5%, savings of $10,000 grow to $70,400 in 40 years. A return of 10% produces a final value of $452,590. As a result, small differences in interest rates often mean the difference between financial success or failure.

Time also plays a crucial role in the valuation process. Time is on the side of the patient investor. Money doubles every 5 years at a 15% rate of return, so that $10,000 becomes $20,000 after 5 years. And it mushrooms into more than $660,000 in 30 years. Obviously patience is still a virtue when it comes to investing.

Present Value

The compound sums or future values given in Table 10-3 provide a useful insight into present values. If 10% is the highest rate of interest that investors can earn on their money, then the sum of $2.594 which will be received in 10 years has a value of only $1 right now. No one will give up more than $1 now to get $2.594 in 10 years (at least no one who understands present value!). Since $1 invested today at 10% grows to $2.594 in 10 years, anyone who gave up more than $1 for a promise of $2.594 would be throwing away money. Similarly, no one who wants to borrow funds now and pay them back later would offer to repay more than $2.594 in 10 years for an immediate loan of $1.

Usually it is more convenient to find the present value of $1 paid out or received in the future. For that reason, present-value tables have been worked out on this basis. Table 10-4 is a present-value table showing how much $1 received at different times in the future is worth right now. It can be seen that $1 received 1 year from now has a present value of $.952 when the interest rate is 5%,

TABLE 10-4   PRESENT VALUE OF $1

End of Period	Present Value of $1 at the Interest Rate of:			
	1%	5%	10%	15%
1	.990	.952	.909	.870
2	.980	.907	.826	.756
3	.971	.864	.751	.658
4	.961	.823	.683	.572
5	.951	.784	.621	.497
6	.942	.746	.564	.432
7	.933	.711	.513	.376
8	.923	.677	.467	.327
9	.914	.645	.424	.284
10	.905	.614	.386	.247
15	.861	.481	.239	.123
20	.820	.377	.149	.061
25	.780	.295	.092	.030
30	.742	.231	.057	.015

whereas the present value is only $.907 when the dollar is received in 2 years. The present value is still less if the money is not received for 3 years. It is $.864. All these figures could have been calculated directly from the compound-sum figures shown in Table 10-3. There it can be seen that $1 invested today at 5% is equal to $1.05 in 1 year, to $1.102 in 2 years, and to $1.159 in 3 years. To find out how much must be set aside now at 5% to have $1 at the end of 1, 2, or 3 years, all that has to be done is divide $1 by each of these future values; that is,

If $1 becomes $1.05 at the end of 1 year then

$$\frac{\$1}{1.102} \text{ or } \$.907 \text{ becomes } \$1 \text{ at the end of 2 years}$$

Therefore, the present value of $1 paid out or received in one year is $.952.
Or if $1 becomes $1.02 at the end of 2 years, then

$$\frac{\$1}{1.102} \text{ or } \$.907 \text{ becomes } \$1 \text{ at the end of 2 years}$$

Therefore, the present value of $1 paid out or received in 2 years is $.907.

In other words, to find the present value of $1, just divide by the corresponding future value. The relationship between interest rates, time, and present values is shown in Figure 10-2.

The following example may be helpful in understanding present value concepts:

Question: A football player signs a contract promising $100,000 a year in salary and a no-strings-attached bonus of $500,000 paid at the end of 6 years. What is the present value of the bonus?

Answer: The present value of the bonus depends upon the best available interest rate that can be earned during the next 6 years. If the interest rate is 15%, the present value of $1 received in 6 years is only about $.43, as can be seen from Table 10-4. The present value of $1 can also be worked out with a calculator. First, the future value of $1 in 6 years' time is found to be $2.313 ($1.15 \times 1.15 \times 1.15 \times 1.15 \times 1.15 \times 1.15$). Then this future value is divided into 1 to find the present value of $1 received in 6 years. The present value is $.432, or 1/2.313. In other words, $0.432 invested at 15% grows to $1 in 6 years' time. The present value of the bonus is therefore $216,000 ($500,000 \times .432$). Any banker who wants to earn exactly 15% on his money can offer the player $216,000 now in exchange for the $500,000 bonus in 6 years.

The interest rate used in finding present values is often called the **discount rate**. And present value is sometimes referred to as the **discounted value**. To

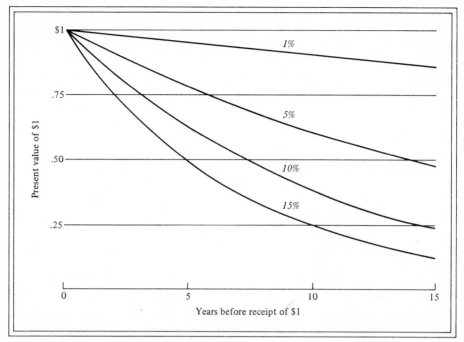

FIGURE 10-2   The impact of time and rate of return on present values.

discount means to make a deduction from a sum or to reduce the full value. A future dollar is discounted because it is worth less to a person than a present dollar.
The amount of the discount reflects the interest lost by having to wait to receive
the future dollar. The higher the interest rate, the greater the discount, since a
greater amount of interest is lost by waiting. The lower the rate, the lower the discount, since less interest is lost.

The following examples demonstrate the use of present- and future-value
concepts:

1 Question: An investor puts $1,000 into a bank account, earns 5% a year on
the money, and keeps it invested for 5 years. At the end of 5 years,
how much money will there be?

Answer: This is a future-value problem, since the investor wants to know
how much he or she will have at some point in the future. Invested
at 5% a year, $1 grows to $1.276 in 5 years, as can be seen from
the future values or compound sums in Table 10-3. Therefore,
$1,000 will grow to $1,276 ($1,000 × $1.276) in 5 years.

The answer can also be worked out very quickly with an electronic calculator as follows:

5,25   1000   (1.05

5%
5yrs

$$\$1.05 \times \$1.05 \times \$1.05 \times \$1.05 \times \$1.05 = \$1.276$$
$$= \text{future value of } \$1 \text{ in 5 years' time}$$
$$\$1,000 \times 1.276 = \$1,276$$
$$= \text{future value of } \$1,000 \text{ in 5 years' time}$$

2 Question: An individual is promised a retirement benefit of $10,000 at the end of 25 years' more service. If the current interest rate is 10%, the present value of that benefit is how much?

Answer: This is a present-value problem, since the investor must determine the value right now of a sum to be received in the future. It can be seen from Table 10-4 that the present value of $1 received in 25 years at 10% is only $.092. Therefore, the present value of $10,000 is $920 ($10,000 times the present value of $1, or $.092).

3 Question: An investor wants to more than double her or his money in 5 years. To do so what rate of return must be earned on the money each year?

Answer: In a sense this is a future-value problem. It can be seen from the compound sums in Table 10-3 that the compound sum of $1 at the end of 5 years is $1.051 at 1%, $1.276 at 5%, $1.611 at 10%, and $2.011 at 15%. At 15% a year for 5 years, the money is more than doubled (every $1 invested becomes at least $2).

4 Question: A taxpayer can select a tax method which permits a delay in paying income tax for 10 years without any penalties. If this method isn't used, the tax must be paid immediately. If the taxpayer can earn 10% on investments and the tax is $5,000, how much is gained at the end of the 10 years by delaying the tax?

Answer: This is a future-value problem, since the investor wishes to know what amount will be accumulated by some date in the future. Whichever tax method is selected, $5,000 in taxes must still be paid. The only difference is when it is actually paid. However, by delaying the payment of the tax, the taxpayer has the use of the money for 10 years. It can be seen from the compound sums in Table 10-3 that if $1 is invested at 10% for 10 years, it grows to $2.594. Therefore, $5,000 invested for 10 years grows to $12,970 ($5,000 × $2.594). After the $5,000 in taxes is paid out at the end of 10 years, there is still $7,970 left. This is $7,970 more than would have been available if the tax had been paid immediately. Obviously, any tax technique which defers taxes can be very valuable. Some of these techniques are described in Chapter Eleven.

5 Question: An investor can borrow $20,000 from one of two institutions. The first charges 12.5% a year and compounds the interest once a year. The second charges 12% a year and compounds the interest every month. Which loan costs the least if the money is borrowed for only 1 year?

Answer: The 1-year future value of $1 at 12.5% is $1.125. That means that the borrower must pay back $22,500 ($20,000 × 1.125). On the second loan the interest is compounded monthly. That is equivalent to charging 1% each month on the loan and on the previously accumulated interest. The future value of $1 invested for 12 months at 1% a month is

$$\$1.01 \times \$1.01 \times \$1.01 \times \cdots \times \$1.01 = \$1.127$$

It can be seen from this that the true annual percentage rate of interest is 12.7%. Therefore, on a $20,000 loan, the future value is $22,540. The second loan costs $40 more than the first loan.

As a rule, the more frequent the compounding, the higher the true annual percentage rate of return. If the loan company compounded interest every day instead of every month, the true rate would be 12.75%. In the most extreme form of compounding, interest is compounded every second. This is called continuous compounding. Of course, no one actually computes the interest every second. Instead, people simply refer to a set of tables based on the assumption of continuous compounding.

VALUE OF ANNUITIES

So far it has been assumed that only a single payment or receipt of money is involved. But sums of money are often received or paid over a number of years. Although the present value or future value of each of these amounts could be determined and the individual values added together, it is much easier to use annuity tables in which this has been done already. An **annuity** is any sequence of equally spaced payments or receipts all of which are for the same amount. Investors often purchase annuities which provide them with a specified number of payments. Or a retirement plan may guarantee them or their survivors a certain percentage of their salary for a fixed number of years. On the other hand, individuals often agree to make a number of payments over time for a home, an automobile, insurance, and a variety of other purchases. Or the investor may want to set aside a fixed amount of money every year through a savings plan for future expenditures.

Two questions arise with regard to annuities—what is the future value of the sum of payments or receipts and what is the present value? In order to answer the

TABLE 10-5   CALCULATING THE FUTURE VALUE
OF AN ANNUITY AT 5%

End of Year 1, $	End of Year 2, $	End of Year 3, $	End of Year 4, $	End of Year 4, $
500	500	500	500	
			× 1.00	500.00
		× 1.05		525.00
	× 1.103			551.50
× 1.158				579.00
				2,155.50

first question, assume a person puts $500 at the end of each year into a savings account paying 5% interest annually. How much will have been saved at the end of 4 years? The answer must be at least $2,000, since $500 has been saved for each of 4 years. In order to find the exact answer, the investor could work out the future value for each amount set aside. This has been done in Table 10-5. The answer shown in the table is $2,155.50. However, it is simpler to consult an annuity table such as Table 10-6. This table shows the future value of a stream of payments of $1 for different time periods and different interest rates. Each of the figures shown in this table is based on the same type of calculations performed in Table 10-5.

According to Table 10-6, $1 a year for 4 years accumulates to $4.31 when the interest rate is 5%. Therefore, $500 a year for 4 years grows to $2,155

TABLE 10-6   FUTURE VALUE OF ANNUITY OF $1*

Number of Years	At the Investment Rate of:			
	1%	5%	10%	15%
1	1.000	1.000	1.000	1.000
2	2.010	2.050	2.100	2.150
3	3.030	3.152	3.310	3.472
4	4.060	4.310	4.641	4.993
5	5.101	5.526	6.105	6.742
6	6.152	6.802	7.716	8.754
7	7.214	8.142	9.487	11.067
8	8.286	9.549	11.436	13.727
9	9.369	11.027	13.579	16.786
10	10.462	12.578	15.937	20.304
15	16.097	21.579	31.772	47.580
20	22.019	33.066	57.275	102.444
25	28.243	47.727	98.347	212.793
30	34.785	66.439	164.494	434.745

* It is assumed that $1 is received or paid out at the end of each year.

TABLE 10-7   CALCULATING THE PRESENT VALUE OF AN
ANNUITY AT 5%

Start of Year, $	End of Year 1, $	End of Year 2, $	End of Year 3, $	End of Year 4, $
	500	500	500	500
476.00	$.952 ×			
453.50		$.907 ×		
432.00			$.864 ×	
411.50				$.823 ×
1,773.00				

($500 × 4.31). If the individual sets aside $500 a year for 20 years at 5%, the savings accumulate to $16,533 ($500 × 33.066) at the end of 20 years. Finally, money set aside at 10% for each of those 20 years grows to $28,638 ($500 × 57.275). Judging from these figures, the rate of interest earned on an annuity has a more and more important effect the longer the money is kept invested.

Now suppose an investor wants to determine the present value of an annuity and plans to receive $500 at the end of each year for 4 years. These four payments are worth at most $2,000 to the investor, who doesn't have the use of the full $2,000 until 4 years have elapsed. In order to find the present value of these receipts, the present value of each separate receipt can be computed as is done in Table 10-7. Or the present value of an annuity table given in Table 10-8 can be used. This table shows the present value of a stream of payments of $1 for

TABLE 10-8   PRESENT VALUE OF ANNUITY OF $1

Number of Years	At the Interest Rate of:			
	1%	5%	10%	15%
1	.990	.952	.909	.870
2	1.970	1.859	1.736	1.626
3	2.941	2.723	2.487	2.283
4	3.902	3.546	3.170	2.855
5	4.853	4.329	3.791	3.352
6	5.795	5.076	4.355	3.784
7	6.728	5.786	4.868	4.160
8	7.652	6.463	5.335	4.487
9	8.566	7.108	5.759	4.772
10	9.471	7.722	6.145	5.019
15	13.865	10.380	7.606	5.847
20	18.046	12.462	8.514	6.259
25	22.023	14.094	9.077	6.464
30	25.808	15.372	9.427	6.566

different time periods and different interest rates. The present value of $1 a year for 4 years is $3.546 when the money is invested at 5%; so $500 a year for 4 years equals $1,773, or $500 × 3.546.

Although there is nothing complicated about annuities, the following examples may be helpful in better understanding them.

1 Question: An investor puts $100 into a bank account at the end of every year for 20 years and earns 5% annual interest on the money. At the end of 20 years, how much money will there be?

Answer: This is a problem on the future value of an annuity, since the investor wants to know the worth of annual deposits at some point in the future. It can be seen from the future values in Table 10-6 that when $1 is set aside every year for 20 years at 5%, the money accumulates to $33.066. Since $100 rather than $1 is deposited each year, the future value of the annuity is $3,306.60 ($100 × $33.066).

2 Question: Some well-known insurance firms advertise that they will return the full amount of money paid for medical insurance if the person buying the insurance never gets sick. The implication is that the insurance costs nothing. Suppose an individual pays the company $300 a year for 30 years and never has to use the insurance, so that the full amount of the insurance premiums ($9,000) is returned at the end of that time. What is the future cost of the medical insurance, assuming that the money paid as premiums could have earned 10%?

Answer: This is also a problem on the future value of an annuity, since the investor wants to know how much the annual deposits are worth at some date in the future. At the end of 30 years, $1 invested each and every year at 10% will accumulate to $164.494. Since the investor is paying $300 a year for medical insurance, this is equivalent to $49,348 ($300 × $164.494). In other words, if the money had been invested in bonds or a savings certificate paying 10%, $49,348 would have accumulated at the end of 30 years. The insurance firm has, of course, done just that. It returns only $9,000 to the individual, who has, in effect, lost the $40,348 in additional funds that would have accrued through investing the money at 10%.

3 Question: A thirty-year-old investor wants to save a total of $500,000 by age sixty. How much must be saved each year at 15% to reach that amount?

Answer: This is another problem on the future value of an annuity. At 15%, $1 set aside each year accumulates to $434.745 in 30 years, an incredibly large increase in the amount invested. To have

$500,000, the person must invest $1,150.10 each year, or $500,000/$434.745. This means that a total investment of only $34,503 (30 payments of $1,150.10) becomes $500,000 through the interest earned on the money.

4 Question: A worker who retires at sixty-five is guaranteed $10,000 a year in pension benefits until death. A sixty-five-year-old man can expect to live approximately 15 more years. What is the present value of his pension benefits if the retiree can earn 5% a year on his money?

Answer: This is a problem on the present value of an annuity. The pensioner is trying to find the value right now of a sequence of future receipts. The present value of $1 a year for 15 years is $10.38 when the interest rate is 5%. Therefore, the present value of the pension benefits is $103,800 ($10,000 × $10.38). This means that a worker would have to accumulate $103,800 by retirement age in order to obtain the same benefits as those paid by the company.

5 Question: A person buys a home for $50,000. The down payment is $10,000, and the balance of $40,000 is borrowed from a savings and loan association at 10% a year. The loan must be paid off in 25 years. Assuming for the sake of simplicity that payments are made at the end of each year, how much will the annual payment be?

Answer: This is a problem on the present value of an annuity. The home buyer is receiving a present amount of $40,000 from the savings and loan association. In return the officers of the institution want to receive a stream of payments which has exactly the same present value when discounted at 10%. That way they earn 10% on their loan. The present value of $1 a year for 25 years equals only $9.077 when the discount rate is 10%. In other words, $9.077 invested immediately at 10% will grow to the exact same amount in 25 years as $1 invested every year for 25 years at 10%. Since $1 a year for 25 years is equal to a present value of $9.077, $4,406.74 a year ($40,000/9.077) for 25 years is equal to $40,000 right now. Therefore, the bank will receive 10% a year on the unpaid balance of the home mortgage if the homeowner pays it $4,406.74 a year.

The amount of interest in each payment varies from year to year. During the early years, most of the annual payments go to pay interest and only a very small part of the loan is repaid. But as the years go by and more and more of the debt is paid off, the amount of interest in each payment decreases. The relationship between the amount of interest in a mortgage payment and the number of years a house is owned is shown in Figure 10-3. During the first year,

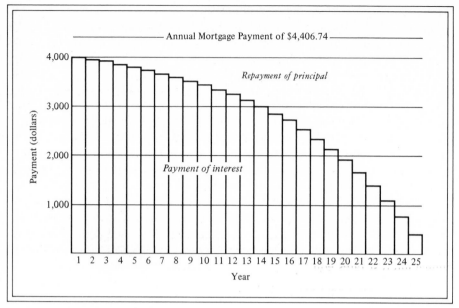

FIGURE 10-3   Payments of interest and principal for a home mortgage.

$4,000 of the $4,406.74 mortgage payment is for interest. This is because the amount of the loan during the first year is $40,000 and the interest rate is 10%. During the twenty-fifth year the amount of interest is only about $300.

Homes offer a partial tax shelter. All interest paid on a mortgage can be deducted from the taxpayer's income. But it can be seen from this last example that the tax shelter aspect of a home becomes less and less important over the years as the mortgage is paid off. Usually, at the same time that the tax deduction for interest is decreasing, the homeowner's income and need for a tax shelter is increasing. For that reason, a mortgage should be periodically refinanced and additional money borrowed on the home. This is the practice followed by most large-scale investors in commercial real estate. Of course, a mortgage should be refinanced only if interest rates have not increased considerably.

VALUE OF PERPETUITIES

Sometimes payments or receipts of equal amounts of money can be assumed to go on "forever". In this special situation, the stream of money is described as a perpetuity, or perpetual annuity. One example of this arises when the dividend paid on a stock can be assumed to be the same for every year in the future. Another example is provided by certain British bonds called **consols**. The British government has pledged to pay the same amount of interest on these bonds forever. A third example is a perpetual-care cemetery, which offers services forever.

At first, it would seem that a promise to pay a certain amount of money forever would be worth a great deal. However, the value of such a promise is equal to just the amount of money that must be set aside at the market rate of interest in order to provide an interest income equal to the promised receipts. An investment which pays $100 a year forever is worth only $1,000 if the interest rate is 10%, since $1,000 invested at 10% will yield $100 forever. If the interest rate is 5%, an investment paying $100 a year forever is worth $2,000, since $2,000 invested at 5% provides an income of $100.

The higher the going interest rate, the less money must be set aside to provide a specific income forever. From these examples it can be seen that the value of any perpetuity is simply equal to the amount received each period divided by the interest rate per period. In the case of a perpetuity paying $100 a year when annual interest rates equal 5%, the value is calculated as follows:

$$\frac{\$100 \text{ amount paid per period}}{0.05 \text{ interest rate per period}} = \$2,000 \text{ value of perpetuity}$$

Changes in the market rate of interest have an important effect on the value of a consol or any other long-lived investment which provides a fixed payment to the investor. If a consol pays $100 and the going rate of interest is 10%, an investor will pay $1,000 for the consol ($100/0.10). Should the market interest rate rise to 20%, the investor will in effect lose $500 of the investment. That is because a security which pays $100 forever is worth only $500 when the interest rate is 20%, since at 20% an investment of $500 yields $100. As a general rule, unexpected increases in market interest rates cause a fall in the prices of bonds and other fixed-income investments. Unexpected decreases in market interest rates have the opposite effect. They cause an increase in bond prices.

The following example may be helpful in understanding perpetuities:

Question: A consol pays $300 in interest every year forever. The market interest rate is 10%. How much is the consol worth?

Answer: Since an investor can earn 10% on any marketable investment, it would be foolish to pay more than $3,000 for the consol. That is because 10% interest on a $3,000 investment is equal to $300. The value of a perpetuity such as this consol can also be calculated as follows:

$$\frac{\text{Amount received each period}}{\text{Market interest rate}} = \frac{\$300}{0.10} = \$3,000$$

Question: The investor buys the consol for $3,000. But because of unexpected inflation, the market interest rate goes from 10 to 20%. As a result, any invested money can earn 20%. What happens to the price of the consol?

Answer: The value of the consol must drop to $1,500, since no one will pay a penny more for it. That is because at a 20% interest rate the amount of interest on any other $1,500 investment is $300. Since the dollar amount of interest paid on the consol is fixed forever at $300, the only way a new investor can make 20% on a consol is to pay $1,500 for the consol. The value of the consol can also be calculated as follows:

$$\frac{\$300}{0.20} = \$1,500$$

PRICE-EARNINGS RATIOS

More than 40 years ago John Williams argued that the value of a stock was equal to the present value of all future dividends. By now, most of Wall Street believes that Williams was right. However, very few investors consciously calculate the present value of the future dividends that they expect to receive from a stock. Instead, they use price-earnings ratios. The price-earnings ratio measures the value an investor attaches to $1 of earnings. For example, IBM usually has a price-earnings ratio of about 20 to 1. That means investors are willing to pay $20 for each $1 of earnings reported by IBM. Therefore, if IBM earns $12 a share, each share will sell for $240. The year-end stock prices, the annual earnings per share, and the year-end price-earnings ratios for IBM for the 5 years from 1971 to 1975 are shown in Table 10-9. It can be seen from this table that actual price-earnings ratios are found by dividing the share price by the earnings per share.

The price-earnings ratio is also called an earnings multiplier. Once the forthcoming earnings of a firm have been estimated, the value of the company's stock can be determined simply by multiplying these earnings by the appropriate price-earnings ratio. If a particular company can be expected to earn $2 a share during the next year and if the price-earnings ratio averages 15 to 1, a share of the stock should sell for about $30.

Price-earnings ratios differ greatly among firms. Whereas the P-E ratio for

TABLE 10-9   P-E RATIOS FOR IBM

Year	Year-End Price, $	Earnings, $	P-E Ratio
1971	336½	7.50	45
1972	402	8.83	46
1973	246¾	10.79	23
1974	168	12.47	13
1975	224¼	13.35	17

IBM is usually more than 20, the P-E ratio for U.S. Steel is often less than 10. Why should $1 of earnings at U.S. Steel bring only $10 in the market when $1 of earnings at IBM sells for $20? The answer depends upon a number of factors. Probably the most important is the expected growth in the company's earnings. The greater the expected growth in earnings, the higher the P-E ratio. That is because dividends are paid out of earnings. And the greater the growth in earnings, the greater the growth in future dividends. IBM is a growth firm; U.S. Steel is not a growth firm.

GROWTH AND VALUE

Dividend projections for two companies are shown in Table 10-10. The first company is expected to experience little or no growth in the future. Management will probably continue to pay a dividend of $1 per share for as long as the company remains in business. If investors are satisfied with a 10% return on their money, they will pay $10 for one share of this stock, since the $1 dividend provides a 10% return. The second company is also paying a $1 dividend, but the payment is expected to increase every year by 6%. As a result, the dividend next year will be $1.06, in the following year $1.124, etc. Shares in this company will sell for $25 each, providing that shareholders expect to earn 10% on their money. This $25 price is fully justified on the basis of present values. In fact, if an investor had a lifetime to spend painstakingly discounting each future dividend back into the present, he or she would arrive at the exact same figure.

Fortunately, there is a much easier way to find present values when steady growth is expected over long periods of time. It can be shown mathematically

TABLE 10-10 PROJECTED DIVIDENDS FOR TWO COMPANIES

Year	Dividends per Share of No-Growth Company, $	Dividends per Share of Growth Company, $
1	1.00	1.00
2	1.00	1.06
3	1.00	1.12
4	1.00	1.19
5	1.00	1.26
6	1.00	1.34
7	1.00	1.42
8	1.00	1.50
9	1.00	1.59
10	1.00	1.69
15	1.00	2.26
20	1.00	3.03
30	1.00	5.42
40	1.00	9.70
50	1.00	17.38

that the present value of any asset which provides a steadily increasing stream of income is equal to:

$$\frac{\text{Current income}}{\text{Desired return} - \text{growth rate}}$$

Judging from this expression, steady growth in future income paid to shareholders assures a firm a high market value. And the higher the growth rate, the greater the price the public is justified in paying. The reason for this is not hard to see. High rates of growth soon transform even the smallest company into an enormous money-maker.

Suppose the dividend on a share is currently $1, the desired rate of return is 10%, and the expected growth in dividends is 6%. Then the present value of a share equals $25 [$1/(0.10−0.06), or $1/0.04]. The value of a perpetuity can also be determined by this same expression. Since the growth rate of a perpetuity is zero, the value of a perpetuity is just the familiar result of the current income divided by the desired return. The no-growth firm described in Table 10-10 has zero growth but is expected to pay $1 a share "forever." Therefore, the value of a share in this firm is $10.

The relationship between a perpetual stream of discounted payments and the growth expression just described appears so tenuous that only a mathematician can accept it immediately. Other people will probably wonder why anyone would pay $25 for a stock that pays only $1 a share. After all, that is a cash return (current yield) of only 4% on the investment. The answer is that the stock should also increase in price by 6% during the year, so that the total return amounts to 10%. This increase in price is the result of being 1 year closer to receiving the very large dividends that the fast-growing company will eventually pay.

The growth-stock expression is remarkable. It demonstrates in just a few words several facts which are still not accepted by millions of investors, thousands of brokers and financial counselors, and the Internal Revenue Service. The first fact is that there is absolutely no reason why growth stocks per se should outperform no-growth stocks. Only if expected growth rates change will unusually large (or small) returns be realized on these stocks. The second fact is that the total return on any investment consists of both dividends and price appreciation. The investor who opts for dividends usually gets just that and little or no growth in value. On the other hand, the investor who purchases a growth stock receives most of the return in the form of increases in the value of the stock. The only difference between the two returns is that the IRS taxes dividends fully but does not tax gains in price at all until they are actually realized. Then if the investment has been held for more than 12 months, gains are taxed at only one-half of the rate applied to dividends.

FINANCIAL DISASTERS

Changes in expected growth rates have a profound effect on the value of an investment. A 1 to 2% change in growth rates can cause a 50 to 100% change in stock prices. Critics of the stock market and of other speculative markets tend to over-look the tremendous impact that these changes have on investment values. Instead they interpret the extreme fluctuations in market prices as evidence of individual irrationality and/or the natural consequence of crowd psychology. Even some professed believers in market efficiency are quick to point out the recurring episodes of speculative fervor. For example, Burton Malkiel has dutifully summarized the tulip mania that eventually bankrupted Holland in the 1600s, the South Sea bubble that wiped out the savings of many Englishmen in the 1700s, and the great stock market crash in the United States in the 1930s.

But how can rationally determined values fluctuate so greatly? The growth-stock expression goes a long way toward explaining these tremendous fluctuations. It can be seen from Table 10-11 that values deviate more and more from current income as expected growth becomes greater and greater. At growth rates which are close to the discount rate, values of 100, 200, and even 1,000 or more times current earnings are justified. Finally, when the growth rate is equal to the discount rate, the value becomes so large that it is impossible to write it down; i.e., the value is infinitely large. The reason for this is that the growth in earnings in each future year more than offsets the reduction in value which occurs because the dividends are received farther into the future. Of course, extremely high rates of growth cannot occur forever, or the fast-growing company or country would someday completely dominate the world economy. The situation is analogous to the growth of bacteria. Should such growth continue unchecked, the earth would quickly become one huge bacteria culture.

High growth rates, even for relatively short periods of time, can justify extremely high investment values. Is it possible then that "speculative manias" are simply the result of rationally expected growth that for some unforeseen

TABLE 10-11   PRICE-EARNINGS RATIOS
AND GROWTH RATES

Growth Rate, %	Price Earnings Ratio*
0	10.0
1	11.1
2	12.5
3	14.3
4	16.7
5	20.0
6	25.0
7	33.3
8	50.0
9	100.0
10	∞

* The price-earnings ratio provides a measure of the market value of $1 of current earnings (assuming all earnings are paid out as dividends). In this case, the discount rate is assumed to be 10%. The price-earnings ratio equals 1 divided by the difference between the discount rate and the growth rate.

reason never materialized? And that values were completely justified on the basis of this expected growth? Of course, the answer will never be known. But it seems at least as likely to be yes as no.

KEYWORDS

asset	future-value concept	annuity
time value of money	compounded interest	perpetuity
time preference	discount rate	consols
present-value concept	discounted value	

QUESTIONS

1   The value of an asset depends upon (1) the stream of future income or benefits, (2) the time value of money, and (3) the uncertainty about future income or benefits. Discuss each of these three factors.

2   An investor buys $3,000 of stocks. The rate of return during the year is a disappointing minus 31%. How much money does the individual have left at the end of the year?

3   Explain why high interest rates produce low present values and why low interest rates result in high present values.

4   A woman has a choice between receiving $1,000 immediately or receiving $1,200 in one year. She takes the $1,000. What does this choice imply about her time value of money?

5   Explain compound interest.

6   As time goes on, interest on the interest becomes more and more important. In 340 years $24 invested at 6% grows to approximately $24 billion. How much of this $24 billion is accounted for by interest on the interest?

7   A trust is a legal arrangement for managing and protecting money. Not too long ago, the United States government went to court to stop a man from creating a perpetual trust, i.e., a trust lasting "forever." He wanted to invest $1 in a perpetual trust at 5%, with all interest reinvested over the years. Why do you suppose the government opposes perpetual trusts? (Hint: Use the rule of 69 to see how long it takes to double your money at 5%. Then try to compute the end result of keeping $1 invested for 500 years.)

8   How much does $2,000 invested at 18% grow to in 8 years? (Hint: Multiply 1.18 by itself 7 times.)

9   Someone offers you a 5% partnership in a 200-acre land development project. The required payments are as follows:

Date	Payment, $
Immediately	8,000
End of year 1	4,000
2	4,000
3	4,000
4	4,000
5	34,000

In effect these payments entitle you to 10 acres of commercial property. What is the present value of the payments at 10%? What is the "present cost" of each acre of land? (Hint: See Table 10-4.)

10 A bond with a face value of $1,000 carries a 5% coupon. Suppose the current interest rate equals 10%. If the bond matures in 10 years, how much should it sell for now?

11 A preferred stock represents a promise to pay a specified income forever. Suppose the preferred stock pays $3.00 a year and the appropriate discount rate equals 10%. What is a fair price for the preferred stock? Explain why.

12 Suppose because of inflationary expectations interest rates increase from 10 to 15%. How does this increase affect the market value of the preferred stock described in question 11?

13 A company earned $4 and paid $1 in dividends during the current year. Investors expect earnings and dividends to grow at a steady rate of 7% a year. And 12% appears to be a reasonable discount rate for this company's dividends. What is the intrinsic value of a share of stock?

14 What is the P-E ratio for the stock in question 13? How would changes in the expected growth rate and in the discount rate change the P-E ratio?

REFERENCES

Gould, John P., and Roman L. Weil: "The Rule of 69," *Journal of Business,* July 1974, pp. 397–398.

Perham, John C.: "The Riddle of the P/E Ratio," *Dun's Review*, September 1972, pp. 39–42.

Williams, John Burr: *The Theory of Investment Value,* Harvard, 1938.

PART THREE

TAXES

CHAPTER ELEVEN

INCOME TAXES

I ncome taxes can be reduced or avoided altogether, and there is nothing immoral or illegal about doing so. The tax structure has been designed to encourage certain types of investments and activities and to discourage others. For the most part, so-called tax breaks are the result of specific legislation—they are not loopholes in that legislation. Investors can take advantage of these tax breaks by knowing certain simple tax concepts and by planning before they invest. But it is important for them to realize that reducing taxes involves costs as well as obvious benefits.

FEDERAL INCOME TAX

Most of America's 82 million taxpayers are painfully aware of two aspects of our tax system. First, income taxes increase with income. According to recent tax tables, a single taxpayer reporting a taxable income of $500 pays the United States government about $70 in taxes. On the other hand, someone earning $50,000 parts with the grand total of $20,170. Second, income taxes increase at a faster rate than income. People making $500 pay 14% of their income in taxes, while those earning $50,000 pay approximately 40%. In other words the federal income tax is a **graduated,** or **progressive, tax**—tax rates increase with income. Not only do the rich pay more, at least in theory, but they also surrender a larger percentage of their incomes to the government.

Things weren't always this way. In fact Americans escaped any form of federal taxation for almost the first 100 years of their nation's existence. Not until the Civil War did the government impose an income tax: 3% on personal incomes over $800. This tax expired in 1872. Then in 1894 Congress passed another income tax law. But the Supreme Court, in a reversal of its Civil War decision, ruled this federal income tax unconstitutional. According to the Court, the Constitution required a uniform tax. The people of the United States finally corrected this situation in 1913 by approving the Sixteenth Amendment. Congress immediately passed a law taxing personal income progressively. Tax rates started at 1% on incomes over $20,000 and rose to a maximum of 6% on incomes exceeding $2 million.

Marginal and Average Tax Rates

Nowadays tax rates start at 14% and go as high as 70%. The strikingly progressive nature of the income tax makes it important for taxpayers to distinguish between **average tax rates** and **marginal tax rates.** The total tax paid by an individual depends upon the average tax rate. But the tax paid by a person on the last, or marginal, dollar of income depends upon the marginal tax rate. The marginal tax rate is usually referred to as the **tax bracket.** It is the marginal tax rate which plays a key role in investment decision making, for reasons explained in this chapter.

The relationship between marginal tax rates and taxable income is displayed in Figure 11-1. By the way, **taxable income** means income after all deductions and exemptions. The government levies a tax of 14% on the first $500 of taxable income, 15% on the second $500, 16% on the third $500, and 17% on the fourth $500. This stair-step increase characterizes a graduated (progressive) income tax. In effect taxpayers climb a series of steps as their income increases. After the first $2,000 in income, the next steps come in intervals of $2,000 rather than $500. The tax rates increase from 19% on any income earned between $2,000 and $4,000, to 21% on income from $4,000 to $6,000, and so forth. Finally, the long climb upward ends at $100,000 for a single taxpayer, because the government taxes all income earned over $100,000 at a rate of 70% (earned income is subject to a maximum rate of 50%). In other words, 70¢ of every additional dollar over $100,000 goes to taxes and only 30¢ remains in the taxpayer's pocket. If individuals in this bracket can somehow reduce taxable income by $1 without changing their actual income, they can save 70¢. This can be done by adopting investment strategies similar to the ones described in this chapter.

A taxpayer making $100,000 pays the government $53,090, not $70,000. So the average tax rate, i.e., the total tax divided by total taxable income, equals 53.1%. This average tax rate consists of a weighted average of marginal tax rates.

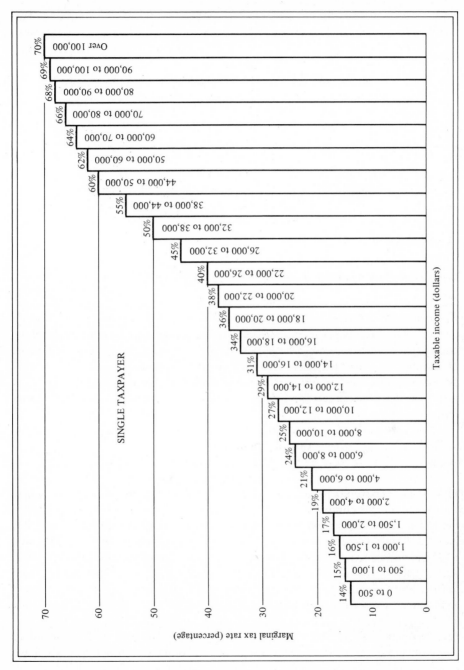

FIGURE 11-1 Marginal tax rates at different levels of taxable income in 1976.

To see why, suppose a single taxpayer earns an income of $4,000 after all deductions and exemptions. The income tax on this amount is computed as follows:

	Taxable Income, $		Marginal Tax Rate, %		Tax, $
1st	500	×	14	=	70
2d	500	×	15	=	75
3d	500	×	16	=	80
4th	500	×	17	=	85
Next	2,000	×	19	=	380
					690

$$\text{Average tax rate} = \frac{\$690 \text{ total tax}}{\$4,000 \text{ total taxable income}} = 17.25\%$$

The same exercise applied to an income of $100,000 produces a tax of $53,090.

Recent tax tables published by the IRS eliminate this drudgery for the average taxpayer. They show the income tax payable on a wide range of incomes. But in the process they make it impossible for the average taxpayer to discover his or her marginal tax rate (tax bracket). For example, according to the 1976 tax tables, a single taxpayer owes $4,879 on an income of $19,000. That amounts to an average tax rate of 25.6% = (4,879/19,000). The crucial marginal tax rate receives no mention in the forms mailed to taxpayers. It equals 36%. Table 11-1 shows the marginal tax rates applying to single taxpayers and to married taxpayers filing joint returns.

STATE INCOME TAXES

Traditionally taxpayers have been primarily concerned with federal taxes. This is a serious oversight. Expenditures by state governments have increased greatly in the last 20 years, and state income taxes have increased accordingly. For example, New York and Minnesota take a hefty 15% of any income over $25,000 and $20,000, respectively. And California claims 11% of any amount over $15,000. State income taxes, like the federal income tax, are progressive. For example, tax rates in Minnesota start at 1.6% on the first $500 and jump quickly to 12.8% on any income between $9,000 and $12,500.

Income tax rates differ greatly from state to state. In Table 11-2 the states have been classified into four groups: those with relatively high, medium, and low tax rates on earned income, and states with no income tax. Although these classifications are somewhat arbitrary, they do make comparisons among the different states easier.

The importance of tax planning to even average investors becomes readily apparent once the federal and state tax rates are combined. Many families earn a

TABLE 11-1   MARGINAL TAX RATES FOR INDIVIDUALS AS OF 1976

Single Return		Joint Return	
Taxable Income, $	Marginal Tax Rate, %	Taxable Income, $	Marginal Tax Rate, %
0–500	14	0–1,000	14
500–1,000	15	1,000–2,000	15
1,000–1,500	16	2,000–3,000	16
1,500–2,000	17	3,000–4,000	17
2,000–4,000	19	4,000–8,000	19
4,000–6,000	21	8,000–12,000	22
6,000–8,000	24	12,000–16,000	25
8,000–10,000	25	16,000–20,000	28
10,000–12,000	27	20,000–24,000	32
12,000–14,000	29	24,000–28,000	36
14,000–16,000	31	28,000–32,000	39
16,000–18,000	34	32,000–36,000	42
18,000–20,000	36	36,000–40,000	45
20,000–22,000	38	40,000–44,000	48
22,000–26,000	40	44,000–52,000	50
26,000–32,000	45	52,000–64,000	53
32,000–38,000	50	64,000–76,000	55
38,000–44,000	55	76,000–88,000	58
44,000–50,000	60	88,000–100,000	60
50,000–60,000	62	100,000–120,000	62
60,000–70,000	64	120,000–140,000	64
70,000–80,000	66	140,000–160,000	66
80,000–90,000	68	160,000–180,000	68
90,000–100,000	69	180,000–200,000	69
Over 100,000	70	Over 200,000	70

combined income of at least $20,000. Assuming they take only the standard deduction and two exemptions, the taxable income reported to the United States government would be about $15,700. Most states define taxable income even more strictly than the federal government.

How much of the family's $20,000 goes to federal and state income taxes? The federal government withholds $3,179 or 16%. And Minnesota, after allowing for federal income taxes, takes $1,620, or 8%. The total average tax rate for both federal and state taxes comes to 24%, and the total marginal tax rate equals 39%–25% federal plus 14% state.

TAXATION OF INVESTMENTS

Most investors share their investment income and/or gains with a silent partner—Uncle Sam. The government taxes all investment income, unless speci-

TABLE 11-2   STATES CLASSIFIED BY INDIVIDUAL STATE INCOME
TAX RATES AS OF 1976

No Income Tax	Low Income Tax*	Medium Income Tax†	High Income Tax‡
Connecticut	Illinois	Alabama	California
Florida	Indiana	Alaska	Delaware
Nevada	Louisiana	Arizona \	District of Columbia
New Hampshire	Maine	Arkansas	Hawaii
South Dakota	Maryland	Colorado	Minnesota
Tennessee	Massachusetts	Georgia	Montana
Texas	Michigan	Idaho	New York
Washington	Mississippi	Iowa	North Dakota
Wyoming	Nebraska	Kansas	Oregon
	New Jersey	Kentucky	Wisconsin
	Ohio	Missouri	
	Pennsylvania	New Mexico	
	Rhode Island	North Carolina	
		Oklahoma	
		South Carolina	
		Utah	
		Vermont	
		Virginia	
		West Virginia	

* 1976 income tax rates are less than 5% on a $20,000 taxable income.
† 1976 income tax rates are greater than 5% but less than 9% on a $20,000 taxable income.
‡ 1976 income tax rates are greater than 9% on a $20,000 taxable income.

fically exempted from taxation, at the same rate as ordinary income. On the other
hand, gains on investments often qualify for reduced tax rates.

Capital Gains

In order to save tax dollars, investors must learn to appreciate the differences
between income and capital gains. A **capital gain** consists of any gain from the
sale or exchange of a capital asset. The federal tax laws define a **capital asset** as
any property not used in a business or trade. For example, if an individual purchases stock for $1,000 and sells it for $2,500, the $1,500 increase in value is
called a capital gain.

Capital gains (and their counterpart, **capital losses**) fall into one of two categories: (1) **short term** or (2) **long term.** Only long-term gains receive favored tax
treatment. Investors pay the full tax on all short-term gains.

Until 1976 the tax laws defined a long-term gain as any gain on an investment held for *more* than 6 months. But Congress revised this definition when it
passed the Tax Reform Act of 1976. Any investment sold in 1977 must have
been held for more than 9 months to qualify as a long-term gain. Beginning with
the 1978 tax year, investments must be held for more than 1 year to achieve
long-term-gain status. (These rules do not apply to options, short sales, or com-

modity futures. All option trades and short sales are automatically classified as short-term. Commodity future contracts need only be held more than 6 months to qualify for treatment as a long-term gain.)

The tax laws carefully spell out the exact technique for measuring the **holding period,** i.e., the length of time an asset is held. As a general rule, the numerical date of the day of purchase marks the end of each holding month in the future. Suppose an investor buys stock on March 23. Then 23 serves as the dividing line in each successive month: April 23 ends 1 holding month, May 23 ends the second month, and March 23 in the following year ends a 12-month holding period. Beginning in 1978, the investor must hold the investment 1 more day than 1 year, in this case until March 24, to satisfy the long-term capital gain requirements.

> EXAMPLE   An individual buys some stock on February 6, 1977, and sells it for a profit on November 7, 1977. The transaction qualifies as a long-term capital gain, since the holding period equals 9 months and 1 day. This just satisfies the rules for the 1977 tax year.

> EXAMPLE   An investor purchases a parcel of land on February 6, 1978, and sells it for a gain on November 7, 1978. The gain is classified as short-term, since the holding period must exceed 1 year beginning in 1978.

> EXAMPLE   An investor buys a bar of gold on March 1, 1978, and sells it on March 2, 1979. The transaction qualifies as a long-term gain (or loss), since the holding period totals 1 year and 1 day.

The government taxes long-term gains at half the ordinary tax rates (subject to certain qualifications). So by taking a long-term gain instead of a short-term gain, investors cut their tax bills substantially. For instance, assume a single person earning a taxable income of $22,000 before any security transactions buys 100 shares of stock at $30 a share, and within 5 months the price climbs to $60. If the stock is sold, with the short-term gain of $3,000, $1,200 of that gain is paid in taxes. If the sale is not made until it qualifies as a long-term gain, only $600 is paid in taxes—a savings of $600.

By the way, the government collects no tax at all on unrealized gains. So the investor completely escapes the tax collector by simply buying and holding the investment.

Capital Losses

The government shares in all gains, but it refuses to split all losses with taxpayers. Taxpayers may write off only a limited amount of capital losses against their other income. The maximum write-offs are as follows:

Tax Year	Short-Term Loss, $	Long-Term Loss, $
1976	1,000	2,000
1977	2,000	4,000
1978 and after	3,000	6,000

After 1977, every dollar of short-term losses (up to $3,000) can be used to reduce ordinary income in any taxable year. If the loss is long-term, every dollar of the loss (up to $6,000) can be used to reduce income by 50¢. Since a short-term loss yields twice the tax exemption as a long-term loss, investors should always strive to realize short-term rather than long-term losses.

> EXAMPLE   An investor earning a salary of $20,000 loses $4,000 on options during the year. She deducts $3,000 of this short-term loss from her income. The remaining $1,000 must be carried forward to another year.

Income

With only a few exceptions, the government taxes investment income like any other income. Tax-exempt interest on municipal bonds provides one welcome exception. And the first $100 in dividends provides another. The so-called **dividend exclusion** permits each taxpayer-investor to exclude the first $100 of dividends from income. These dividends can be paid on either common stock or preferred stock (payments on savings and loan association savings accounts do not qualify). For that reason every investor should consider holding some dividend-paying stocks.

Tax Year

Investors often wait until the end of the year to take their gains or losses. For this reason, it is very important to know the exact rules for determining the tax year of a transaction. Taxpayers elect to report their income on either a cash or accrual basis—most individuals use a cash basis. Taxpayers on a **cash basis** must report income in the year they actually receive payment and deduct expenses in the year they actually pay them. On the other hand, taxpayers on an **accrual basis** must report income in the year it becomes receivable and deduct expenses during the year they become payable.

> EXAMPLE   A consultant works all December for a company and receives a check for services rendered on January 3. If the consultant reports on a cash basis, the December earnings go on the tax return for the new year. If the consultant reports on an accrual basis, the earnings go on the old year's return. This is because work was performed and the consultant's claim for payment was accumulated (accrued) during December.

These rules have important implications for investors. Investors on a cash basis must actually receive payment before they report any gains on investments. Usually there is some delay between the execution of a sale and the receipt of money. For instance, an investor who sells a particular stock on December 28 does not receive payment until January in the following year because of the 5-day waiting period imposed by the securities exchanges. Therefore, no gain can be reported until the following year. For some reason, this only holds true for gains. A loss is reported in the year in which the transaction is made, regardless of whether or not payment is actually received then or in the following year. On the other hand, accrual taxpayers report the gain or loss in the year in which the investment is sold, regardless of when they receive payment.

TAX STRATEGIES

Despite the complexity of the tax laws, one simple investment strategy can save most investors tax dollars—cut your losses short, let your profits run. Unfortunately, this policy suffers from two serious shortcomings. First, most investors find it so simple and so straightforward that they can't believe it. Second, only investors make money following this policy. On the other hand, brokers, accountants, lawyers, and the government all stand to lose money. After all, anyone adhering to this strategy pays almost no commissions or taxes and needs little or no advice.

Modified Buy-and-Hold Policy

The "cut your losses short, let your profits run" philosophy represents a slight variation on the familiar buy-and-hold policy. Buying and holding minimizes commissions and other transactions costs. But in the world of taxes, a buy-and-hold policy fails to maximize shareholder wealth. Some sales are justified just because the tax laws permit investors to write off a certain amount of their losses against other income. As a result, investors need to modify the buy-and-hold policy accordingly. The new strategy is, (1) don't take gains (let your profits run); (2) take losses, providing the savings in taxes more than offset commissions and other costs (cut your losses short). When expressed this way, the buy-and-hold policy finds ready acceptance. However, investors usually agree with this philosophy because of a belief in trends rather than in generally efficient markets. If stocks or other investments trend upward to downward, it only makes sense to sell the losers and hold on to the winners.

To take taxable gains in a generally efficient market is senseless, unless absolutely necessary. The price at any one point in time provides the best indication of the value of an investment, regardless of how the investor feels about the future. Despite this fact of investment life, many people take gains simply because they believe other investments offer better prospects for appreciation. For example, someone buys 200 shares of a $10 stock and watches it climb to $15 within a few months. Because of the size and speed of the move, the individual thinks future gains will be limited or the stock price will return to a lower level. She sells, taking a $1,000 short-term gain. If she earns a taxable income of $22,000, she has assured herself of a loss of 40% of this gain just by paying federal income taxes. Here's why:

Don't Take Gain		Take Gain	
Taxable income without gain	$22,000	Taxable income without gain	$22,000
		Short-term capital gain	1,000
		Taxable income with gain	23,000
Income tax	$ 5,990	Income tax	$ 6,390

In this case the gain increases the investor's income tax by $400.

Unfortunately, no amount of logic will convince some people that they are wrong to take taxable gains. But one simple experiment can. Anyone who occasionally sells an investment which has a ready market can keep a running total of how he would have done by holding these investments rather than selling them. The transactions record in Table 11-3 provides an example of how this can be done. The first half of the table resembles the usual trading record kept by some investors. It seems to support the belief that the investor was justified in buying and selling, since each sale took place at a considerable gain and the overall results are impressive. The second half of the table shows how a buy-and-hold strategy would have performed in comparison. The taxes and commissions paid while

TABLE 11-3   A BUY-AND-HOLD STRATEGY VERSUS
A TRADING STRATEGY

Date	Decision	Price, $	Profit before Taxes and Commissions, $	Taxes, $	Commissions, $
Results from a Trading Strategy*					
Dec. 1974	Buy 1,000 shares of UAL	14			258
May 1975	Sell 1,000 shares of UAL	19	5,000	2,214	314
May 1975	Buy 644 shares of Pizza Hut	29½			292
June 1975	Sell 644 shares of Pizza Hut	31⅛	1,047	226	303
June 1975	Buy 978 shares of UAL	20½			326
Aug. 1975	Sell 978 shares of UAL	22	1,467	402	337
Aug. 1975	Buy 1,096 shares of Pizza Hut	19⅝			344
Nov. 1975	Sell 1,096 shares of Pizza Hut	22¼	2,877	1,084	366
Nov. 1975	Buy 938 shares of UAL	26			358
Dec. 1975	Sell 938 shares of UAL	28⅜	2,230	748	375
Totals			12,621	4,674	3,273
Results from a Buy-and-Hold Strategy†					
Dec. 1974	Buy 1,000 shares of UAL	14			258

* The investor is in a 50% tax bracket. During 1 year this individual spends $4,674 on taxes and another $3,273 on commissions. The profit before commissions and taxes equals $12,621. After commissions and taxes it amounts to only $4,674.

† 1,000 shares of UAL were worth $28,375 at the end of December 1975. The purchase price was $14,000. The increase in value was $14,375.

following the trading strategy and the buy-and-hold strategy are also shown. When the results are presented in this way, even the most avid trader has difficulty arguing against a buy-and-hold policy.

Taking taxable gains is senseless unless absolutely necessary. The opposite is true of tax losses. Short-term capital losses of up to $3,000 and long-term capital losses of up to $6,000 can be used to reduce income taxes. Before deciding to sell an investment and take a tax loss, the investor should consider all the costs and benefits incurred by selling.

> EXAMPLE   An investor purchases 100 shares of stock on July 9, 1978, for $30 a share. On December 30, 1978, the stock is worth only $20 a share. If the investor sells the stock, there is a short-term capital loss of $1,000. Here are the tax results if the investor pays taxes at a marginal rate of 32%:
>
> | | |
> |---|---:|
> | Tax savings if stock is sold (32% × 1,092.50 loss)* | $349.60 |
> | Less commission on sale of stock and reinvestment of proceeds | − 92.50 |
> | Savings from taking a tax loss | $257.10 |
>
> * This loss also includes commissions of $92.50.

Criticisms of the Modified Buy-and-Hold Policy

The modified buy-and-hold policy has some obvious advantages. It lowers federal and state income taxes, reduces commissions and other transactions costs, and saves the investor time. Does the policy suffer from any disadvantages? Many investors think so. Here are the usual criticisms together with possible rebuttals:

1   *Criticism*   With the modified buy-and-hold policy you never realize gains, only losses. Why bother investing if you never make any money?
Rebuttal   Trading one investment for another does not make gains or losses any more real. What counts is the market value of the investor's portfolio. A modified buy-and-hold policy maximizes this market value. As a result, the individual has more money to spend.

2   *Criticism*   Investors following a modified buy-and-hold policy resemble gamblers letting all their winnings ride on a single spin of the roulette wheel. These people are bound to lose eventually. Remember the old Wall Street saying, "Bulls and bears both make money, but not hogs."
Rebuttal   The gambling analogy is totally incorrect. But for the sake of argument, suppose the investor does take the gains and then reinvests the money in other stocks. The net effect is to switch from one roulette wheel to another. And in doing so, the investor drops a large number of chips which disappear into cracks in the floor (namely taxes and commissions).

3   *Criticism*   The modified buy-and-hold policy never lets the investor recover losses by holding on to investments which have declined in value. By the same token, there is no way to protect profits by selling. Investors adhering to a modified buy-and-hold policy violate the old Wall Street rule, "You never go broke taking profits."

Rebuttal   The idea of protecting profits or recovering losses on specific investments makes no sense at all. Investors must stop keeping score of individual investments and instead concentrate on overall results. Look at the following portfolio:

Stock	Purchase Price, $	Current Price, $	Change in Value, $
Interco	2,000	4,000	2,000
Dow Jones-Irwin	2,000	6,000	4,000
Polaroid	8,000	14,000	6,000
Control Data	6,000	4,000	−2,000
Genesco	10,000	5,000	−5,000

An investor with a score-card mentality probably views this portfolio as follows:

Stock	Won, $	Stock	Lost, $
Interco	2,000	Control Data	−2,000
Dow Jones-Irwin	4,000	Genesco	−5,000
Polaroid	6,000		

There is an obvious temptation to sell Interco, Dow Jones-Irwin, and Polaroid in order to "finalize" gains. On the other hand, the investor avoids selling Control Data and Genesco. After all they may eventually end up in the win column.

But this strategy ignores the bottom line—the profit or loss on the entire portfolio. Buying and selling can't change the fact that the stocks in the portfolio sell for $5,000 more than their cost. Nor can buying and selling change the fact that past prices provide few clues to future prices. For this reason, the "winners" and "losers" in the portfolio, together with any prospective entries, stand an equal chance in the future. All buying and selling can do is increase taxes and commissions (unless the stock is sold for a tax loss).

4   *Criticism*   The modified buy-and-hold policy completely overlooks the fact that some investors possess considerable insights into market values.

Rebuttal   Not really. Investors adhering to the modified buy-and-hold policy simply play the odds. They know that taxes on capital gains are a certainty, whereas above-average performance in a generally efficient market is very unlikely.

Even the tiny percentage of investors gifted with special insights or information can use the modified buy-and-hold policy. They should always balance the expected value of their knowledge against the taxes and commissions resulting from a trade. This will bias their behavior in the direction of taking losses, not gains—once they come to grips with their egos.

Alternatives to Taxable Gains

Tax-wise investors employ a number of techniques for avoiding or reducing taxable gains while at the same time selling or switching investments. These methods include:

1   Tax-free exchanges
2   Matching losses and gains
3   Identification of specific investments
4   Installment sales

Tax-free Exchanges   Tax-free exchanges apply to real estate, coins, art, antiques, and other tangible investments but not to securities. In order to avoid the recognition of a gain (or loss), the investment must be exchanged for property of a like kind. For example, an investor can trade an apartment building for another apartment building, or for a ranch, farm, or shopping center. However, the IRS does not permit the exchange of livestock of the opposite sexes—apparently the differences between the two sexes are just too great!

Tax-free exchanges usually involve at least three parties. For example, suppose Jones wants to sell an apartment building and buy a large ranch in New Mexico. The building originally cost Jones $200,000 and now it's worth $500,000; so a sale would create a very substantial capital gains tax. Jones avoids the problem by going to a realtor who arranges the following series of transactions:

Smith owns a ranch in New Mexico.	Thompson wants to buy Jones' apartment building.	Jones wants to sell the apartment building and buy a ranch in New Mexico.

First Thompson buys Smith's ranch in New Mexico. Then Jones trades Thompson the apartment building for the ranch. That way, everyone satisfies their original objectives and Jones pays no capital gains tax on the building.

Congress liberalized the tax-free-exchange rules for personal residences. A homeowner can actually sell his or her residence and delay any capital gains tax by building or purchasing another home. But the two transactions must take place within a period of 18 months before or 18 months after the sale of the original residence.

> EXAMPLE   A couple purchased a home for $40,000 in 1976. They sell it in 1980 for $60,000 and within a month buy another home costing $70,000. By doing so, they avoid recognizing a $20,000 capital gain.
>
> On the other hand, if they had purchased a new home costing only $55,000, they would have had to pay a capital gains tax on the $5,000 difference between the sales price of the original home and the purchase price of their new home.

Matching Gains and Losses   Taxpayers must match capital gains with losses and report the total on their tax returns. First the taxpayer offsets all short-term losses and short-term gains (including any carried over from previous years). Then the individual compares long-term losses and long-term gains. Finally both the short- and long-term categories are combined. Investors with large portfolios can almost always take a loss in the year they take a gain, thus avoiding any capital gains tax.

Identification of Specific Investments   Suppose an investor buys shares in a mutual fund or stock over a long period of time. Perhaps the transactions record looks as follows:

Date	Transaction	Price	Amount Invested
1/10/74	100 shares of General Engineering	$30	$3,000
6/15/74	100 shares of General Engineering	40	4,000
3/21/75	100 shares of General Engineering	50	5,000
4/30/76	100 shares of General Engineering	60	6,000

The average cost of the General Engineering shares equals $45 (the total investment of $18,000 divided by 400 shares). If the investor sells 100 shares in 1979 at $60 a share, the IRS assumes the first 100 shares purchased at $30 were sold, and therefore, taxes must be paid on a capital gain of $3,000. But the investor can specifically identify the shares sold by asking a broker to "sell the 100 shares purchased on 4/30/76 at $60 a share." This completely eliminates the capital gain and the capital gains tax. (By the way, the broker must acknowledge in writing the investor's request before executing the sale.)

Installment Sale   The **installment-sale** procedure does not really eliminate taxable gains. It simply delays the agony of payment. With an installment sale, the investor prorates the gain on the sale over the life of the installment contract. But the seller can receive no more than 30% of the sale price during the year of the sale.

INCOME STRATEGIES

There is a second simple strategy for reducing or eliminating taxes—don't receive taxable income. Income from investments usually gets taxed at ordinary tax rates. Unless the investor falls in a low tax bracket, it makes no sense to hold investments paying a considerable taxable income.

Municipal Bonds

One alternative is to invest in tax-exempt municipal bonds. But these bonds are not appropriate for every investor. The rationale for this statement is a familiar

TABLE 11-4 A COMPARISON OF BEFORE-TAX YIELDS ON TAX-EXEMPT
AND TAXABLE BONDS

Date	Yields on Aaa Taxable Bonds, %	Yields on Aaa Tax-exempt Bonds, %	Difference in Yields, %
October 1969	7.33	5.80	1.53
October 1970	8.03	6.05	1.98
October 1971	7.39	4.75	2.64
October 1972	7.21	5.03	2.18
October 1973	7.60	4.76	2.84
October 1974	9.27	6.21	3.06
October 1975	8.86	6.67	2.19
October 1976	8.32	5.29	3.03

Source: Reprinted from Moody's Investors Services, Inc., *Moody's Bond Record,* February 1977.

one—competition. People in high tax brackets compete for the available tax-exempt bonds by bidding up their prices and/or by agreeing to lower pretax incomes.

The end result of this competition can be seen by comparing the yields on tax-exempt and non-tax-exempt bonds of similar quality. Table 11-4 shows the average yield on bonds rated Aaa (the highest rating given by Moody's). On October 1969, taxable bonds yielded 7.33%. At the same time tax-exempt bonds yielded only 5.8%. That's a difference of 1.53%. In more recent years the yield spread widened still further. By 1974 taxable bonds were offering 9.27%, while tax-exempt bonds were yielding only 6.21%.

Judging from these figures, investors usually sacrifice several percentage points in yield by holding tax-exempt bonds. For that reason, only individuals and institutions in higher tax brackets should purchase tax-exempt bonds. The taxes these investors save on interest income more than offset the lower pretax yields.

In order to determine whether to purchase tax-exempt or taxable bonds, the investor must compare the **marginal after-tax returns** on both types of bonds. Marginal refers to the last dollar of income. And the after-tax return equals the return after paying all taxes. So the marginal after-tax return equals the return after taxes on the last dollar of income. For example, if an investor falls in a 40% tax bracket, 40¢ of each additional dollar of income must be paid in taxes and only 60¢ remains. Therefore, the after-tax return from a taxable investment amounts to only 60% of the pretax return. For example, the marginal after-tax return on a bond paying 10% equals 6%. As a general rule, the marginal after-tax return to any investor equals 1 minus the investor's marginal tax rate times the return before taxes.

Given this information, any investor can determine whether or not to purchase tax-exempt bonds. Obviously, individuals or institutions in a zero-tax bracket, such as pension funds, have no business buying such bonds. This advice also holds true for investors in low tax brackets. Suppose tax-exempt bonds yield

7% and taxable bonds 10%. Only if the investor pays taxes at a marginal rate of 30% or more does it make sense to buy tax-exempt bonds. An investor in a 30% tax bracket realizes the same after-tax return from a taxable bond as from a tax-exempt—in this case 7%. This can be seen as follows:

	Before-Tax Return, %	*After-Tax Return, %*
Tax-exempt bond	7	7
Taxable bond	10	$(1 - 0.30) \times 10 = 7$

Any investor paying a marginal tax rate of 50% receives an after-tax return from tax-exempt bonds of 7%, whereas the after-tax return on taxable bonds equals only 5%. These after-tax returns are calculated as follows:

	Before-Tax Return, %	*After-Tax Return, %*
Tax-exempt bond	7	7
Taxable bond	10	$(1 - 0.50) \times 10 = 5$

The after-tax returns from taxable bonds purchased at face value are shown in Table 11-5.

TABLE 11-5   AFTER-TAX RETURNS TO INVESTORS IN DIFFERENT TAX BRACKETS

% Bracket	32	36	39	42	45	48	50	53	55	58	60	62	64
					Before-Tax Returns								
4.25	6.25	6.64	6.97	7.33	7.73	8.17	8.50	9.15	9.56	10.24	10.75	11.32	11.94
4.50	6.62	7.03	7.38	7.76	8.18	8.65	9.00	9.57	10.00	10.71	11.25	11.84	12.50
4.75	6.99	7.42	7.79	8.19	8.64	9.13	9.50	10.11	10.56	11.31	11.88	12.50	13.19
5.00	7.35	7.81	8.20	8.62	9.09	9.62	10.00	10.64	11.11	11.90	12.50	13.16	13.89
5.25	7.72	8.20	8.61	9.05	9.55	10.10	10.50	11.17	11.67	12.50	13.12	13.82	14.58
5.50	8.09	8.59	9.02	9.48	10.00	10.58	11.00	11.70	12.22	13.10	13.75	14.47	15.28
5.75	8.46	8.98	9.43	9.91	10.45	11.06	11.50	12.23	12.78	13.69	14.38	15.13	15.97
6.00	8.82	9.37	9.84	10.34	10.91	11.54	12.00	12.77	13.33	14.29	15.00	15.79	16.67
6.25	9.19	9.77	10.25	10.78	11.36	12.02	12.50	13.30	13.89	14.88	15.63	16.45	17.36
6.50	9.56	10.16	10.66	11.21	11.82	12.50	13.00	13.83	14.44	15.48	16.25	17.11	18.06
6.75	9.93	10.55	11.07	11.64	12.27	12.98	13.50	14.36	15.00	16.07	16.87	17.76	18.75
7.00	10.29	10.94	11.48	12.07	12.73	13.46	14.00	14.89	15.56	16.67	17.50	18.42	19.44
7.25	10.66	11.33	11.89	12.50	13.18	13.94	14.50	15.43	16.11	17.26	18.13	19.08	20.14
7.50	11.03	11.72	12.30	12.93	13.64	14.42	15.00	15.96	16.67	17.86	18.75	19.74	20.83
7.75	11.40	12.11	12.70	13.36	14.09	14.90	15.50	16.49	17.22	18.45	19.37	20.39	21.53
8.00	11.76	12.50	13.11	13.79	14.55	15.38	16.00	17.02	17.78	19.05	20.00	21.05	22.22

Left margin label: After-Tax Returns

Example: A person in a 64% tax bracket who makes a before-tax return of 22.22% will keep only 8% after taxes. Therefore, a tax-exempt bond yielding 8% provides the same after-tax return as a taxable bond yielding 22.22%.

Growth Stocks

Another alternative to receiving taxable income is to buy investments in which the income is retained rather than paid out. The best example of this is stock in a growth company. As a rule, growth companies reinvest most of their earnings. For example, McDonald's earned $2.20 a share in 1975 but paid no dividends. In contrast, firms experiencing low growth have little need to retain their earnings. McGraw-Edison, a manufacturer of heavy electrical equipment, earned $2.05 a share in 1975 and paid a dividend of $1.28.

Of course, it does no good to just buy stock in a firm paying no or low dividends. The stock must also increase in value. Generally speaking, the lower the dividend payment, the greater the increase in the value of the firm. After all, the firm usually makes additional profits on reinvested earnings. The price of the stock goes up as a reflection of these increased earnings and the prospect of larger future dividends.

Because of the considerable tax advantage in receiving capital gains as opposed to dividends, one would expect people to prefer stocks paying low dividends. As a result, the prices of low-dividend stocks should be bid up until the before-tax returns fall below those on high-dividend stocks. This is true of tax-exempt and taxable bonds. Strangely enough, it does not appear to be the case with stocks. According to Black at M.I.T. and Scholes at the University of Chicago, both professors of finance, the before-tax returns are apparently just as large for low-payout stocks as for high-payout stocks. No one can explain why this is so. But investors not needing the income would do well to avoid buying stocks paying sizable dividends. Instead, they should hold stocks paying low dividends and appreciating in price. These price gains are not taxed at all while they remain unrealized. Should an investment have to be sold, advance planning can ensure that the capital gain is long term, so that the gain is taxed at only one half the rate of dividends.

Series E Government Bonds

Government bonds provide another example of reducing taxes by not taking income. Interest on Series E bonds is not paid to the investor; instead it is added to the redemption value of the bond. This build-up in value of the bond is shown in Table 16-6. When held to maturity, a government savings bond yields 6% before taxes.

The holder of a Series E bond can report the yearly increase in the value of this bond as interest received during the year or wait until cashing the bond in and then report the entire increase as interest. Since the increase in value is still taxed as interest, the tax benefits of this latter course of action are not as marked as in the case of growth stocks, where the appreciation resulting from retained earnings is a capital gain. However, being able to defer taxes for a considerable period of time is a valuable right in itself. Any money held even temporarily can be invested and earn interest. Moreover, this deferment of taxes can go on for a long time if so desired. Even the death of the owner of a Series E bond need not result in the payment of income taxes on the accrued interest.

Deferring taxes has another advantage. Often an investor's income declines considerably with age and then retirement. If taxes are not paid until the low-income years, tax rates and consequently taxes may be considerably lower than they would have been otherwise.

Government securities, including savings bonds, have another advantage. Interest paid on these bonds is exempt from state income taxation.

Despite these advantages, government savings bonds are not a very attractive investment for most investors. The yields are usually just too low compared with those on similar securities.

Pension Funds

Pension funds provide many investors with another means for deferring taxation on investment income. Any income paid into a qualified pension plan is not taxed until paid out. In addition, pension funds have several other attractions: payments of taxes on realized capital gains are deferred, and when taxes are finally paid, the investor can select an averaging technique which reduces his total tax bill. The effect that the deferment of income taxes can have is shown in Table 12-1 in Chapter Twelve.

Income Averaging

Since the federal income tax is a graduated tax, it penalizes the individual with a fluctuating income. For example, someone who makes $40,000 one year and zero the next pays considerably more in income taxes than someone who makes $20,000 in each of 2 years.

To some extent Congress has recognized the inequity which exists when taxpayers who make the same total income pay grossly different taxes. As a result, the government permits **5-year income averaging** on tax returns. But the rules for income averaging are unnecessarily complicated and are somewhat restrictive.

Not everyone is eligible to use income averaging. Only individuals (not firms) who have been citizens or residents of the United States for 5 years and who can pass a **support test** are allowed to use income averaging. In order to pass the support test, an individual must have provided 50% or more of his or her own support during each of the 4 years previous to the year for which income averaging is used. If a joint return is filed, both the husband and the wife must meet this test. (There are some complicated exceptions to these rules.)

To see how income averaging can be used, imagine that an individual had a taxable income of $38,000 during the current year, which is called the **computation year.** Income in each of the 4 previous years, which are referred to as the **base years,** was $8,000. Without income averaging the income tax on $38,000 equals $13,290. The amount of the tax paid on the current income can be reduced by computing the tax on the basis of income averaging. Here are the necessary calculations:

1	30% of total income received in the 4 base years (0.30 × $32,000)	$ 9,600.00
2	20% of difference between current income of $38,000 and $9,600	5,680.00
3	Sum of items *1* and *2*	$15,280.00
4	Income tax on income shown on line *3*	$ 3,606.80
5	Income tax on income shown on line *1*	1,990.00
6	Difference in taxes on items *4* and *5*	$ 1,616.80
7	Four times the amount on line *6*	$ 6,467,20
8	Total tax for the current year (sum of items *4* and *7*)	$10,074.00

If income averaging hadn't been used, the tax on $38,000 would have been $13,290 instead of $10,074.

With income averaging, a taxpayer earning $38,000 in 1 year and $8,000 in each of 4 years pays a total tax of $16,434 on $70,000 in income. On the other hand, an individual who makes $14,000 a year for each of 5 years for the same total income of $70,000 pays a total of $16,050 in taxes. So income averaging almost provides for equal taxes on equal incomes.

Income Splitting

Income averaging can save taxpayers tax dollars. Another technique called **income splitting** works on the same principle. But with income splitting, income is averaged over different individuals rather than over different time periods. Imagine a family of four making $30,000 a year. If the husband and wife file a joint return, their tax bracket equals 39% and the tax amounts to $7,880. The fact that this family is in a 39% tax bracket means that 39¢ out of every additional dollar of income goes to the government. If they could only shift some of their income to a lower tax bracket, they could hold on to much more of it.

For example, if the parents can somehow shift $1,000 to each of their two children, the family will save $640 in taxes. Here's how: The children must each pay $70 in taxes on their $1,000 incomes or a total of $140. (They each have an exemption of $750. That leaves a taxable income of $250, which is taxed at 14%.) On the other hand, their parents reduce their taxable income by $2,000 and save $780 = ($2,000 × 0.39).

Unfortunately, income cannot be shifted by simply giving children part of the parents' income. Nor can the parents use some subterfuge like paying their children $1,000 each for doing household duties. Instead income shifting must be accomplished by (1) transferring income-producing property to the children, or (2) incorporating a family business and paying the children for assisting in its operation. Since few families have real business operations, the transfer of income-producing property has become the most popular means of shifting income. For example, United States savings bonds can be bought in a child's name alone. Then all interest on the bonds is taxable to the child, even though the parents can redeem the bonds if necessary. However, many people make the mistake of buying bonds for their children and registering the bonds in the name of the child with themselves as co-owners. As a result, they must pay the income tax on the interest.

Gifts of securities can also be made to children in order to transfer income-producing property. If the child is a minor, the appropriate form in which to make this gift is called **statutory custodianship.** This arrangement makes it possible for the custodian—usually the person making the gift—to manage the property. The custodian can sell the property, reinvest the proceeds, pay over to the minor any income or property for the support, maintenance, benefit, and education of the minor, etc. Statutory custodianship is a very flexible form of transfer which involves little or no cost. It is far superior to an outright gift of securities or shares in a mutual fund to a minor, since the future sale or transfer of this property can be blocked.

When a substantial transfer of property is being considered, a trust should probably be used. A **trust** is a legal arrangement which provides for control of property. The most widely used type of trust for income shifting is a 10-year-1-day trust, sometimes called a **Clifford trust.** This type of trust makes it possible for a person to be an "Indian giver" and only temporarily give away property. The property can be recovered at the end of a stated period of time or upon the death of the person to whom the property was given. Moreover, some control can even be retained over the property during the period of the "gift." The following example shows how a trust can be used to reduce income taxes:

EXAMPLE John and Mary Davis have saved $20,000, which they plan to use for the education of their 5-year-old son, John, Jr. At the present time, the money is invested in corporate bonds which yield 10%; so the yearly income on the bonds equals $2,000. Since the Davises already make $30,000 a year, they must pay $780 in taxes on the $2,000 in interest. And as the years go by and the interest accumulates, they will pay higher and higher taxes on the increased interest.

John and Mary have considered putting the bonds in a custodial account for John, Jr., at their local brokerage firm. But they have three reservations. First, they may someday need the money for themselves. Second, $20,000 is a lot of money for an eighteen-year-old to have. Third, in the event of their death, the custodial account might be managed badly. For these reasons, they decide to create a trust for John, Jr. The trust must last for at least 10 years and 1 day or until the death of the beneficiary (John, Jr.) in order to qualify for an income-shifting tax break. This presents no problem, since John, Jr., won't start college for 13 more years. John and Mary decide to have the trust last until John, Jr., turns 18, at which time the bonds revert to them. All accumulated income will be paid out to John, Jr., at that time.

TAX SHELTERS

Very few investors appreciate the fact that common stocks paying low dividends provide an excellent tax shelter. Probably still fewer recognize the tax savings possible with Series E government bonds. And only recently have individuals begun to learn about the unique tax-saving features of pension funds. Instead, the phrase "tax shelters" invokes images of real estate, oil and gas, cattle feeding, equipment leases, citrus and almond groves, and vineyards.

Tax-sheltered investments offer two important tax advantages: (1) conversion and (2) deferral. **Conversion** consists of the opportunity to incur deductions against ordinary income while at the same time earning income taxed at reduced rates. **Deferral** involves the postponement of taxes to a later date. Some experts on tax shelters add a third possible tax advantage to the list—**guaranteed deductibility** of investment losses. In other words, investors in some tax shelters can write off the full amount of their capital losses rather than being limited to a specific amount during any one year.

Cattle Feeding Cattle feeding provides a good example of deferral. The "feeding" process begins with the purchase of young cattle weighing from 400 to 750 pounds. These cattle are housed in feedlot pens, where they are fed a special diet for 4 to 6 months. The "finished" cattle, each weighing about 1,000 pounds, are then sold at public auctions to meat packers.

By purchasing cattle and feed near the end of the year, taxpayers create deductions against the current year's income. This defers income taxes until the following year, when the owners sell the cattle for a profit. However, by investing more and more money in cattle-feeding operations, taxpayers can presumably defer the receipt of taxable income forever.

The deferral of income taxes benefits investors in three ways. First, deferral provides the taxpayer with an interest-free loan from the government equal to the amount of the tax. Suppose the investor owes $50,000 in taxes. By deferring the payment for 1 year, the investor can invest the $50,000 and earn a return on the money. Second, deferral makes it possible for the taxpayer to shift income into a later year, when he or she falls in a much lower tax bracket. Third, deferral enables the taxpayer to delay the payment of taxes until he or she has the necessary cash.

Equipment Leases Equipment leases also provide a deferral of taxes. Most leases involve long-term rental agreements. These leases cover a wide variety of equipment, including computers, trucks, planes, railroad cars, and drilling rigs. Suppose a group of investors decides to buy a computer and lease it to a company. By writing off accelerated and bonus depreciation on the computer, the investors realize substantial tax losses in the early years of the lease. Then as the allowance for depreciation declines, taxable income from the lease increases. The net effect—a deferral of taxable income to a later year.

EXAMPLE   A group of doctors buys a computer and leases it to a company. The government permits taxpayers to depreciate computers over a 5-year period—the assumed useful life of a computer. By the way, the word **depreciate** means to reduce the estimated value. Supposedly the value of an asset declines each year because of obsolescence and wear and tear. For that reason, the government allows taxpayers to write off depreciation on any income-producing asset.

Taxpayers can elect a number of different depreciation techniques. The simplest is **straight-line depreciation.** With straight-line depreciation, taxpayers deduct an equal portion of the assumed loss in value each year. Suppose the computer costs $50,000. Then with the straight-line technique, the taxpayers deduct one-fifth, or 20%, of the $50,000 cost each year, that is, $10,000. Why one-fifth? Because the assumed life of the computer equals only 5 years. At the end of that period the computer is assumed to be worthless.

Instead of taking straight-line depreciation, the doctors decide to use **double declining-balance depreciation.** With the double declining-balance method, the taxpayer applies twice the straight-line rate, in this case 40%, to the undepreciated balance.

In addition to the regular depreciation, taxpayers claim 20% bonus depreciation on new equipment.

Real Estate   Real estate tax shelters offer conversion and/or deferral. Taxpayers can obtain these benefits by investing in a wide variety of real estate projects, including apartments, office buildings, industrial parks, shopping centers, mobile-house parks, and raw land.

To see how conversion works, assume a group of 10 investors purchases 200 acres of land. The acreage lies alongside a major highway about 20 miles from a large city. If the city continues to grow, the land should double in value in 5 years. Here are the complete details of this land deal:

Purchase price	$1,000,000
Down payment	$100,000
Loan at 10%	$900,000
Annual interest payment	$90,000

The buyers agree to divide all costs and gains equally.

Interest payments can be deducted against ordinary income. So each of the investors deducts $9,000 a year in interest. If the investor pays taxes at the 70% marginal rate, this deduction reduces taxes by $6,300. Then at the end of the fifth year the group sells the property, but for $1,450,000 instead of $2,000,000. Now each investor reports a long-term capital gain of $45,000. Despite the fact that total interest payments exactly equal the increase in the land price, the investor benefits. This can be seen as follows:

	Benefits	Costs
Total interest payments (5 years × $9,000)		$45,000
Savings in income taxes (5 years × $6,300)	$31,500	
Long-term capital gain	$45,000	
Increase in taxes		15,750
	$76,500	60,750
Net gain from investment	$15,750	

Apartment buildings offer deferral as well as conversion. First, the investor converts interest payments on the mortgage into long-term capital gains (if all goes well). Second, the investor writes off large amounts of depreciation in the early years, thereby shifting income taxes into the later years.

Oil and Gas Probably the most publicized tax shelters involve oil and gas. Getting oil and gas out of the underground rock where it accumulates takes large amounts of money. Nowadays a single well costs upward of $250,000 to drill. And only 1 in every 10 exploratory wells results in a discovery of a new field. Perhaps more important, only 1 well in every 40 or 50 becomes a commercial success.

In order to encourage the search for oil and gas, Congress has long provided the oil and gas industry with favorable tax treatment. Investors in oil wells can deduct intangible drilling costs from income. And depletion allowances (similar to depreciation) shelter part of the gross income. Finally the owners can sell a producing property for a capital gain.

Limited Partnerships

Tax-sheltered investments like oil and gas, cattle feeding, and real estate require constant supervision and expert management. For these reasons, most of these tax shelters are operated as limited partnerships. The word "limited" refers to the limited liability offered by this type of partnership.

There are two categories of partners in a limited partnership: a **general partner** and **limited partners.** The limited partners are the investors. They assume a strictly passive role in the partnership, simply providing the money and hoping for a satisfactory outcome. The general partner is an individual and/or a company with expertise in managing a specific type of tax shelter. The general partner seeks out investors, invests their money, keeps the partnership books, reports the financial results, and distributes any profits. For these services, the general partner receives a management fee from the limited partners and quite often shares in the profits.

Why structure tax-sheltered investments as limited partnerships and not corporations? Because all losses and gains from a partnership flow through to the partners. As a result, partners can deduct their share of the losses. With a corporation the losses can only be used to offset corporate income. (The Subchapter S corporation provides an exception to this rule.)

THE COSTS OF REDUCING TAXES

There are costs as well as benefits in reducing taxes. One of the most obvious costs has already been mentioned—the lower pretax returns available on most tax-sheltered investments. There is another significant cost associated with tax-sheltered investments which many investors overlook because it is nonmonetary. Since tax-sheltered investments are financed with large amounts of debt, they are usually quite risky. Although this debt makes it possible for investors to obtain larger tax benefits from the investment, at the same time it exposes them to considerable fluctuations in the value of the investment. It is no coincidence that investors in tax sheltered ventures often lose their entire investment and sometimes are even forced to provide additional funds to make up the losses.

Complex tax laws and ever-changing legislation add to the risks of tax shelters. Probably the most serious risk arises from the fact that the tax laws can be interpreted in numerous ways. What may seem to be a perfectly valid tax shelter to investors and their lawyers can be turned into a tax liability by the Internal Revenue Service. Beauty is definitely in the eyes of the beholder. In an effort to eliminate some of this risk, the IRS used to issue what became known as **safe-harbor rulings.** These rulings stated certain conditions which tax-sheltered investments should satisfy. If a tax shelter met these conditions, investors could be reasonably certain that the IRS would not rule adversely on the investment. Unfortunately, Congressional pressure has resulted in the IRS discontinuing its issuance of safe-harbor rulings, so that the risk of an adverse judgment is ever present.

The complexity of the tax laws also imposes costs on taxpayers seeking tax shelters. It is now quite possible that a tax-sheltered investment will increase taxes rather than reduce them. For instance, a tax shelter may result in a shifting of income out of the 50% maximum tax bracket on earned income into tax brackets as high as 70%. In addition, the tax shelter may substantially increase so-called preference items, such as interest, capital gains, and accelerated depreciation. The government imposes a minimum tax of 15% on excessive deductions. Obviously, the taxpayer should rely on expert tax advisers, who coincidentally command high fees. But even experts make mistakes.

Investors playing the tax-shelter game face one additional risk—they increase the chances of being scrutinized by the Internal Revenue Service. A good example of this increased audit risk is provided by a specialized audit program referred to as the IRS Drilling Fund Program, which was directed at oil and gas tax shelters. With computer assistance, this program identified 200 drilling funds which had an estimated 24,000 investors in various parts of the United States. The tax returns of these investors were then audited by the IRS. The IRS supposedly plans to expand the program on a national basis and to operate similar programs for real estate and other tax shelters.

SUMMARY

Every investor can save tax dollars by following two simple rules. The first is not to take capital gains unless absolutely necessary. This can be accomplished by adopting a buy-and-hold policy and by using tax-free exchanges whenever possible. If gains must be taken, every attempt should be made to realize only long-term gains. On the other hand, losses should always be taken whenever it is possible to reduce taxes or whenever funds are needed. Investors who believe in the efficient-market concept will have no difficulty following these policies. The second rule investors should follow is not to take taxable income unless it is needed.

There are other ways to reduce taxes. Two of the simplest are income averaging and income splitting. Income splitting can easily be accomplished by transferring income-producing property to family members who are in lower tax brackets, through making outright gifts or creating trusts. Income averaging can only be used by investors whose income varies greatly from year to year.

Investors who are in higher tax brackets will want to explore other strategies for reducing taxes. But they should do so with the realization that there are costs as well as benefits in investing in most tax shelters. And these trade-offs should be considered in any investment strategy.

KEYWORDS

graduated (progressive) tax	cash basis	Clifford trust
average tax rates	accrual basis	conversion
marginal tax rates	tax-free exchanges	deferral
tax bracket	installment sale	guaranteed deductibility
taxable income	marginal after-tax returns	depreciate
capital gain	5-year income averaging	straight-line depreciation
capital asset	support test	double declining-balance
capital losses	computation year	depreciation
short term	base years	general partner
long term	income splitting	limited partners
holding period	statutory custodianship	safe-harbor rulings
dividend exclusion	trust	

QUESTIONS

1 Distinguish between marginal and average tax rates.

2 Use the rates shown in Figure 11-1 to calculate the income tax paid by a single person on an income of $10,000. What is the average tax rate? What is the tax rate on the last dollar earned by the taxpayer?

3 Do you believe in a graduated income tax? Why or why not?

4 What are your own state income tax rates? For a general idea, refer to Table 11-2. Otherwise look at an old state income tax return or call the local office of the State Commissioner of Revenue.

5 Define a long-term capital gain. Does the definition depend upon the year the taxpayer realizes the gain?

6 How much of a short-term loss can a taxpayer write off in 1978 and each year thereafter? What if the loss exceeds these limits?

7 Why should individual investors hold enough common or preferred stock to receive $100 in dividends?

8 Consider the following situation: A single taxpayer expects to earn $20,000 in the current year and $40,000 in the following year. Suppose the taxpayer has a sizable loss on a stock. Should the loss be taken this year or next?

9   Do you think most investors follow a modified buy-and-hold policy? Why or why not?

10 How would you have fared in your own investment program by adhering to a modified buy-and-hold policy?

11 Discuss the alternatives to taking taxable gains.

12 Suppose tax-exempt bonds yield 6% and taxable bonds return 9%. Should a married couple living in Minnesota and earning $40,000 purchase tax-exempt bonds? (What condition do these bonds have to satisfy in order to be exempt from the state income tax?)

13 Devise an income-splitting strategy for your own family.

14 Explain why tax-favored treatment reduces the cost of beef and oil and lowers the rent on apartments.

15 Why are most tax shelters structured as limited partnerships?

REFERENCES

Black, Fischer, and Myron Scholes: "The Effects of Dividend Yield and Dividend Policy on Common Stock Prices and Returns," *Journal of Financial Economics,* May 1974, pp. 1–22.

Break, George F., and Joseph A. Pechman: *Federal Tax Reform: The Impossible Dream,* Brookings, Washington, D.C., 1975.

Commerce Clearing House Editorial Staff: *1977 U.S. Master Tax Guide,* 60th ed., Commerce Clearing House, Chicago, Ill., 1976.

"Could a Trust Fund Save You Money?" *Changing Times: The Kiplinger Magazine,* July 1975, pp. 37–40.

Facts and Figures on Government Finance, Tax Foundation, New York, 1975.

Hitchings, Bradley, ed.: "Real Estate Swapping: A Complex Tax Shelter," *Business Week,* Feb. 7, 1977, pp. 81–82.

*Greisman, Bernard, ed.: *1977 Edition of J. K. Lasser's Your Income Tax,* Simon and Schuster, New York, 1977.

The J. K. Lasser Tax Institute: *J. K. Lasser's Saving Tax Money with Trusts,* Business Reports, Larchmont, N.Y., 1975.

Main, Jeremy: "Trusts Are More than a Means to an End," *Money,* August 1974, pp. 66–71.

*National Retired Teachers Association and American Association of Retired Persons: *Tax Facts 1976,* Washington, D.C., March 1976.

Reid, Peter C., and Gustave Simons, eds.: *Corporate and Executive Tax Sheltered Investments,* Presidents Publishing House, New York, 1972.

"Take Your Tax Return Step by Step," *Changing Times: The Kiplinger Magazine,* February 1975, pp. 18–22.

U.S. Advisory Commission on Intergovernmental Relations: *Inflation and Federal and State Income Taxes,* November 1976.

U.S. Department of Treasury, Internal Revenue Service, *Statistics of Income: Individual Income Tax Returns,* 1976.

* Publications preceded by an asterisk are highly recommended.

CHAPTER TWELVE

TAX-SHELTERED RETIREMENT PLANS

Because of earlier retirement and longer life expectancies, the amount of money needed for retirement has increased significantly over the last several decades. Many people now retire at fifty-five to sixty years of age. And these individuals can confidently expect to live until they are between seventy-five and eighty. Since most retirees earn very little from part-time jobs, they must rely on either their own savings or society for the necessary income.

An increasingly large part of these savings is being placed in private retirement (pension) plans. Most plans qualify for important tax advantages. Contributions to an IRS-approved plan are considered to be deductions from taxable income and result in substantial savings in taxes. In addition, income and capital gains earned on pension assets escape taxation until paid out as retirement benefits. The **Pension Reform Act of 1974** makes it possible for all employees to share in these benefits. No wonder the assets of private pension plans now total more than $200 billion and continue to grow rapidly.

MAJOR ADVANTAGES OF TAX-SHELTERED RETIREMENT PLANS

Nearly everyone earning either a salary or self-employed income can participate in a tax-sheltered retirement plan. The four major types of tax-sheltered retirement plans are:

1 **Individual Retirement Account** (usually abbreviated IRA and pronounced I-RAH)
2 HR-10 or **Keogh** (pronounced KEY-OH) **plan**
3 **Tax-sheltered annuity** program
4 Qualified corporate pension and/or profit-sharing plan

Generally speaking, anyone earning a salary and not taking part in another type of tax-sheltered pension plan can start an IRA. In order to participate in a Keogh plan, the individual must have some self-employed income or work for an employer with a Keogh plan. Tax-sheltered annuities are available to employees of schools and universities, hospitals, and other nonprofit institutions. And many companies provide their employees with pension and/or profit-sharing plans.

Tax-deductible Contributions

Tax-sheltered retirement plans offer two important advantages over ordinary savings plans. First, contributions (the amount paid) to these plans qualify as deductions from taxable income. Second, interest and/or gains on money invested in these plans are not taxed until withdrawn. As a result, pension plans grow tax-free.

To see how a contribution to an IRA, Keogh, or tax-sheltered annuity reduces an individual's income taxes, suppose a woman earns a taxable income of $10,000 a year. In other words, her income after all deductions and exemptions totals $10,000. If she contributes $1,500 to an IRA, the impact on her tax bill is as follows:

Taxable income without plan	$10,000
Average tax rate[1]	20.9%
Income tax without plan	$ 2,090
Taxable income without plan	$10,000
Contribution to plan	1,500
Taxable income with plan	$ 8,500
Average tax rate	20.2%
Income tax with plan	$1,717
Income tax savings	$ 373

Contributions by an individual to an IRA, Keogh, or tax-sheltered annuity qualify as a tax deduction. But workers already covered by a company plan are not able to take advantage of these individual retirement plans. In most company pension and/or profit-sharing plans, the employer makes the contribution and the employee pays nothing. For that reason, the employee is not allowed to deduct the contribution from his or her income.

Even so, the impact on the individual's tax bill compares favorably with that of other tax-sheltered retirement plans. An employer must usually choose between making contributions to a pension plan or not making contributions and paying higher salaries to employees. For example, an employer can either pay a $10,000 salary to each employee or pay $8,500 and contribute $1,500 to the pension plan of each. With a qualified pension plan, none of this $1,500 gets reported as income. And it grows tax-free, just as a contribution to an individual retirement plan does.

Tax Deferral on Interest and Gains

Contributions to tax-sheltered retirement plans not only reduce today's taxes, they also reduce taxes in the future. No tax is paid on any interest or gains until money is withdrawn from the plan. By then the taxpayer usually falls in a much lower tax bracket and can take advantage of other tax-saving devices soon to be described.

This tax-free buildup can be very important. For example, someone with a taxable income of $10,000 pays taxes of $192 on $800 interest. With a tax-sheltered retirement plan, the full $800 is retained until it is withdrawn from the plan. The tax savings are still more substantial for someone with a taxable income of $40,000. Without the plan this individual pays the government $440 of the $800 interest and keeps only $360. Again, with a tax-sheltered retirement plan, the full $800 is retained until the money is withdrawn.

Long-Term Results

So far only the 1 year results of a tax-sheltered pension plan have been examined. What effect do these tax-shelter features have over a long period of time? The exact answer depends upon the investor's own personal situation. Investors save more in taxes:

1   The higher their tax brackets
2   The more they earn on their investments
3   The larger their contributions
4   The longer they keep their money in a plan

The following examples demonstrate the savings possible with a tax-sheltered retirement plan:

A twenty-five-year-old man has a taxable income of $10,000. He sets aside $500 a year every year in a tax-sheltered retirement plan until he is sixty-five. He earns 8% on his money. Here are the results (calculated with a computer) over the 40-year period:

End of Year	Amount in Tax-sheltered Plan, $	Amount in Ordinary Savings Plan, $	Difference, $
10	9,909	7,646	2,263
20	29,667	20,881	8,786
30	71,722	45,338	26,384
40	161,432	89,126	72,306

A forty-five-year-old business woman with a taxable income of $40,000 sets aside $6,000 a year in a Keogh plan until she is sixty-five. Here are the results over the 20-year period:

End of Year	Amount in Tax-sheltered Plan, $	Amount in Ordinary Savings Plan, $	Difference, $
5	63,905	39,612	24,293
10	140,604	79,795	60,809
15	248,363	127,494	120,869
20	400,718	183,388	217,330

BASIC MECHANICS OF RETIREMENT PLANS

Regardless of whether a person participates in a company, government, or individual retirement plan, the basic determination of the amounts necessary to pay retirement benefits remains the same. The key factors affecting this determination are (1) the expected life of the individual, (2) the expected return on the investments, (3) the desired pattern of contributions to the fund, and (4) the benefits from the plan.

The impact of each of these factors is best analyzed by referring to a simple example. Suppose a thirty-five-year-old man wants to receive a lifetime retirement income of $20,000 a year beginning at age sixty-five, to be paid entirely from his own savings. Having decided upon the benefits to be paid by the plan, he must next determine how long those benefits will be paid. If he lives until age sixty-five, he can then expect to live for 15 more years, or until he reaches eighty. (This life expectancy comes from special tables prepared by the Internal Revenue Service.) Therefore, his savings together with the interest earned on them must be sufficient to provide at least 15 payments of $20,000 each.

At a 10% rate of interest, 15 annual payments of $20,000 have a present value of $167,340 ($1 received at the start of every year for 15 years has a present value at 10% equal to $8.367). In other words, the prospective retiree must save $167,340 by the time he reaches sixty-five. Knowing the amount needed for retirement, he has one final decision to make concerning the desired pattern of contributions. If he decides to set aside, or "fund," the same amount every year, it is a simple matter to calculate how much this amount must be. Since $1 a year invested at the start of each year at 10% accumulates to $180.94 in 30 years, $924.84 a year grows to $167,340. Thus, by saving $924.84 each year at 10%, the investor assures himself of an annual pension of $20,000 for 15 years, providing he continues to make 10% on his savings after he retires.

A number of important assumptions were made in the preceding example. The first concerns the rate of return on investments. If the investor earns only 2% a year instead of 10%, he must save $6,335 a year rather than $924.84. On the other hand, if he earns 16%, it is necessary to set aside only $210 a year. Obviously the government, a company, or an individual can arrive at radically different answers about the contributions needed to pay retirement benefits, depending upon the assumptions they make about future interest rates. Moreover, it should be apparent by now that a fixed-contribution pension plan can never by itself provide a guaranteed benefit. Even though an annual contribution of $924.84 may initially appear to be enough to provide an annual benefit of $20,000 for 15 years, any change in the returns actually earned on those contributions changes the benefits that can be paid from pension assets. For example, if pension assets grow at only 2% a year, contributions of $924.84 for 30 years provide only $2,919.96 a year in pension benefits.

The contributions required to fund a pension plan also depend upon the expected lifetime of the individual. If a man lives to be ninety instead of eighty, annual contributions of $924.84 invested at 10% will provide only $16,761 per year in benefits during the 25 years of retirement. In order to provide the full benefit of $20,000 for 25 years, an annual contribution of $1,103.55 must be made. Obviously the longer the retiree lives after retirement, the larger the contributions that he must make to his pension plan during his working life. For that reason, the longer retirement periods made possible through increased life expectancies and early retirement have placed great financial strains on individual, company, and government pension plans.

INDIVIDUAL RETIREMENT ACCOUNTS

The Pension Reform Act of 1974 (the real name is actually the Employment Retirement Income Security Act or ERISA for short), makes it possible for wage earners not already participating in a tax-sheltered pension plan to create their own plans. The plan is called an Individual Retirement Account. An individual starting an IRA simply fills out the necessary forms with a bank, savings and loan association, mutual fund, life insurance company, or other financial institution offering this arrangement.

An IRA offers some important tax advantages to investors who would otherwise be unable to participate in a qualified retirement plan. The most important advantage that it has over an ordinary savings plan is that contributions to an IRA are viewed by the federal government as a deduction from the individual's ordinary income. As a result, no income tax is paid on salary contributed to an IRA. Unfortunately, the government currently limits contributions to 15% of each year's salary, up to a maximum of $1,500 ($1,750 if certain special conditions are satisfied).

To see how an IRA works, assume a person is employed by a firm which has no qualified pension plan. The individual makes $8,000 a year. Since Social Security and Railroad Retirement are not considered to be pension plans for purposes of creating an IRA, she can start an Individual Retirement Account. Because the maximum contribution equals 15% of her salary or $1,500, whichever is less, she can contribute up to $1,200 ($8,000 × 0.15). Or she can contribute less than that. In fact, since contributions to an IRA are completely voluntary, she does not need to make any contribution.

If she puts $1,200 into an IRA, she will deduct this amount from her income, so that she pays taxes on only $6,800. If she gets a raise and makes $10,000 in the following year, she can contribute up to $1,500 to the IRA. Or she can contribute zero or any amount between zero and $1,500. Should her salary later increase to $20,000, she would be limited to a maximum contribution of $1,500.

Despite the low level permitted for contributions, an IRA can still save the investor a significant amount of taxes. A single taxpayer with a taxable income of $20,000 who contributes the maximum of $1,500 to an IRA calculates the tax as follows:

Without an IRA
$20,000   taxable income
  5,230   income tax
With an IRA
$20,000   taxable income
− 1,500   contribution to an IRA
$18,500   taxable income
$ 4,690   income tax

Tax savings with an IRA = $5,230 − $4,690 = $540

By putting money into an IRA rather than into an ordinary savings plan, the investor saves $540 in taxes. This reduction in the taxes that would otherwise have been paid means that the out-of-pocket costs for the IRA total only $960 rather than $1,500. And there are other savings. No income taxes are paid on interest earned on funds invested in the IRA or on capital gains as long as the money remains in the IRA. Unfortunately, taxes are not avoided forever. They are only deferred until a later date when the funds are withdrawn. At that time, the full amount of the withdrawal is taxed as ordinary income.

TABLE 12-1   THE IMPACT OF DEFERRING TAXES ON INTEREST*

Number of Years	Savings without Tax Deferral, $	Savings with Tax Deferral, $	Number of Years	Savings without Tax Deferral, $	Savings with Tax Deferral, $
1	1,050	1,080	21	2,764	5,034
2	1,102	1,166	22	2,901	5,437
3	1,156	1,260	23	3,045	5,871
4	1,214	1,360	24	3,196	6,341
5	1,274	1,469	25	3,354	6,848
6	1,337	1,587	26	3,521	7,396
7	1,403	1,714	27	3,695	7,988
8	1,473	1,851	28	3,879	8,627
9	1,546	1,999	29	4,071	9,317
10	1,623	2,159	30	4,273	10,062
11	1,703	2,332	31	4,485	10,868
12	1,788	2,518	32	4,707	11,737
13	1,876	2,720	33	4,941	12,676
14	1,969	2,937	34	5,186	13,690
15	2,067	3,172	35	5,443	14,785
16	2,170	3,426	36	5,713	15,968
17	2,277	3,700	37	5,996	17,246
18	2,390	3,996	38	6,294	18,625
19	2,509	4,316	39	6,606	20,115
20	2,633	4,661	40	6,934	21,724

* Based on the assumption that an investment of $1,000 is held by an individual in a 38% tax bracket, i.e., a single person with a taxable income of $20,000.

But this delay in the payment of taxes greatly increases the amount of money available to the investor upon retirement. For example, a single person with a taxable income of $20,000 lands in a 38% tax bracket—38¢ of each additional dollar over $20,000 goes to pay taxes. A qualified retirement plan temporarily shelters any interest income. So instead of paying out 38¢ of each dollar of interest earned, the investor reinvests the full amount of the interest. The importance of this delaying action to an individual making $20,000 a year is shown in Table 12-1.

RULES AND REGULATIONS ON IRAs

An IRA can save an investor a great deal of tax money. Or if government regulations are not followed, an IRA can actually end up costing additional tax dollars. The government apparently believes that the early withdrawal of funds from an IRA defeats its purpose. For that reason, the IRS assesses a 10% penalty tax on any funds an individual withdraws from an IRA before reaching fifty-nine and a half years of age. And this withdrawal is also taxed as ordinary income.

EXAMPLE   An individual needs $1,000 which she cannot obtain anywhere else. She withdraws this amount from her IRA bank account even though she has not yet reached fifty-nine and a half years of age. If she has a taxable income of $20,000 during the year of withdrawal, her total tax is computed as follows:

$20,000	taxable income without distribution
1,000	amount received from IRA
$21,000	taxable income with distribution
$ 5,610	income tax on $21,000
100	penalty tax of 10% on premature distribution of $1,000
$ 5,710	total tax

The early distribution of IRA assets costs the taxpayer in the preceding example an additional $100 for the penalty tax. This penalty tax is not deductible from the taxpayer's income.

In addition, the taxpayer pays the regular income tax on the distribution. This is not an additional tax, since it would have been paid earlier if the money had not been put in the IRA. But the early withdrawal of funds from an IRA sometimes results in an increase in ordinary income taxes. As a rule, salaries increase over time. An individual earning a taxable income of $10,000 saves approximately $250 in taxes by contributing $1,000 to an IRA. If that $1,000 is withdrawn from an IRA 5 years later when the individual's taxable income equals $20,000, income taxes of $380 must be paid. Why the $130 difference in the ordinary income tax? Because the tax bracket jumps from about 25% on an income of $10,000 to about 38% on $20,000. As a result, the early distribution of the $1,000 has actually cost the investor the penalty tax of $100 plus the additional income tax of $130 for a total of $230. Of course, the exact opposite result occurs if the individual's income drops in later years. Then the withdrawal is taxed at lower, not higher, tax rates.

Effect of Early Withdrawal

Because of the 10% penalty tax on premature withdrawals, no one should make contributions to an IRA which cannot be kept invested for at least several years. The exact amount of time required to break even on an IRA contribution withdrawn prematurely depends upon the individual's tax bracket and the rate of interest earned on the contribution. The higher the tax bracket and rate of return, the shorter the length of time a contribution need be kept in the IRA. If an individual in a 50% tax bracket takes just $1,000 as ordinary income and invests it in an ordinary savings plan rather than an IRA, the result will be $670 at the end of 6 years after all income taxes are paid. On the other hand, $1,000 invested in an IRA at 10% grows to $1,772 in 6 years. If the $1,772 is then withdrawn from the IRA, a penalty tax of $177 and an ordinary income tax of $886 must be paid, leaving $709. Because of the early withdrawal, the person is almost no better off with an IRA.

Figure 12-1 shows the results of investing in an IRA and paying the early

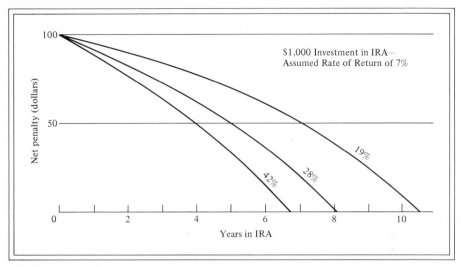

FIGURE 12-1 Minimum holding periods for an IRA.

withdrawal tax as compared with making an ordinary investment. It can be seen from these figures that investors who earn 7% and are in the 19 to 42% tax brackets must retain their money in an IRA for at least 6 years and as much as 10 years in order to do as well as they would have done by simply investing in a non-tax-sheltered savings plan.

The rules on early distributions from an IRA do not apply in two cases. Should an individual be disabled or die, the full amount can be withdrawn without the payment of the 10% penalty tax. This provision actually makes it possible for an IRA to provide a combination of retirement, disability, and death benefits. Of course, the ordinary income tax must still be paid on any withdrawals upon disability or death.

Distribution of Benefits

There is another penalty tax associated with IRAs. If some of the savings that have accumulated in an IRA are not distributed to the individual by the age of seventy and a half years, the IRS assesses a penalty tax of 50%. This 50% tax is on the amount that should have been paid out of the IRA.

There are several alternative methods for determining the amount that should have been paid out of an IRA by the end of the year in which the individual reaches seventy and a half. The first is to determine the expected life of the person participating in the IRA. At seventy years of age, a man can expect to live for about 12 more years. Therefore, by the end of his seventieth year, he should have withdrawn one-twelfth of the balance in the IRA account. If the balance is $200,000, the exact distribution during his seventieth year should be $16,667. If instead he withdraws only $10,000, he will be assessed a penalty tax of $3,334, which is equal to 50% of the difference between $16,667 and $10,000. In each successive year he should withdraw at least enough so that the balance is exhausted at the end of his expected lifetime.

Prohibited Transactions

One other rule is of special importance to anyone thinking of starting an IRA. Certain transactions between an individual and his or her IRA are prohibited. In particular, anyone who borrows money from an IRA or uses it to secure a loan enters into a **prohibited transaction.** As a result, the government automatically disqualifies the IRA as of the first day of the year in which the transaction took place. Upon disqualification, the full value of the IRA is deemed to have been distributed to the participant, who pays the ordinary tax on that amount as well as the penalty tax of 10% (if under fifty-nine and a half years of age or not disabled). Since the savings in the IRA can be very large, the penalty tax and additional income tax incurred can be sizable.

Excess Contributions and Rollovers

Two other regulations apply to IRAs. The first is that excess contributions to an IRA are penalized by being taxed at 6% for each year that the **excess contribution** exists. An excess contribution is defined as any payment to a pension fund in excess of that permitted by law. Second, participants are allowed to make tax-free transfers, usually called **rollovers** of investments from one IRA to another IRA. But such rollovers cannot occur more often than once every 3 years. This provision gives added flexibility to participants in IRAs, since they can switch money out of a bank or other fixed-income investment into stocks or other variable-income investments.

Tax-free rollovers may also be made between an IRA and a company or self-employed plan. However, care must be exercised in doing this, since the tax treatment of IRAs is less favorable than that of these other plans.

SELECTING APPROPRIATE INVESTMENTS FOR AN IRA

An Individual Retirement Account can be established with a bank, savings and loan, life insurance company, and mutual fund as well as with other types of financial institutions. As a result, almost any type of investment can be made through an IRA. Even the government sells retirement bonds which can be purchased for individual retirement plans.

Because of the tax-shelter features of IRAs, some investments are much more appropriate than others. Capital gains and interest on investments in an IRA are not taxed at all until they are paid out, and then both are taxed as ordinary income.

The eventual taxation of capital gains at the full tax rate makes stocks and real estate less attractive as IRA investments. Many investors hold stocks and real estate because increases in value are not taxed until realized and then at only half the ordinary tax rates. The existing rules by which IRAs are taxed completely remove this advantage.

Stocks versus Bonds

Most investors want to hold both variable-dollar assets, such as stocks or real estate, and fixed-dollar securities, such as bonds or savings certificates. Moreover, they will probably divide their savings between an IRA (or other tax-sheltered retirement plan) and other investments held outside the IRA. Given the existing system of taxation, it appears best to hold high-yield, fixed-income securities in the IRA and to hold stocks outside of the IRA. By doing this, the full amount of interest is temporarily sheltered in the IRA, while gains on stocks are taxed at only one-half the ordinary tax rates. To see how important a difference this can make, consider an investor who earns a taxable income of $30,000 weighing the following two investment strategies:

Strategy 1	*Strategy 2*
Make a $1,500 annual investment in bonds paying 8%. These bonds are held in an IRA.	Make a $1,500 annual investment in stocks held in an IRA.
Also	Also
Make a $1,500 annual investment in low-yield stocks which are held outside the IRA.	Make a $1,500 annual investment in bonds paying 8%. These are held outside the IRA.

Strategy 1 provides the investor with much better results than Strategy 2. If the stocks yield 2% in dividends and 10% in capital gains, the resultant wealth after 30 years is $400,000 if Strategy 1 is followed. With Strategy 2, it is $300,000.

Insurance

Insurance policies, like stocks and real estate, ordinarily provide certain tax advantages. In particular, the investment (cash) value of a life insurance policy builds up tax-free until the policy is surrendered. At times this tax advantage makes the purchase of a life insurance annuity or endowment contract worthwhile despite the high cost and inflexibility usually associated with this type of savings plan. But with an IRA, increases in the value of every investment grow tax-free, so that annuities or endowments offer no special tax advantages. Since the disadvantages of an annuity or endowment contract outweigh the remaining advantages, life insurance annuities and endowments usually make a poor investment for IRAs. Despite this fact, one-fourth of the money invested in IRAs goes to purchase annuity or endowment contracts.

Annuity and endowment contracts have one outstanding shortcoming—most of the first year's premium goes to commissions and other sales expenses. For example, an investor who purchases a retirement-income endowment policy which has an annual premium of $1,500 probably never sees any part of that first $1,500. It pays for the "total sales and administrative costs of the company." Nor is that the end of these costs. On a typical endowment policy offered by one of the largest insurance companies in the United States, the sales and administrative expenses in the second year equal $780 (in the first year, $1,500) and in both the third and fourth years they amount to $200. In each succeeding year until the end of the life of the contract, the sales and administrative costs total at least $120. The magnitude of these costs would no doubt deter many prospective purchasers of annuity and endowment contracts if only they knew about them. Unfortunately, most insurance company presentations make no explicit mention of these costs.

But the insurance company presentations do show total cash values at age sixty-five or later. This cash value is usually very impressive and often implies that contributions to an individual retirement annuity more than quadruple in value in a 30- to 40-year period. Without exception, this projected cash value receives a prominent place in the sales presentations, together with a correspondingly large projected monthly life income upon retirement. And, again without exception, there is a footnote to these figures stating that the projections are for illustrative purposes only and are not guaranteed. What this means is that the actual experience of an individual who purchases an annuity or endowment contract can differ greatly from the illustration.

Insurance firms guarantee only a minimal return on money invested in their contracts. This guaranteed rate is often as low as $2\frac{1}{2}$ to 3% in later years. Apparently because this guaranteed rate is so low, it is seldom openly mentioned. Instead, it is usually buried in the insurance contract, which the investors eventually receive after they have already committed themselves to purchasing an annuity or endowment. For this reason, the present merchandising practices of some insurance firms in the IRA market border on misrepresentation.

The variable annuities offered by insurance firms for use in IRAs are also costly. Again, there is usually a sales and administration charge which is subtracted from the individual's contributions. This charge averages about 9.3% of the amount invested. However, if an installment contract is signed, as it usually is with an IRA, the first year's sales and administration charge is 25% of the amount invested. In the second and third years, an additional charge of 21.95% is assessed. In the fourth year, it is 7.53%. And in all the following years, it is 4.17%. In contrast with this, no-load mutual funds make equity investments available to the investor at no charge.

Individual Retirement Bonds

There is still one other type of asset which can be held by an IRA. The government sells individual retirement bonds. These bonds yield 6% a year, compounded semiannually, if they are held to maturity and can be bought in denominations of $50, $100, and $500. Individual retirement bonds have one advantage—they are sold in small amounts. But the returns on individual retirement bonds are substantially below those of any other long-term federal obligation. Long-term Treasury bonds currently yield more than 8%, and, of course, they are completely marketable. These bonds can be purchased indirectly by buying shares in a bond mutual fund.

SOME QUESTIONS AND ANSWERS ABOUT IRAs

Because Individual Retirement Accounts are relatively new, most people have a number of questions about what they can and can't do with an IRA. Here are the answers to some commonly asked questions about IRAs:

1 Question: Can I put money into an IRA if I work for a company that already has a qualified pension plan?

Answer: You cannot contribute to an IRA during any year in which you participate in another qualified pension plan. The government defines **participation** as the actual accumulation of retirement benefits.

2 Question: My income consists solely of interest on bonds. Can I contribute part of this income to an IRA?

Answer: No. Contributions to tax-sheltered retirement plans are based on earned income. Interest, capital gains, rents, and oil royalties are not considered to be earned income.

3 Question: Suppose that I start contributing to an IRA and then take a job with a company that has a qualified pension plan. What do I do?

Answer: Simply stop making contributions to your IRA. The money you have already set aside will continue to grow in the IRA tax-free. Do not withdraw any money from the IRA unless you are disabled or have reached fifty-nine and a half years of age.

4 Question: Can I have more than one IRA?

Answer: Apparently there is no limit to the number of IRAs you can have. But your maximum contribution to all of them cannot exceed $1,500 per year.

5 Question: I am married and make $20,000 a year. My wife does not work. Can I start an IRA for my wife as well as for myself?

Answer: Yes. But you must follow 1 of 2 procedures: (1) make a contribution to two separate IRAs—one for yourself and one for your wife or (2) make a contribution to a single IRA owned jointly by you and your wife. By the way, the government permits a maximum deduction of $1,750 instead of $1,500 for contributions involving a taxpayer and an unemployed spouse.

SELF-EMPLOYED RETIREMENT PLANS

Even though they have been widely publicized, IRAs have several distinct disadvantages compared with qualified company plans and self-employed plans. For that reason, most self-employed individuals who have no employees would probably be better off selecting a Keogh retirement plan for themselves.

Keogh versus IRA

One distinct advantage that a Keogh plan has over an IRA is that contributions of up to $7,500 can be made, even though the limitation is still 15% of salary. For instance, a self-employed person who earns $50,000 can contribute as much as $7,500 to a Keogh plan, whereas the maximum he or she could invest in an IRA would be only $1,500. Another advantage is that the retirement income which is received from a Keogh plan can be taxed at lower rates. The Pension Reform Act makes it possible to apply a special **10-year income-averaging** method to lump-sum distributions from a self-employed plan. Although the rule is somewhat complicated, it works more or less as follows:

> An individual retires at sixty-five, having accumulated $200,000 in a Keogh plan by that time. The retiree withdraws this entire amount during the tax year in order to treat the withdrawal as a lump-sum distribution for tax purposes and use the special 10-year averaging method.

> $200,000   lump-sum distribution from pension plan
> $\underline{\times \quad .10}$
> $ \ 20,000   10% of distribution

> The income tax on $20,000 at the single-taxpayer rate (which is required regardless of the marital status of the recipient) is $5,230. This tax is always computed separately from any other income the taxpayer has earned during the year. Multiplying this by 10 gives a total tax of $52,300.

> If a lump-sum distribution of $200,000 had been made from an IRA, the 10-year averaging method could not have been used. The tax then would have been $123,090, providing that the standard 5-year income-averaging method discussed in Chapter Eleven was not used.

It is apparent from the preceding example that the special 10-year averaging method can save a retiree a great deal of tax money if a lump-sum distribution is desired.

Keogh plans are similar to IRA plans in the following respects: There is a 6%

penalty tax for excess contributions, a 10% penalty tax for withdrawals from the plan before fifty-nine and a half years of age, a 50% penalty tax for insufficient withdrawal after seventy and a half, and a strict prohibition against using the pension plan assets as collateral for a loan or borrowing money from the pension plan. However, an individual who has a Keogh plan can still make contributions after seventy and a half years of age. With an IRA, no contributions are permitted after that age.

Fixed-Contribution and Fixed-Benefit Plans

Most Keogh plans are set up as **fixed-contribution plans.** That means that a fixed percentage of the individual's salary is contributed to the plan each year. Since the maximum contribution is fixed regardless of the rate of return earned on pension investments, it is impossible to determine ahead of time the retirement benefit which will eventually be received. The higher the return realized on the Keogh investments, the greater the benefits will be. The lower the return, the lower the benefits.

For that reason, a retirement plan can pay a guaranteed benefit only when contributions are allowed to vary from year to year. A plan which pays guaranteed benefits is called a **fixed-benefit or defined-benefit plan.** It is now possible to create a fixed-benefit Keogh plan. The maximum retirement benefit depends upon the age at which the individual starts to participate in the plan. The maximum benefits as a percentage of salary that can be provided by a Keogh plan are as follows:

Fixed-Benefit Keogh Plan

Age when Participation Began in the Plan	Maximum Retirement Benefit as a Percentage of Salary*
30 or less	6.5
35	5.4
40	4.4
45	3.6
50	3.0
55	2.5
60 or over	2.0

* The maximum salary to which these percentages can be applied is $50,000.

EXAMPLE If an individual who is forty years old starts a Keogh plan, a benefit of 4.4% of each year's salary between the ages of forty and forty-five can be realized, 3.6% of each year's salary from forty-five to fifty, etc. If the salary stays at $30,000 until retirement at age sixty-five, the total retirement benefit can equal $23,250. The person can make whatever contribution is necessary to provide this sum, even though the contributions exceed 15% of salary or $7,500.

Some Questions and Answers

Most taxpayers have a number of questions about Keogh plans. Here are the answers to some commonly asked questions:

1 Question: Must I pay Social Security taxes on any income contributed to a Keogh plan?

   Answer: Yes, and the same is true of any other type of tax-sheltered retirement plan.

2 Question: All self-employed individuals who start a Keogh plan must base their contributions on some percentage of their income or net profits. What percentage should they select? Must they always contribute this percentage of their income or profits?

   Answer: The maximum percentage is 15%. Since this percentage cannot be revised upward, it is usually best to select the maximum rate of 15%, providing the self-employed individual has no employees. Despite the misleading wording of most Keogh plans, the self-employed individual who has no employees can always contribute less than the percentage specified in the Keogh agreement. If the self-employed individual has employees, this flexibility in contributions is lost.

3 Question: I have a full-time job with a company that has a qualified retirement plan. I also work part time for myself repairing appliances. Can I start an IRA or Keogh?

   Answer: You can start a Keogh, since you have self-employed income. Your contributions to the Keogh plan must be based only upon the amount of your self-employed income. You cannot start an IRA, since you are not allowed to contribute to an IRA during any year in which you participate in another tax-sheltered retirement plan.

4 Question: How do you tell if you are self-employed?

   Answer: If you work for yourself or with one or more partners, then you are probably self-employed. As a general rule, people who pay their own Social Security taxes are self-employed.

5 Question: I am self-employed. Should I start an IRA or a Keogh plan?

   Answer: The answer depends upon whether or not you have any employees. If you have no employees, you are better off with a Keogh plan. If you have one or more employees, they will probably have to be included in the Keogh plan. This will impose additional costs which you may not want to incur. In that case, the IRA may be better, since you do not have to include your employees.

TAX-SHELTERED ANNUITIES AND CUSTODIAL ACCOUNTS

Anyone who earns income and is not covered by a qualified pension plan can have an IRA. Individuals who are self-employed or who earn some self-employed income can have a Keogh plan. And there is still one other alternative. Employees of tax-exempt charitable, educational, and religious organizations as well as of public educational institutions can have their own tax-sheltered annuities or custodial accounts. This is true even if they participate in regular pension plans offered by their employers.

Before ERISA, employees of tax-exempt organizations or of public schools could purchase only tax-sheltered annuities. The high commissions and low returns on most of these annuities discouraged many people from starting their own retirement plans. But now the law permits the purchase of mutual funds as well as annuities.

Tax-sheltered Annuity versus IRA or Keogh Plan

The tax-sheltered annuity or custodial account is superior to either the IRA or Keogh plan. There are several reasons why this is so. First, employees are allowed to make larger contributions to their annuity or custodial account. The law states that the annual contribution can be 20% of total "includable" compensation. **Includable compensation** is usually equal to the individual's total salary (including sick pay and bonuses) minus the contribution made to the tax-sheltered retirement plan.[2] In contrast with the IRA and Keogh plans, the limit on contributions is $25,000 a year.

An individual tax-sheltered plan with a nonprofit institution or public school has another distinct advantage over an IRA or Keogh. With an IRA or Keogh, a contribution can be based only on the current year's income. If no contribution is made during the year, the possibility of deferring the tax on that year's income is lost forever. But with a tax-sheltered annuity or custodial account, the employee is allowed to catch up on past contributions. In other words, a contribution based on a particular year's salary can be made in later years. The following shows how this can be done:

> A woman has taught in a public school system for 5 years. Although she participates in the regular retirement plan, she can also have her own tax-sheltered retirement plan. But until now she has made no contributions to such a plan.
>
> At the start of her sixth year of teaching she marries. Her husband's income is $28,000, and her own income is $10,000. Their combined income puts them in a 42% tax bracket, and her husband has considerable savings. They decide that the best way to reduce taxes and save additional money is for her to immediately contribute as much as possible to a tax-sheltered retirement plan. The maximum contribution cannot exceed her **exclusion allowance** for the current year. The exclusion allowance for the current year is calculated in two steps: (1) Multiply the number of years

worked times the employee's includable compensation and times 20%; (2) From the figure determined in step 1, subtract all previous contributions made to a qualified retirement plan which were not included in the employee's taxable income. Her exclusion allowance is calculated as follows:

Step 1   6 years × $10,000 (income) × 20% $12,000
Step 2   The school board has a qualified retirement plan. Each year
           it contributes $500 to this plan for each teacher. These
           contributions are not included in the teachers' salaries.   − 3,000
                 Maximum contribution possible $ 9,000

It appears that the teacher can have $9,000 of her salary withheld for the purchase of a tax-sheltered annuity or a mutual fund. But if she contributes $9,000, the includable compensation figure used in Step 1 will drop from $10,000 to $1,000 and the maximum contribution will be zero. By using the trial-and-error method to see how different contributions affect the final results, the maximum contribution can be estimated to be approximately $4,500. The exact answer in this case is determined as follows:

Maximum contribution = [6 years × ($10,000 − contribution) × 20%] − $3,000
Maximum contribution = $4,090.90

Limits on Catch-up Contributions

ERISA now limits catch-up contributions to tax-sheltered annuities and custodial accounts. The general rule is that a contribution cannot be greater than 25% of total compensation during the year. However, after reviewing ERISA, the IRS has decided that the legislation implies that the contribution made during the year cannot exceed the amount determined by any one of the following three rules:

1   In the year of separation from an employer, an employee can compute the maximum allowable contribution on the basis of the most recent 10 years of employment. The maximum contribution is $25,000. This alternative can be used only once in a lifetime.
2   The maximum contribution is limited to 25% of current compensation plus $4,000. The maximum contribution is $15,000.
3   The employee can elect to use the 25% limitation every year and not even use the exclusion allowance. The last rule becomes very complicated when the individual participates in a regular pension plan as well as having a tax-sheltered annuity or custodial account.

The preceding rules apply only to employees of educational institutions, hospitals, and home health-service agencies. Other employees who have tax-sheltered annuities or custodial accounts must abide by the general rule that contributions must be the lesser of the exclusion allowance or 25% of compensation.

Calculating the maximum permissible contribution is difficult. But once this figure has been determined, the employee simply fills out a **salary reduction**

agreement with the employer. This agreement instructs the employer to withhold a specified amount from the individual's salary. The withheld amount is used to purchase an annuity or mutual fund. A tax deduction cannot be taken if the employee purchases the annuity or mutual fund directly.

Tax-sheltered annuities and custodial accounts have still one other advantage over a Keogh or IRA plan. If the employer is a religious organization or a private educational institution, any money withheld from the employee's salary and contributed to the plan passes to the employee's beneficiaries completely free of estate taxes.

COMPANY RETIREMENT PLANS

Tax-sheltered retirement plans operated by companies for their employees are still the most important private source of retirement savings in this country. At the end of 1973, more than 368,000 companies had obtained approval from the IRS for their plans. And $132 billion was held in these company plans.

The Pension Reform Act of 1974 mandated significant changes in the way these plans must be operated. As a result of these changes, employees participating in qualified company pension plans may obtain important new benefits, providing companies are not forced to cut back on their plans because of the additional expense of satisfying the new rules.

Vesting

Probably the most important provision of the Pension Reform Act concerns **vesting.** *Vesting* occurs when a participant in a pension plan obtains a claim on benefits which cannot be taken from that person even in the case of dismissal or resignation from the job. Until the Pension Reform Act, many pension plans paid no retirement benefits to an employee who left before retirement age. As a result, employees were often locked in by their pension plans—if they left for another job, they had to leave behind significant amounts of money which had accumulated. Now the government requires companies to follow one of three alternative vesting schedules: (1) **10-year vesting,** (2) **15-year graded vesting,** and (3) **rule-of-45 vesting.**

Ten-year vesting is the simplest to understand. If a company pension plan has 10-year vesting, every employee who participates in the plan must be fully vested after working for the company for 10 years. This means that any benefits that would be paid during retirement, given the number of years worked, must be paid regardless of whether or not the employee leaves the company. Never again can an employee who has worked for more than 10 years be fired or laid off and lose all pension benefits.

Companies have a choice as to how they allocate the percentage of benefits which vest over the 10-year period. The least costly method of allocation is 100%

vesting at the end of the tenth year. Since the full amount of benefits vests in the tenth year, an employee leaving after 9 years of employment receives nothing. Or, the firm may have benefits vest at 10% a year for each of the 10 years, so that regardless of when the employee leaves, she or he has some vested benefits. Whatever the annual percentages selected, only one requirement must be satisfied: the participant must be fully vested at the end of 10 years of service.

With 15-year graded vesting an employee must be at least 25% vested in pension benefits by the end of 5 years of service. The percentages vested during each of these 5 years can be any amount as long as they total 25%. In the sixth through the tenth years at least an additional 5% must be vested at the end of each year. In the tenth through the fifteenth years at least an additional 10% must be vested each year. The following table gives the minimum vested benefits permitted with graded vesting:

Years of Service	Nonforfeitable Vested Percentage
5	25
6	30
7	35
8	40
9	45
10	50
11	60
12	70
13	80
14	90
15 or more	100

Rule-of-45 vesting requires that participants in a plan be at least 50% vested when the total of their years of service with the employer and their age equals forty-five or more and they have at least 5 years of service. For each year of service after they are 50% vested, the employees' vested percentage must not be less than the amount shown in the following table:

Years of Service	Sum of Age and Service	Lowest Nonforfeitable Vested Percentage
5	45	50
6	47	60
7	49	70
8	51	80
9	53	90
10	55	100

An additional requirement of the rule-of-45 is that each employee with 10 years of service, regardless of age, must be at least 50% vested, with 10% additional vesting for each extra year of service.

Employee Participation

Vesting gives employees a nonforfeitable right to the pension benefits earned as a participant in a plan. But if they are not participants in the plan, they earn no benefits. For this reason, ERISA sets forth strict rules on employee participation in pension plans. No worker can be excluded from a plan because of age except when within 5 years of retirement age. And employers must select between 1 of 2 participation standards: (1) every employee who is twenty-five years of age and has 1 year of service must be allowed to participate, or (2) every employee who has 3 years of service must be allowed to participate and must be given 100% vesting at the time of participation. No matter which standard is used, all the time worked by the employee previous to participation in the plan is still counted in determining vesting and the amount of pension benefits.

Accrual of Benefits

Despite these regulations, it might still be possible for employers to exclude certain employees from benefits. After all, a vested right to pension benefits is meaningless if the worker accumulates no benefits. For this reason, ERISA also sets standards that must be met by qualified pension plans in regard to accrued benefits. The **accrued benefit** is the retirement benefit that an employee accumulates over the years of service; i.e., it is the balance in the employee's account at any moment in time. It is conceivable that some unscrupulous employers might set up pension plans in which employees accrued only very small benefits during most of their years of employment. This could be done by having the pension-benefit formula state that for each year of service up to 20 years only a small percentage, say one-half of 1%, of the average salary would be paid in retirement income. For every year of service over 20, a much higher percentage, say 4% a year, might be paid. In that way, only the few employees who stayed on for more than 20 years would collect substantial retirement benefits. In order to eliminate this possibility, ERISA states that accrual rates must meet one of the following three tests:

1 The rate at which retirement benefits are accrued in later years cannot be more than a third greater than that in earlier years.
2 Each employee accrues benefits each year of not less than 3% of the total benefit which would have been earned had the employee joined the plan at the earliest possible age and remained in it until age sixty-five.
3 The minimum accrued benefit for each year is a fraction of what would be received at normal retirement. This fraction is equal to 1 divided by the total number of years that would have been accumulated in the plan if the employee remained until retirement age.

Advantages of Company Plans

The Pension Reform Act imposes strict standards on the qualified pension plans of employers as well as requiring that employers complete a multitude of forms and other paperwork. In drafting the law, Congress seems to have viewed the employer-employee relationship as though the two were adversaries. Actually a qualified pension plan can benefit both the employer and the employees. An employer is allowed to deduct contributions to a pension plan just as if they were compensation to the employees. On the other hand, employees who participate in the plan do not have to pay taxes on these contributions until they are actually received as pension benefits. And any increases in the invested value of these contributions are also tax-free until benefits are paid. As a result, there are substantial tax savings to employees. For these reasons, a company's contribution to a qualified pension plan grows to a much higher value than does the same amount invested by an individual in an ordinary savings plan. The exact amount of these tax savings was shown in earlier examples. For instance, a twenty-five-year-old employee who makes a taxable income of $10,000 and whose income will grow by 2% a year would have to set aside $2.26 in order to match the growth in value of $1 invested in a company pension plan. A thirty-year-old individual who makes $20,000 and whose income will grow by 4% a year would have to invest $3.33 to match a $1 contribution made on his or her behalf. An executive who makes a taxable income of $40,000 and whose income will grow by 2% a year would have to save $2.68 to match the $1 invested in the plan by his or her employer.

Even though company pension plans offer substantial benefits to employees, very few prospective employees ever inquire about these plans. In the past, that may have been because no one could imagine working for the same company until retirement. Now, with many firms offering partial vesting in 5 years and full vesting in 5 to 10 years, it pays to compare the pension benefits (and other benefits) as well as the salaries offered by different companies.

To see how important pension benefits can be, imagine a thirty-five-year-old woman who must decide which of two job offers to accept. Both jobs pay $30,000 a year, but the job with Company B seems to offer more promise. The pension plans at the two companies are as follows:

Company A	*Company B*
100% vesting in pension benefits at the end of 10 years. No vesting until then. A monthly contribution of 2% of the first $400 of earnings and 4% of earnings over $400 required of every employee.	10% vesting each year. No contributions required of employees.
Monthly benefits upon retirement at age sixty-five equal $1^1/_4$% of the first $400 of average monthly earnings plus 2% of all earnings in excess of $400 for each year worked.	Monthly benefits of $1^1/_2$% of the first $500 monthly average earnings and 2% of monthly earnings in excess of $500 for each year.

Neither plan offers any death benefits. In the case of death, all the employee's contributions to the plan at Company A are returned with 2% interest. Since there are no employee contributions to the plan at Company B, there is nothing to return.

ANALYSIS   The plan at Company B offers the employee greater total benefits, and no contributions are required. If she lives to retirement age in 30 years' time and makes $2,500 a month, or $30,000 every year, she will collect benefits as follows:

At Company A	At Company B
$ 400 × 1¼% × 30 = $ 150	$ 500 × 1½% × 30 = $ 225
2,100 × 2% × 30 = 1,260	2,000 × 2% × 30 = 1,200
Total monthly retirement benefit = $1,410	Total monthly retirement benefit = $1,425

Monthly contributions
$ 400 × 2% = $ 8 $0
$2,100 × 4% = $84 $0
$92 a month, or $1,104 a year

If the employee earned 8% on her money and invested it in a tax-sheltered IRA, she would have to put aside $1,292 to provide herself with a monthly retirement benefit of $1,425 at age sixty-five. Therefore, the retirement benefits at the Company B job are worth at least $1,292 a year. The benefits at Company A are worth only about $212 a year more than their costs.

Since companies must compete on the basis of their product prices, they can seldom afford to offer both excellent pension benefits and high salaries. Some firms choose to compete for better employees by offering higher salaries; others offer better pension benefits; and some offer neither. There is only one way to tell which of these categories a firm falls in, and that is to analyze the retirement benefits offered by the company.

Integration of Benefits with Social Security

There is one feature of company pension plans which has attracted considerable unfavorable publicity. Some employees have retired from firms thinking their pension plans would provide a specific dollar income each month. After retirement, they found their benefits reduced at the same time that inflation pushed the cost of living higher and higher. This reduction occurred because their company pension plans were integrated with Social Security benefits. **Integration of benefits** means that the company views its pension plan as only one part of a larger retirement system. The other part of this system is the government's Social Security program.

This seems to be a reasonable view on the part of companies, since they contribute 5.85% of each employee's base earnings to Social Security. On the 1976 Social Security base salary of $15,300, that amounts to a contribution of $895.05 a year. Moreover, the contribution rate and the base salary are scheduled to increase in the future, so that contributions made by both companies and individuals will increase. One way for a company to take this payment into account is to provide that retirement benefits paid by the company will be reduced, or offset, by benefits paid by Social Security. For example, the benefits book of one large company states:

An employee who has 10 or more years of service and meets the participation requirements of the plan is entitled to a yearly benefit at age 65 of 1²/₃ percent times the years of service and times the average annual earnings for the highest five consecutive years. This amount is reduced by 50 percent of the Social Security benefits the employee is eligible to receive at the time of his retirement. Subsequent increases in Social Security benefits will not affect retirement benefits.

In this case, the firm is offsetting its benefits by 50% of Social Security benefits. It might have selected an offset of 100%, in which case the firm would pay out only that part of the benefit which exceeds the total Social Security benefits received by an individual. By doing this, it would be able to give all employees the same retirement benefits as a percentage of their salary. This can be better understood by referring to the benefits shown in Figure 12-2. Another way

FIGURE 12-2   Integration of Social Security with company retirement benefits.

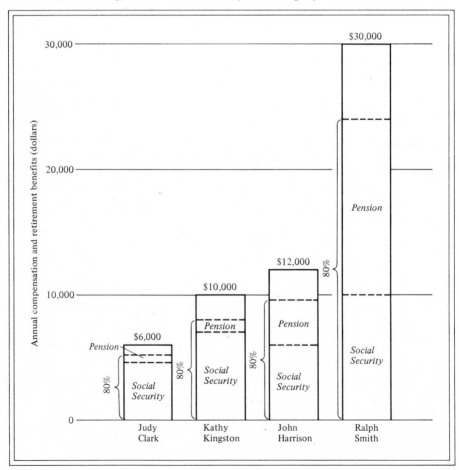

to do this would be to have benefits accrue at different rates, depending upon the individual's salary. For example, the company might give retirement credits equal to $1^1/2\%$ of each year's earnings up to the Social Security wage base plus 2% of each year's earnings in excess of that wage base.

The most important phrase in the company plan just described is the statement that "subsequent increases in Social Security will not affect retirement benefits." This means that future increases in Social Security benefits will not result in a reduction in company benefits *after* the individual has retired. Much to the dismay of some retirees, not all companies have followed this policy in the past. Some firms have tied the retiree's benefits to Social Security payments *after* retirement. If this is the case, an individual can retire with a Social Security benefit of perhaps $600 a month and a company benefit of $400. If the Social Security benefit is raised to $800 or even $1,000 in later years, the retiree's company benefits, given a 100% offset, will decrease to $200 or $0. This might be satisfactory if the increase in Social Security benefits were a real increase. But usually it is simply a reflection of the fact that inflation has made it necessary to increase pension benefits in order to make up for the higher cost of living. By decreasing its benefits as Social Security benefits are increased, the company holds total dollar benefits constant, even though the purchasing power of a dollar is declining. The net effect can be a serious decline in the retiree's standard of living.

Rights of Employees under ERISA

ERISA requires that every participant in a qualified company pension plan be provided with a summary description of the plan. This description must be written in plain language which can be understood by the average employee. Moreover, at least once every 12 months, the employee is entitled to receive up-to-date information on the retirement benefits that he or she has earned. This information should help considerably in making retirement plans and in determining whether or not to take another job.

IMPLICATIONS FOR INVESTMENT STRATEGY

Company retirement plans have come a long way in the past 50 years. Instead of a gold watch, many employees now receive lump-sum payments of $100,000 or more when they retire.

These generous company benefits are necessary because people are living longer and retiring earlier. And with the changing family structure in this country, retirees can no longer rely on their families for support. To some extent, Congress has recognized the greatly increased need for retirement savings by extending significant new tax advantages to individual retirement plans. As a result, a substantial part of most workers' savings will probably be vested in some type of tax-sheltered retirement plan. For that reason, retirement plans must be considered in developing an investment strategy.

Tax-sheltered retirement plans provide funds for retirement and for emergencies such as death and disability. In addition, certain types of individual retirement plans can conceivably be used to satisfy long-term objectives, such as a college education for a family's children, despite the penalty tax on early withdrawals. Since taxes are deferred on any interest earned in a tax-sheltered retirement plan, the investor earns additional interest on savings. If the money that is withdrawn from the plan has been held for a long enough time, this additional interest will more than offset the penalty tax.

Individual retirement plans can also be viewed as a source of unemployment benefits. Workers who are unemployed for long periods of time are usually in very low tax brackets. As a result, their premature withdrawals from a plan are taxed at such low rates that the 10% penalty tax becomes inconsequential. In effect, their plans have made it possible for them to shift income from a period of high taxes to a time of low taxes.

Over the years, Congress has passed legislation granting numerous tax advantages to qualified retirement plans. The net effect of this legislation is to pay people to save money for certain purposes. Investors can now purchase retirement, death, and disability benefits at bargain prices. Benefits that would ordinarily cost $2 or $3 or even more can be acquired with only a $1 contribution to a tax-sheltered retirement plan. The individual's investment strategy should be modified to reflect the large payoffs of such contributions.

With individual tax-sheltered retirement plans, investors often have complete control over how their contributions are invested, and there appears to be a very good possibility that many firms will eventually permit employees to set their own investment policies for company pension plans. The policies chosen should be consistent with the investor's overall investment strategy. For example, the assets held in the individual's portfolio should probably provide capital gains or nontaxable income. And a buy-and-hold policy should be carefully followed with regard to these investments. The assets held in the individual's retirement plan should yield the highest income possible. By adopting this asset mix, the investor minimizes taxes and diversifies the total portfolio.

KEYWORDS

Pension Reform Act of 1974 (ERISA)
Individual Retirement Account (IRA)
Keogh plan (HR-10)
tax-sheltered annuity
prohibited transaction
excess contribution

rollovers
participation
10-year income averaging
fixed-contribution plans
fixed-benefit or defined-benefit plan
includable compensation
exclusion allowance

salary reduction agreement
vesting
10-year vesting
15-year graded vesting
rule-of-45 vesting
accrued benefit
integration of benefits

QUESTIONS

1 What are the four major types of tax-sheltered retirement plans?
2 What are the two major advantages of tax-sheltered retirement plans over ordinary savings plans?
3 Suppose you pay taxes at a marginal rate of 30%. How much are the out-of-pocket costs for a $1,500 contribution to an IRA?
4 Explain how the expected life of an individual and the expected return on savings affect the potential benefits from a retirement plan.
5 Suppose an individual wants to retire in 40 years with an annual salary of $20,000 and expects to live for 25 years after retirement. How much must she set aside each year in a TSRP (tax-sheltered retirement program) at 5, 10, and 15% rates of return?
6 A worker makes $20,000 a year. How much can he contribute to an IRA?
7 Describe and explain the penalties for premature withdrawal of funds from an IRA, a prohibited transaction, and late distribution of benefits.
8 Suppose you want to hold both bonds and stocks. Which would you purchase through an IRA or other TSRP? Why?
9 Would you purchase insurance annuities or endowments through an IRA or other TSRP? Why or why not?
10 A twenty-five-year-old woman starts a defined-benefit Keogh plan. Suppose she makes $25,000 every year until she retires at sixty-five. What is the maximum retirement benefit she can collect from her Keogh plan?
11 Suppose you qualify for either an IRA or Keogh. Debate the pros and cons of both types of plans.
12 Can a public school teacher participate in a tax-sheltered annuity and custodial program if she already takes part in the regular school retirement program?
13 Describe the various types of vesting schedules. Now suppose you had to design a vesting schedule which minimizes the benefits received by a company's employees. How would you do it?
14 Suppose you pay taxes at a 30% marginal rate. How much do you have to save on your own in order to match a company contribution of $1 to a fully vested tax-sheltered retirement plan?
15 How do tax-sheltered retirement plans affect your own investment strategy?

REFERENCES

Allen, Everett T.: *Pension Planning,* Irwin, Homewood, Ill., 1976.

Bildersee, Robert A.: *Pension Regulation Manual,* Warren, Gorham and Lamont, Boston, 1975.

Buppert, William I., III: "Vesting and Funding: The Props under ERISA," *The Personnel Administrator,* September 1975, pp. 48–50.

"Congress, Regulators Tussle over ERISA Costs," *Employee Benefit Plan Review,* August 1976, pp. 50–52.

Forseter, Bernard: "Integration of Pension and Profit-sharing Plans," *Taxes: The Tax Magazine,* September 1973, pp. 517–524.

Glasser, Stephen A.: *A Practical Guide to the New Pension Reform Legislation,* Law Journal Press, New York, 1975.

Hobman, Richard J.: "Setting Investment Policy in an ERISA Environment," *Journal of Portfolio Management,* Fall 1975, pp. 17–21.

Individual Retirement Plans, Commerce Clearing House, New York, 1975.

McGill, Dan M.: *Fundamentals of Private Pensions,* Irwin, Homewood, Ill., 1964.

Moffitt, Donald: "How Persistent Investors Found Way to Trade in Securities with Tax-deferred Keogh Money," *The Wall Street Journal,* Jan. 10, 1977, p. 26.

U.S. Department of Labor, Labor-Management Services Administration, *Often-asked Questions about the Employee Retirement Income Security Act of 1974,* 1976.

U.S. Department of Treasury, Internal Revenue Service, *Tax Information on Individual Retirement Savings Programs,* Pub. 590, April 1975.

_____, *Tax Information on Pension and Annuity Income,* Pub. 575, 1975.

_____, *Tax Sheltered Annuity Plans for Employees of Public Schools and Certain Tax-exempt Organizations,* Pub. 57, 1973.

PART FOUR

INSTITUTIONS

CHAPTER THIRTEEN

INVESTMENT COMPANIES

Diversification eliminates much of the risk of investing, but because of high commission costs, most small investors find it difficult to acquire well-diversified portfolios. Both small and large investors face another problem—they often lack the time and/or the desire to invest their own money. Or they may still suffer from an inferiority complex when it comes to competing with investment professionals, despite all the evidence about market efficiency.

Mutual funds and other investment companies provide an alternative for these investors. These companies make it possible for investors to combine their money and then invest in stocks, bonds, and other securities. Each investor then shares in all the income, gains, and expenses realized on this pool of funds.

A Columbia economist named Roger Murray claims investment companies provide investors with the best overall results. According to Murray, "The picture of the individual as a direct owner of securities has been romanticized almost beyond recognition." And Paul Samuelson tells people, "You give up your claim to boast about your luck. . . . But you'll know your money is being handled in an efficient and expeditious way."

THE INVESTMENT COMPANY CONCEPT

The **investment company** concept dates back to 1868, when the British founded the Foreign and Colonial Government Trust. The promoters of the trust promised "the investor of moderate means the same advantages as the large capitalist, in diminishing the risk of investing in Foreign and Colonial Government Stocks, by spreading the investment over a number of different stocks." Apparently investors liked the idea. By 1875, 18 different trusts had been formed in England and Scotland, many of them holding substantial amounts of American securities.

Not much has changed in the more than 100 years since then. Investment companies still offer the investor opportunities for diversification by pooling the funds of many investors and buying a large number of securities. Some of the bigger investment companies hold stocks in more than 100 companies. This diversification increases the expected return of the portfolio without increasing the risk or reduces the risk without decreasing the return. Figure 13-1 compares the risks and returns of individual stocks with those of several investment companies.

Investment companies generally operate like ordinary corporations. They raise money by selling shares. The shareholders vote for directors, who in turn

FIGURE 13-1 Comparison of the risks and returns of mutual funds and individual stocks. (From Haim Levy, and M. Sarnat, "Investment Performance in an Imperfect Securities Market and the Case for Mutual Funds," *Financial Analysts Journal,* March–April 1972, p. 80.)

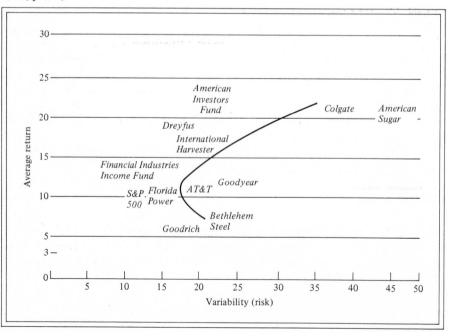

4)

appoint officers to manage the company. And the shareholders partake in the profits and losses of the investment company.

But there are several important differences between an investment company and a regular corporation. First, instead of buying machinery and equipment and producing a product or service, investment companies simply invest their shareholders' money in passive investments like stocks or bonds. Second, the shareholders usually hire an investment advisory firm to manage these investments and to operate the company. Third, investment companies pay no taxes on any income or gains, providing they pass these through to their shareholders.

Many investors believe investment companies offer more than just diversification. One of the most commonly cited advantages is lower transactions costs. Because of their size, investment companies pay lower commissions when buying and selling investments. Of course, it is this reduction in transactions costs which makes diversification possible in the first place.

Another frequently mentioned benefit is professional management. Apparently many people think that the "highly qualified portfolio managers" employed by investment companies possess the ability to outperform the market. Professional management also frees investors from the time and effort required to select and manage investments. And it probably reduces anxiety in investors who find direct involvement with the ups and downs of the market extremely frustrating or who lack the self-control necessary to follow a successful investment strategy on their own.

TYPES OF INVESTMENT COMPANIES

Investment companies fall into two general categories: (1) open-end and (2) closed-end companies. **Open-end investment companies,** usually called **mutual funds, buy and sell their own shares.** As a result, the amount of capital invested in a mutual fund changes from day to day, as investors buy new shares or redeem (sell) their old shares. In other words, the open-end company is always "open" to new money or to withdrawals. The Investment Company Institute follows these flows of capital closely and periodically publishes the sales, redemptions (repurchases), and net redemptions (sales minus redemptions) of the mutual funds. Some of these figures are shown in Table 13-1.

Unlike mutual funds, **closed-end investment companies** do not stand ready to buy and sell their own shares on demand. Instead, investors trade these shares with other investors, just as they do the shares of GM, IBM, and other corporations. Since closed-end companies refuse to buy or sell their shares (except on special occasions like a new-issue offering), the total amount of money contributed by investors remains fixed. In other words, the closed-end company is "closed" to new money or to withdrawals.

Judging from Figure 13-2, the last three decades have been years of spectacular growth for investment companies in the United States. In 1948, investment company assets totaled only about $2 billion. By 1976, these companies were

TABLE 13-1   GROSS SALES AND REDEMPTIONS OF MUTUAL FUNDS

Year	Gross Sales, $	Redemptions, $	Net Sales or Redemptions, $
1975	10,056,547	9,570,236	486,311
1974	5,320,627	3,936,958	1,383,669
1973	4,359,288	5,651,064	1,291,776
1972	4,892,502	6,562,876	1,670,374
1971	5,147,186	4,750,222	396,964
1970	4,625,802	2,987,572	1,638,230
1969	6,718,283	3,838,682	3,056,637
1968	6,819,763	3,661,646	2,981,081
1967	4,669,575	2,744,197	1,925,378
1966	4,671,842	2,005,079	2,666,763
1965	4,358,144	1,962,432	2,395,712
1964	3,402,978	1,874,094	1,528,884
1963	2,459,105	1,505,335	953,770
1962	2,699,049	1,122,695	1,576,354
1961	2,950,860	1,160,357	1,790,503
1960	2,097,246	841,815	1,255,431

Source: Reprinted from Wiesenberger Services, Inc., *Investment Companies,* 1976.

shepherding nearly $60 billion. Most of this money found its way into mutual funds rather than closed-end investment companies. Mutual funds currently account for about 85% of all investment company assets. Why the great difference in popularity between open- and closed-end companies? Probably because the mutual funds employ widespread advertising and a large sales force, as well as providing a ready market for their shares.

FIGURE 13-2   Growth in investment company assets. (From Wiesenberger Services, Inc., *Investment Companies,* 37th ed., 1977, p. 12.)

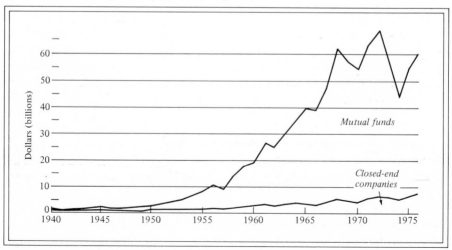

Net Asset Value per Share

The investor in a mutual fund or closed-end investment company buys a proportional share in the assets and liabilities in the company's portfolio. Nearly all these assets consist of the securities of other firms. Take the Rowe Price New Era Fund, for example. On December 31, 1974, its assets consisted of the following:

Investments in securities at value	$188,130,371
Cash	1,296,743
Receivables	1,889,049
Total assets	$191,316,163

The securities included stocks in 62 companies as well as bonds and certificates of deposit. The receivables consisted of dividends and interest earned but not yet collected and money due on fund shares and securities recently sold. The fund's liabilities equaled $1,275,439 and consisted of payables for securities purchased, shares redeemed, and accrued expenses.

The crucial figure to the shareholder is the **net asset value per share,** i.e., the net asset value of the investment company divided by the number of shares outstanding. On December 31, 1974, the net asset value per share of the Rowe Price New Era Fund equaled $8.47. This number is calculated as follows:

Assets	$191,316,163
Liabilities	− 1,275,439
Net assets	$190,040,724

$$\text{Net asset value per share} = \frac{\$190,040,724 \text{ net assets}}{22,437,159 \text{ outstanding shares}}$$

$$= \$8.47$$

Load and No-Load Mutual Funds

Mutual funds come in two distinct varieties—load and no-load. Investors with a do-it-yourself bent can probably save thousands of dollars over their lifetimes by knowing the difference. **No-load funds** sell their shares at no charge to investors. **Load funds,** on the other hand, charge investors a commission for purchasing their shares. This sales charge can indeed be a heavy "load" for the investor to bear. Usually, it equals 8.5% of the offering price of the fund's shares, but it varies from a low of 1% to a high of 8.5%. The sales charges on several hundred load funds are shown in Table 13-2.

Load funds report their sales charges as a percent of the offering price of their shares. Critics of load funds prefer to state the sales charge as a percent of the amount actually invested in the fund, i.e., as a percentage of the net asset value per share. For instance, an investor who pays $1,000 for shares in a load fund with an 8.5% sales charge invests only $915 in the fund. The other $85 goes to the individuals and firms selling the shares, with the dealer responsible for the sale probably receiving 60% of the commission. As far as the investor is con-

TABLE 13-2   SUMMARY OF SALES
CHARGES ON LOAD FUNDS

Sales Charge, %*	Number of Funds
1.00	1
1.50	1
3.00	2
7.00	1
7.25	3
7.50	12
7.55	1
8.00	17
8.50	180

* Sales charge quoted as a percentage of total money involved.

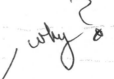

cerned, this $85 disappears forever. In this case, the sales charge as a percent of the amount invested equals 9.3% ($85/$915) as opposed to the stated rate of 8.5%.

Investors interested in buying mutual funds can find a daily listing in *The Wall Street Journal* or in the financial pages of most newspapers. Figure 13-3 provides a sample of these mutual fund quotes. The *Journal* lists the name of the fund, the net asset value per share (abbreviated NAV), the offering price, and the change in the net asset value per share from the preceding day.

No-load funds stand ready to buy and sell their shares at the net asset value per share. For example, the Acorn Fund (the first fund listed in Figure 13-3) sells its shares for their net asset value of $14.30. This is indicated by the letters "N.L." in the offering-price column. The letters stand for No-Load, indicating that investors in Acorn receive a net asset value per share exactly equal to the price they pay—$14.30.

The *Journal* arranges funds by their investment advisory organizations. For example, the American Funds group sponsors 10 different funds. The first fund in this group, the American Balanced Fund (abbreviated Am Bal) carries a NAV of $7.98 but sells for $8.72. This is obviously a load fund, since the investor pays $8.72 for a share valued at only $7.98. The load equals $0.74 ($8.72 − $7.98) on each share. As a percent of the cost of a share, the load amounts to 8.49% ($0.74/$8.72).

Closed-End Investment Companies

The February 21, 1977, issue of *Barron's* disclosed some interesting "bargains." On that date the shares of scores of investment companies were selling for less than their net asset values. Look at the price list in Table 13-3. The discount ranged from a low of 9.7% for Niagara shares to 47% for the Value Line Development Corporation. In other words, investors could purchase shares in these

Mutual Funds

Wednesday, March 2, 1977

Price ranges for investment companies, as quoted by the National Association of Securities Dealers. NAV stands for net asset value per share; the offering includes net asset value plus maximum sales charge, if any.

	NAV	Offer NAV Price	Chg.
Acorn Fnd	14.30	N.L.−	.03
Adv Invest	9.96	N.L.−	.03
Aetna Fnd	7.23	7.90−	.03
Aetna InSh	12.87	14.07+	.03
Afuture Fd	9.10	N.L.−	.01
AGE Fund	5.27	5.38	...
Allstate	8.42	N.L.−	.01
Alpha Fnd	10.56	N.L.−	.01
Am Birthrt	9.75	10.66+	.01
Am Equity	4.90	5.36	...
American Funds Group:			
Am Bal	7.98	8.72+	.01
Amcap F	5.43	5.93−	.01
Am Mutl	9.73	10.63+	.03
Bnd FdA	15.24	16.66+	.01
Cap FdA	6.25	6.83	...
Gth FdA	4.47	4.89−	.03
IncF Am	16.23	17.74	...
I C A	13.71	14.98−	.03
Nw Prsp	15.84	17.31−	.03
Wash Mt	7.01	7.66+	.02
American General Group:			
A GenBd	8.98	9.81+	.01
A GC Gr	4.08	4.46	...
A Gn Inc	6.51	7.11+	.01
A GnVen	10.83	11.84−	.06
Eqty Gth	6.51	7.11−	.01
Fd Amer	6.58	7.19	...
Prov Inc	3.96	4.27+	.01
Am Grwth	5.57	6.01	...
Am Ins Ind	4.89	5.34	...
Am Invest	5.30	N.L.−	.01
AmInv Inc	12.32	N.L.−	.02
AmNat Gw	2.74	2.99	...
Anchor Group:			
Daily Inc	1.00	N.L.	...
Growth	6.40	6.90−	.01
Income	7.45	8.03	...
Spectm	4.42	4.77	...
Fund Inv	6.72	7.25−	.01
Wa Natl	9.83	10.60	...
Audax Fnd	7.56	8.26+	.03
Axe-Houghton:			
Fund B	7.84	8.52+	.01
Income	4.93	5.36	...
Stock Fd	5.93	6.48−	.03
BLC Gwth	10.24	11.19	...
Babsn Inc	1.77	N.L.	...
Babsn Inv	9.36	N.L.−	.02
Beacon Hll	8.41	N.L.	...
Beacon Inv	9.35	N.L.−	.02
Berger Group Funds:			
100 Fund	7.19	N.L.+	.02
101 Fund	9.13	N.L.−	.02
Brksh Cap	7.81	8.54−	.03
Bondsk Cp	4.85	5.30	...
Bos Found	9.52	10.40+	.02
Brown Fnd	3.43	3.70	...
Calvin Bullock Funds:			
Bullock	12.88	14.08−	.01
Canadn	7.56	8.26+	.01
Div Shrs	3.10	3.39−	.01
Income	14.78	16.15	...
Ntwide	10.03	10.96	...
NY Vent	11.04	12.07−	.01
C G Fund	9.58	10.36−	.03
CG Inc Fd	8.51	9.20+	.01
Cap Presv	1.00	N.L.	...
Century Sh	10.52	11.34+	.01
Chalng Inv	10.13	11.07−	.01
Charter Fd	13.85	15.14−	.02

	NAV	Offer NAV Price	Chg.
Resrch	14.87	16.25	...
LifeIns Inv	6.98	7.62	...
Lincoln National Funds:			
Selct Am	7.04	N.L.+	.01
Selct Spl	12.54	N.L.	...
Loomis Sayles Funds:			
Cap Dev	9.98	N.L.+	.01
Mutual	12.88	N.L.+	.01
Lord Abbett:			
Affilatd	8.15	8.79+	.01
Bond Deb	11.30	12.35+	.02
Income	3.54	3.82+	.01
Lutheran Brotherhd Fds:			
Broth Fd	10.50	11.48+	.01
Broth Inc	9.31	10.17+	.02
Bro MBd	10.11	11.05−	.02
Broth US	9.87	10.79+	.01
Mass Company:			
Freedm	8.05	8.80−	.01
Indep Fd	7.11	7.77−	.03
Mass Fd	10.60	11.58	...
Mass Financial Svcs:			
MIT	10.59	11.42−	.02
MIG	8.37	9.02−	.02
MID	14.44	15.57−	.02
MFD	11.74	12.66−	.02
MCD	12.67	13.66−	.06
MFB	15.56	16.78+	.01
Mather Fd	12.93	N.L.−	.07
ML CapFd	12.95	13.85−	.02
ML RdyAs	1.00	N.L.	...
Mid Amer	5.13	5.61	...
Money Mkt	1.00	N.L.	...
MONY Fd	9.11	9.96−	.03
MSB Fund	(z)	(z)	(z)
Mutl BnFd	8.88	9.70−	.02
M I F Fd	8.54	9.23−	.01
M I F Gro	3.77	4.08	...
Mutual of Omaha Funds:			
Amer	11.68	11.86+	.03
Growth	4.00	4.35−	.02
Income	9.38	10.20	...
Mutl Shars	28.44	N.L.+	.03
Natl Indust	10.62	N.L.+	.01
National Securities Funds:			
Balanc	9.46	10.20+	.02
Bond	4.62	4.98	...
Dividnd	4.13	4.45	...
Preferd	7.47	8.05+	.03
Income	5.41	5.83−	.02
Stock	8.23	8.87+	.01
Grwth	5.49	5.92−	.02
New Eng Life Fds:			
Equity	16.74	18.20+	.02
Grwth	8.49	9.23+	.02
Income	13.95	15.16	...
Side	13.10	14.24+	.01
Neuberger Berman Mngt:			
Energy	14.48	N.L.−	.03
Guardn	27.82	N.L.+	.02
Partner	9.28	N.L.+	.02
N E A Mut	8.16	N.L.−	.01
Neuwirth	8.09	N.L.+	.01
Newton Fd	11.13	N.L.−	.06
Newtn Inv	9.93	N.L.−	.02
New World	10.89	N.L.−	.02
Nichlas Fd	13.91	N.L.+	.01
Nomura C	9.54	10.26−	.04
Noeast Inv	x14.75	N.L.−	.31
Nuveen BF	9.59	10.04	...
Omega Fd	9.97	10.09	...
One Wll St	13.55	N.L.−	.01

FIGURE 13-3 Sample mutual fund quotations. (Reprinted with permission of *The Wall Street Journal*, © Dow Jones & Company, Inc., Mar. 3, 1977, p. 32. All rights reserved.)

TABLE 13-3   SAMPLE PRICES AND NAVs OF CLOSED-END FUNDS

	NAV, $	Stock Price, $	% Difference
Diversified Common Stock Funds			
Adams Express	14.65	$11^7/_8$	−18.9
BakerFen	55.44	$34^1/_4$	−38.2
aCarriers	16.54	$13^3/_4$	−16.9
GenAInv	12.26	$10^1/_4$	−16.4
Lehman	12.97	$11^1/_8$	−14.2
Madison	16.95	$12^1/_4$	−27.7
NiagaraSh	12.73	$11^1/_2$	−9.7
OseasSec	4.59	$3^3/_8$	−26.5
Tri-Contl	24.14	$20^1/_2$	−15.1
United	12.31	$10^7/_8$	−11.6
US&For	21.72	$16^3/_4$	−22.9
Specialized Equity and Convertible Funds			
AmUtils	14.51	$11^7/_8$	−18.1
bASA	16.09	20	+24.3
Bancroft Conv	22.32	$16^1/_4$	−27.2
Castle	23.81	18	−24.4
CentSec	8.46	6	−29.1
ChaseCvBs	11.51	$8^1/_2$	−26.2
Claremont	9.32	$6^1/_2$	−30.2
CLIC	8.05	—	—
aDrexelUtl	21.48	$17^1/_4$	−19.7
Japan	11.63	$8^3/_4$	−24.8
KeysnOTC	9.86	$7^3/_8$	−25.2
NatlAvia	22.63	15	−33.7
NewAmerFund	17.90	14	−21.8
PetroCp	24.82	$26^1/_4$	+5.8
RetIncC	2.70	$1^7/_8$	−30.6
S-GSecInc	1.82	$1^1/_2$	−17.6
Source	17.21	14	−18.7
StdSh	40.83	$25^1/_2$	−37.5
VILmDvCp	4.22	$2^1/_4$	−47.0

a—ex-dividend; b—as of Thursday's close.

companies for substantially less than their NAVs. For example, Niagara shares valued at $12.73 sold for $11^1/_2$—9.7% less than their NAV. And investors looking for a real loss leader could have purchased shares in Value Line for only $2^1/_4$, a 47% discount from the NAV of $4.22.

To beginning investors, these discounts probably sound like someone offering dollar bills for less than a dollar. Surely such a sale would attract an enormous crowd of buyers. Actually, experienced investors greeted the day's quotes with only a yawn. Closed-end companies frequently sell at substantial discounts from their net asset values. Unlike mutual funds, these companies adopt a passive role with respect to their own shares, neither buying nor selling them. Instead, pro-

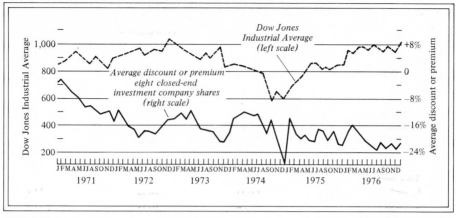

FIGURE 13-4 Discounts and premiums on the shares of eight closed-end investment companies. (From Wiesenberger Services, Inc., *Investment Companies,* 37th ed., 1977, p. 20.)

spective investors must find willing sellers. As a result, the forces of supply and de-mand determine day-to-day prices, just as these forces set the prices of shares of GM, GE, and IBM.

Figure 13-4 shows the discount or premium on the shares of eight closed-end investment companies during the period from 1970 to 1977. Why the sub-stantial discounts over such long periods of time? A number of researchers and investment professionals have suggested possible answers. Wiesenberger Ser-vices, Inc., the publisher of a widely used advisory service on investment compa-nies, cites the absence of a redeemability feature similar to that offered by mutual funds and a lack of sales effort as the reasons for the discount.

Wiesenberger's explanation fails on two counts. First, there is no reason why the absence of a redeemability feature should cause investment shares to sell at a discount. These shares can and occasionally do sell at a premium. Take American South African, a company holding mostly gold-mining stocks, for example. Ac-cording to Table 13-3, shares in American South African (abbreviated ASA) sold at a 24.3% premium over their net asset value on February 17, 1977.

Second, Wiesenberger's view of the investment world clashes with the gen-erally efficient market concept. Security prices seldom deviate for very long from intrinsic values. So the lack of a sales effort by the closed-end companies implies nothing about the prices of their shares.

Rodney Roenfeldt and Donald Tuttle, professors of finance at the University of South Carolina and Indiana University, focus instead on the market's expecta-tions about the ability of fund managers to predict security prices. Roenfeldt and Tuttle show that funds with substantial discounts over long periods of time per-formed significantly worse than other funds and the overall market. Apparently the discount in the price of the shares reflects this poor performance.

OBJECTIVES

Different investors have different objectives; so no one investment company completely satisfies the needs of everyone. As a result, some companies emphasize income, others attempt to achieve the largest capital gains possible, and still others seek to balance income with capital gains.

In order to avoid disappointment or confusion, the managements of most investment companies publicly state their investment objectives. At the end of 1975, nearly one-fourth of all mutual funds had adopted the "go-go" objective of obtaining **maximum capital gains** for their investors. A maximum capital gains objective has several important implications for the investment strategy of the fund. Most of the stocks purchased and held by this type of fund pay low or no dividends. After all, the lower the dividend, the higher the expected appreciation, other things being equal. In addition, these funds purchase more risky stocks—a reflection of the fact that higher returns usually accompany higher risks. The risk taken may be further increased by investing in small, unknown companies, by using borrowed money to provide financial leverage, and by concentrating money in only a few industries rather than diversifying among many. Furthermore, the management of a maximum capital gains fund may frequently buy and sell stocks, may request that compensation be partially based upon performance, and may employ such techniques as selling short, buying unregistered securities (called "letter stock"), and writing uncovered options.

Obviously, the policies followed by most capital gains funds do not appeal to every investor. In fact, most of the money invested in mutual funds goes to either growth or growth-income funds. Growth and growth-income funds follow more conventional investment policies than maximum capital gains funds. According to Wiesenberger, **growth funds** generally view income as only a secondary or incidental objective. On the other hand, **growth-income funds** have a record of relatively stable income over the years, probably because they usually buy stocks paying "reasonable" dividends.

Another type of fund is termed a balanced fund. Whereas the maximum capital gains, growth, and growth-income funds invest primarily in common stocks, **balanced funds** hold bonds and preferred stocks as well as equities. They do this in order to achieve their objective of minimizing risk while at the same time retaining some possibilities for long-term growth and current income. Today less than 4% of all mutual funds "balance" their portfolios.

Investors always face a trade-off between capital gains and income. The higher the expected capital gain, the lower the expected income and vice versa. Maximum capital gains funds attempt to maximize appreciation. On the other hand, **income funds** attempt to provide "as liberal a current income from investments as possible," according to Wiesenberger. These investment companies achieve their objectives in various ways. Take the money market funds, for example. They invest in money market instruments like negotiable certificates of deposit, commercial paper, Treasury bills, and bankers' acceptances. Other in-

vestment companies with an income objective invest in tax-free municipal bonds
or in preferred stocks or in corporate bonds.

Risk and Return

The stated objectives of funds provide the investor with qualitative guideposts to
follow in selecting a fund. In particular, these objectives indicate the risk and return that can be expected from a fund. From the description of the policies followed by the funds, the most risky group appears to be the maximum capital
gains funds; the least risky, the income funds. The funds can be arrayed in order
of increasing risk and return as follows:

Income

Balanced

Common Stocks { Growth-income

Growth

Maximum capital gains

increasing

risk and return

Stated objectives can aid investors in selecting a fund. But these objectives
are qualitative and therefore somewhat ambiguous. Just what does growth-
income really mean? And are all the funds in one group more or less risky than all
the funds in another group?

Professor John McDonald of Stanford University provided some answers to
these questions in a recent study of the relationship between the stated objectives
and the actual market risk of mutual funds. He classified the funds as maximum
capital gains, growth, growth-income, income-growth (slightly more emphasis on
income than on growth), balanced, and income. Then McDonald calculated the
beta (systematic risk) of each fund as well as the average betas for all funds in a
group.

The results are shown in Figure 13-5. The general pattern is consistent with
the graph on the previous page: the greater the emphasis on capital gains, the
greater the risk. The maximum capital gains group displayed the greatest volatility, the income funds the least. The average beta for the maximum capital gains
funds equaled 1.22. In other words, for every 1% change in the market, these
funds moved by about 1.22%. The average beta declined steadily over the other
groups, reaching a low of 0.55 for the income group of investment companies.
For every 1% change in the market, the average income fund moved by 0.55%.

The stated objectives of the funds coincide well with their average betas, but
there is considerable overlap between funds in different groups. Indeed, some of
the funds in the lowest-risk group (income) possessed considerably higher betas
than funds in the second most risky group (growth). And funds in the growth,
growth-income, and income-growth categories often displayed more risk than
funds in the highest-risk category of maximum capital gains. McDonald also com-

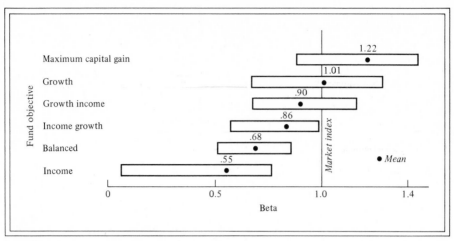

FIGURE 13-5   Stated objectives and betas of mutual funds. (From J. G. McDonald, "Objectives and Performance of Mutual Funds, 1960–1969," *Journal of Financial and Quantitative Analysis,* June 1974, p. 316.)

puted the standard deviation of monthly returns for each of the funds. These standard deviations are illustrated in Figure 13-6. They follow the same general pattern as the betas. In fact, in this case the greatest overall fluctuation is found in the growth group, rather than in the maximum capital gains group. Judging from these results, an investor selecting mutual funds solely on the basis of their stated objectives sometimes faces considerable disappointment.

FIGURE 13-6   Stated objectives and standard deviations of monthly returns of mutual funds. (From J. G. McDonald, "Objectives and Performance of Mutual Funds, 1960–1969," *Journal of Financial and Quantitative Analysis,* June 1974, p. 316.)

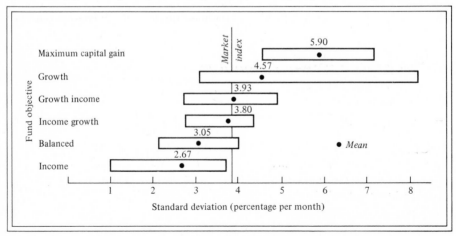

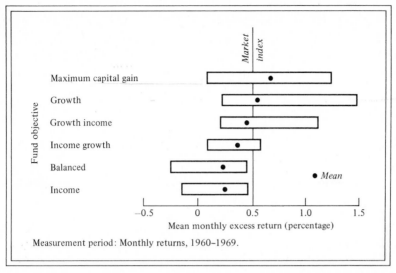

FIGURE 13-7   Stated objectives and excess returns of mutual funds. (From J. G. McDonald, "Objectives and Performance of Mutual Funds, 1960–1969," *Journal of Financial and Quantitative Analysis,* June 1974, p. 317.)

Since return is closely related to risk, it should come as no surprise that the highest average returns were earned on the most risky funds. The excess returns (over what could have been earned on 30-day commercial paper) on the funds is shown in Figure 13-7. The group with the highest overall risk had the highest average return; the group with the lowest overall risk had almost the lowest average return. But again the results for the individual funds are somewhat discouraging. The overlap in the rates of return on individual funds in different groups is marked. The worst-performing fund in the high-risk (and supposedly high-return) group had a lower return than funds in every other group. And some of the funds in the lowest group outperformed funds in the highest group.

INVESTMENT COMPANY SERVICES

Mutual funds and some closed-end companies offer investors a wide variety of services. These include:

1 Open account
2 Systematic withdrawal plans
3 Automatic dividend reinvestment
4 Monthly dividend checks
5 Tax-sheltered retirement plans
6 Exchange privileges

7   Insurance against long-term loss
8   Accumulation plans

Most investors find the **open account** the most useful service. Rather than issue share certificates, the mutual fund opens an "account" for the investor with its custodian. The custodian maintains a continuous record of the investor's purchases and sales of fund shares. The custodian provides the investor with a financial statement documenting every transaction and with a summary statement at the end of the year for tax purposes.

With an open account, there are no stock certificates for the investor to safeguard or redeem (unless the fund is specifically requested to issue the certificates). And the individual can ask the fund to add capital gains distributions and dividends to the account. By the way, closed-end investment companies do not offer open accounts, since they do not buy and sell their own shares.

Systematic withdrawal plans make it possible for investors to receive a steady income from their investment companies. For example, a woman might instruct her fund to pay out $100 every month. Some funds even allow investors to withdraw a fixed percentage of the current value of the account.

Many funds and several of the closed-end investment companies provide for automatic reinvestment of dividends. Of course, some investors prefer to receive the cash instead. Investment companies usually pay dividends every 3 months, but a few of them pay dividends monthly.

Investment companies also offer special accounts satisfying all the rules for IRA and Keogh plans and for tax-sheltered custodial accounts.

The **exchange privilege** sometimes applies to a group of funds sponsored by one investment advisory firm. For example, the T. Rowe Price organization permits investors to shift money among its six different funds. According to a recent prospectus, the exchange may be requested by telephone, telegram, or letter, subject to certain conditions. Unfortunately, investors must still pay an income tax on any capital gains realized by the exchange. In other words, the IRS views this exchange as a simultaneous sale and purchase of shares.

Insurance against Loss

One of the most interesting new services offered by some mutual funds involves insurance against long-term loss in the value of fund shares. For a small premium, investors can purchase insurance guaranteeing the redemption value of fund shares at the end of 10, $12^1/_2$, or 15 years. Here's how the insurance works. The insurance firms make up any difference between the starting value of the investment (including the full amount of the premium) and the ending value (with all dividends and capital gains distributions reinvested). The insurance costs a total of 6% of the investment, with premiums payable in equal installments over the life of the policy. A 10-year policy costs 0.6% per annum, a $12^1/_2$-year policy 0.48% per annum, and a 15-year policy 0.4% per annum.

EXAMPLE   Steve Williams buys $10,000 of mutual fund shares. The fund offers insurance on the redemption value. Steve takes a 10-year policy and pays six-tenths of 1% each year in premiums. He reinvests all dividends and capital gains distributions, and at the end of 10 years the investment totals $11,200. This $11,200 ending value exceeds the $10,600 starting value (including the total cost of the insurance); so the insurance firm pays nothing. If the value of the account had equaled only $9,000, the insurance firm would have paid Steve $1,600 = ($10,600 − $9,000).

Accumulation Plans

Accumulation plans can be either voluntary or contractual. A **voluntary accumulation plan** simply consists of an informal arrangement to make a periodic purchase of the fund shares. The fund mails the investor a reminder just before each payment date. Some investors apparently appreciate this gentle nudge toward increased savings.

A contractual plan represents more of a disservice than a service, at least when offered by a load fund. Over the years the sales charge on a load mutual fund consumes a considerable part of the investor's savings. A **contractual accumulation plan** depletes the investor's capital even more quickly. In fact, commissions on funds purchased through this type of plan sometimes amount to as much as 50%. By the way, the phrase "contractual plan" is somewhat misleading. An investor agreeing to a contractual plan never signs a legally enforceable contract, despite the fact that the document reads like a legal contract, but simply agrees to purchase a specific dollar amount of the fund. For example, a plan issued by one of the largest mutual funds in the country reads as follows:

> Planholder agrees to make _____ equal payments, hereafter referred to as "Plan Payments," of $ _____ each, due on the _____ day of every month hereafter, in the aggregate amount of $ _____.

The investor and the mutual fund representative fill in the appropriate blanks and the investor then signs the document.

If a contractual plan does not really commit investors to a definite payment program, what does it do? Wiesenberger glowingly describes contractual plans as a "Goad to a Goal." And it lists in detail the incentives to perseverance associated with such plans. Wiesenberger's view coincides nicely with that of the mutual fund industry it serves.

In reality, contractual plans amount to a declaration of "open season" on the individual's money. With a contractual plan, the mutual fund and its agents are free to bag unusually large commissions as a percent of the total amount invested. Suppose an individual agrees to purchase $12,000 of a mutual fund in 200 equal monthly installments of $60 each. If the mutual fund charges a commission of 8½% on its shares, the total commission on $12,000 equals $1,020. Because of the contractual plan, the mutual fund feels free to load most of this sales charge onto the early payments—a so-called **front-end load**. This imposes a severe penalty on investors unable or unwilling to continue payments, since most of their early payments go to sales charges.

Congress recognized this fact several years ago and provided specific relief for contract investors in the Investment Company Amendments Act. This law grants people the right to demand a complete refund of all their money within a period of 45 days from the mailing of the contract certificate. The law also limits the sales charge to a maximum of 50% of the first year's installments or to a so-called spread-load averaging 16% over the first 48 payments. If the investment company opts for the 50% front-end load, the investor automatically receives the right to a refund for a period of 18 months. If the initial 45-day period has passed, the refund is limited to the net asset value per share and any sales charges in excess of 15% of all payments.

OPERATIONS OF INVESTMENT COMPANIES

Most investment companies incur substantial costs in the pursuit of performance and diversification. Probably the greatest outlay consists of the **advisory fee** paid to the investment adviser. This fee usually equals one-half of 1% of all investment company assets under $100 or $200 million. For example, Fidelity Trend Fund pays its investment adviser one-half of 1% of the first $200 million in daily net assets. If Fidelity keeps an average of $100 million invested during the year, its adviser collects $500,000 for managing the portfolio. If its investments average $200 million, the compensation jumps to $1 million.

Many investment advisory firms set their fees on a sliding scale. As the amount managed increases, the fee as a percentage of these assets decreases. At Fidelity Trend, the adviser's fee starts at 0.5% for the first $200 million, drops to 0.45% on the next $100 million, to 0.4% on the next $400 million, to 0.35% on the next $300 million, and finally slides to 0.3% on any amount over the $1 billion mark. Why the decline in rates? Because of the economies associated with large size; i.e., it doesn't take twice as much effort to manage twice as much money.

Advisory Fees

There are two ways to view advisory fees. Many investors think the fee a small price to pay for professional management. After all, they reason, a good investment advisory firm pays for itself many times over by searching out undervalued investments. On the other hand, a growing number of investors are taking a "show me" attitude toward fund managers. For years they have watched funds underperform the general market. And now the efficient-market concept provides them with further reason for questioning the worth of most investment advisers. Since investment companies trade almost exclusively in the stocks of very large, well-known companies, fund managers have little chance of beating a simple buy-and-hold policy.

The efficient-market concept provides one reason for doubting the wisdom of paying large advisory fees. The intimate relationship between many investment companies and their advisory firms provides another. Investment companies too often appear to be held captive by their investment advisers. Directors and/or major shareholders of management firms usually dominate the boards of directors of the funds. For example, a quick survey of the board of directors of a $2-billion mutual fund reveals that 4 of the fund's 7 directors also work for the advisory firm. This is the maximum number of **inside directors** permitted by the government. (The Investment Company Act limits the number of inside directors to 60% of the board.) The other directors of the fund are officers of large business corporations. These outside directors own a total of only 1,300 shares—hardly an important position. Overlapping directorships lead to a serious conflict of interest. Fund directors should attempt to minimize costs, but in their role as employees of the advisory firm, they quite naturally want to maximize fees or some other measure of profits. For that reason, the compensation paid to the advisory firm may be excessive. And the fund may tie itself to the adviser regardless of the quality of the advice received.

Total Expenses

Investment companies have other expenses in addition to advisory fees. These expenses include the salaries of investment company officers and personnel, the fees of accountants, attorneys, and the custodian, and perhaps rent for office space and other facilities (most advisory firms provide these facilities as part of their service). Finally there are expenditures for printing, postage, mailing, and advertising. The total expenses, including the advisory fee, of most investment companies seldom exceed 1%.

About the only generalities that can be made about investment company expenses are that (1) they have remained fairly stable over the last 10 years, (2) the larger the fund the smaller they are, and (3) they are approximately the same for load and no-load funds. The expense ratios for different sizes and types of funds are as follows:

Assets in Millions, $	No-Load, %	Load, %
1,000 plus	0.51	0.38
300–1,000	0.57	0.53
100–300	0.60	0.70
50–100	0.92	0.82
20–50	1.02	0.93
10–20	1.08	1.02
5–10	1.34	1.14
1–5	1.91	1.34

Turnover

The expense ratio does not reflect all the costs of operating an investment company. There is one very important exclusion—the brokerage commissions and other transactions costs involved in buying and selling investments. Most funds report the commissions paid during each of the most recent 3 years somewhere in their prospectuses, together with the **portfolio turnover.** This turnover figure indicates the percentage of the portfolio bought or sold during the year, i.e., turned over. Higher turnover implies more frequent transactions and larger brokerage commissions.

Portfolio turnover rates vary greatly from investment company to investment company. The David L. Babson Investment Fund reported a turnover rate of 2.8% during 1975. In the same year, Istel Fund had a portfolio turnover rate of 95.3% of average assets. In other words Istel held its investments an average of only 1.05 years (1 year/0.953). During 1975, Istel handed out $1.2 million in commissions, not to mention the other costs of transacting. They paid only $800,000 for all other expenses (about 0.73%), including the advisory fee during the same year. So turnover has a tremendous impact on costs.

In contrast to operating expenses, portfolio turnover rates seldom receive much attention, despite their importance. This disparity between operating expenses and commission costs probably exists because investment companies add commission costs to the value of their assets rather than deducting them from income. As a result, these costs disappear into the balance sheet.

Believers in generally efficient markets and those just skeptical of the ability of advisers to select superior investments want to minimize these transactions costs. They view portfolio turnover as a double-edged sword. It not only increases out-of-pocket expenses but also produces a significant tax liability in the form of increased capital gains taxes.

On the other hand, the management and directors sometimes benefit from high rates of turnover. Either the commissions go to a "friendly" brokerage firm controlled indirectly by these people or the commissions serve as indirect payment for investment advice provided by an independent brokerage firm. The more free advice the advisory firm receives from a brokerage house, the less time, effort, and money it needs to expend on its own research for the investment company and the higher its profits. Whatever the case, the shareholders lose.

Taxation of Investment Companies

In a sense an investment company resembles a communal brokerage account, with investors sharing in the gains, losses, and expenses in direct proportion to their holdings. The government recognizes this fact by permitting these companies to qualify for special tax treatment. Ordinarily, companies first pay taxes on any income or gains and then the shareholders pay taxes on all dividends. Treating investment companies this same way would discriminate against investors wishing to pool their funds rather than invest on their own. For that reason the government does not tax investment companies if 90% of their gross income comes from dividends, interest, and gains on securities and if they distribute 90% of their net income to shareholders. (Actually the government imposes several additional restrictions.)

Any dividends and interest received by an investment company go first to cover its operating expenses. The company then pays the remainder to shareholders, who report these dividends as income on their personal tax returns. Investment companies also realize capital gains periodically. Usually the companies distribute these gains to their shareholders, who then pay capital-gains taxes. But some investment companies retain all gains and pay the maximum capital gains tax themselves. This procedure involves the shareholders in some complex calculations. First, they report their share of the capital gains on their income tax returns and determine the amount of tax. Then they claim their share of the capital gains tax already paid by the investment company. And, finally, they claim any difference between the tax paid by the company and the tax they would have had to pay themselves.

At the end of the year, every investment company mails its shareholders an information return similar to the one shown in Figure 13-8. This return provides shareholders with all the information needed to complete their income tax returns.

Chapter Eleven emphasized the importance of taxes in selecting investments. Investors minimize income taxes by following a policy of cutting their losses short and letting their profits run. Unfortunately, very few investment companies follow that policy. Instead, they take profits in stocks and distribute the gains to their shareholders. The mutual fund summarized in Figure 13-9 provides a good example of this costly practice. Assume an investor purchased $10,000 of shares in this fund on January 1, 1967. The sales charge equaled 8½%; so the individual

FIGURE 13-8   Sample of tax information provided by investment companies.

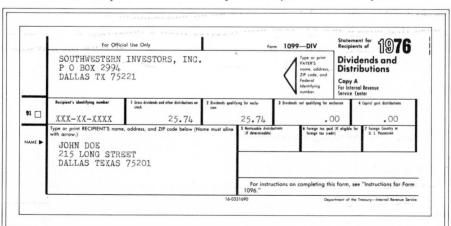

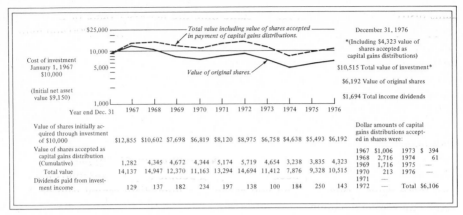

FIGURE 13-9   "Maximizing taxes" with a mutual fund. (From Wiesenberger Services, Inc., *Investment Companies,* 37th ed., 1977, p. 193.)

immediately lost $850. The fund distributed capital gains in 6 out of the next 10 years. Several of these distributions were very large, relative to the amount initially invested. For example, the distribution in 1968 amounted to $2,716. By the end of 1974, the shareholder had received a total of $6,106 in capital gains distributions and of course had paid the resulting capital gains taxes. Despite this fact, the shares showed almost no increase in value over the 10-year period. Assuming complete reinvestment of all distributions, the value of the shares increased from $10,000 at the start of 1967 to only $10,515 at the end of 1976. Therefore, the true capital gains amounted to only $515. However, because of the fund's perverse policy of taking profits and letting losses run, shareholders paid taxes on $6,106 of capital gains.

Such undesirable situations can and should be avoided. One solution is to select a fund which attempts to minimize taxes. A case in point is the T. Rowe Price Growth Fund. Because T. Rowe Price is a no-load fund, $10,000 actually buys $10,000 of investments. A $10,000 investment at the start of 1962 grew to $28,603 by the end of 1972, assuming the reinvestment of all distributions. Despite this very large increase in value, the management of the fund distributed only $3,585, a fraction of the actual gains. As a result, shareholders were spared the unnecessary payment of capital gains taxes.

Inept selection of investment companies often results in the payment of real tax dollars on phantom gains. These tax liabilities sometimes materialize almost overnight for the unsuspecting investor. Most funds distribute gains once a year. Imagine the plight of investors who unwittingly purchased shares on October 30, 1968 in the fund illustrated in Figure 13-9. They experienced the following series of events:

First they each spent $10,000 for shares worth only $9,150, the remainder going to pay the sales charge of $8\frac{1}{2}\%$. One day later the fund declared a capital gains distribution of $2,716. At the same time the net asset value of the shares dropped by the exact same amount. A single investor earning $20,000 and living in an "average" state as far as income taxes are concerned probably falls in a 40% tax bracket. Assuming all the distribution qualified as a long-term capital gain, this investor unexpectedly had to mail the IRS an additional $543 in taxes for the year. The net result of the purchase of shares was a total loss of $1,393 ($543 in increased taxes and $850 in sales charges).

No wonder the Securities and Exchange Commission has asked mutual fund sales people to warn investors about the tax consequences of buying a fund near the date of a capital gains distribution or dividend payment. (Apparently some sales personnel had actually been encouraging people to purchase funds just before these dates. "Buy now and you receive an immediate capital gain or dividend," they argued, failing to point out the equal and offsetting change in the net asset value of each share produced by the distribution.)

Evaluating Performance

Everybody loves a winner. And the 10 million or more Americans holding shares in investment companies are no exception. But telling the winners from the losers in the performance derby takes a trained eye.

Traditional techniques for gauging investment company performance rely upon either a measure of average return or a comparison of beginning and ending values. Suppose an investor wants to measure the performance of a mutual fund during the 10-year period from December 31, 1966, to December 31, 1976. Wiesenberger provides a chart similar to the one shown in Figure 13-10. This chart displays the beginning value, usually assumed to be $10,000, and several ending values.

These terminal values vary, depending upon the assumptions made about the reinvestment of dividend and capital gains distributions. According to Wiesenberger, the original shares in the Johnston Mutual Fund had increased in value to $12,330 at the end of 10 years. Assuming reinvestment of all capital gains distributions, the total value of the investment in the Johnston Fund equaled $14,963. Wiesenberger also presents the results from reinvesting all dividends and distributions in shares of the investment company. These figures are shown in Figure 13-10. They are:

Initial investment at offering price, Jan. 1, 1967	$10,000
Total dividends from income reinvested	2,300
Total amount invested	12,300
Total value, Dec. 31, 1976	$17,499

The terminal value of $17,499 includes all dividends and capital gains; so it provides a measure of the total performance of the fund.

The information in Figure 13-10 can also be used to calculate average returns for different periods of time. The 1-year return on Johnston from December 31, 1975, to December 31, 1976, is calculated as follows:

Value of original shares at the end of 1976	$12,330
Value of original shares at the end of 1975	10,877
Change in value	1,453
Plus annual investment income dividend	218
Plus capital gains distributions	216
Total gain	$ 1,887

$$1976 \text{ return} = \frac{\$1,887 \text{ total gain}}{\$10,887 \text{ value of original shares at end of 1974}}$$

$$= 17.3\%$$

The annual returns for other years can be computed in the same way and then combined to form 5- and 10- year average returns. Or the compounded annual returns can be derived. And if greater precision is desired, the exact dates of the dividend and capital gains distributions can be included in the analysis.

Average returns and the comparisons of beginning and ending values receive wide publicity. But they provide an incomplete picture of investment company performance. Most investors like return but dislike risk. As a result, high-risk investments generate higher returns on average than low-risk investments. This higher return serves to compensate people for the mental (and sometimes physical) anguish associated with risk.

Traditional measures of investment performance completely ignore this fundamental trade-off between risk and return. They award the blue ribbons to the fastest-growing funds, regardless of how that growth took place. More modern measures consider not only who won or lost the race, but how the race was run. In other words, they balance the returns against the risk to arrive at a risk-adjusted rate of return.

Before calculating these risk-adjusted returns, some decisions must be made about (1) the period of time to be covered and (2) the **differencing interval** to be used. The term "differencing interval" refers to the period for which the returns are calculated, i.e., the time interval over which the values are differenced. Most experts in the field of portfolio measurement appear to prefer either a quarterly or monthly differencing interval, since it makes possible more exact measurement.

Risk-Return Measures of Portfolio Performance

Judging from the capital-asset pricing model, the expected return on a security or a portfolio equals the risk-free return plus a risk premium. Since all investments earn the risk-free return, it makes sense to exclude the risk-free return from the performance measure and focus on the **excess return.** The excess return equals

Statistical History

						% of Assets in								
Year	Total Net Assets ($)	Number of Share-holders	Net Asset Value Per Share ($)	Yield (%)	Cash & Equiv-alent	Bonds & Pre-ferreds	Com-mon Stocks	Income Div-idends ($)	Capital Gains Distribu-tion ($)	Expense Ratio (%)	Offering Price ($) High	Low		
1976	286,236,631	49,329	21.80	1.4	14	6	80	0.32	0.32	0.63	21.80	19.34		
1975	274,481,051	55,612	19.23	2.2	7	3	90	0.42	—	0.64	21.23	15.14		
1974	206,899,889	56,735	14.93	3.6	21	—	79	0.54	0.25	0.65	23.00	13.35		
1973	297,332,193	56,631	22.69	1.6	15	5*	80	0.37	0.80	0.63	30.54	21.27		
1972	332,510,881	48,046	30.01	0.7	10	11*	79	0.22	0.59	0.62	30.37	24.43		
1971	221,361,130	37,496	24.75	0.8	8	12*	80	0.21	—	0.64	24.85	19.58		
1970	155,026,800	31,752	19.75	1.7	8	12*	80	0.338	0.37	0.70	21.88	15.21		
1969	143,181,147	27,143	21.71	1.4	6	9*	85	0.31	0.73	0.72	23.00	19.88		
1968	123,730,349	23,344	22.66	1.4	6	8*	86	0.32	0.75	0.71	24.24	18.83		
1967	100,669,393	19,015	22.00	1.3	3	11*	86	0.29	0.70	0.67	22.57	17.55		
1966	64,634,579	14,607	17.68	1.7	5	3*	92	0.31	0.65	0.68	19.66	15.12		

*Includes a substantial proportion in convertible issues.

Directors: Nathan H. Garrick, Jr., Pres.; Fentress Hill II, Exec. V.P.; Ruth Marie Adams; David L.Beckedorff; Francis P. Brennan; Richard A. Crowell; Leslie Rollins; James L. Stone; William W. Wolbach.

Investment Adviser: Douglas I. Johnston & Co., Inc. Compensation to the Adviser is 1/8 of 1% quarterly on the first $100 million of average net assets, reducing to 1/10 of 1% quarterly on assets in excess of $100 million.

Custodian and Transfer Agent: The Bank of New York, New York, N.Y.

Distributor: None. Shares are sold directly by the fund.

Sales Charge: None. Shares are issued at net asset value. Minimum initial investment is $250; subsequent open account investments must be at least $50.

Dividends: Income dividends are paid semi-annually in the months of January and July. Capital gains, if any, are paid optionally in shares or cash in January.

Shareholder Reports: Issued quarterly. Fiscal year ends December 31. The 1976 prospectus was effective in May.

Qualified for Sale: In all states and DC.

Address: 460 Park Ave., New York, NY 10022.

Telephone: (212) 679-2700.

An assumed investment of $10,000 in this fund, with capital gains accepted in shares, is illustrated below. The explanation on page 153 must be read in conjunction with this illustration.

THE JOHNSTON MUTUAL FUND, INC.

Cost of investment January 1, 1967 $10,000

(Initial net asset value $10,000)

$40,000 / 30,000 / 20,000 / 15,000 / 10,000 / 5,000

Total value including value of shares accepted in payment of capital gains distributions.

Value of original shares.

Year end Dec. 31 1967 1968 1969 1970 1971 1972 1973 1974 1975 1976

December 31, 1976

*(Including $2,633 value of shares accepted as capital gains distributions)

$14,963 Total value of investment*

$12,330 Value of original shares

$2,133 Total income dividends

	1967	1968	1969	1970	1971	1972	1973	1974	1975	1976
Value of shares initially acquired through investment of $10,000	$12,443	$12,817	$12,279	$11,171	$13,999	$16,974	$12,834	$8,445	$10,877	$12,330
Value of shares accepted as capital gains distribution (Cumulative)	403	837	1,253	1,375	1,723	2,537	2,327	1,645	2,120	2,633
Total value	12,846	13,654	13,532	12,546	15,722	19,511	15,161	10,090	12,997	14,963
Dividends paid from investment income	164	187	187	211	133	142	244	363	284	218

Dollar amounts of capital gains distributions accepted in shares were:

1967	$396	1973	$ 520
1968	438	1974	167
1969	440	1975	—
1970	231	1976	216
1971	—		
1972	375	Total	$2,783

Results taking all dividends and distributions in STOCK.

Initial investment at offering price, Jan.1, 1967	$10,000
Total dividends from income reinvested	$ 2,300
Total amount invested	$12,300
Total value, Dec. 31, 1976	$17,499*

*Includes value of shares received in payment of $2,944 capital gains.

Results taking all dividends and distributions in CASH.

Initial investment at offering price, Jan. 1, 1967	$10,000
Total value, Dec. 31, 1976	$12,330
Distributions from capital gains	$ 2,550
Dividends from investment income	$ 1,887

FIGURE 13-10   Typical description of investment company performance. (From Wiesenberger Services, Inc., *Investment Companies,* 37th ed., 1977, p. 279.)

the difference between the actual return and the return on a riskless security like a Treasury bill.

Jensen, Treynor, and Sharpe have all proposed methods for adjusting these excess returns for differences in risk. Sharpe concentrates on the total variability of portfolio returns, measured by the standard deviation of historical returns. Treynor and Jensen both use beta as their measure of risk.

Sharpe calls his measure of portfolio performance the **reward-to-variability ratio**. The reward equals the average excess return provided by a portfolio. The variability, or standard deviation, of excess returns represents the risk experienced by the investor. The ratio of reward to variability indicates the reward per unit of risk; i.e.,

$$\text{Reward-to-variability ratio} = \frac{\text{average excess return}}{\text{standard deviation of excess returns}}$$

$$= \text{reward per unit of risk}$$

 The higher the reward-to-variability ratio, the better the performance of the portfolio. And portfolios with high reward-to-variability ratios provide the most return for the least risk.

The misleading nature of performance measures based solely on the average return is illustrated in Figure 13-11. Mutual fund A earned an average excess return of 4%, whereas mutual fund B provided an excess return of only 2%. But B gave the investor much more return per unit of risk than A. The reward-to-variability ratio of A is $1/2$ (4%/8%); for B it is 1 (2%/2%). By the way, the reward-to-variability ratio of a portfolio equals the slope of the line connecting two points: one point represents the portfolio and the other depicts a zero-excess-return combination (point 0). So the steeper the slope, the better the portfolio.

These lines also show the various combinations of risk and return available to an investor who purchases some of the portfolio with cash and invests the rest

FIGURE 13-11   Measuring the risk-adjusted performance of investment companies.

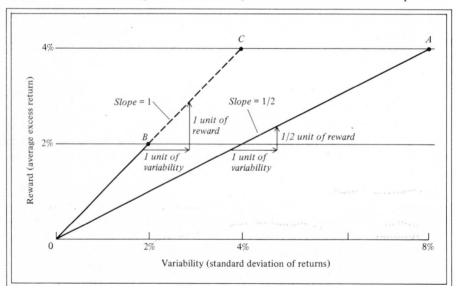

in Treasury bills. Treasury bills offer zero risk and provide no excess return. Investors holding half their money in portfolio A and half in T-bills experience exactly half the excess return of portfolio A (since the excess returns on T-bills equals zero). And they confront exactly half the risk of portfolio A (again since the risk of T-bills equals zero). Therefore the risk-return combination of a portfolio consisting of 50% of Mutual Fund A and 50% of T-bills plots halfway between point 0 and point A.

Now assume investors can borrow unlimited amounts of money at the risk-free rate of return. By buying shares in Fund B on a 50% margin, investors could have attained the risk-return combination shown by point C. (See Chapter Eight for a description of the risk and return on leveraged portfolios.) This portfolio dominates Fund A since it provides an excess return of 4% and has a variability of only 4%.

Unlike Sharpe, Jensen, and Treynor, both base their performance measures on nondiversifiable risk (beta). They first fit a fund's returns to the market model. This adjusts the returns for nondiversifiable risk. Jensen then uses the intercept from the market model, or alpha, to measure the ability of a fund's manager to outperform the market. In the absence of forecasting ability, alpha equals zero and the excess return on the portfolio depends solely upon its nondiversifiable risk. Treynor uses a combination of alpha and beta to calibrate performance.

SELECTION

Mutual funds and closed-end investment companies operate in generally efficient markets. Most of their holdings consist of the securities of *Fortune* 500 companies like IBM, Xerox, GM, and GE. As a result, the odds of their beating the market appear to be very small—a fact attested to by most performance studies.

For that reason, investors who are window-shopping for funds should probably adopt the following selection process:

1   *Load versus no-load funds*   Immediately eliminate all load funds from consideration. Anyone who has read this far probably knows more about investments than most mutual fund salespeople. So why pay for the "guidance" provided with load funds? The do-it-yourself investor can select from hundreds of no-load funds and perhaps save thousands of dollars over the years.

2   *Objectives*   Match your own personal objectives with those of the various funds. Most funds declare their investment objectives in their prospectuses, which, by the way, should be required reading for all would-be investors. Wiesenberger also reports these objectives. And the investor can learn the fund's beta from Wiesenberger, Fundscope, or some other advisory service.

3   *Operating expenses*   Eliminate any funds with operating-expense ratios in excess of 0.75% a year. There is absolutely no need to pay any more than

this for professional management. The state of California even goes so far as to protect its residents from excessive management fees. It forbids the sale of shares in mutual funds with expense ratios over 1% a year.

4   *State laws*   Eliminate funds not approved for sale in your state. Open-end funds continually sell new securities; so they must satisfy the blue-sky laws in each state in which they are sold. Because of the expense, few funds register in every state. Try to select a fund approved for sale in most of the states. That way you can continue your purchases if you move to another state.

5   *Turnover rate*   Compare the turnover rates of the various funds. High turnover rates imply large commission costs and unnecessary taxes. The one exception to this rule concerns money market funds. Because of the short-term nature of their holdings, these funds must turn their portfolio over frequently.

6   *Unrealized capital gains*   Avoid companies with large unrealized capital gains. Why buy someone else's tax liability? When the fund sells these appreciated stocks, the shareholders must pay capital gains taxes.

   Always time purchases after the scheduled date of any capital gains distributions. Most investment companies report these dates in their prospectuses.

7   *Size*   Consider the size of the fund. Large funds usually offer better diversification and lower operating costs. But some investors feel large funds lack nimbleness in shifting their assets. And several studies show a direct relationship between size and liquidity costs. Unloading large blocks of stock apparently depresses stock prices temporarily.

8   *Minimum investment*   Some investment companies require initial investments of as much as $5,000 to $10,000. Others ask for only a few hundred dollars. By the same token, the minimum subsequent investments range from $10 to $1,000 or more. Investors planning to make small initial or subsequent investments may face a sudden reduction in the number of their possible candidates.

9   *Services*   Most open- and some closed-end investment companies offer a wide variety of services, including open accounts, withdrawal plans, and tax-sheltered retirement plans.

10   *Performance*   Past studies of performance provide only a glimmer of hope for any investment company persistently outperforming the market. But if an excellent track record can be purchased at no extra cost, why not select the better-performing (at least historically) fund?

11   *Age*   Funds come and funds go. Generally speaking, new funds and investment companies should be avoided. This is especially true of closed-end investment companies. Almost without exception, the shares of these companies eventually sell at substantial discounts from their new-issue prices.

12   *Portfolio*   Different investment companies concentrate their holdings in different industries and stocks. For example, the David L. Babson Investment Fund held most of its money in the following five industries at the end of 1975: drugs and hospital supplies, petroleum, consumer products, chemi-

cals, and life insurance. In addition, it held nearly 15% of its assets in five stocks. Investors interested in playing the beat-the-market game can do so at low cost by simply studying the various portfolios. Obviously, anyone bearish on the drug and hospital business would have done well to avoid shares in the Babson Fund.

13 *Litigation*   Not even mutual funds are immune from litigation in this age of lawsuits. Avoid funds involved in law suits. (This does not imply that investors should sell their shares whenever legal troubles arise.)

14 *Net redemptions*   A fund's net redemptions equal its sales of new shares minus its repurchases of old shares. Some investors think a steady flow of money into a fund produces better performance. This seems debatable. These flows probably reflect the public's perception of the fund's management. Good management attracts additional money; poor management drives it away.

Positive cash flows (more sales than redemptions) may have one beneficial effect. These flows make it possible for the fund to steadily add to its assets, thereby practicing time diversification. In other words, the fund doesn't place all its funds into the market at one point in time.

15 *Open-end versus closed-end funds*   Open- and closed-end funds both have their proponents. For example, Burton Malkiel strongly recommends the purchase of closed-end companies in his book *A Random Walk down Wall Street*. According to Malkiel, these companies provide investors with the opportunity to buy shares at a substantial discount. On the other hand, Donald Rugg and Norman Hale, authors of the *Dow Jones–Irwin Guide to Mutual Funds*, totally dismiss closed-end companies as a feasible alternative. They ask their readers, "Why pay commissions when you can buy no-load funds at no cost?" As a general rule, it does appear that small investors should favor the open-end investment companies in order to reduce their transactions costs.

INDEX FUNDS

A recent cartoon in *Fortune* pictured nine greyhounds chasing a mechanical rabbit labeled the S&P 500. The cartoon symbolizes the failure of professional money managers—the greyhounds—to beat the overall market—the mechanical rabbit.

Greyhounds never learn the folly of their chase. But according to A. F. Ehrbar, the author of the *Fortune* article accompanying the cartoon, some investors do. As a result, "Index funds, and the idea behind them, now threaten to reshape the entire world of professional money management. That world includes hundreds of investment counselors, mutual fund management companies, and insurance companies, and is dominated by the trust departments of the big New York banks."[1] Altogether these institutions manage more than $300 billion in securities.

Index funds seek to match the market, no mean feat, as most performance studies illustrate. They accomplish this objective by buying the averages. In other words, the funds hold portfolios designed to almost duplicate movements in broad-based averages like the Standard and Poor's Index, hence the name "index fund." Index-fund managers appear to be taking the view that "if you can't beat them, join them."

The idea behind the index funds is a familiar one by now—the efficient-market concept. Ehrbar comments on why investors ignored the concept for so long:

> *The findings appeared mainly in scholarly journals of limited circulation—especially the* Journal of Business *and the* Journal of Finance—*and were presented in mathematical terms that few laymen could decipher. Those on Wall Street who were exposed to the evidence paid little attention because it came at the height of a bull-market euphoria. Managers were promising returns of 12 or 15 percent, and investors assumed that the pros knew what they were doing.*[2]

Ehrbar also explains why the "compelling logic" of the efficient market is suddenly making converts among the professionals. According to Ehrbar,

> *More recently, investors have been paying closer attention to the case against trying to beat the averages. Their second thoughts have been stimulated by the managers' woeful performance over the past three years. They have also been stimulated by the sales pitches of three relatively small players in the management game who have been trying to lure customers away from their huge New York competitors by selling index funds. The three: the Wells Fargo Bank of San Francisco, the American National Bank & Trust Co. of Chicago, and Batterymarch Financial Management Corp. in Boston.*[3]

The Wall Street Journal provides further evidence of the switch to index funds. The *Journal* quotes Virginia Sirusas, a vice-president of Bankers Trust in New York, as saying, "The movement is a serious one. The funds aren't a fad; they're here to stay." In 1975, index funds claimed only $300 million in assets. At the end of 1976, assets totaled $2 billion. And the *Journal* forecasts holdings of $5 billion by the end of 1977.

Nearly all this money comes from pension funds. At the end of 1977, only one investment company offered an index fund strategy—The First Index Investment Trust. The original prospectus describes the trust as follows:

> *First Index Investment Trust (the "Trust") is a new open-end investment trust designed as an "index fund," and is the first of its kind to be offered to the public. The Trust's investment objective is to provide investment results that correspond to the price and yield performance of publicly traded common stocks, as represented by the Standard & Poor's 500 Composite Stock Price Index (the "Index").*

As new products go, the First Index Trust can hardly be rated an overwhelming success. The original offering of $30 million of shares had to be reduced to

$15 million because of a lack of public interest. And yet, this no-load fund offers an extremely low expense ratio of about two-tenths of 1% of assets and rarely turns over its portfolio. In fact, the fund expects the turnover rate to be less than 5%, "a figure far lower than for most other investment companies."

Index funds represent the ultimate in funds, at least as far as modern investment theory is concerned. They provide nearly perfect diversification at extremely low cost. And investors can easily adapt them to numerous different strategies. Here are just a few of the possible strategies:

Passive strategy—hold shares in an index fund, buying and selling only to take tax losses or to adjust the desired combination of risk and return.

Market timing strategy—buy and sell the index funds (at no cost) when the market is believed too high or too low.

Core, noncore strategy—split the portfolio into two components, one consisting of the index fund and the other of stocks believed to be undervalued.

Option strategy—write options on overvalued stocks and cover them by holding shares in an index fund.

All these strategies are discussed in Chapter Twenty. Obviously, index funds have an important role to play in the investment world—if investors can learn new ways of chasing mechanical rabbits.

KEYWORDS

investment company	growth funds	contractual accumulation
open-end investment companies (mutual funds)	growth-income funds	plan
	balanced funds	front-end load
closed-end investment companies	income funds	advisory fee
	open account	inside directors
net asset value per share	systematic withdrawal plans	portfolio turnover
no-load funds		differencing interval
load funds	exchange privilege	excess return
maximum capital gains (funds)	voluntary accumulation plan	reward-to-variability ratio index funds

QUESTIONS

1 Explain the investment company concept.
2 How does a closed-end investment company differ from an open-end investment company (mutual fund)? Which type controls more assets?
3 The Pro Fund has assets of $100 million and liabilities of $1 million. It has 10 million shares outstanding. What is the net asset value per share of the fund?
4 Would you buy shares in a load fund? Why or why not? Name at least three no-load funds. (See Figure 13-3.)

5   Why do closed-end investment companies usually sell at a discount? Does this imply that closed-end companies are a good or a bad buy?

6   List five different mutual fund objectives. Which one most closely corresponds to your own investment objective?

7   How well do the stated objectives of mutual funds coincide with quantitative measures of risk like beta and the standard deviation of returns? Does this create a problem for the investor? Would buying shares in several different funds help solve this problem?

8   List the most important services offered by mutual funds. Which ones would you use?

9   What do you think of contractual plans? What has the government done to protect investors against contractual plans?

10   How does portfolio turnover affect shareholders in a fund?

11   Suppose you want to minimize your income taxes. How would you go about selecting a fund that meets this objective?

12   Would you use Sharpe's reward-to-variability ratio or Jensen's alpha in evaluating mutual funds? Why?

13   Use the following information to select 1 of 2 funds:

	Fund A, %	Fund B, %
Average quarterly excess return	2	1.5
Beta	1.2	0.8
Alpha	0	0

Explain your selection.

14   Comparisons of mutual funds with the overall market (as measured by Standard and Poor's 500) generally show the market beating the funds. Why is this an unfair comparison? (Hint: The average mutual fund has a beta of 0.8.)

15   Suppose you wanted to buy a mutual fund. How would you go about selecting a fund?

16   Would you consider buying an index fund? Why or why not?

REFERENCES

Ambachtsheer, Keith: "Profit Potential in an 'Almost Efficient' Market," *The Journal of Portfolio Management,* Fall 1974, pp. 84–87.

*Arbit, Harold L., and James E. Rhodes: "Performance Goals in a Generally Efficient Market," *The Journal of Portfolio Management,* Fall 1976, pp. 57–61.

Babson, David L.: "Index Funds: Why Throw in the Towel," *The Journal of Portfolio Management,* Spring 1976, pp. 53–55.

Belliveau, Nancy: "Here Come the Index Funds. Which School Do They Represent? Misery-Loves-Company or Safety-in-Numbers?" *Town and Country,* January 1977, pp. 48, 151.

Bent, Bruce R.: "Sorting Out the Money Market Funds," *Trusts and Estates,* June 1976, pp. 408–415.

Bicksler, James L., and Paul A. Samuelson, eds.: *Investment Portfolio Decision-Making,* Heath, Lexington, Mass., 1974.

Black, Fischer: "Can Portfolio Managers Outrun the Random Walkers?" *The Journal of Portfolio Management,* Fall 1974, pp. 32–36.

Boudreaux, Kenneth J.: "The Pricing of Mutual Fund Shares," *Financial Analysts Journal,* January–February 1974, pp. 26–32.

Bullock, Hugh: *The Story of Investment Companies,* Columbia, New York, 1959.

"Closed-End Bond Funds: Investing for Income," *Changing Times: The Kiplinger Magazine,* September 1973, pp. 37–39.

Dacey, Norman F.: *Dacey on Mutual Funds,* Crown, New York, 1970.

Dreyfus, Patricia A.: "Tying Your Investments to the Indexes," *Money,* May 1976, pp. 87–88, 94.

*Ehrbar, A. F.: "Index Funds—An Idea Whose Time Is Coming," *Fortune,* June 1976, pp. 144–150, 154.

_____: "Some Kinds of Mutual Funds Make Sense," *Fortune,* July 1975, pp. 57, 61–62.

Ferguson, Robert: "Active Portfolio Management: How to Beat the Index Funds," *Financial Analysts Journal,* May–June 1975, pp. 63–72.

Friend, Irwin, Marshall Blume, and Jean Crockett: *Mutual Funds and Other Institutional Investors: A New Perspective,* McGraw-Hill, New York, 1970.

"The Funds: For Leverage Lovers," *Forbes,* Feb. 1, 1976, p. 68.

Good, Walter R., Robert Ferguson, and Jack Treynor: "An Investor's Guide to the Index Fund Controversy," *Financial Analysts Journal,* November–December 1976, pp. 27–36.

Gray, William S., III: "Index Funds and Market Timing: Harris Trust's Approach," *Trusts and Estates,* May 1976, pp. 314–318.

"How to Choose a Money Market Fund," *Forbes,* Dec. 15, 1975, pp. 57–58.

Jensen, Michael C.: "The Performance of Mutual Funds in the Period 1945–1964," *Journal of Finance,* May 1968, pp. 389–419.

Lamb, Robert: "A Wary Look at Those Tax-exempt Mutual Funds," *Fortune,* December 1976, pp. 50–59, 67.

McDonald, John G.: "Objectives and Performance of Mutual Funds, 1960–1969," *Journal of Financial and Quantitative Analysis,* June 1974, pp. 311–333.

Madrick, Jeffrey G.: "Finding a Mutual Fund that Fits," *Money,* August 1974, pp. 41–43, 46.

*"Money Management—Wall Street Goes Slow," *Business Week,* Oct. 11, 1976, pp. 100–104, 109.

"Mutual Funds—A Cold Hard Look," *Changing Times: The Kiplinger Magazine,* September 1975, pp. 24–28.

Nevans, Ronald: "REITs: Those to Buy and Those to Bury," *Financial World,* Apr. 23, 1975, pp. 9–12.

Raw, Charles, Bruce Page, and Godfrey Hodgson: *Do You Sincerely Want to Be Rich? The Full Story of Bernard Cornfeld and IOS,* Viking, New York, 1971.

Rugg, Donald D., and Norman B. Hale: *The Dow Jones–Irwin Guide to Mutual Funds,* Dow Jones–Irwin, Homewood, Ill., 1976.

*Sharpe, William F.: "Adjusting for Risk in Portfolio Performance Measurement," *The Journal of Portfolio Management,* Winter 1975, pp. 29–34.

_____: "Mutual Fund Performance," *Journal of Business,* January 1966, pp. 119–138.

Smith, Keith V., and David Shulman: "The Performance of Equity Real Estate Investment Trusts," *Financial Analysts Journal,* September–October 1976, pp. 61–66.

Springer, John L.: *The Mutual Fund Trap,* Regnery, Chicago, Ill., 1973.

Treynor, Jack L.: "How to Rate Management of Investment Funds," *Harvard Business Review,* January–February 1965, pp. 63–75.

U.S. Department of the Treasury, Internal Revenue Service, *Tax Information on Mutual Fund Distributions,* Pub. 564, 1976.

Voorheis, Frank L.: "How Well Do Banks Manage Pooled Pension Portfolios?" *Financial Analysts Journal,* September–October 1976, pp. 35–40.

Williamson, J. Peter, and Allan Silver: "Sideways Betas: Criticism and Response," *Journal of Portfolio Management,* Winter 1976, pp. 68–70.

* Publications preceded by an asterisk are highly recommended.

CHAPTER FOURTEEN

LIFE INSURANCE

Although life insurance is seldom thought of as an investment, more than 70% of the individual insurance sold in the United States provides an investment medium as well as protection. This investment component of life insurance accounts for a substantial part of the average person's portfolio. Indeed, most people acquire life insurance long before they purchase stocks or bonds. Despite the fact that two out of three Americans own insurance, apparently only a handful of them are aware of the tremendous variations in the types and costs of life insurance. And still fewer know the true returns on money invested in life insurance or the actual price of the protection provided by insurance.

DESCRIPTION OF LIFE INSURANCE

Life insurance is usually classified as term, straight life, or endowment. **Term insurance** provides protection only—there is no element of savings. Term has been compared to the insurance policies purchased on automobiles, homes, etc. These policies pay off only if one of the events specified in the policy occurs—such as a car accident or damage to the house. No investment builds up in the policy; the insured simply pays for coverage for a certain period. When that period ends, either the policy expires or another payment must be made to keep the coverage in force.

In contrast to this, both **straight life insurance**—also known as ordinary, whole, or permanent life insurance—and **endowment insurance** combine a savings plan with insurance protection. Of course, this does not mean that the purchaser gets both for the price of one. In fact, the combination of savings and protection in a life insurance policy often costs more than the two do when purchased separately.

Pooling of Risks

In order to better understand the different types of life insurance, it is important to know how insurance firms operate. Insurance basically involves a pooling of risks. In the case of life insurance, the risk is the possibility of death. This possibility can be very accurately estimated by referring to past **mortality rates.** For example, the odds that a man who just turned twenty-five will die before reaching twenty-six are approximately 2 out of 1,000. This means that 2 out of every 1,000 twenty-five-year-old men alive at the start of the year will die during the year.

In order to protect their families against this possibility, 1,000 twenty-five-year-olds could band together, with each member of the group contributing some amount of money to a common fund—perhaps $2. They could then agree to distribute the proceeds of this fund to the families of the deceased. Under normal conditions, two individuals in this group of males will die; so each person contributing money can expect his family to receive $1,000 upon his death. In effect, everyone has purchased $1,000 of life insurance. Of course, few people today would be satisfied with a paltry $1,000 in life insurance. So they might agree to pay $20 for a $10,000 policy or $200 for a $100,000 policy.

A pooling of risks results when each person accepts the small loss of $2 (the payment for the insurance, usually called the **premium**) in order to protect against the larger but uncertain loss of income associated with death. The amount of this loss is presumably measured by the amount of the life insurance. In actuality, individuals do not join together in informal groups to obtain protection against the losses associated with death. Instead, they purchase life insurance from insurance companies. However, insurance companies still base their premiums upon the odds or probability of a person dying during the year. Some of these odds are presented in Table 14-1. They are taken from the Commissioners 1958 Standard Ordinary Mortality Table, which is used by many insurance firms to establish rates for their policies. According to Table 14-1, the probability of death increases with age. But these year-to-year probabilities remain very low, regardless of the person's age. For instance, less than one-half of 1% (approximately 32 out of every 1,000) of the sixty-five-year-old males will die during a year. Actually, the probabilities in the commissioners' table considerably overstate the true probability of a male dying during any one year. That is because the table includes a margin of safety for the insurance firms.

TABLE 14-1   MORTALITY RATES

Age at Beginning of Year	Number of Males per 1,000 Dying during Year
18	1.69
19	1.74
20	1.79
21	1.83
22	1.86
25	1.93
30	2.13
35	2.51
40	3.53
45	5.35
50	8.32
55	13.00
60	20.34
65	31.75
70	49.79
75	73.37

Source: S. S. Huebner, and Kenneth Black, Jr., *Life Insurance,* 9th ed., 1976, p. 239. Adapted by permission of Prentice-Hall, Inc., Englewood Cliffs, New Jersey. This chart appeared in the Commissioners 1958 Standard Ordinary Mortality Table.

Because the probability of death increases with age, insurance costs must also increase with age. It costs a group of twenty-five-year-old males approximately $2 a person to provide themselves with $1,000 of insurance. It costs each individual in a group of sixty-five-year-old males approximately $32 for the same amount of insurance. To see why, imagine a group of 1,000 sixty-five-year-olds. If the expected number of deaths (32) occurs during the year, the family of each of the deceased collects $1,000. Total contributions to the life insurance fund amounted to $32,000, or 1,000 × $32. Assuming no expenses, this fund is divided equally among the families of the deceased, with each family receiving $32,000/32, or $1,000.

Insurance Lingo

By the way, several words appear frequently in every discussion of insurance: insured, beneficiary, policyholder, and face amount of insurance. The **insured** is the person covered by the life insurance policy. In the event of the death of the insured, the life insurance company (or association) pays a death benefit to the **beneficiary** or beneficiaries named in the policy. The **policyholder** owns the policy, makes the payments, and possesses all the privileges of ownership, including the right to cancel the policy or to change the beneficiary. Usually the policyholder and the insured are one and the same person. Finally, the **face amount** of the policy refers to the amount of the death benefit.

One other phrase deserves clarification. Life insurance protects against losses from death, not life. Therefore life insurance should really be called death insurance, just as accident, fire, and disability insurance all refer to specific calamities. But given the unpleasant connotations of the word death, the "life" insurance industry can probably be forgiven for its lack of candor.

Term Insurance

Yearly term insurance provides protection only. Every person contributes an amount based upon the probability or odds of dying during the year. This probability depends upon age, sex, and race and is determined by the insurance company from **actuarial** (statistical) **tables.** Of course, usually far more than 1,000 people purchase policies, and there are also numerous age groups. As a result, insurance firms can be almost certain that the actual number of deaths will be equal to the expected number. After all, they have the law of large numbers working in their favor. Insurance firms can be even more certain of the outcome if they reinsure some of their policies with other insurance companies, thereby sharing the risk. Insurance firms also have a surplus, consisting of invested capital and profit, which they can fall back upon. And, of course, they charge more for insurance than will be needed to pay off their policies in normal times. For all these reasons, most firms can more or less guarantee that anyone who purchases insurance will receive the full amount specified in the policy.

How do the cost figures in the previous section compare with the premiums actually charged by insurance firms? Old Line Life of Milwaukee consistently ranks among the lowest-cost firms (for term insurance) in consumer reports. According to the *1977 Life Rates and Data,* published by the National Underwriter Company, Old Line sold 1-year term insurance (also called annual term) during 1977 for the following premiums:

Age	Old Line Premiums per $1,000 of Term Insurance, $*
25	2.19
35	2.46
45	4.95
55	12.40
65	33.20

* Add $10.00 maximum per policy.
Source: *Life Rates & Data, 1977,* rev. ed., published by The National Underwriter Company, Cincinnati, Ohio.

The above rates apply to policies of $25,000 or more. At these premiums a twenty-five-year-old male can purchase $100,000 of life insurance for 1 year for $219.

Insurance companies sell 5- and sometimes 10-year term insurance, as well as 1-year term. For 5-year term, the owner of the policy pays a steady premium during each of the 5 years. This annual premium reflects the average mortality

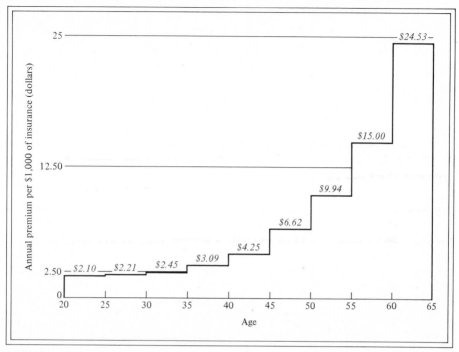

FIGURE 14-1 Sample premiums for 5-year term insurance.

rate over the 5-year period. At the end of 5 years, the policyholder usually has the option of renewing the policy, but the premium jumps to a higher level. The Old Line premiums on a 5-year term policy are shown in Figure 14-1.

If a fixed amount of term insurance is purchased, premiums increase year after year. Apparently many individuals view these increases in premiums with dismay. They prefer to pay the same amount each year, despite the fact that their own incomes usually increase over time. There are really only two ways for this to be done. The first is to continue paying the same amount of money every year and simply get less insurance each year, since insurance costs more with increasing age. This type of payment plan is provided by **decreasing term insurance.** The amount of life insurance coverage provided by a decreasing term policy is illustrated in Figure 14-2. Because the cost of providing protection increases every year, the amount of insurance which can be purchased with a specific amount of money decreases every year.

Straight Life and Endowment Insurance

The other approach to buying insurance is to overpay in the early years and underpay in the later years. This is essentially how straight life and endowment

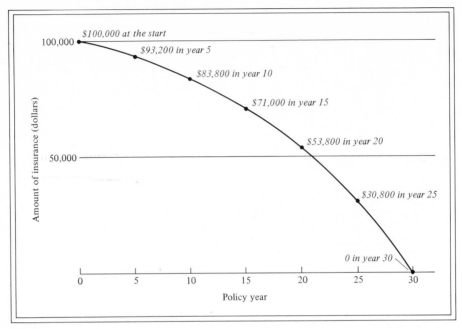

FIGURE 14-2   Sample death benefits provided by decreasing term insurance.

insurance work. Too much is paid for protection in the early years of the policy. This excess is invested by the insurance company. The interest on these funds and/or the funds themselves are then used in later years to make up the difference between the true cost of insurance and the premium paid.

An Old Line straight life policy and a 1-year term policy are compared in Figure 14-3. For the sake of simplicity, premiums are shown per $1,000 of insurance. In the first year of the policy, the straight life premium exceeds the term premium by $8.11. As the years go by, this difference narrows, until finally, between the ages of fifty-two and fifty-three, the term premium surpasses the straight life premium.

What happens to the excess payments straight life policyholders turn over to their insurance companies? Part of this money goes for commissions and expenses. The insurance companies, acting on behalf of their policyholders, invest the remainder. Policyholders have the right to claim some of these invested proceeds, called the **cash value,** at any time. They can do so by either surrendering their policies and demanding the refund of their cash values or borrowing the cash values. Figure 14-4 shows the gradual buildup in the cash value of the straight life policy described in Figure 14-3. It also shows the results of investing the difference between the straight life and term policies at an interest rate of 5% a year.

Straight life insurance policies usually provide coverage until the insured

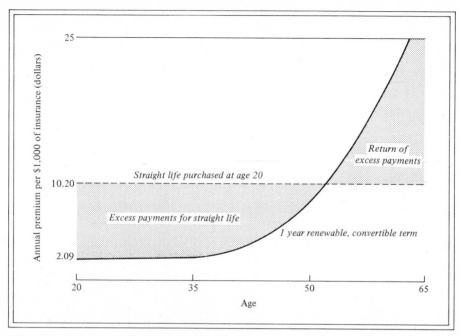

FIGURE 14-3   Comparison of 1-year term with straight life insurance.

reaches one hundred years of age. On the other hand, term policies can almost never be renewed beyond the age of sixty-five or seventy. How do insurance companies provide coverage for so many years for a level premium? The answer to this crucial question is also shown in Figure 14-4. Despite the confusion surrounding insurance, the basic concept is surprisingly simple. A straight life policy actually provides a decreasing amount of protection as the years go by. By the age of fifty, a $1,000 policy provides only $800 of protection. The other $200 consists of the cash value of the policy, which belongs to the policyholder—dead or alive. Insurance companies include the cash value in the death benefit. In other words, beneficiaries receive only the face amount of the policy, not the face amount plus the cash value. By the age of sixty-five, the policy provides only $449 of protection, with the remainder consisting of the cash value. This amount of protection costs about $14.91 a year when purchased through term insurance, and yet the straight life policyholder pays only $10.20. How is this possible? The insurance company uses some of the interest on the policyholder's investment to make up the difference.

Endowment insurance works on the same principle as straight life insurance. The only difference between the two forms of insurance is that endowment insurance combines even more of a savings element. Usually by the end of a limited period of time, say 20 years, this savings element equals the face value of the policy.

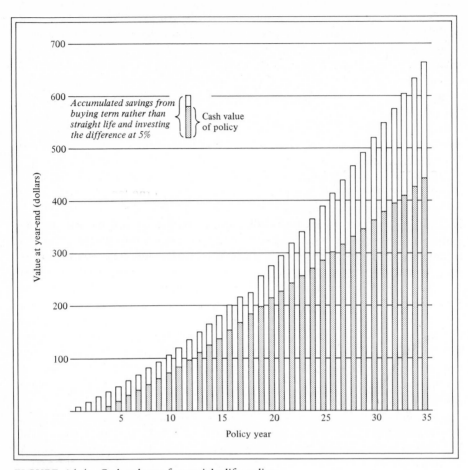

FIGURE 14-4   Cash values of a straight life policy.

PARTICIPATING VERSUS NONPARTICIPATING POLICIES

Most of the insurance policies sold today are **participating (par) policies.** Anyone buying a participating policy shares or "participates" in the investment and operating performance of the insurance company. In setting their premiums, insurance companies must forecast rates of return on investments, mortality, and costs far into the future. Since forecasts are seldom exactly right, the premium may be too high or too low. Insurance companies selling participating policies prefer to err on the high side in setting their rates, i.e., overcharge for their product. Later they refund part of the excess premium in the form of a **policy dividend.** *"Dividends"* on insurance policies are obviously not dividends in the ordinary sense of the word. Such payments are simply a refund of an overpayment. For this reason the Internal Revenue Service does not tax insurance dividends.

Not all policies are participating. Some are **nonparticipating (non-par) policies** and pay no dividends. Instead of refunding overpayments, a company issuing this type of policy selects the best premium possible, based on expectations of the future, and charges exactly that price. The premium provides for a profit in the ordinary course of events, but there is no intentional overcharge. If the premiums turn out to be too high, the company makes a greater than average profit. On the other hand, if they are too low, the company makes less than usual or even loses money on those particular policies. Nonparticipating insurance is like nearly every other product sold in this country—companies determine the best price possible and then sell at that price.

One has to wonder how a product as unique as the participating life insurance policy ever evolved. Part of the answer may lie in the long-term nature of the insurance contract. Policies issued on young children may not be paid off for 80 or 90 years. Much can happen in that time to change the original assumptions upon which the policy prices and rates of return were based. But this is not a completely satisfactory explanation, since government and corporate bonds are also issued for very long periods of time at fixed rates of interest.

It seems more appropriate to compare the holder of a participating policy to a shareholder. In effect, the dividends on shares fluctuate with the fortunes of the company issuing the policy. On the other hand, the holder of a nonparticipating policy occupies a position similar to that of a bondholder. Regardless of what happens, the premium paid to the company remains unchanged. As a consequence, the investment is less risky. It should come as no surprise, then, that the average cost of a nonparticipating policy is slightly higher than that of a participating policy.

The participating policy has one important disadvantage. It is very difficult to determine the true cost of such a policy, since dividends vary from year to year and seldom exactly equal the projections made by the company issuing the policy. This task is made even more difficult by the fact that insurance companies never make dividend projections part of the actual policy and seldom provide prospective purchasers with a record of how well the firm has done in meeting its past projections. This practice stands in marked contrast to the readily available record of dividends paid on the common stocks of industrial companies.

Should the prospective buyer of life insurance purchase a participating or a nonparticipating policy? Joseph Belth, a professor of insurance at Indiana University and a respected analyst of life insurance, recommends that a participating policy be bought if the purchaser thinks future interest rates will increase. That is because premiums are based on the lower current interest rates. Once the higher interest rates are realized, premiums can be reduced by the company. This reduction takes the form of increased dividends. On the other hand, Belth advises the purchase of a nonparticipating policy if future interest rates will be lower than current rates. (Since premiums are based on high current interest rates, these premiums will eventually be too low to cover all costs.)

Although there is nothing incorrect about this approach to buying life insurance, it does have several mildly ridiculous implications. First, it implies that individuals who purchase insurance are able to do a better job of predicting future interest rates than experienced professionals who work for insurance companies. And, even more important, it also implies that the future rates revealed in the term structure of interest rates are biased estimates. In effect, the purchaser of insurance is being told to speculate on future interest rates. For people who associate the savings element of insurance with bank accounts and government savings bonds, such advice would probably come as quite a surprise.

Probably the most sensible conclusion that can be reached about par and non-par insurance is that there is little difference in the average cost of the two. Since non-par insurance has a fixed cost, the policyholder incurs less risk in that he knows the exact cost.

MEASURING THE COST OF INSURANCE

Perhaps no topic has been more debated or publicized than the cost of life insurance. And yet many investors are still ignorant of the tremendous variations that exist in the prices of substantially identical policies. The most important reason for this widespread ignorance is the difficulty in measuring the true cost of life insurance.

The greatest cost-measurement problems are associated with straight life

TABLE 14-2   PREMIUMS, DIVIDENDS, AND CASH VALUES FOR A $10,000 STRAIGHT LIFE INSURANCE POLICY (MALE, AGE 30)

Policy Year	Premium, $	Dividend, $	Cash Value, $
1	215.50	3.80	9.30
2		15.50	119.50
3		19.30	301.50
4		23.70	485.30
5		28.20	674.90
6		33.00	860.90
7		37.50	1,051.10
8		42.00	1,242.20
9		46.80	1,438.70
10		51.80	1,635.00
11		57.30	1,826.30
12		63.30	2,021.50
13		69.30	2,212.20
14		75.20	2,402.80
15		81.30	2,598.40
16		86.80	2,794.00
17		92.90	2,991.70
18		99.20	3,191.20
19		105.40	3,393.40
20		111.40	3,593.60

insurance. Purchasers of straight life policies pay for a savings plan as well as for protection. Unraveling the cost of each of these elements is especially difficult, since payments are made over a long period of time, dividends are often paid on the policies, and there is a buildup in the cash value of the policy over the years. Obviously the time value of money should be a primary consideration in any analysis of insurance. But the traditional method for calculating the cost of an insurance policy is based on a **net cost concept**—a technique which fails to give any consideration to the time value of money. With the net cost method, all outlays and all receipts from the policy are simply added together, regardless of when they occur.

Net Cost Technique

The best way to understand the net cost method is to apply it to an actual policy. The figures in Table 14-2 show the premiums, dividends, and cash values for a straight life insurance policy. The face value of the policy is $10,000, so that in the event of the death of the insured, the insurance company will pay $10,000 to the beneficiary of the policy. Since the policy is participating, dividends are paid to the policyholder. If the person insured by the policy is thirty years old, the annual payment for the policy is $215.50. If this particular policy is held for 10 years and then surrendered for its cash value, the net cost is calculated as follows:

Payments for 10 years (10 × $215.50)		$2,155.00
Receipts:		
Dividends for 10 years	$ 301.60	
Cash value of policy at end of 10 years	1,635.00	−1,936.60
Net cost for 10 years		$ 218.40
Annual net cost ($218.40/10)		$21.84

The net cost of the policy when surrendered after 10 years is only $218.40, or an average annual cost of $21.84. This is approximately $2.18 for each $1,000 of insurance.

The net cost method often gives strange results. For instance, it is not unusual to find that the net cost of a policy is negative. In other words, total receipts from the policy exceed total payments. For example, the net cost of owning the policy described in Table 14-2 for 20 years and then surrendering it for the accumulated cash value is:

Payment for 20 years (20 × $215.50)		$4,310.00
Receipts:		
Dividends for 20 years	$1,143.70	
Cash value of policy at end of 20 years	3,593.60	− 4,737.30
Net cost for 20 years		−$ 427.30
Annual net cost (−$427.30/20)		−$21.37

The ridiculous implication of the preceding figures is that the insurance firm is paying people to buy insurance. The problem, of course, is that the net cost method does not consider the time value of money. An investor who lends money to someone for 20 years should earn a considerable amount of interest. But according to the net cost method, the investor is no worse off if simply repaid the same amount of money at the end of 20 years. For that reason, the net cost method has been discredited in recent years and has been labeled a deceptive sales practice by some well-informed critics of the insurance industry. However, many insurance firms still reveal only net cost figures to their prospective customers.

Interest-adjusted Techniques

In order to determine the true cost of a life insurance policy, the time value of money must be considered. This can be done by calculating the present or future values of the payments and receipts associated with the policy. The simplest application of these **interest-adjusted techniques** is to a nonparticipating (no dividends paid) straight life policy. Suppose the annual payment equals $150 a year for a $10,000 policy and the policyholder surrenders the policy for its cash value of $3,000 after 20 years. The net cost method indicates a total cost of $0 (total payments of $3,000 and a cash value of $3,000) and an annual net cost of $0.

But the purchasers of such insurance might well ask themselves how well they would fare over the next 20 years if they simply invested the $150 a year in a bank account instead of purchasing life insurance. If they made 6% a year on the invested money, their annual payments would accumulate to $5,849 at the end of 20 years. If they earned 8%, the payments would accumulate to $7,413, and if 10%, they would accumulate to $9,450. Since the policyholders receive a cash value of only $3,000 at the end of 20 years, the total future cost of the protection element of the insurance at 6% is $2,849, ($5,849 − $3,000 cash value) or $4,413 at 8% or $6,450 at 10%. These costs are shown in Figure 14-5. Of course, there are those who argue that individuals do not have the willpower to save money on their own. But that does not change the fact that the money sacrificed for the insurance is the future value of all payments less the future value of all receipts. Nor does it change the fact that the insurance firm does invest the premiums and therefore does have the $2,849 or $4,413 or $6,450 at the end of 20 years.

The future cost of insurance which was just calculated is a total-cost figure. In order to compare policies over different periods of time it is necessary to determine an **interest-adjusted annual cost**. This figure gives full recognition to the time value of money. Once the total future cost for a policy has been calculated, it is simple to determine the amount that must be set aside every year at a particular interest rate to accumulate to that figure. If the total future cost is $2,849 and the interest rate is 6%, the annual cost is $73.07. In other words, an annual payment of $73.07 for 20 years grows to $2,849 when invested at 6% a year. Therefore, the annual interest-adjusted cost of the insurance is $73.07 for a

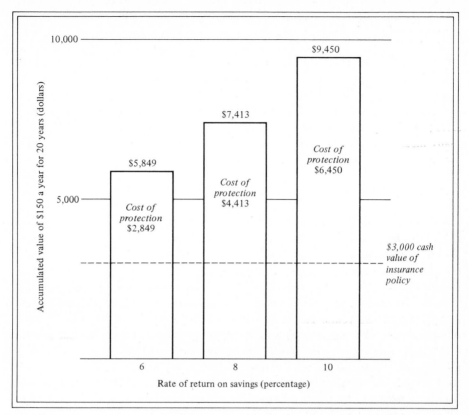

FIGURE 14-5   Future costs of life insurance at different rates of return.

$10,000 policy or $7.31 per $1,000 of insurance. This is also known as the 20-year **surrender cost index,** since it is based on the assumption that the policy is held for 20 years and then surrendered for its cash value.

Problems in Measuring Cost

There are still other problems in measuring the cost of an insurance policy, especially a participating policy. The cash values and dividends vary from year to year. As a result, the same policy can be a high-cost or low-cost policy, depending upon how long it is held and upon whether it is surrendered or held until death occurs.

A second problem in measuring the cost of insurance policies is the interest assumption. Different investors have different amounts to invest and are in different tax brackets. Moreover, their preferences for present as opposed to future income vary greatly. As a result, the interest rate that is appropriate for them differs considerably. But most interest-adjusted cost presentations are based upon the assumption that a single interest rate, usually 4 or 5%, is appropriate for all individuals. The effect of changing the interest rate used in calculating the interest-adjusted cost figure can be dramatic.

Cost Variations

Now that a method for measuring the true cost of a policy has been developed, the cost of different straight life policies can be compared. The interest-adjusted costs to a thirty-five-year-old male of the 10 lowest- and the 10 highest-cost straight life policies sold in Pennsylvania in 1973 are shown in Table 14-3. The lowest-cost policy was sold by USAA Life Insurance. It had an annual cost of $3.24 per $1,000 of insurance when held 10 years. The most expensive policy had an annual cost of $10.54 per $1,000, or more than three times as much for a substantially identical policy! Term policies also differ dramatically in price. Old Line Life sold a 5-year term policy to twenty-five-year-old males for $2.21 per $1,000. A similar policy from Pioneer Mutual of Fargo, North Dakota, cost $9.50.

How can such large price variations exist? The answer seems to lie in the complexity of insurance products. Until very recently, it was almost impossible for the average person to determine the true cost of insurance. Instead, people had to rely upon their own intuition in comparing the effect that different premiums, dividends, and cash values had upon the cost. Unfortunately, intuition can seldom be relied upon to solve difficult problems involving the time value of money. For example, in 1973 Northwestern Mutual had the third lowest priced policy sold in Pennsylvania, with a premium of $235 a year for $10,000 of straight life insurance. At the same time, the policy sold by Occidental Life of North Carolina was among the 10 most expensive policies sold by the 152 companies operating in Pennsylvania. But the premiums on the Occidental policy were only $226, $9 a year *less* than the premiums on the Northwestern Mutual policy.

Obviously, premiums are not a very satisfactory measure of the true cost of insurance. This is why the chairman of a Senate committee investigating the life insurance industry declared that with life insurance "what you see is what you get, but what you pay isn't what it costs." The large difference in the true cost of the policy is a reflection of the fact that the "dividends" paid to policyholders by the lowest-cost companies are much larger than those paid by the highest-cost companies, or they are paid much earlier, or the cash values in the policies increase more rapidly.

Although the cost variations are enormous, they might be rationalized away if only a few policies were sold at high prices. But that is not the case. Even with the policies sold by the largest insurance companies in the country, costs vary greatly. The interest-adjusted cost for the policies of the 35 largest insurance companies operating in Pennsylvania during 1973 are shown in Table 14-4. The lowest-cost policy on a 10-year basis is $4.65 per $1,000; the highest-cost policy is $10.61. The most expensive policy costs about 150% more than the least expensive. And the variation from company to company is substantial. The average

TABLE 14-3 DATA FOR THE LOWEST- AND HIGHEST-COST PARTICIPATING POLICIES SOLD IN PENNSYLVANIA IN 1973 (MALE, AGE 35)*

Lowest-Cost $10,000 Straight Life Policies

Rank	Company	Annual Premium, $	Cash Value 10/20 Year, $	Cost Index 10/20 Year
1	USAA Life Ins. Co.	161	1,370 / 3,130	3.24 / 3.51
2	The Ministers Life & Casualty Union	198	1,510 / 3,400	4.16 / 3.48
3	The Northwestern Mutual Life Ins. Co.	235	1,732 / 3,751	4.65 / 4.13
4	Presbyterian Minister's Fund	177	1,680 / 3,530	3.71 / 5.12
5	Central Life Assur. Co. (Iowa)	196	1,600 / 3,422	4.39 / 4.48
6	Connecticut Mutual Life Ins. Co.	218	1,600 / 3,421	4.74 / 4.45
7	Bankers Life Co. (Iowa)	188	1,430 / 3,440	4.98 / 4.40
8	Massachusetts Mutual Life Ins. Co.	222	1,600 / 3,676	5.11 / 4.63
9	Provident Mutual Life Ins. Co. of Phila.	210	1,570 / 3,400	4.94 / 4.94
18	Phoenix Mutual Life Ins. Co.	234	1,760 / 3,930	6.07 / 4.64

Highest-Cost $10,000 Straight Life Policies

Rank	Company	Annual Premium, $	Cash Value 10/20 Year, $	Cost Index 10/20 Year
152	Great Commonwealth Life Ins. Co. (Texas)	237	1,547 / 3,569	9.91 / 10.41
151	All American Life & Casualty Co. (Ill.)	242	1,466 / 3,422	10.38 / 9.07
150	Security Life & Accident Co. (Colo.)	250	1,460 / 3,430	10.25 / 8.83
149	United Presidential Life Ins. Co.	247	1,381 / 3,342	10.54 / 8.42
148	The Baltimore Life Ins. Co.	258	1,540 / 3,610	9.95 / 8.73
147	The Capitol Life Ins. Co. (Colo.)	238	1,466 / 3,422	10.13 / 8.21
146	Government Personnel Mutual Life Ins. Co. (Texas)	238	1,410 / 3,430	10.34 / 7.91
145	The Chesapeake Life Ins. Co.	240	1,355 / 3,246	9.96 / 8.15
142	Occidental Life Ins. Co. of North Carolina	226	1,466 / 3,422	9.27 / 8.32
140	Standard Mutual Life Ins. Co. (Kansas)	238	1,401 / 3,369	9.48 / 7.96

* Insurance costs change from year to year. For this reason, the Pennsylvania Insurance Department cautions consumers against using the figures reported in Table 14-3 and 14-4. They are for illustration only. Ranked according to the average of the cost indexes over 10 years and over 20 years.

Source: Reprinted from the Shopper's Guide to Straight Life Insurance, 2d ed., Commonwealth of Pennsylvania Insurance Department, Harrisburg, Pa., 1973.

TABLE 14-4 INTEREST-ADJUSTED COSTS FOR POLICIES OF THE 35 LARGEST INSURANCE COMPANIES OPERATING IN PENNSYLVANIA IN 1973 (MALE, AGE 35)

$10,000 Straight Life Policy

	Company	Annual Premium, $	Cash Value 10/20 Year, $	Cost Index 10/20 Year
1	The Northwestern Mutual Life Ins. Co.	235	1,732 / 3,751	4.65 / 4.13
2	Connecticut Mutual Life Ins. Co.	218	1,600 / 3,421	4.74 / 4.45
3	Bankers Life Co. (Iowa)	188	1,430 / 3,440	4.98 / 4.40
4	Massachusetts Mutual Life Ins. Co.	222	1,600 / 3,676	5.11 / 4.63
5	Provident Mutual Life Ins. Co. of Phila.	210	1,570 / 3,400	4.94 / 4.94
6	Home Life Ins. Co. (NY)	220	1,200 / 3,210	6.03 / 4.31
7	National Life Ins. Co. (Vt.)	228	1,687 / 3,749	6.01 / 4.64
8	Mutual Benefit Life Ins. Co.	230	1,656 / 3,510	5.59 / 5.09
9	Phoenix Mutual Life Ins. Co.	234	1,760 / 3,930	6.07 / 4.64
10	The Canada Life Assur. Co.	214	1,610 / 3,570	5.67 / 5.30
11	New York Life Ins. Co.	231	1,540 / 3,380	5.93 / 5.23

$25,000 Straight Life Policy

	Company	Annual Premium, $	Cash Value 10/20 Year, $	Cost Index 10/20 Year
1	Massachusetts Mutual Life Ins. Co.	545	4,218 / 9,373	3.97 / 3.60
2	The Northwestern Mutual Life Ins. Co.	578	4,331 / 9,378	4.29 / 3.77
3	Connecticut Mutual Life Ins. Co.	534	3,999 / 8,552	4.24 / 3.95
4	Bankers Life Co. (Iowa)	459	3,575 / 8,600	4.50 / 3.92
5	Provident Mutual Life Ins. Co. of Phila.	512	3,925 / 8,500	4.46 / 4.46
6	Home Life Ins. Co. (N.Y.)	538	3,100 / 8,025	5.21 / 3.81
7	Sun Life Assur. Co. of Canada	579	4,289 / 9,007	4.33 / 4.74
8	Mutual Benefit Life Ins. Co.	559	4,141 / 8,774	4.94 / 4.44
8	Nationwide Life Ins. Co.	563	4,313 / 9,034	4.52 / 4.86
10	The Penn Mutual Life Ins. Co.	537	4,250 / 9,400	5.42 / 4.02
11	The Equitable Life Assur. Society of U.S. (N.Y.)	556	4,000 / 8,575	5.03 / 4.55

12	Sun Life Assur. Co. of Canada	234	1,495 3,525	6.16 5.01	
13	The Guardian Life Ins. Co., of America	210	1,585 3,726	6.27 5.10	
14	The Great-West Life Assur. Co.	229	1,640 3,570	5.80 5.58	
15	New England Mutual Life Ins. Co.	232	1,638 3,602	6.34 5.05	
16	Nationwide Life Ins. Co.	235	1,601 3,613	6.20 5.47	
17	State Mutual Life Assur. Co. of America (Mass.)	220	1,600 3,421	6.32 5.35	
18	The Penn Mutual Life Ins. Co.	202	1,350 3,310	6.06 5.75	
19	Crown Life Ins. Co.	189	1,330 3,210	6.39 5.46	
20	The Manufacturers Life Ins. Co.	197	1,280 3,170	6.82 5.18	
21	State Farm Life Ins. Co.	227	1,487 3,437	6.91 5.28	
22	Occidental Life Ins. Co. of Calif.	229	1,610 3,980	7.28 5.22	
23	The Lincoln National Life Ins. Co.	236	1,581 3,569	7.10 5.57	
24	The Prudential Ins. Co. of America	243	1,660 3,570	6.90 6.22	
25	The Equitable Life Assur. Society of U.S. (N.Y.)	230	1,530 3,430	7.20 5.97	

12	Phoenix Mutual Life Ins.	572	4,400 9,825	5.59 4.16	
13	The Guardian Life Ins. Co. of America	508	3,963 9,315	5.55 4.38	
14	National Life Ins. Co. (Vt.)	561	4,218 9,373	5.69 4.32	
15	State Mutual Life Assur. Co. of America (Mass.)	530	3,999 8,552	5.52 4.55	
16	New York Life Ins. Co.	564	3,850 8,450	5.43 4.73	
17	New England Mutual Life Ins. Co.	574	4,288 9,004	5.42 4.75	
18	The Great-West Life Assur. Co.	501	3,550 8,500	5.63 4.68	
19	Continental Assur. Co.	570	4,100 9,500	6.00 4.50	
20	The Canada Life Assur. Co.	504	3,350 8,075	6.10 4.42	
21	Crown Life Ins. Co.	458	3,325 8,025	5.79 4.86	
22	Occidental Life Ins. Co. of Calif.	551	4,025 9,950	6.38 4.32	
23	Mutual Life Ins. Co. of New York	574	4,300 9,025	5.89 4.83	
24	The Lincoln National Life Ins. Co.	590	4,251 8,926	5.97 4.87	
25	The Manufacturers Life Ins. Co.	479	3,200 7,925	6.28 4.64	

TABLE 14-4 (Continued)

TABLE 14-4 CONTINUED

$10,000 Straight Life Policy

	Company	Annual Premium, $	Cash Value 10/20 Year, $	Cost Index 10/20 Year
26	The Western & Southern Life Ins. Co.	236	1,250 3,340	6.27 6.96
27	Franklin Life Ins. Co.	226	1,496 3,525	7.41 5.90
28	The Mutual Life Ins. Co. of New York	234	1,660 3,610	7.36 6.03
29	Connecticut General Life Ins. Co.	220	1,740 3,720	6.35 7.07
30	Continental Assur. Co.	239	1,550 3,830	8.13 5.62
31	John Hancock Mutual Life Ins. Co.	231	1,320 3,370	7.52 6.57
32	Metropolitan Life Ins. Co.	248	1,660 3,700	7.89 6.24
33	American National Ins. Co.	242	1,530 3,650	8.43 6.22
34	Republic National Life Ins. Co.	222	1,500 3,530	7.91 7.57
35	Aetna Life Ins. Co.	244	1,510 3,610	10.61 6.51

$25,000 Straight Life Policy

	Company	Annual Premium, $	Cash Value 10/20 Year, $	Cost Index 10/20 Year
26	State Farm Life Ins. Co.	554	3,718 8,593	6.31 4.68
27	Republic National Life Ins. Co.	574	3,475 9,225	6.88 4.26
28	John Hancock Mutual Life Ins. Co.	548	3,300 8,425	6.32 5.37
29	The Prudential Ins. Co. of America	580	4,325 9,075	6.45 5.63
30	The Western & Southern Life Ins. Co.	580	3,125 8,350	5.94 6.58
31	Franklin Life Ins. Co.	557	3,740 8,814	7.05 5.54
32	Metropolitan Life Ins. Co.	605	4,150 9,250	7.29 5.64
33	Connecticut General Life Ins. Co.	546	4,350 9,300	6.15 6.87
34	American National Ins. Co.	588	3,825 9,125	7.70 5.50
35	Aetna Life Ins. Co.	606	4,175 9,025	8.01 5.43

Source: Reprinted from the *Shopper's Guide to Straight Life Insurance*, 2d ed., Commonwealth of Pennsylvania Insurance Department, Harrisburg, Pa., 1973.

individual who randomly selected a $10,000 policy from 1 of these 35 companies paid about 60% more than the cost of the cheapest policy.

Although the differences between the costs for a 20-year holding period are also large, they are not as marked as the 10-year costs. The cheapest policy on a 20-year basis is $4.13 per $1,000 of insurance; the most expensive is $7.57. The individual who purchases the most expensive policy pays 83% more than the cost of the cheapest policy.

FINANCIAL STRENGTH OF LIFE INSURANCE COMPANIES

Price should be the primary consideration in selecting a life insurance policy, but other factors must also be considered. Probably the most important is the financial strength of the insurance company. Insurance protects against catastrophe. If the insurance company is unable to pay death benefits in such a circumstance, this protection is lost at the worst possible time. Moreover, many individuals have a substantial part of their savings in insurance policies in the form of cash values. The bankruptcy of the insurance company or its involvement in financial difficulties might result in the loss of some or all of these savings. Or the policyholders' access to their cash values might be restricted. And if it were necessary for the company to cancel its policies, some of the policyholders might be unable to obtain insurance from another company because of bad health or increased age.

Fortunately, insurance firms seldom fail. But it does happen. A case in point is the Century Life Insurance Company of Texas. It went bankrupt in 1969. The Texas Insurance Department arranged to have another company take over its outstanding policies, so that all policyholders were able to have continued coverage, and death benefits were paid out. But a claim was placed against 35% of the cash values of all policies. As a result, anyone surrendering an insurance policy received only 65% of the supposed cash value.

Most investors are at least vaguely aware of the risk associated with their investments. But very few ever stop to think about the risk of one insurance policy as compared with another. Investors demand and get a higher expected return for taking on more risky investments. They should also demand and get a higher return (or pay a lower price) on life insurance policies sold by more risky companies. The results presented in Chapter Nine on bonds demonstrate that differences in risk need not be very great in order to justify large differences in rates of return.

Ratings of Insurance Firms

Information about the financial strength of insurance companies is generally not made available to prospective purchasers of insurance. However, insurance companies are rated in *Best's Insurance Reports: Life-Health,* which can be found in most libraries. The ratings are included in *Best's* recommendations of each insurance company. The ratings are "most substantial," "very substantial," "substantial," "considerable," and "no description." The words used in reporting each firm's financial quality have an obvious shortcoming—only the initiated can tell a good rating from a bad rating. In particular, the wording implies that insurance companies are of the fine, good, better, and best categories. No mention is made if the company does not fall into one of these four categories. In fact, it is the absence of a recommendation which reveals that the company is of low quality. The recommendation for an insurance firm in the safest category is as follows:

Policyholder's Recommendation

The results achieved by the company have been most favorable. In our opinion, it has most substantial over-all margins for contingencies. Upon the foregoing analysis of its present position we recommend this company.

Beginning with its 1976 edition *Best's* changed its recommendations to alphabetical ratings. Prior to the 1976 edition, only 25 to 30% of the insurance firms analyzed by *Best's* had earned a recommendation. Now almost all the companies receive one of the following ratings: A+ and A (excellent), B+ (very good), B (good), C+ (fairly good), and C (fair). Judging from figures compiled by Joseph M. Belth, the A+ rating is similar to a recommendation of "most substantial" or "very substantial." In 1976, 203 companies received the top rating of A+.

There is no reason for a prospective purchaser of insurance to buy a policy from a firm which is rated lower than A+ (a recommendation of "most substantial" or "very substantial") unless the price is also significantly lower. But financial strength, or the lack of it, seems to have little or no bearing on the price of a policy. Indeed, there is some indication that lower-quality firms actually charge more for their policies.

Financial strength provides an assurance that the policyholder will be covered for as long as desired and will receive all benefits promised. It also has an impact on whether or not dividends are paid as originally indicated. Insurance companies never guarantee the dividends they will pay on participating policies. Instead, the rate of return the insurance company earns on its investments determines whether dividends will be large or small. An insurance company which adopts an aggressive investment policy should earn a higher return on the average and be able to pay out larger dividends. But returns can also be much lower than average, with the result that dividends are smaller. In other words, the more risky the investment policy, the more uncertain the policyholder is of the return on the savings element of insurance and on the cost of protection. Again, it appears that the person is usually not reimbursed for this uncertainty.

PROVISIONS IN INSURANCE POLICIES

Most insurance companies offer a wide variety of options on their policies for a modest additional cost. The most important are renewability, convertibility, waiver-of-premium for disability, and guaranteed insurability.

Renewability and **convertibility** options are strictly associated with term insurance policies. Term policies usually last for a limited period of time, such as 1, 5, or 10 years. At the end of this period, the policyholder may wish to renew the policy. For a few additional dollars, the purchaser of a term insurance policy can obtain a guarantee from the insurance company that it will renew the policy without a medical examination. The renewability provision also protects the individual against a change in rates for any other reason. Without the renewability provision, the company can require a medical examination before renewing the policy. Depending upon the results, the company can refuse to renew the policy or can increase the rates because of the individual's poor health. Even if the results from the medical examination prove satisfactory, the company can still refuse to renew the policy for other reasons, such as a change in occupation. As a result, the individual may be unable to obtain insurance at reasonable rates. The renewability provision eliminates this unfortunate possibility.

The convertibility provision permits a policyholder to exchange a term policy for a straight life policy, without having to provide any evidence of insurability. By paying for a convertibility provision, the individual is assured of being able to switch to a different type of policy at a later date. Of course, if there is no intention of purchasing a straight life insurance policy, it would be pointless to pay additional money for the conversion privilege. For most people, the convertibility option is much less important than the renewability option.

The **waiver-of-premium** provision applies to all types of policies. It is a very popular option—more than half the policies issued include this type of benefit. Essentially, the waiver-of-premium provision states that the insurance company will make all policy payments for an individual who becomes disabled. Disability can be defined in the insurance contract in a number of ways. Generally, it refers to the inability to engage in any occupation for remuneration or profit. Moreover, the disabled person must usually remain in that condition for 6 months before the waiver-of-premium provision becomes effective.

The **guaranteed insurability** provision also applies to all types of policies. It permits the insured individual to buy additional insurance at the existing rates without having to take a medical examination.

LAPSE RATES

Straight life insurance is often described as permanent insurance. Many life insurance sales people emphasize this permanence. According to them, straight or so-called whole life insurance provides protection for the "whole life" of the insured. And the insured need not die in order to collect benefits, since a savings element is an integral part of every straight life policy. Furthermore, straight life insurance supposedly provides a weak-willed individual with the incentive to save money which would be squandered otherwise.

These are strong arguments in favor of straight life insurance. Unfortunately, they are not entirely valid. Many of the "permanent" insurance policies lapse, i.e., are canceled or surrendered within several years. And only a very small percentage of all straight life policies are maintained for as long as 20 years. This high lapse rate has two implications for consumers. First, it implies that many people who buy insurance are either not content with the product or probably didn't need the insurance. Second, it means that those who purchased insurance lost a substantial amount of money in life insurance commissions as well as having paid for insurance they didn't need.

The lapse rates of policies sold by insurance companies are not common knowledge. However, a Senate subcommittee chaired by Philip Hart, a Democrat from Michigan, collected detailed information from a number of insurance companies on the lapse rates of their policies. A summary of these data is presented in Table 14-5. The lapse rates are for policies issued to thirty-five-year-old males. By the end of 1 year, 15% of the policies sold by Aetna (the first company in the table) had lapsed. By the end of the second year approximately 7% more had lapsed; so the total lapse rate equaled 22%. By the end of the tenth year, 42% of the policies had lapsed. These lapse rates specifically exclude policies terminated by death.

Not all companies have lapse rates as good as those of Aetna. For example, 34% of the "permanent" policies sold by Fidelity Union were canceled within a year. And 66% had been canceled by the end of the tenth year. Moreover, the lapse rates displayed in Table 14-5 understate true lapse rates, since these figures exclude life insurance purchased by younger individuals, who are more apt to cancel their straight life policies. Total lapse rates for the twenty-one- to twenty-five-year age group can be as much as 15 to 25% higher than the rate for thirty-five-year-olds.

Senator Hart's subcommittee did not ask for information on the lapse rates of term policies. But one insurance company, Allstate Life Insurance, voluntarily provided data. People held their term policies an average of 5.847 years. In contrast to this, purchasers of straight life policies held them an average of only 4.790 years. Judging from these figures, forced savings does not seem to work very well. And "temporary" term insurance is held for a longer period of time than "permanent" straight life insurance.

TAXATION OF INSURANCE POLICIES

Misconceptions about insurance abound, but they seem especially prevalent with regard to the taxation of insurance policies. The first misconception concerns the taxation of insurance death benefits, which are not taxed as income to the recipient. But that does not make insurance unique. No money, land, or other asset bequeathed by an individual is taxed as income to the recipient.

However, insurance proceeds are often taxed as part of the estate of the deceased. Whether or not they become part of the estate depends upon whether or not the deceased owned the policy. There has been considerable discussion about what constitutes ownership of a policy, and there have also been a number of court cases. To date the issue is still not settled.

Straight life insurance is often recommended as a tax shelter. But, generally speaking, the tax-shelter aspects are of value only if the individual also needs the insurance. The tax-shelter aspect of life insurance arises from the fact that part of the premiums for providing protection are paid from interest on the reserves held by the insurance company (and contributed by the policyholders). Since this interest is never paid out to the policyholders, it is never taxed. In contrast to this, the individual who buys term insurance and invests the difference must pay all the term premiums with after-tax dollars.

There is a second tax advantage to straight life insurance. Part of the increase in the cash value of the policies is the result of the interest earned on reserves. This increase in cash value is not taxed until the policy is surrendered for its cash value, at which time the excess of cash value over premiums paid is taxed as ordinary income.

Tax deferral is not unique to straight life insurance. Even government savings bonds possess this feature. And there are substantial costs in owning a life insurance policy. First, the expenses of the insurance company must be considered. Second, there are the costs of protection. Third, most states tax insurance companies on life insurance premiums. For these reasons, a straight life policy should never be purchased solely as a tax shelter. Instead, the tax-shelter aspects should be considered in determining whether or not to buy term and invest the difference.

INSURANCE AS AN INVESTMENT

The savings element of life insurance policies constitutes the most important asset of the under-twenty-five age group. Apparently most people buy straight life insurance long before they even consider purchasing stocks or bonds. Given the importance of insurance as an investment, it is surprising that almost no information is available about the returns from investing in it. Unlike banks and savings and loan companies, insurance companies do not tell individuals what rate of return they earn on their money. Instead, sales presentations emphasize the safety and permanence of life insurance savings.

This silence on the part of the official spokesmen of the life insurance industry has fostered a number of myths. The first is that straight life insurance policies pay high returns when held for long periods of time. It is not unusual to find insurance salespeople arguing that these returns exceed 30%. And they support their arguments with actual figures taken from policies. On the other hand, critics of the insurance industry have attacked these same policies on the grounds that the return is only 2 to $2^1/2\%$. To prove their statements, these critics point to clauses buried in the fine print of most policies which guarantee returns of only 2 or $2^1/2\%$.

TABLE 14-5   LAPSE RATES FOR STRAIGHT LIFE INSURANCE POLICIES ISSUED TO THIRTY-FIVE-YEAR-OLD MALES*

Company	Of Initial 100,000 Policies, Cumulative Percent[1] Lapsed at End of Year—				
	1	2	10	20	30
Aetna	15	22	42	53	62
American General	10	17	46	62	73
American Heritage	28	36	64	77	85
American National	24	30	54	65	73
Bankers (Iowa)	20	27	47	61	71
Central Life Assurance	13	17	32	41	47
Combined (MDO)	29	35	53	69	79
Confederation (Can.)	5	19	54	70	80
Conn. General	11	18	38	52	64
Conn. Mutual	16	21	38	50	58
Crown (Can.)	9	14	34	45	54
Equitable Assur. Society	19	25	47	60	69
Farmers New World	29	38	59	70	78
Fidelity Union	34	50	66	76	NA
General American	17	24	44	56	64
General United	20	30	60	73	82
Georgia Inter.	18	29	61	75	84

Company	Of Initial 100,000 Policies, Cumulative Percent[1] Lapsed at End of Year—				
	1	2	10	20	30
Mutual Benefit (N.J.)	7	13	43	57	67
Mutual of N.Y.	18	24	48	60	69
National Investors	20	30	61	75	83
National Life and Accident	26	35	59	69	76
National of Vermont	10	14	32	47	59
National Old Line	20	28	46	56	64
Nationwide	25	33	52	63	70
New England Mutual	10	16	40	51	61
New York Life	19	23	45	57	69
Northwestern Mutual	6	8	21	34	45
Northwestern National	20	26	47	58	65
Occidental (Calif.)	18	24	36	48	58
Ohio State	29	37	62	75	83
Pacific Mutual	22	26	41	52	61
Penn Mutual	22	30	40	56	67
Phoenix Mutual	15	22	46	59	71
Pilot	15	21	42	54	66

Company					
Hamilton National	22	32	63	76	84
Home	10	15	37	49	58
Interstate Life and Acc	30	47	64	72	77
Jefferson Standard	15	21	40	53	65
John Hancock	28	35	52	63	69
Lafayette	20	26	45	55	59
Lamar (non-par)	21	24	38	46	51
Liberty Life	23	31	54	66	74
Liberty National	28	38	59	70	78
Lincoln National	18	24	46	59	70
Mass. Mutual	6	9	30	44	55
Metropolitan	19	26	48	58	66
Minnesota Mutual	12	17	45	62	72
Monumental (Prm. Not.)	29	36	59	69	75
Monumental (MDO)	31	43	57	64	68

Company					
Provident Life and Acc	9	17	44	59	67
Provident Mutual	13	17	37	49	58
Prudential	10	19	44	51	55
Republic National	15	24	59	73	78
Southland[2]	20	29	47	61	71
Southwestern	10	15	29	42	53
State Farm	18	28	43	51	59
State Life	20	28	50	63	73
State Mutual[3]	9	15	41	55	63
State Mutual[4]	6	11	31	42	50
Travelers	19	26	48	60	71
Union Central	25	30	48	62	72
United Benefit	22	32	59	69	76
Western and Southern[5]	17	27	52	61	67

* Derived from company responses to life insurance questionnaire No. 1 (Feb. 8, 1973) question 33. Although terminations by death were included in question 33, they have been excluded in this particular analysis.

[1] Rounded.

[2] Ordinary business only; "executive preferred" excluded.

[3] Regular straight life business.

[4] Noncigarette smoker straight life policy.

[5] Premium notice, debit business.

NA—Not available.

Source: The Life Insurance Industry. Hearings before the Subcommittee on Antitrust and Monopoly of the Committee on the Judiciary, United States Senate, 93rd Congress, Second Session, July 16, 1974.

Calculating Rates of Return
on Insurance Cash Values

Because of the complexity of the insurance product, most investors are unable to determine for themselves the true returns on their policies. The difficulty is that it is almost impossible to untangle the protection element from the savings element. One solution to this problem is to compare the outcome from buying straight life insurance with that from buying term insurance from the same company and then investing the difference between the two premiums.

In the early years a term policy costs substantially less than a straight life policy. For example, a thirty-five-year-old man can actually buy a $25,000 non-par 5-year renewable term policy for about $85 a year. A $25,000 non-par straight life policy from the same company costs $400 a year. These figures are presented in Table 14-6. The yearly difference in the insurance premiums of $315 could be invested in a bank account or in bonds. At the end of 5 years, the term policy could be renewed for another 5 years at an annual premium of $112.50. The premiums on the straight life policy would remain at $400 a year. If the individual continued to invest the difference between the term and the straight life, $287.50 a year could be set aside for the second 5 years.

Now the important question for prospective purchasers of insurance is, What rate of return must be earned on their savings to exactly match the performance of the insurance company? The answer for a 10-year period is shown in Table 14-6. Anyone who earns 3% on these savings can accumulate $3,569.07 by investing the difference between the straight life and the term premiums. This is slightly more than the $3,560 cash value of the straight life policy at the end of 10 years. Therefore, any investor earning 3% on his or her money should equal the performance of the life insurance company. And investors earning more than 3% on their side funds should outperform this insurance company.

TABLE 14-6   BUYING TERM AND INVESTING THE DIFFERENCE*

Policy Year	Straight Life Premium, $	5-Year Term Premium, $	Difference, $	Total Savings at Start of Year, $	Interest on Savings at 3%, $	Total Savings at End of Year, $
1	400.00	85.00	315.00	315.00	9.45	324.45
2		85.00	315.00	639.45	19.18	658.63
3		85.00	315.00	973.63	29.21	1,002.84
4		85.00	315.00	1,317.84	39.54	1,357.38
5		85.00	315.00	1,672.38	50.17	1,722.55
6		112.50	287.50	2,010.05	60.30	2,070.35
7		112.50	287.50	2,357.85	70.74	2,428.59
8		112.50	287.50	2,716.09	81.48	2,797.57
9		112.50	287.50	3,085.07	92.55	3,177.62
10		112.50	287.50	3,465.12	103.95	3,569.07

* Rates are for a $25,000 non-par policy for a thirty-five-year-old male. This policy has a cash value of $3,560 at the end of 10 years.

This example represents a considerable simplification of the actual steps involved in computing the return on the savings element of a life insurance policy. Since most policies are participating rather than nonparticipating, dividends must also be considered. And to be absolutely correct, some adjustment for the declining amount of protection offered by straight life insurance must be made. An individual who buys a $25,000 term policy and invests the difference at 3% has accumulated $3,569 at the end of 10 years. Should he or she die on the last day of the tenth year, the heirs will inherit the $3,569 as well as receiving $25,000 from the insurance company. But if a straight life policy had been purchased instead, the heirs would receive only $25,000 from the insurance company. They would not receive both the $25,000 face value of the policy and the cash value that had accumulated on that policy. For this reason, the person who buys term and invests the difference can buy less than $25,000 of insurance and still be as well off as the individual who buys a $25,000 straight life policy.

Actual Rates of Return

Stuart Schwarzschild, a professor of business administration at Georgia State University, recently published the findings of an extensive study of the rates of return on participating straight life insurance. He based his calculations on policy data for 67 randomly selected life insurance companies for the year 1971. These 67 firms accounted for 75% of all straight life insurance sold in the United States during that year. Schwarzschild's results are shown in Table 14-7. It appears that the average person who buys a large policy can expect to make about 4% a year on the savings element, providing the policy is held for 20 years. Schwarzschild does not present any results for shorter holding periods. But his data can be used to calculate rates of return on the average $100,000 policy held for 1-, 5-, and 10-year periods, as shown in Table 14-7. All these returns are based upon the assumption that the individual needs the protection element of the insurance policy. If that is not the case, the returns are much lower, since any money spent on the protection element is wasted.

TABLE 14-7   RATES OF RETURN ON THE AVERAGE $25,000 AND $100,000 PARTICIPATING LIFE INSURANCE POLICY

Holding Period, Years	$25,000 Policy			$100,000 Policy		
	Age 25, %	Age 35, %	Age 45, %	Age 25, %	Age 35, %	Age 45, %
1	NA*	NA	NA	−95.2	−92.0	−85.1
5	NA	NA	NA	−5.6	−3.4	−1.5
10	NA	NA	NA	2.3	2.7	3.5
20	4.1	4.0	4.2	4.0	4.2	4.5

* NA—not available.

Source: Stuart Schwarzschild, "The 20-Year Yield on Life Insurance Cash Values," *Best's Review,* November 1975, pp. 10, 12, 71–73.

The returns on life insurance appear to be very low and even negative when the policy is held for less than 10 years. That is because insurance policies have a large **front-end load.** In other words, the greatest part of the commissions and other sales costs comes out of the first premiums. According to Schwarzschild's figures, thirty-five-year-olds who purchase a $100,000 straight life policy pay an average premium of $2,155. If they surrender the policy at the end of the first year, they receive a cash value of only $93 and dividends of $38 for a whopping out-of-pocket cost of $2,024. On the other hand, those individuals who purchase term policies pay only $535 and receive dividends of $9. Their out-of-pocket costs amount to only $526.

Insurance versus Other Investments

The savings element in life insurance has approximately the same risk as a high-quality bond. How do the returns on these two investments compare? During 1970, the yield to maturity on government bonds with maturities of less than 1 year, 3 to 5 years, and more than 10 years averaged 6.5, 7.4, and 6.6% a year, respectively. In 1971, the average returns on these securities equaled 4.7, 5.8, and 5.7%. Government bonds are considered the safest investment there is. The yield on 20-year AAA corporate bonds, another low-risk investment, averaged 8.04% a year in 1970 and 7.4% in 1971. Banks and savings and loan associations were paying $5^3/_4$ and 6% on 2-year savings certificates during that same period. Apparently policyholders earn substantially lower returns than bondholders.

Despite their low returns, straight life policies have one marked advantage over government and corporate bonds and the obligations of savings institutions. Policyholders pay no tax on the interest earned on the savings element of these insurance policies until they surrender them. And then they pay taxes only on the excess of the cash value over the total of all premiums. As a result, most of the interest on life insurance is usually tax-exempt.

Whether or not this exemption can offset the low returns on the policy depends on the tax bracket of the policyholder as well as the amount of money invested. At the start of 1971, the highest-grade tax-exempt municipal bonds carried a yield to maturity of at least 5.2%. This tax-free return was substantially in excess of the return on an average straight life policy. In addition, most people have the option of investing a considerable part of their earnings in tax-sheltered retirement plans. These plans also make it possible for individuals to defer taxes on any interest earned.

Judged solely on the returns earned by policyholders, straight life insurance is not a very good investment. If people need protection, they would be better off buying term rather than straight life insurance and investing the difference elsewhere. If people don't need protection, they should never buy insurance solely as an investment. Perhaps that is the reason that the insurance industry has been silent regarding rates of return.

The next question about insurance concerns the safety and permanence of the savings element. Insurance companies invest their policyholders' money primarily in bonds and mortgages. The investment holdings of United States life insurance companies at the end of 1975 are shown in Table 14-8. Two types of investments—long-term corporate debt and mortgages—accounted for nearly 69% of all assets.

Holders of participating insurance policies share in the actual investment results experienced by insurance firms. For that reason, it is only natural to conclude that the future returns on the savings element of straight life policies will be similar to those on long-term, fixed-income obligations. And by the same token, the policyholder should be exposed to about the same risk as the person who buys long-term bonds and mortgages. The only difference in the risk and returns is due to the fact that insurance firms usually follow conservative investment practices. They do so by retaining a substantial part of the policyholders' money in the form of reserves. As a result, policyholders experience considerably less risk and substantially lower returns than they would on a portfolio of bonds and mortgages.

There are three more points which should be made about insurance as an investment. First, because of their conservative practices, the dividends that insurance firms project for their policies are sometimes less than they actually pay. As a result, the rates of return that have been presented here may be a low estimate of the actual returns that can be earned on participating policies. Second, the record of insurance firms during the Depression was admirable, in that very few firms went bankrupt. However, during 1 year most insurance firms did block the

TABLE 14-8 ASSETS OF UNITED STATES LIFE INSURANCE COMPANIES AT THE END OF 1975

Type of Investment	Value (in millions), $	Total Assets, %
Cash	1,925	0.7
Government securities:		
1 year or less	1,284	0.4
Over 1 year	13,893	4.8
Corporate debt:		
1 year or less	4,813	1.7
Over 1 year*	108,781	37.6
Mortgages	89,167	30.8
Loans to policyholders	24,467	8.5
Other assets	15,049	5.2
Common stocks	20,304	7.0
Real estate	9,621	3.3
Total assets	289,304	100.0

* Includes preferred stocks.

withdrawal of cash values for from 4 to 6 months. Third, straight life policies offer an important advantage if the individual files for bankruptcy. Most state bankruptcy courts permit policyholders to retain some or all of the cash values they have accumulated in their life insurance policies.

HOW MUCH INSURANCE?

According to figures released by the Bureau of the Census in 1972, every new worker entering the labor force is a potential millionaire. Recent college graduates can expect to earn at least $711,000 during their working lives. And other workers, regardless of their age and education, will probably earn hundreds of thousands of dollars before they retire. Obviously, the most important asset that most families have is their future earning power.

Economic Value of Life

Life insurance makes it possible to protect this asset. The question is, How much protection is necessary? One answer is to estimate the individual's **economic life value,** usually called **human life value** in the insurance literature. The term "human life value" implies that people attach a dollar valuation to human life itself—a grotesque distortion of life. In actuality, the economic- or human-life-value concept simply refers to the valuation of the earning capacity of a man or woman.

In theory, the determination of this value is simple. All that has to be done is to calculate the particular individual's earnings and personal living costs for each year in the future until retirement. These net income figures can then be converted into a present value by discounting them at some interest rate. For example, a thirty-five-year-old man takes home a salary of $17,000 which is not expected to change in the future. His own basic living costs are $7,000 a year, leaving $10,000 for expenditures by the family and for savings. He plans to retire at sixty-five. The present value of this $10,000 a year for 30 years is $137,650 when discounted at 6%. Therefore, his economic life value equals $137,650. In the event of his death, that would be the economic loss suffered by his family.

As people grow older, their economic life value decreases, since there are fewer and fewer years of future earnings remaining until retirement. The thirty-five-year-old described in the previous example is worth $137,650. One year later this present value drops to $135,900. At forty-five, it equals $114,700. And at fifty-five years of age, it amounts to only $73,600. Finally, at sixty-five it is $0, because of retirement from the work force, and it is assumed that Social Security payments cover only the person's living costs. The decline in economic life values from year to year implies that decreasing term insurance or a steadily declining amount of renewable term insurance is the most appropriate form of life insurance for individuals. This life insurance makes it possible to guarantee the collection of economic life values by completely diversifying away the risk of death.

The explicit recognition of the economic value of a human life radically changes the analysis of investments. If a husband and a wife are viewed as a partnership, their investment portfolio might be described as follows:

Investments	
Cash	$ 300
Savings account	4,700
Stocks and bonds	5,000
Personal property	10,000
Economic life values	300,000
Total	$320,000

For younger individuals, life values usually totally dominate other investments. As people grow older, they convert these life values into more tangible assets, such as a home, stocks and bonds, and pension plans.

Needs Approach to Insurance

Few individuals hardheartedly calculate their life values and then buy insurance for their families in these amounts. Even if they wanted to, it would be very difficult for them to predict future incomes and to define basic living costs. One alternative is to estimate the family's needs and the costs that would be incurred by the individual's death. Then the present value of the needed income can be determined. This approach to buying insurance is sometimes called **programming insurance,** or the **needs approach** to buying insurance.

Most insurance agents use the following simplified presentation in calculating life insurance needs:

Needs Approach to Insurance

John and Judy Kirby are thirty and twenty-five years of age, respectively. They have two children, one 5 and one 3 years old. John takes home $20,000 a year. Judy doesn't work. In the event of John's death, the family could expect to receive $9,000 a year in tax-free Social Security benefits until the children had reached eighteen or graduated from college at twenty-two. They would also have a mortgage of $40,000, personal debts of $5,000, and the final expenses associated with John's death of $5,000. Finally, there would be college costs of approximately $10,000 to consider for each child. Judy has decided that she would take a part-time job for about $3,000 a year if John dies. John and Judy both agree that the family would need still another $3,000 a year to maintain their present life-style, providing that all debts have been paid and a college fund has been created for the children.

They calculate their insurance needs as follows:

1	Total debts:		
	Mortgage	$40,000	
	Debts	5,000	
	Final expenses	5,000	
	College fund	20,000	
		$70,000	
	Minus assets available to pay off these debts:		
	Social Security death benefits	$ 255	
	Savings account	4,700	
	Stocks and bonds	5,000	
		−9,955	
	Extra cash needed to pay debts		$ 60,045
2	Desired annual income	$15,000	
	Anticipated income:		
	Social Security benefits	9,000	
	Wife's part-time job	3,000	
		$12,000	
	Additional annual income needed	$ 3,000	
	Extra cash needed to provide an annual income of $3,000 if invested at 6%		50,000
	Total amount of insurance needed at present		$110,045

The solution presented above is considerably simplified, since the time value of money has not been considered in calculating the funds needed for the children's education. In addition, it is totally subjective, since it is based on this particular family's perceived needs. The Kirby family appears to require a substantial amount of insurance—more than $100,000. At John's age, $100,000 of term insurance can be purchased for an annual payment of about $250 a year.

IMPLICATIONS FOR INVESTMENT STRATEGY

Insurance is seldom mentioned by investment advisers or by the authors of investment books. This is a serious oversight, for two reasons. First, the cash values associated with straight life insurance policies make up a substantial percentage of many investors' portfolios. Second, by far the most important asset possessed by most people is their future earnings potential. This earnings potential can be protected with life insurance.

Deciding how much insurance to buy can be a difficult process. As we have seen, the costs of substantially identical insurance policies differ greatly and the true returns on the savings element of life insurance policies are seldom mentioned. Despite the complexities of insurance, or perhaps because of them, a few generalizations are necessary. They are as follows:

1   Straight life insurance combines both protection and savings. It is very difficult, and perhaps impossible, to determine the exact cost of each element. Any estimate of the separate costs should be based upon a consideration of the time value of money. A technique for doing this was presented in this chapter.

2   Life insurance can be purchased which provides protection only. This is called term insurance. The costs of most term insurance policies are relatively easy to measure. Therefore, comparison of different term policies is not too difficult.

3   The savings element of straight life insurance represents an investment in the insurance company's portfolio. The performance of this savings element is more or less tied to the performance of that portfolio. The portfolios of most insurance firms are invested primarily in mortgages and bonds. Therefore, it probably does not matter whether investors hold a bond mutual fund or a life insurance policy. If the cash value of a straight life insurance policy appears to be more stable than an investment in a bond mutual fund, it is because the insurance company withholds a substantial part of the returns.

4   Since the transactions costs associated with straight life insurance are relatively large, the investor who purchases life insurance should probably plan to hold the policy for at least 10 years or more. However, statistics indicate that many people hold their policies for considerably less than 10 years. These people should probably never have bought straight life policies.

5   The costs of different policies vary considerably. Substantial savings are possible if the individual shops around and understands how to measure the true cost of insurance.

6   Insurance firms have gained substantial tax advantages for their cash value life insurance policies. The most important advantage is the tax-free buildup of cash values. However, this tax advantage appears to be largely offset by (1) high transactions costs, (2) substantial administration fees, (3) the large reserves retained by companies, and (4) other taxes paid by insurance companies. Certainly a cash value life insurance policy should never be purchased solely as a tax shelter.

7   By paying for life insurance, the policyholder guarantees that the beneficiaries will receive the insured "insurable value." By its very nature, the protection element of insurance can never create wealth. It can only preserve it.

KEYWORDS

term insurance	endowment insurance	premium
straight life insurance	mortality rates	insured

beneficiary	nonparticipating (non-par)	convertibility
policyholder	policies	waiver-of-premium
face amount	net cost concept	guaranteed insurability
actuarial tables	interest-adjusted tech-	front-end load
decreasing term insurance	niques	economic life value
cash value	interest-adjusted annual	human life value
participating (par)	cost	programming insurance
policies	surrender cost index	needs approach
policy dividend	renewability	

QUESTIONS

1 Use the mortality rates in Table 14-1 to estimate the cost of a $100,000 term insurance policy for someone twenty years old. About how much should the same policy cost a forty-five-year-old individual? Why the difference?

2 Debate the following statement: People save money by buying insurance while they are still young.

3 Explain the difference between the policyholder, the beneficiary, and the insured.

4 What are the principal types of term insurance? Describe each.

5 How do term and straight life insurance differ?

6 People often borrow the cash values of their straight life insurance policies. Some critics of the life insurance industry condemn the companies for charging interest on these policy loans. Is this criticism justified?

7 Explain the true nature of life insurance dividends. Does the IRS tax these dividends? Why or why not?

8 Compute the 5- and 10-year net cost of the following $100,000 straight life insurance policy.

Year	Premium, $	Dividend, $	Cash Value, $
1	2,155	38	93
2	2,155	155	1,195
3	2,155	193	3,015
4	2,155	237	4,853
5	2,155	282	6,749
6	2,155	330	8,609
7	2,155	375	10,511
8	2,155	420	12,422
9	2,155	468	14,387
10	2,155	518	16,350

9 Use the same information provided in question 8 to compute the 5- and 10-year surrender indexes. What do these figures measure?

10 Explain the following statement about life insurance: "What you see is what you get, but what you pay isn't what it costs."

11 How much do life insurance costs vary?

12   What ratings does *Best's* assign to life insurance companies? Look up the ratings of the
      10 lowest-cost companies in Pennsylvania in 1973 (see Table 14-3). Do you have to
      sacrifice quality to obtain low-cost insurance?

13   Some insurance salespeople caution against buying term. "It's only temporary," they
      argue, "and you lose the chance to buy straight life insurance." Can these arguments
      be justified in the light of the renewability and convertibility provisions available with
      term?

14   How do average lapse rates affect your decision about what type of insurance to pur-
      chase?

15   Discuss the risk-return characteristics of insurance. How does straight life insurance
      compare with other investments?

16   Contrast the economic value of life and the needs approach to insurance. Reread the
      example of the needs approach. Do you think John and Judy Kirby really need
      $110,045 of insurance? Why or why not?

REFERENCES

Aponte, Juan B., and Herbert S. Denenberg: "A New Concept of the Economics of Life
    Value and the Human Life Value: A Rationale for Term Insurance as the Cornerstone
    of Insurance Marketing," *Journal of Risk and Insurance,* September 1968, pp.
    337–356.

*Belth, Joseph M.: *Life Insurance: A Consumer's Handbook,* Indiana University Press,
    Bloomington, Ind., 1973.

Best's Insurance Reports: Life-Health, 1976, 71st ann. ed., A. M. Best Co., Morristown,
    N.J., 1976.

Buley, R. Carlyle: *The American Life Convention: 1906–1952,* Appleton-Century-Crofts,
    New York, 1953.

Colberg, Marshall: "Age-Human Capital Profile for Southern Men," *Review of Business and
    Economic Research,* Winter 75/76, pp. 63–73.

Dacey, Norman R.: *What's Wrong with Your Life Insurance,* Collier Macmillan, New York,
    1963.

*Denenberg, Herbert S.: *The Shopper's Guidebook to Life Insurance, Health Insurance, Auto
    Insurance, Homeowner's Insurance, Doctors, Dentists, Lawyers, Pensions, etc.,* Consumer
    News, Inc. Washington, D.C., 1974.

———, and Spencer L. Kimball, eds.: *Insurance, Government, and Social Policy: Studies in
    Insurance Regulation,* Irwin, Homewood, Ill., 1969.

The Editors of Consumers Reports, *The Consumers Union Report on Life Insurance,* Bantam,
    New York, 1972.

"FTC Will Study Whether Life Insurers Disclose Enough about Cost of Policies," *The Wall
    Street Journal,* Dec. 16, 1976, p. 6.

Gaines, Price, Jr., ed.: *1976 Interest Adjusted Index: Life Insurance Premium Outlay and Sur-
    render Comparisons,* The National Underwriter Company, Cincinnati, Ohio, 1975.

Guarino, Richard, and Richard Trubo: *Your Insurance Handbook,* Doubleday, Garden City,
    N.Y., 1975.

Harper, Victor L.: *Handbook of Investment Products and Services,* New York Institute of
    Finance, New York, 1975.

* Publications preceded by an asterisk are highly recommended.

Huebner, S. S., and Kenneth Black: *Life Insurance,* 8th ed., Appleton-Century-Crofts, New York, 1972.

Life Insurance Fact Book 1975, Institute of Life Insurance, New York, 1975.

"Life Insurance: How Costs Compare, Company by Company," *Changing Times: The Kiplinger Magazine,* June 1974, pp. 25–32.

The Life Insurance Industry, Hearings before the Subcommittee on Antitrust and Monopoly of the Committee on the Judiciary, 93d Cong. 1st Sess., pt. 3, Feb. 23, 1973, and pt. 4, July 16, 1974.

McGill, Dan: *Life Insurance,* Irwin, Homewood, Ill., 1967.

McLean, Ephraim R.: "An Appraisal of Computerized Life Insurance Estate Planning," *The Journal of Risk and Insurance,* September 1974, pp. 497–509.

Moffitt, Donald: "Citibank Devises Simple Chart to Figure How Much Life Insurance Families Need," *The Wall Street Journal,* Dec. 6, 1976, p. 36.

1975 Life Rates and Data, The National Underwriter Company, Cincinnati, Ohio, 1975.

*Schwarzschild, Stuart: "The 20-Year Yield on Life Insurance Cash Values," *Best's Review,* November 1975, pp. 10, 12, 71–73.

Statistical Abstract of the United States, U.S. Government Printing Office, Washington, D.C., 1972.

U.S. Bureau of the Census, "Annual Mean Income, Lifetime Income, and Educational Attainment of Men in the United States, for Selected Years, 1956 to 1972," *Current Population Reports,* ser. P-60, no. 92, 1974.

U.S. Department of Health, Education, and Welfare, *Actuarial Tables Based on United States Life Tables: 1969–71,* vol. 1, no. 2, National Center for Health Statistics, Rockville, Md., May 1975.

————, *Comparability of Mortality Statistics for the Seventh and Eighth Revisions of the International Classification of Diseases, United States,* ser. II, National Center for Health Statistics, Rockville, Md., 1975.

————, "Mortality," *Vital Statistics of U.S. 1973,* vol. II, National Center for Health Statistics, Rockville, Md., 1975.

————, Social Security Administration Office of Research and Securities, "1972 Lifetime Earnings by Age, Sex, Race, and Education Level," *Research and Statistics Note,* Sept. 30, 1975.

CHAPTER FIFTEEN

SOCIAL SECURITY

Claims on Social Security benefits constitute one of the most important assets in an individual's portfolio. According to recent government projections, today's worker can reasonably expect to collect more than $1 million from the Social Security program (assuming continued inflation). And yet, most people appear to know little or nothing about these benefits, probably because of the complexity of the system.

BACKGROUND OF SOCIAL SECURITY

Congress passed the first Social Security Act in 1935. The revolutionary new program offered both retirement and unemployment benefits. Some observers of the political scene think the legislation passed only because of the Great Depression. Americans, long-time believers in the Puritan work ethic and self-reliance, suddenly found themselves powerless to fend off the effects of widespread economic disaster.

Today Social Security plays a vital role in the lives of millions of Americans. In 1974 more than 100 million men and women worked in jobs covered by Social

Security. And during the same year more than 30 million people—1 out of every 7 Americans—collected cash benefits from the program. These benefits totaled approximately $5 billion a month.

The Social Security Act provides for social insurance, public assistance and welfare services, and children's services. However, most people associate the phrase "Social Security" with the **OASDI** program. These letters stand for Old Age, Survivor's, and Disability Insurance. This chapter focuses on OASDI, since it relates most directly to investment decisions.

Despite its longevity and all-encompassing nature, few people really understand Social Security. Robert Myers, for years the chief actuary of the Social Security Administration and now a professor of insurance at Temple University, says, "The general public has a number of misconceptions about the basic nature of the program along with a surprisingly good understanding of its purpose." According to Myers, Social Security differs from private insurance in a number of important ways. And Social Security bears no similarity to a savings account.

Myers, like most experts, agrees that the fundamental purpose of OASDI is to provide a floor of protection under the covered risks. Over the years, the covered risks have been expanded to include death and disability as well as old age. All these events lead to a loss of income and to economic insecurity. Social Security benefits replace part of this lost income.

COVERAGE

The Social Security umbrella covers 9 out of 10 people employed in the United States. The only large categories of workers not included in the program are those in the federal civil service and employees of certain state and local governments.

In order to qualify for OASDI benefits, people need credit for a certain amount of covered employment. The Social Security system refers to these credits as **quarters of coverage.** Most employees accumulate one quarter of coverage for each calendar quarter in which they earn $50 or more in wages. Or they automatically receive four quarters of coverage for every year their salaries exceed the maximum earnings recognized by Social Security ($15,300 in 1976 and higher in later years).

The self-employed receive work credit for four calendar quarters in every year they report a net profit of $400 or more. Farmers, ranchers, farm laborers, and domestic employees also build up quarters of coverage for their work, but the rules differ slightly.

Status

Quarters of coverage serve as a stepping-stone to the receipt of OASDI benefits. The Social Security Administration recognizes the following hierarchy of participants:

1   Fully insured
2   Currently insured
3   Transitionally insured
4   Not insured

A **fully insured** status virtually guarantees the individual and his or her family all OASDI benefits—obviously a very important right. Anyone with 40 quarters (10 years) of coverage falls in this desirable category. But some older people (those born before 1929) satisfy the requirements with fewer quarters of coverage. Table 15-1 shows the number of quarters of coverage required for fully insured status.

The **currently insured** status entitles the worker's family to some Social Security benefits. Anyone with 6 or more quarters of coverage in the most recent 13-quarter period is considered to be currently insured.

The **transitionally insured** status applies to people who reach the age of seventy-two without achieving a fully insured status. It entitles them to receive limited benefits with only a few (sometimes zero) quarters of coverage.

TABLE 15-1   QUARTERS OF COVERAGE NEEDED
FOR FULLY INSURED STATUS

Year of Birth*	Quarters Needed		Year of Birth*	Quarters Needed	
	Men	Women		Men	Women
1892 or earlier	6	6	1911	24	22
1893	7	6	1912	24	23
1894	8	6	1913	24	24
1895	9	6	1914	25	25
1896	10	7	1915	26	26
1897	11	8	1916	27	27
1898	12	9	1917	28	28
1899	13	10	1918	29	29
1900	14	11	1919	30	30
1901	15	12	1920	31	31
1902	16	13	1921	32	32
1903	17	14	1922	33	33
1904	18	15	1923	34	34
1905	19	16	1924	35	35
1906	20	17	1925	36	36
1907	21	18	1926	37	37
1908	22	19	1927	38	38
1909	23	20	1928	39	39
1910	24	21	1929 or later	40	40

* The SSA assigns people born on the first day of a year to the previous year of birth. For example someone born on January 1, 1925 needs 35 quarters of coverage—the number corresponding to a birth date of 1924.

CONTRIBUTIONS

Ever since its initiation in 1935 the Social Security program has been based on workers' **contributions.** For some reason the Social Security Administration insists upon using the word "contribution," even though such payments are neither voluntary nor refundable. The government collects the **Social Security payroll tax** from both employees and their employers under the authority of the Federal Insurance Contributions Act, part of the Internal Revenue Code. The initials of this act—**FICA**—appear on almost every paycheck.

Although very few Americans know exactly what those letters mean, they do know that FICA deductions get bigger nearly every year. The maximum Social Security tax totaled only $30 a year between 1937 and 1949. By 1965 it had jumped to $174. And in the next decade FICA taxes climbed nearly 500% to $824.85 a year. The complete historical record of payroll taxes is shown in Table 15-2.

Many Americans forget that their employers match their own contributions. And the Social Security Administration (SSA) does nothing to correct this over-

TABLE 15-2   MAXIMUM SOCIAL
SECURITY TAXES, 1937–1977

Years	Social Security Taxes, $*
1937–1949	30.00
1950	45.00
1951–1953	54.00
1954	72.00
1955–1956	84.00
1957–1958	94.50
1959	120.00
1960–1961	144.00
1962	150.00
1963–1965	174.00
1966	277.20
1967	290.40
1968	343.20
1969–1970	374.40
1971	405.60
1972	468.00
1973	631.80
1974	772.20
1975	824.85
1976	895.05
1977	965.25

* Since Social Security taxes are paid by both the employee and
the employer, the total Social Security taxes collected for each
employee are actually double the amounts shown here.

sight, focusing instead on employee contributions. For example, a recent study by the SSA compares OASDI benefits to employee contributions and completely ignores the matching contributions. It is probably no coincidence that the Social Security program appears to be a much better bargain when viewed in this way. On the other hand, most economists argue that the employer's costs are passed through to the employee in the form of lower wages and/or higher product costs. Eliminate the Social Security tax and the employee's real wages would soon increase by the amount of the employer's contribution. So workers really paid double the figures shown in Table 15-2.

The Social Security tax depends upon two factors: the **tax rate** and the maximum Social Security **earnings base.** The earnings base refers to the maximum wage covered by Social Security (and therefore the maximum figure used in computing benefits). In 1975 the earnings base equaled $14,100. At the same time the tax rate equaled 5.85%. So anyone earning $14,100 during 1975 paid $824.85 ($14,100 × 0.0585) in Social Security taxes. No one, regardless of how much he or she earned, paid more than this in such taxes in 1975. By the same token, no one can base his or her benefits on any earnings in 1975 in excess of $14,100. Table 15-3 shows the maximum earnings base for the period 1937–1977. These figures will later be used in calculating Social Security benefits.

Table 15-4 shows the Social Security tax rates over the same period of time. These rates include the payment for hospital insurance, another part of the Social Security program. The self-employed pay higher tax rates than people working for an employer. For example, the self-employed contributed 7.9% of their net earnings in 1975. This rate represents a mysterious compromise between the 5.85% rate paid by the employee and the combined rate of 11.7% paid by the employee and employer.

TABLE 15-3   MAXIMUM WAGES
COVERED BY SOCIAL SECURITY,
1937–1977

Years	Maximum Earnings Base, $
1937–1950	3,000
1951–1954	3,600
1955–1958	4,200
1959–1965	4,800
1966–1967	6,600
1968–1971	7,800
1972	9,000
1973	10,800
1974	13,200
1975	14,100
1976	15,300
1977	16,500

TABLE 15-4   OASDI TAX RATES

Calendar Year	OASDI Rate, %	Hospital Insurance Rate, %	Total Rate, %
1937–1949	1.00	—	1.00
1950–1953	1.50	—	1.50
1954–1956	2.00	—	2.00
1957–1958	2.25	—	2.25
1959	2.50	—	2.50
1960–1961	3.00	—	3.00
1962	3.12	—	3.12
1963–1965	3.62	—	3.62
1966	3.85	0.35	4.25
1967	3.90	0.50	4.40
1968	3.80	0.60	4.40
1969–1970	4.20	0.60	4.80
1971–1972	4.60	0.60	5.20
1973	4.85	1.00	5.85
1974–1977	4.95	0.90	5.85

EXAMPLE   Todd Wheeler earned a salary of $10,000 during 1977. He paid a Social Security payroll tax of $585 ($10,000 × 0.0585) during the year. His employer matched this contribution.

SOCIAL SECURITY BENEFITS

The government first began paying Social Security benefits in 1940. By the end of 1976 total benefit payments had grown more than a thousandfold. Now they account for more than 20% of the entire federal budget. The beneficiaries include approximately 12 million retired workers, 3 million husbands and wives, 6 million survivors of workers, and 2 million disabled workers and their dependents. Altogether, 1 in every 7 Americans looks for a monthly Social Security check. By the way, Social Security benefits qualify as tax-free income.

According to Pechman, Aaron, and Taussig—economists with the Brookings Institution and authors of *Social Security: Perspectives for Reform*—"The relationship between individual contributions (that is, payroll taxes) and benefits received is extremely tenuous. Within any age group, including those persons presently retired and those still working, the values of individual benefits and taxes (appropriately discounted) vary greatly. . . ." The twofold nature of the Social Security system creates this disparity between contributions and benefits. Social Security attempts to provide our citizens with economic security by partially replacing income lost because of retirement, disability, or death. At the same time the program tries to correct deficiencies in income.

Estimating Benefits

If employer contributions are included, the average American pays more for Social Security than for all other insurance. And annual contributions to the program exceed annual savings. Despite the substantial costs of Social Security, apparently very few people know exactly what they are getting for their money. Most Americans seem to be unable to answer one or more of the following questions:

1 Are you presently eligible for:

   a Retirement benefits?   Yes_____   No_____

   b Survivor's benefits?   Yes_____   No_____

   c Disability benefits?   Yes_____   No_____

2 How much would you and/or your family receive in Social Security payments in the event of your:

   a Retirement? $_____

   b Disability? $_____

   c Death? $_____

The Social Security Administration must bear much of the blame for this widespread ignorance of benefits. It makes almost no attempt to communicate prospective benefits to individuals. Moreover, some Social Security personnel callously disregard people's questions about future benefits, taking the attitude that "When you die, your spouse can come down here and find out his or her benefits."

As a result, most people must calculate their own prospective benefits. The first step in doing this is to obtain a history of covered earnings and quarters of coverage. The W-2 (income tax withholding) forms carry Social Security earnings, but few people retain these forms for more than a couple of years. Fortunately, a detailed record of earnings can usually be obtained from a Social Security office. But the individual must either file a special form titled "Request for Detailed Earnings Information" and pay a fee or request a detailed earnings record (for free) from a representative of the Social Security Administration. After receiving the year-by-year earnings record, the individual can estimate her or his Social Security benefits. By the way, the widely advertised "Request for Statement of Earnings" does not provide sufficient information to calculate benefits.

RETIREMENT BENEFITS

The sixty-fifth birthday marks a momentous occasion in most people's lives. That's the age at which American men and women become eligible to receive full retirement benefits from Social Security.

The exact amount of these benefits depends upon the individual's average earnings over a specific number of years, called **elapsed years.** Table 15-5 shows the number of years used by the Social Security Administration in calculating these average earnings. For example, 33 years of wages must be included for any-one born in 1927.

Table 15-6 shows how to calculate retirement benefits for a man born in 1912 and retiring in 1977 at the age of sixty-five. The second column of the table contains the maximum Social Security earnings base mentioned earlier. The third column lists earnings in work covered by Social Security. These earnings cannot exceed the earnings base shown in column 2. (Remember the individual never makes "contributions" on any amount in excess of the earnings base.)

According to Table 15-1, a man born in 1912 needs 24 quarters of work credit to qualify for all retirement benefits. And, judging from Table 15-5, the Social Security Administration counts 19 years of covered earnings in determin-ing his benefits. The fourth column shows the highest earnings. The number of years' earnings in this column equals the number required for the calculation of the individual's average annual earnings under Social Security. In order to maxi-mize benefits, the SSA selects only the years of highest earnings. This has been done in column 4 of Table 15-6. The sum total of the earnings listed in column 4 equals $156,900. So the average wage for the purpose of calculating retirement benefits amounts to $8,258 ($156,900/19 years).

Retirement benefits depend upon average earnings. Table 15-7 shows the relationship between these earnings and benefits. According to this table, average

TABLE 15-5   NUMBER OF YEARS' SALARY CONSIDERED IN CALCULATING SOCIAL SECURITY RETIREMENT BENEFITS

Year of Birth	Years Counted		Year of Birth	Years Counted	
	Men	*Women*		*Men*	*Women*
1896 or earlier	5	5	1913	19	19
1897	6	5	1914	20	20
1898	7	5	1915	21	21
1899	8	5	1916	22	22
1900	9	6	1917	23	23
1901	10	7	1918	24	24
1902	11	8	1919	25	25
1903	12	9	1920	26	26
1904	13	10	1921	27	27
1905	14	11	1922	28	28
1906	15	12	1923	29	29
1907	16	13	1924	30	30
1908	17	14	1925	31	31
1909	18	15	1926	32	32
1910	19	16	1927	33	33
1911	19	17	1928	34	34
1912	19	18	1929 or later	35	35

TABLE 15-6 CALCULATION OF RETIREMENT BENEFITS

Step 1 Find the number of elapsed years considered in calculating retirement benefits. (See Table 15-5.) Enter this number in box B.

Step 2 Add the earnings figures listed in column 4 and enter the total in box A.

Step 3 Divide the figure in box A by the figure in box B. The result equals the average annual earnings. Use this number to find the primary monthly benefit in Table 15-7.

Year (1)	Maximum Social Security Earnings Base, $ (2)	Earnings (or Estimates of Future Earnings) in Work Covered by Social Security, $* (3)	Years of Highest Earnings, $† (4)
1951	3,600	3,600	
1952	3,600	3,600	
1953	3,600	3,600	
1954	3,600	3,600	
1955	4,200	4,200	
1956	4,200	4,200	
1957	4,200	4,200	
1958	4,200	4,200	
1959	4,800	4,800	4,800
1960	4,800	4,800	4,800
1961	4,800	4,800	4,800
1962	4,800	4,800	4,800
1963	4,800	4,800	4,800
1964	4,800	4,800	4,800
1965	4,800	4,800	4,800
1966	6,600	6,600	6,600
1967	6,600	6,600	6,600
1968	7,800	7,800	7,800
1969	7,800	7,800	7,800
1970	7,800	7,800	7,800
1971	7,800	7,800	7,800
1972	9,000	9,000	9,000
1973	10,800	10,800	10,800
1974	13,200	13,200	13,200
1975	14,100	14,100	14,100
1976	15,300	15,300	15,300
1977	16,500	16,500	16,500

$$\boxed{\$156,900} \div \boxed{19} = \boxed{\$8,258}$$

Box A   Box B   Average Annual Earnings

* If earnings exceed those in column 2, list the maximum for that year. Insert 0 for no earnings under Social Security.

† Select the highest earnings in column 3 and enter here. Number of years selected must equal number in box B.

TABLE 15-7   SOCIAL SECURITY BENEFITS BY AVERAGE EARNINGS

Average Annual Earnings, $	Primary Insurance Amount per Month, $	Maximum Family Benefits per Month, $
1,200	147.10	220.70
1,500	169.30	254.00
1,800	181.70	272.60
2,100	196.30	294.50
2,400	208.80	313.20
2,700	221.20	331.80
3,000	236.40	361.40
4,000	278.10	475.30
5,000	322.50	595.10
6,000	364.50	668.60
7,000	408.40	727.80
8,000	453.10	792.90
9,000	478.90	838.20
10,000	502.00	878.50
11,000	525.10	918.50
12,000	546.60	956.40
13,000	567.30	992.50
14,000	587.90	1,028.90
15,000	606.10	1,060.60

Note: The actual Social Security benefit table is based upon monthly earnings defined over very small intervals, like $606 to $609.

annual earnings of $8,258 roughly correspond to a monthly Social Security retirement benefit of $453.10. The SSA refers to this monthly benefit as the **primary insurance amount.**

The American people display a distressing lack of knowledge of Social Security benefits. According to one survey, less than one-half the nonretired men and women over fifty-five years of age know how much they will eventually receive in Social Security retirement benefits. And yet this group faces retirement within 10 years. Obviously, younger workers possess still less knowledge of retirement benefits. No wonder Pechman, Aaron, and Taussig claim Americans suffer from "widespread myopia with respect to retirement needs." This myopia has sad consequences.

> Many people fail to save enough to prevent catastrophic drops in post-retirement income. In 1962, the median amount of investment income of all aged persons was less than $300. Not only do people fail to plan ahead carefully for retirement; even in later years of their working life, many remain unaware of impending retirement needs. Unfortunately, the mistakes of youth are to a large degree irreversible, since it is generally impossible to accumulate in a short period just before retirement sufficient assets to provide adequate retirement income.[1]

Today's investors can avoid these mistakes by estimating their future retirement benefits and structuring their investment portfolios accordingly.

Early Retirement

Regular retirement under the Social Security system comes at age sixty-five. But many people opt for **early retirement.** Retirement can begin as early as age sixty-two, in which case the retiree receives only 80% of the regular retirement benefit. This reduction in benefits remains in effect for as long as the retiree lives.

The benefit reduction of 20% for retirement at sixty-two is not really a penalty. It simply reflects the increased number of payments received by people retiring early. The longer a person waits to retire after reaching sixty-two, the smaller the necessary reduction. This reduction can be calculated as follows:

$$\text{Percentage reduction in benefits for early retirement} = 20\% \times \frac{\text{number of months before age 65}}{36 \text{ months}}$$

Look at the right-hand side of the above expression. The second term equals the number of months between the actual retirement age and the regular retirement age of sixty-five divided by 3 years. Judging from this expression, an individual retiring at sixty-three and a half years of age receives 10% less than the regular retirement benefit.

Should a person retire at sixty-two or at sixty-five? A healthy person, especially a woman, probably accumulates more Social Security benefits over the retirement years by retiring at sixty-five rather than sixty-two. Since the reduced benefit at sixty-two amounts to only 80% of the full benefit at sixty-five, 15 years of reduced benefits equal 12 years of full benefits. Therefore, anyone who expects to live to be at least seventy-seven gains by waiting until sixty-five to retire and then collecting the full benefit each month. On the other hand, someone who does not expect to live until seventy-seven should retire at sixty-two and start receiving benefits as soon as possible.

The normal life-span of a sixty-two-year-old man supposedly amounts to about 17 years. Women of the same age look forward to more than 20 years of life. So healthy men and women collect more dollar benefits if they delay retirement until age sixty-five. Of course, the time value of money has been completely ignored so far. Suppose the retiree earns 6% on his or her investments. Then the break-even point for selecting between retirement at age sixty-two or age sixty-five comes at an expected lifetime of seventy-nine. In other words, anyone who expects to live to be more than seventy-nine should retire at age sixty-five, not at sixty-two.

Late Retirement

Only a small percentage of the working population delay their retirement past the age of sixty-five. Those doing so receive a slight increase in their eventual retirement benefits. The increase equals one-twelfth of 1% for each month that the individual delays the receipt of benefits. The maximum increase amounts to 7% and corresponds to the postponement of retirement until the age of seventy-two.

Some people may wonder at the arithmetic of Social Security. After all, the government reduces benefits by 20% if a man or woman retires 3 years early but increases the benefits by only 3% for retiring 3 years later. Whatever the rationale, the net effect is to encourage mass retirement at age sixty-five.

Family Benefits

Social Security pays family benefits. Table 15-8 illustrates which members of the worker's family qualify for retirement and disability benefits. According to this table, a retired worker with a sixty-five-year-old spouse collects 50% more than a single worker. These extra benefits reflect the added needs of the family; i.e., they satisfy the objective of social adequacy. At the same time, they violate the objective of individual equity, since contributions depend only on salary and not on family size.

The government sets a ceiling on the total Social Security benefits collected by a family. As a rough approximation, the maximum benefit collected by an entire family (including the worker) equals 175% of the individual worker's benefit, i.e., of the primary insurance amount.

TABLE 15-8   FAMILY RETIREMENT AND DISABILITY BENEFITS

Recipient	Status Required	Amount of Benefit
Disabled worker	Fully insured	100% of primary insurance amount
Retired worker sixty-two or over	Fully insured	100% of primary insurance amount. Benefit permanently reduced by five-ninths of 1% for each month collected before age sixty-five
Wife or divorced wife	Fully insured	50% of primary insurance amount. Benefit permanently reduced by $25/36$ of 1% for each month collected before age sixty-five
Dependent husband sixty-five or over	Fully insured	Same as above
Wife of any age caring for child under eighteen or disabled before twenty-two	Fully insured	50% of primary insurance amount
Dependent child or grandchild: (1) under age eighteen, (2) a full-time student under twenty-two, or (3) disabled before age twenty-two.	Fully insured	50% of primary insurance amount

Note: The worker must satisfy additional requirements for disability benefits. In addition, some workers with transitionally insured status and their wives qualify for a small fixed benefit.

Retirement Test

The so-called **retirement test** probably causes more complaints than any other aspect of the Social Security system. This test imposes limits on the amount of income people can earn while collecting benefits. If earnings exceed the exemption, the government reduces Social Security benefits. In 1976 this reduction equaled $1 for every $2 earned above $2,760. So anyone making $3,760 during the year lost $500 in Social Security benefits.

The retirement test does not apply to nonwage income like interest, dividends, or rent.

Replacement Rate

Critics complain about the low level of benefits provided by the Social Security program. It is an unfair complaint. The designers of the Social Security system never intended to completely eliminate private savings programs. Instead, they chose to replace only part of the worker's income.

Discussions of the Social Security system often center on so-called replacement rates. The **replacement rate** is defined as the ratio of Social Security benefits to preretirement earnings. For example, if a person earns $10,000 and collects $6,000 after retirement, the replacement rate equals 60%. Replacement rates understate the retiree's welfare, since recipients of Social Security checks pay no income taxes on such payments.

As a general rule, Social Security benefits vary inversely with previous earnings. In other words, the lower the preretirement earnings, the higher the replacement rate. This again reflects the twofold nature of the program—individual equity and social adequacy. Replacement rates also depend upon the family structure.

SURVIVOR'S BENEFITS

Social Security fulfills some of the roles of life insurance. In particular, the program pays survivor's benefits to certain members of the family. A fully insured status guarantees survivor's benefits to:

1 Your widow or dependent widower when sixty or older
2 Your dependent parents when sixty-two or older

A fully insured and/or currently insured status (only 6 quarters out of the most recent 13 covered) ensures benefits to:

1 Your widow, regardless of age, provided she is caring for your children. The children must be under the age of eighteen.

TABLE 15-9   SURVIVOR'S BENEFITS

Recipient	Status	Amount of Benefit
Widow or surviving divorced wife sixty or over	Fully insured	100% of primary insurance amount. Benefit permanently reduced by nineteen-fortieths of 1% for each month collected before age sixty-five. If disabled, reduced benefits available as early as age fifty (reduction equals $^{43}/_{240}$ of 1% for each month before sixty).
Dependent widower sixty or over	Fully insured	Same as above
Widow or surviving divorced wife under sixty-two if caring for child either (1) under eighteen or (2) disabled before twenty-two	Fully or currently insured	75% of primary insurance amount
Dependent child or grandchild: (1) under eighteen, or (2) a full-time student under twenty-two, or (3) disabled before age twenty-two	Fully or currently insured	75% of primary insurance amount
Dependent parent sixty-two or over	Fully insured	82^1/$_2$% of primary insurance amount or 75% to each of both parents

2 Your unmarried dependent children younger than eighteen or under twenty-two if full-time students.

3 Your disabled children, regardless of their age, if their disability began before age twenty-two.

4 Your dependent parents if sixty-two or older.

5 Your surviving divorced wife, providing she was married to you for at least 20 years before the divorce. In addition, she must be at least sixty or be caring for your children under the age of eighteen.

Table 15-9 lists the survivor's benefits available to a worker's family. And Table 15-10 lists the number of quarters needed to be insured for survivor's benefits.

Social Security also pays the family or next of kin a lump sum of $255—not enough even to bury the deceased. Obviously, Social Security does not completely eliminate the need for private life insurance.

DISABILITY BENEFITS

Disability poses a more serious threat to the economic security of most people than death. One large insurance firm publishes the following statistics:

1 At age forty, disability occurs 3.3 times more often than death.

2 At age forty, the odds of disability are 3 times those of death.

3 At age fifty, disability occurs 2 times as frequently as death.

TABLE 15-10   QUARTERS OF COVERAGE NEEDED AND NUMBER OF
YEARS' SALARY CONSIDERED FOR SURVIVOR'S OR DISABILITY BENEFITS

Age at Death or Disability*	Number of Quarters	Number of Years Counted	Year of Death or Disability†
21	6	2	—
22	6	2	—
23	6	2	—
24	6	2	—
25	6	2	—
26	6	2	—
27	6	2	—
28	6	2	1957
29	7	2	1958
30	8	3	1959
31	9	4	1960
32	10	5	1961
33	11	6	1962
34	12	7	1963
35	13	8	1964
36	14	9	1965
37	15	10	1966
38	16	11	1967
39	17	12	1968
40	18	13	1969
41	19	14	1970
42	20	15	1971
43	21	16	1972
44	22	17	1973
45	23	18	1974
46	24	19	1975
47	25	20	1976
48	26	21	1977
49	27	22	1978
50	28	23	1979
51	29	24	1980
52	30	25	1981
53	31	26	1982
54	32	27	1983
55	33	28	1984
56	34	29	1985
57	35	30	1986
58	36	31	1987
59	37	32	1988
60	38	33	1989
61	39	34	1990
62	40	35	1991

* Individuals born on January 2, 1930, or later should use the Age at Death or Disability column.
† People born before January 2, 1930 should refer to the Year of Death or Disability column.

Given the frequency of disability, people should be aware of Social Security disability benefits. And they should be certain they qualify for these benefits. In order to receive disability payments they must be fully insured (see Table 15-10 for the necessary number of quarters covered) and unless blind must also satisfy one of the following conditions:

1 Anyone thirty-one years or older at the time of disability needs at least 20 quarters of coverage out of the most recent 40 calendar quarters.
2 Anyone under thirty-one at the time of disability needs work credit for at least half of the calendar quarters between the twenty-first birthday and the date of disability. (If the number of elapsed quarters is an odd number, reduce it by 1.) In addition, men or women in this age category need at least 6 quarters of coverage as a minimum.

The Social Security program imposes strict **disability standards.** The government pays benefits only when the individual is so severely disabled that he or she is unable to engage in "any substantial gainful activity." In other words, the person must be unable to perform any type of work. Moreover, the disability must be expected to last at least 12 months or eventually cause death. Since no absolute definition of disability is possible, the Social Security Administration gives a specific governmental agency in each state the power to decide whether or not people qualify for disability benefits.

Certain members of the disabled worker's family also receive benefits. Table 15-8 shows who qualifies for these payments.

INFLATION AND SOCIAL SECURITY BENEFITS

Inflation severely penalizes people receiving a fixed income. As prices rise, the same number of dollars purchases fewer and fewer goods. Several years ago Congress recognized the plight of individuals trying to live on fixed Social Security checks during times of severe inflation and provided for automatic increases in benefits. Now Social Security benefits increase every June if the cost of living increased by at least 3%.

This **escalator provision** ties benefits to the Consumer Price Index. Generally speaking, the percentage increase in monthly benefits equals the percentage increase in the CPI during the previous year. With each automatic increase in benefits, the maximum earnings base also rises.

How have Social Security recipients fared in real terms over the years? Figure 15-1 answers that question for the period from 1940 to 1975. It shows minimum, maximum, and average retirement benefits in 1975 dollars. The retirement benefit collected by an individual (excluding any family benefits) in 1975 amounted to slightly more than $200. This corresponds to retirement benefits of less than $100 in 1940. So Social Security benefits more than doubled, even after adjusting for the tremendous decline in the purchasing power of the dollar.

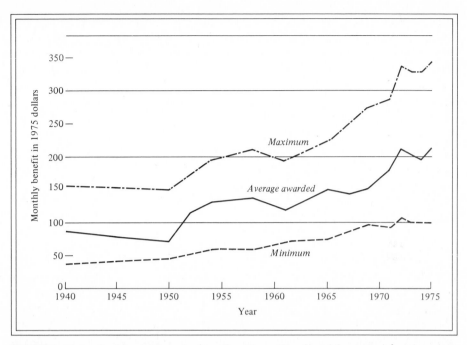

FIGURE 15-1 Real Social Security benefits. (From The Social Security Administration, Bureau of Labor Statistics, Consumer Price Index. This chart appeared in Greenough/King, *Pension Plans and Public Policy,* Columbia University Press, New York, 1976, p. 87.)

Decoupling Benefits

The automatic escalator provision of the Social Security program suffers from a serious flaw. Replacement rates for annual wages vary drastically, depending upon actual inflation rates. For example, under the present system people retiring in the year 2025 will receive a benefit equal to 130% of their final salary if inflation averages 4%, but the benefit amounts to only 49% of their salary if inflation averages 2%.

In the first case, people find themselves retiring with a higher salary than they earned on their jobs. Although this may sound wonderful, it would probably bankrupt the system (and whatever remains of the Puritan work ethic). In the second case, the replacement rate falls substantially below the current replacement rate of 61%; so retirees would face an impoverished future.

The problem stems from the fact that the automatic escalator not only increases the checks of people already collecting benefits, it also increases the future benefits of present workers. At the same time, inflation pushes up wages and the maximum earnings base. This raises average earnings and causes a further increase in benefits.

Many experts on Social Security recommend **decoupling** the system. In other words, they want to eliminate the ties between benefit increases for those still working and those already receiving Social Security checks. This would stabilize replacement rates and save billions and perhaps trillions of dollars.

THE FUTURE OF SOCIAL SECURITY

For nearly 40 years the Social Security system performed miracles. It promised people far more than they paid into the program and then somehow delivered the benefits. No wonder there has been almost universal acclaim for the OASDI program.

But now those "miracles" appear to have been nothing more than sleight of hand, with the Social Security system simply transferring money from one group of workers to another. This discovery proved to be a painful one for the American people. Witness the stream of articles and books with titles like: *Social Security: The Fraud in Your Future,* "The Squeeze Ahead for Social Security," "Why So Many Feel They're Shortchanged by Social Security," "Farewell to Ponzi?" and "Propping Up Social Security: The System Doesn't Have to Go Broke if Congress Would Stop Playing Politics."

Warren Shore's *Social Security: The Fraud in Your Future* probably strikes the hardest at the present system. He claims the Social Security Administration has deliberately misled the American people with statements like the following:[2]

> *The basic idea of social security is a simple one: During the working years employees, their employers, and self-employed people pay social security contributions which are pooled in special trust funds. When earnings stop or are reduced because the worker retires, becomes disabled, or dies, monthly cash benefits are paid to replace part of the earnings the family has lost.*

The words "trust fund," as Shore points out, usually imply property held by one party for another. Because of the repeated use of these words in the Social Security literature, most Americans believe they own the money "contributed" to Social Security. But the "trust funds" are virtually nonexistent.

Shore also attacks continued attempts by the Social Security Administration to sell the American people on the insurance aspects of the system. According to Shore,[3]

> *. . . The administration's vast public relations staff never misses a chance to drive home the idea that Social Security and insurance are the same thing.*
>
> *In the administration pamphlet describing the Social Security card, we are told, "Your card is the symbol of your insurance policy under the federal Social Security law."*
>
> *At least thirty-five times in the sixty-one current Social Security Administration booklets describing the system, taxes, removed from payroll checks before a worker ever sees them, are referred to as either "contributions," or "premiums"!*

Contrary to the misleading advertising of the government, Social Security bears only a vague resemblance to private insurance programs. Unlike private insurance, Social Security attempts to achieve both (1) income replacement and (2) income maintenance. Income replacement involves the partial replacement of income lost because of retirement, death, and disability. The program provides for a pooling of these risks, as does private insurance.

The income-maintenance objective involves correcting deficiencies in income, i.e., improving the welfare of people. The emphasis here is on social adequacy, meaning that the benefits paid by the program provide at least the minimum standard of living. This aspect of Social Security bears absolutely no relationship to insurance of any sort. (But there appears to be a distressing tendency on the part of some people to base their definitions of "social insurance" on the most current version of the Social Security program.)

Benefits versus Contributions

Because of these twin objectives, the Social Security program differs from private insurance in one fundamental respect—benefits often differ from contributions. This raises a rather obvious question: Who gets the most (or least) from Social Security? The difference between benefits and contributions depends largely upon the age of the individual. *Money* magazine printed a rather revealing analysis of the costs and benefits of OASDI in 1974. It created an imaginary family named the Smiths, assumed each Smith earned the maximum taxable wage during each working year, and then projected all Social Security contributions and benefits for each member of the family. The family consists of five generations of Smiths: a great-grandfather, a grandfather, a father, a son, and a grandson.

The great-grandfather, now ninety years old, retired in 1950. Since the government did not begin collecting Social Security taxes until 1937, he made contributions for 13 years. His contributions over those years totaled only $390, even though he earned the maximum wage covered by Social Security. *Money's* actuaries expect great-grandfather Smith to collect $64,279. At that rate, he receives $164.80 in benefits for every dollar originally paid into Social Security. Of course, his contributions would have earned interest and grown to a larger amount. After discounting for this interest, the payoff still amounts to $58.40 for each $1 of cost.

The grandfather, at age sixty-four, is not quite so lucky. When he retires at sixty-five, he will have paid Social Security taxes of $5,519 in the last 38 of his 45 working years. Expected benefits over his lifetime come to $127,957—a return of $23.20 for each dollar. With interest included, the return drops to $5.90 for every $1.

The thirty-nine-year-old father experiences a still smaller return for his contributions. He pays a total of $40,299 and receives benefits worth $513,872—a payoff of $12.80 per $1 or of $2.70 per dollar with interest added.

His nineteen-year-old son faces the dismal prospect of paying $136,554 in Social Security taxes. But he supposedly receives $1,542,863, a payoff of $11.30 for each dollar or of $2.10 with interest included.

And no wonder the newly born grandson comes into the world crying. According to the actuaries, the government expects him to pay more than $430,000 in payroll taxes. In return it promises him about $4,000,000 in benefits. The payoff rate for the youngest Smith equals $9.30 to $1, or $1.80 to $1 with the adjustment for interest.

Judging from the results reported in *Money,* the Social Security system penalizes young workers (at least relative to old workers). Other, more authoritative, studies reach the same conclusion. In addition, the Social Security system "discriminates" against certain individuals within any one generation. Single people pay much more for each dollar of benefits than married workers. Remember, Social Security pays family benefits without any increase in the "contribution" rate. Social Security also discriminates against other groups of people, such as married working women.

Financing the System

The second difference between Social Security and private insurance concerns the technique for financing benefit payments. The government requires insurance companies and firms with pension plans to hold reserves against all promised payments. These reserves consist of bonds, stocks, and other income-producing assets. Any firm violating these reserve rules faces severe penalties. On the other hand, the government operates the Social Security system on a pay-as-you-go basis, taking from Peter to pay Paul. At the present time the "reserves" in the "trust funds" total less than 1% of outstanding commitments.

Contrary to popular belief, the present system of financing Social Security benefits in no way implies impending bankruptcy. In fact, many economists prefer a pay-as-you-go basis (technically referred to as **current-cost financing**) to the buildup of enormous reserves. They argue that the present system is justified on the following grounds:

1 OASDI is compulsory. In contrast to private insurance firms, the Social Security system can always rely on new entrants for "contributions."
2 The taxing power of the federal government can always be used to provide additional revenues.
3 Large trust funds might constitute a fiscal drag on the economy.

Other economists provide some convincing arguments against the pay-as-you-go basis, including the following:

1 Substantial reserves improve the chances of collecting promised benefits.
2 Large trust funds reduce the dependence of current generations on future generations.
3 A pay-as-you-go basis fails to reflect true costs. As a result, political expediency generally rules in the determination of benefits.
4 Real capital (productive resources) must be accumulated in order to provide for retirement. The formation of real capital makes it possible for the retired generation to receive goods and services (because of increased production)

without having to take them away from other members of society through taxation.

Current State of the System

Nowadays critics often compare the Social Security system with a **Ponzi scheme.** Charles Ponzi gained immortality by fraudulently collecting $16 million from the American public in 1920. He promised to pay people 100% interest on their money every 90 days. He confounded skeptics by doing just this for a few months. But the interest came from other investors and not from the purchase of international postal money orders, as Ponzi claimed.

Ponzi schemes rely upon a continuing stream of new investors to provide the funds needed to pay off the old investors. To see why, suppose a promoter promises to double people's money every year. In order to meet this promise, the number of participants in the scheme must be doubled each year (assuming the original investors always withdraw at the end of a year).

Early participants in a Ponzi scheme often earn large returns on their investments. But as time goes on, it becomes more and more difficult to add the ever-increasing number of participants vital to the operation of the system. As a result, the last investors usually get little or nothing for their money.

The Securities and Exchange Commission cautions investors about Ponzi schemes in a booklet titled *How to Avoid Ponzi and Pyramid Schemes.* The SEC tells people to watch out for the following characteristics:

1 Reliance on funds from new investors to pay returns . . . to old investors
2 Need for an inexhaustible supply of new investors
3 Absence of a profitable product or efforts to make profits through productive work
4 Lack of assets

There are some striking similarities between the United States Social Security system and a Ponzi scheme. First, the money used to pay benefits to old workers comes from the "contributions" of new workers. Second, the system needs an inexhaustible supply of new workers to make good its promises to pay the old workers benefits far exceeding their contributions. Third, the system fails to provide for investment in the productive assets necessary to increase output. Fourth, the "trust funds" are so small relative to promised payments that there are virtually no assets.

Ponzi schemes always collapse because new entrants fail to materialize in sufficient numbers. For a long time, the Social Security program appeared to be immune from this shortcoming. But the recent sharp decline in birth rates has sent a shudder throughout the system. Arthur E. Hess, deputy commissioner of the Social Security Administration, told William Mead, a reporter for *Money* magazine that[4]

The people born during the post-World War II baby boom will eventually retire, and the current decline in the birth rate will reduce the relative number of wage earners to foot the Security bill. The ratio of working taxpayers to nonworking pensioners is crucial to the system; it varies with the year-to-year birth rate and mortality rates and it will get much worse, as illustrated by the Social Security Administration's records and projections:

Ratio of Wage Earners to Pensioners

1950	11.7 to 1	1980	2.6 to 1
1960	4.0 to 1	1990	2.4 to 1
1970	2.8 to 1	2020	1.9 to 1
1974	2.5 to 1	2040	1.8 to 1

Judging from these figures, the baby-boom-and-bust problem appears very far away in the future. But, in reality, the people whose retirement incomes are now at stake are those in the fifteen- to thirty-year age group. And older workers will no doubt feel the repercussions.

Without pyramiding, current and future workers must pay ever-increasing Social Security taxes in order to support those collecting benefits. Already the Social Security Administration has promised over $3 trillion more in benefits than it expects to receive in contributions (discounting all benefits and contributions back to the present). This amounts to more than 30 times the total amount of money collected for Social Security in 1975. Moreover, these figures depend upon the realization of certain optimistic assumptions made by the SSA.

Some of the more pessimistic forecasters see the Social Security tax bite eventually increasing to 20 to 25% of income from the present 5.85%. Probably long before then people will refuse to make these "contributions." Then the system would be bankrupt, but only in the sense of needing a transfusion from general tax revenues. Of course, that leaves the voters with 1 of 2 painful choices, either to increase income taxes or to reduce Social Security payments.

Solving the Problems

What can be done to solve these problems? The Social Security Advisory Council, a prestigious group of business people, labor leaders, and private citizens propose a change in the benefit formula. The council wants to "decouple" benefits and stabilize replacement rates. Under this approach, Social Security would pay future retirees the same percentage of their recent wages as it now pays to retirees. Since real wages rise over the years because of increased productivity, pension benefits in real dollars would actually increase over time.

Another approach, recommended by Harvard University economist William Hsiao, involves guaranteeing a constant purchasing power pension. Benefits would be tied to the cost of living rather than to earnings. As a result, people would receive pensions with the same purchasing power as today's retirees. Hsiao's proposal reduces the costs of the program even more than the simple decoupling recommended by the Advisory Council, since it ignores the increase in real wages made possible by increased productivity. According to Hsiao, "The approach would not only eliminate the threat of a deficit, but with a few other adjustments would result in stable tax rates for the foreseeable future—reducing the chance that future generations would refuse to pay the tax bill for today's workers."

Other economists suggest correcting the fiction that Social Security is really an insurance program. If the voters want an insurance program, a definite relationship between contributions and benefits should be arranged. If such a program does not provide sufficient benefits for low-income and elderly workers, then citizens should consider alternative methods for providing more directly for these groups. Some of the steps that might be taken in making the Social Security system a true social insurance program are:

1 Permit individuals to apply their compulsory contributions toward private savings and insurance programs.
2 Require that employees' contributions actually be invested for them rather than being used to pay other peoples' benefits. This would considerably reduce the uncertainty about the future of the program.
3 Change the present regulations so that there is a direct tie between contributions made and benefits received. Until that is done, the program has strong elements of a welfare system, with future generations having to bear the costs of present generations and with those paying the most in any one generation receiving the least per dollar of contributions. If an income-maintenance program is desired, and there are some persuasive arguments why it might be, operate a separate program.
4 Recognize the unfair treatment of families with more than one worker. Many women workers receive larger benefits through their husbands than through their own contributions. And yet they must still pay Social Security taxes.
5 Eliminate the practice of reducing Social Security checks when the recipient works. At the present time, the government reduces benefits by 50¢ for each $1 the individual earns in excess of $2,760 a year. Moreover, both Social Security and income taxes must be paid on these excess earnings. As a result the marginal tax rate on any income earned over $2,760 exceeds 56%—a prohibitive rate.

IMPLICATIONS FOR INVESTMENT STRATEGY

Social Security benefits and costs are too substantial to be ignored in any investment strategy. Investors should have a general understanding of the Social Security program. And they should have some idea of their disability, survivor's, and retirement benefits. Although the rules may at first appear complicated, these benefits can be easily determined. The real problem comes in estimating retirement benefits, which may not be received until far into the future.

In projecting retirement benefits, investors face the usual uncertainties about future inflation rates, rates of return, and salaries. In addition, they confront the serious question of whether or not the Social Security system can pay the retirement benefits which have been promised to participants. Persistent trends towards lower population growth, earlier retirement, and longer lifetimes may eventually cripple the system. Of course, the taxing power of the government can always be used to subsidize the program. But when benefits cease to be even remotely related to contributions and are determined strictly by votes, the outcome will probably become even more uncertain than it is now.

In addition to knowing how the system works and what costs and benefits to expect, investors can take an active role in maximizing their benefits and minimizing their costs. In order to do this they must accept the fact that the Social Security program attempts to satisfy the two diverse and somewhat inconsistent goals of providing a social insurance program and of correcting deficiencies in incomes. Because of this second objective, individuals who make only a small contribution to the program receive relatively large benefits. For example, a person who earns $50 a calendar quarter can become fully insured for all Social Security benefits in 10 years or less. As a result, the individual collects a retirement benefit of at least $1,200 a year and perhaps as much as $1,800 for life, as well as obtaining disability and survivor's insurance. The total cost of all these benefits comes to at most $117. (A quarterly wage of $50 adds up to $2,000 over a 10-year period, and the worker pays 5.85% of this $2,000 in Social Security taxes.)

Federal employees have long taken advantage of this aspect of the system by so-called double-dipping. They are not required to pay Social Security taxes, since they have their own retirement system. After they retire, they can obtain any type of covered employment which pays at least $50 a calendar quarter and thereby qualify for Social Security benefits as well. Like federal employees, employees of state and local governments and of certain nonprofit institutions can elect not to take part in the Social Security program. If recent figures are any indication, more and more of these workers will probably make this selection in the future.

Generally speaking, any worker not covered by Social Security should attempt to qualify for at least the minimum Social Security benefits. This is especially true for women. Those married for less than 20 years lose the right to their husband's Social Security benefits in the event of divorce. Only by qualifying for Social Security on their own can they be certain of receiving any benefits.

Although it is a good idea for women to qualify for minimum Social Security benefits, it sometimes makes little sense for them to qualify for larger benefits. The government does not allow working women to collect benefits based on their own employment record as well as on their husband's record. They must select one or the other. Because many women earn considerably lower salaries than men, the benefits they collect as wives often exceed their own Social Security benefits. So in a sense their own Social Security contributions are wasted. These Social Security taxes can be avoided if a wife and/or children are employed in a family business which is unincorporated.

Because the Social Security Administration ties benefits to a person's family status, recipients of Social Security benefits sometimes find their very lives being altered drastically. Remarriage of a widow or widower or divorced wife or marriage of a dependent child can result in a reduction or complete loss of benefits. In addition, dependent children and grandchildren may find it profitable to remain in school solely because of the extensive Social Security benefits they continue to receive while full-time students under the age of twenty-two.

Any retirement decision will also have to be based upon a careful consideration of the benefits gained or lost by retiring at a certain age. Individuals who retire early receive reduced benefits. On the other hand, those who delay retirement until after they are sixty-five add little to their retirement benefits. Moreover anyone who starts collecting benefits and works at the same time often does so at a very high cost. For example, every $1 earned over $2,760 in 1976 reduced Social Security benefits by 50¢. Since this reduction applies only to earned income, retireees may be able to redirect their earnings so that they escape this penalty. One way to do so is to incorporate a business and distribute any earnings as dividends. Another way is to buy real estate which pays rental income and spend the time managing the property instead of working at a regular job. Rental income is considered to be exempt for purposes of Social Security. A third technique for avoiding the loss of benefits is to arrange to receive income in only a few months of the year. Regardless of the amount earned during a year, the SSA reduces benefits only for those months in which wages exceed $230.

KEYWORDS

OASDI	FICA	replacement rate
quarters of coverage	tax rate	disability standards
fully insured	earnings base	escalator provision
currently insured	elapsed years	decoupling
transitionally insured	primary insurance amount	current-cost financing
contributions	early retirement	Ponzi scheme
Social Security payroll tax	retirement test	

QUESTIONS

1   Why is a knowledge of Social Security benefits vital to investment strategy?
2   What is the primary purpose of the Social Security Program?
3   Are all jobs covered by Social Security? How do people accumulate quarters of coverage under the system?
4   How many quarters of coverage does someone born in 1958 need to be fully insured for retirement benefits? How about a woman born in 1934? (Hint: Use Table 15-1.)
5   Suppose a man earned $16,000 in 1977. How much did he pay in Social Security taxes? How much did his employer pay? (The tax rate equaled 5.85% in 1977.)
6   Use the following information to estimate the benefits Samuel Adams received when he retired in 1976 at the age of sixty-five:

Year	Earnings, $	Year	Earnings, $
1951	3,000	1964	8,600
1952	3,600	1965	10,000
1953	4,000	1966	10,500
1954	5,000	1967	11,000
1955	5,500	1968	12,000
1956	5,000	1969	13,000
1957	6,000	1970	14,000
1958	7,000	1971	15,000
1959	7,000	1972	16,000
1960	7,000	1973	17,000
1961	7,000	1974	18,000
1962	8,000	1975	18,000
1963	8,200	1976	18,000

7   Bill Townsend plans to retire in a few years at the age of sixty-two. Bill's wife will also be sixty-two at that time. How much of the primary insurance amount will Bill and his wife receive?

8   Ted Springate attends college part-time. He is married and has two young children. Before buying a life insurance policy, he asks you to estimate his survivor's benefits. Use the following information for a twenty-three-year-old man with 16 quarters of coverage:

Covered Earnings, $
1977	5,000
1978	6,000
1979	7,000
1980	8,000
1981	9,000

9   Nora Kaplan graduated from law school at the age of twenty-five. One month after graduation she was totally disabled. Use the following information to compute her disability benefits, given her age at date of disability as twenty-five, the number of quarters between her twenty-first birthday and date of disability as 17, with 5 quarters of coverage (from working during summers):

Covered Earnings, $
1974	1,000
1975	1,100
1976	1,200
1977	1,300
1978	1,500

(Be certain to check to see if Nora satisfies all the requirements for disability benefits.)

Next assume Nora worked for 2 full years after graduation and then became disabled at the age of twenty-seven. She earned $12,000 in 1979 and $15,000 in 1980. How much does she collect in disability benefits?

10 Do you feel the Social Security Administration has been entirely forthright in its public statements about the nature of the Social Security program? Why or why not?

11 Who receives the most from Social Security relative to their contributions? Who receives the least? Do you feel some participants in the Social Security program should be required to subsidize the income of other participants? Why or why not? Are there any alternatives?

12 Debate the pros and cons of current-cost financing of Social Security.

13 Do you think Social Security resembles a Ponzi scheme? Does a government-run Ponzi scheme differ from a privately operated Ponzi scheme in any crucial respects?

14 What caused the sudden concern about the ability of the Social Security system to meet its promises?

15 What changes do you recommend in the current Social Security program? Why?

REFERENCES

Bell, Carolyn Shaw: "Social Security Myths and Inequities," *The Washington Post,* Sept. 2, 1973, pp. D1, D4.

Biossat, Bruce: *Medicare and Social Security: What You've Got Coming,* Dolphin Books, Garden City, N.Y., 1974.

Booth, Philip: *Social Security in America,* Institute of Labor and Industrial Relations, The University of Michigan–Wayne State University, 1973.

Bowen, William G., et al., eds.: *The Princeton Symposium on the American System of Social Insurance: Its Philosophy, Impact, and Future Development,* McGraw-Hill, New York, 1968.

Brown, J. Douglas: *An American Philosophy of Social Security: Evolution and Issues,* Princeton, Princeton, N.J., 1972.

Cohen, Wilbur J., and Milton Friedman: *Social Security: Universal or Selective,* American Enterprise Institute for Public Policy Research, Washington, D.C., 1972.

"Farewell to Ponzi? Must Come to the Social Security System," *Barron's,* Jan. 3, 1977, p. 7.

Friedman, Milton: "On Social Security," *Newsweek,* Apr. 3, 1967, p. 81.

Greenough, William C., and Francis P. King: *Pension Plans and Public Policy,* Columbia, New York, 1976.

Laffer, Arthur B., and R. David Ranson: "Some Economic Consequences of the U.S. Social Security," unpublished manuscript.

*Mead, William B.: "The Squeeze Ahead for Social Security," *Money,* October 1974, pp. 32–35.

Munnell, Alicia Haydock: *The Effect of Social Security on Personal Saving,* Ballinger Publishing, Cambridge, Mass., 1974.

*1976 Social Security and Medicare Explained, Commerce Clearing House, Chicago, Ill., 1976.

*Pechman, Joseph A., Henry J. Aaron, and Michael K. Taussig: *Social Security: Perspectives for Reform,* Brookings, Washington, D.C., 1968.

"Propping Up Social Security," *Business Week,* July 19, 1976, pp. 34–38, 43.

Rejda, George E.: *Social Insurance and Economic Security,* Prentice-Hall, Englewood Cliffs, N.J., 1976.

* Publications preceded by an asterisk are highly recommended.

Samuelson, Paul: "On Social Security," *Newsweek,* Feb. 13, 1967, p. 88.

Shore, Warren: *Social Security: The Fraud in Your Future,* Macmillan, New York, 1975.

U.S. Board of Trustees, Federal OASDI Trust Funds, *1972 Annual Report,* 92d Cong., 2d Sess., House Doc. 92–307, June 6, 1972.

U.S. Board of Trustees, Federal OASDI Trust Funds, *1975 Annual Report,* 95th Cong., 2d Sess., House Doc., 1975.

U.S. Bureau of the Census, *Current Population Reports: Projections of the Population of the United States: 1975 to 2050,* ser. p. 25, no. 601, 1975.

U.S. Treasury Department, Saltonstall Report, "Statement of Liabilities and Other Financial Commitments of the United States Government as of June 30, 1973," unpublished.

"Why So Many Feel They're Shortchanged by Social Security," *U.S. News and World Report,* July 26, 1976, pp. 37–39.

PART FIVE

COSTS OF INVESTING

CHAPTER SIXTEEN

TRANSACTIONS COSTS

Academicians often describe the investments markets as if these markets were perfect. A **perfect market** is a market in which (1) there are no costs to buying and selling, (2) information is free and readily available to everyone, and (3) there are no taxes. In this ideal environment it is difficult to imagine investors getting themselves into much trouble.

Unfortunately, no market is perfect. Probably the single most serious obstacle to developing a successful investment strategy and then following it through is the cost of buying and selling investments. Numerous investors have been wiped out by paying excessive brokerage commissions. For example, one small investor placed $3,000 with a brokerage firm and authorized the broker to buy and sell at the broker's own discretion. After only 1 month, total purchases in the account amounted to $31,000, total sales to $26,000, and the commissions collected by the brokerage firm on these transactions amounted to $1,022. The investor's overall loss for the month equaled $2,900.

This story illustrates one of the dangers inherent in the present investments markets. Most individuals who provide investment advice make money only when their customers pay commissions. As a result, even the most sincere brokers face a serious conflict of interest. Their job is to generate commissions.

In order to do this, they must encourage their customers to buy and sell, regardless of the costs of such trading.

COSTS OF BUYING AND SELLING STOCKS

Trading costs have escalated in the last decade. In 1964 an investor could buy 100 shares of stock at $10 a share and pay only $17 in commissions. By 1975 commission costs at most brokerage houses had almost doubled; so it cost at least $27.50 in commissions to buy the same stock. A **round trip** in the stock, that is, buying and selling it, cost $55. And by 1976 the round trip costs had increased to $66. At these prices an investor must make at least 6.6% on a $1,000 investment just to recover the money paid in commissions. Since the return on stocks averages about 10% a year, most investors must wait more than 8 months just to break even on their investments.

The commissions on lower-priced stocks account for an even higher percentage of the stock price. Anyone buying 100 shares of a $2 stock for a quick profit has to be a real optimist. In 1975 the round-trip commission on this $200 purchase equaled $22.88, or more than 11% of the purchase price. And by 1976 commissions charged by many brokers were consuming about 17% of the total amount invested.

Brokerage commissions now amount to a very substantial part of the first year's returns on stocks. This burden falls unevenly on investors for reasons soon to be explained. It is especially heavy on the small investor. Before May 1, 1975, all member firms of the New York and American Stock Exchanges charged the same commission rates. Some of these rates are shown in Table 16-1. According to the figures in this table, a small investor purchasing 10 shares of a $10 stock had to pay $7.04 in commissions on a $100 investment. In other words, for every $1 invested in stocks, 7.04¢ went to commission costs. On the other hand, a large investor buying a thousand shares at $10 a share paid $213.62, or 2.14% of the amount invested. In other words, only 2.14¢ of every $1 invested was paid in commissions.

After May 1, 1975, the exchanges abandoned fixed commission rates and the Securities and Exchange Commission required every brokerage house to set its own commission rates. Despite the increased price competition, most brokers continue to follow the same rate structure for individual accounts. The commission rates charged by one of the largest brokerage firms in the country are shown in Table 16-2. The table is broken down into two sections giving the rates for (1) an odd lot or one round lot and (2) multiple round lots. A round lot is an order for exactly 100 shares. And a multiple round lot is any multiple of 100 shares.

According to Table 16-2, the commission on an order of 10 shares at $10 a share now equals 10% of the $100 investment; that is, 10¢ out of every $1 goes to commission costs. The commission on 1,000 shares at $10 a share is $213.62. This figure is calculated as follows:

TABLE 16-1 SAMPLE OF FIXED COMMISSION RATES CHARGED BY
MEMBERS OF THE NYSE AND AMEX BEFORE MAY 1, 1975

Share Price, $	Number of Shares						
	5	10	20	50	100	500	1,000
1					9.24	46.20	92.40
2				7.04	11.44	57.20	107.80
3				8.14	13.64	67.65	119.90
4				9.24	15.84	74.80	129.80
5			7.04	10.34	18.04	81.95	139.70
6			7.48	11.44	20.24	86.90	168.91
7			7.92	12.54	22.44	91.85	180.09
8			8.36	13.64	24.64	96.80	191.27
9			8.80	14.74	26.07	101.75	202.45
10		7.04	9.24	15.84	27.50	106.70	213.62
20	7.04	9.24	13.64	25.30	41.80	176.36	325.40
30	8.14	11.44	18.04	32.45	53.90	232.25	399.92
40	9.24	13.64	22.44	39.60	63.80	288.14	449.60
50	10.34	15.84	25.30	46.75	71.50	325.40	499.28
60	11.44	18.04	28.16	51.70	80.73	362.66	548.96

Basic fee	$ 27.32
+ 1.1178% × $10,000	111.78
+ $7.452 per round lot × 10	74.52
Total commission	$213.62

The commission on the $10,000 order amounts to 2.14¢ of each $1 invested. So
the small investor pays nearly 5 times as much per dollar invested as the large
investor.

Nature of Commissions

The present system of commission rates puts small investors at a considerable
disadvantage. But the fact that commissions are a larger percentage of the investment the smaller the amount invested is in no way the fault of brokerage houses.
These differences exist because the costs of buying or selling investments are primarily **fixed costs.** Costs are said to be fixed when they remain the same regardless of the quantity produced or ordered. For instance, no matter how many
shares or how much money is involved in any one order, a brokerage firm still
incurs certain costs. The registered representative must spend time on the phone
taking the order and must then transmit the order to other personnel who wire it
to the firm's New York office. The New York office transmits the order to the
floor of the exchange, wires back the details of the completed transaction, and

TABLE 16-2   SAMPLE OF COMMISSIONS ON STOCKS AFTER MAY 1, 1975

Money Involved, $	Commission
Orders for 100 Shares or Less	
1.00–162.50	10% of funds
162.51–1,099.99	$13.00 + 2% of funds
1,100.00–2,499.99	21.25 + 1.25% of funds
2,500.00–5,000.00	25.50 + 1.1% of funds
5,000.01 and above	$80.73*
Orders for More than 100 Shares	
200.00–1,099.99	$ 13.00 + 2% of funds
1,100.00–2,499.99	21.25 + 1.25% of funds
2,500.00–5,000.00	25.50 + 1.1% of funds
5,000.01–19,999.99	27.324 + 1.1178% of funds
20,000.00–29,999.99	101.844 + .7452% of funds
30,000.00–300,000.00	176.364 + .4968% of funds

Plus for Each Round Lot:

Lots	Money Involved		
	$200.00–$2,000.00	$2,000.01–$5,000.00	$5,000.01–$300,000.00
1–10	$5.50 ea.	$7.25 ea.	$7.452 ea.
11 and over	5.50 ea.	4.75 ea.	4.968 ea.

* The maximum commission for a single round lot or an odd lot is $80.73.

then bills the customer. Probably the rep calls the customer to report how the order went. Finally, the firm has to process the customer's payment and perhaps receive and hold the customer's share certificate. These steps and the time and money involved remain more or less the same whether 1 or 10,000 shares are involved. As a result, most of the costs of executing a buy or sell order are fixed.

Because of the fixed costs for transacting, the average commission paid by a buyer or seller varies with the size of the order. The larger the dollar amount of the order, the lower the average cost of exchanging a dollar of stock. For example, if transactions costs are completely fixed and equal $15 an order, the cost of buying and selling each $1 of stock in an order is described in Figure 16-1. If $100 of stock is bought or sold, the commission cost is 15¢ per $1 of stock. If the order size is $1,000, the cost per $1 of stock is only 1.5¢. And for an order of $10,000 (not shown on the graph), the cost amounts to only a fraction of 1¢ for each $1 exchanged.

Fixed transactions costs are an economic fact of life. The high commission

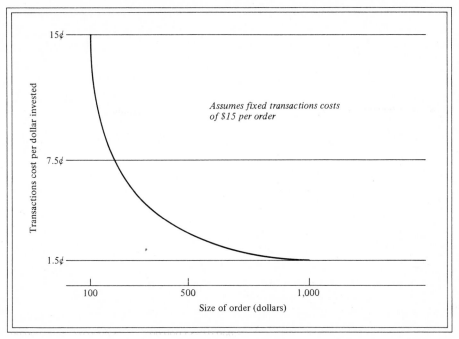

FIGURE 16-1   Transactions costs per dollar invested.

rates paid by small investors on each dollar invested simply reflect these fixed costs. They are not the result of brokers taking unfair advantage of small investors. If anything, it appears that the old commission rates charged by members of the organized stock exchanges discriminated against large buyers and sellers rather than against small investors. Before May 1, 1975, the commission on 100 shares priced at $10 was $27.50, whereas it was $71.50 on 100 shares priced at $50. Since most of a brokerage firm's costs are the same regardless of the price of the shares, this large increase in commissions is difficult to explain. Many individuals have argued that such increases were not a reflection of economic reality, but were instead the result of the monopoly power of the exchanges. If the exchanges were truly competitive, commissions would increase very little with larger dollar amounts, since no additional work is required to process the order.

The same criticism can be made of the rates set by individual firms after May 1, 1975. According to the competitive rate schedule summarized in Table 16-2, the commission on 100 shares priced at $10 a share is now $33. It is $80.50 for 100 shares at $50 a share. The question remains, What additional cost does the broker incur on $50 shares that he does not incur on $10 shares? The answer appears to be none. And that is the reason why so many large buyers and sellers have refused to pay the published commissions and have bargained with individual brokers for special discounts. These discounts reportedly range from 30 to 40% or more of the quoted rates. Other investors have turned to discount brokers who openly publish more realistic rates.

Specialist Fees

There are other costs in buying and selling stocks which are less obvious than brokerage commissions. Both the New York Stock Exchange and the American Stock Exchange have specialist systems. Specialists make a market in stocks by standing ready to buy or sell shares. By doing this, they provide almost immediate execution of any buy or sell order.

Specialists act like any retailer. Like a used-car dealer, they provide a ready market. And like the car dealer, they must maintain an inventory, since purchases and sales very seldom come at exactly the same moment. For keeping this inventory and providing the customer with the opportunity to buy and sell without delay, they collect a markup which covers their costs and provides a profit. For example, they may buy a stock for $40 and then sell it a little later for $40^1/$_2$. If the original seller and buyer had been willing to wait to transact with each other, they would probably have compromised on a price of $40^1/$_4$. Thus, the buyer and the seller have together paid 25¢ a share to the specialist for being able to buy and sell immediately rather than having to wait.

This difference between buying and selling prices is more apparent in stocks traded over the counter. The over-the-counter market is unlike the New York and American Stock Exchanges in that there is no centralized meeting place. Instead, numerous dealers located in banks, brokerage firms, and other financial institutions around the country stand ready to buy and sell shares in certain stocks. Like the specialists on the exchanges, they charge a markup. For instance, the bid-and-asked prices on Dairy Queen on February 26, 1975, were $3^1/$_4$ and $4. Since investors always buy at the high price and sell at the low price, they would have had to pay $4 for each share of stock. If they bought the stock at $4 a share and then immediately had a change of mind about the prospects of the company and sold the stock back to the dealer, they would have received only $3^1/$_4$ for each of the shares. The difference between the bid price of $3^1/$_4$ and the asked price of $4 is called the bid-ask spread; the spread in this case equals 75¢. It is the cost of buying and selling 1 share. If the investor had purchased 100 shares, the difference between the buying and selling prices would have been equal to $75 (100 shares times the bid-ask spread of 75¢) on this $400 purchase, plus the standard brokerage commissions.

State Tax

There is one other cost to trading stocks. Every time a share is sold on the New York Stock Exchange, a tax is assessed by the State of New York. The tax depends on the sales price of the stock and at most amounts to only 2.5¢ per share for out-of-state residents.

REDUCING TRANSACTIONS COSTS

Investors seldom think about the costs of buying and selling shares, and brokers never mention them. But a knowledge of these costs can be very important in formulating an investment strategy. It is immediately apparent that anyone who can invest large amounts of money has a distinct advantage over another person with only small amounts to invest. After all, the large investor pays much lower commission costs as a percent of the amount invested. For example, an investor buying 5 shares of a $20 stock probably pays 10% of the money invested in commissions. On the other hand, someone purchasing 100 shares, pays only about 2%. Small investors seem to have a good reason for leaving the stock market: it appears to be uneconomical to buy shares from a broker. But there are numerous ways to reduce these costs if they do not buy and sell through a regular brokerage account. And even if they do, there are still several techniques for reducing commission costs.

Buy and Hold

The first approach to cutting transactions costs is simply to buy and hold the investment. Once a stock is purchased, it is held regardless of its future price behavior. The investor sells the stock only when the money is needed. The investor never sells just in order to reinvest in another stock or bond or the like.

By using a buy-and-hold approach, even small investors can greatly reduce commission costs by averaging commission costs over a long period of time rather than over a large number of dollars. For example, investors who purchase $100 of stocks pay approximately 10% of that amount in brokerage fees. When they sell the stock, they pay another 10%. And if they buy an odd lot, they also give up an extra eighth of a point for the odd lot differential on each share bought and sold. In addition, they may also pay a bid-ask spread. As a result, the transactions costs probably total 25% of the amount invested. If the stock is held for only 1 year, the costs of transacting are 25% a year.

Since these costs far exceed the expected return on stocks, the small investor who plans to buy and sell stock in 1 year is almost certain to lose on the transaction. By holding the stock for 5 years, the investor reduces the costs of transacting to 5% a year—still a very large percentage of the expected annual returns on the investment. By holding the stock 10 years, the individual cuts transactions costs to 2.5% a year—a much more reasonable figure. On a larger investment of $1,000, the round-trip transactions costs would be approximately 7% for 1 year, 1.4% per year for a 5-year holding period, and 0.7% for a 10-year holding period.

Though investors can save substantial amounts of money on transactions costs by employing a buy-and-hold policy, most of them have a difficult time accepting such a policy. When their investments start dropping in price, they want to sell out in order to avoid imagined future losses. Or if they decide to hold their stocks and then suffer a substantial loss, they become determined to get out once prices recover. Or if their stocks go up rapidly, they sell them to "protect" their gains and then reinvest the money in other stocks. Or they buy and sell in the hopes of getting in at the lows and selling at the highs. All these actions appear somewhat ridiculous in the light of the efficient-market concept.

According to the efficient-market concepts, stocks are priced fairly in that they are neither too high nor too low on average. The current price of any stock traded in a generally efficient market reflects almost all that is known about the company, the economy, etc. That price is the consensus of opinion of numerous knowledgeable shareholders and potential market participants. Anyone who buys or sells solely because of a belief that the current price is to high or too low is betting against the market. And the evidence on the efficient market indicates that such bets seldom pay off.

Since frequent buying and selling does not improve investment performance, every investor should consider adopting a buy-and-hold policy in order to reduce transactions costs. Of course, some individuals will ask why they should invest their money in stocks or other investments if they never plan to sell them at a profit. The answer is that taking a profit on a stock or other investment and then reinvesting the funds elsewhere does not make that profit any more real than it was before the sale. People invest in order to be able to spend money in the future. With a buy-and-hold policy, the odds are that they will have more to spend when they finally do sell than they would have had with a policy of actively buying and selling investments.

Proper Timing of Orders

There is another way for small investors to reduce their commission costs. By placing their orders infrequently, they can accumulate enough money to be able to purchase larger dollar amounts of stock. For instance, an investor who follows a plan of buying 10 shares of a $10 stock every month from a broker pays commissions of $10 on this $100 investment. If instead the money is placed in the bank and then 30 shares are bought at the end of 3 months, commissions total only $19. They would have been $30 if 10 shares had been bought for each of 3 months in a row. If the person waits 10 months in order to buy a full 100 shares, the commission is only $33 compared with the $100 it would have been under a monthly purchase plan—an annual reduction of $67 in commission costs.

Small investors buying or selling shares in odd lots suffer from another handicap. They must pay a one-eighth-point differential to an odd-lot dealer for each share. This differential is added to the effective purchase price and taken off the selling price. For instance a person buying five shares at $20 per share would actually pay $20\frac{1}{8}$ per share. If these shares were sold for $20 each, the investor would get only $19\frac{7}{8}$ per share. This cost is in addition to brokerage commissions. The only way investors can eliminate this odd-lot differential is by placing orders for round lots. Investors should also give careful consideration to buying high-priced shares in order to save on commissions. As a rule, a larger commission per dollar invested is paid on low-priced shares than on high-priced shares.

Listed versus Over-the-Counter Shares

It has already been mentioned that transactions costs consist of more than the brokerage commission. The bid-ask spread on securities is especially important. The bid-ask spread is stated explicitly for over-the-counter stocks—it is usually at least one-half of a point regardless of the price of the stock. The bid-ask spread is not stated explicitly for stocks traded on organized exchanges, but it does exist. It is the price charged by the specialist for standing ready to buy and sell immediately. Because of the greater size and efficiency of the exchanges, this difference between the buying and selling price is probably smaller for stocks traded on the exchanges than for over-the-counter stocks. Therefore, any investor trying to choose between two stocks with equal potential—one listed on the NYSE or AMEX and one traded over the counter—should reduce costs by buying the stock traded on the organized exchange.

Stocks traded over the counter should be purchased only when they can be held for a long time or if there is reason to believe they offer above-average returns. If over-the-counter stocks are purchased, every attempt should be made to select only higher-priced stocks, since the bid-ask spread is a smaller percentage of the share price, again because of those fixed costs. For example, on February 26, 1975, the bid-ask prices on Dairy Queen were $3^{1}/_{4}$ and 4. On Pabst Brewing they were $26^{1}/_{8}$ and $26^{3}/_{8}$. The markup or bid-ask spread on Dairy Queen shares was greater than that on Pabst, despite the fact that Pabst shares sell for almost 8 times the price of Dairy Queen. As a result, investors who bought Dairy Queen paid 10 times as much in dealer's fees as investors who bought an equal dollar amount of Pabst. This is shown in Table 16-3.

Although the bid-ask spread does not change much with share prices, it does vary with the activity of the stock. If the stock is actively traded and there are a large number of shares outstanding, the bid-ask spread will be lower than if the stock is infrequently traded. This is simply a reflection of the fact that the over-the-counter dealer can lower the markup on each share as volume increases, since the dealer's merchandise (shares of a particular stock) sits on the shelves for less time. At the same date that the bid-ask on Pabst was $26^{1}/_{8}$–$26^{5}/_{8}$, the bid-ask on Kansas City Life Insurance was $26^{1}/_{2}$–$27^{1}/_{2}$, a markup of one full point on each share. To see why this was so, one need only look at the number of shares sold on that day—47,700 of Pabst and 600 of Kansas City Life Insurance. As in

TABLE 16-3   COSTS OF BUYING OVER-THE-COUNTER STOCKS

Stock	Buying Price, $	Selling Price, $	Bid-Ask Spread, $	Spread per $1 Invested, $ *
Dairy Queen	$3^{1}/_{4}$	4	.75	.188
Pabst Brewing	$26^{1}/_{8}$	$26^{5}/_{8}$	.50	.0188

* Based on buying price.

the case of supermarkets, the greater the volume, the lower the markup or bid-ask spread on the merchandise.

Special Accounts

There are other ways for investors to reduce the commissions they pay. Small investors can participate in special discount plans offered by several brokers. For instance, Merrill Lynch, Pierce, Fenner, and Smith has a "Sharebuilder Plan" for individuals investing less than $5,000 at any one time. The Sharebuilder Plan permits the purchase of fractional shares (for example, a person can buy $3^1/_2$ shares of a stock) and also provides for automatic reinvestment, at no cost, of dividends in the same stock as that paying the dividend. The savings possible with the Sharebuilder Plan range from almost 40% off the regular commission on a $100 order to about 15% off the commission on a $5,000 order. Probably the only disadvantages to the plan are that orders can be placed by mail only (by restricting orders to the mail, the brokerage firm reduces costs) and stocks selling for less than $3 cannot be purchased.

No-Load Mutual Funds

Investors have another alternative. They can buy shares in a no-load mutual fund. There is no sales charge for purchasing shares in such a fund. And because the funds are able to invest large sums of money, they pay much smaller commissions per dollar invested. Of course, since these funds do charge management fees, the investor must balance the reduced commissions against these costs. In addition, many funds turn over their holdings frequently and, as a result, incur greater transactions costs than small investors who buy and hold. This is discussed in Chapter Thirteen. As a general rule, investors who plan to purchase less than several hundred dollars of stock at a time are better off buying shares in a well-managed no-load mutual fund.

Discount Brokerage Plans

For active traders, there is still another way to reduce commission costs. **Discount brokerage firms**—sometimes called discounters, boutiques, or unbundled brokerage firms—offer savings of from 20 to 80% on regular brokerage fees. These savings are possible because of the bare-bones operations of the discount brokers. The average discount brokerage firm has no registered representatives, offers no investment advice, and executes trades in the over-the-counter market or in the newer third market rather than on an organized exchange. Most of the discount firms are very small, whether measured in terms of the number of employees, the number of accounts, or the capital invested in these companies.

Even when a discount broker is used, the amount of money invested has an important impact on the possible savings. One discount broker offers a straight 20% reduction on commission charges for any transaction involving up to

$9,999. On larger orders, the reduction is as much as 50% or more. Another discount broker says plainly that "the more money you have to spend, the more you save—like everything else." The small investor saves about 20%, the large investor up to 80%. Another discount brokerage firm requires that customers subscribe to its service. Investors pay a flat fee of at least $250. This covers the commissions on 1,000 shares of stock in a series of up to 10 transactions. Moreover, the transactions can be in different securities, and no limits are placed on the value of the securities. There are several other plans available at this same discount brokerage firm. They are as follows:

Plan	Number of Shares that Can Be Traded	Plan Fee, $	Average Fee per 100 Shares, $	Allowable Transactions
A	1,000	250	25.00	10
B	2,500	525	21.00	25
C	5,000	900	18.00	43
D	10,000	1,600	16.00	76
E	25,000	3,750	15.00	179

Regardless of the type of trade or the plan used, the firm guarantees a savings of at least 30% of regular brokerage commissions.

Despite the reduced commission costs offered by discount firms, most investors continue to use ordinary brokerage firms. There are important reasons for this. First, because of the discounters' small size and relative newness, many investors know little about these firms. Second, some investors prefer to work through salespeople and want the investment advice offered by standard brokerage firms. Third, and probably most important, the discounters do not trade on the organized exchanges, but instead transact in the third market. As a result, the investor may have to pay more or sell for less than would have been possible if the trade had been executed on an organized exchange.

In addition to the discounters, several small brokerage firms with seats on the NYSE offer commission discounts. During 1977, Icahn & Co., Quick & Reilly, Murial Siebert & Co., and Kingsley, Boye & Southwood all advertised substantial reductions in the pre-1975 NYSE fee schedule. But this is a far cry from the widespread discounting expected after fixed commission rates ended in May 1975.

Investment Clubs

Many investors have been encouraged by brokerage firms to form investment clubs as a means of reducing transactions costs. One investor buying $100 of stock pays at least 10% of that amount in commissions. Twenty investors working together in an investment club can combine their money and buy $2,000 of stock. These investors will pay only about 2% for transactions costs. This pooling of funds to buy larger amounts of securities is the same principle as that behind mutual funds. But the investment clubs make it possible for each person to retain some say-so over investment policies as well as providing a social and educational function.

Automatic Dividend Reinvestment and New Issues

Usually the cheapest way to buy merchandise is to purchase it directly from the manufacturer. Shares of stock are no different. Investors who attempt to reduce transactions costs by using mutual funds, discount brokers, or special investment plans offered by regular brokers must still rely on agents. It would probably be cheaper for them to transact directly with the company which issues the shares.

Unfortunately, only one company in the United States, American Telephone and Telegraph, sells securities directly to the general public. But there are numerous companies that sell stock to their own employees through stock purchase plans. And over 300 companies have **automatic dividend reinvestment (ADR) plans.** With an ADR plan, shareholders can opt to have dividends automatically reinvested for them in additional shares at little or no extra cost. Instead of receiving cash dividends, they simply use the money to purchase new shares.

Offerings of new issues also provide the investing public with the opportunity to buy securities without paying any transactions costs. Usually when a company decides to sell a large number of new shares to the public, it pays all the costs of selling the securities. As a result, the investor acquires shares without paying any commissions.

Direct-purchase plans, special-discount programs available through brokers, and no-load mutual funds make it possible to reduce transactions costs. Even more importantly, they give small investors an opportunity to buy stocks which they might not have purchased otherwise. Many small investors have attempted to open regular brokerage accounts only to find that brokerage firms don't want their business. Although there is seldom an outright rejection of their accounts, a brief discussion with a registered representative can be sufficiently negative to discourage even the most ardent small investor. And perhaps this is the fairest way to treat the small investor, since the costs of investing small amounts of money through a regular brokerage account are such a large percentage of the amount invested.

MINIMUM-COST TRADING STRATEGIES

Despite the evidence supporting the efficient-market concept, some investors still select investment strategies which require frequent trading. These individuals usually base their trades on techniques they believe will either (1) improve their overall market timing or (2) enable them to select individual stocks which are under- or over-valued. No-load mutual funds provide an ideal investment medium for investors who want to concentrate on market timing. Instead of attempting to get into and out of individual stocks as the market moves up and down, the investors simply exchange one no-load mutual fund for another at little or no cost. When they think the market is poised for new highs, they acquire shares in a mutual fund which invests in stocks. When it appears the market will decline, they redeem their shares in the stock mutual fund and buy shares in a fund which invests only in bonds, Treasury bills, savings certificates, and other fixed-dollar investments. Since there is no sales charge on no-load funds and usually no redemption fee, transactions costs are minimized.

Options

No-load mutual funds are of limited use to investors who want to actively trade individual stocks. But these investors can probably reduce their commission costs substantially by trading options on the stocks rather than the stocks themselves. An option gives an individual the right to buy or sell a stock at a specific price within a fixed period of time. In effect, an investor gains all the advantages of owning the stock by buying an option on that stock.

The commissions on options traded on the Chicago Board Options Exchange are shown in Table 16-4. Since options sell for substantially less than the actual stock, the commissions that must be incurred are also less than the commissions on stocks. For example, a May 70 option on 100 shares of Coca-Cola cost $850 on February 16, 1977. On that same day, shares of Coke sold for $77³/₄, so that 100 shares of Coke cost $7,775. The commission on the option equaled $23.05; the commission on the shares amounted to $80.73, or more than 3 times as much money. Any investor planning to buy and sell Coke during a 3-month period can save a substantial amount in commissions by buying and selling stock indirectly through the use of options. If the stock goes up, the option does too; so the option can be sold for a profit. There is no need to ever buy the stock.

TABLE 16-4   STANDARD COMMISSIONS ON CBOE OPTIONS

Money Involved, $	Commission
Single Option for 100 Shares	
Less than 2,500	1.3% of money involved + $12
2,500 or more	0.9 of money involved + 12
Several Options in One Order	
Less than 2,500	1.3% of money involved + $12
2,500 up to 20,000	0.9 of money involved + 22
20,000 or more	0.6 of money involved + 82

Plus $6 commission for each of the first 10 options bought or sold in one order and $4 for each option over 10.

TABLE 16-5   COMPARISON OF STOCK AND OPTION TRADES

Stock	Price, $	Round-Trip Commission, $	Option	Price, $	Round-Trip Commission, $
AT&T	65	161.46	April 55	$10^{1}/_{8}$	50.32
Atlantic Richfield	57	161.46	April 45	$12^{3}/_{8}$	56.18
Fluor	$34^{3}/_{4}$	127.46	April 30	5	37.00
Homestake	39	136.80	April 25	14	60.40
International Harvester	$31^{3}/_{4}$	120.86	April 25	$6^{3}/_{4}$	41.56
Safeway	$49^{1}/_{4}$	159.36	March 45	$4^{1}/_{4}$	35.06

Investors attempting to reduce commission costs by trading options rather than stocks need to remember that:

1   The risk-return characteristics of options differ from those for stocks.
2   Not all option prices move in an exact 1-to-1 relationship with stock prices. As a general rule, investors following this trading strategy should buy in the money options with near-term expiration dates. These options provide the same price movement as the underlying stocks.

Table 16-5 shows a sample of the trades available on February 16, 1977. For example, the investor wishing to buy and sell Safeway stock within a 4-week period could have bought the March 45 option instead of the stock and saved nearly $125 in commissions (more if the option expired worthless). By the same token, anyone trading Homestake over a 2-month period should have dealt in the options rather than the stock. The difference in the commissions amounted to $76.

By going the option route, traders saved more than $100 in commissions on Atlantic Richfield. But they sacrificed $37.50 in premiums, because the exchange value of the April 45 options equaled only $12, not $12³/₈. Actually the interest earned on the surplus funds left over from the option purchase probably more than made up for this loss. And the option transaction involved less risk than the outright purchase of the stock.

COSTS OF BUYING AND SELLING OTHER INVESTMENTS

Buying and selling costs are often much larger for other types of investments than stocks. For instance, an investor who decides to auction off art or antiques will probably have to pay the auctioneer 20 to 25% of the sales price. And a landowner who attempts to sell a $40,000 tract of land will usually pay from 7 to 10%

of the sales price, or, in this case $2,800 to $4,000 in commissions. If instead this person had bought and sold 1,000 shares of a $40 stock, the commissions would have totaled about $900, or 2.3% of the $40,000. On the other hand, some transactions costs are even lower than those on stocks. Anyone buying and selling $40,000 of corporate bonds through a broker would probably pay $15.00 for each $1,000 bond bought and sold, or $600 in total. The commissions on the bonds as a percent of the investment are about $1^1/2\%$.

The transactions costs of most investments, unlike those for stocks and bonds, are seldom stated explicitly. Usually, these costs are simply added to the purchase price. For instance, individuals who invest in diamonds buy at retail prices and sell at wholesale prices. Since the markup on diamonds often exceeds 100%, the transactions costs can be enormous. A person who pays $400 for a diamond will be lucky to get $200 for it a month later. But because the transactions cost is included in the price, that fact will seldom become known until the diamond is sold.

Government Savings Bonds

Even the United States government charges the investor buying and selling costs. With government savings bonds, these costs take the form of a price penalty for surrendering the bond before the maturity date. Series-E savings bonds cannot even be redeemed within 2 months of the purchase date. If these bonds are redeemed between 2 and 6 months after purchase, the investor gets back exactly what was paid—but not 1¢ of interest. If the bonds are held for a year, the redemption value is so low that only a 4.54% return is earned on the bond, despite the government's claim that the bonds yield 6%. The longer the bond is held before being redeemed, the closer the return comes to being 6%. The complete schedule of redemption values, together with the annual rate of return earned by holding the bonds is given in Table 16-6.

The government does not provide the buyer of Series-E bonds with this redemption table, and no mention is made in government savings bond advertisements of the possible loss associated with redeeming bonds before they mature. Since the investment costs are buried in these redemption figures, it seems likely that very few investors recognize the costs of early redemption and the importance of holding their savings bonds until maturity. This might be all right if most people bought and held savings bonds for the full 5 years. But a recent Congressional study reveals that 43% of all savings bonds are cashed in before the 5 years have passed.

Series-E bonds have one other unique but unpublicized feature. The person cashing in bonds loses nearly 6 months' interest by redeeming the bonds on the wrong day. It can be seen from Table 16-6 that redemption values increase only once every 6 months. Those who redeem a $10,000 savings bond after owning it for 364 days will receive $7,640. By waiting 1 more day, so that a full year has passed, they will collect $7,844, or $204 more. But the greatest 1-day difference occurs in the last 6-month period. A bondholder who unknowingly cashes in a

TABLE 16-6 REDEMPTION VALUES AND RATES OF RETURN ON SERIES-E BONDS BEARING ISSUE DATES BEGINNING DECEMBER 1, 1973

Period (Years and Months after Issue)	Issue Price, $ — Denomination, $								Approximate Investment Yield (Annual Percentage Rate)		
	18.75 / 25.00	37.50 / 50.00	56.25 / 75.00	75.00 / 100.00	150.00 / 200.00	375.00 / 500.00	750.00 / 1,000.00	7,500.00 / 10,000.00	From Issue Date to Beginning of Each Half-Year Period	From Beginning of Each Half-Year Period to Beginning of Next Half-Year Period	From Beginning of Each Half-Year Period to Maturity
	Redemption Values during Each Half-Year Period, $ (Values Increase on First Day of Period)										
0-0 to 0-6	18.75	37.50	56.25	75.00	150.00	375.00	750.00	7,500.00	—	3.73	6.00
0-6 to 1-0	19.10	38.20	57.30	76.40	152.80	382.00	764.00	7,640.00	3.73	5.34	6.25
1-0 to 1-6	19.61	39.22	58.83	78.44	156.88	392.20	784.40	7,844.00	4.54	5.00	6.37
1-6 to 2-0	20.10	40.20	60.30	80.40	160.80	402.00	804.00	8,040.00	4.69	4.98	6.57
2-0 to 2-6	20.60	41.20	61.80	82.40	164.80	412.00	824.00	8,240.00	4.76	5.24	6.83
2-6 to 3-0	21.14	42.28	63.42	84.56	169.12	422.80	845.60	8,456.00	4.86	5.39	7.15
3-0 to 3-6	21.71	43.42	65.13	86.84	173.68	434.20	868.40	8,684.00	4.95	5.53	7.59
3-6 to 4-0	22.31	44.62	66.93	89.24	178.48	446.20	892.40	8,924.00	5.03	5.92	8.29
4-0 to 4-6	22.97	45.94	68.91	91.88	183.76	459.40	918.80	9,188.00	5.14	6.09	9.48
4-6 to 5-0	23.67	47.34	71.01	94.68	189.36	473.40	946.80	9,468.00	5.25	12.93	12.93
5-0*	25.20	50.40	75.60	100.80	201.60	504.00	1,008.00	10,080.00	6.00	—	—

* Maturity value reached at 5 years and 0 months after issue.

$10,000 savings bond 1 day before the 5 years ends receives $9,468. One day later the bond would have been worth $10,080.00—a difference of more than $600. Judging from the figures in Table 16-6, the best time to redeem a bond is the first day of the new 6-month period.

Savings Accounts and Certificates

Series-E bonds, of course, are not the only investment which pays higher returns if held for a long period of time. The same is true of savings accounts at banks and savings and loan associations. These institutions incur considerable costs by constantly accepting deposits and paying out money. The fewer times that such transactions are made in an account, the lower the costs of maintaining the account. In order to offset the costs associated with deposits and withdrawals, banks and savings and loan associations pay low interest rates on short-term accounts and higher interest rates on long-term accounts. During 1976, many savings and loans paid 5.25% on passbook accounts which could be added to or withdrawn from at any time. At the same time, these savings and loans offered the following returns on long-term accounts:

Stated Return	Type of Account	Actual Return*
5.75	90–day account	5.91
6.50	1–year maturity	6.72
6.75	2¹/₂–year maturity	6.98
7.50	4–year maturity	7.79
7.75	6–year maturity	8.06

* The actual return reflects the compounding of interest.

Since the higher yields on long-term accounts reflect reduced transactions costs, frequent withdrawals from these accounts would defeat the whole purpose of having such accounts. For that reason, savings and loans and banks impose substantial penalties for early withdrawals. In particular, the first 3 months' interest is lost and the accounts are then credited with the lowest interest paid by the institution—that on passbook accounts—for the remaining time they were held. Obviously, careful planning is necessary even with savings deposited in banks and savings and loans.

Transactions costs have still another effect on the interest rates paid on savings accounts. The government permits savings and loans to pay one-quarter of 1% more on deposits than banks pay. This difference is presumably a reflection of the fact that many investors find it easier to deposit money in a bank at which they have their checking account; i.e., they incur lower costs by using a bank rather than a savings and loan. In order to offset this advantage, the regulatory authorities have allowed savings and loans to pay slightly higher rates.

Life Insurance

No discussion of the costs of buying and selling investments would be complete without some mention of life insurance costs. There are three principle types of life insurance—straight life, endowment, and term. Only term insurance is pure life insurance. Both straight life and endowment include a savings element as well as protection. This savings element is referred to as the cash surrender value and is explained in detail in Chapter Fourteen. The combination of a savings element with protection in the same insurance policy makes it difficult to break down the true cost of the protection and the actual return being earned on savings. And most insurance companies fail to disclose price information which would help the prospective purchaser of insurance. As a result, several state commissioners of insurance and members of the United States Congress have taken an active role in unraveling these costs. The results of their investigations have been widely publicized.

Probably one of the most surprising findings was the size of the commissions received by insurance salespeople. Although commissions vary widely from company to company, most insurance firms pay their sales personnel at least 100% of the first year's premium. Since the premium on a $10,000 straight life policy for a thirty-five-year-old male averages about $230, the commission on such a policy would be at least $230. Insurance firms usually spread this commission out over a 5-to-10-year period, with only part of the commission paid out in the first year. A typical pattern of fees is 55% of the annual premium in the first year, 10% in the second through the fifth years, and then 2% in the sixth through the twentieth years. Like any other sales charge, this money is lost by the investor.

The salesperson is not the only one who receives a commission on insurance sales. Many insurance firms have general agents who supervise sales in a particular region of the country and who receive a commission on every policy sold in the region.

The commissions on term insurance have not been mentioned yet. Since term insurance contains no savings element, it is not an investment in the usual sense of the word. But term insurance, together with an independent savings program, is often suggested as an alternative to straight life or endowment insurance. Term commissions are generally much lower than the commissions on either straight life or endowment insurance. Commissions paid in the first year average about 35% of the first year's premium. Usually 5% is paid in the second through the fifth years and nothing in the later years. Thus, term commissions consume a much lower percentage of the premium. In addition, the initial premium on a term life insurance policy is much less than the premium on a straight life insurance policy with the same face value. A twenty-five-year-old who buys a $10,000 straight life policy will pay about $180 a year for the policy, but would pay only $50 in the first year for a term policy. The insurance agent would probably get about $180 in commissions for the straight life policy, but only $28 for the term policy.

Tax Shelters

Higher average incomes and the increasingly severe tax burden have led many investors to seek out tax-sheltered investments. They have not had far to look. Garden-apartment projects have been heavily promoted in many states, and most securities salespeople at brokerage houses know of at least one oil-drilling venture or cattle-feeding and/or -breeding partnership which they will recommend. Despite this widespread interest in tax shelters, investors show little awareness of the large costs sometimes associated with tax shelters. By law, tax-sheltered investments sold in more than one state must be registered with the Securities and Exchange Commission. Anyone buying shares in these tax shelters must also be provided with a prospectus describing the security being offered.

A prospectus for the Hanover Drilling Program provides a good example of the cost of investing in a tax shelter. Like most tax shelters, Hanover is organized as a limited partnership, so that individual investors can write off losses on their own income tax returns. The limited partners are the ordinary investors. They take no part in managing the partnership. Instead, all operations are handled by the general partner, which is either an individual or a company.

Hanover Planning, a subsidiary of the company operating the drilling program, sells shares in the program. Hanover Planning receives a cash commission of $8^1/2\%$ of the value of the shares sold to the limited partners. Although this commission is not paid directly by the limited partners, it is paid indirectly in the form of a management fee of 10%, which is collected by the general partner during the first 4 months of partnership operations. In addition, the limited partners must pay all expenses associated with the offering of shares in the program.

There are no explicit costs for selling partnership shares in most tax shelters, probably because the sale of shares is usually restricted. One of the conditions the Treasury Department has set for a tax shelter to qualify as a limited partnership is that investors' interests not be freely transferable. Most limited partnerships satisfy this requirement by completely prohibiting the sale of a partner's interest until some future date. For example, the Hanover Drilling prospectus states that there will be no market for the shares during the first 3 years. At the end of 3 years of operations, the general partner agrees to purchase up to 20% of the shares outstanding. According to the prospectus, the purchase price of these shares will be computed by a formula which "might well represent an amount less than the fair value of the property interests underlying the Units."

Gold, Art, Antiques, and Coins

During times of unexpected inflation, investors owning art, antiques, gold, silver, and stamps, and other "real" investments often realize enormous returns. For example, in the 3-year period from 1972 to 1974, gold bullion more than quadrupled in price, going from approximately $40 an ounce to more than $180 an ounce. Certain gold coins widely sought after by collectors did even better—they increased by 800%. And the increases in the prices of art, antiques, and silver coins were no less phenomenal. For example, between 1970 and 1973, eighteenth-century British art doubled in value, Italian baroque and eighteenth-century art increased by 250%, and seventeenth-century Dutch and Flemish art tripled. Lured on by these high returns and frightened by the possibility of runaway inflation, many investors decided to invest at least part of their savings in one or more real investments. Unfortunately, most investors have little or no knowledge of the large costs which are often associated with this type of investment.

United States citizens have been permitted to own gold bullion since December 1974. Gold can be bought in many sizes, ranging from a 1-ounce wafer to the 40-ounce gold bars traded on the metal exchanges. Most of the brokerage firms that sell gold charge a commission of 12%. Banks often sell gold for less than that—about 7%. But the commission costs are not the only costs of buying gold. There is also a markup on smaller purchases. A 40-ounce gold bar might sell for a price of $7,200, or $180 an ounce, whereas a 1-ounce bar will sell for $193. The commissions on silver are similar. The individual who invests in gold and silver may do better by buying coins instead of bullion. No explicit commission is charged on most coins. Instead, the coin dealer makes a profit on the spread between buying and selling prices.

Art and antiques can be bought and sold at auctions or through a dealer. Auctioneers usually receive about 25% of the proceeds. However, for large sales of more than $25,000, commissions go as low as 12 1/2%. The art collector who sells a collection through a dealer pays a much higher price. As a rule, dealers get about 40% of the asking price.

There is an additional cost to buying and selling investments such as art, antiques, and bullion. Many states have sales taxes, which are assessed on all merchandise bought by residents of the state. As an example of these sales taxes, any California resident buying a painting would pay the state a tax of 5% of the price. On the other hand, a resident of Montana would pay no sales tax.

TRANSACTIONS COSTS AND HOLDING PERIODS

Some investments have high buying and selling costs associated with them, whereas others have low costs. As a rule, investments which have high transactions costs also have higher returns when held for long periods of time. In a sense, these higher returns reimburse investors for the additional transactions costs. On the other hand, investments which have low transactions costs provide lower returns in the long run. The most extreme example of this is a checking account. There is almost no cost to depositing or withdrawing money from a checking account, but any money kept in such an account normally earns no return.

Because of transactions costs, investors can make much greater profits on their investments by planning ahead. Advance planning is necessary because there is usually a trade-off between flexibility and rates of return. Investments that must be held for long periods of time generally pay higher rates of return. But if a long-term investment is sold after only a short period of time, substantial transactions costs are incurred and the returns are less than could have been earned on a short-term investment.

One example of the trade-off between flexibility and returns is a 6-year savings certificate issued by a bank or savings and loan association. A 6-year certificate yields nearly 3% a year more than a passbook account. As a result, savers collect nearly 60% more interest income each year on the certificates. And the difference becomes even more dramatic if this interest is reinvested over a long period of time. An investment of $1,000 in 6-year certificates grows to $25,339 in 42 years. The same $1,000 invested in a passbook account at 5% grows to only $7,762 at the end of 42 years. However, a 6-year certificate does have one marked disadvantage. The investor's funds are immobilized for 6 years. Early withdrawal of this money results in the loss of 3 months' interest, and only the passbook rate is earned for the remainder of the time that the money was on deposit.

Many people have missed the opportunity to earn high returns on their money because they have overlooked long-term investments such as savings certificates, stocks, art, and real estate. On the other hand, numerous investors have incurred substantial costs because they were forced to liquidate these same investments after holding them for only short periods of time. Both groups of investors could have reduced their transactions costs and increased their returns by planning their investments more carefully. Investors should always attempt to determine for how long their money can be kept invested. This can be done by forecasting future cash receipts and expenditures and giving careful consideration to certain personal factors. Both of these topics are discussed in Chapters Eighteen and Nineteen. The expected length of time that an investor's money can be tied up is called the **expected holding period.** Once both the expected holding period and transactions costs are known, an appropriate investment strategy can be determined.

For example, a couple may be considering the purchase of a home. Future cash receipts are believed to be more than sufficient to meet all expenditures. But there is a good possibility that they will have to move to another city in 3 years. Therefore, the expected holding period for the home is approximately 3 years. The typical costs of buying and selling a home are shown in Table 16-7. Although these costs vary from one area of the country to another, the total transactions costs on a home usually equal about 9% of the price. After considering all the costs of owning a home, the cost of renting a similar home, and the expected increase in home prices, the couple decides to rent. This is consistent with the general rule of thumb that a house must be owned for at least 3 years just in order to recover transactions costs.

TABLE 16-7   TYPICAL COSTS OF BUYING AND SELLING A $75,000 HOME*

Item	Paid by Buyer, $	Paid by Seller, $
Broker's commission (6% of sales price)		4,500.00
Loan origination fee (1% of loan)	600.00	
Loan discount (1¹/₂% of loan)	900.00	
Credit report	18.50	
Photos	10.00	
Closing fee	15.00	15.00
Document preparation	30.00	40.00
Title insurance	30.00	405.00
Recording fees	13.50	2.50
Survey	65.00	
Pest inspection		15.00
Home inspection	60.00	
Total costs	1,742.00	4,977.50

* Purchased in Dallas, Texas in 1977 with a $15,000 down payment.

TRANSACTIONS COSTS AND INVESTMENT ADVICE

Transactions costs have another important effect on the investor's behavior. They often result in the investor being sold the wrong type of investment. Obviously, a salesperson has no incentive to sell no-load mutual funds. Only load funds pay a commission. As a result, any visitor to a brokerage office will find stacks of prospectuses on different investment companies. But all these mutual funds have one thing in common—they are load funds. For the same reason, almost every financial planning firm and salesperson for such a firm will do their best to recommend a load mutual fund. Whether or not the fund satisfies the objectives of the investor often receives only a secondary consideration.

The same is true of insurance. Since insurance salespeople make much larger commissions on straight life insurance than they do on term insurance, they usually make every attempt to sell a straight life policy rather than a term policy. This has been shown time and again in studies conducted by consumers' magazines. In most of these studies, several "average" households discuss their insurance needs with insurance salespeople and ask for recommendations. Almost invariably, each salesperson recommends the purchase of straight life insurance, even though term insurance is much better suited to the family's needs.

The behavior of mutual fund and insurance salespeople is in no way unique, of course. Most financial advice is provided by people who earn a commission on the sale of a particular type of investment. No matter how conscientious they are, these sales personnel face a fundamental conflict of interest. Their goals seldom coincide completely with the goals of their clients and/or customers. As a result, it is only natural to expect them to occasionally sacrifice their customer's welfare for their own.

For these reasons, investors would do well to follow a few simple rules. The first rule is to recognize the ever-present conflict of interest which exists when anyone provides advice and also earns commissions on the investments that are bought or sold on that advice. The second and third rules follow from the first. The second rule is that only the investor can be entrusted with the determination of her or his own investment strategy. The third rule is that every investor should rely on independent financial advice whenever possible.

In conclusion, there is nothing wrong with the present system of investment sales and advice. Nor is there anything reprehensible in the behavior of investments salespeople. The system can and does work well—if the investor is well informed. If the investor is not well informed, it is difficult to conceive of any system that will perform completely satisfactorily.

SUMMARY

According to Simon Ramo, author of *Extraordinary Tennis for the Ordinary Tennis Player,* the secret to winning can be summed up in two words—not losing. Ramo has assembled detailed statistics on thousands of tennis games to support his point of view. Judging from these figures, amateur tennis players are seldom defeated by their opponents. Instead, they beat themselves by aggressively hitting the ball out of the court or into the net. For this reason, Ramo concludes that anyone who wants to win at tennis should play a steady game and eliminate as many mistakes as possible. The player who follows this strategy usually wins because the opponent makes more errors.

It appears that investors, like tennis players, often beat themselves. There seems to be no other explanation for the continued failure of so many people. Investors have every opportunity to take part in a "fair game" when they invest their money. It is fair for two reasons. First, they can buy stocks, bonds, and other securities which are traded in generally efficient markets. Since the prices of these securities reflect nearly all available information, the average person cannot be "beaten" by other investors who have more expertise or knowledge. Second, the returns on investments have been positive over long periods of time. In fact, substantial profits could have been made on stocks, real estate, art, and other investments during the last 20, 30, 40, and more years. So the secret to a winning investment strategy must be simply not losing.

One way for an investor to stop losing and start winning is to recognize the importance of transactions costs. Transactions costs should be minimized whenever possible. Numerous techniques for reducing the costs of buying and selling stocks, bonds, and other investments have been described in this chapter.

KEYWORDS

perfect market
round trip
fixed costs

discount brokerage firms
automatic dividend rein-
    vestment (ADR) plans

expected holding
    period

QUESTIONS

1   Use Table 16-2 to calculate the round-trip commission on 100 shares bought and sold at $20 a share.
2   Why are some of the costs of transacting fixed? How do fixed costs affect the small investor's chances of making a quick profit? How about a quick loss?
3   What other transactions costs are there for stocks besides commissions?
4   A buy-and-hold strategy spreads fixed costs over a long period of time. How does this help the investor?
5   A small investment club buys $200 of stock every month. Suggest a more appropriate investment strategy for the club. Where can the club treasurer invest the funds in between stock purchases?
6   Why do the bid-ask spreads vary on over-the-counter stocks?
7   How can special accounts and no-load mutual funds reduce transactions costs?
8   Do discount brokerage firms offer much promise for small investors? Who do you think should patronize these firms? Why?
9   Options provide an excellent means of reducing stock trading costs. Describe a trading strategy based on options. Answer the following criticisms of this strategy: (1) Option commissions are very high as a percent of the amount invested, and (2) the investor usually loses money on option trades.
10 Look at the rates of return on government savings bonds held for different periods of time. Judging from these returns, what are the costs of buying and selling a bond? (Hint: How much money do you sacrifice by cashing the bond prematurely?)
11 The rates of return on savings certificates differ greatly depending upon their maturity. Do you feel all this difference is caused by transactions costs? (Hint: Does the government in any way regulate these rates?)
12 How do the commissions on straight life and term insurance differ?
13 Tax shelters often turn into tax traps because of transactions costs. Discuss these costs.
14 Rank the following investments with regard to transactions costs: stocks, bonds, real estate, art, and gold.
15 How do transactions costs affect the desired holding period of an investment?
16 Debate the following statement: Investors should never take advice from those who benefit from their purchases and sales.

REFERENCES

Acheson, Alex: "How to Find Your Blue Chip Home," *D Magazine*, January 1977, pp. 75–87.
Dreyfus, Patricia A.: "A Better Break for the Small Investor," *Money*, March 1976, pp. 41–43.

Ellis, Charles D.: "The Loser's Game," *Financial Analysts Journal,* July–August 1975, pp. 19–26.

Fredman, Albert: "'Discount' Broker Tells How It's Done," *The Media General Financial Weekly,* Dec. 23, 1974, p. 4.

———: "'Discounters' Open Way to Third Market," *The Media General Financial Weekly,* Dec. 16, 1974, p. 4.

"How Do Brokers Treat the Small Investor?" *Changing Times: The Kiplinger Magazine,* July 1973, pp. 25–28.

Ramo, Simon: *Extraordinary Tennis for the Ordinary Tennis Player,* Crown, New York, 1970.

The Source Book of Base Commission Tables, Source Securities Corporation, New York, 1976.

U.S. Department of Housing and Urban Development, *Settlement Costs,* Washington, D.C., May 1975.

CHAPTER SEVENTEEN

OTHER INVESTMENT COSTS

I n a perfectly efficient market, only one price can exist for any one investment at a single point in time, and that price reflects everything known about the investment. In less efficient markets, prospective buyers and sellers often confront different prices for the same investment. A $100,000 term insurance policy will cost some people $240 a year. Others who are either less fortunate or less informed will pay nearly twice as much for a similar policy. And the quality of the investment can also vary substantially. In 1974, $1,000 could have been used to buy a high-quality corporate bond. Or the investor might have purchased a bond in a fraudulent Florida land operation.

Finding the lowest price and/or the highest quality takes time and effort. This time and effort constitute a very real but often ignored cost of investing. Moreover, there are a multitude of other investment costs. Antiques, art, Scotch, wine, diamonds, commodities, and numerous other investments must be stored somewhere, and most people insure them against theft or damage. Although storage and insurance costs seldom amount to much in the short run, they can become a burden over the years. In addition, appraisal fees must often be paid when buying or selling more exotic investments. Finally, there are management fees. Real estate, cattle, and oil properties all require time and/or talent. As a result, many investors pay someone to manage these investments.

TIME

The old saying that time is money has never been truer than today. Every hour spent seeking out and evaluating investments represents lost income. This loss is most obvious for business and professional people. They can earn additional income for every hour they work, almost without limit. As a result, every hour devoted to investments reduces the incomes earned in their professions.

Even employees on a fixed salary sacrifice income by spending time investing money. These people can devote additional hours to their regular jobs, thereby inviting faster promotions or larger pay raises. Or they can moonlight on a second job or spend time repairing a home, car, or boat for possible resale. Finally, they can reduce costs, perhaps by spending more time shopping for household goods or by commuting further distances to work from a less expensive home in the suburbs or by providing services to the family which might otherwise have been purchased, such as maintenance, financial planning, cooking, etc.

As a result, every hour spent evaluating investments represents a very real cost. This cost is measured by the **opportunity cost** or **alternative cost** of the time. The opportunity cost depends upon what the investors could have done with their time. If they could have worked for $50 an hour, that is the amount forgone by spending time making investments. The higher the salary, the greater the opportunity cost and the more expensive the time.

Prospective investors should give careful consideration to the opportunity cost of their time and select their investments accordingly. A busy doctor who spends 5 hours a week selecting stocks probably forgoes $250 to $500 a week in additional income from his or her practice. Obviously doctors must have very substantial investments in order to justify spending their own time managing them. For the same reason dentists who drive around the countryside buying up vacant land may actually lose money despite their success in selecting good properties.

Some investors devote many hours each month to the stock market. Others completely avoid stocks simply because they are unwilling to spend the time. Still others pay large management fees to investment advisers who assume all the investment duties for them. Apparently, numerous individuals believe that stocks are a complex investment medium requiring considerable time, effort, and knowledge. They are making a serious mistake. The stocks and bonds of large companies trade in generally efficient markets. Both amateurs and experts compete on equal terms in such markets. And there is almost no return on time spent in seeking out undervalued or overvalued investments. Therefore, investors need not spend much time in supervising or managing these stocks and bonds. Investors who have avoided stocks because of the considerable amount of time believed necessary to select appropriate issues should reconsider their positions.

This is not to say that everyone should spend little or no time on their investments. Many stocks and bonds trade in generally efficient markets, so that their prices serve as valid guideposts to their true value. But the stocks and bonds of small, closely held corporations and the bonds of small municipalities trade in less efficient markets. The same is true of real estate, insurance, coins, silver bars, art, antiques, and numerous other investments. The prices of these investments not only differ from place to place; they also differ from investor to investor. And their prices may be very poor indicators of their true value. Some insurance policies sell for 200 to 300% more than other policies offering exactly the same benefits. Or a gold coin may cost $270 at one dealer's and only $250 at another dealer's in the same city. More specialized investments, such as small silver bars, usually vary in price by 10 to 50%. And homes are seldom sold for their asking price. Usually the seller sets the asking price considerably higher than the desired price. Depending upon the timing and bargaining skills of the buyer and seller, the actual sales price can be 10, 15, or even 25% lower than the asking price.

Obviously, some investments require time and effort, and others do not.

THE ECONOMICS OF INFORMATION

The prices and quality of nearly identical investments often vary tremendously. Perhaps the most publicized examples of price variations involve life insurance. But there are very few investments that don't differ in price, depending upon where and from whom they are purchased. The reason that prices and quality differ is a simple one: There are costs to obtaining information. In the absence of these costs everyone would know the exact price and quality of each investment. Eager purchasers would converge on the sellers with the lowest prices and/or best quality. These sellers would almost immediately raise their prices or reduce their quality. At the same instant, other sellers would find their customers deserting them. These sellers would reduce their prices or raise the quality of their goods. The end result would be that only one price would exist for a particular quality of investment and that price would be a fair price.

In reality both buyers and sellers incur costs in obtaining information about prices and quality. For that reason, buyers and sellers seldom know all the price and quality differences in an investment. As a result, different prices exist at the same time for the same investment.

A number of factors determine whether or not an investor gets a bargain or pays too high a price. Chance plays an important role. Just by coincidence some people are in the right place at the right time. Another very important factor is knowledge or education. Merely by knowing that substantial price and quality differences exist, investors improve their bargaining positions and buying techniques. Numerous studies of consumer behavior show a strong tie between education and the price paid for a good. The higher the level of education, the lower the price paid and/or the higher the quality of the good purchased.

Winning and Losing in Inefficient Markets

What separates the winners from the losers in inefficient markets? The winners appear to search more for the lowest prices. Other things being equal, the person who spends the most time looking for investments will get the best price. For some reason many people seem to lose sight of the fact that investments, like any other product, vary in price and quality. The same people who scan the newspaper daily for the best food prices buy the first insurance policy presented to them. Or after only 5 days of looking for homes, they purchase a house. Or they buy a lot for a second home in a part of the country which they have never seen. Or they purchase valuable stamps or coins without attempting to validate the quality of those stamps or coins. Whatever the investment, this failure to search for the best price and quality almost always results in their paying a higher price than necessary. And in some cases fraud is involved.

Costs and Benefits of Search

How much time and effort should investors spend in searching for the best investments? The answer to this question depends upon the cost of searching and the expected benefits. The cost depends upon the value of the investors' time and whether or not they view searching as recreation or work. The higher their hourly salary, the higher their search costs and the less time they should spend looking for investments, other things being equal. An individual who makes $10,000 a year ($5 an hour) can much more easily justify a search for low-priced properties than a person who runs and owns a company and makes $60,000 a year ($30 an hour). Similarly, an individual who really enjoys looking at homes, antiques, or art should spend more time investing in these assets than someone who views traveling from prospective home to home or from store to store as work and not pleasure.

The expected benefits from searching for an investment depend upon how much the prices and quality of that investment vary and upon how much money will eventually be invested. The greater the variation in prices, the better the chance the would-be buyer can save a considerable amount of money. And the more money to be invested, the more important those savings become. A 10% reduction in price saves a person who invests $100 only $10; it saves $5,000 for the person who invests $50,000.

The amount of variation in the price and/or quality of an investment depends upon:

1 The complexity of the investment
2 The size of the average purchase
3 The frequency of the purchase
4 The price volatility of the investment
5 The competitiveness of the sellers
6 The personal characteristics of would-be investors

The more complex the investment, the more difficult (and therefore more costly) it is to evaluate. Probably the most difficult investment for the small investor to evaluate is straight life insurance. An exact evaluation of a straight life policy can be done only with a computer. As a result, substantially identical policies sell for widely different prices.

The size of the average purchase also affects the degree of price variation. The smaller the average purchase, the less it pays to search for the best price or quality. And the less information investors possess about prices, the more those prices vary.

The frequency of purchase has an offsetting effect. The more frequent the purchase, the greater the chance the buyer has to encounter different prices. In addition more frequent purchases increase the total amount invested and justify more search.

The more volatile investment prices are, the more short-lived is any information about prices and the less worthwhile is the search. It does no good to know which coin dealer has the lowest prices in the country at a given moment if coin dealers change their prices every week in a completely arbitrary fashion.

The competitiveness of sellers also affects price variation. As a general rule, competition goes hand in hand with price variation. This may seem contrary to common sense, since the existence of a wide range of prices penalizes some investors and consumers. But price variation usually proves even more detrimental to firms attempting to charge monopolistic prices. Price variation makes it very difficult for firms to police their price-fixing agreement. This in turn provides each seller with the incentive to reduce excessive prices in order to obtain additional business at the expense of other firms. Price-cutting eventually destroys any monopolistic agreement. As a result, price-fixers almost always attempt to establish a single fixed price and/or ban the advertisement of prices. That is why the courts have recently ruled against the fixed-fee schedules of lawyers and other professionals. And it is why the FTC has attacked the medical profession's ban on advertising.

Implications for Investors

The economics of information has some important implications for investors. These implications are as follows:

1   High-income investors should spend relatively little time investing their money since their opportunity costs are so high. They can do this by selecting investments traded in the most efficient markets. The stocks and bonds of large, well-known corporations, the bonds of large tax-exempt borrowers, such as states and cities, options on the stocks of large firms, and futures contracts for important commodities, all trade in generally efficient markets. Therefore, high-income investors would do well to seriously consider these investments. In fact, all investors, no matter what their income, can minimize the time they spend investing their money by following a similar strategy.
2   Individuals who have considerable free time (a low opportunity cost) and/or enjoy bargain hunting will probably make the greatest profit by investing in assets such as real estate, which are traded in less efficient markets.

3   Investors should consider the amount of money they can invest both now and in the future. It does not make much sense to acquire an extensive knowledge about a particular type of investment if the most money that will ever be invested is $1,000. The exceptions to this rule are people who can sell their advice. Would-be experts would probably be wise to specialize in investments which are traded in relatively inefficient markets.

4   Every investor should be aware of the fact that prices and quality can vary considerably at any point in time for different types of investments. The less efficient the market in which the investment is traded, the greater the possible variation and the better the chances that a person will purchase either a bargain or a rip-off.

PRICE VARIATION

If the market for an investment is inefficient, different people will pay different prices for the same type of investment. Straight life insurance probably provides the most striking example of this fact. But prices also vary substantially for real estate, loans, antiques, art, coins, and stamps. The existence of numerous prices at one point in time should not be confused with price variation over time.

Loans on Securities

Price variation exists even for securities loans. Most brokerage firms lend money to their customers to carry securities. The interest rates on these loans vary from firm to firm. One brokerage house charges 2% above the **call loan rate** to brokers. The call loan rate is the interest rate which brokerage firms pay banks for the money they borrow. Another large brokerage house charges $1^1/2\%$ above the call loan rate. A third brokerage company openly publishes the following schedule of interest rates:

Average Daily Debt, $	% Added to Call Money Rate
over 50,000	$^1/_2$
30,000–50,000	1
10,000–29,999	$1^1/_2$
below 10,000	2

Banks often lend money to investors for even less than brokerage firms do. This is not surprising, since banks lend the money to the brokers in the first place. Usually investors can borrow at the call loan rate or at even lower rates from banks where they do business. Over a number of years the difference in the rates charged by some brokerage firms and some banks can amount to thousands of dollars.

Consumer Loans

The rates on consumer loans differ even more dramatically than do loans on securities. According to a 1975 survey, rates on $1,000 secured loans (loans backed by some collateral) varied from a low of 11% to a high of 14% at New Orleans banks. Many of these loans were made as second mortgages or on automobiles. The lowest rate charged by a finance company on a secured loan was 15%, and the highest was 36%. Obviously a little shopping around for the best rates could have saved a borrower a considerable amount of money. Even a 1% reduction in the interest rate paid on a $5,000 loan equals $50. A careful search for the best rates charged for unsecured loans would have produced even greater savings. The best rate charged by a bank for a $1,000 unsecured loan was 14%; the worst rate was 20%. The best rate quoted by a finance company for an unsecured loan was 30%; the worst rate was 60%. While some of these differences can be attributed to the lenders' different perceptions of the riskiness of the borrower, many of these variations simply reflect different pricing policies.

Mortgages

Interest rates on home mortgages also vary from lender to lender but not by as much as other loans. There are two reasons why the difference between the highest and lowest rates quoted by banks and savings and loan associations seldom exceeds 1%. First, mortgages are secured by the home itself as well as by the borrower's down payment; so there is very little risk of loss. Second, home loans usually involve a great deal of money, so that borrowers can be expected to engage in considerable search for the lowest interest rates. A 1% difference in interest rates on a $40,000 mortgage amounts to $400 a year. If a mortgage is paid off over a 30-year period, a 1% reduction in the mortgage rate results in total savings of $12,000. The savings obviously justify at least several days of search by the borrower for the best rate available.

Prospective borrowers looking for the best terms on a home mortgage confront one problem. Many lenders have a separate charge for making the loan in addition to the regular interest payments. Usually the charge for making a loan is expressed in terms of points. One **point** equals 1% of the amount of the loan; two points equals 2% of the loan. If a bank agrees to a mortgage loan of $40,000 with four points, it is asking to be paid 4% of the mortgage, or $1,600, for making the loan. The borrower must pay the $1,600 when the loan agreement is signed and the loan obtained.

The existence of loan charges in the form of points makes it difficult for prospective borrowers to compare the cost of alternative home loans. For example, is an 8% loan with four points better than an 8¹/₂% loan with no points? The answer to such a question is far from obvious. Not only must some detailed calculations be made, but these calculations also depend upon how long the borrower lives in the home and upon his or her tax bracket. The average purchaser of a home sells it after 6.3 years and pays back the mortgage. Given a 20% tax bracket and this duration of the loan, the borrower would be better off taking the $8^1/_2\%$ loan with no points. So interest rates on home loans can be misleading.

House Prices

The home buyer who has the good sense to seek out the lowest mortgage rate will probably have searched carefully for the best-priced house. Prices often differ considerably for substantially identical houses. And to make the quest for value still more challenging, the asking price is seldom identical with the actual sales price. The usual discount from the asking price of a used home is approximately 10%, and it can exceed 25% on more expensive homes. Since sales at the asking price are the exception rather than the rule, the buyer who offers to pay the asking price is usually either naive and/or uninformed. The following is a sample of list prices and actual sale prices for a sample of houses put on sale between 1969 and 1975 in New Orleans:

List Price, $	Actual Price, $	Discount, %
28,500	25,000	12.3
43,500	39,000	10.3
33,750	31,000	8.1
22,000	18,600	15.5
135,000	115,000	14.8
64,000	58,000	9.4
48,500	40,000	17.5
25,000	25,000	0.0
225,000	170,000	24.4
75,000	65,500	12.7
79,500	76,000	4.4

An examination of listings (houses offered for sale by realtors) reveals another very important aspect of investments in real estate. The average time required to sell a home is about 3 months, and many homes take from 6 to 9 months or even longer to sell. As a general rule, the more expensive the home and the more unique the style, the longer it takes to sell. And, of course, the reasonableness of the asking price plays an overwhelmingly important role in how quickly the house sells.

The economics of information provides an explanation of why price, style, and reasonableness have such an important effect on the time required to sell a property. Higher-priced homes and homes with a distinctive style appeal to a smaller number of buyers. For that reason, it takes longer to find a buyer. The reasonableness of the price also affects the number of buyers. The lower the price relative to similar homes, the greater the number of prospective buyers. In fact, the best-priced homes often sell on the first day they are listed. For that reason, knowledgeable home buyers make every attempt to obtain the new listing sheets as soon as they are available. And personal contacts play an important role in the search for undervalued real estate. The old saying that the best farms never leave the county appears to be true. In other words, people who live in the local area snap up the best properties before outsiders even know they are being offered for sale. And the same holds true of houses.

QUALITY VARIATION

Price variation is fairly obvious once the investor is aware that it exists, but quality variations can sometimes be very difficult to detect. As a result, there are numerous instances of fraud. Even in the absence of fraudulent sales practices, many people misjudge the quality of investments and unknowingly pay more than they are worth. Amateur art investors seem especially given to this shortcoming. They often discover famous paintings stuck away in the backs of small shops and buy them at what seem incredibly low prices. After taking their discoveries home and paying an expert to appraise them, they usually find out that the painting is either a forgery or is the work of an authentic but relatively unknown and unvalued painter.

Unfortunately, there is no easy way to learn how to judge quality. Usually, sufficient expertise can be acquired only after thousands of hours of experience in one narrow field of investments. For that reason, people searching for undervalued antiques, art, jewels, or even properties had better be prepared to spend considerable time learning the intricate details of their chosen fields.

Individuals who are content to pay a fair price for these investments have another alternative. They can purchase their investments through reputable dealers and rely primarily on them for assurance of the quality of the investment. Even then, they should attempt to measure the quality of their investments, since well-known dealers have been known to make mistakes and/or act against the best interests of their clients.

Coins

The quality of an investment is obviously very important. But can its importance be measured in dollars and cents? The answer is definitely yes. Coins provide a good example of the close tie between quality and price. Most coin dealers and coin collectors use from six to eight quality ratings for coins: fair, good, very good, fine, very fine, extremely fine, uncirculated, and proof. Proof coins are specially struck for coin collectors and have a mirrorlike surface. Each of the other ratings indicates some degree of wear and tear on the coin. The highest quality nonproof coin is called uncirculated, meaning that it has never been placed in circulation. A price list showing the importance of coin quality to price is presented in Table 17-1.

Prices for the same type of coin differ greatly depending upon its quality. An

TABLE 17-1   COIN QUALITY AND PRICE

	Good, $	Very Good, $	Fine, $	Very Fine, $	Extremely Fine, $	Uncirculated, $
1915 Lincoln cent	.50	1.00	4.00	8.50	18.00	65.00
1921 Lincoln cent	.25	.35	.60	1.50	4.50	21.00
1926-D buffalo nickel	2.00	4.00	8.50	26.00	55.00	320.00
1931 mercury dime	.75	1.25	2.00	3.00	6.50	45.00
1939-S Washington quarter	2.00	2.50	3.50	NA*	10.00	40.00
1921-S walking Liberty half dollar	15.00	25.00	57.00	70.00	450.00	4,000.00

* NA—not available.

Source: R. S. Yeoman, *The Red Book of United States Coins —1976: A Guidebook of United States Coins,* 29th ed., © 1975 Western Publishing, Inc., Racine, Wisconsin, 1976, pp. 83, 84, 93, 110, 124, and 141.

investor who purchases a very fine 1926-D buffalo nickel pays about 300% more than another investor who selects the next lower quality coin. The physical difference between a fine and a very fine coin is not very substantial. The fine buffalo nickel is described as having two-thirds of the buffalo's horn showing. On the very fine coin the full horn shows.

Stamps

Quality is no less important in stamps. *Scott's Stamp Guide,* probably the most authoritative source of prices for stamps, publishes prices for two grades of stamps. Unused stamps usually sell for a substantial premium over postage stamps which have been canceled. Moreover, the publishers of *Scott's* in the introduction to their guide state that:

> *Condition is the all-important factor of price. Prices quoted are for stamps in fine condition. Slightly defective stamps which are off-center, heavily canceled, faded or stained are usually sold at large discounts. Damaged stamps which are torn or mutilated or have serious defects seldom bring more than a small fraction of the price of a fine specimen.[1]*

Gems, Antiques, and Scotch

Quality is also crucial in other types of investments. The casual investor in diamonds seldom realizes that a tiny flaw in a diamond which cannot even be seen by the naked eye reduces the value of the stone by about 80%. In addition, a stone's color, cut, and brilliance strongly affect its value. Similarly the cost of antique furniture depends greatly upon its patina and its condition. Investors in Scotch whisky who occasionally sample their investment probably know that Scotches not only taste different but also sell at widely varying prices. But the purchaser probably doesn't realize that there are several hundred different distilleries in

Scotland which produce Scotch and that the product of each distillery is not only distinctive but also sells at different prices. Moreover, the length of time that these spirits have been stored affects both their flavor and their value.

Overgrading Investment Quality

The wide variation in prices associated with different grades of investment quality presents a very real danger to uninformed investors. There is a good chance they will purchase investments which have been overrated and by doing so will pay too much. This is apparently not uncommon in coin investing, where some less scrupulous dealers and individuals persistently overgrade the coins they sell. The temptation to describe a 1926-D buffalo nickel as very fine rather than fine is obvious. Buyers who pay a price corresponding to the higher grade may not discover what has happened until years later when they attempt to sell the coins.

There is no completely satisfactory solution to the problem of establishing quality. One way to judge quality is to compare coins with photographs of the different grades of coins to determine if there has been any consistent overgrading. In addition, some of the large dealers will provide repurchase agreements, guaranteeing that they will buy back the coin, or at least will certify the quality of the coin. Finally, the investor may attempt to resell some of the newly purchased coins to other dealers. By doing so, the coin collector not only finds out if the coins were graded correctly but also determines the amount of transactions costs. This eliminates any unpleasant surprises which might arise at a less opportune moment and also prevents a large loss from accumulating over the years. Similar tactics can be used with other types of investments.

FRAUD

In 1975 investigators uncovered an enormous land-fraud scheme based on the sale of Florida property. Although the exact toll remains unknown, swindlers apparently bilked thousands of investors out of as much as $1 billion. Despite the amount of money involved, the fraud was a relatively simple one. A number of small companies sold corporate notes guaranteeing interest of 12 to 14% a year. According to the security salespeople, these notes were backed by first mortgages on valuable Florida real estate.

The high returns were advertised extensively and attracted numerous small investors, many of them retirees desperately trying to live on the interest from their meager investments. Since the inflation rate often exceeded the maximum interest rates paid by banks, the land notes seemed to offer an attractive alternative.

In actuality, the land notes were almost a guaranteed loss. Banks and other financial institutions already held the first mortgages on the property. The land consisted of a central Florida swamp not worth a tenth of the value of the notes. Finally, there was no way for the companies issuing the notes to earn sufficient income to pay the interest. Instead, the proceeds from the sale of new notes went to pay the interest on the old notes and salespeople's commissions and expenses. In addition, the organizers of the companies skimmed off a large part of the funds for themselves.

In retrospect, the Florida land-note fraud followed an easily recognizable pattern. The state of Florida has a long history of land frauds. Miami–Fort Lauderdale, the headquarters of many of the companies selling land notes, has even been called the con artist's capital. One Scotland Yard inspector sarcastically observed that "I don't see how any businessman can give a Fort Lauderdale address and expect to be taken seriously any more."

Like other frauds, an intensive sales effort promising abnormally large returns accompanied the land-note sales. People displayed their usual gullibility by believing that these high returns could be earned with little or no risk. Perhaps every investor in this country should have a reminder tattooed on the back of her or his check-writing hand. It would read as follows: "Warning. The higher the expected return, the greater the risk—no matter what anybody says to the contrary." Any company or salesperson attempting to argue this point can probably be classified as naive, overenthusiastic, or dishonest.

The 1974–1975 recession had a more important role in ending the land-note fraud than did law enforcement agencies. Sales of land notes declined so sharply that the companies were unable to pay the promised interest payments. Only then did investigators seek injunctions to stop the sale of these securities.

In order to bolster sales during the last year, the companies issuing the notes announced that an insurance firm had agreed to guarantee certain transactions. Again, the techniques used to defraud investors were disturbingly familiar. Phony offshore insurance companies, banks, and mutual funds often serve as impressive stage props in swindles. To the financially sophisticated, **offshore** means a place where a business can avoid the commercial restrictions and taxes imposed by most industrialized countries. During the 1960s, the Bahamas, Bermuda, Panama, British Honduras, the British Virgin Islands, and the Netherlands Antilles attracted hundreds of legitimate corporations. Because of the almost complete lack of regulation, these tax havens also became the headquarters of numerous paper empires used by swindlers.

Bank of Sark

The Bank of Sark provides an impressive demonstration of the power of paper corporations to defraud investors. Sark is a dot of land inhabited by 600 people and located in the English Channel. Although officially part of England, Sark qualifies as a tax haven because of its relative independence in setting taxes and commercial laws. Since the people of Sark are law abiding, only one constable resides on the island.

In 1969, a $72.5 million bank, the Bank of Sark, sprang from the island's rocky soil. Forty million dollars of checks drawn on the Bank of Sark were soon accepted by Braniff International Airways, the Dallas Bank and Trust and Mercantile National Bank in Dallas, Southern State Bank of South Houston, South-western Bell Telephone, and many other banks, companies, and individuals. But the Bank of Sark existed solely in the imagination of the swindlers and their victims. Its only assets, other than the impressive bank stationery, were a post office box, a telex, and a rented office in a small building shared by an optician and a hairdresser. The perfect swindle has apparently been committed. Despite the magnitude of the fraud, no one has yet been prosecuted for the crime.

Other Fountain Pen Creations

The power of the pen has become more and more evident during the last 15 years. Hundreds of impressive-sounding but phony corporations and foundations have been created solely on paper. The Baptist Foundation of America, American Fidelity Money Order, Cumberland Insurance Investment Group, Inc., Trans-Continental Casualty Company, and Continental Investment Bankers are but a few of the many fountain pen creations. Each of these concerns supposedly had millions of dollars of assets. In reality almost all their assets existed only on paper.

Take for example the $4.9 million of Tennessee land shown on the books of the Cumberland Insurance Investment Group. The title to the land was based on land grants first issued by the United States government in the 1800s. Tennessee courthouses still register deeds to property on the basis of these land grants, even though the grants are worthless. Jonathan Kwitney, a reporter for *The Wall Street Journal* and author of the *Fountain Pen Conspiracy,* showed how easily anyone can become a land baron overnight. He obtained title to 80,000 acres in Fentress County, Tennessee, for the grand total of $5. His deed is officially registered on page 313 of Book 5-4 of the county land records. For anyone with criminal instincts, the next step is obvious. Value the land described in the phony deed at the going price of $65 an acre and to all intents and purposes become a millionaire. Then borrow money from banks, corporations and investors on the basis of that value, never intending to repay the loans.

Despite the simplicity of this ruse, it has worked many times. One North Carolina bank lent $900,000 on the security of a Tennessee land-grant deed. The title was even authenticated by a nationally known title insurance firm. But the North Carolina bank had to share its ownership with several hundred million people—the land consisted of the publicly owned Great Smoky Mountains National Park.

Corporate-Shell Game

Tennessee land even helped swindlers promote the **corporate-shell** game. A corporate shell is simply the legal remains of a once-active corporation. These corporate shells are as inert as the dried seashells on a beach. All activity has ceased and all that remains are the outstanding shares, a name approved by the SEC and/or a state government, and possibly a tax loss. Because these are valuable attributes, an active market in corporate shells exists. In the hands of a clever swindler, one of these corporate shells can be worth a fortune.

Imaginative con artists breathed life into one corporate shell named EDP Learning Systems. The promoters first injected millions of dollars of paper assets into the company. These assets consisted of (1) closed-down race tracks assigned a value of $5.2 million but worth only $25,000; (2) mining property listed at $2.5 million but never located because of the vagueness of the deed; (3) a deed to 5,000 acres in Imperial Valley, California, based on a Spanish land grant—the property actually consisted of part of a U.S. Army gunnery range; (4) an old claim to 3.5 million acres of offshore land near the Arctic Circle acquired for $10,000 but valued at $31.5 million; and (5) a strange assortment of other imaginary properties and assets. The only thing missing from this list of assets was the official seal of approval from a certified public accountant. In a short time an eager but dishonest CPA was found to provide this approval.

After the infusion of these new "assets," EDP Learning Systems was renamed Picture Island Computer Company, Inc. (The company also owned several drive-in photo kiosks.) Picture Island Computer soon provided further proof that a good salesperson can sell almost anything. The crooks operating the company recruited brokers and market makers around the country. Although some were dishonest, many simply believed the stories they heard and passed them on to their customers. The big lie worked. Prices bounded upward from 10¢ in January 1970 to a high of $11 a share several months later. Numerous investors heard the glowing reports, saw the stock moving up steadily day after day, and bought. Many small businesspeople also sold their companies to Picture Island for shares of stock. Some banks even made secured loans on the basis of shares in Picture Island.

Picture Island ended as it had begun—worthless. Society incurred a high cost for the fraud. But the score or more of swindlers who were involved in the creation and distribution of shares paid almost none of their debt to society. Two of them were sentenced to several months in jail. In that respect, the Picture Island stock fraud resembles the Bank of Sark swindle and most of the other fraudulent schemes that have been foisted on the American public. Nonviolent crime is seldom punished. And, when it is, the sentence is so lenient that con artists are soon back promoting new schemes. Several congressional hearings into crime have revealed that most of the investment frauds in this country are perpetrated by fewer than 500 people. The same names appear repeatedly in injunctions and indictments. Active prosecution and more realistic sentencing of these criminals would eliminate much of the fraud. At the present time, shoplifters are sometimes punished more severely than crooks who steal millions.

Preventing Fraud

Millions of investors have lost billions of dollars in fraudulent investments, proving that no investment market is completely efficient.

The purchaser of land, the buyer of car and life insurance, the investor in securities, the small businessperson, and the banker must all confront this reality. That is the first step in protecting themselves from fraud. There are other actions they can take, but none will guarantee them against all losses. Diversification can at least reduce the seriousness of any one loss. And an awareness of the immutable nature of the risk-return relationship should also help. Anyone who promises to pay a high return with no risk to the investor should immediately be suspect. As we have seen, Ponzi fooled thousands of investors by promising to pay them interest of 50% every 45 days and then doing just that—with their own money—but the efforts of a few die-hard skeptics resulted in his early exposure.

Whenever sizable amounts of money are involved in any investment, some effort should be made to examine the actual physical assets. Paper empires boast almost no real assets. A single trip to Picture Island's closed-down race tracks or to the Bank of Sark's office would have saved people millions of dollars. Many fraudulent investments have another telltale sign—they have almost no past histories as active enterprises. Both the Bank of Sark and Picture Island literally appeared out of nowhere. It may be old-fashioned to do business only with firms that are well established and well known, but it could save money in the long run. There is one final precaution to follow. Bargains, by their very nature, are never extensively advertised. If they were, they would soon cease to be underpriced. Anytime an extensive sales effort is coupled with a supposed bargain, caution is recommended.

It may not be worth the individual investor's time and effort to carefully screen each of many investments, since fraud losses are infrequent and account for only a small percentage of the total money invested. But fraud prevention is justified on a national scale. Investors can help eliminate fraud by demanding stricter penalties for fraud and requesting that a single law enforcement agency be made responsible for the investigation and prosecution of fraud. Many of the con artists operate in different states and countries. Because of overlapping jurisdictions, coordination among law-enforcement agencies has been minimal.

HIDDEN COSTS IN REAL ESTATE

Modern-day fairy tales have tremendous appeal. All that they need is a title like *How I Turned $1,000 into $10,000,000 in My Spare Time.* Despite the seeming sophistication of some of these stories, most are simply updated versions of the old "frog turns into a prince" theme. In the last 10 years the frog has been increasingly cast as undervalued real estate—a dilapidated home, apartment building, trailer court, or commercial property.

The scenario of these real estate fairy tales goes as follows:

1   Investor discovers undervalued property which badly needs improvements. (Frog appears.)

2 Investor undertakes the very unpleasant task of renovating the property. (Princess kisses frog.)
3 Property is transformed into a handsome investment which can be sold for a large profit. (Frog becomes prince.)

There is nothing wrong with fairy tales. Not only are they entertaining, but they also contain much truth. But the modern-day versions usually eliminate or understate the vital link between the frog and the prince. That vital link is the thoroughly unpleasant task of kissing the frog, or renovating the property. Perhaps because property renovation is so unpleasant, the search for the property and its subsequent sale dominate each story. As a result, today's fairy tales are only shallow reproductions of the originals.

Costs of Renovation

The truth is that property renovation done by experts is a costly, time-consuming task. When undertaken by an investor, it is often tedious, sometimes exhausting, and occasionally dangerous. And, of course, there is always the risk that the renovation will not be completely successful.

To see what this can mean to the average investor, assume that a suitably shabby but "undervalued" property has been located. The ad for this particular property describes it as a "handyman's special" needing "TLC." It costs only $40,000, but the yard has been neglected for years, the paint is peeling off the exterior, the interior is in a state of disrepair, and there is no central air conditioning. The investor buys the property, moves the family in, and goes to work immediately. Evenings and weekends are spent scraping paint and toiling in the yard. The entire inside of the house is scrubbed down and the floors sanded. Bids are obtained for central air conditioning, and a suitable unit is eventually selected and installed. A multitude of other improvements are made.

At the end of the year the house looks like new. A "For Sale by Owner" sign is put in the front yard, and an ad is inserted in a newspaper. In 2 months someone appears on the front step and buys the house for $52,000. The investor-renovator realizes an enormous profit of $12,000 on a $8,000 down payment. Right?

Wrong. The profit on the investment is far less than $12,000. Paint, wallpaper, plants, sod, and the central air conditioning cost a total of $5,000. Closing costs and advertising add another $1,000. But the profit is still $6,000 on a $14,000 investment. Right?

Wrong. The investor spent an average of 20 hours a week working on the home and selling it. Over 14 months that amounts to nearly 1,200 hours. Assuming that this person can always make at least $2.50 an hour in a part-time job, $3,000 in income has been sacrificed by working on the home. So the real profit is at most $3,000.

By comparison, a new $65,000 home could have been bought with the $13,000 invested in the renovated home. Because of inflation, all homes increased in value by 5% during the year. So the new home would have appreciated by $3,750—more than was made on the renovation. And the family would have enjoyed a much easier life. Moreover, the new home would have had a 2-year warranty. Fortunately for the investor-renovator, the plumbing in the old home didn't fail, nor was the foundation cracked, etc. Repairing any of these possible defects would have completely eliminated the profit.

Management Costs

Renovations promise extremely high returns over short periods of time. These high returns are questionable. To some extent the returns on ordinary rental properties also appear to be overstated. The reason for the overstatement is the same—failure to consider some of the more intangible investment costs. Again the most important cost is time spent in managing the property. Duplexes and four-flats have gained great popularity. Many investors imagine that they can achieve high returns with low risk by investing in these small rental properties. What they forget or refuse to recognize is that time is a very valuable commodity. And time is just what it takes to properly manage a rental property.

Maintenance is an ongoing process—there is grass to cut, snow to shovel, windows to wash, floors to scrub, appliances to repair, etc. And the properties must be rented. The higher the turnover in even a small property, the more ads that must be placed and the more calls taken and apartments shown. Certainly no way to spend a pleasant weekend! Moreover, some of the costs, although very real, are even more difficult to measure. Who can really describe the cost of fixing a stopped-up toilet in an irate tenant's apartment early on a Sunday morning? Who can imagine the fear, and the legal difficulties in certain states, involved in evicting a tenant who refuses to pay the rent on time and who is several months in arrears? Will the tenant destroy the apartment, throw a brick through the owner's window, make threatening phone calls? No one can tell.

Despite the ambiguity of renovation and management costs, people can put a price tag on them. They can do so by soliciting professional renovators and apartment managers. Renovating fees vary greatly, but in most states labor costs exceed $10 an hour. Management fees for real estate vary with the size of the property, but usually equal 5 to 10% of the rent collections. For small rental properties they may be as high as 15%, if a manager can even be found. Although that may not sound like very much as a percent of sales, it is a very large percent of profits.

None of this criticism is meant to imply that $1,000 cannot be turned into $10 million by investing in real estate. But to do so the investor probably needs to have tremendous leverage and/or talent and work very hard. Does the chance of making $10 million really justify all this trouble? There is no right or wrong answer. Every investor must live with his or her own decision. But at least that decision should be made with a clear understanding of the factors involved.

TABLE 17-2   TYPICAL MANAGEMENT FEES* IN TAX SHELTERS

Tax Shelter	Management Fee
Drilling program	One-time fee of 12½% plus 40% of partnership revenue
Cattle breeding and feeding	Annual fee of 4% of investment plus 20% of partnership net income
Real estate	4% of all cash distributions plus property management fee of 5% of all gross rentals plus 4% of all profits

* In addition to management fees, these tax shelters involve transactions costs ranging from 8 to 16.75%.

MANAGEMENT FEES FOR OTHER INVESTMENTS

Management fees are also an important cost of owning most tax shelters. Searching for oil, raising cattle, or leasing railroad cars takes specialized talents. For that reason, busy investors prefer to leave the management of these tax shelters to experts. A sample of management fees from recent offerings of tax shelters is presented in Table 17-2. To the uninitiated, these fees may appear low. But they are a very considerable proportion of the actual income and gains expected from the tax shelter. Moreover, the fees differ greatly, depending upon the particular investment selected.

Professional management is also available for individuals who want to invest in securities. The fees for small accounts usually average 2% of the total assets entrusted to investment advisers. Since the expected return on stocks during noninflationary times totals only about 10%, the management fee represents a substantial percentage of the return. Bank trust departments and mutual funds charge less for their advice. Their fees seldom average more than 1% of assets and can be as low as three-tenths of 1% on portfolios of $50,000 or more.

In an efficient market, investment managers are as fallible as anyone else. But for some people, bank or mutual fund management fees can still be a bargain. It all depends upon their personality. Investors subject to guilt feelings or anxiety about their own selection of investments are almost certain to benefit from professional investment management. It is much less taxing on the psyche to blame an "expert" for investment setbacks than to fault oneself. Investors who view the stock market as the best roulette wheel in town can also gain from professional management—providing they don't switch to some other game at the same time they turn their money over to the managers. And individuals who pride themselves on their own in-depth research, time-consuming though it is, could probably more than make up the management fee in higher salaries and/or increased leisure time.

BARGAINING

Individual buyers and sellers seldom play an active role in efficient markets. Like spectators at a play, they watch from the balcony as prices unfold. Even though their collective action determines these prices, each buyer or seller becomes a **price taker,** either accepting the going market price and transacting at that price or not. There is no in-between. On the other hand, personalities often dominate price setting in inefficient markets. Because of information costs, prices in these markets seldom reflect all known information. Indeed investors often face considerable uncertainty about current prices.

This uncertainty produces an inherent conflict between every buyer and seller. A "right" price no longer exists. Instead, participants in every transaction must somehow determine the fair price. Although both parties benefit from any voluntary exchange, one of them now benefits more than the other, with the greatest gains going to the better bargainer. Benjamin Franklin summarized the situation very well when he said, "Trades would not take place unless it were advantageous to the parties concerned. Of course, it is better to strike as good a bargain as one's bargaining position admits. The worst outcome is when, by overreaching greed, no bargain is struck, and a trade that could have been advantageous to both parties does not come off at all."

Franklin's comment sets the guidelines for successful negotiation or bargaining. Negotiators, and by the nature of the world this description probably includes everyone, must first recognize that there can be no complete winner or loser. In a successful negotiation everybody wins. But two questions remain: Who wins the most? And by what techniques?

Judging from the numerous books, articles, and seminars on bargaining, the ideal negotiator possesses many diverse qualities. According to Fred Ickle,[2] "The complete negotiator . . . should have a quick mind but unlimited patience, know how to dissemble without being a liar, inspire trust without trusting others, be modest but assertive, charm others without succumbing to their charms, and possess plenty of money and a beautiful wife while remaining indifferent to all temptation of riches and women." Obviously, very few people satisfy Ickle's description. But most can improve their negotiating abilities. And they can do so by cultivating one trait not even mentioned by Ickle—curiosity.

Role of Knowledge in Bargaining

Knowledge is power, at least in bargaining. Without detailed information on prices and quality, even the most skilled negotiator must eventually fall prey to the unscrupulous or to the better informed. Tourists attempting to shop in foreign countries without knowing the appropriate exchange rates can woefully attest to this fact of life.

Most of the research published on bargaining ignores the importance of information and concentrates instead on the personal characteristics of the bargainer. For example, one veteran negotiator tells the prospective bargainer to:

1 Appear well-dressed and eliminate mannerisms and bad habits.
2 Speak clearly and plainly but have a good vocabulary.
3 Be very observant and try to observe personal traits.

4 Avoid anger.
5 Listen carefully.

Although such advice may be helpful to some individuals, it certainly does not provide a general framework for the development of bargaining strategies. Moreover, there is absolutely no evidence that successful negotiators invariably follow these procedures.

Despite the importance of negotiations, no social scientist or mathematician has yet produced a satisfactory theory of bargaining. Interpersonal conflicts are just too complicated to be realistically explained with today's techniques. But the prospective investor need not give up hope of ever bargaining effectively for real estate, insurance, antiques, art, etc. Anyone can devise an informal approach to bargaining simply by understanding several general concepts.

First, every product possesses a number of different characteristics. Since price is only one of the many factors in a transaction, it should never become all-important. John Ruskin makes this point very bluntly when he says, "There is hardly anything in the world that some man cannot make a little worse and sell a little cheaper, and the people who consider price only are this man's lawful prey."[3]

Second, in the absence of an efficient market, people possess widely divergent views about price and quality. Past experience, personality, preferences, and specific knowledge of comparable prices and qualities all have their impact. The resulting mental image seldom assumes a well-defined form; i.e., few people appear to carry price tags around in their minds. Instead, each person has a rather fuzzy conception of current market values. The negotiating process apparently alters that concept.

Imagine two people confronting each other over the bargaining table—in this case a kitchen table. One of them is a homeowner attempting to sell the house without an agent; the other is a prospective buyer. Both possess mental images of the house, its general characteristics, and the going price of similar houses. No one knows the exact nature of these images or how they are formed. Presumably, the less information the person has, the more blurred the image. In the complete absence of information, the individual believes anything to be possible.

By accepting this point of view, the buyer's and seller's beliefs about the fair price can be expressed as follows:

$55,000	$65,000	seller
$50,000	$70,000	buyer

Judging from this diagram, the seller knows more about current market prices, or perhaps about the home itself, than the buyer. The prospective buyer believes the current market price falls anywhere between $50,000 and $70,000—a wide range of possibilities. The seller thinks that similar homes sell for between $55,000 and $65,000.

This representation of the beliefs of the buyer and seller about the appropriate price rests upon several important assumptions. First, both participants must remain reasonably objective and separate their personal desires from their views of the world. Wishful thinking on the part of the buyer or seller must not shape their estimates of the characteristics of the home or the range of prices. Otherwise the buyer would expect a zero price and the seller millions of dollars. Second, there are times when information will broaden the range of price possibilities rather than narrow it. Many antiques appear to be worthless pieces of junk to the average person. Only the experienced collector knows their true value.

Now suppose both the prospective buyer's and seller's image of prices coincide with the range of prices they will accept. If the seller holds fast to his concept of a fair price, the prospective buyer may purchase the home for as little as $55,000 or as much as $65,000. Any price in this range is completely acceptable to both the buyer and seller, and both will benefit from the transaction. But considerable room exists for bargaining. In fact, the skilled negotiator may gain at least an extra $10,000 from the other participant in the transaction, depending upon the tactics used.

Bargaining Tactics

According to Chester Karass, author of *Give and Take: The Complete Guide to Negotiating Strategies and Tactics,* one of the most successful bargaining tactics is to make low offers when buying and high demands when selling. High and low offers have their greatest impact on uninformed buyers and sellers. The less a person knows about prices, the greater the weight given to any single offer. For that reason, tourists usually face a difficult period of adjustment in a foreign country. Their concepts of a fair price depend almost entirely on prices in their own country. When these prices differ considerably from those in the country visited, they often give considerable credence to extreme offers. As a result their counteroffers are biased upward.

Many people fail to recognize the importance of making extreme offers. Instead they base their quotes on their own concepts of a fair price. This may be an important face-saving device. But anyone following such an approach does so at a high dollar cost. Assume the would-be buyer asks the would-be seller how much is wanted for the home. The seller can quote the highest price that seems reasonable—$65,000—or demand much more—say $80,000. By quoting an extremely high price the owner retains the opportunity of selling for $70,000—a price the buyer believes reasonable—and may even shift the buyer's range of acceptable prices to a higher level, say to $75,000.

The buyer can now respond in a number of ways. The very worst thing to do is to candidly say, "Eighty thousand dollars is too much for me. I had planned to spend only $70,000 at the most. But I suppose I can go as high as

$75,000." This exposes the buyer's position completely and concedes all gains to the seller. Instead the buyer must:

1   Negotiate so that the seller's own goals and beliefs are revealed
2   Attempt to modify those goals and beliefs to the buyer's advantage

In this case the buyer is definitely handicapped by a comparative lack of information. Other things being equal, the better-informed person will do a better job of bargaining. The buyer, feeling inherent weakness in this case, decides to rely on personality, and, rather than respond with a counteroffer, attempts to embarrass the seller with the unreasonableness of the price. "Eighty thousand dollars!" the buyer says. "You know that is an unfair price. I'm going to look elsewhere."

Suddenly two new factors have entered the negotiations. One involves the ego of the seller. The other concerns the possible loss of the prospective buyer. The next step in bargaining depends upon the seller's strength of purpose, personality, and perception of the buyer. Some people would immediately collapse under these pressures and attempt to accommodate the prospective buyer. In this case, the seller does just that by saying, "Perhaps you're right. I don't really know much about home prices. What do you think is a fair price?"

The prospective buyer grasps this opportunity to take the offensive and responds with a bluff. "Well, I've been looking at homes for some time now and your home seems to fall in the $50,000 category."

The weakened seller can barely muster the courage to plaintively say, "But I had hoped to get at least $55,000 for the home."

This last statement completely reveals the owner's bargaining position and gives the prospective buyer a tremendous advantage. The latter can move to close the sale at that price or bargain further and attempt to lower the price still more. Having gained so much so quickly, the buyer chooses the second course of action and says, "Fifty-five thousand seems like a reasonably fair price. But it looks like the house will need to be painted next year. If you knock off $2,000 from your price to pay for the painting, I think we have a deal."

The seller has already lost the war but continues the battle by negotiating the painting cost and eventually convinces the prospective buyer that $500 will cover the painting. Later the owner proudly relates to the family the details of the negotiations, emphasizing his or her success at holding the buyer close to the $55,000 price. Such is life.

Obviously, bargaining is an art, not a science. For that reason, natural talents and experience play important roles in bargaining. But even the neophyte can improve in skill by remembering certain fundamental concepts.

1   Establish personal goals and objectives before bargaining.
2   Collect enough information to form reasonable estimates of price and quality.
3   Never reveal personal goals, objectives, or estimates of price and quality

unless absolutely necessary. The opposition will sometimes go to great extremes to obtain this information.

4   Always attempt to determine and perhaps even alter the personal goals, objectives, and estimates of price and quality of the opposing bargainers.

5   Recognize that price is only one item in the bargain.

6   Accept the fact that people, not machines, do most of the bargaining. Skilled negotiators attempt to discover the personal needs of the participants and then satisfy those needs. They also recognize the importance of negotiating while mentally alert and physically healthy and even attempt to select the best time and place for bargaining.

7   While bargaining, always remain a skeptic. Some people will say or do almost anything to achieve their own ends. And remember that friendships formed during bargaining usually exist to further the other person's goals.

8   Always impose costs of failure on the other negotiator, who otherwise has nothing to lose by attempts to bargain.

9   Negotiate only with those who have the authority to negotiate.

Unfair Bargaining

No set of rules can solve every problem. But the preceding concepts can clarify many issues when applied imaginatively. In *Give and Take,* Chester Karass discusses several hundred bargaining strategies. One of these strategies involves nonperformance. Unscrupulous negotiators often use this strategy to trap the unsuspecting. For example, instead of feigning indignation, the prospective home buyer might say, "Eighty thousand dollars. That seems like a reasonable price. When can I move in?" Pleased by this easy success, the seller relaxes and admits to a plan to relocate on the West Coast within 5 weeks, where a commitment to buy an expensive home has already been made. To all intents and purposes, the buyer then proceeds to close the deal. But "unexpected problems" soon arise which delay the closing. Constant reassurances by the buyer keep the anxious seller patiently waiting for the money. And then, only 2 days before the seller intends to move, the buyer calls and very apologetically says that unexpected circumstances will prevent the completion of the transaction.

The seller faces an impossible situation. Shouts, pleas, and threats of legal action are all to no avail. But, fortunately, one of the people who originally looked at the home calls the next day and asks, "Is the home still for sale?" Clutching at this last opportunity, the seller quickly agrees to a price of $55,000, never realizing that the "last-minute" buyer originally paid a friend, relative, or business associate to fake the $80,000 offer.

Karass cites another bargaining technique sometimes used by unethical bargainers. He calls it "low balling." The seller realizes the prospective buyer is shopping for the best price possible and so quotes an unrealistically low figure. Then when the buyer returns, the price is raised. Car salespeople sometimes "low ball" by citing impossibly low prices. When the bargain hunter returns, they add on costly extras or shift the prospective buyer to a more expensive automobile.

SUMMARY

Price and quality variations exist in many markets. Indeed, the securities markets seem to be the exception to the rule of market inefficiency. Certainly real estate prices vary considerably, depending upon the individual circumstances surrounding the sale. And there seldom exists a single "right" price for insurance, coins, stamps, art, and other collector's items. Even the market for consumer loans exhibits considerable variation at any one point in time.

These price and quality variations present the well-informed investor with the opportunity for substantial gains. In order to capitalize on this opportunity, investors need to understand the economics of information and they have to acquire bargaining skills. Moreover, they must somehow avoid falling prey to con artists.

The economics of information is based upon one very important assumption—that time is money. The search for the lowest investment price and/or for the best quality takes time. Therefore, every individual must balance the possible benefits from this search against the costs.

Some investors can justify more search than others. As a rule, the higher their earnings, the more their time is worth. Therefore, high-income investors (or those who greatly enjoy leisure) should spend relatively little time investing their money.

The amount of money being invested, both now and in the future, also plays a role in selecting the appropriate search strategy. The larger the amount to be invested, either now or in the future, the greater the possible benefits from search.

The price and quality variation inherent in inefficient markets often result in a confrontation between the buyer and the seller. Since no one knows the "right" price, the prospective buyer and seller must often bargain over the final price. The end result depends primarily upon the knowledge of the parties to the transaction and their respective bargaining skills.

Knowledge is power in bargaining. But other techniques also serve a purpose. Successful bargainers take care to avoid exposing their own objectives, goals, or estimates of price. At the same time they strive to determine and perhaps even modify the underlying objectives of the opposing party.

Skilled negotiators often play on the personal needs of the participants in a transaction. For that reason, every participant in the bargaining process should always remain skeptical of friendships or promises made during bargaining. Skilled negotiators also try to confine negotiations to the time and place of their choosing. Finally, they always impose costs of failure on the other party.

Inefficient markets present a serious challenge to investors. There is the ever-present danger of fraud. Unfortunately, no one is completely immune from this possibility. Even investors in reasonably efficient markets sometimes suffer from fraudulent transactions. The Equity Funding fraud cost investors more than $100 million. Many of these investors represented the Who's Who of Wall Street, and Equity Funding stock traded on the NYSE, the largest and best-known stock exchange in the world.

The possibility of fraud cannot be eliminated. But investors can reduce this possibility and/or mitigate the consequences. First, they must diversify. Second, they should be wary of new ventures with almost no past history as a going enterprise. Third, they should avoid heavily advertised "bargains." And, fourth, they should lobby for stricter enforcement of existing laws and the establishment of a single law enforcement agency to deal with investment fraud.

Investors can more or less select their own habitat. Some invest almost exclusively in assets traded in generally efficient markets. Others devote their time and energies to trading in inefficient markets. Despite the claims of many investment advisers and salespeople, there is no "right" or "wrong" investment medium. Individuals and institutions must base their decision upon their own resources, goals, abilities, etc.

KEYWORDS

opportunity cost (alterna-
    tive cost)
call loan rate
point

offshore
corporate shell
price taker

QUESTIONS

1   Does the opportunity-cost concept explain why doctors seldom spend much time investing their money?

2   Suppose a woman spends 10 hours a week following the stock market. By doing so, she beats the market by 5% a year. Is this expenditure of time justified? (Hint: Make some assumptions about the amount of money she has invested and the opportunity cost of her time.)

3   Investments traded in inefficient markets require a larger expenditure of the investor's time than investments traded in generally efficient markets. Explain why.

4   List the factors affecting price and/or quality variation. Discuss the impact each has on price variation.

5   How much do the sales prices of houses differ from the asking prices? Why do large and/or distinctive homes take longer to sell and vary more in price?

6   What danger awaits the beginning investor in coins? How can collectors protect themselves?

7   What general characteristics do most fraudulent schemes have in common?

8   Do you still believe in real estate "fairy tales"? Why or why not?

9   Many small investors pridefully tell of their high returns on rental properties. And

they laugh at the idea of buying stocks. Do you think the rate-of-return figures cited by these investors tell the whole story?

10   Why should anyone pay for advice about investments traded in generally efficient markets? Which investment advisers charge the lowest fees?

11   How important do you think personal characteristics are in bargaining?

12   Why does information play such a key role in bargaining?

13   Why do good bargainers generally ask the other person to "Make me an offer" or to "Name your price"?

14   You are thinking of buying several acres of undeveloped land. You have carefully researched the sales prices of comparable parcels and feel the land is worth $3,000 an acre. The seller asks you to make an offer. What do you tell her?

15   Does a knowledge of bargaining techniques play any role in your own investment strategy? (What percent of your portfolio "trades" in inefficient markets? Be certain to include your human capital.)

REFERENCES

Becker, Gary: "A Theory of the Allocation of Time," *Economic Journal,* September 1965, pp. 493–517.

"Buying Vacation Land—Nine Ways Not to Get Stung," *Changing Times: The Kiplinger Magazine,* August 1973, pp. 7–10.

"Can Scotch Whiskey Really Make You Rich?" *Changing Times: The Kiplinger Magazine,* May 1973, pp. 45–47.

Dirks, Raymond L., and Leonard Gross: *The Great Wall Street Scandal,* McGraw-Hill, New York, 1974.

Ehrbar, A. F.: "The Home-Stake Case: Where Was the SEC?" *Fortune,* September 1974, pp. 95ff.

Hershman, Arlene: "The Cash Play in Real Estate," *Dun's Review,* August 1975, pp. 53–55.

Ilich, John: *The Art and Skill of Successful Negotiation,* Prentice-Hall, Englewood Cliffs, N.J., 1973.

Karass, Chester L.: *Give and Take: The Complete Guide to Negotiating Strategies and Tactics,* Thomas Y. Crowell, New York, 1974.

Kwitney, Jonathan: *The Fountain Pen Conspiracy,* Knopf, New York, 1973.

"Let a Professional Manage Your Investments?" *Changing Times: The Kiplinger Magazine,* March 1973, pp. 7–12.

Mayer, Alan J., and William Schmidt: "Florida: Biggest Fraud Yet?" *Newsweek Magazine,* May 26, 1975, pp. 69–70.

Modigliani, Franco, and Gerald A. Pogue: *A Study of Investment Performance Fees,* Heath-Lexington Books, Lexington, Mass., 1974.

Montgomery, Jim: "Florida Officials Ask U.S. Assistance in Investigating Huge Securities Swindle," *The Wall Street Journal,* May 15, 1975, p. 2.

Nierenberg, Gerard I.: *Fundamentals of Negotiating,* Hawthorn, New York, 1973.

Ozga, S. A.: "Imperfect Markets through Lack of Knowledge," *Quarterly Journal of Economics,* February 1960, pp. 29–52.

Randall, Robert: "The Carat and the Shtick of Buying Diamonds," *Money,* April 1974, pp. 52–56.

"What Good Are Financial Advisers?" *Dun's Review,* September 1975, pp. 45–47, 87–88.

Williams, J. D.: *The Compleat Strategyst,* McGraw-Hill, New York, 1966.

Yeoman, R. S.: *The Red Book of United States Coins—1976: A Guide Book of United States Coins,* 29th ed., Western Publishing Company, Racine, Wis., 1976.

Young, Oran, ed.: *Formal Theories of Negotiation,* University of Illinois Press, Champaign, Ill., 1975.

PART SIX

APPLICATIONS

CHAPTER EIGHTEEN

RISK TAKING

A dam Smith gained fame and probably fortune from *The Money Game.* *The New York Times* described it as "the best book there is about the stock market and all that goes with it." And M.I.T. economist Paul Samuelson called *The Money Game* "a modern classic."

Just what did Smith do to justify this acclaim? For one thing, he gave the world the following invaluable advice about the market: "If you don't know who you are, this is an expensive place to find out." Then he explored the emotional aspects of investing in an entertaining and insightful summary of stock market happenings.

Smith's book represents one of the few attempts to probe into actual investment decision making. Academicians and practitioners all agree upon the importance of knowing "who you are" before investing. But because of the complexity of human behavior, they have been able to provide investors with only a few guidelines. Some of these guidelines are set forth in the coming pages.

PORTFOLIO SELECTION

Looking for a universal rule of human behavior? Then search no further. The answer in less than 25 words is, <u>Maximize expected utility</u>.

Many economists believe this single phrase provides an excellent description of individual choice under uncertainty. But flesh-and-blood investors need more than the maximize-expected-utility rule to guide them in their decision making. No one can possibly examine the expected utility associated with every possible decision. Moreover, the unadorned expected-utility concept leaves economists unhappy and/or underemployed. To quote from Fama and Miller's *The Theory of Finance,* "The expected utility model per se provides no observable or testable propositions about consumer behavior. In order to make the model practicable and to give it economic substance, we must impose more structure on the problem."[1]

Risk and Return Preferences

Fama and Miller do just this. They assume that people find it possible to summarize their investment opportunities solely in terms of means and standard deviations of rates of return. In other words, the individual can rank one portfolio over another by simply looking at its risk and return.

Fama and Miller go on to say that:

> One special case in which such an approach is legitimate is when distributions of returns on all portfolios are normal. A normal distribution can be fully described once its mean (expected value) and standard deviation are known. Thus all the differences between any number of normal distributions can be determined from their means and standard deviations. In the consumption-investment model this implies that all portfolios can be ranked by the individual on the basis of these two parameters of their return distributions.[2]

Now suppose the following very general statements describe investors:

1   They behave like expected-utility maximizers.
2   They always prefer more return to less.
3   They dislike risk.

Fama and Miller show that any investor satisfying these three conditions behaves in a very consistent fashion. In particular, the individual's expected utility increases with the expected return of a portfolio and <u>decreases with the standard deviation.</u> In other words, the investor prefers more expected return to less, while at the same time disliking risk. Figure 18-1 provides a graphic description of this individual's tastes or preferences in the form of indifference curves. Each **indifference curve** shows a particular level of satisfaction. By design, the individual views all the risk-return combinations along a single indifference curve with "indifference." For example, risk-return combination A provides the same satisfaction as combination B.

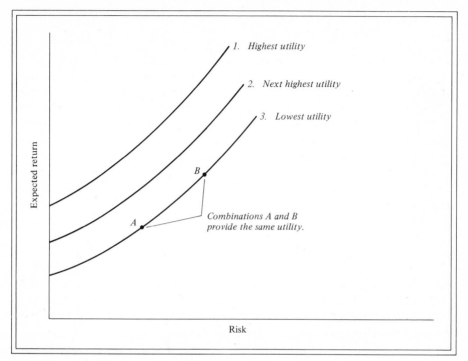

FIGURE 18-1   Risk and return preferences.

Higher indifference curves represent greater utility. After all, the higher the curve, the greater the expected rate of return. Investors prefer all combinations of risk and return on the first indifference curve in Figure 18-1 to those on the second and third curves. And they prefer all combinations on the second indifference curve to those on the third curve.

By the way, the indifference curves slope upward rather than downward, because people view risk as bad rather than good. They demand higher returns in order to compensate them for taking on more risk.

Risk and Return Objectives

The essential ingredients in any decision-making process always fall into two major categories:

1   Tastes or preferences
2   Opportunities, usually referred to as the **opportunity set** or constraint set

The indifference curves just described portray the personal tastes or preferences of the investor in terms of risk and return. They show what investors want to do. On the other hand, the opportunity set shows what they can do. In this particular case, the opportunity set consists of all possible risk-and-return combinations available to the individual—literally billions of possible portfolios! But given the assumption that people prefer more return than less and dislike risk, the possible choices can be narrowed down considerably. Indeed, the efficient frontier (discussed in Chapter Seven) shows all the best risk-return combinations. Anyone sincerely interested in maximizing his or her expected utility, i.e., obtaining the most return for the least risk, views the efficient frontier as the relevant opportunity set. Line *ABC* in Figure 18-2 represents the efficient frontier. Each portfolio on this line provides the maximum return for a given degree of risk.

Now would-be investors know what they want to do and what they can do. That leaves one vital question unanswered: What should they do? The answer is found by meshing together an investor's preferences and opportunities. Judging from the investor's preferences, portfolio *B* in Figure 18-2 provides the greatest satisfaction. By investing in this portfolio, the individual attains the greatest expected utility possible, i.e., reaches the highest indifference curve. Any other portfolio, for example portfolio *A* or *C*, produces a lower level of satisfaction.

Different investors select different portfolios. For example, the indifference curves in the first half of Figure 18-3 characterize someone who hates uncertainty. This fear of the unknown shows up as a demand for very high returns for risk bearing. The optimal portfolio for this individual consists of risk-free assets, like passbook accounts or Treasury bills. On the other hand, the individual in the

FIGURE 18-2   Preferences, opportunities, and optimal portfolio.

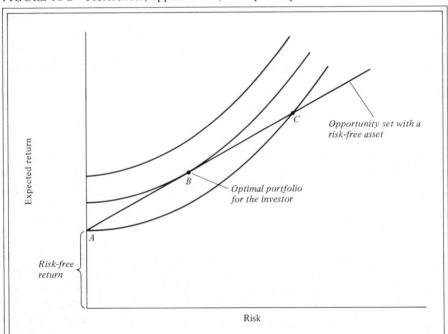

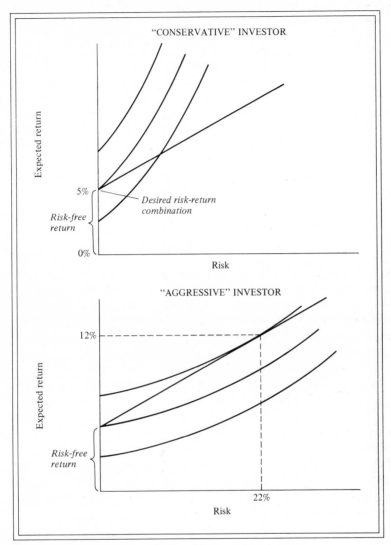

FIGURE 18-3 "Conservative" and "aggressive" investors.

second half of Figure 18-3 displays a much greater willingness to assume risk, providing some compensation is received for risk bearing. This investor selects a much riskier portfolio.

The preceding analysis makes it clear that investors can express their portfolio objectives solely in terms of risk and return. The first individual, a timid sort, attempts to avoid all risk while at the same time earning about 5% a year. The second investor, considerably more courageous, hopes to average 12% a year while at the same time limiting risk (the standard deviation of returns) to about 22% a year. By adopting these widely divergent objectives, both investors adhere to the age-old maxim, "To thine ownself be true." In the process, they satisfy the more general goal of maximizing expected utility.

This "investment-by-objectives" approach—call it IBO as opposed to MBO for management by objectives—promises to become more and more commonplace in future years. Already the findings on the efficient-market concept have prodded some institutional investors into setting risk-and-return objectives. These investors accept the fact that the security markets provide very few free lunches. But the markets do offer a tremendously varied "cuisine" in terms of risk and return. As a result, the most important investment decision facing both institutional and individual investors today involves the selection of the risk-return combination providing the greatest satisfaction.

RISK-TAKING PROPENSITY

Look at Figure 18-3, which shows the interaction between the investor's risk-return preferences and the opportunity set. The opportunity set, at least in terms of financial securities, has been explored in thousands of articles, books, and dissertations. But preferences remain an uncharted area, even though equally important to investment decision making.

For some reason, financial theorists and investment professionals give only lip service to these preferences. The theorists casually sketch indifference curves representing make-believe investors. And brokers and investment advisers half-heartedly ask people to categorize themselves as "income oriented, conservative, aggressive, or speculative." As a result, investors must turn elsewhere for information about their own tastes and preferences.

The field of psychology appears to be a logical source of information about personal tastes and preferences. But as Adam Smith observed, most psychologists show more interest in why "call girls take up their trade" than in trying to explain risk taking. Smith describes his difficult search for knowledge about the psychological aspects of investing as follows:

> I set out after market people who had occasionally used a term such as "mass masochism" in a sentence such as "Everyone knows that odd-lot purchases demonstrate mass masochism on the part of the public." But when I talked to them, all that appeared were the usual generalizations about markets, buttered lightly with a few cocktail party psychiatrisms. Then I began to correspond with a few psychologists and social scientists. Here, in an area where, if there is any Truth to be found, there is certainly a commercial application, only a handful of people were even interested.[3]

Judging from the articles published by this "handful of people," many psychologists view risk taking as a general personality characteristic. They frequently refer to **risk-taking propensity,** i.e., the individual's natural inclination toward risk. Risk-taking propensity serves as a possible explanation of problem-solving

ability, creativity, accidents, vocational choice and entrepreneurship, and crimi-
nality. A variety of techniques have been proposed for the assessment of this
risk-taking propensity.

Tests of Risk-taking Propensity

Psychologist Paul Slovic, one of the most energetic researchers in risk-taking
behavior, has provided a detailed summary of attempts to measure RTP, or
risk-taking propensity. According to Slovic, these tests fall into three categories:
(1) response-set and judgmental, (2) questionnaires, and (3) probability and preference measures. A review of these tests may help the investor satisfy another
age-old maxim: "Know thyself."

Response-Set and Judgmental Measures   As early as 1936, psychologists
noted a tendency for people to gamble on tests. One type of gamble involves
guessing in ability tests when there is a greater penalty for mistakes than for blank
answers. Studies of test guessing show it to be independent of ability, but more
common among boys than girls. Several psychologists have used an index of test
gambling in an attempt to measure RTP, including preferences for risky occupations. Apparently people interested in sales occupations (supposedly a risky profession) gamble more on tests than those seeking careers in civil engineering.

Another type of gambling on tests involves sacrificing accuracy for speed. Test
takers exhibit considerable consistency in speed versus accuracy scores. One study
of the personality differences between fast and slow deciders shows that fast
deciders score higher on masculinity. However, none of this evidence relates
directly to risk taking.

A final type of response involves category ranges. People display marked differences in their estimates of the maximum and minimum values of items like the
length of whales or the annual rainfall in Washington, D.C. Most of the studies
done to date attempt to link broad categorizing with high risk taking. Males
appear more apt than females to use broad categories.

Unlike the response-set measures, judgmental measures of risk taking focus
on one's confidence in one's own judgments. In the "Desire for Certainty Test,"
people first complete sentences like, "The chances that such and such an event
will occur are about _____ in 100." Then they rate their confidence in these
estimates. Individuals with less confidence in their judgments apparently tend to
view risk taking as more "hostile, cold, and tense" than more confident people.

Questionnaire Measures   Supposedly the way men and women conduct their
lives reflects upon their general attitudes toward risk taking. Therefore, a questionnaire about life experience should provide some measure of risk-taking pro-
pensities. Psychologists employed by the U.S. Air Force used this approach to
study fighter pilots. The psychologists first asked each pilot about his early life
experiences and then administered a test of risk-taking behavior.

The psychologists' conclusions about risk taking coincide surprisingly well with the uninformed opinions of the general public. They found that so-called "high riskers" engaged early in "masculine status giving activities" like smoking, driving a car, playing with snakes, hitchhiking, and drinking. They also gave expression to their aggressive drives by fighting more frequently, by taking dares, and by doing cruel things. Always active participants in sports, high riskers especially enjoyed rough sports like football, boxing, wrestling, hunting, and fishing. Finally high riskers frequently engaged in dangerous activities like auto racing and motorcycling and participated in gambling games like poker, blackjack, and craps.

Another questionnaire, called the "Job Preference Inventory," has been used to measure people's attitudes toward their jobs. High-risk takers prefer jobs in which they are almost always on their own and can make decisions by themselves. Moreover, they readily accept positions leading to either success or failure. Finally, high-risk takers place more emphasis on promotions based upon merit than low-risk takers.

Probability- and Variance-Preference Measures   Gambling provides a rich opportunity for observing risk-taking behavior. Numerous psychologists have studied people's reactions to gambles—both artificial and real. In the quest for realism, one enterprising psychologist even enlisted the support of a Las Vegas casino for his experiments.

Nearly all these probability studies involve their subjects in choices between different bets. For example, the subjects might be asked to choose between pairs of bets like the ones shown in Table 18-1. Men and women tend to show preferences for probabilities as well as variances in these experiments. In other words, the subjects favor some probabilities over others.

This probability preference contradicts much of the work done in finance and economics. Remember, investors supposedly base their selections only upon expected returns and standard deviations (or variances). Probabilities as such play no role in investment theory.

One psychologist explains these probability preferences in terms of motivation. Atkinson proposes a risk-taking model based upon the explicit consider-

TABLE 18-1   SAMPLE BETS ON A PSYCHOLOGICAL TEST

First Bet

Win	$4.00	Probability	$8/10$
Lose	.50	Probability	$2/10$

Second Bet

Win	$40.00	Probability	$1/10$
Lose	1.00	Probability	$9/10$

ation of (1) the subjective probability of success, (2) the subjective probability of failure, (3) the incentive value of success, (4) the negative incentive value of failure, (5) the achievement motive, and (6) the motive to avoid failure. Atkinson predicts that people with greater achievement motives relative to the desire to avoid failure will prefer tasks with intermediate probabilities of success. On the other hand, individuals dominated by the fear of failure prefer tasks with either extremely high or extremely low probabilities of success.

A number of early tests provided strong support for Atkinson's motivation theory. For example, people with a high motivation to succeed preferred to shoot from a moderately difficult distance in experimental shuffleboard games, while those motivated to avoid failure took either close or faraway shots. (Close shots assure success; faraway shots, because of their extreme difficulty, eliminate any possibility of being blamed for failure.) Other experimentation related probability preference to a real gambling situation and reported similar results—subjects with a strong need for success chose gambles with intermediate payoffs and probabilities of success.

Gambling experiments reveal other disturbing (at least to economists) aspects of decision making. Most important, subjects in these experiments often violate every existing theory of decision making. For example, look at the bets in Table 18-1. Many people say they prefer the first of the two bets. Then when asked to set a selling price for each of these bets, they turn around and put a higher price tag on the second bet, thus reversing their choices.

Slovic and Amos Tversky of Hebrew University show that other subjects steadfastly violate one of the axioms underlying expected-utility theory in experiments like the following:

Imagine an urn known to contain 90 balls. Thirty of the balls are red, the remaining 60 are black and yellow in unknown proportion. One ball is to be drawn at random from the urn. Consider the following actions and payoffs:

Situation X

	30 Red	60	
		Black	Yellow
Act 1—Bet on red	$100	$0	$0
Act 2—Bet on black	$0	$100	$0

If you bet on red, Act 1, you win $100 if a red ball is drawn and nothing if a black or yellow ball is selected. If you bet on black, Act 2, you win $0 if a red ball is drawn, $100 if a black ball appears, and $0 for a yellow ball.

Select either Act 1 or 2. Next, consider the following two actions under the same circumstances:

	Situation Y		
	30	60	
	Red	Black	Yellow
Act 3—Bet on red or yellow	$100	$0	$100
Act 4—Bet on black or yellow	$0	$100	$100

Now select either Act 3 or 4.[4]

The right set of answers to these questions is either acts 1 and 3 or acts 2 and 4. Other selections contradict a general rule of behavior referred to as the independence, or "sure-thing," principle.

The gambling experiments disclose another fact about human decision making. Most people find it difficult to process all of the information involved in even these straightforward selections. As a result, they often select simple strategies to guide them in their choices. This probably explains much of their "inconsistent behavior." In addition, people appear to be very sensitive to the conditions surrounding their choices. For example, boredom often plays an important role in experiments. Bored subjects adopt simple strategies, whereas highly motivated subjects often adopt extremely complex strategies.

Not all of the probability measures of risk taking rely upon gambling situations. Kogan and Wallach devised a measure called the "Dilemmas of Choice Questionnaire." The 12 "dilemmas" on this frequently used questionnaire all involve a choice between two alternatives: one safe and the other risky. Naturally, the risky alternative offers a much greater payoff—in terms of either money, happiness, health, or some other type of success. Here is a sample dilemma from the test:

1   *Mr. A, an electrical engineer, who is married and has one child, has been working for a large electronics corporation since graduating from college 5 years ago. He is assured of a lifetime job with a modest, though adequate, salary, and liberal pension benefits upon retirement. On the other hand, it is very unlikely that his salary will increase much before he retires. While attending a convention, Mr. A is offered a job with a small, newly founded company which has a highly uncertain future. The new job would pay more to start and would offer the possibility of a share in the ownership if the company survived the competition of the larger firms. Imagine that you are advising Mr. A. Listed below are several probabilities or odds of the new company's proving financially sound.*

   PLEASE CHECK THE LOWEST PROBABILITY THAT YOU WOULD CONSIDER ACCEPTABLE TO MAKE IT WORTHWHILE FOR MR. A TO TAKE THE NEW JOB.

   _____*The chances are 1 in 10 that the company will prove financially sound.*
   _____*The chances are 3 in 10 that the company will prove financially sound.*
   _____*The chances are 5 in 10 that the company will prove financially sound.*
   _____*The chances are 7 in 10 that the company will prove financially sound.*
   _____*The chances are 9 in 10 that the company will prove financially sound.*

_____*Place a check here if you think Mr. A should not take the new job no matter what the probabilities.*[5]

Each person taking the test must indicate the lowest probability of success he or she needs in order to take the more risky alternative. According to Kogan and Wallach, older people demand higher probabilities of success before agreeing to undertake a risky act. In addition, men require lower probabilities of success than women for choices involving the risk of death, loss of income, or a football defeat. However, women show greater risk-taking propensity for artistic careers and marriages.

Generality of Risk Taking

Can risk taking be viewed as a general personality characteristic? The answer so far, according to Slovic, is no. Or at least, no one has yet found a satisfactory measure of risk-taking propensity. Most recent studies fail to find that risk taking in one situation is related to risk taking in other situations. As Slovic says, "only those tasks highly similar in structure and involving the same sort of payoffs have shown any generality" in risk preferences.

One of the few exceptions to this rule concerns certain subgroups of individuals. According to Kogan and Wallach, men and women with a high degree of defensiveness and anxiety display a substantial degree of consistency in their risk taking in various situations. In addition, women show more consistency in their preferences than men.

As a result of the generally negative findings about RTP, some psychologists are now concentrating their attention on multidimensional measures of risk taking. They classify risk in three or more categories, like financial, physiological (danger to the person), and social (loss of prestige or self-esteem). According to this view, a man might adopt a life-style full of physiological risk, say washing windows on a 50-story building, while at the same time completely avoiding financial risk.

GAMBLING

Strangely enough, most public relations people on Wall Street and financial economists share a common view of risk taking. They believe that people must be paid for their risk bearing. In other words, no investor gambles.

But not everyone agrees. Thomas Schelling, a Harvard economist and an expert on strategy claims that, "The greatest gambling enterprise in the United States . . . is the stock market." Schelling's comment strikes a responsive chord in the millions of Americans who refuse to buy stocks. And it vaguely resembles the indictment of the markets brought by Congress and the Securities and Exchange Commission after the Great Crash.

Who Gambles? Why?

Gambling is too widespread to ignore. Estimates of annual expenditures on gambling range from $22 billion a year to $500 billion. The first figure comes from the authoritative Commission on the Review of the National Policy toward Gambling. The second is from John Scarne, an expert on gambling and author of numerous books including *Scarne on Cards*. Whatever the actual dollar figures, there is no denying that many millions of Americans gamble every year. According to the Survey Research Center at the University of Michigan, nearly 60% of all adults participate in some type of gambling.

By the way, gambling officially covers a wide range of activities, including dog and horse races, lotteries, bingo, sports cards, numbers, roulette, and card games. Indeed, gambling appears to be limited only by peoples' imagination, since men and women bet on the hour of a child's birth, the date of the first snowfall, and even on their paycheck numbers.

Does gambling mark the individual as abnormal? Definitely not. Studies done at the psychological laboratory at Colgate University confirm the normality of most gambling behavior. Psychologists at Colgate administered three sets of tests to students at several colleges. These tests measured psychoneurotic tendencies, introversion and extroversion, and intelligence. Judging from the results, gambling can be considered as much a function of the normal (at least in the sense of being average) personality as nongambling.

Who gambles? According to the Survey Research Center,[6] "Betting is not confined to a few groups or a few areas. Betting is a universal phenomenon in the United States. A sizable majority of adults in most major subgroups say they bet—men and women, whites and non-whites, from one ocean to another." The Center goes on to make the following points:

1 Despite a substantial level of participation by all groups, there are meaningful differences. More males say they bet than females (68 percent vs. 55 percent).
2 The higher the income and education, the more likely the individual is to bet.
3 Single people, with the exception of widows and widowers, reported more betting than married folk. The widowed are least likely to bet.
4 Gambling is a young person's pursuit. Betting participation goes down as age goes up.

Why do people gamble? The answer depends upon the type of game played. Table 18-2 shows the primary reasons given for gambling. Casinos, race tracks, and bingo games apparently attract a fun-loving crowd. And the same is true of friendly bets on sporting events. Most of the participants in these games "have a good time." On the other hand, relatively few off-track bettors claim to be having fun. Instead, as incredible as it may seem, 68% of these misguided souls say they are in it to "make money." Indeed, regardless of the gambling activity, numerous people cite monetary reasons—either "to make money" or "a chance to get rich"—as a primary motivating factor for their wagering. Whatever happened to risk aversion?

TABLE 18-2 MAJOR REASONS FOR GAMBLING

Specific Reasons*	Legal Games					Illegal Games			
	Horses at Track, %	Casinos, %	Sports with Friends, %	Bingo, %	Lottery, %	Sports, %	Horses with Bookie		Numbers, %
							Track Bettors, %	Nontrack Bettors, %	
Have a good time	86	78	63	62	15	48	33	2	6
Excitement	51	46	46	27	23	38	35	12	19
Challenge	40	41	50	20	33	67	39	60	20
Make money	33	36	27	19	55	56	66	68	43
Chance to get rich	7	7	2	3	40	8	13	0	0
Pass the time	13	26	18	37	7	10	5	58	5
Something to look forward to	16	13	31	14	40	26	2	25	14

* Respondents chose 1, 2, or 3 reasons from a list of 11 reasons provided.
Source: Commission on the Review of the National Policy toward Gambling, Gambling in America: Appendix 2, Survey of American Gambling Attitudes and Behavior, Washington, D.C., 1976, p. 46.

Compulsive Gambling

Gambling dates back to antiquity. Archaeologists found stick dice in the cliff ruins of Colorado, gaming boards in the excavations at Ur and Crete, and dice in the pyramids of Egypt. The pervasiveness of gambling, coupled with a belief in its basic irrationality, has provoked many a psychiatrist into theorizing on its possible causes. Most of these theories are cloaked in ids, superegos, egos, oedipal complexes, and sexual impulses. Probably the clearest explanation, at least for the layperson, comes from Edmund Bergler—the first psychoanalyst to extensively study and treat compulsive gamblers.

Bergler reserves the term **gambler** for compulsive or pathological gamblers. According to Bergler, pathological gamblers exhibit some or all of the following characteristics:[7]

1 *Gambling is a typical, chronic, and repetitive experience.*
2 *Gambling absorbs all other interests.*
3 *The gambler displays persistent optimism about winning.*
4 *The gambler never stops while winning.*
5 *The gambler eventually risks more than he or she can afford.*
6 *The gambler seeks and enjoys a strange thrill from gambling, a combination of pleasure and pain.*

Bergler distinguishes between the conscious and unconscious motivations of the gambler. The gambler's conscious response to the question, "Why do you gamble?" is usually, "Because I want to win money" or, "The game gives me thrills and excitement." Bergler reports that "Further probing into the gambler's conscious motivation reveals this line of reasoning: The possibility of earning real money by normal work is greatly restricted, if not impossible. On the other hand, there are people who make fortunes quickly through gambling. Why not try that way?"

Despite these rationalizations by gamblers, most psychiatrists believe the answer to compulsive gambling lies in the unconscious. Bergler argues very convincingly that gamblers unconsciously *want* to lose. This probably seems like a ridiculous desire. But in their own confused way, compulsive gamblers apparently transform pain into pleasure; i.e., they suffer from masochism.

Fortunately, only a very small (but still too large) percentage of the population falls in the compulsive gambling category. Popular estimates range from 2% to the often-quoted figure of 6% provided by Gamblers Anonymous. But the Survey Research Center study suggests a figure of 1.1% for men and 0.5% for women, with another 2 or 3% of the population potentially compulsive gamblers. Here are some of the questions the center used to screen its sample for compulsive and potentially compulsive gamblers:[8]

1 *When playing a game, I prefer to play for money.*
   a   True   b   False

2   *The higher the stakes, the more I enjoy the bet.*
   a   True   b   False
3   *When gambling, I would go for broke rather than play it safe.*
   a   True   b   False
4   *Once in a while I put off until tomorrow what I ought to do today.*
   a   True   b   False
5   *I would never put* all *of my money into a venture, even though the possible profits were great.*
   a   True   b   False

Compulsive gamblers tend to answer true to the first three questions. For some reason, they also showed a marked tendency to say false to the fourth question. Judging from the answers to question 5, even compulsive gamblers sincerely believe in some diversification. The actual responses to these survey questions were as follows:

PERCENTAGE ANSWERING TRUE

Question	Total Sample	Potential Compulsive Gambler, %	Compulsive Gambler, %
1	16.5	51.4	62.6
2	12.9	18.8	47.6
3	7.6	20.2	31.4
4	85.3	23.5	20.4
5	79.9	80.5	76.1

Investments, Speculation, and Gambling

Traditional investment textbooks almost always devote a page or two to a sober discussion of the differences between **speculation** and investments. For example, Frederick Amling, author of one widely read investments text, says "The distinction between investment and speculation must be made clear, even though it is easier to state what an investment is and what a speculation is than to distinguish one from the other. At times it is impossible to make the distinction."[9] With this less than auspicious start, Amling, like other authors, goes on to say that speculators take on considerably more risk than investors.

Fred Schwed—author of *Where Are the Customers' Yachts?*—provides one of the most amusing definitions of speculation and investment. According to Schwed:

> *Speculation is an effort, probably unsuccessful, to turn a little money into a lot.*
>
> *Investment is an effort, which should be successful, to prevent a lot of money from becoming a little.*[10]

So much for the largely arbitrary distinction between speculation and investment.

Now what about the similarities between gambling and investing? Most dictionaries refer to a gamble as "an act involving an element of risk." That definition certainly applies to investments. But it also describes most of life's activities—from walking across the street to selecting a marriage partner. Therefore, it seems unfair to degrade investing by calling it gambling. Instead, it seems more appropriate to reserve that term for the "unnecessary taking on of risk." In particular, a gamble involves taking on risk without demanding compensation in the form of increased expected return. Bank accounts and stocks involve risk, but in greatly different degrees. However, both promise the investor positive returns. People buy stocks for the increased expected return; i.e., they take on additional risk because they expect to receive additional compensation.

By now it comes as no surprise that some individuals use the investments markets to gamble. In other words, they take on risk without expecting or demanding a positive return. At the turn of this century, so-called bucket shops flourished. These shops offered people the opportunity to bet a few cents or a much larger sum on stocks. Rather than actually invest the money, the bucket shops took the other side of the bets and paid off the winners. Some cynics say legitimate brokerage firms forced the closing of these bucket shops in order to reduce competition.

Whatever the cause, more traditional forms of gambling now claim the $2 bets. The investment markets are reserved for larger wagers. At least, that appears to be the opinion of no less an authority on the stock market than Adam Smith. According to him:

> *The list of roles investors play could go on and on, but the Australopithecus jawbone is still missing. Perhaps, as the savants say, the investors are in the market for something else. I have a friend who runs a small clearing-house shop, and this is what he says:* "I don't care whether they're big investors or little investors. If they make a little money, they're happy, if they lose a little money, they're not too unhappy. What they want to do is to call you up. They want to say, 'How's my stock? Is it up? Is it down? What about earnings? What about the merger? What's going on?' And they want to do this everyday. They want a friend, they want someone on the telephone, they want to be a part of what's going on, and if you gave them a choice between making money, guaranteed, or staying in the game, and if you put it in some acceptable face-saving form, every last one of them would pick staying in the game. *It doesn't make sense, or the kind of sense you expect, but it makes a nutty kind of sense if you see it for the way it is.*"[11]

Reconciliation

Economists almost always cast the investor in the role of a risk averter. Risk averters live by a simple code of conduct—they demand more return for taking on more risk.

Judging from the success of Las Vegas and the popularity of Smith's *Money Game,* not every investor fits this mold perfectly. But the overall market does seem to be dominated by people who expect a positive return and invest primarily for this reason. Nearly every study done to date reports a direct tie between return and risk over long periods of time. Moreover, investors switch to other investments when they fail to receive adequate compensation for risk bearing. Nearly 5 million stockholders left the marketplace between 1970 and 1975, when returns stayed persistently negative. Given a choice "between making money, guaranteed, or staying in the game," many investors opted for the money—contrary to Smith's conclusion.

So the fundamental force motivating investors appears to be a desire for greater return with greater risk. But at the same time, people display a fun-loving nature and often sacrifice some return just for the privilege of playing the game. Here are some guidelines for investors to follow in deciding whether or not they are sacrificing returns for excitement:

1 Active trading almost guarantees negative expected returns. A pattern of active trading suggests a tendency to gamble in the market (or ignorance of the facts of investment life).
2 Certain investment media bear a striking resemblance to more traditional forms of gambling. For example, commodity futures probably yield zero or negative expected returns despite their considerable risk.
3 The refusal to diversify almost surely signals a desire to gamble, not to invest.

Of course, there is no reason why investing must be a deadly serious business. Some investors consciously opt for an investment strategy which provides the opportunity to play the money game. This possibility is considered in Chapter Twenty.

ASSESSING RISK-RETURN PREFERENCES

Fischer Black, one of the leading proponents of the efficient-market theory says, "For an individual, the main investment policy decision is how much risk to take in his portfolio." Black's comment summarizes the views of most financial theorists. But why the recent emphasis on risk rather than return?

The answer, of course, is the convincing evidence on the efficiency of markets. In a generally efficient market, expected returns depend almost totally upon risk. This presents investors with a very real dilemma. They like high returns but dislike risk. And yet, in order to capture large profits they must sacrifice some safety.

In a sense, the efficient-market concept marks the end of an age of innocence (or perhaps gullibility). No longer can the investor realistically hope to realize consistently high returns by devoting time and effort to the discovery of under- (or over-) valued stocks. Nor do market-timing techniques promise to shelter investors from the ravages of broad market movements.

Consequently the success and happiness of the investor depends upon the proper selection of risk and return objectives. But unfortunately, financial theory appears to have outstripped financial reality. Stock tips still abound, but not one financial theorist or investment institution stands ready to guide individual investors along the newly discovered path to rational investing.

Adam Smith's statement to the contrary, a number of psychologists have attempted to explore the "emotional" area of investing. But most of their efforts—some of them very ingenious—have met with failure. About all that can be concluded from a study of the psychology of risk taking is that no technique has yet been devised to measure risk-taking propensity, if it exists.

Actually, the failure of repeated attempts to find a general risk-taking characteristic qualifies as a very important finding. For one thing, it totally contradicts popular belief. And it alerts the investing public to the need for carefully assessing its desire for financial risk taking. Stereotyped labels like "conservative" or simple generalizations based on general behavior have no place in portfolio selection.

Just what can the investor do in selecting the appropriate combination of risk and return? There are three possible solutions to the problem:

1 Compute a personal utility function.
2 Review the risks and returns of alternative portfolios and rely upon the subconscious to somehow put the pieces together properly.
3 Learn the trade-offs between risk and return and consciously make a choice.

Computing a Personal Utility Function

The indifference curves describing risk and return preferences come from a utility function. So why not compute the investor's utility function? Harry Markowitz gives one answer: "Real investors these days usually seem more comfortable with the idea of examining risk-return trade-offs, than with psychoanalyzing their utility function and letting the computer pick a portfolio that maximizes its expected value." Psychologists like Amos Tversky give another answer: "After more than fifteen years of experimental investigation of decisions under risk, the evidence on the descriptive validity of the SEU (subjective expected utility) model is still inconclusive." Despite these difficulties, Teweles, Harlow, and Stone plunge ahead in the *Commodity Futures Game* and tell investors how to compute their own utility functions (they call these functions "personal trading curves"). They are to be complimented on trying to find a practical application for an important segment of financial theory.

Review of Risk and Returns

A less ambitious and therefore perhaps more useful procedure involves a simple review of the risks and returns of various portfolios. Figure 18-4 shows the probability distributions of three different investment portfolios—Treasury bills, long-term government bonds, and stocks. The expected returns and standard deviations of returns in this figure come from the Ibbotson-Sinquefield study of returns over the period 1926–1976. (For a discussion of this study see Chapter Nine.)

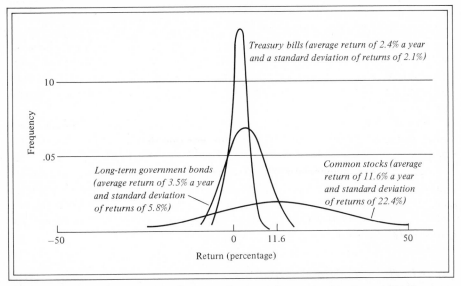

FIGURE 18-4   Probability distributions of returns for stocks, bonds, and T-bills.

Many investors find these probability distributions "unnatural." They prefer to think in terms of distinct possibilities. The information in the probability distribution of returns on stocks can be condensed as follows:

Loss or Gain, %	Probability of Loss, %	Probability of Gain, %
0 to 10	13.3	17.1
10 to 25	11.7	25.4
25 to 50	4.9	23.0
50 to 75	0.2	4.2
75 or more	very small	0.2
Total	30.1	69.9

In other words, investors holding a broadly diversified portfolio of high-grade common stocks (the market portfolio) can expect to lose money about one-third of the time (30.1% to be exact). These losses will exceed 25% of the amount invested about 5% of the time, or approximately once in every 20 years. Of course, the portfolio also offers the possibility of some very large returns. The gains will exceed 50% about 4% of the time.

EXAMPLE   The expected return and standard deviation of returns can be used to calculate the probability of specific losses or gains. For example, suppose some investors want to calculate the probability of making 25% or more on their money. If the standard deviation of annual returns equals 22.4% and the expected return equals 11.6%, a gain of 25% corresponds to .6 standard deviations; that is,

$$\frac{25\% \text{ actual return } - 11.6\% \text{ expected return}}{22.4\% \text{ standard deviation}} = .6 \text{ standard deviations}$$

Figure 18-5 shows the probability of realizing various returns. According to this figure, a gain of 25% or more (which in this case corresponds to a return at least .6 standard deviations above the expected return) will occur about 27.4% of the time.

Still another way of reviewing the distribution of possible returns is to set confidence intervals for common odds or probabilities. This has been done in Figure 18-6.

Now suppose an investor wants to know the possible outcomes from investing $10,000 in the market portfolio. The confidence intervals in terms of gains or losses are also presented in Figure 18-6. Judging from these confidence intervals, the chances of either doubling the investment or losing the entire sum are very small indeed.

Paper Portfolios and Computer Simulation

As we have noted, people show a tremendous ability to learn by trial and error. In fact, with complex mechanical tasks, only "practice makes perfect." But with investments, practical experience sometimes comes at a very high cost. Moreover, the nature of the investments world often precludes a broad understanding of risk and return. There are two reasons for this. First, there are an enormous

FIGURE 18-5   Probabilities of realizing various rates of return.

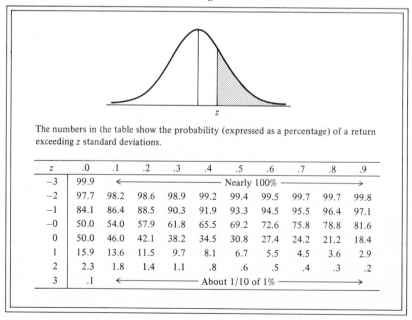

The numbers in the table show the probability (expressed as a percentage) of a return exceeding z standard deviations.

z	.0	.1	.2	.3	.4	.5	.6	.7	.8	.9
−3	99.9	←				Nearly 100%				→
−2	97.7	98.2	98.6	98.9	99.2	99.4	99.5	99.7	99.7	99.8
−1	84.1	86.4	88.5	90.3	91.9	93.3	94.5	95.5	96.4	97.1
−0	50.0	54.0	57.9	61.8	65.5	69.2	72.6	75.8	78.8	81.6
0	50.0	46.0	42.1	38.2	34.5	30.8	27.4	24.2	21.2	18.4
1	15.9	13.6	11.5	9.7	8.1	6.7	5.5	4.5	3.6	2.9
2	2.3	1.8	1.4	1.1	.8	.6	.5	.4	.3	.2
3	.1	←			About 1/10 of 1%					→

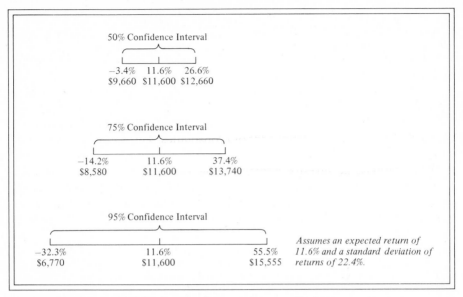

50% Confidence Interval

-3.4% 11.6% 26.6%
$9,660 $11,600 $12,660

75% Confidence Interval

-14.2%   11.6%   37.4%
$8,580 $11,600 $13,740

95% Confidence Interval

-32.3%   11.6%   55.5%   *Assumes an expected return of*
$6,770 $11,600 $15,555 *11.6% and a standard deviation of*
                                     returns of 22.4%.

FIGURE 18-6   Confidence intervals for various rates of return.

number of possible investments. Second, the laws of chance often work in a very heavy-handed way. Depressions, at least great depressions, mercifully occur very infrequently. On the other hand, bull markets (and more recently bear markets) occasionally last for a decade or more. Any investor relying completely on market experience often gains a very distorted image of reality.

Paper portfolio games solve one of these problems. They provide practical experience at almost zero cost. Rather than invest real money, the individual merely pretends to invest. By recording all imaginary trades and periodically noting the value of the portfolio, the prospective investor lives vicariously. Of course, paper-money gains and losses lack the excitement of real gains and losses. Even so, several large mutual funds require their employees to manage imaginary portfolios as a prelude to supervising actual portfolios. And there would probably be far fewer mourners on Wall Street if people played options and commodity futures on paper before risking their cash on an unknown quantity.

Computers provide the ultimate in simulated investing. With a computer, the prospective investor can experience a lifetime of returns in only a few minutes. And these returns reflect the same probability distributions underlying the returns on real investments.

SUMMARY

By investing in generally efficient markets, people can shape their own financial destinies. If they desire high returns, they simply seek out high-risk investments. If it is security they want, they settle instead for low returns.

This freedom of choice creates a serious problem for investors. An old German saying, "Die Wahl ist die Qual," describes the situation best. Translated it means "Choice is frustration." In order to achieve the greatest satisfaction, every investor must somehow select the specific combination of risk and return most suited to her or his own needs.

Investors looking for an easy answer to the question of how much risk to take face considerable disappointment. Economists and investment professionals offer no advice at all. And psychologists, despite repeated attempts, have met with little success in measuring risk-taking propensity. Judging from the results of their studies, stereotyped images of risk takers as young or old, male or female, professional or blue collar, aggressive or introverted have almost no validity. Moreover, risk taking can and does differ in different activities. Therefore, any attempt by brokers or investors to draw inferences about financial risk taking from other types of behavior seems almost certain to fail.

So much for paper and pencil tests of risk taking. What does the real world tell us about risk taking? First, gambling is widespread. So not all people try to avoid all financial risk. Apparently the excitement of the game more than makes up for the negative expected return. Second, a small percentage of the population appears to be compulsive gamblers. No doubt this explains the apparently irrational behavior of some investors.

A review of gambling and of psychological tests provides a deeper understanding of the complexity of risk taking. But how does the investor actually decide how much risk to take? One answer, albeit not an easy one, is to become familiar with the risk and returns inherent in the marketplace. This can be done by studying probabilities or by playing with paper portfolios or by taking part in computer simulations.

KEYWORDS

indifference curve	gambler
opportunity set	speculation
risk-taking propensity	paper portfolio

QUESTIONS

1 Justify the use of only the mean and standard deviation in describing the opportunity set.

2 Explain why indifference curves like those in Figure 18-1 can never cross. Why do the indifference curves slope upward? Why do higher indifference curves indicate greater investor satisfaction?

3 Look at the "conservative" and "aggressive" investors described in Figure 18-3. How would you measure investors' attitudes toward risk, assuming you know their indifference curves?

4 Brokerage firms and investment advisers often ask investors to declare whether they

are income-oriented, conservative, aggressive, or speculative. Then they select securities corresponding to these risk categories. Can anyone select an appropriate portfolio for an investor just by considering the individual's preferences? (Hint: The opportunity set also plays a role. Show why, using Figure 18-2.)

5 Why is it so important to set risk-return objectives when investing in an efficient market?

6 Why do you think the so-called emotional aspects of investing (personal preferences) have been ignored for so long by economists and financial theorists?

7 Describe the three categories of tests used by psychologists to measure risk-taking propensity.

8 Explain Atkinson's theory of risk taking.

9 The Kogan and Wallach "Dilemma of Choice Questionnaire" appears to provide a very convenient way of measuring risk-taking propensity. In actuality, it suffers from several shortcomings. Explain these shortcomings in terms of the expected-utility model.

10 Do you think risk-taking propensity is a general personality characteristic? Explain your answer in terms of your own behavior.

11 Who gambles? Why?

12 Describe some of the characteristics of the pathological gambler.

13 Explain the differences between investment, speculation, and gambling. Do you think some people use the investments markets as a gambling casino?

14 List three possible solutions to the problem of selecting the appropriate risk-return combination.

15 Look at the probability distributions in Figure 18-4. Which comes closest to matching your own investment objective?

REFERENCES

Amling, Frederick: *Investments: An Introduction to Analysis and Management,* Prentice-Hall, Englewood Cliffs, N.J., 1974.

Atkinson, J.W.: "Motivational Determinants of Risk Taking Behavior," *Psychological Review,* November 1957, pp. 359–372.

Bergler, Edmund: *The Psychology of Gambling,* Bernard Hanison Ltd., London, 1958.

Black, Fischer: "The Investment Policy Spectrum: Individuals, Endowment Funds and Pension Funds," *Financial Analysts Journal,* January–February 1976, pp. 23–30.

Commission on the Review of the National Policy toward Gambling, *Gambling in America: Appendix 2, Survey of American Gambling Attitudes and Behavior,* Washington, D.C., 1976.

Fama, Eugene F., and Merton H. Miller: *The Theory of Finance,* Dryden Press, Hinsdale, Ill., 1972.

Lichtenstein, Sarah, and Paul Slovic: "Response-induced Reversals or Preference in Gambling: An Extended Replication in Las Vegas," *Journal of Experimental Psychology,* November 1973, pp. 16–20.

_____: "Reversals of Preference between Bids and Choices in Gambling Decisions," *Journal of Experimental Psychology,* July 1971, pp. 46–55.

Markowitz, Harry M.: "Markowitz Revisited," *Financial Analysts Journal,* September–October 1976, pp. 47–52.

_____: *Portfolio Selection: Efficient Diversification of Investments,* Wiley, New York, 1959.

*Schwed, Fred, Jr.: *Where Are the Customers' Yachts?* John Magee, Mass., 1960.

Slovic, Paul: "Assessment of Risk Taking Behavior," *Psychological Bulletin,* March 1964, pp. 220–233.

_____: "Convergent Validation of Risk Taking Measures," *Journal of Abnormal and Social Psychology,* July 1962, pp. 68–71.

_____: "Information Processing, Situation Specificity, and Generality of Risk-taking Behavior," *Journal of Personality and Social Psychology,* April 1972, pp. 128–134.

_____, and Amos Tversky: "Who Accepts Savage's Axiom?" *Behavioral Science,* November 1974, pp. 368–373.

_____, and Sarah Lichtenstein: "Relative Importance of Probabilities and Payoffs in Risk Taking," *Journal of Experimental Psychology Monograph,* November 1968, pp. 1–18.

_____, and Ward Edwards: "Boredom-induced Changes in Preferences among Bets," *The American Journal of Psychology,* June 1965, pp. 208–217.

*Smith, Adam: *The Money Game,* Vintage Books, New York, 1976.

Teweles, Richard J., Charles V. Harlow, and Herbert L. Stone: *The Commodity Futures Game: Who Wins? Who Loses? Why?* McGraw-Hill, New York, 1974.

Wallach, M.A., and N. Kogan: "Aspects of Judgment and Decision Making: Interrelationships and Changes with Age," *Behavioral Science,* January 1961, pp. 23–36.

Weinstein, Malcolm S.: "Achievement Motivation and Risk Preference," *Journal of Personality and Social Psychology,* October 1969, pp. 153–172.

* Publications preceded by an asterisk are highly recommended.

CHAPTER NINETEEN

CONSUMPTION-INVESTMENT DECISIONS

J udging from the contents of most investments books, people invest solely for the joy of making money. Actually, nothing could be further from the truth. Investments serve merely as a means to an end. And that end is consumption. As a result, both the amount invested and the types of investments selected depend on more fundamental decisions about consumption. In fact, the entire investment process rests upon a series of consumption-investment decisions individuals make over their lifetimes.

A FRAMEWORK FOR CONSUMPTION-INVESTMENT DECISIONS

In studying consumption and investment, economists have found one assumption about human behavior to be especially useful. They refer to it as the **nonsatiation axiom.** That is a polite way of saying that people are greedy, i.e., they always prefer more goods to less. But in this world of limited resources, people never completely satisfy their unlimited wants. Instead they must choose between different goods and services. In doing so, consumers make two types of decisions.

515

The first involves the selection of specific goods and services during any one period of time, say a year. For example, do they go skiing in Colorado or surfing in Florida? The second type of decision involves the allocation of consumption over different periods of time. For example, do they take a short vacation every year or do they forgo taking a vacation for 5 years, save $10,000, and then take a 2-month cruise?

Consumption-investment theory focuses on the second type of decision— the allocation of consumption over time. (By the way, consumption includes donations to charity as well as cruises on the Mediterranean.) Economists assume that men and women attempt to spend money in such a way as to obtain the greatest satisfaction during their lives. In other words, the consumer seeks to maximize the expected utility of his or her lifetime consumption.

Two-Period Consumption-Investment Model

Before exploring consumption-investment decisions in more detail, it is worth detouring to a simple two-period model. The two-period model focuses on only two points in time—now and later:

Period 1   Period 2

Now   Later

What this model lacks in realism, it makes up for in simplicity. Moreover, it serves to illustrate the most important aspects of consumption-investment decisions.

Here is the scenario economists usually create for this two-period world:

1 Everyone knows the future.
2 People can borrow and lend at a single rate of interest.
3 All consumption and all financial transactions take place at the start of each period.

Just as in the previous chapter, the essential ingredients in the decision-making process fall into two categories:

1 Tastes or preferences
2 Opportunities, usually referred to as the opportunity set or constraint set

But now these categories are defined in terms of consumption rather than risk and return.

The opportunity set consists of all possible consumption choices available to the decision maker. Obviously these choices depend heavily on how much money a person possesses and the rates of return on investments. Laws and technology also set limits. For example, one cannot sell oneself into slavery or buy a perpetual-motion machine.

In order to better understand the opportunity set, suppose an inhabitant of this two-period world starts the year with $20,000. If the interest rate equals 10%, the line from A to C in Figure 19-1 shows all possible patterns of consumption during the two periods. Point C shows one possibility—forgoing all consumption during the first year (a difficult choice, since it means certain starvation) and then spending the initial $20,000 plus $2,000 interest at the start of the next year. Or the consumer may allocate only $10,000 to investments and spend the rest immediately. The person is thus guaranteed a $10,000 standard of living now and an $11,000 standard in 1 year (point B).

Now assume that a would-be investor comes into this two-period world with no money, but expects to receive $22,000 at the end of 1 year in salary, wages, or an inheritance. By borrowing against this future income at a 10% rate of interest, the individual "slides down" the curve from C to A. For example, the man or

FIGURE 19-1   Consumption opportunities.

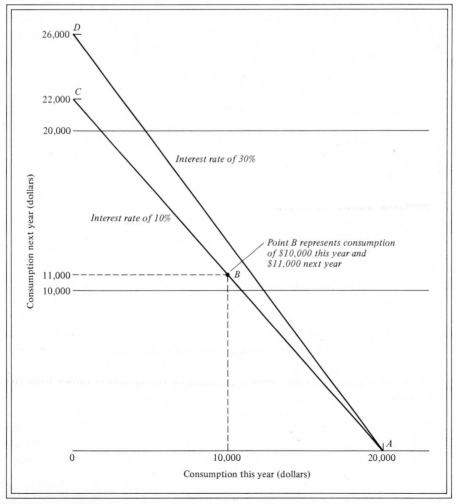

woman can borrow $20,000 now, spend the money, and then repay the lender with the $22,000 received at the start of the following year. This consumption pattern is represented by point A (again, a difficult choice, since it results in starvation). Or the individual can borrow only $10,000 now and repay the loan plus $1,000 interest in 1 year's time. This consumption-investment decision results in spending $10,000 now and $11,000 next year (point *B*).

How do changes in the interest rate and resources affect the individual's opportunity set? Higher rates imply greater opportunities. This can also be seen in Figure 19-1. The slope of the line showing the opportunities reflects the rate of return—the higher the rate, the steeper the slope. If the interest rate equals 30%, the consumption possibilities associated with immediate resources of $20,000 are shown by the line from *A* to *D*. This is a much larger opportunity set than that which existed at a 10% rate of interest. As a result, the individual starting with $20,000 can consume as much as $26,000 worth of goods and services in the second period.

Changes in resources have an obvious impact on the opportunity set, as every winner of the Irish Sweepstakes knows. The greater the resources, the greater the consumption possibilities, both now and in the future. The most important financial resources consist of:

1   Accumulated wealth
2   Future wages, salaries, and other earnings
3   Future receipts from company pension plans, Social Security, and other government programs
4   Inheritances, prizes, and gifts

Each of these resources will be discussed later in this chapter.

Tastes or Preferences

Tastes or preferences constitute the other set of elements in the decision problem. An individual's tastes are highly subjective and depend upon personality, upbringing, education, health, age, and a host of other factors. Figure 19-2 shows an imaginary investor's preferences. The objects of choice are standards of living (consumption) in 2 different years. Each indifference curve shows a particular level of satisfaction. Points *A, B,* and *C* on the lowest indifference curve represent various consumption patterns over the 2 years which provide the individual with the same degree of satisfaction. Suppose these consumption patterns consist of the following standards of living:

	A, $	B, $	C, $
This year	4,000	7,500	13,000
Next year	14,000	7,500	4,500

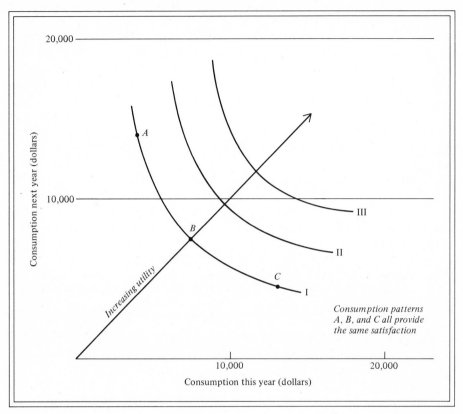

FIGURE 19-2   Consumption preferences.

The fact that these possibilities all lie on the same indifference curve indicates that the individual views them as providing the same utility.

Unlike indifference curves defined in terms of risk and return, these curves slope downward. Now the individual must select between two goods—consumption this year and next—rather than one good and one bad—return and risk. But higher indifference curves still imply greater utility. That's because the consumer spends more. And money does bring happiness, at least in economic theory.

Opportunities and preferences can be combined into one diagram like that in Figure 19-3. Suppose someone plans to make a salary of $20,000 this year and $10,000 next year. How much should he spend and how much should he save? Point *A* shows one possibility—matching consumption to income. But judging from the indifference curves, the consumer achieves the greatest satisfaction (represented by the highest indifference curve) by spending $15,000 this year and $15,500 next year (point B). Since he earns $20,000 and spends only $15,000, he must save the remaining $5,000. This $5,000 grows to $5,500 when invested at

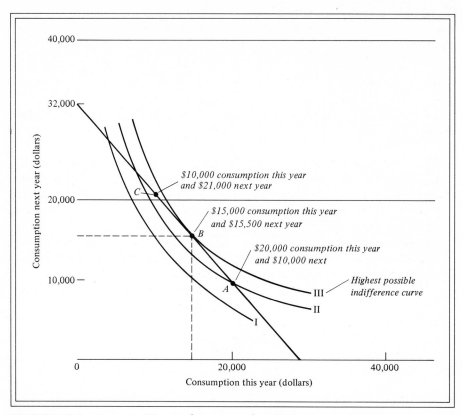

FIGURE 19-3   Opportunities, preferences, and optimal consumption patterns.

10%, which he spends the next year, together with his salary of $10,000, for a total expenditure of $15,500. Here are his exact consumption-investment decisions:

Year	Resources at Start of Year, $	Consumption, $	Investment, $
1	20,000	15,000	5,000
2	15,500	15,500	0

On the other hand, suppose a young medical intern with identical preferences expects to make only $10,000 this year and $21,000 next year (point *C*). She prefers to spread her consumption evenly over the 2 years; so she borrows $5,000 and spends it. Then she repays the loan at the end of the year from her salary of $21,000. As a result, she winds up spending $15,000 this year and $15,500 next year (point *B*). Here are her exact consumption-investment decisions:

Year	Resources at Start of Year, $	Consumption, $	Investment, $
1	10,000	15,000	−5,000 (debt)
2	21,000	15,500	0

The two-period model of consumption and investment demonstrates the following truths:

1   There is nothing wrong with borrowing per se, despite widespread publicity to the contrary. Borrowing makes it possible to spread income and consumption over time. This smoothing of expenditures increases the consumer's welfare by eliminating the need to live like a pauper one day and a prince the next as income fluctuates.
2   Consumption-investment decisions depend upon the proper meshing of opportunities with tastes and preferences. This requires self-knowledge on the part of the investor and advance planning.
3   Different people need to follow different consumption-investment strategies.
4   Happiness, or at least utility, depends heavily on future as well as present consumption.

RATIONAL MAN

People invest in order to consume. And optimal consumption-investment decisions require extensive knowledge of both present and future resources. But strangely enough, authors of investment books never tell investors how to incorporate these resources into their decision making. This oversight appears to result from their too-ready acceptance of the **rational-man assumption.** According to Harry Markowitz, "This rational man is unlike you or me in that he makes no errors in arithmetic or logic in attempting to achieve his clearly defined objectives." Markowitz goes on to say that every action taken by a rational man "is perfectly thought out; every risk is perfectly calculated."

Very few men or women even come close to satisfying this ideal. The famous French essayist Montaigne probably spoke for most people when he said, "I find it more trouble to take care of money than to get it."

Financial counselors claim the fundamental problem faced by most people in managing their money is the lack of a coherent plan, i.e., clearly defined objectives. Apparently even executives fail to set goals. Financial advisers offer to correct this lack of foresight—but at a high price. According to *The Wall Street Journal,* "Typically, the counselors charge between $4,000 and $5,000 per executive for one-time financial analysis and advice, plus $1,500 a year for follow-up service that includes tax-return preparation."

Here's how various financial institutions justify these high fees:

"Coordination is the key word. An individual can get input from several sources but never put them together to look at the total picture." (United States Trust)

"What's important is to get an accurate overview although you may have expert advice in several specific areas." (Wells Fargo Bank)

"Most executives don't really know how to deal with their own financial affairs." (First National City Bank)

In order to improve this abysmal situation, firms offering financial planning use detailed personal and financial questionnaires to identify an individual's preferences and opportunities. Their computers then spew out detailed printouts showing future cash flows, taxable income, and an income statement and balance sheet. Finally, the counselors make their recommendations about everything from taxes to retirement living.

The remainder of this chapter describes some of the tools and techniques used by the best of these financial advisers.

BALANCE SHEET

A personal balance sheet provides people with a snapshot of their resources. It shows them what they own (assets) and owe (liabilities) at a specific moment in time. Investors, be they complete neophytes or hardened veterans, need to base their decisions on this list of resources.

A personal balance sheet differs from the standard accounting statement issued by companies in an important way. The former carries resources at their market value, i.e., what they will supposedly fetch in the marketplace. On the other hand, company balance sheets almost always show the firm's assets and liabilities on an historical cost basis, i.e., at the original purchase price and not the market value.   *ACCOUNTING STATEMENT*

Why the difference? Because accountants and the governmental agencies regulating business feel more secure in using historical costs. Despite the fact that market values provide more current information, they often involve subjective estimates. Imagine an accountant trying to place a market value on a 50-ton machine cemented to the floor of a factory! It's much simpler to record just the cost of the machine.

Fortunately, the average investor faces a much easier job than the average accountant. First, most people can trust themselves to value their belongings as fairly as possible. Second, most of an individual's assets possess a ready market; so there is little doubt about their true worth.

Market values offer several advantages over historical cost figures. Most important, they show investors what they can do at a particular moment in time. Suppose someone purchased 100 shares of stock at $5 a share for a total cost of $500. Now the stock sells for $50 a share; so the market value equals $5,000. Aside from taxes, the original cost of the stock serves only as a point of historical interest. The investor wants to know what can be done with the stock. And the current price tag of $5,000 answers that question.

TABLE 19-1   INVESTOR'S BALANCE SHEET AS OF JUNE 30, 1978

Assets (what is owned)		Liabilities (what is owed)	
Cash and checking account	$ 300	Loan	$ 3,000
Savings account	3,000	Mortgage on home	35,000
Cash value of life insurance	1,000	Total liabilities	$38,000
Stocks	5,000	Net Worth (what is owned after	
Automobile	3,000	all debts have been paid)	$22,300
Home	45,000	Total liabilities and net worth	$60,300
Personal property	3,000		
Total assets	$60,300		

Market values also simplify record keeping. Most people tend to forget about depreciation. Assets like cars and other durable consumer goods get used up in day-to-day living. Market values automatically incorporate these changes.

The balance sheet displays the market values of assets and liabilities. But sometimes it takes a considerable amount of time to sell an asset. That's why most accountants list assets and liabilities on a balance sheet by their degree of **liquidity,** with the most liquid mentioned first. Liquidity measures the speed and ease with which an asset can be sold. The more liquid the asset, the more easily and quickly it can be sold for a fair price. Look at the sample balance sheet shown in Table 19-1. Cash, demand deposits (checking accounts), and savings accounts can all be exchanged almost immediately. Stocks and bonds also sell easily at their current price. But real estate suffers from illiquidity. Homes usually take from 3 to 6 months to sell. And vacant land often remains on sale for years. Forced sales of real estate almost always result in the owner accepting a substantial reduction in value. So this ranking by liquidity serves a purpose. The less liquid the asset, the more uncertain the investor is of its current market value.

Completing a Balance Sheet

The balance sheet provides people with an objective portrayal of their resources. Although considerable detail can be sacrificed in completing a balance sheet, no sizable asset or liability should be overlooked. The following checklist may prove helpful in filling out a balance sheet like the one shown in Table 19-2.

Assets
1   *Cash and checking account*   Cash includes all coin and currency, whether carried in a wallet, kept in a cookie jar, or under a mattress, or buried in the backyard. The amount of cash in a checking account equals the balance recorded in the checkbook, assuming all checks have cleared and all deposits have been recorded.
2   *Savings account*   The savings account should be listed as the amount shown in the passbook. Certificates of deposit constitute a special form of savings account. They can be carried on the balance sheet at face value, unless the

TABLE 19-2   SAMPLE PERSONAL BALANCE SHEET

Balance sheet for _____ (name)
As of _____ (date)

	Amount, $	% of Total Assets
Assets (what is owned)		
Cash and checking account	_____	_____
Savings account	_____	_____
Cash value of life insurance	_____	_____
U.S. government securities	_____	_____
Stocks and bonds	_____	_____
Accounts and notes receivable	_____	_____
From friends and relatives	_____	_____
From other sources	_____	_____
Automobiles	_____	_____
Home	_____	_____
Other real estate	_____	_____
Retirement plans	_____	_____
Business interests	_____	_____
Personal property	_____	_____
Other assets	_____	_____
Total assets	_____	_____
Liabilities (what is owed)		
Accounts and bills due	_____	_____
Notes payable	_____	_____
Unpaid income tax	_____	_____
Other unpaid taxes and interest	_____	_____
Mortgage on home	_____	_____
Mortgages on other property	_____	_____
Other debts	_____	_____
Total liabilities	_____	_____
Net Worth (total assets minus total liabilities, or the excess of what is owned over what is owed)	_____	_____
Total liabilities and net worth	_____	_____

unpaid interest is substantial, in which case this interest should be added to the face value.

3 *Cash value of life insurance*   This is not the face amount of the insurance policy; i.e., it is not the amount the insurance company pays in the event of death. The balance sheet lists the investor's resources at a particular point in time. The policyholder does not own or have access to death benefits until the insured dies. But the policyholder does have access to the cash surrender value of the life insurance policy. Most policies show the cash values at various points in time. Or the exact cash value can be determined by calling the insurance agent or writing the company.

4 *United States government securities*   Most investors think of government securities as government savings bonds, which have fixed redemption values.

If a bond was purchased recently, the redemption value comes very close to the amount originally paid, and this figure can be used on the balance sheet. If the bonds are already several years old, a table of redemption values (available at any Federal Reserve bank) must be used to determine the market value. Other government securities trade in public markets. The prices of these securities can be obtained by calling a bank or a brokerage firm.

5 *Stocks and bonds*   Since stocks and bonds fluctuate considerably in price, anyone completing a balance sheet must use up-to-date prices. *The Wall Street Journal* and most large daily newspapers carry the daily prices of many stocks and bonds. Prices for stocks or bonds not listed in the papers can be obtained from a bank or brokerage firm.

6 *Accounts and notes receivable*   Accounts and notes receivable consist of money owed to the investor. They should be carried on the balance sheet at face value, together with any substantial amount of interest. Any excess withholdings for taxes or Social Security should be listed as an account receivable from the government. In addition, banks often require owners of rental property to hold extra money in their accounts for the payment of future taxes and insurance premiums on the property. These amounts can also be entered as an account receivable. Finally, personal IOUs, whether from friends and relatives or other people, should be recorded at a realistic figure.

7 *Automobiles*   Car prices are readily available. A trip to a used-car dealer and/or a survey of the classified ads usually provides a good estimate of the market value of a car in average condition. However, these prices probably exceed the actual price that could be obtained, since people nearly always ask for higher prices than they expect to receive. The *NADA Official Used Car Guide* shows wholesale prices and is therefore more realistic.

8 *Home*   Valuing a home is difficult. Unless there is good evidence to the contrary, a recently purchased home should be carried on the balance sheet at its purchase price. If the house has already been owned for several years, a check of neighborhood prices may be helpful in estimating value. A realtor or an insurance agent who sells home insurance may also be willing to help assess the sale value. Their estimates will probably exceed the true market value.

9 *Other real estate*   The original purchase price may be the only practical way of valuing such property.

10 *Retirement plan*   Many people overlook this extremely important asset. Although access to a retirement plan may be restricted, it should still be listed at its market value.

11 *Business interests*   More than 8 million Americans own their own companies. An accurate valuation of most of these firms is nearly impossible, but insurance agents or valuation experts can provide estimates. Or the owner may simply multiply the company's profits by an "appropriate" multiple.

12 *Personal property*   This category includes appliances, tape recorders, stereos, CB radios, TV sets, clothes, furniture, etc. Clothes have almost no

market value, regardless of their original purchase price. Since the balance sheet describes what the investor can do, not what was done, clothes should be carried at their true market value, even though it may be very low. Durable consumer goods, such as stereos, possess ready marketability and can be valued by referring to want ads or from personal experience. Furniture may or may not have a ready market value. Modern furniture has a very low resale value; antiques retain their value much more.

13   *Other assets*   This is a very important category for some investors. It may include a valuable coin or stamp collection, art, or money held in special accounts.

Liabilities

1   *Accounts and bills due*   Any amounts payable on charge accounts and any unpaid bills should be listed at their face value.

2   *Notes payable*   This category includes personal loans, student loans, and money borrowed on life insurance policies. Notes should be carried at the unpaid balance.

3   *Unpaid income tax, other unpaid taxes, interest, and mortgages*   All of these are carried on the balance sheet at the unpaid balance. Future interest payments should not be included.

4   *Other debts*   For many investors the most important debt consists of money borrowed to buy securities in a margin account. This amount can be found on the latest brokerage statement—it includes any accrued interest.

The difference between assets and liabilities equals **net worth**; i.e.,

$$\text{Net worth} = \text{assets} - \text{liabilities}$$

No other number says so much about the financial status of an individual or family. Suppose a person has a net worth of $20,000. That means that assets exceed liabilities by $20,000. In other words, if the person sold off all his or her assets and paid all debts, there would remain $20,000 in cash.

Despite the relative shortness of life, some people show an amazing ability to pile up great fortunes. The latest list of the richest people in the world includes:

Name	Estimated Net Worth, $	Principal Source of Wealth
Daniel Ludwig	3 billion	Oil tankers
John MacArthur	1 billion	Insurance—Banker's Life and Casualty
Ray Kroc	Over 600 million	Hamburgers—McDonald's
Paul Mellon	500 million to 1 billion	Inheritances
Leonard Stern	Over 500 million	Pets—Hartz Mountain

And according to the Internal Revenue Service, there are now more than 180,000 millionaires in the United States. That's a lot of net worth!

Other Purposes of a Balance Sheet

The balance sheet does more than help in planning. First, it provides a record of assets and liabilities in the case of theft or loss. Too many insurance policies, bank accounts, stocks, and other securities are lost by their owners and their heirs because of a lack of records. Second, it places investors in a much better position to turn over their affairs to their spouses or trustees in the event of death or serious illness. As one financial planner melodramatically puts it, "Remember that many wives who are uninformed about financial matters are only one heartbeat away from total financial dependence on others."

For these reasons, everyone should make several copies of the balance sheet and other important documents. These copies can be stored in a safe-deposit box and/or in a desk or fireproof cabinet in the home or office.

HUMAN CAPITAL

Despite its seemingly all-inclusive nature, the typical balance sheet ignores a very important asset. Over their lifetimes most people earn hundreds of thousands of dollars. No wonder economists refer to a person's earnings capacity as human capital. This human capital produces a return in the form of wages and salaries.

Several factors contribute to the amount of lifetime income earned by individuals. Aside from the relatively few people born with silver spoons in their mouths, the primary factors influencing an individual's lifetime income include education, sex, socioeconomic background, natural ability, race, health, the economic state of the world, and chance.

Education

Education plays a vital role in future earnings. According to projections by the U.S. Bureau of the Census, the average male college graduate can expect to make 50% more than a high school graduate and twice as much as a person who dropped out of school after the eighth grade. These increased earnings reflect the time and money spent in the pursuit of education, i.e., the investment in human capital.

Figure 19-4 shows the lifetime earnings corresponding to different levels of education. These future earnings figures can be discounted back to the present to provide estimates of human capital. This has been done by economists at the Social Security Administration. Table 19-3 shows the present value of expected lifetime earnings by years of school completed. Someone in the twenty to twenty-four age category who expects to graduate from college possesses a present value of $227,423—a sizable investment! On the other hand, the present value of someone in the same age group who never graduated from high school averages only $106,944.

Elementary school:	
Less than 8 years	$280,000
8 years	$344,000
High school: 1 to 3 years	$389,000
4 years	$479,000
College: 1 to 3 years	$543,000
4 years	$711,000
5 or more years	$824,000

FIGURE 19-4   Education and projected lifetime earnings of men, 1972. (From U.S. Bureau of the Census, *Current Population Reports: Annual Mean Income, Lifetime Income, and Educational Attainment of Men in the U.S., for Selected Years, 1956 to 1972,* ser. P-60, no. 92, 1974.)

Sex

The median annual income of women falls far below that of men. Female college graduates make only about 50% as much as male graduates. And the same holds true for men and women with less education. Table 19-4 shows the difference in income by education and age. Judging from these numbers, sex is an inherent resource, at least if one happens to be a man!

These differences apparently exist because of the occupations or professions of the respective sexes. Louise Kapp Howe, author of *Pink Collar Workers,* cites example after example of the lower-paying jobs available to women, like school

TABLE 19-3   *PRESENT VALUE OF EXPECTED EARNINGS BY AGE AND EDUCATION*

| Age Group | Education | | |
	Elementary, $	High School, $	College, $
1–4	36,656	58,570	74,819
10–14	65,937	105,356	134,584
20–24	106,944	158,411	227,423
30–34	123,538	167,274	271,681
40–44	103,857	145,207	246,244
50–54	71,924	102,470	178,765
60–64	27,306	45,184	84,789
70–74	6,441	13,412	26,718
80–84	2,085	4,751	7,896

Source: Social Security Administration, "1972 Lifetime Earnings by Age, Sex, Race, and Education Level," *Research and Statistics Note,* Office of Research and Statistics, September 30, 1975.

TABLE 19-4   MEDIAN INCOME OF FULL-TIME
WORKERS* BY EDUCATION AND SEX

Education	Women, $	Men, $
Elementary school		
less than 8 years	5,109	8,647
8 years	5,691	10,600
High school		
1 to 3 years	6,355	11,511
4 years	7,777	13,542
College		
1 to 3 years	9,126	14,989
4 years or more	11,359	18,450

* Persons 25 years old and over as of March 1974.
Source: U.S. Bureau of the Census, *Current Population Reports: Money Income and Poverty Status of Families and Persons in the United States: 1975 and 1974 Revisions,* ser. P-60, no. 103, September 1976, pp. 22–23 (advance report).

teaching, social work, and secretarial positions. More recently, stories of some exceptional woman who has become the first female commercial pilot, truck driver, or TV anchorperson have appeared in the news. But to date, this "invasion" of the traditionally male professions has had little or no impact on the incomes of most women.

Other Resources

Inheritances benefit a small number of people. In one study of inheritances, researchers asked men and women, "Have you ever inherited any money or property? If yes, when and how much?" On the average, less than 1% of the individuals in any particular age group became heirs during any single year. And the median inheritance totaled only $3,500.

The right to receive government payments also constitutes an important resource. Over the years the federal budget has increased tremendously. The fastest-growing section of that budget goes by the name of "income security." Income security includes Social Security payments, unemployment compensation, and welfare payments. Some of these payments depend upon the individual's contributions. Others are only remotely tied to wages and salaries.

CASH FLOW STATEMENT

A balance sheet is static—it does not portray change. Like a snapshot, it captures only one moment in time. For this reason, the balance sheet must be supplemented with a statement of expected cash flows. A cash flow statement shows all cash receipts and expenditures. In effect, it measures the flow of dollars into and out of the individual's pocket.

A cash flow statement, when combined with a balance sheet, provides an indication of the individual's present and future resources. Table 19-5 shows a sample 1-year cash flow statement for a recent college graduate. The statement resembles the ones used by many banks, financial counseling firms, and insurance agencies. Most people who fill out cash flow statements do so for the entire family. Usually the statement covers a period of 1 year.

Cash flow statements require a considerable expenditure of time and effort to complete. But the end results usually justify this expenditure. Here are some steps to follow in completing a cash flow statement:

1 Sit down in a quiet place.
2 Assemble all canceled checks, checkbooks, bills, credit card statements, receipts, and paycheck records for the past year.
3 Start with the cash receipts section of the cash flow statement. Take the most recent paycheck. Do you expect your salary to remain the same during the

TABLE 19-5 PROJECTED CASH FLOW STATEMENT FOR AN INVESTOR FOR THE YEAR JULY 1, 1977, TO JULY 1, 1978

Receipts		
Salary	$10,000.00	
Bonus	500.00	
Dividends and interest	12.50	
Total receipts		$10,512.50
Payments		
To the government		
Federal taxes	1,780.56	
Social Security	585.00	
State taxes	99.84	
Total payments to the government		$ 2,465.40
Fixed		
Rent	1,920.00	
Insurance		
Car	420.00	
Home or apartment	72.00	
Medical	180.00	
Life	109.20	
Total fixed payments		$ 2,701.20
Variable		
Food	1,200.00	
Car repairs, gas, etc.	444.00	
Clothing	360.00	
Entertainment and travel	1,500.00	
Utilities	120.00	
Miscellaneous	660.00	
Total variable payments		$ 4,284.00
Total payments		$ 9,450.60
Discretionary income (total receipts minus total payments)	$ 1,061.90	

coming year? If so, simply record the salary. Otherwise, add estimated cost-of-living adjustments and raises. If the salary is based on commissions or if the bonus is tied to performance, a rough estimate will have to suffice.

Dividends and interest can be estimated from the income tax return filed for the previous year. Or better still, future dividends and interest payments can be based upon projections taken from *The Wall Street Journal* or *Barron's.* Payments to the government consist of taxes (both federal and state) and Social Security. Usually the monthly withholding for taxes and Social Security can be taken off the latest paycheck stubs, or the yearly figures from the previous year's W-2 forms can be used. Estimated taxes should also be included, taking into consideration changes in the tax rates and Social Security payments.

Payments can be segregated into two categories, as in the table: (1) fixed and (2) variable. Fixed payments, like a mortgage payment, rent, or insurance premiums, seldom change from month to month. On the other hand, variable expenditures, like clothing, medical bills, and entertainment, fluctuate considerably over the months or years.

The difference between planned cash expenditures and receipts equals **discretionary income.** Many people incorrectly view this figure as savings. Actually the word "savings" refers to the difference between income and consumption. Part of the mortgage and straight life insurance payments go to savings. And, of course, the investor can save all discretionary income if so desired.

LIFETIME EARNINGS

There are two ways to integrate wages and salaries into the consumption-investment decision. The simplest is to discount all future earnings back to the present and then focus on human capital. The other approach involves explicit consideration of all future earnings. The next section takes this cash flow approach and studies the time pattern of income.

Lifetime Income Profiles

Salaries gradually increase with work experience. In 1972 the *Harvard Business Review* conducted a survey of 6,000 graduates of 16 MBA granting universities. Their findings confirm this pattern. The median salaries received by MBA graduates relative to their year of graduation appear on the top of the next page. Judging from these figures, a year of experience translates into a raise of about $1,000.

Unfortunately, salaries seldom increase indefinitely with increasing age and experience. Usually, at around fifty years of age, the individual's earnings level off or even decrease because of lessened ability and/or desire to perform the tasks required by the job. The *Harvard Business Review* study stopped short of this age

MEDIAN SALARY FOR MBAs

Graduating Class	Salary, $	Years after Graduation
1947	36,000	25
1952	31,000	20
1957	29,000	15
1962	25,000	10
1967	20,000	5
1969	17,000	3

Source: John E. Steele, and Lewis B. Ward, "MBAs: Mobile, Well Situated, Well Paid," *Harvard Business Review,* January–February 1974, © 1973 by the President and Fellows of Harvard College. All rights reserved.

group. But a Bureau of Labor Statistics survey shows average annual incomes for people up to age sixty-four. The findings are summarized in Figure 19-5.

Judging from Figure 19-5, semiskilled, skilled, clerical, self-employed, and professional workers all begin their careers making more or less the same income. And all but the self-employed peak at more or less the same time—about

FIGURE 19-5 Lifetime income profiles by occupational category. (From U.S. Department of Labor, Bureau of Labor Statistics, *Survey of Consumer Expenditures: Consumer Expenditures and Income.*)

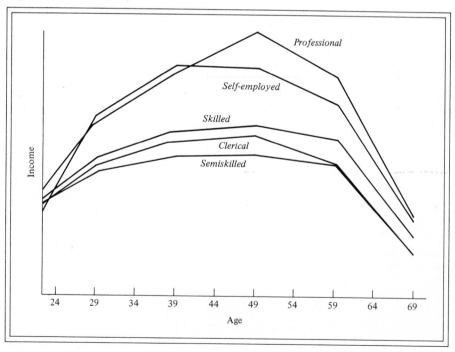

fifty years of age. However, the rates of growth in earnings differ substantially over the years. The professional's earnings increase at a fast rate until age forty-nine. (The BLS shows income after taxes. Before-tax earnings probably show even greater increases.) On the other hand, the semiskilled realize little economic benefit from their increased experience.

Uncertainty

Uncertainty complicates the consumption-investment decision in numerous ways. Investors must guess their future salaries and invested wealth, their changing tastes and preferences, the future prices of goods and services, and even their lifetimes. Previous chapters discussed the expected returns on securities, changes in the price level, and mortality rates. This section focuses on uncertainty about future earnings.

Table 19-6 shows the distribution of incomes among individuals in the United States. Incomes show a surprising dispersion. And adjustments for race, sex, and the amount of time worked fail to eliminate this variation. Incomes differ substantially even among people in the same occupation. Despite the fact that the average physician and surgeon earned $33,000 in 1974, 6% of this group earned less than $10,000. The same holds true for salespeople, with more than 15% earning at least $15,000, while at the same time more than 10% earned less than $6,000. Narrowing the employment category down still further, full-time male

TABLE 19-6   MONEY INCOME IN 1975

Income, $	% of Income Recipients
Under 2,000	14.1
2,000–2,999	15.6
3,000–3,999	12.4
4,000–4,999	8.9
5,000–5,999	7.3
6,000–6,999	5.8
7,000–7,999	5.7
8,000–9,999	9.1
10,000–14,999	13.0
15,000–24,999	6.6
25,000–49,999	1.3
50,000 and up	0.2
Median 4,882	
Mean 6,623	

Source: U.S. Bureau of the Census, Current Population Reports: Money Income and Poverty Status of Families and Persons in the United States: 1975 and 1974 Revisions, ser. P-60, no. 103, September 1976, p. 2 (advance report).

auto mechanics from the ages of thirty-four and forty-four recorded the following yearly incomes:

Income, $	% of Auto Mechanics
0 to 1,999	2.4
2,000 to 3,999	5.1
4,000 to 5,999	16.0
6,000 to 6,999	11.4
7,000 to 7,999	14.5
8,000 to 9,999	23.7
10,000 to 14,999	22.2
15,000 and up	4.7
Median 8,050	

Even within this narrow category, earnings still exhibit a tremendous dispersion. Because of this large in-group variation, Christopher Jencks—the author of a book titled *Inequality*—claims that earnings depend largely upon unknown factors conveniently summarized by the term "luck." Lester Thurow, an economist at M.I.T., offers another more socially acceptable explanation—on-the-job training. Some people obtain much better training than others, and this accounts for substantial differences in money income. Whatever the reason, people face considerable uncertainty about the exact magnitude of their salary. This uncertainty varies from occupation to occupation and from age group to age group.

BUDGETING

Apparently society now offers people so many opportunities that the proper pursuit of happiness requires some well-defined objectives. Since individuals invest in order to consume, it seems only natural to express these personal objectives in terms of actual consumption items. This goal-setting process goes by the name of budgeting. *Webster's Dictionary* defines a **budget** as a "plan for the coordination of resources and expenditures." Why is such a plan necessary? Because without one the consumer's unlimited wants often crash head on into his or her limited resources.

One form of budgeting simply involves listing all future expenditures. Such a list represents the consumer's vision of the ideal consumption pattern, given her or his predictions of future income, prices, product qualities, etc.

In real life, consumers somehow solve this complicated choice problem. But the very idea of explicitly planning each and every expenditure borders on the absurd. The adequacy of any decision-making process must be judged on the basis of its costs as well as its benefits. Extremely detailed budgets consume so much time (a very valuable good) that the costs probably far exceed the increased satisfaction.

TABLE 19-7   TRIAL BUDGET

Expenditure Category	Average Monthly Expenditures, $	% of Expenditures
Food	100	11.4
Housing	160	18.3
Car and repairs	80	9.1
Insurance	80	9.1
Clothing	40	4.6
Entertainment and travel	75	8.6
Utilities	10	1.1
Miscellaneous	30	3.4
Savings	96	11.0
Government	205	23.4
	876	100.0

A more practical alternative is to simply budget general categories of expenditures, like housing, utilities, food, and transportation. This appears simple enough, but many would-be budgeteers find the process of setting limits on expenditures a painful process. Actually the sole purpose of the budget is to enhance utility by improving consumption patterns.

The logical first step in creating a budget is the study of past consumption patterns. These past patterns provide one measure of the individual's own unique tastes and needs. The cash flow statement in Table 19-5 provides a convenient summary of past expenditures. These figures provide the basis for a trial budget, perhaps like the one shown in Table 19-7. After a month, the individual or family can make any necessary adjustments. Budgeting should always be viewed as an ongoing process.

Table 19-8 shows "average" figures for expenditures by United States families. Financial counselors sometimes attempt to mold their clients to these

TABLE 19-8   "AVERAGE" BUDGET

Expenditure Category	Percentage of Expenditures
Food at home	20.9
Food away from home	3.8
Housing, including furniture	22.6
Transportation	7.3
Clothing	7.6
Personal care	2.1
Medical care	3.7
Taxes	22.6
Life insurance, gifts, and contributions	5.4
Recreation, education, entertainment, and miscellaneous	6.2

Figure based on an intermediate budget of $14,333.
Source: U.S. Department of Labor, Bureau of Labor Statistics.

averages. Indeed, budgeting practice too often resembles the iron bed of Procrustes. Procrustes, according to Greek mythology, was a much-feared highway robber. Not just content to steal people's money, Procrustes placed his victims on an iron bed. If they fit the bed perfectly, he freed them unharmed. Otherwise he shortened them by cutting off their legs or lengthened them by stretching them on the rack.

Allocation of Time

Despite widespread recognition of the fact that time is money, economists long ignored the question of the proper allocation of time by consumers. According to Gary Becker, an economist at Columbia University:

> Economic development has led to a large secular decline in the work week, so that whatever may have been true of the past, today it's below fifty hours in most countries, less than a third of the total time available. Consequently, the allocation and efficiency of non-working time may now be more important to economic welfare than that of working time; yet the attention paid by economists to the latter dwarfs any paid to the former.[1]

Becker's article, "A Theory of the Allocation of Time," represents one of the first and perhaps most influential attempts to "redress the balance." Becker and other economists view the family or household as combining "time and market goods to produce more basic commodities that directly enter their utility functions. One such commodity is the seeing of a play which depends on the input of the actors, script, theater, and the playgoer's time; another is sleeping, which depends on the input of a bed, house (pills) and time."[2] It is these more basic commodities, not the goods themselves, which enter the utility function.

This approach makes clear the constraint on utility maximization imposed by time. People devote their time to either work or consumption activities. By working more hours, the consumer increases the amount of income (and therefore goods) available, but at the expense of time spent on consumption. Therefore, it only makes sense to focus on the maximum money income achievable by the individual. According to Becker, this full income "could in general be obtained by devoting all the time and other resources of a household to earning income with no regard for consumption. Of course, all the time would not usually be spent at a job: sleep, food, even leisure are required for efficiency." The consumer spends this "full income" either directly on market goods or indirectly by forgoing money income. So a complete budget requires the statement of expenditures on leisure time as well as on more tangible goods.

Leisure time falls into two general categories: active participation or passive participation (spectator activities). Spectator activities supposedly account for most leisure time. David Blank, vice-president of economics and research at CBS, estimates that the average adult spends about 50 hours a week in spectator activities. Not surprisingly, television accounts for nearly half of this total. Another third is spent listening to the radio. Newspaper and magazine reading come in a distant third and fourth. According to Blank, only a tiny fraction of spectator time goes to reading books or attending cultural events.

By the way, working hours vary greatly depending upon the profession. More than two-fifths of all managers, officials, and proprietors of companies work 49 hours or more a week. An incredible 24% of this group claim they labor more than 60 hours a week! But farmers and farm managers prove that Mother Nature is the most demanding of them all: 63% report working more than 60 hours a week.

LONG-TERM FINANCIAL PLANNING

People save for a variety of reasons. According to consumer surveys, retirement heads the list of savings objectives. And with good reason, since the resources needed for a happy retirement have escalated with earlier retirement and longer life expectations. Next to retirement, emergencies receive the most attention from savers. Many feel the need for protection against the proverbial rainy day. Possible emergencies include the loss of a job, disability, and medical costs. Other frequently cited savings objectives revolve around children's education, bequests, and consumer durables, like a home, boat, or car.

The next two sections provide a brief description of financial planning for retirement and an emergency like the loss of a job. These techniques can easily be applied to other objectives.

Retirement

Mandatory retirement at age sixty-five dominates United States employment policy. And many companies and governmental agencies now encourage earlier retirement. Despite the inevitability of retirement, too few men and women consciously plan for this momentous event in their life. The principal retirement objectives concern (1) when and (2) at what standard of living. These decisions are intertwined, since a delay in retirement usually makes it possible to accumulate increased resources.

A nationwide survey conducted by the Social Security Research Institute provides some important insights into the retirement decision. According to the institute, the major finding is that "financial factors—primarily expected retirement income—are of principal importance in the retirement decision." Other factors playing a role in the retirement decision include (1) health, (2) interest in recreational activities, and (3) job satisfaction. Individuals with poor or declining health usually prefer early retirement, as do those people with a strong interest in hobbies, sports, travel, and other recreational activities. On the other hand, job satisfaction seems to result in a desire to delay retirement.

The institute reports that three-fourths of retirees describe themselves as either "satisfied" or "very satisfied" with retirement. Apparently, retirement can "be a genuinely satisfying time of life for many, if not most, people." By the way, financial resources in the form of adequate retirement income again appear to have a substantial impact on happiness. And another survey by the National Institute of Mental Health confirms these findings.

> EXAMPLE   Roger and Carolyn Etherington both plan to retire at the age of sixty-five. They want to receive a total retirement income equal to at least 80% of their income immediately before retirement (with both computed on an after-tax basis). Assuming a 2% a year real increase in their incomes until the age of fifty, they expect to be earning $50,000 a year immediately before retirement. Taxes will take $10,000, leaving a $40,000 after-tax income.
>
> They estimate their retirement income (again in real terms) at the age of sixty-five to be as follows:

Company pension benefits	$16,000
Social security benefits (tax free)	13,000
Total retirement income before taxes	$29,000
Taxes	−4,000
Total retirement income after taxes	$25,000

> It appears that their after-tax retirement income will be equal to only $25,000 or 62.5% of preretirement income. This falls short of their objective of 80% of $40,000, or $32,000.
>
> Where will the additional $7,000 a year come from? One answer is savings. Here are the amounts needed at different rates of return:

4%	6%	8%	10%	12%
$80,942	$72,065	$64,709	$58,567	$53,397

> These figures are based upon the assumption that both Etheringtons die exactly 15 years after retirement.
>
> There are numerous ways to achieve the necessary amount of savings. If the Etheringtons opt for a low-risk–low-return investment strategy, they will have to save considerably more than with a high-risk and high-return strategy. For example, at 4% a year, $1,000 a year for 35 years grows to $73,650. At 12% it takes only $171 a year to accumulate this sum. By the way, these figures show the advantage of planning far into the future. Given enough time, even small savings grow into large amounts of money.

The previous example ignores the impact of inflation. Most financial advisers attempt to incorporate their own forecasts of inflation into their projections. But this approach suffers from two shortcomings. First, inflation forecasts are notorious for their inaccuracy. Second, inflation-adjusted figures confuse most people. To see why, suppose a job currently pays $20,000 a year. At an annual rate of inflation of 8% a year, the same job pays an incredible $434,500 a year in 40 years. And yet the real salary remains unchanged.

Rather than employ these astronomical figures, it appears best to work with real numbers. For example, salary increases are expressed in real terms as are all rates of return.

Emergencies

Many financial counselors advise their clients to maintain at least 6 months' salary in reasonably liquid assets. This money supposedly protects the family in the event of unemployment. In reality, the necessary reserves depend upon a number of factors, including:

1 The size and flexibility of cash expenditures and receipts
2 The state of the job market
3 The amount of unemployment compensation available
4 The career objectives of the individual
5 The available line of credit

> **EXAMPLE**   David and Cheryl Sawyer both work. Dave earns $16,000 a year and Cheryl $10,000. According to their cash flow statement, they spend only $12,000 a year (not including payments to the government). And because they own their car and furniture outright, they have few fixed payments. If the Sawyers had to, they could cut their expenditures back to $10,000 a year for a short time.
>
> Because of the small probability of both losing their jobs, Dave and Cheryl decide that an emergency fund of $6,000 in liquid assets suffices. (They already have this money invested in mutual funds.) In addition, the Sawyers apply for and receive a **line of credit** from their local bank. This line of credit entitles them to automatically borrow up to $2,000 at any time.

SUMMARY

Every investor must answer two basic questions:

1 How much should I invest?
2 Where should I invest?

In answering these questions, people make some incredibly complicated decisions. Indeed, even mathematically sophisticated economists cringe at the thought of providing exact solutions to these everyday problems.

But economists do know how to describe the investment process. They view consumption as the be-all and end-all of any investment activity. The two-period consumption-investment model demonstrates the impact of consumption on investment (and vice versa). It also serves to illustrate the importance of properly coordinating personal preferences with available resources. Finally, it provides a justification for borrowing (under the right circumstances).

The coordination of preferences with resources requires financial planning—unless the investor qualifies as a completely rational man or woman. The balance sheet and cash flow statement aid in this planning process. They describe present resources and expected changes in these resources. For most people, human capital represents the most important resource. College graduates can expect to earn nearly $1 million during their lifetimes. These earnings translate into a present value of nearly $300,000.

Budgets, despite their unpleasant connotations, play a vital role in channeling these resources to their best uses. In order to achieve the greatest satisfaction during their lifetimes, individuals must mesh their opportunities with their tastes and preferences. This requires a clearly defined set of objectives, i.e., a budget. Consciously or unconsciously, everyone follows a budget. But given the complexity of modern-day life, a written budget probably provides the most appropriate guidelines.

People invest for many reasons. According to consumer surveys, retirement is the most-often-cited objective. Other important objectives include provisions for emergencies, children's education, bequests, and the purchase of consumer durables, like a home, boat, or car. Given the long-time horizon involved with these expenditures, financial planning becomes especially important.

KEYWORDS

nonsatiation axiom	net worth	line of credit
rational man assumption	discretionary income	
liquidity	budget	

QUESTIONS

1 Draw the two-period opportunity set for an investor starting the year with $10,000 and receiving no other income. Assume the interest rate equals 8%.
2 Draw some indifference curves for an imaginary investor (perhaps yourself). Now explain why (1) none of these curves should cross each other; (2) higher curves indicate higher levels of satisfaction; (3) indifference curves usually slope downward; and (4) these curves usually bend inward. (See Figure 19-2 for an example.)
3 Now combine the indifference curves from question 2 with the opportunity set from question 1. How much should this imaginary investor consume in year 1 and year 2? Next imagine that this individual expects to receive an inheritance of $100,000 at the end of 1 year. How does this change the optimal consumption-investment pattern?
4 Debate the pros and cons of borrowing money. (Does the two-period model provide any justification for borrowing? On what terms?)
5 Explain the need for personal financial planning. (Or do you qualify as a completely rational man or woman?)
6 Use the balance sheet in Table 19-1 to answer the following questions:
   a Suppose the investor needed to raise $9,000 within a week. Could this be done without substantial costs?
   b How do you rate this portfolio as far as riskiness?
   c What percent of the portfolio consists of real assets? Of nominal assets? How should this investor fare during a time of unexpected inflation?
   d Suppose the $3,000 loan on the balance sheet represents credit card charges and

the interest rate equals 18%. What would you recommend? What if the loan represents the unpaid balance on a car and the interest rate amounts to 12%?

7 Many people confuse discretionary income with savings. Explain the difference.

8 Look at the cash flow statement in Table 19-5 and answer the following questions:
   a How much does this individual actually take home after paying all taxes?
   b Do any of the variable expenses appear to be unusually high or low?
   c Do you think this person should consider buying a new car if the annual payments equal $1,500?

9 Most academicians and investment advisers believe that investors become increasingly risk-averse as they grow older. In fact, the almost classic example compares the cautious investment policy of an elderly widow with the speculative objectives of a young doctor. Can you explain this difference in terms of resources rather than tastes and preferences? (Hint: Does the human capital of these two investors differ?)

10 What real (as opposed to nominal) growth rate do you expect in your own salary? Why?

11 How much uncertainty surrounds your future earnings?

12 Prepare a state of the world analysis for yourself for each of the following possibilities: death, disability, and unemployment. What probabilities do you attach to these states of the world?

REFERENCES

Bailard, Thomas E., David L. Biehl, and Ronald W. Kaiser: *Personal Money Management,* Science Research Associates, Chicago, 1977.

Barlow, Robin, Harvey E. Brazer, and James N. Morgan: *Economic Behavior of the Affluent,* Brookings, Washington, D.C., 1966.

Fama, Eugene F., and Merton H. Miller: *The Theory of Finance,* Dryden Press, Hinsdale, Ill., 1972.

Howe, Louise Kapp: *Pink Collar Workers,* Putnam, New York, 1977.

Kreps, Juanita M.: *Lifetime Allocation of Work and Income: Essays in the Economics of Aging,* Duke, Durham, N.C., 1971.

Lang, Larry R., and Thomas H. Gillespie: *Strategy for Personal Finance,* McGraw-Hill, New York, 1977.

Markowitz, Harry M.: "Markowitz Revisited," *Financial Analysts Journal,* September–October 1976, pp. 47–52.

_____: *Portfolio Selection: Efficient Diversification of Investments,* Wiley, New York, 1959.

Neal, Charles: *Sense with Dollars,* Doubleday, Garden City, N.Y., 1967.

Porter, W. Thomas, and Durwood L. Alkire: *Wealth: How to Achieve It!* Reston Publishing, Reston, Va., 1976.

Soltow, Lee, ed.: *Six Papers on the Size Distribution of Wealth and Income,* National Bureau of Economic Research, New York, 1969.

Steinem, Gloria: "Where the Women Workers Are . . . . The Rise of the Pink Collar Ghetto," *Ms.,* March 1977, pp. 51–52.

Stillman, Richard J.: *Guide to Personal Finance: A Lifetime Program of Money Management,* Prentice-Hall, Englewood Cliffs, N.J., 1975.

Thurow, Lester C.: *Generating Inequality: The Distributional Mechanisms of the Economy,* sponsored by the U.S. Department of Labor, Employment and Training Administration, Office of Research and Development, Washington, D.C., 1975.

U.S. Bureau of the Census, *Current Population Reports: Annual Mean Income, Lifetime Income, and Educational Attainment of Men in the United States, for Selected Years, 1956 to 1972,* P-60, no. 92, 1974.

U.S. Department of Health, Education and Welfare, Social Security Administration, Office of Research and Statistics, "1972 Lifetime Earnings by Age, Sex, Race, and Education Level," *Research and Statistics Note,* Sept. 30, 1975.

U.S. Department of Labor, Employment Standards Administration, Women's Bureau, *1975 Handbook on Women Workers,* 1975.

CHAPTER TWENTY

INVESTMENT
STRATEGY

Not long ago institutional investors and brokerage firms discovered the words "investment strategy." This phrase possesses tremendous appeal, since most people think of a strategy as a particularly clever or skillful plan. Small wonder the investment community quickly adopted the term and began referring to most of its recommendations as investment and/or portfolio strategies.

THE STRATEGY CONCEPT

Historically the word "strategy" referred to war and the direction of military forces. Karl von Clausewitz, a Prussian army officer and author of the classic *On War,* defined strategy as "the art of the employment of battles as a means to gain the object of war. . . ." Another famous military strategist, Helmuth Moltke, chief of staff of the Prussian army under Bismarck, described strategy as "the practical adaption of the means placed at the general's disposal to the attainment of the object in view."

Game Theory

Until 1944, strategy retained this blood and bullets emphasis. Then John von Neumann and Oskar Morganstern, two mathematicians at Princeton University, published their famous book, *The Theory of Games and Economic Behavior.* By the way, the word "game" does not imply any lack of seriousness. **Game theory,** also called the theory of games of strategy, actually involves a mathematical approach to conflict. Games like checkers, chess, and bridge happen to offer the purest examples of conflict situations. In other words, the battlefield and the parlor are never very far removed. Both display a common denominator—conflict.

Game theorists all agree on the definition of a **strategy.** They describe it as any complete plan. Here are some more detailed definitions.

"A strategy is a plan so complete that it cannot be upset by enemy action or Nature. . . ." (J. D. Williams, author of the *Compleat Strategyst*)

A strategy "means a complete program given by a player before the game begins (say to a referee), stating what he will do in every conceivable situation in which he may find himself in the course of the game." (Anatol Rapoport, author of *Fights, Games and Debate*)

". . . A detailed specification of actions is called a (pure) strategy." (R. Duncan Luce and Howard Raiffa, authors of *Games and Decisions*)

By the way, nothing in the game-theory definition of strategy suggests cleverness or skill. A strategy is simply a complete plan—perhaps clever, perhaps foolish. Nor does the choice of a strategy imply that the decision maker is adopting a rigid set of actions, regardless of future events. For example, an individual might adopt the following investment strategy:

Invest $2,000 in stock options.

If the options increase in value, hold them until the final trading day and then sell them and reinvest all the proceeds in new options.

If the options decline in value by more than 50%, immediately sell them and never buy another option.

If the options decline in value by less than 50%, continue to hold them. Close out the trade on the final day and then toss a coin to decide whether or not to buy more options. If the coin lands heads, invest another $2,000 in options. If it lands tails, wait 5 years before buying another option.

Obviously a properly defined strategy leaves the investor free to adapt to circumstances.

Decision Making

The money game far exceeds the capabilities of present-day game theory. As a result, investors must continue to rely upon their own wits. But at the same time they can structure their investment decisions in a reasonable fashion. Figure 20-1 shows the basic elements in any decision problem.

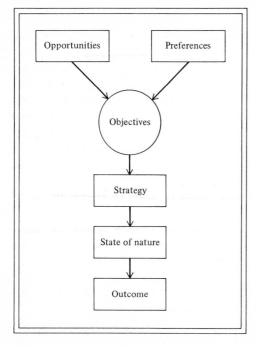

FIGURE 20-1 Basic elements in a decision problem.

David Miller and Martin Starr, professors at Columbia University and authors of the *Structure of Human Decisions,* provide one of the clearest explanations of human decision making. According to Miller and Starr, "The decision maker wants to achieve something—call it his goal, purpose, objective, or any other synonymous word." In order to achieve this objective, the individual selects a specific combination of resources from among all those available. Miller and Starr then go on to say, "For convenience we will call any such specific utilization of resources under the decision maker's control a strategy. His decision will consist of the selection of one of his available strategies." This strategy, together with the **state of nature,** determines the final outcome.

INSTITUTIONAL INVESTING

Merrill Lynch, the country's largest brokerage firm, provides institutions with detailed advice on investment strategies. For example, their asset-management group publishes a monthly release called *Monitored Investment Strategies.* Here are three of the "monitored" strategies included in this release, together with the objectives they are designed to achieve:

> *Appreciation Strategy. The objective is above average appreciation on an intermediate term basis. This approach best suits active investors willing to accept greater risk in order to capitalize on rapidly changing market trends.*

Total Return Strategy. *The objective is a total return in excess of inflation. Investors interested in total return are conservatively oriented and seek a combination of income and moderate appreciation.*

Growth Strategy. *The objective is long-term growth of capital at a rate in excess of that attained by the market as a whole. This approach is best suited to those investors willing to accept a greater measure of risk associated with the premium price earnings multiple accorded growth stocks in an effort to achieve a more substantial reward over the longer term.*[1]

These objectives imply radically different portfolios. For example, in April 1977 Merrill Lynch recommended the following asset allocations for each strategy:

	Asset	Percentage of Portfolio
Appreciation Strategy	Cash Reserve	0%
	Basic Industry/Capital Spending	30%
	Consumer Goods	35%
	Energy	20%
	Financial Services	15%
Total Return Strategy	Reserves (Money Market Instruments)	15%
	Intermediate Term Debt	20%
	Good Quality Common Stocks	65%
Growth Strategy	Cash Reserves	0%
	Growth Stocks	100%

The reasons for these commitments also differ considerably. Generally speaking, Merrill Lynch, like many other investment institutions, structures its forecasts on an economy-industry-firm basis. First, it predicts the overall economic outlook. Its April 1977 forecast read as follows:

The correction in stock prices could continue for a while longer as time will be required for investors to realize that profits, inflation, and the energy situation are not as negative as they now appear. For example, our economists are estimating a 14% increase in capital spending during 1977 and a further rise of 13% in 1978. Recent surveys indicate that consumers remain optimistic as reflected in the sharp rise in consumer credit during February. As evidence accumulates that the background is improving, investors should become more favorably disposed towards common stocks, and the market environment will begin to improve. Given this outlook, we suggest utilizing near term weakness to position stocks for intermediate term appreciation.[2]

Then they forecast industry performance. And finally they single out specific firms for special attention. A typical industry and firm forecast looks like this:

As detailed last month, leading indicators showed mounting strength in capital spending plans. Recent surveys suggest a robust environment over the next two years with particular strength in the equipment sector helping companies such as Harris Corp. and Combustion

Engineering. Further, Combustion should be a prime beneficiary of the likely promotion of coal as a substitute for oil and natural gas in electricity generation. Pollution control stocks will be aided by a pick-up in capital spending and Wheelabrator will also be favorably impacted by its recent acquisition of a specialty bearings manufacturer.[3]

ACTIVE/PASSIVE STRATEGIES

The investment strategies recommended by Merrill Lynch, like those of most brokerage houses, are based upon a belief in inefficient markets. But some institutions now appear to be accepting the generally efficient market concept. The April 1977 issue of the *Institutional Investor* carried a remarkable story by Chris Welles titled "Modern Portfolio Theory: Reprogramming the Money Manager." The article is remarkable because the *Institutional Investor* caters almost exclusively to professional investors. Many of these professionals see the new investment technology as a threat to their existence. One pension consultant, John Casey says, "I feel sorry for a lot of these guys. They were trained to do things a certain way. They've spent years working hard to do it that way. Now suddenly they're beginning to discover that what they've been doing all their life hasn't worked and that they've been doing it the wrong way. Think of the psychological shock these guys must be going through. Sometimes I wonder how they manage to get up in the morning."[4]

Despite these misgivings, the editors of the *Institutional Investor* introduced Welles's article by saying:

Instead of destroying money management as we know it, the new technology promises to make investing more disciplined, systematic, precise, efficient, and, hopefully, more effective. It will bring about an historic division of the business into passive management, purely for diversification, and active management, for performance. Though computer analysis and quantitative techniques will be more widely used, human judgment will continue to be extremely important, particularly in the search by active managers for undervalued opportunities. And to the extent that it is successful, active management, freed of many of the constraints of the past, could experience a major rejuvenation.[5]

Much of Welles's article concentrates on **active/passive investment strategies**—the newest buzzword in the investment community. An active/passive strategy represents a compromise between two very different views of the world. Traditional investors pursue undervalued (or overvalued) securities in an "active" attempt to increase their returns. Perhaps because of their belief in their predictive abilities, they pay only limited attention to risk. On the other hand, believers in efficient-market theory forsake security analysis (at least in its traditional form) and "passively" accept market prices. Rather than spend time searching out individual securities, they concentrate on diversification and the selection of the appropriate combination of risk and return.

An active/passive strategy combines both the active and passive approaches to investment selection. In effect, the individual or institution invests money in two separate portfolios. One is designed to achieve diversification. This passive portfolio closely resembles the overall market and usually goes by the name index fund or **core portfolio.** (See Chapter Thirteen for a further description of index funds.) The index fund provides near optimal diversification at a very low cost. After all, the managers of an index fund spend little time or effort in selecting individual securities, and they seldom turn over the portfolio.

Instead, portfolio managers attempt to beat the market with an active portfolio—sometimes called a **noncore portfolio.** Here the name of the game is still timing and selection. But with the passive portfolio already providing much of the needed diversification, the managers can now take greater risk and invest more heavily in their favorites.

Incidentally, the phrase "passive portfolio" refers only to attempts to select under- and over-valued securities. It implies nothing about the activity of the investor or portfolio manager with regard to selecting appropriate objectives, minimizing taxes, etc.

Innovative investment managers like Harold Arbit, a vice-president of the American National Bank in Chicago, recommend passive management for 80 to 85% of the institutional investor's money. The other 15 to 20% goes into an actively managed portfolio with performance as the goal. But even here, progressive institutions like American National recognize the impossibility of achieving performance with traditional investment techniques. Arbit stresses innovation in the search for inefficiencies in the market. "First you have to know what information has already been reflected in existing prices," says Arbit. In other words, simply forecasting the future accurately is not enough. Forecasts must also differ from those already impounded in prices. And that takes creativity. It probably also involves investing in a wide variety of assets like options, convertible bonds, foreign securities, and real estate.

THE INDIVIDUAL INVESTOR

So much for the latest activities of institutional investors. Before sketching investment strategies for individual investors, it would be helpful to know more about their attitudes and attributes. Fortunately, a recent joint effort by a large brokerage firm and several professors of finance—Ronald Lease, Wilbur Lewellen, and Gary Schlarbaum—provides just that information. Lease, Lewellen, and Schlarbaum collected questionnaires from 1,000 randomly selected customer accounts at the brokerage house. The questions on the survey represent the combined efforts of behavioral scientists at Purdue University, the research staff of the NYSE, officers and employees of the brokerage firm, and of course Lease, Lewellen, and Schlarbaum.

Table 20-1 shows some of the findings of the study vis-à-vis the attitudes of the individual investor. Most of the investors in the sample appear to enjoy investing their money. Perhaps because of the "recreational aspects" of the money game, these people manage their own money rather than relying completely

TABLE 20-1 *ATTITUDES OF THE INDIVIDUAL INVESTOR*

Attitude	*Rating**
I enjoy investing and look forward to more such activity in the future.	4.09
Relying exclusively upon mutual fund investments reduces personal satisfaction I obtain from making my own investments.	3.94
Security prices are not predictable in the short run.	3.88
To make money, an investor must be prepared to take substantial risks.	3.61
I am substantially better informed than the average investor.	3.31
The individual investor tends to be a more important force in the financial markets than the institutional investor.	2.21
The individual investor who regularly trades securities is likely to fare better financially than the individual who holds out for the long run.	2.56

* Explanation of ratings: 5 = strongly agree; 4 = moderately agree; 3 = neither agree nor disagree; 2 = moderately disagree; 1 = strongly disagree.
Source: Ronald C. Lease, Wilbur G. Lewellen, and Gary G. Schlarbaum, "The Individual Investor: Attributes and Attitudes," *Journal of Finance,* May 1974, p. 431.

upon mutual funds. At the same time they accept the fact that short-term fluctuations in security prices are impossible to predict. And a substantial number of these investors agree that in order to make money, an investor must be prepared to take substantial risks. Finally, respondents in the survey feel they are slightly better informed than the average investor. This is not surprising, since the customers in the sample averaged fifty-seven years of age and all of them had maintained an account with the brokerage house for at least 7 years. In addition, more than half the group owned over $40,000 of stocks apiece.

Given the age, experience, and amount of money invested by these people, the survey findings on investment decision making come as quite a surprise. In response to the question, "Approximately how many hours do you spend per month on your securities portfolio?" investors answered as follows:

Percentage of Sample	*Amount of Time Each Month, hours*
34	Less than 3
21	3–5
18	5–10
12	10–20
6	20–30
9	More than 30

More than half the respondents spend less than 5 hours a month on their investments!

Of course, there is always the possibility that these well-to-do participants in the market relied extensively upon professional advice. The questionnaire raises just this question. Investors were asked, "During the last year, approximately how much money did you spend for: (1) Subscriptions to investment and business periodicals; (2) Subscription advisory services; (3) Professional investment counseling?" Here are the results:

Expenditure, $	Periodical Subscriptions, %	Subscription Advisory Services, %	Professional Counseling, %
0	31	71	92
Less than 15	16	6	1
15–50	34	8	2
50–100	15	7	1
100–250	3	6	1
Over 250	1	2	3

Again the results fail to support many people's preconceptions of the cost of investing in securities. Despite the fact that investment counseling fees and expenditures for investment and business periodicals and advisory services qualify as tax deductions, few investors sought much advice. Many of them spent less than $15 during the year for all forms of investment advice. Of course, another possibility is that investors expect their brokerage commissions to pay for all their investment research.

Two questions in the survey bear directly on investment strategy. One concerns the techniques used by investors in making their decisions. Here are the replies to a question about the approaches most frequently used in evaluating securities:

Sample, %	Approach Used to Evaluate Securities
42	Fundamental approach, i.e., analysis of such fundamental factors as general business conditions, industry outlook, earnings, dividends, quality of management, etc.
4	Technical approach, i.e., analysis of market factors such as stock price movements, supply versus demand, amount of odd-lot trading, resistance levels, short interest, charts, etc.
23	Combination of fundamental and technical approaches
20	Rely primarily on brokerage firm or account executive for recommendations
7	Rely primarily on paid investment newsletters or investment counselor's advice
4	Other

The other question concerns expected returns. Asked to give the returns they expected to earn before taxes by holding common stocks, investors replied as follows:

Sample, %	Expected Average Annual Return, %
20	0–5
49	6–10
20	11–15
7	16–20
2	21–25
2	Above 25

The mean value for the sample comes to 9.3%, leading Lease, Lewellen, and Schlarbaum to jokingly observe that most brokerage house customers must have subscriptions to the *Journal of Business* (that's where the Lorie-Fisher study of rates of return originally appeared).

SAMPLE INVESTMENT STRATEGIES

How does an individual select an appropriate investment strategy? The answer hinges upon a number of factors, including:

1   Amount to invest
2   Forecasting ability
3   Degree of belief in market efficiency
4   Knowledge
5   Opportunity cost of time
6   Tax rate
7   Projected cash flows
8   Time horizon (expected holding period)
9   Risk-return preferences
10 Desired liquidity
11 Transactions costs
12 Personality
13 Other considerations

A carefully devised investment strategy reflects all these factors. Take the case of Jim Pickard, for example. He wants to invest a total of $10,000. Jim possesses no forecasting ability, at least so far as he knows, and he believes in the general efficiency of the securities markets. Moreover, his job never brings him into contact with inside information, and his only knowledge of investments and taxes consists of what he learned in this book.

This year he expects to earn $25,000 as a salesman. That means his time is worth about $12.50 an hour. He derives no enjoyment from investing, preferring to spend most of his leisure time watching TV, participating in sports, and dating.

At his present salary Jim falls in a federal tax bracket of 36%. And the marginal tax rate at the state level equals 5%. So the combined marginal tax rate equals 41%. He expects to remain in this tax bracket for the next 5 years.

Jim plans to save $2,400 a year, in addition to making voluntary contributions to his company pension plan. He has no need for additional income from his investments. Moreover, he foresees no need for funds within the next 5 years, unless an emergency occurs. As a result, he is willing to accept a time horizon (holding period) of at least 5 years.

Jim finds it difficult to describe his feelings about risk and return. He always thought of himself as a risk taker, but now he realizes that financial risk often differs considerably from other types of risk. Given the historical relationship between risk and return described in Chapter Nine, he believes the overall stock market provides a reasonable combination of risk and return.

Investment Strategy for Jim Pickard

Jim should adopt a passive investment strategy, at least in regard to selecting investments. The choice of a passive strategy seems logical given (1) his admitted lack of forecasting ability, (2) his belief in generally efficient markets, (3) his lack of contact with people possessing special knowledge about investments, and, perhaps most important of all, (4) his lack of interest in investing.

Given his risk-return preferences, an index fund appears best suited to his investment needs. An index fund coincides with his own views about market efficiency. And, in addition, it offers low turnover, low management costs, and excellent diversification.

However, the index fund idea suffers from two drawbacks. First, very few index funds are available to individuals. Second, no mutual fund passes tax losses through to its shareholders.

For that reason, Jim decides to invest an equal amount of money in each of 10 stocks, with each stock selected from a different industry. Commissions on these purchases will total more than 3% of the amount invested. But Jim plans to spread these costs over a number of years by adopting a modified buy-and-hold policy. In other words, he intends to sell stocks only to take tax losses.

Rather than invest the full $10,000 all at one time, Jim decides to employ time diversification and purchase one stock each month. And despite his belief in general market efficiency, he relies upon the *Value Line* service at a local library for ideas about specific stocks. *Value Line*'s performance ratings offer a small chance of outperforming the market. And *Value Line* also lists the stock's beta, its safety factor and stability index, and any insider buying or selling. Finally, the brief descriptions in *Value Line* give Jim a chance to indulge in crystal-ball gazing at no cost.

Jim's projected cash flow statement indicates a discretionary income of $200 a month, all of which he plans to save. This monthly cash flow can go either into a bank account or into a no-load mutual fund until it accumulates to $1,000. Then the money can be invested in another stock.

With no current need for extra income, Jim decides to select stocks paying low or no dividends. The first $100 of dividends from stocks are tax-free. Additional dividends are taxed at Pickard's combined marginal tax rate of 41%.

Investment Strategy for Beth Collins

Beth plans to graduate from college in a year with a business-school major. She has saved $2,000 from part-time jobs. She played with a paper portfolio in a recent investments course and discovered that she really enjoys the money game.

Although Beth doubts her forecasting ability, the fair-game prospects of the securities markets appeal to her. At first, the idea of a generally efficient market sounded pretty farfetched, but now she accepts the logic behind the concept. After all, the broker's tips she got from a friend did even worse than her own selections.

At the present time, her tax bracket is only 14%. And she has no need for income or liquidity, since her parents provide all the necessities of life.

Beth's time horizon is less than 1 year. As she puts it, she hates to just sit and watch her stocks. Instead, she wants to actively participate in buying and selling, and she wants to obtain the greatest gains—regardless of risk—in the shortest time possible.

Given Beth's short time horizon, her desire for constant involvement in ups and downs of the markets, and her goal of a high return, stock options or futures appear to be the logical investment media. Beth decides to invest in options rather than futures since options offer a positive expected return.

Now the trick is to avoid losing all her money in only a few trades. Probably 8 out of 10 options expire worthless. And transactions costs usually amount to about 10% of each option trade. Beth decides to never invest more than $1,000 at a time in options. Moreover, she plans to always hold options in four different stocks in completely different industries.

INVESTMENT STRATEGY IN THE FUTURE

At a recent meeting of the American Finance Association, the president, Professor John Lintner of Harvard University, told the assembled members:

> *In historical perspective, progress in academic disciplines has typically been marked by a series of seminal conceptual breakthroughs, followed by often long periods of consolidation, refinement, testing and implementation. . . .*
>
> *Happily, our field of finance has had its share of such seminal breakthroughs.*[6]

Not everyone shares in Lintner's jubilation. Indeed, many professional investors view the new financial technology with a mixture of contempt and fear. John Schulz, a columnist for *Forbes* magazine and a well-known technical analyst, says, "the stock market is too serious a business to be left to the academics." And

Paul Wilson, executive vice-president at Fidelity Bank, and Robert Cummins of Lloyd Investments talk of "confounding the Academia nuts who deny the possibility of superior performance."

But the investments profession bestows its harshest criticism on those in its own ranks who break with tradition. Becker Securities supposedly lost millions of dollars in commissions when it started its now widely used portfolio-evaluation service. And investment managers at Wells Fargo Bank, probably the first large bank to adopt the new investment technology, initially found themselves branded as "beta freaks" and "moon men."

Despite these difficulties, large institutional investors are increasingly recognizing the advantages of the new techniques. And, as further proof that money talks, at least some investment managers are responding to these needs. Many of them are paying $10,000 a year or more for computer programs like those developed by Barr Rosenberg and Associates. Rosenberg, a professor of business administration at the University of California at Berkeley, has parlayed his technical expertise into some incredibly sophisticated products. His computer programs forecast portfolio risk, analyze the determinants of risk within a portfolio, and predict the effect of portfolio modifications upon risk. For example, an investment manager can ask for a computer listing of the contributions of individual assets to total portfolio risk and to the diversifiable and nondiversifiable risk of the portfolio.

Rosenberg also offers a "Portfolio Optimization System," which chooses the best portfolios for institutional investors. Here's a typical problem solved by Rosenberg's computer program:

> A prospective client is dissatisfied with the performance of his present investment adviser and wants to change management. He seeks a well-diversified portfolio with a low level of risk. His present portfolio includes a number of small companies which are not in the S&P 500 as well as 20% cash.
>
> The prospective client is aware of the undesirability of excessive transactions. Indeed, the client specifically requires that portfolio turnover not exceed 40%.
>
> Examination of the assets in the current portfolio reveals three investments which should be eliminated. The other investments should only be sold if the resulting reduction in residual risk warrants the necessary transaction costs. Finally, one of the holdings must be maintained at its present level since it represents a controlling interest in a company.
>
> This problem includes many of the common features of a major portfolio revision: some assets must be sold, others must be retained; a number of assets presently included in the portfolio are unsuitable for further purchase but need not be sold; an existing cash holding must be invested in common stock; further diversification is needed; and transaction costs incurred in revising the portfolio must be controlled.[7]

What does all of this imply for the future? Rosenberg says, "Someday the individual investor will probably be able to walk into a brokerage firm, pay $25, and have his utility function calculated right on the spot." Then one of the firm's investment strategists, aided by a computer, will help the investor define his or her objectives and select an optimal portfolio.

KEYWORDS

game theory   active/passive investment   core portfolio
strategy   strategies   noncore portfolio
state of nature

QUESTIONS

1 Describe the basic elements in a decision problem (see Figure 20-1).
2 Active/passive strategies represent a compromise between two extreme views of the securities markets. Discuss these views.
3 How much of your portfolio would you devote to active management? What does this imply about your belief in efficient markets?
4 Some people enjoy playing the money game more than others. Will these investors devote more or less of their funds to actively managed portfolios? Why?
5 Describe the "average" investor.
6 Debate the following statement: "Individuals generally devote little time or effort to their investments."
7 List the most important factors in devising an investment strategy. How do these factors apply to you?
8 Use the information in the previous question to design your own investment strategy.
9 What role should the broker and/or institution play in helping to set individual investment strategies?
10 What techniques do you think individuals will use in selecting investments within the next 10 to 20 years?

REFERENCES

Ambachtsheer, Keith: "Profit Potential in an 'Almost Efficient' Market," *Journal of Portfolio Management,* Fall 1974, pp. 84–87.
Arbit, Harold L., and James E. Rhodes: "Performance Goals in a Generally Efficient Market," *Journal of Portfolio Management,* Fall 1976, pp. 57–61.
Black, Fischer, Yale Hirsch, and John Westergaard: "Nuggets," *Journal of Portfolio Management,* Winter 1977, pp. 71–77.
Fisher, Lawrence, and Roman Weil: "Coping with the Risk of Interest Rate Fluctuations: Returns to Bondholders from Naive and Optimal Strategies," *Journal of Business,* October 1971, pp. 408–431.
*Garrone, François, and Bruno Solnik: "A Global Approach to Money Management," *Journal of Portfolio Management,* Summer 1976, pp. 5–14.
Hoffman, Richard J., and Steven R. Resnick: *Investment Strategy,* Merrill Lynch, Pierce, Fenner, and Smith, Inc., New York, March 1977.

Lease, Ronald C., Wilbur G. Lewellen, and Gary G. Schlarbaum: "The Individual Investor: Attributes and Attitudes," *Journal of Finance,* May 1974, pp. 413–433.

Lorie, James H., and Mary T. Hamilton: "Long Range Risk Policy," *Financial Analysts Journal,* July–August 1973, pp. 46–50.

Luce, R. Duncan, and Howard Raiffa: *Games and Decisions: Introduction and Critical Survey,* Wiley, New York, 1957.

Merrill Lynch Asset Management, Inc.: *Monitored Investment Strategies,* New York, April 1977.

Miller, David W., and Martin K. Starr: *The Structure of Human Decisions,* Prentice-Hall, Englewood Cliffs, N.J., 1967.

Rapoport, Anatol: *Fights, Games, and Debates,* University of Michigan Press, Ann Arbor, Mich., 1960.

Rosenberg, Barr, and Andrew Rudd: "Portfolio Optimization Algorithms: A Progress Report," Research Program in Finance Working Paper No. 42, University of California, Berkeley, May 1976.

Schulz, John W.: "Technician's Perspective: Not by Math Alone," *Forbes,* Nov. 1, 1973, p. 86.

Sharpe, William F.: "Likely Gains from Market Timing," *Financial Analysts Journal,* March–April 1975, pp. 60–69.

Smith, Rodger F., and Thomas M. Richards: "Asset Mix and Investment Strategy," *Financial Analysts Journal,* March–April 1976, pp. 67–71.

*Treynor, Jack L., and Fischer Black: "How to Use Security Analysis to Improve Portfolio Selection," *Journal of Business,* January 1973, pp. 66–86.

Upson, Roger B., Paul F. Jessup, and Keishiro Matsumoto: "Portfolio Diversification Strategies," *Financial Analysts Journal,* May–June 1975, pp. 86–88.

*Welles, Chris: "Modern Portfolio Theory: Reprogramming the Money Manager," *Institutional Investor,* April 1977, pp. 35–52.

Williams, J. D.: *The Compleat Strategyst,* McGraw-Hill, New York, 1966.

Wilson, Paul N., and Robert I. Cummin: "Pension Officers, Are You Wasting Management and Transaction Costs?" *Financial Analysts Journal,* March–April 1977, pp. 58–62.

* References preceded by an asterisk are highly recommended.

NOTES

CHAPTER ONE

[1] Louis Engel, *How to Buy Stocks,* 5th ed., Bantam, New York, 1972, p. 5.

[2] This is a quote from Richard M. Hexter, Executive Vice President of Donaldson, Lufkin, & Jenrette. It appeared in *A Complete Guide to Making a Public Stock Offering,* 2nd ed., by Elmer Winter © 1972 by Prentice-Hall, Inc., Englewood Cliffs, N.J., p. 41.

[3] John Brooks, *Business Adventures,* Weybright and Talley, New York, 1969, p. 279.

[4] Ibid., p. 280.

CHAPTER TWO

[1] The article subsequently appeared in book form in John Brooks, *Business Adventures,* Weybright and Talley, New York, 1969, pp. 1–2.

[2] William J. Baumol, *The Stock Market and Economic Efficiency,* Fordham, New York, 1965, p. 3.

[3] Richard R. West, and Seha M. Tinic, *The Economics of the Stock Market,* Praeger, New York, 1971, pp. 50–51.

[4] Lawrence A. Armour, "Making A Market; NASDAQ Has Opened a New Competitive Era on Wall Street," *Barron's*, Mar. 8, 1971, p. 3.

[5] Letter of Donald Weeden to the Securities and Exchange Commission, Dec. 19, 1969.

[6] Gustave L. Levy, Address before the Dean's Council Dinner, UCLA Graduate School of Management, Los Angeles, May 14, 1974.

[7] Securities and Exchange Commission, *Report of the Special Study of Securities Markets,* Part 2, July 17, 1963, pp. 170–171, 247.

[8] Henry G. Manne et al., *Wall Street in Transition,* New York University Press, New York, 1974, p. 25.

[9] Ibid., pp. 44–45.

[10] Ibid., p. 205.

[11] "Big Board Disciplines 3 Firms for Violations of Net-Capital Rules," *Wall Street Journal,* © Dow Jones & Company, Feb. 15, 1974, p. 18. All rights reserved.

CHAPTER THREE

[1] Moody's Investor's Service, Inc., *Moody's Industrial Manual,* vol. 1, 1977, p. 167.

[2] Abba Lerner, "The Burden of the National Debt," *Income, Employment and Public Policy,* 1948, p. 255. This quote appeared in *Public Principles of Public Debt* by James M. Buchanan, Irwin, Homewood, Ill., p. 12.

[3] Michael L. Gezci, "The Rating Game: Credit-grading Firms Wield Greater Power in Public Debt Market," *Wall Street Journal,* Oct. 26, 1976, p. 1.

CHAPTER FOUR

[1] Max G. Ansbacher, "Near-Total Wipe-Out," *Barron's,* © Dow Jones & Company, Inc., August 1974, p. 9. All rights reserved.

[2] Bache Halsey Stuart Shields, Inc., *Commodity Report/Weekly Digest,* Nov. 4, 1976, p. 4.

[3] Thomas A. Hieronymus, *Economics of Futures Trading,* Commodity Research Bureau, New York, 1971, p. 6.

[4] Bruce G. Gould, *Dow Jones–Irwin Guide to Commodities Trading,* Dow Jones-Irwin, Homewood, Ill., 1973, p. v.

CHAPTER FIVE

[1] Eugene F. Fama et al., "The Adjustment of Stock Prices to New Information," *International Economic Review,* February 1969, pp. 1–21.

[2] Fred Schwed, Jr., *Where Are the Customers' Yachts?* John Magee, Mass., 1960, pp. 159–161. Reprinted by permission of Simon & Schuster, Inc., New York, © 1945, 1955 by Fred Schwed, Jr.

[3] B. F. Skinner, "Superstitions in the Pigeon," *Journal of Experimental Psychology,* April 1948, pp. 168–172.

CHAPTER SEVEN

[1] Amos Tversky, and Daniel Kahneman, "Judgment under Uncertainty: Heuristics and Biases," *Science,* vol. 185, Sept. 27, 1974, p. 1125.

CHAPTER EIGHT

[1] Constantino Bresciani-Turroni, *The Economics of Inflation,* George Allen & Unwin Ltd., London, 1953, p. 260.

CHAPTER NINE

[1] Maury Seldin, and Richard Swesnik, *Real Estate Investment Strategy,* Wiley-Interscience, New York, 1970, p. 4.

CHAPTER TWELVE

[1] Tax rates and tax laws change frequently. For the sake of simplicity, 1975 income tax rates are used throughout this chapter.

[2] The maximum contribution per year is sometimes stated as 16 2/3% of total salary (including the contribution). This can be shown to be equivalent to 20% of includable compensation (total salary minus the contribution).

CHAPTER THIRTEEN

[1] A. F. Ehrbar, "Index Funds—An Idea Whose Time Is Coming," *Fortune,* June 1976, p. 145.

[2] Ibid., p. 146.

[3] Ibid., p. 146.

CHAPTER FIFTEEN

[1] Joseph A. Pechman, Henry J. Aaron, and Michael K. Taussig, *Social Security: Perspectives for Reform,* The Brookings Institution, Washington, D.C., 1968, pp. 61–62, 69.

[2] Warren Shore, *Social Security: The Fraud in Your Future,* © 1975 by Warren Shore, Macmillan Publishing Co., New York, 1975, pp. 5–6.

[3] Ibid., p. 19.

[4] William B. Mead, "The Squeeze Ahead for Social Security," *Money,* October 1974, p. 34.

CHAPTER SEVENTEEN

[1] *Scott's Stamp Guide,* Scott's Publishing Co., New York, vol. II, 1968, p. iii.

[2] This quote appeared in Gerald I. Nierenberg, *Fundamentals of Negotiating,* Hawthorn Books, Inc., New York, 1973, p. 29. This quotation is from *How Nations Negotiate* by Fred Charles Ikle.

[3] This quote by John Ruskin appeared in Gerald I. Nierenberg, *Fundamentals of Negotiating,* Hawthorne Books, Inc., New York, 1973, p. 205.

CHAPTER EIGHTEEN

[1] Eugene F. Fama, and Merton Miller, *The Theory of Finance,* Dryden Press, Hinsdale, Illinois, 1972, p. 217.

[2] Ibid., p. 217.

[3] Adam Smith, *The Money Game,* © 1976 by Adam Smith, Random House, New York, p. 31.

[4] Paul Slovic, and Amos Tversky, "Who Accepts Savage's Axiom?" *Behavioral Science,* November 1974, p. 369.

[5] M. A. Wallach, and N. Kogan, "Aspects of Judgment and Decision Making: Interrelationships and Changes with Age," *Behavioral Science,* January 1961, vol. 6, p. 27.

[6] Commission on the Review of the National Policy toward Gambling, *Gambling in America: Appendix 2, Survey of American Gambling Attitudes and Behavior,* U. S. Government Printing Office, Washington, D.C., 1976, pp. 1, 4 & 7.

[7] Edmund Bergler, *The Psychology of Gambling,* Bernard Hanison, Ltd., London, 1958, pp. 7–8.

[8] Commission on the Review of the National Policy toward Gambling, op. cit., pp. 432–433.

[9] Frederick Amling, *Investments: An Introduction to Analysis and Management,* 3rd ed., Prentice-Hall, Englewood Cliffs, N.J., 1974, p. 8.

[10] Fred Schwed, Jr., *Where Are the Customers' Yachts?* John Magee, Mass., 1960, p. 172. Reprinted by permission of Simon & Schuster, Inc., New York, © 1945, 1955 by Fred Schwed, Jr.

[11] Smith, op. cit., p. 68.

CHAPTER NINETEEN

[1] Gary Becker, "A Theory of the Allocation of Time," *The Economic Journal,* September 1965, p. 493.

[2] Ibid., p. 495.

CHAPTER TWENTY

[1] Merrill Lynch Asset Management, Inc., *Monitored Investment Strategies,* New York, April 1977, p. 2.

[2] Ibid., p. 3.

[3] Ibid., p. 4.

[4] Chris Welles, "Modern Portfolio Theory: Reprogramming the Money Manager," *Institutional Investor,* April 1977, p. 36.

[5] Introduction by editors to Chris Welles' "Modern Portfolio Theory: Reprogramming the Money Manager," *Institutional Investor,* April 1977, p. 35.

[6] John Lintner, "Inflation and Security Returns," *Journal of Finance,* May 1975, p. 260.

[7] This is paraphrased from Barr Rosenberg and Andrew Rudd, "Portfolio Optimization Algorithms: A Progress Report," Research Program in Finance, Working Paper No. 42, University of California, Berkeley, May 1976, pp. 1–103.

INDEX